Abraham in
the New Testament

Abraham in the New Testament

John Eifion Morgan-Wynne

◆PICKWICK *Publications* · Eugene, Oregon

ABRAHAM IN THE NEW TESTAMENT

Copyright © 2020 John Eifion Morgan-Wynne. All rights reserved. Except for brief quotations in critical publications or reviews, no part of this book may be reproduced in any manner without prior written permission from the publisher. Write: Permissions, Wipf and Stock Publishers, 199 W. 8th Ave., Suite 3, Eugene, OR 97401.

Pickwick Publications
An Imprint of Wipf and Stock Publishers
199 W. 8th Ave., Suite 3
Eugene, OR 97401

www.wipfandstock.com

PAPERBACK ISBN: 978-1-7252-5829-7
HARDCOVER ISBN: 978-1-7252-5830-3
EBOOK ISBN: 978-1-7252-5831-0

Cataloguing-in-Publication data:

Names: Morgan-Wynne, J. E., author.

Title: Abraham in the New Testament / John Eifion Morgan-Wynne.

Description: Eugene, OR: Pickwick Publications, 2020 | Includes bibliographical references and index.

Identifiers: ISBN 978-1-7252-5829-7 (paperback) | ISBN 978-1-7252-5830-3 (hardcover) | ISBN 978-1-7252-5831-0 (ebook)

Subjects: LCSH: Abraham—(Biblical patriarch)—in the New Testament | Abraham—(Biblical patriarch) | Judaism—Relations—Christianity

Classification: BS580.A3 M67 2020 (print) | BS580.A3 (ebook)

Manufactured in the U.S.A.   MAY 20, 2020

Translations of New Testament passages are the author's. Other quotations from the Bible and the Apocrypha are from the text of the Holy Bible, New Revised Version, copyright 1987, by the Division of the Christian Education of the National Council of Churches in the USA, used by permission.

Dedicated to Enid,
Wife and Best Friend,
Loyal Supporter,
Fellow Pilgrim on life's journey.

Contents

Preface | ix
Abbreviations | xi

1 Abraham in Paul's Letter to the Galatians | 1
    1.1. General Introduction | 1
    1.2. Introduction to the Letter to the Galatians | 2
    1.3. Paul's Use of Abraham in the Letter to the Galatians | 36
    1.4. Summary | 85

2 Paul's Letter to the Romans | 90
    2.1. Introduction | 90
    2.2. Paul's Use of Abraham in the Letter to the Romans | 98
    2.3. A Comparison of the Use of Abraham in Galatians and Romans | 141

3 Abraham in the Letter to the Hebrews | 165
    3.1. Introduction | 165
    3.2. Abraham in the Letter to the Hebrews | 168
    3.3. Summary | 201

4 Abraham in the Letter of James | 204
    4.1. Introduction | 204
    4.2. Abraham in the Letter to James | 206
    4.3. The Relation of James and Paul and Their Respective Use of Abraham | 223

5 Abraham in Luke-Acts | 231
   5.1. Introduction | 231
   5.2. The Birth Stories | 232
   5.3. Abraham elsewhere in Luke-Acts | 262
   5.4. Individuals as Children of Abraham | 263
   5.5. The Fulfilment of God's Promise to Abraham/the Fathers | 263
   5.6. The Post-Mortem Existence of the Patriarchs | 268
   5.7. Conclusion. | 269

6 Abraham in the Gospel of John | 270
   6.1. Introduction | 270
   6.2. Abraham in the Gospel of John. | 271
   6.3. Summary | 287

7 Abraham in the Gospel of Matthew | 291
   7.1. Introduction | 291
   7.2. The Genealogy | 291
   7.3. Jesus as the Messiah and Son of David | 294
   7.4. Jesus as Son of Abraham | 305
   7.5. Summary | 310

8 Summary and Concluding Reflections | 314

Excursus: Abraham in the Apostolic Fathers | 328
   1. The First Epistle of Clement | 328
   2. The Letters of Ignatius | 333
   3. The Epistle of Barnabas | 335
   4. Summary | 340

Bibliography | 343
   Bibliography for Excursus on Abraham in the Apostolic Fathers | 373

Index of Modern Scholars | 375
Index of Biblical and Extra Biblical Writings | 383

Preface

SOON AFTER I BECAME NT Tutor at Regent's Park College, Oxford, the syllabus for the Honours School of Theology in the University was altered, and Romans and Hebrews in Greek became the set texts for the second NT paper. During my work, this faced me with some of the differences between Paul and the unknown author of Hebrews, not least in their understanding of faith. Erik Grässer's *Glaube im Hebraerbrief* made a considerable impression on me. At the same time, I was intrigued by the different emphases in the use of Abraham in these two authors and also in the letter of James. I never had the time, or did not make the time, to pursue this while I was actually teaching. It was not till I had actually left teaching in the Baptist theological colleges at Oxford and Bristol that I was asked to give four talks to the annual retreat of the ministers of the URC Eastern Province, held at Westminster College, Cambridge. This provided the stimulus to look at the use of Abraham in Paul, Hebrews, James, and John. Then in retirement more time has become available to take up this theme.

Some justification is needed for the appearance of another work on Abraham in the NT. Just a few monographs dealing with the use of Abraham in the whole of the New Testament have appeared, while there have been a number of monographs and articles on Paul's use of Abraham, not to mention that commentaries on Galatians and Romans have to deal with this in the course of their exegesis of these letters. Commentaries on the Letter of James deal with similarities and differences between its author and Paul on justification and their respective use of Abraham figures as part of this. The use of Abraham in Hebrews has not attracted as much attention, though obviously commentaries deal with this in the exegesis on chapters 6 and 11 especially.

So what does justify another treatment? Some justification exists in pulling together a great deal of discussion by scholars of different countries and confessional backgrounds and making this available. The main reason in pursuing this study has not been just an academic one, though I hope that what is offered commands the respect of scholars. In the end, I am particularly concerned with the implications of the study, not as regards Jewish-Christian dialogue, but in respect of preaching. What implications do the differences in the variety of depictions of Abraham have for the way in which the preacher today handles the New Testament? Has each writer manipulated the story of Abraham for their own purposes? Or do the materials about Abraham offer springboards for the way in which the different writers apply Abraham to the Christian congregations to which they wrote? Were they reapplying tradition in a purely arbitrary manner, or was the story itself so rich as to be conducive to different applications? That is the issue which I try and discuss in the closing chapter. I have been preaching since I was about fifteen years of age and continued still regularly doing so until recently. I suppose that it could be said that preaching is in my life blood! I believe that what I do in the study must be the foundation of what I do in the pulpit. I cannot leave behind what I do in the study when I preach, for that would be intellectual dishonesty, and Jesus did after all command us to love God with our minds as well as with our hearts and our wills. Conversely, it has always been the message and the theology of the Biblical writers which holds the greatest attraction for me. For me study and preaching mutually interact, each in a sense feeding the other.

I, therefore, hope that the scholar may find this volume useful and that those who preach may also find that what is offered here impels them to their own reflection on how they handle the word of truth today and the manner in which they show themselves to be a herald of the good news of God.

I would like to place on record my indebtedness to the many scholars whose works I have read, even where I may not always have agreed with their conclusions.

I wish to thank my editor at Wipf and Stock, Dr. Robin Parry, for his kind patience and prompt answer to all my queries. Thanks also to Zane Deren, Zechariah Mickel, and Calvin Jaffarian for their patience and kindness. I would also like to thank Savannah Landerholm and Mike Surber who designed the cover for Abraham in the OT & Early Judaism and Abraham in the NT respectively.

On a practical level, my daughter, Leri-Anne, and grandson, Samuel, have given me tremendous help when I ran into difficulties with the computer, and I am most grateful to them.

The dedication indicates something of what I owe to my wife, Enid, over the fifty-seven years of our marriage.

Abbreviations

AGAJU	Arbeiten zur Geschichte des antiken Judentums und des Urchristentums
AJ AAU	Acta Jutlandica. Aarsskrift for Aarhus Universitet
AK	Arbeiten zur Kirchengeschichte
ALGHJ	Arbeiten zur Literatur und Geschichte des Hellenistischen Judentums
AOTC	Apollos Old Testament Commentary
ASNU	Acta Seminarii Neotestamentieri Upsaliensis
ATANT	Abhandlungen zur Theologie des Alten und Neuen Testaments
ATD	Acta Theologica Danica
ATD	Das Alte Testament Deutsch
BA	Baker Academic
BBB	Bonner Biblische Beiträge
BET	Beitrage zur Evangelischen Theologie
BETL	Bibliotheca Ephemeridum Theologicarum Lovaniensium
BFT	Biblical Foundations in Theology
BGBH	Beiträge zur Geschichte der biblischen Hermeneutik

BHT	Beiträge zur Historischen Theologie
BJS	Brown Judaic Studies
BO	Biblica et Orientalia
BRS	The Biblical Resource Series
BS	Bibel Studien
BSL	Biblical Studies Library
BTS	Biblisch-Theologische Studien
BVB	Beiträge zum Verstehen der Bibel
BWANT	Beiträge zur Wissenschaft vom Alten und Neuen Testament
BZ	Biblische Zeitschrift
BZAW	Beihefte zur Zeitschrift für die altestamentliche Wissenschaft
BZNW	Beiheft zur Zeitschrift für die neutestamentliche Wissenschaft
CB	Coniectanea Biblica
CBC	Cambridge Bible Commentary
CBQMS	Catholic Biblical Quarterly Monograph Series
CHB	Cambridge History of the Bible
CJAS	Christianity and Judaism in Antiquity Series
CNT	Commentaire du Nouveau Testament
CRINT	Compendia Rerum Iudaicarum ad Novum Testamentum
CSHJ	Chicago Studies in the History of Judaism
DBSJ	Detroit Baptist Seminary Journal.
DJD	Discoveries in the Judean Desert.
ECB	Die Neue Echter Bibel
ECC	Early Christianity in Context
EH	Europäische Hochschulschriften
EKKNT	Evangelisch-Katholischer Kommentar zum Neuen Testament
ESEC	Emory Studies in Early Christianity
ET	English Translation
EvTh	Evangelische Theologie
ExT	Expository Times

FFNT	Foundations and Facets: New Testament
FOTL	The Forms of the Old Testament Literature
FRLANT	Forschungen zur Religion und Literatur des Alten und Neuen Testaments
FTS	Frankfurter Theologische Studien
FzB	Forschung zur Bibel
GAP	Guides to the Apocrypha and Pseudepigrapha
GTA	Göttinger Theologische Arbeiten
HBS	Herders Biblische Studien
HBT	Horizons in Biblical Theology
HCS	Hellenistic Culture and Society
HDR	Harvard Dissertations in Religion
HM	Heythrop Monographs
HNT	Handbuch zum Neuen Testament
HTKNT	Herders Theologischer Kommentar zum Neuen Testament
HTS	Harvard Theological Studies
ICC	International Critical Commentary
IKZ	Internationale Kirchliche Zeitschrift
IRT	Issues in Religion and Theology
JCC	Jewish Culture and Contexts
JSOTSS	Journal for the Study of the Old Testament Supplement Series
JSPS	Journal for the Study of the Pseudepigrapha Supplement
JSPSS	Journal for the Study of the Pseudepigrapha Supplement Series
KAV	Kommentar zu den Apostolischen Vätern
KBANT	Kommentare und Beiträge zum Alten und Neuen Testament
LHB/OTS	Library of Hebrew Bible/Old Testament Studies
LCL	Loeb Classical Library
LNTS	Library of New Testament Studies
LQHR	London Quarterly and Holborn Review
LSJ	Liddell et al., *Greek-English Lexicon*

LSTS	Library of Second Temple Studies
LTJ	Lutheran Theological Journal
MNTS	McMaster New Testament Studies
MTS	Münchener Theologischer Studien
NA	Neutestamentliche Abhandlungen
NEB	New English Bible
NSBT	New Studies in Biblical Theology
NTC	New Testament in Context
NTOA	Novum Testamentum et Orbis Antiquus
NTR	New Testament Readings
NTM	New Testament Monographs
OBO	Orbis Biblicus et Orientalis
OBT	Overtures to Biblical Theology
OTG	Old Testament Guides
OTKNT	Ökumenischer Taschenbuchkommentar zum Neuen Testament
OTL	Old Testament Library
PA	Philosophia Antiqua
PACS	Philo of Alexandria Commentary Series
PBM	Paternoster Biblical Monographs
QD	Quaestiones Disputatae
RB	Revue Biblique
RNT	Regensburger Neues Testament
SANT	Studien zum Alten und Neuen Testament
SAP	Sheffield Academic Press
SBA AT	Stuttgarter Biblische Aufsatzbände Altes Testament
SBA NT	Stuttgarter Biblische Aufsatzbände Neues Testament
SBL	Society of Biblical Literature
SBLDS	Society of Biblical Literature Dissertation Series
SBLEJL	Society of Biblical Literature Early Judaism and its Literature
SBLMS	Society for Biblical Literature Monograph Series

SBLSS	Society of Biblical Literature Semeia Series
SBS	Stuttgarter Bibel-Studien
SBT	Studies in Biblical Theology
SBTS	Sources for Biblical and Theological Study
SD	Studies and Documents
SDSSRL	Studies in the Dead Sea Scrolls and Related Literature
SFSHJ	South Florida Studies in the History of Judaism
SGKA	Studien zur Geschichte und Kulter des Alterums
SJSJ	Supplements to the Journal for the Study of Judaism
SHAW	Sitzungsberichte der Heidelberger Akademie der Wissenschaft
SKPAWB	Sitzberichte der Königlichen Preussischen Akademie der Wissenschaften zu Berlin
SN	Studia Neotestamentica
SNTSMS	Society for New Testament Studies Monograph Series
SOTBT	Studies in Old Testament Biblical Theology
SNTW	Studies of the New Testament and its World
SP	Sacra Pagina
SPB	Studia Post-Biblica
SPM	Studia Philonica Monographs
STDJ	Studies on the Texts of the Desert of Judah
SUNT	Studien zur Umwelt des Neuen Testaments
SVTP	Studia in Veteris Testamenti Pseudepigrapha
TANZ	Texte und Arbeiten zum Neutestamentlichen Zeitalter
TB	Theologische Bucherei
TBC	Torch Bible Commentaries
TDNT	Theological Dictionary of the New Testament
TF	Theologische Forschung
THE	Theologische Existenz Heute
THNT	Theologischer Handkommentar zum Neuen Testament
TSAJ	Texte und Studien zum Antiken Judentum
TTZ	Trierer Theologische Zeitschrift

WANT	Beiträge zur Wissenschaft vom Alten und Neuen Testament
WMANT	Wissenschaftliche Monographien zun Alten und Neuen Testament
WUNT	Wissenschaftliche Untersuchungen zum Neuen Testament
ZAW	Zeitschrift für Alttestamentliche Wissenschaft
ZB	Zürcher Bibelkommentare
ZNW	Zeitschrift für Neutestamentliche Wissenschaft
ZTK	Zeitschrift für Theologie und Kirche

1

Abraham in Paul's Letter to the Galatians

1.1. General Introduction

ABRAHAM IS DISCUSSED AT some length by the apostle Paul in two of his writings: the Letter to the Galatians and the Letter to the Romans. But the phrase "the seed of Abraham" occurs outside these two letters in 2 Corinthians, in a passage where Paul refers to a rival apostolate who had arrived at Corinth, and whose members were clearly calling themselves members of the "seed of Abraham" as part of the commendation of themselves. Very reluctantly Paul "took them on" on their own approach and, at the beginning of what has come to be known as "the Fool's Speech" (11:1–12:13), matched their claims, for he too was a Hebrew, an Israelite, a member of the seed of Abraham, a servant of Christ (11:22). The first three items are relative to Jewishness and refer to the position of one who is a member of the elect people of God, who shares in the benefits of all God's mighty acts on behalf of His people and His promises to them, acts and promises which go back to the founding patriarch of the nation.[1]

---

1. For detailed discussion of these three titles, see Georgi, *Die Gegner des Paulus im 2. Korintherbrief*, 63–82; *Opponents*, 41–60; Berger, *Abraham in den paulinischen Hauptbriefen*, 88–89; Wieser, *Die Abrahamvorstellungen im Neuen Testament*, 36–40; Niebuhr, *Heidenapostel*, 129–32.

While the statement of being a servant of Christ was the climax of this short list, this did not mean that his Jewish advantages were thereby called in question; rather, they were subordinated to what Paul said in explanation of his being a servant of Christ. He went on to point to the persecutions, trials, and dangers which he had suffered as pointers to his weakness which in turn was based on the pattern of Jesus' own ministry.[2]

For our purpose, the passage is of interest because it shows how important the figure of Abraham and descent from him was regarded in some circles of the early church.[3] It presumably also helped to impress the members of the Corinthian congregation who in all probability comprised some Hellenistic Jews and a majority of Gentile converts.[4] For Paul it was subordinated in significance to living out the death and resurrection of Christ—specifically, of knowing the dying of Christ, or weakness, and, in that very state, also knowing the risen power of Christ given to those who believe, to strengthen them.[5]

1.2. Introduction to the Letter to the Galatians

We shall, then, concentrate on Galatians and Romans. Scholars are in agreement that they were written in that order, but they differ as to the exact chronological relationship of the two letters. Broadly speaking, probably a majority of scholars accept that Galatians was written after Paul had learned about the arrival and activity among the Galatian churches of people representing a decidedly conservative Jewish Christian stance (or the activity of people representing the local Jewish community).[6] This activity had apparently made inroads among Paul's converts, to his considerable dismay. Romans was written a few months later, and draws up a balance sheet, so to speak, of his thoughts and arguments. Other scholars dissent from this viewpoint and believe that Galatians is probably the earliest extant letter of Paul, written before the Jerusalem Council which was convened to sort out the problems which had arisen because of the mission of the Jewish Christians both to Galatia and to the city of Antioch where Paul was based. In this way,

---

2. As Niebuhr, *Heidenapostel*, 132, rightly maintains.

3. Martin, *2 Corinthians*, 375, after referring to Paul's usage in Galatians, points to the fact that the phrase had a wider currency elsewhere in the early church.

4. Berger, *Abraham*, 89, suggests that being a Jew might have been one of the criteria in attempts to determine the genuineness and legitimacy of an apostle = missionary preacher. This probably goes too far, but it might have found mention in the letters of recommendation with which these visitors were furnished.

5. See 4:10-12; 12:1-10; 13:3-4.

6. See Nanos, *Irony of Galatians*.

these scholars also hoped to solve one of the problems occasioned by differences between Paul's accounts of his visits to Jerusalem in Galatians 1–2 and the account of Paul's visits to Jerusalem in Acts 9, 11, and 15.

It is not necessary for us to get involved in a discussion of this particular knotty problem, which would take up far too much space.[7] Both viewpoints share the conviction that Galatians was written at the height of the crisis in the Galatian churches and with great passion,[8] in order to fend off the influence of some who wanted the Galatians to be circumcised with all that that entailed as regards keeping the Law of Moses, and in order to defend the right of Gentile converts to be part of God's people without having to submit to all the requirements of the Law. That is sufficient for our purpose.

1.2.1. The Situation in the Galatian Congregations

Since the letter is addressed to the Galatians, it seems appropriate methodologically to enquire about them and their situation as Paul saw it, first of all, and not to leap into a discussion of those whom Paul described as unsettling the Galatians.[9]

Paul looked back at the time of their conversion and the time immediately following it, and commented favorably on it. They had come to know God (4:8), which suggests a pagan background, and they had received the Spirit (3:2). They had received Paul most warmly as a messenger of God and of Christ Jesus, even though there were certain circumstances about him (he has not specified what these were) that might have put them off receiving him (4:14-15). He commented that they had begun well (5:7a); however, things had changed, so much so that Paul can even ask "Who prevented you from obeying the truth?" (5:7b).

That all is not well with the Galatians had been obvious from the start of the letter in the way that Paul, dispensing with the customary thanksgiving for the recipient(s) at the beginning of a Greek letter, expressed his amazement that the Galatians had so quickly turned away from the

---

7. Nor the issue of whether the letter was written to the churches of south Galatia (the so-called "provincial [i.e., Roman] hypothesis") or of north Galatia (the so-called "territorial hypothesis").

8. This does not mean that Galatians is full of ill-thought out, exaggerated statements which Paul later had to correct in the letter to the Romans. See the comments on this on page 42.

9. See Nanos, *Irony*, 62–72, 75–85; Kwon, *Eschatology in Galatians*, 28–50, both of whom make this point. Cf. Cosgrove, *Cross and the Spirit*, 16, who argues that what Paul sees as the real issue must form the presupposition of exegesis.

God who called them in Christ Jesus, to another gospel, which he denied actually merited the designation "gospel." He referred to some who were unsettling them and wanting to pervert the gospel of Christ (1:6-7). He addressed the letter's recipients in 3:1: "O foolish Galatians, who has bewitched you?" At the beginning of the letter, Paul had pronounced a curse on all who deviated from the gospel of God's grace shown in Jesus Christ (1:8-9),[10] and, later, warned that whoever was unsettling them would incur God's judgement, whoever they were (5:10). He even wished that they would castrate themselves (5:12).

So, who were these people who were unsettling the Galatians and what was the basis of their effect on them?[11] Can we form an "identikit" of those whom Paul criticized? Recent warnings about the dangers of "mirror reading" of the views of Paul's opponents must be heeded.[12] Nevertheless, we can suggest certain features of their teaching. That Paul referred to attempts to persuade the Galatians to accept circumcision (5:2-4, 12; 6:12-13[13]) suggests an approach which believed circumcision to be a vital feature of God's covenant with His people, Israel, and that would carry with it the need to obey God's Law as mediated through Moses (it is a priori unlikely that Paul's opponents would only require circumcision by itself).[14]

---

10. See Morland, *Rhetoric of Curse in Galatians*, for a thorough exploration of the significance of Paul's utterance of a curse.

11. My phraseology is based on the assumption that those whom Paul describes as unsettling the Galatians had come from outside, rather than being indigenous Galatians (i.e., Gentile), whether Christians (as some have argued, e.g., Munck, *Paul and the Salvation of Mankind*, 87-134; Gaston, *Paul and the Torah*, 7-8, 25, 209n8), or proselytes (so Nanos, *Irony*).

12. E.g., Lyons, *Pauline Autobiography*, 96-105; Barclay, *Mirror Reading a Polemical Letter*, 73-93. To give an example, Longenecker, *Triumph of Abraham's God*, 150-56, is right that Paul's language has connotations of the evil eye (3:1) and sorcery (4:16). That would be Paul's interpretation of his opponents' attitude and tactics. They themselves would no doubt be horrified by such accusations. See Esler, *Galatians*, 64-68, for a cautious defense of a careful mirror reading.

13. The exact meaning of οἱ περιτεμνόμενοι is disputed: it could mean "those who advocate circumcision" or "those who have got, or let themselves be, circumcised." In the latter case, they would be former Gentiles who had become proselytes. See Nanos, *Irony*, 234-42, for a full discussion of the various possibilities.

14. Kwon, *Eschatology*, 207-211, believes that the opponents were selective in what they taught of the demands of the Law: they stressed the privileges of the Jews in terms of the history of salvation without sufficient attention to God's moral demands, but this is unconvincing in view of the high value placed on the Law in Judaism. Sanger, *Die Verkündigung des Gekreuzigte und Israel*, 267, thinks that the Galatian Christians believed that circumcision and the observance of Jewish festival days was sufficient. This takes account of the specific references in the letter to circumcision (5:2-4, 12; 6:12-13) and the reference to special days (4:10), but why should the Galatian Christians have

Given the link between Abraham and circumcision, which was a sign of the eternal covenant made by God with him and his descendants in the passage at Genesis 17, and given that Paul discussed the question of who was a true descendant of Abraham (3:6-29), we may feel on firm ground in thinking that the opponents appealed to God's eternal covenant with Abraham as the basis of belonging to the people of God. For them, the coming of Jesus the Messiah did not in any way invalidate that covenant. Therefore, Gentile people like the Galatians, in order truly to enjoy the blessings given to the people of God and to be counted among the descendants of Abraham, needed to be circumcised. In that way they would receive the full blessings which Jesus the Messiah had brought. Circumcision was to be a mark of Abraham's descendants forever. This much suffices for our purposes.

Paul referred to the Galatians observing certain special days, months, and seasons, and this could refer to the regulations about Israel's days of worship included in the Law (4:10). Indeed, Paul charged them with a desire, having begun initially with the experience of the Spirit, to achieve "perfection" through doing what the Law required (3:2-5; cf. 4:21, where Paul referred to those who desire to be under the Law).

There is a remarkable charge made by Paul against the Galatians in 4:9: that they were returning to "the weak and poverty-stricken στοιχεια," to whom they wished to be in subjection all over again (4:9). This is predominantly seen as one of Paul's most severe criticisms of the Law in Galatians: that, in effect, by putting themselves under the Law, the Galatians would be coming under renewed subjection to angelic powers. It would be factually equivalent to going back to the slavery of their pagan days.[15] Nanos (in accordance with his view that the "influencers" were non-Christian representatives of the Jewish Synagogue authorities in Galatia) takes a literal view of the charge: he believes that the "influencers" had encouraged the Galatian believers in Jesus, who were a sub-group of the Jewish community, before they received circumcision, to return to participating in pagan religious ceremonies in order not to offend the local authorities and thus create difficulties for the Synagogue vis-à-vis those local authorities.[16] This view has its attractions, but it raises the question of whether the

---

thought that the food laws were not that important?

15. Schlier, *Der Brief an die Galater*, 203; Bonnard, *Galates*, 90; Betz, *Galatians*, 216-17; Mussner, *Der Galaterbrief*, 303; Longenecker, *Galatians*, 181; Dunn, *Epistle to the Galatians*, 225-26; Martyn, *Galatians*, 411. Bruce, *Epistle to the Galatians*, 203, speaks of legalism as the enslaving power (following Caird, *Principalities and Powers*, 53).

16. Nanos, *Irony*, 257-63. Esler, *Galatians*, 92, also believes that some were at risk of crossing back over into the realm of Gentile idolatry, appealing to 4:9 and 5:20 but without discussion.

Christian believers were a sub-group of the Jewish community and under its jurisdiction.[17] As Bird has remarked, the contours of the debate possess an intra-Christian character.[18]

That the Galatians were coming under some pressure could be suggested also by 4:17, where Paul indicated that those who "*seek*" to persuade them are motivated by a desire to exclude the Galatians so that they will "*seek*" these people. The unsettlers (to use Paul's phrase) could thus have indicated that the Galatians were not fully members of the people of God (hence "exclude" them), and Paul interpreted this as motivated by the aim of making the Galatians covet this status all the more and so come to depend on these people.[19]

Clearly, Paul hoped by his letter to nullify the effect of these "unsettlers." We, of course, do not know whether any or how many, if any, Galatians had actually taken the step of becoming circumcised; if some had, then Paul was aiming at those who had not taken the step. There is a reference to rivalry and back-biting among them, and this could be an indication that a competitive spirit, in terms of keeping the regulations of the Law, had begun to operate in the congregation (5:15).[20] But caution is needed in case we over-interpret, and scholars are divided as to whether there is a concrete or general reference behind 5:15.[21]

---

17. Bird, *Crossing Land and Sea*, 141. He asks whether in this case Paul would characterize the teaching which he opposed as "another gospel" (1:6–9) and doubts whether the charge of avoiding persecution on account of the cross (6:12) would fit non-Christian Jews.

18. Bird, *Crossing*, 141.

19. This suggestion by Paul seems more consonant with people coming from outside the Galatian congregations rather than the problem arising from Galatian Christians themselves feeling uncertain about their status and so wanting circumcision in order to come within the eternal covenant with Abraham and his descendants.

20. So Bonnard, *Galates* 109; Mussner, *Galaterbrief*, 373–74, are prepared to entertain the possibility that Paul is warning against what *might* happen if the Galatians turn to Judaism, for a casuistic legalism all too easily destroys αγαπη.

21. Those who think that this is a general remark include Betz, *Galatians*, 277; Dunn, *Galatians*, 292–93; cf. Merk, *Handeln aus Glauben*, 70n35. On the other hand, Schlier, *Galater*, 246; Bruce, *Galatians*, 242; Longenecker, *Galatians*, 244; Martyn, *Galatians*, 491; Barrett, *Freedom and Obligation*, 74; Barclay, *Obeying the Truth*, 153; *Gift*, 432–34 (pointing to how self advertisement, rivalry, and public competition were a perpetual cause of tension in everyday life, while warning against too speculative assessments); Esler, *Galatians*, 92, 225–26 (who sees some of Paul's Gentile converts falling back into the viciously competitive practices characteristic of the Mediterranean region); Cummins, *Paul and the Crucified Christ*, 104–5; Hoppe, *Paranese und Theologie im Galaterbrief*, 214, 225–27, all do see a reference to contentiousness in the congregations. Martyn thinks that the agitators have attributed this trait to the work of the "Impulsive Flesh," which can only be corrected by adherence to the Law. Nanos,

1.2.2. Galatians 1:6–17

Having mentioned that Paul dispensed with the customary thanksgiving for the recipients, we need also to mention how Paul spent a fair amount of space maintaining that he had not received his gospel from human sources but through a revelation from God about Jesus Christ (1:11–12; cf. 1:15) and how he proceeded to give a rough outline of his life story before and after this revelation.[22] He had been a persecutor of the church of God and had been zealous for the ancestral traditions of Judaism,[23] but then God revealed His Son to (or in) him with the purpose that he should preach the gospel to Gentiles (1:15–16); i.e., the decision to preach the gospel to Gentiles had not been a purely personal decision by Paul under his own initiative, but by divine purpose and command.

In giving an account of his life in Judaism before the revelation concerning Jesus, Paul had his eyes on the situation in Galatia. As one who once was deeply immersed in a life given over to obeying the Torah, he knew what he was talking about and could speak with authority about matters pertaining to the Law, circumcision, and other regulations. Those years in Judaism had a negative relevance for his work as an apostle in general and in Galatia in particular.[24]

We may at this point seek to discern the consequences for Paul's future as a result of this "revelation" given by God to Paul.[25] In the first place, Paul

---

Irony, 113, 218–25, 272–73, takes this verse as applying to what he calls the "influencers": they had a competitive spirit, and so it becomes a warning of what could happen if the Galatians accept circumcision and, thus, proselyte status.

22. A widespread view among scholars has been that Paul was defending himself against the charge that he was inferior and subordinate to the Jerusalem church leaders. Phrased like this, this view has some cogency. If, however, it is argued that his opponents criticized Paul for being *dependent* on Jerusalem, then such a view is open to the criticism that the opponents would hardly criticize Paul for such a dependence, as Ruth Schäfer, *Paulus bis zum Apostelkonzil*, 42, cogently points out. (She mentions W. Lütgert and A. Fridrichsen as having earlier pointed to this weakness.) More recently, the view has been put forward that Paul is not giving a defense of his apostleship but rather was seeking to show that the Gospel is not based on human effort but how God lays hold of individuals and changes them. See Lyons, *Pauline Autobiography*, 123–76; Gaventa, *Galatians 1 and 2*, 309–326; Lategan, *Is Paul Defending His Apostleship in Galatians?*, 411–30; Martyn, *Galatians*, 157; Witherington, *Grace in Galatia*, 73–74. Cf. Barclay, *Paul's Story*, 133–56, esp. 138–46.

23. For an extremely detailed examination of Galatians 1:13–14, see Niebuhr, *Heidenapostel*, 19–43.

24. Niebuhr, *Heidenapostel*, 20–21.

25. The list of consequences mentioned by Kraus, *Gottes Gerechtigkeit und Gottes Volk*, 337–38, differs slightly from what is offered here. Kraus lists a new view of the person and way of Jesus; Paul's zeal for the Law had to be pondered on; and the revelation

clearly *learned a new estimate of Jesus*.²⁶ Previously, he had in all probability regarded Jesus who had been crucified as someone cursed by God.²⁷ On the Damascus Road, he learned that this Jesus was none other than God's Son and that God had clearly vindicated him by raising him from the dead and glorifying him. The one whom he had previously regarded as cursed by God and an apostate outside the community of the people of God, had been declared in the right by God.²⁸ This "Christology" was bound to involve a considerable rethink of Paul's previous attitudes, both of the person of Jesus and the meaning of his death on the cross.

Here is a suitable place to mention that Wright has argued, against the case asserted by Sanders that Paul moved from solution (Christ) to the problem (people were sinners needing to be saved), that the pre-Christian Paul already had a problem: viz. that Israel's "exile" remained even though physically (many) Jews had returned from Babylon centuries before. Pagans ruled over Israel and the Holy Land; and many Jews collaborated with these pagan rulers; evil seemed rampant the world over. Yet God had not intervened to right these wrongs and vindicate His own holiness. Now in the Damascus Road experience, Paul learned that God had intervened to right the wrongs in the world, even though He had done so in an unprecedented and astonishing manner in the crucified Jesus.²⁹

Secondly, *he learned afresh the sense of the grace of God*. He who had been opposing God's purposes expressed through Jesus, and, then, through the followers of Jesus, had, nonetheless, been forgiven and taken up into the service of God and His Son. If, as we may readily grant, Paul knew about the grace of the God of Israel in electing Israel to be His people, his experience on the Damascus Road brought home to him in a vivid, personal way just how gracious God was ("called me by His grace" [Gal 1:15; 2:9; cf. 1 Cor 3:10; 15:10; Rom 1:5]). No wonder that we find Paul

---

was the ground on which the legitimation of his apostleship to the Gentiles was based.

26. Donaldson, *Paul and the Gentiles*, 16, 18, 27, 45–46, 76–78, 150, 169, 213, 250–51, 271, 289, 297, 304, constantly stresses this point.

27. Dietzfelbringer, *Die Berufung des Paulus*, 33–37; Hengel, *Pre-Christian Paul*, 83–84; Niebuhr, *Heidenapostel*, 72; Donaldson, *Remapping*, 288; Dunn, *New Perspective on Paul*, 351.

28. If we draw in also 1 Corinthians 9:1–2; 15:3–8; 2 Corinthians 4:4–6, then the titles or designations Lord, Christ, and Image/radiance of God's glory flowed from the experience on the Damascus Road. Cf. Dietzfelbringer, *Berufung*, 64–74. (Dietzfelbringer refers to Paul's momentous experience as his "Damascus experience." In the English speaking world, the phrase "Damascus Road experience" has become the standard terminology. I retain this without entering into a discussion of whether Paul's experience took place en route for Damascus or at Damascus itself.)

29. Wright, *Pauline Perspectives*, 201, 296–97.

emphasizing the grace of God in his message (e.g., Rom 3:24; 5:15–21)! But we can go a step further. If he who had resisted God's purposes could receive God's grace, then who among sinners could be excluded from being recipients of that same grace? In his experience of the grace of God, there was *the seed of universalism*.

Thirdly, he *learned that he had a new task for the future—to preach the gospel of this Jesus to the Gentiles*.[30] There is no need to postulate that this conviction only dawned on Paul several years later.[31] On this point, the narratives in Acts about Paul's Damascus Road experience (9:15; 22:15, 21; 26:17–23) cohere with what Paul says here in Galatians 1:16. A further point to be borne in mind is the fact that Paul says that after God's revelation of His Son, "*immediately*" without conferring with any human beings, he went to Arabia. The old view of spending time in Arabia in a kind of spiritual retreat to work out what his experience meant is now abandoned, and there is scholarly consensus that Paul preached the Gospel of Jesus Christ in Arabia. This suggests that Paul had already concluded that his future work lay in taking the Gospel to the wider world, even if there was a Jewish population there.

It is clear that Paul described his call in terms drawn from the passage in Isaiah 49:1–6, where the servant of God was given a task to take the light of God's salvation to the end of the earth.[32] Dietzbringer sees this as confirmation for a close link between Paul's call and his actual mission work which included Gentiles as well as Jews. He also believes that Paul's reference (2 Cor 11:32–33) to the fact that the ethnarch of Damascus, an officer of King Aretas, wanted to arrest Paul and guarded the city gates with the aim of preventing

---

30. Ruth Schäfer, *Paulus*, 109, points out that revelation and sending form for Paul an indissoluble unity, and that his becoming a disciple of Jesus and becoming an apostle could not be separated in his experience. She goes on to comment that it is impossible in Paul's view to recognize his conversion as worked by God without in the same breath attributing this quality to his commission to preach the Gospel among the Gentiles.

31. Caird, *Apostolic Age*, 120, maintained, "The period of readjustment was probably quite short." Dietzfelbringer, *Berufung*, 137–46, also argues for a close link between Paul's call and his missionary work which embraced Gentiles. See also Dunn, *Light to the Gentiles*, 258–65; Blaschke, *Beschneidung*, 365–66, 367. On the other hand, Watson, *PJG*, 59–60, denies that his call had a fairly immediate effect on Paul's understanding of his life's work, and believes (79–82, 96–99) that it was Jewish resistance to the preaching of the Gospel which led to a self-conscious Gentile mission. Barclay, *Gift*, 361, suggests that Paul's interpretation of the Christ-gift took place over many years alongside Gentile converts gifted with the Spirit. He lists a number of factors—Paul's experience, his rereading of Scripture, reflection on the story of Jesus, and extended interaction with "un-judaized" believers—which led to his formulation.

32. E.g., Dietzfelbringer, *Berufung*, 141. If the account of Jeremiah's call (1:4–10) has also exerted some influence, then it should be borne in mind that God appointed him to be "a prophet to the nations."

his departure, probably means that Paul's preaching of a law-free gospel had aroused opposition among the Jewish population of the city.[33]

Here we might mention a point which Wright has stressed in respect to the impact which Paul's Damascus Road experience made on him in relation to the manner in which the work of God should be carried out. Prior to the Damascus Road experience, he had been extremely zealous for the traditional customs of his people. His role model would have been men like Phinehas and Elijah of old who had been willing to resort to violence in defence of Yahwism. Paul himself had employed violent methods against the followers of Jesus. Wright suggests that through the revelation on the Damascus Road, Paul surrendered the ideal of violent zeal for the role of the servant of Isaiah.[34]

In the fourth place, there is another aspect, one which is not overtly stated but which we may legitimately deduce from what Paul said. He referred to his zealous pursuit of the ancestral customs and traditions of his people, and that obviously means striving to keep the Law, no doubt in accordance with the Pharisaic tradition (see Phil 3:5). It was because of this zeal for the Law and tradition that Paul persecuted the followers of Jesus, seeing in them a threat to Israel's heritage. And where had this zeal brought him? He found out that he was resisting God's purposes, rejecting God's chosen Messiah and Son, and persecuting "the church of God"! Zeal for the Law had brought him into collision with God. Zeal for the Law had made him into an enemy of God.[35] *It is not putting the matter too strongly to say that inevitably, given his personal history, the Law was going to be a "problem" for Paul.*[36] There is the additional factor that—accepting the historicity of a

---

33. Dietzfelbringer, *Berufung*, 143–44. Thurén, *Derhetorizing Paul*, 155–64, has suggested that the OT concept of universal monotheism (e.g., Isa 45:21–23; Zech 14:9), which would come to pass at the End, was seen by Paul as in the process of realization, because Jesus had opened up the way to the God of Israel for all nations, and for this to become a reality the barrier between Israel and the nations which the Law constituted needed to be eliminated. "Active Gentile mission can be seen as an unavoidable result of this theological turn" (Thurén, *Derhetorizing Paul*, 164).

34. See Wright, *Pauline Perspectives*, 152–59; cf. *Pauline Perspectives*, 568.

35. See Caird, *Apostolic Age*, 122; Dietzfelbringer, *Berufung*, 96.

36. Cf. Caird, *Apostolic Age*, 122. I personally heard Caird say this sort of thing in lectures in Oxford in the early 1960s. It is only hinted at in his *New Testament Theology*, 15, 92. Haacker, *Verdienste und Grenzen*, 9, makes the comment that the encounter with Christ showed that Paul's concept of a life of Pharisaic zeal and persecution of the church of God was wrong. See also Stolle, *Nomos zwischen Tora und Lex*, 60. Thus, we dissent from the view of Esler, *Galatians*, 178, who thinks that Paul's interest in the Law was reactive and that he was dragged into discussion about it when difficulties arose over relationships between Jewish and Gentile Christians in his mixed congregations. Tobin, *Paul's Rhetoric*, 55, even goes so far as to say that the Damascus Road experience

trial of Jesus before the Sanhedrin and their condemnation of him—Jesus had been condemned in some sense or other as a breaker of the Law in Jewish eyes, and yet God had vindicated him in the resurrection and glorified him. The members of the Sanhedrin, representatives of the Jewish nation, had in the name of the Law and the nation rejected their Messiah. A still further aspect of this issue is the fact that the Law had pronounced the curse on Jesus who was the obedient Son of God. How had it come about that this had happened?[37] These were some of the issues in relation to the Law with which Paul had to grapple as a result of his momentous encounter with the risen, glorified Jesus on the road to Damascus. We shall assume that the revelation, given to Paul on the Damascus Road, was going to raise questions for him about the place and purpose of the Law in God's dealings with Israel and the world. Paul would have been forced to have worked out a different understanding of how the Law fitted into God's purposes after his experience.[38] This would be part of a new interpretation of biblical traditions,[39] of which his use of Genesis 15:6 is a striking example.

The impact, then, of his conversion/call must be borne in mind when we consider some of Paul's statements about the Law and its relation to Jesus Christ.[40]

Fifthly, and finally, *Paul received what we can call a new identity* through his encounter with the risen Jesus on the Road to Damascus.[41] Previously, he had been zealous for the Law and the ancestral traditions of

---

showed Paul that the Law was no longer obligatory for believers.

37. This point is especially stressed by Dietzfelbringer, *Berufung*, 98–100. He speaks of the Torah's being possessed by the curse and how the cross reveals its curse-character. As we see from Romans, Paul held on to the fact that the Law was God's Law and yet argued in Romans 7 that Sin had got hold of it and used it for its own ends, against the original intention of the Law. The seeds of this dialectic are there in the Damascus Road experience.

38. Cf. Donaldson, *Remapping*, 268, 292. We can see this revision in what Paul said later (Phil 3:7–11).

39. Cf. Haacker, *Verdienste und Grenzen*, 9.

40. For studies of Paul's conversion/call, see esp. Wilckens, "Die Bekehrung des Paulus," 11–32; Dupont, *Conversion of Paul*, 176–94; Luz, *Das Geschichtsverständnis des Paulus*, 216–20, esp. 218–20; Kim, *Origins of Paul's Gospel*. In his *Paul and the New Perspective*, 1–84, Kim responds with a severe critique of Dunn's criticism of his own interpretation of the Damascus Road experience, for which, see Dunn, *Jesus, Paul, and the Law*, 89–107; Stuhlmacher, *Purpose of Romans*, 344–45; Dietzfelbringer, *Berufung* (to which Dunn, *Jesus, Paul, and the Law*, 105–6, responds). The comment of Wright in his Tyndale Lecture of 1978 is one which he repeats in several other places: "Paul's life and thought flow consistently from his vision on the Damascus Road" (*Pauline Perspectives*, 20; cf. 8–9). See also Sprinkle, *Paul & Judaism Revisited*, 244–49.

41. Barclay, *Gift*, 356–60.

Israel. Now, the Law was no longer central to that identity, but rather the Jesus who had been crucified and whom God had raised. Paul described this transformation as having been crucified with Christ to the Law, and, as a consequence, it was no longer he but Christ who lived in him and was the influence and motivating power of Paul's motives, thoughts, and actions (2:19–20). Barclay puts it thus: "The revelation of God's Son undercut his loyalty to the cultural norms he once considered authoritative."[42]

1.2.3. Galatians 1:18–2:10

Resuming Paul's story in Galatians, after the statement that he, without consulting with any human authority, had gone to Arabia and had no immediate contact with those in Jerusalem who were apostles before him (1:16b–17), there follows the reference to his first visit to Jerusalem, which in fact occurred three years later, and then lasted only a fortnight, during which he only saw[43] Cephas (Peter) and James the Lord's brother. The brevity of the stay was far too short for any prolonged training.[44] After this brief stay in Jerusalem (he does not appear to have visited any of the churches in Judea, to judge by verse 22), Paul went off and preached the gospel in Syria and Cilicia (v. 21), a report of which reached the ears of the Judean churches who praised God as a result (vv. 23–24).

Thus far, Paul had sought to establish the assertion that he had made at 1:11–12. Then he went on to mention his second visit to Jerusalem which took place either after or during[45] the fourteen years after this revelatory experience.[46] Paul appears here to be distancing himself from any suggestion that he had submitted to the Jerusalem church leaders (the "Pillars").[47] There

---

42. Barclay, *Gift*, 359.

43. See Hofius, "Gal 1:18," 255–67, for convincing arguments that ιστορησαι means to get to know Cephas personally rather than "to get information about" (against Kilpatrick and Dunn).

44. DeSilva, *Interpreting Galatians*, 138.

45. See Schäfer, *Paulus*, 163–67, for arguments in favor of taking δια with a genitive referring to time, here as meaning "during" rather than "after:" Paul went up at some point during the fourteen years, probably nearer the end of this time span. See Bauer, *Lexicon*, 178–79, for the two possibilities, though Bauer himself lists Galatians 2:1 under passages denoting an interval *after*.

46. It is not absolutely certain whether the fourteen years is exactly after the revelatory experience or fourteen years after the three years. For our purposes, it does not really matter.

47. On the "Pillars," see Barrett, "Paul and the 'Pillar' Apostles," 1–19.

appears to be something of a shift in the direction of the flow of the argument in 2:1–10 (even if Jerusalem figures in both 1:15–24; 2:1–10).[48]

Paul's account not only began by saying that he went up to Jerusalem on the basis of a revelation from God (and, by implication, not because of any command from the Jerusalem church leaders), but it also emphatically maintained that the Jerusalem apostles had not added anything to his version of the gospel (v. 6d),[49] nor had one of his colleagues, a Gentile called Titus, been forced to be circumcised (vv. 3–5). (We note that at this point Paul referred specifically to the Galatians—he had successfully resisted all demands and/or suggestions that Titus should be circumcised "in order that the truth of the gospel might continue with *you*.")[50]

The main point of the account is that Paul's apostleship to the Gentiles had been recognized by the pillars[51] of the Jerusalem church as equally valid as Peter's apostleship to the Jewish people; and they had exchanged the right hand of fellowship with him and Barnabas (vv. 7–9). By implication, the agreement recognized that Gentiles brought to faith in Paul's mission should not be required to be circumcised, while those Jews coming to belief in Jesus would still be expected to observe the requirements of the Law even if such compliance did not contribute to gaining salvation.[52] It is worth pointing out that many interpreters believe that the issue of sharing table fellowship, including the Lord's Supper, between law-observant Jewish Christians and Gentile Christians in mixed congregations was not dealt

---

48. See DeSilva, *Interpreting Galatians*, 99–100, 138. In varying ways, Schlier, *Galater*, 64; Bonnard, *Galates*, 35; Mussner, *Galaterbrief*, 100, see a shift from proving that his gospel did not stem from humans to official recognition by the Jerusalem authorities of Paul's "independent" gospel. Cf. Longenecker, *Galatians*, 44, 61; Schäfer, *Paulus*, 160, who heads the section Galatians 2:1–10, "Recognition of the Pauline Gospel in Jerusalem by the Pillars." Those who think that Paul is still defending his assertion that his gospel was not of human origin include Betz, *Galatians*, 83; Dunn, *Galatians*, 87.

49. The request that Paul and Barnabas should "remember the poor" within the Jerusalem Christian community (v. 10) clearly in Paul's mind did not constitute any diminution of the recognition of the gospel which he preached.

50. The JB gets the sense of this with a paraphrase: "To safeguard the true meaning of the Good News for you." Esler, *Galatians*, 130, believes that as soon as Paul took Titus with them to Jerusalem, the issue of table fellowship was inevitably raised (for Esler, table fellowship is sharing the eucharist). He may be right, but there might be a Greek-speaking Christian group in Jerusalem, where Titus could have shared worship and the Lord's Supper. According to Acts 21:16, Paul and his colleagues lodged in Jerusalem with Mnason of Cyprus (so Haenchen, *Acts*, 607; Marshall, *Acts*, 341).

51. See Walter, *Die "als Säulen Geltenden" in Jerusalem*, 78–92, for the suggestion that "pillars" picks up a general Jewish designation for outstandingly pious observers of the Law rather than pillars of the church conceived of as the eschatological temple.

52. See Schnelle, *Mutz ein Heide*, 98–101.

with, and that this "blew up" a little later and then had to be dealt with. If this view is correct, the agreement involved either a deliberate fudging of the issue or an extraordinary naivety on the part of the participants. A number of scholars, including Ruth Schäfer believe, on the other hand, that the Jerusalem pillars did accept that the recognition of the Antiochene mission would involve close fellowship between Jewish and Gentile followers of Jesus in the Syria-Cilicia area.[53] What the Jerusalem agreement did not deal with was what would happen if law-observant Jewish Christians visited mixed congregations, and claimed the right to live as law observant Jews.[54] We shall return to this issue later.

We may pause here and consider why Paul was so concerned to lay out the account of what had happened at Jerusalem. It may be that the opponents in Galatia had insinuated that Paul was not of the same standing as the leaders of the Jerusalem church. These leaders had, after all, been personal followers of Jesus. They had had that personal contact with him, whereas Paul had not had that privilege. They also had been recipients of an appearance of the risen Jesus after his resurrection. There is a certain defensive tone in this section (1:17–2:10) which could justify this interpretation. On the other hand, it could be that Paul stressed that his gospel originated from God because that gospel was under attack, rather than that he was personally.[55] Yet another explanation is possible: that Paul narrated how he had withstood the pressure to have Titus circumcised in order to encourage the Galatians to follow his own example and resist the pressure on them to be circumcised.[56] It could be a case of both/and in respect of the second and third explanations.

We may also raise the question of who were behind those who were active in the Galatian churches and were preaching there? Did they in fact have backers or senders to whom they were responsible? The answer to that will depend on whether we think of those in Galatia whom Paul attacks as Jewish Christians or Jews. If they were Jewish Christians, did they come from within the Jerusalem church? Those whom Paul called "the false brothers" (2:4) come to mind. They presumably had never accepted the agreement made between the "pillars" of the Jerusalem church and the Antioch church represented by Barnabas and Paul.[57] They may have grown in

53. Schäfer, *Paulus*, 229.
54. Schäfer, *Paulus*, 233.
55. So Wisdom, *Blessing*, 133; Cummins, *Paul*, 109–114.
56. Nanos, *Irony*, 152.
57. Esler, *Galatians*, 132, goes so far as to assert that their defeat would have left the advocates of Gentile circumcision wanting revenge.

influence subsequent to the meeting in Jerusalem. They may have exerted some—even if not a dominant—influence on James, and this would be congruous with the reference to James's request to Peter and the other Jewish Christians at Antioch in the incident recorded by Paul (2:11–14). On the other hand, Paul did not draw a direct link between the false brothers of 2:4 and those in Galatia whom he attacked. The latter could have been answerable to Jewish authorities in Galatia, and Paul's purpose could have been to encourage the Galatian believers to resist the demand for circumcision as he had done in the case of Titus.[58]

1.2.4. Galatians 2:11–21

Following this account of visits to Jerusalem, Paul told the story of what has come to be known as the "Antioch incident" (from 2:11 onwards). Peter had come to Antioch, where he had fitted in with the practice in the Antioch congregation and had had table fellowship with Gentile Christians.[59] However, messengers from James (who, we may assume, had by this time, in the absence of Peter from Jerusalem, become leader of the church there) had arrived and, presumably as a result of a message from James,[60] Peter and other Jewish Christians, including Barnabas, had withdrawn[61] from table fellowship with Gentile Christians (thus, in effect, bringing a division into the church, which, up till then, had apparently[62] enjoyed harmonious relationships among its members).

An immense amount of literature has been written on this incident, and, indeed, it has been described as one of the most important events in

---

58. So Nanos, *Irony*, 147–58.

59. The συνησθιεν in verse 12 has an iterative sense: "He used to eat." Paul does not say why Peter behaved as he did. Had he been influenced by the approach of Jesus, who dined with tax-collectors and sinners, or had he, now a travelling missionary preacher to his Jewish compatriots, adopted the kind of approach which Paul assumed and which he outlined in 1 Corinthians 9:19–23?

60. Peter's change of behavior, plus that of Barnabas, would be hard to explain unless James was behind those who had come from Jerusalem. See Dunn, *Dialogue Progresses*, 421–22.

61. Schäfer, *Paulus*, 235, 239–43, takes the imperfects υπεστελλεν και αφωριζεν in verse 12b as conatives, believing that Paul reacted swiftly to avert the damage to the fellowship of the Antiochene congregation.

62. I say apparently, because it *could be* that there were Jewish Christians in the church at Antioch who were unhappy about the table fellowship current in the church and communicated their reservations to James and the Jerusalem church, and possibly asked for a ruling or some intervention. This is a possibility canvassed in Wehnert, *Die Reinheit*, 126, 266.

the story of the earliest church.⁶³ Most scholars probably assume that James exerted pressure on Peter and the other Jewish Christians out of either hostility towards Paul or deep reservations about his version of the gospel, despite the Jerusalem agreement. (Romans 15:30-31 is certainly evidence that towards the end of his ministry as a free man Paul was aware of suspicions about him at Jerusalem both among unbelieving and believing Jews alike.) This view entails a picture of a growing rift in the nascent Christian movement between an increasingly conservative Jerusalem church under James and the Pauline wing of the church.

There is another possibility which was suggested by the late T. W. Manson⁶⁴ and which has been also put forward in a sharpened form by a number of other scholars without necessarily mentioning Manson's contribution.⁶⁵ Manson maintained that in view of how suspicious the devout Jew was of partaking of Gentile hospitality, many in the Jerusalem church were shocked at Peter's behavior, and that James was concerned that, if news got around generally in Jerusalem that Peter and other Jewish Christians were having table fellowship with uncircumcised Gentiles, this would redound unfavorably upon the Christian community in Jerusalem and would expose it to criticism from the Pharisees and other ultra-orthodox Jews.⁶⁶ Subsequent contribu-

---

63. So Dunn, "Incident at Antioch," 162.

64. See Manson, "Problem of the Epistle to the Galatians," 168-89, esp. 180-81. This was originally a lecture given at the John Rylands Library in 1940 and published that same year in *BJRL* 24. Manson gave no indication that he was here agreeing with a view expressed earlier by any scholar. On the continent, Munck, *Paul*, 106-7; Schmithals, *Paul and James*, 61-78, esp. 66-67, reached a conclusion similar to that of Manson, though they were unaware of Manson's work. The *BJRL* article would be unavailable in Denmark and Germany because of the War, and it was not published in Manson's *Studies* until 1962. In England, Dix, *Jew and Greek*, 41-43, (not available to me) also maintained that "those of the circumcision" were non-Christian Jews.

65. E.g., Reicke, *Der geschichtliche Hintergrund*, 176-83; Nickle, *Collection*, 64-66; Jewett, *Agitators and the Galatian Congregation*, 198-212, esp. 294-96; Schütz, *Paul and the Anatomy of Apostolic Authority*, 153-54; Hengel, *Acts and the History of Earliest Christianity*, 113; Roloff, *Die Apostelgeschichte*, 312-13; Bruce, *Galatians*, 130; Marxsen, *Sündige tapfer*, 81-82; Pesch, *Die Apostelgeschichte*, 2:222; Wehnert, *Reinheit*, 253, 267; Watson, *PJG*, 106-7, have all argued in varying degrees for the increasing pressure of Jewish nationalism as the background of James's intervention. See Dunn, "Incident at Antioch," 137-48, for a discussion of Jewish attitudes to table fellowship in Second Temple Judaism in the first century; of the deteriorating political situation in Palestine; of the increasingly polemical responses by Jews to this situation; and of the potential consequences of this for the new Christian movement there; more briefly in *Galatians*, 123. See Nanos for criticism of Dunn's view of Jewish attitudes to table fellowship with non-Jews in this period.

66. Cf. the exhortation in the book of Jubilees: "Separate yourself from the Gentiles, and do not eat with them . . . and do not become associates of theirs, because all their deeds are defiled and all of their ways are contaminated and despicable and abominable" (22:16).

tions have pointed to the increasing nationalistic atmosphere, from the 40s AD on, among Jews in Israel in opposition to Roman rule, and the consequent pressure this exerted on the Jerusalem believers. Manson thought that James acted without thinking of what the effect of his request might be on the Antioch church itself. His sole concern was with his own church's position. Manson actually took the phrase φοβουμενος τους εκ περιτομης (literally "fearing those of the circumcision") as referring to both Christian and non-Christian Jews back in Jerusalem. The latter could find in Peter's behavior an extra ground of complaint against the Christian community that they were being unfaithful to the ancestral faith, while the former would share that kind of viewpoint. Indeed, the former group would be ultra-conservative Jews, precisely the kind of people who had visited Galatia. Manson's view is certainly possible. As mentioned, a number of scholars have argued along somewhat similar lines, and something like it now figures in Dunn's most recent attempt to explain James's conduct.[67]

It would have the advantage of not envisaging a virtual split between Jewish and Gentile Christianity, the latter as represented by the Pauline mission. In the intervening decade, the increasing number of Gentile converts, perhaps beginning to outnumber Jewish Christians in churches founded by Paul, began to set alarm bells ringing in the minds of conservative Jewish Christians[68] and to deepen already held suspicions of Paul. These deepened suspicions would then be in his mind when he wrote Romans 15:30–31.

If, however, Nanos is right and those whom Paul attacks were Galatian Jews seeking to persuade the Galatian Christians to accept circumcision, then the purpose behind narrating 2:11–21 would be to insist that as Paul had stood up to Peter, so in Galatia there should be no capitulation to this demand for circumcision.[69] But, against Nanos's view, as Watson has pointed out,[70] it is difficult to see why chapters 1–2 were included if the opposition came from local Jews in Galatia.

An exegetical problem is where does Paul's account of what he said to Peter finish? Furthermore, how far is what he wrote conditioned by the situation in Galatia itself? Clearly Paul had his eyes on that situation as well as the incident at Antioch. Rhetorically speaking, he is building up to his case against the Galatians, so that there are good grounds for supposing that verses 14–21 blends the two situations together.[71]

---

67. Dunn, *Beginning from Jerusalem*, 1084–85.
68. This phrase is used in Dunn, *New Perspective*, 38.
69. Nanos, *Irony*, 152–54.
70. Watson, *PJG*, 113n37.
71. So, e.g., Mussner, *Galaterbrief*, 145–46; Martyn, *Galatians*, 229–30. Barclay, *Gift*,

Paul tackled Peter on the grounds of inconsistent behavior which was not in accord with the heart of the gospel, nor with the agreement reached between the Jerusalem pillars and the Antiochene delegation. Peter had as a Jew lived in table fellowship with Gentiles and not in accordance with strict Jewish dietary rules (2:14a); so, Paul asked, how could he now compel Gentiles to live like Jews? (2:14b). The phrase "compel Gentiles to live like Jews" refers to the actual practical consequences of Peter's conduct (and that of the other Jewish Christians, including Barnabas) if a united church was to be maintained at Antioch and if two separate churches, one of Jewish Christians and the other of Gentile Christians, were not to arise.

Paul did not say what the result of his remonstration to Peter was. Probably the majority of scholars assume that Paul was unsuccessful in getting Peter and the other Jewish Christians, including Barnabas, to change.[72] In support, they generally point to the fact that Paul's association with Barnabas came to an end and Paul seems to have become less linked with the Antioch church but began to branch out with new colleagues who were not members of the congregation there. On the other hand, if Paul had "lost the day," would he have mentioned the episode? Presumably his opponents in Galatia would be aware of what had happened at Antioch (the event would inevitably become known). There is surely cogency in the view that he would hardly have mentioned the event if it had turned out unfavorable.[73]

Then Paul wrote "we who are Jews by birth and not Gentiles sinners" (2:15).[74] This description of Gentiles would be regarded by many Jews as a "given": Gentiles were sinners, but Jews were not to be so classified.[75]

366, points out that the whole passage (2:11–21) is a literary unit and explains Paul's challenge to Peter and unfolds the truth of the Gospel, irrespective of how much (if any) Paul actually said to Peter.

72. See the long list (forty-five names!) in Schäfer, *Paulus*, 240n73.

73. See Schäfer, *Paulus*, 240–43. Her list of those who had previously espoused this view includes thirteen names. She believes that Paul did prevail and that the breach in fellowship was a short intermezzo in the story of the Antiochene congregation. In his account Paul did not enlarge on the outcome as he did not wish to push the disagreement with Cephas into a definitive break between Cephas and himself nor did he want it to lead to a break-up of the agreement reached in Jerusalem.

74. This is probably a nominative pendens construction, with the language drawn from Jewish polemic (see, e.g., Kümmel, *Individualgeschichte*, 159; Dunn, *Galatians*, 132–33). The suggestion that verses 15 and 16 should be taken as two antithetical sentences is to be rejected as syntactically incorrect (rightly Kümmel, *Individualgeschichte*, 158).

75. When Jews sinned, they could obtain forgiveness through repentance and sacrifice. The author of 2 Maccabees draws a distinction between the way that God has dealt with the nations and with Israel. He lets the sins of the nations reach their full extent and then intervenes with His judgement; with Israel, however, He intervenes before

Gentiles were sinners not only because of the fact that they did not possess the Law but also, and above all, because of their behavior, especially their polytheism and immoral conduct.[76] (Of course, sectarian Judaism saw the distinction between righteous and sinners running through Israel.)[77]

Paul continued (the subject is "we who are Jews by birth" [2:15]) "knowing[78] that no person[79] is in the right with God on the basis of works required by the law but only[80] through faith in Jesus Christ (δια πιστεως Ιησου Χριστου), we also believed[81] in Christ Jesus in order that we might be declared in the right with God on the basis of faith in Christ (εκ πιστεως Χριστου) and not

---

such a point has been reached and by chastisements He disciplines Israelites in order to bring them back to Himself. He never deserts Israel or withdraws His mercy from Israel (6:12–17). See also Wisdom of Solomon 11:8–10; 12:20–22.

76. Cf. Westerholm, *Perspectives Old and New*, 370n52, who states that Gentiles were sinners because they did not do what was right or acceptable to God, not because they were outside the Covenant per se.

77. Dunn, *Galatians*, 133, believes that Paul is echoing language used by those from James. Martyn, *Galatians*, 209, suggests that the use of this language is like setting a trap which will be sprung in verse 16.

78. Some manuscripts do not have δε, including P46 A D2 syr (hel) cop, thus treating verses 15–16 as one sentence. The δε introduces something of an adversative note: "But we know"; Gaston, *Paul*, 70, considers it doubtful whether in fact Cephas or the Jerusalem church would have agreed with this formulation. But what about Paul's assertion (1 Cor 15:1–11) that he and the early witnesses of the resurrection of Jesus were agreed on the gospel as contained in the formulation of verses 3–5 (and possibly Romans 4:25 if, as is widely held, this was a pre-Pauline formula)? In another essay, entitled "Paul and Jerusalem," Gaston himself itemizes the expiatory and sacrificial meaning of Jesus' death as part of the Jerusalem church's theology (*Paul*, 111–12).

79. Kümmel, *Individualgeschichte*, 160–61, is right to deny that Paul is here emphasizing ανθρωπος, as Klein, *Rekonstruktion*, 184–85, maintains.

80. I here take the εαν μη in verse 16 to be strongly adversative (but only) and to indicate an antithesis to "works of the law," rather than exceptive "apart from faith, etc.," which would indicate that Christian faith is a necessary addition to keeping the Law. The adversative sense is supported by the immediately following clause beginning with και ημεις with its sharp contrast between justification by faith in Christ Jesus and doing works required by the Law.

There is rather a complicated solution, held by de Boer and Das, according to Ulrichs, *Christusglaube*, 122n179, which suggests that in verse 16a Paul was quoting a Jewish Christian view, with εαν μη exceptive, only to contradict it in verse 16b. Dunn, *Galatians*, 137–38, thinks that Paul is being conciliatory here in the hope of keeping Peter and the others with him, but would he not thereby have weakened his case in the Galatian situation?

81. Ulrichs, *Christusglaube*, 111–12, takes the aorist here as an ingressive one, pointing to conversion, and so maintains that there is no redundancy in the use of the noun πιστις after the verb in verse 16bc.

on the basis of works required by the Law, because no human being will be justified on the basis of works required by the Law" (2:16).[82]

Paul thus claims by implication that his fellow Jewish Christians through their conduct in withdrawing from table fellowship with their Gentile fellow believers had changed their viewpoint. That viewpoint had been a *shared conviction* that right standing with God did not in fact rest on human performance but on God's action through Jesus Christ. The knowing which has altered their viewpoint had clearly come about because of the revelation from God through Jesus Christ. As a result of the ministry, death, and resurrection of Jesus, they know that no one has kept the Law sufficiently to find acceptance before God and that they depend on what God has done in and through Jesus, especially his death on the cross.[83]

We need to notice that Paul has not only repeated the subject mid-sentence but written και ημεις. Why did he write "we also" (or "even we")? The και implies in addition to some others: in other words, *believers in Jesus from among non-Jews*. "We also"—like them—"have believed in messiah Jesus in order to be justified by faith in Christ and not by works of the Law."[84]

If this is so, the implication is that Paul's fellow Jews were in no better position than the Gentiles.[85] Indeed, there is a substantial amount of evidence in the literature of Second Temple Judaism that many Jews *did* believe that their nation was sinful, was incapable of keeping the Law, and, therefore, merited God's judgment.[86] This evidence seems to go a long way to challenge the view, often expressed from Sanders on, that Jews did not in fact expect that people would succeed in obeying the Law completely.[87]

---

82. See Excursus 2 at the end of this chapter (53–54) for a discussion of the phrases in Greek, because whether they mean faith directed to Jesus Christ (objective genitive), as we have translated them, or the faith/faithfulness of Jesus Christ (subjective genitive), has been the subject of renewed controversy of late.

83. We may think of the pre-Pauline formula quoted by Paul (1 Cor 15:3), together with other passages where Paul has possibly utilized pre-Pauline material (e.g., Rom 3:24-25; 4:25; 1 Cor 6:11).

84. A number of scholars have made this point—Klein, "Individualgeschichte und Weltgeschichte," 185; Kümmel, *Individualgeschichte*, 162–63; Bruce, *Galatians*, 139; Betz, *Galatians*, 115; Dunn, *Galatians*, 137; Martyn, *Galatians*, 252; Witherington, *Grace*, 182–83.

85. "The hamartological difference between Jews and Gentiles is now deemed as abolished, insofar as in the light of justification in Christ the not-being-sinners of former Jews over against former Gentiles does not exist any more" (Schnelle, *Heide*, 106).

86. See Elliott, *Survivors*; Thielman, *From Plight to Solution*, 28–45; *Paul and the Law*, 49–55. Barclay, *Gift*, 405–6, points in particular to the Hodayot, Pseudo-Philo, and *4 Ezra*.

87. Paul is, of course, himself evidence that some in Judaism did think that it was possible to keep the Law fully (Phil 3:6b).

To this point we may add one to which Stuhlmacher[88] has drawn attention: the living Christ had accepted *Peter and James* as well as Paul after severe failures and had enlisted them into his service.[89] In other words, *all three had experienced gracious acceptance* (which means, in effect, justification) by the risen Christ.

Paul did not say anything here about trying to establish a claim on God, nor was he opposing doing, in contrast to believing, at some philosophical level.[90] There is no hint here in Paul's wording, either, that Paul has in mind *only* such things as circumcision, the food laws, and observance of the Sabbath, regarded as signs of national identity as God's people, as badges of the covenant.[91] That appears to be unduly restrictive an interpretation.[92]

The knowing that has been attained through God's revelation in Jesus Christ is confirmed by the witness of Scripture. All along Scripture had witnessed to the fact that no human being would be justified by works of the Law (v. 16d). Paul quoted Psalm 143:3 LXX in a form edited by himself: "Because no human being will be justified on the basis of doing the works required by the Law." The main alteration is Paul's addition of εξ εργων νομου, which secures the point which he was making.[93] So, experience of revelation and the witness of Scripture had combined to convince Jewish Christians that they were sinners just like the Gentiles and that they needed to believe in Jesus in order to be justified before God.

Excursus on Paul's Phrase τα εργα του νομου

In an effort to take on board the thrust of Sanders's work in *Paul and Palestinian Judaism* (that the Jews believed that they were in the covenant with God entirely because of God's mercy and grace) and yet come up with a

---

88. Stuhlmacher, *Revisiting Paul's Doctrine*, 26-27. Apparently independently, Mayer, *Early Christians*, 179, makes a similar point.

89. Peter had denied his master, while the Gospels of Mark and John suggest that James along with the rest of the family had not thought much of Jesus' activities during his earthly ministry (Mark 3:21; John 7:1-9). Both had experienced an appearance of the risen Jesus (Luke 24:34; 1 Cor 15:5, 7), while Luke 22:31-32 and John 21:15-17 point to a commission given to Peter for the period after the resurrection.

90. Thielman, *Plight*, 62.

91. So Dunn has argued in several publications (see, e.g., *Galatians*, 134-38).

92. Klein, *Rekonstruktion*, e.g., 188, has strongly maintained this.

93. The two other alterations are the omission of "before You"—which was unnecessary as it would be taken for granted—and the alteration of πας ζων into πασα σαρξ. Was Paul justified in adding "on the basis of works of the Law" or has he radically altered the sense to suit his purpose?

more satisfactory explanation of why Paul broke with Judaism than Sanders's own view (Judaism isn't Christ), Dunn has argued in many publications that what Paul meant by the phrase τα εργα του νομου was those specific parts of the Law which in effect served as badges of Jewish consciousness of being the elect nation, chosen by God, and different from other races. In particular, he instances circumcision, the food laws, and sabbath observance. These were very much identity markers, serving to mark off Jews from other races. He lays great stress on the evidence of a concern to maintain Jewish separateness over against other nations, of which a passage from the Letter of Aristeas is a striking illustration: "In his wisdom the legislator . . . surrounded us with unbroken pallisades and iron walls to prevent our mixing with any other peoples in any matter. . . . So, to prevent our being perverted by contact with others or by mixing with bad influences, he hedged us in on all sides with strict observances connected with meat and drink and touch and hearing and sight, after the manner of the Law."[94]

In both his commentaries on Galatians and Romans Dunn consistently applies this understanding of the phrase and draws the implications for how he understands Paul's teaching on justification by faith. It becomes primarily a tool to defend the inclusion of Gentiles in the people of God without their having to observe all the requirements of the Law, particularly those aspects which were bound up with Jewish national distinctiveness. The question is how far is he right? Dunn has now produced a new essay to accompany the republishing of the numerous articles written by him over the last few decades.[95] In it he responds to criticisms, defines more clearly points not made as succinctly in previous articles, and hones others. Modifications and clarifications made by Dunn will be taken into consideration in the ensuing discussion.

We may begin by pointing to the fact that particularly Deuteronomy, but also Leviticus, stressed that it was Israel's obligation to observe *all* the statutes which God had given to it through Moses.[96] Thus, Deuteronomy 27:26, which Paul quoted at Galatians 3:10 is typical: Israel is to do all that is contained in the book of the law. (This verse in Deuteronomy rounds

---

94. *Letter of Aristeas* 139, 142.

95. Dunn, *New Perspective on Paul*, 1-97. The new essay to introduce the collection is entitled, "The New Perspective on Paul: Whence, What, and Whither?"

96. A number of scholars have made this point, e.g., Thielman, *Plight*, 63; *Law*, 275; Das, *Paul, the Law, and the Covenant*, 155-60; DeSilva, *Faith versus Works of Law*, 221-22. We may quote Westerholm, *Perspectives*, 368: "Paul has little to say about those [distinctively Jewish] practices per se. Everything in his response indicates that, to his mind, the issue could only be addressed by assessing the adequacy of the Sinaitic covenant to provide a framework within which its adherents could enjoy God's blessing, inherit God's promises, and be found righteous before God."

off a section comprised of the curses pronounced on those who do certain prohibited things, and these prohibitions appear in other parts of the Torah, or, as we might say, other streams of tradition about the laws which Israel should observe once they were in the promised land.) This fact could indicate that Paul was thinking of obedience to the Law in general.[97] From Leviticus we might mentioned the instruction: "You shall keep all my statutes and all my ordinances, and observe them, so that the land to which I bring you to settle in may not vomit you out. You shall not follow the practices of the nations that I am driving out before you. Because they did all these things, I abhorred them. . . . You shall be holy to me; for I the LORD am holy, and I have separated you from the other peoples to be mine" (20:22-23, 26). The passage from Leviticus 18:5, quoted by Paul in Galatians 3:12, "The person who does them shall live by them," is preceded by "And keep all my commandments and all my decrees and do them." Dunn's rejoinder to all this is, nonetheless, while accepting that works of the Law mean what the Law requires to be done, to point out that the general principle can be put to the test by particular works of the Law, and that these are circumcision and the laws about clean and unclean which are the issue behind Galatians 2:4-5 and 11-14, respectively.[98]

Returning to Deuteronomy 27:15-26, Das has made two points which are worth noticing. Firstly, the prohibitions, apart from the first one about not making images, in no way involve Israel's distinctiveness as a nation. If we are prepared to grant that Paul had in mind the whole passage, or to invoke the principle of intertextuality, then this does not support the idea that Paul was only concerned with identity markers. Secondly, some of the prohibitions involve private sins or sins done in secret (particularly sins of sexual activity within the prohibited degrees of relationship and of bestiality).[99]

The most important argument against Dunn's position is that in the contexts where Paul used the phrase he seems to be thinking of the Law as a whole and not just parts of it. Thus, for example, in Galatians 2:16, it would have been perfectly possible for Paul to have used with the verb "justified" a qualifying phrase like "through circumcision" or "by means of food" (διὰ βρώματος).[100] He could have used language similar to 1 Corinthians 8:8: "But food will not present us to God; we are neither worse off

---

97. Suggested by Das, *Paul*, 158
98. Dunn, *New Perspective*, 25-27.
99. Das, *Paul*, 157-58.
100. Paul uses βρῶσις two times in 1 Corinthians 8 and three times in Romans 14, when discussing the issue of eating food offered to idols.

if we do not eat, nor are we better off if we do eat." It is significant that he uses the entirely general phrase "works of the Law." Furthermore, when a few sentences later, he said that he has died to the Law (v. 19), it is more natural to assume that Paul was thinking of the Law in its entirety than a limited range of laws bound up with Israel's sense of identity surrounded by a sea of paganism. The same would apply when he asked the Galatians whether they received the Spirit by doing the works required by the Law or by hearing the Gospel message and believing (3:2-5).

Dunn's rejoinder is that what sparked the confrontation with Peter and other Jewish Christians at Antioch was the issue of table fellowship with Gentile Christians (i.e., laws about food and clean/unclean issues were being exalted as absolutely necessary). He maintains that the general principle [the Law should be kept] may come to a head or be focused on the keeping of particular laws [food laws, purity regulations].[101]

When we turn to Galatians 3:10 (to be considered in more detail later), the whole thrust of verses 10-12 is the contrast between Law and faith, between doing the whole of the Law and believing, between the curse threatened on those who do not keep all the Law and the promise of life to those who believe. The quotation from Habakkuk about faith indicates that life comes through faith, not through keeping the Law which (so it is implied) no one has achieved.[102]

The picture is no different really in Romans (we are aware that many scholars think that Paul changed his mind between Galatians and Romans and modified some of the extreme statements made in Galatians when writing to the Roman church). God will reward every one according to their works (2:6). God is impartial in His judgment, and this means that the Jew cannot plead special privileges to avoid judgment. "It is not the hearers of the Law who are in the right with God, but the doers of the Law will be declared in the right" (2:13). Nothing in the context would incline us to limit carrying out the Law to those laws which were identity markers. Later, in the same chapter, Paul criticized the Jew for teaching not to steal while stealing, and not to commit adultery while doing so, and, while abhorring idolatry, robbing temples (2:21-22). These are not identity markers! He then went on to say that circumcision was profitable if one kept the Law (v. 25). This further step in Paul's argument does indeed show that circumcision was regarded by Jews as important, but what he had said previously shows that keeping the Law was to be concerned with

---

101. See Dunn, *New Perspective*, 25-28.

102. Das, *Paul*, 157n34, points out that the history of Israel would have shown Paul that the promise of life through the observance of the Law was an illusory one.

ethical issues as well as what has been termed "boundary markers." The catena of OT quotations, by which Paul sought to show that the Jews stand condemned by their own Scriptures, deals with moral faults: i.e., Paul here did not criticize his fellow country men and women for their concentration on "badges of Jewish nationalism."[103]

Likewise, when Paul said that some Gentiles (possibly Christian Gentiles, but probably not),[104] although not possessing the Law, kept what was required by the Law (τα του νομου), he was not thinking of things like circumcision or the food laws, but, to borrow a phrase from Matthew's Gospel, "the weightier matters of the Law." Paul went on to say that by doing what the Law required Gentiles showed that το εργον του νομου had been written on their hearts (v. 15). The use of the singular here is significant: Paul was not thinking of knowledge of the individual laws but rather of the basic knowledge of the will of God. What was revealed to Israel in the Law given at Sinai was also revealed to the Gentiles. This can explain why later Paul would say that "what the Law says it says to those under Law so that *every* mouth may be silenced and the *whole* world held accountable to God" (3:19).[105]

Another point is what in the long run is the effect of Dunn's interpretation on the significance of the death of Jesus? If "getting in" to God's people is now based on faith in Jesus but not keeping such prescriptions as circumcision etc, to what purpose did Christ die? Dunn appears to interpret the "curse of the Law" as Jewish misunderstanding of the Law by using it to restrict God's grace in nationalistic terms and so to exclude others and preventing God's blessing reaching non-Jews. Westerholm asks, "Were all Jews guilty of racism—or were the select Jews who escaped this sin in no need of Christ's death? Was the death of Christ the only way Jews could be disabused of their misunderstanding? Had it no broader function? . . . [Dunn's view] coheres ill with Pauline claims that all the world is "under sin" and culpable before God, that Jews no less than Gentiles are "sinners," God's "enemies," the "ungodly" who need to be declared righteous by faith."[106] Dunn

---

103. See Westerholm, *Perspectives*, 317-19, for his criticism of Dunn on this point.

104. So Minear, *Obedience of Faith*, 51; Cranfield, *Romans*, 1:155; Watson, *PJG*, 215, but denied by Wilckens, *Römer*, 1:133; Dunn, *Romans*, 1:98; Ziesler, *Romans*, 86.

105. Heiligenthal, *Werke*, 282-83, quotes Bornkamm, *Studien zu Antike und Urchristentum*, 99, 101, with approval: "[Verses] 14f. are in no way interested in whether there are non-Jews who will be saved, but solely in the fact that even the Gentiles have a knowledge of God's Law, because of which they are also answerable to God. . . . Nomos means also the one and same Law of God, which is given to Jews and Gentiles only in different ways."

106. Westerholm, *Perspectives*, 318, believes that Das's judgment on Paul's understanding of the death of Christ is broadly similar (Das, *Paul*, 160). We might also mention

has acknowledged that his phrase was less than happy, and affirms that he in no way wishes to undermine Paul's analysis of the radical helplessness of the human situation and his concern for the salvation of the individual, but that he continues to wish to remind us of the fact that the there is a social and ethnic dimension of Paul's understanding and expression of the Gospel and his defence of justification by faith.[107]

Mention ought to be made of the fact that we now know that the phrase "works of the Law" was used in two documents at Qumran. 4Q174 interprets 2 Samuel 7. The "house" which God would build is a temple, probably to be interpreted as the Qumran community itself. It is built to offer "works of the law" for God. What the Law requires are the sacrifices which the Qumran community can offer to God. A little later, in a reference to the time of trial in the last days, it is said that "a remnant of the people shall be left according to the lot (assigned to them) and they shall practice the whole law" (2:2-4). The reference here to the whole Law suggests that the earlier reference to "works of the law" should be given a comprehensive sense.

4QMMT, which was addressed to the leader of a group other than the Qumran community itself and commended the Qumran interpretation of the Law to this person and his group, refers to the "works of the Law" performed by pious kings, especially David, which the addressee and his group must imitate. To perform these "works of the Law" would mean that righteousness would be reckoned (an allusion to either Genesis 15:6 [Abraham] or Psalm 106:31 [Phineas]) to the one who does them, and this would accrue to the benefit also of Israel. This suggests that doing the works of the law can have an atoning function. The crucial issue for interpretation is whether the fact that ritual issues dominate the preceding sections means that "works of the law" must be restricted to ritual matters, or would the whole Law, ritual and ethical, be in mind?[108] The writer did say, however,

---

the declaration at the beginning of Galatians — that Jesus Christ died "that he might deliver us from this present evil age according to the will of our God and Father" (1:4), which cannot be limited in its scope to Jewish nationalistic misunderstanding of the Law.

107. Dunn, *New Perspective*, 30.

108. See the careful study of de Roo, *Works of the Law*, esp. 4-41, 72-98. De Roo challenges the contention of both Dunn and Bachmann that "works of the Law" are ritual observances and that the Hebrew *m'sh* means precept or ruling. Rather, the Hebrew *m'sh* means act or deed, as indeed previously Martinez, "4QMMT in a Qumran Context," 23-25, had assumed. Actually, Dunn maintained that the term refers to both precept and action. See his 1997 essay "4QMMT and Galatians," reprinted in Dunn, *New Perspective*, 339-45, esp. 342-43, and reiterated in *New Perspective*, 23-24n93. de Roo further believes that there is no reason to restrict these works of the Law to parts of it; rather, they embrace the whole of the Law.

De Roo draws into her discussion the Damascus Document. At 5:5-6, there is a reference to the works of David, which, apart from the murder of Uriah, God "left to

that he had written concerning some of the works of the Law, and he holds out David as a model of royal piety. He believed that kings of Israel who were obedient to the Torah were saved from troubles, like David himself. It is fairly obvious that the author of 4QMMT did not think that someone who kept the specific halakoth mentioned but ignored the rest of the Torah would be counted as a true Jew.[109] In context, ritual matters seem to be uppermost in the author's mind when he used the phrase "works of the law,"[110] while clearly keeping the rest of the Law would be axiomatic. Wright puts it this way: the works of the law advocated in 4QMMT will indicate now in the present and at the final judgment who really belongs to the people of God, who are the ones with whom the God of Israel is in Covenant.[111]

Dunn sees this passage from 4QMMT as indicating what were, in the view of the author, the specific requirements of the Law which must be fulfilled for others to be acceptable to God.[112] The author is setting forth instances as test cases of others' acceptability to God. It is a question of obeying the Law as interpreted by the author and his fellow members of the Qumran community. The author draws a boundary line excluding others, if they do not accept these rulings.

There remains here, then, a difference of exegetical conclusions to be drawn from 4QMMT, while a recognition that it has a significance for the debate over Paul's understanding of "works of the Law."

Without in any way claiming to have covered the whole range of passages involved in the debate, enough has been said to show that when Paul

---

him," i.e., God remembered David's works for his benefit and that of Israel. De Roo (11-16) takes David's works to be works in accordance with the Law and God counted them to the benefit of those coming after him, which would be, in the author's view, the Qumran community (earlier, the author had stated that God, in recognition of the covenant with the ancestors, had left a remnant to Israel, which was of course the Qumran community itself [1:4-5]).

Schwartz, *MMT, Josephus, and the Pharisees*, 79, believes that 4QMMT was addressed to the party in power and its ruler in the early Hasmonean period in an effort to revise the laws of the Temple and priesthood in line with the positions of the Qumran community (cf. Schiffman, *Place of 4QMMT*, 95–96). If this were correct, the fact that ritual issues play such an important part need occasion no surprise. On the other hand, the writer does not seem to be completely at odds with the person to whom he is writing, as Wright, *Perspectives*, 335, has pointed out, and this would hardly be the case in respect to the Hasmoneans and/or the Temple establishment.

109. Wright, *Pauline Perspectives*, 343.
110. Wright, *Pauline Perspectives*, 312, 332–43.
111. Wright, *Pauline Perspectives*, 341.
112. Dunn, *New Perspective*, 25n99.

used the phrase τα εργα του νομου, he had the whole range of what the Law demands, rather than a particular section of the Law.[113]

Mention might be made finally of the view of Gaston.[114] Gaston acknowledges indebtedness to the work of E. Loh-meyer[115] who stated that the natural meaning was "the works worked by the Law," with του νομου being a genitive of performer (genitivus auctoris), though Lohmeyer himself went on to assume that it must, however, mean "works which the Law demands." Gaston takes Romans 2:15 and 4:15 as offering clues. The latter states that the work performed by the Law was to unleash the wrath of God (Rom 4:15), while the former maintains that the Gentiles were aware of this (Rom 2:15, as in 1:32). But do not Galatians 3:10 and 12 weigh against Gaston's view? Paul asserted in Galatians 3:10 that the curse of the Law falls on those who do not continue to do what is written in the Law (i.e., the Law lays down what must be done, failure to do which will result in a curse), the implication being that to do the Law means to enjoy life which God intended for His people. This is confirmed by verse 12, where Paul quoted the principle that it is *doing* the law which leads to the life which God intended. Also, at Romans 2:14, the sense is surely that Gentiles who do not have the Law do what the Law requires (τα του νομου ποιωσιν). Then again, Paul asserted in Romans 7:10 that the purpose of the Law was to lead to life, but that sin had used the Law as a base of operations to stimulate sinful behavior. Gaston's view is unconvincing.

1.2.4. Continued

Returning to Galatians 2:16, Jewish Christians, then—including those who had appeared in Galatia—would have accepted that, given Israel's sins, there was a need for acquittal at the bar of God's judgment, and that God had provided this acquittal, the forgiveness of sins, through Christ's sacrificial death and that, therefore, faith in Jesus was crucial for ultimate justification.[116]

---

113. Watson, *PJG*, 19–21, 121, 124, 202–3, 212, 346, has reiterated his position that "works of the law" refers to the distinctive way of life of the Jewish community, without any necessary orientation towards "boundary markers," and he himself then goes on to draw sociological consequences from the Pauline antithesis of works and faith—that members of the Christian community in Rome, especially Jewish Christians, should separate themselves from the Jewish community. Barclay, *Gift*, e.g., 373–74, is also critical of Dunn's attempt to limit the meaning to boundary markers.

114. Gaston, *Paul*, 69–70.

115. Lohmeyer, *Gesetzewerke*, 177–207.

116. Martyn, *Galatians*, 266. Klein, *Rekonstruktion*, 191, suggests that the identity of Jewish and Gentile Christians is worked out here as an equality of believers. But, as

We note that here there is for Paul an unequivocal link between justification, Christology, and the atoning death of Christ.[117] There is, then, no need to drive a wedge between the ideas of justification and participation in Christ. They belong together.

Why, then, given this agreement, does Paul go on immediately to say "But if seeking to be justified in Christ, we ourselves (καὶ αὐτοί) have been found to be sinners, is Christ then a minister[118] of sin?" (v. 17). The phrase καὶ αὐτοί picks up the "we" of the verb εὑρέθημεν and is comparable to the καὶ ἡμεῖς of verse 16b—Jewish Christians.[119] How can "seeking to be justified in Christ" be regarded as ending up "found to be sinners"? One possible explanation is to assume that the charge of being found to be sinners must have been levelled at Paul, probably by the opponents in Galatia.[120] What can explain the charge? Their thought may have run along the following lines. In their coming to commitment to Jesus, Jewish Christians admitted that they were sinners. They discovered, found out (εὑρέθημεν),[121] that in fact they also were sinners—"we also," i.e., alongside Gentiles.[122] This would mean, so the charge would run, that Christ was being made responsible for

---

Kümmel, *Individualgeschichte*, 166, points out, this does not say anything about "the promise structure of Judaism," whether the promises of God are still valid for Jews when they become Christians.

117. See Stuhlmacher, *Revisiting*, 44, for a criticism of the New Perspective for its failure to allow for a clear relationship between Christology and justification. Previously, his teacher, E. Käsemann, had also vigorously defended the link between justification and Christology, in "Justification and Salvation History" (*Perspectives on Paul*, 60-78). See especially: "The Pauline doctrine of justification is entirely and solely Christology, a Christology, indeed, won from Jesus' cross and hence an offensive Christology" (73) and the extended 76-78n27, added to the original lecture for publication.

118. Greek διάκονος. Translations vary between "minister" (Lightfoot, *St. Paul's Epistle to the Galatians*, 116; Burton, *Galatians*, 125; Longenecker, *Galatians*, 88-90; Barrett, *Freedom*, 19) and "servant" (Bruce, *Galatians*, 141; Dunn, *Galatians*, 141; Martyn, *Galatians*, 253). Witherington, *Grace*, 186, has minister/servant. If "servant" is used, then it must be in the sense of agent or helper.

119. So Klein, *Rekonstruktion*, 190; Bruce, *Galatians*, 137, 139; Witherington, *Grace*, 185.

120. A number of scholars accept that verse 17 contains a charge made by Paul's opponents—Betz, *Galatians*, 120; Martyn, *Galatians*, 255; Barrett, *Freedom*, 19; Westerholm, *Perspectives*, 372. Dunn, *Galatians*, 142, regards this as "not impossible." We see in Romans 3:8 a further indication that Paul was criticized on the score that his emphasis on God's free gift of justification apart from doing the works required by the Law was injurious to ethical standards. Cummins, *Crucified Christ*, 206-212, without linking it to the opponents in Galatia, comes to a similar interpretation of the meaning of 2:17.

121. Klein, *Rekonstruktion*, 187, 190, maintains that εὑρέθημεν suggests a new discovery; cf. Dunn, *Galatians*, 141.

122. Barclay, *Gift*, 384n93, calls this "the traditional reading."

convicting even those who were Jews by birth of being sinners, and so he had increased the amount of sin, and was thus a minister of sin.[123] This "discovery" by Jewish Christians would also mean that the distinction between Jews and Gentiles, enumerated in verse 15, had collapsed. It was no longer tenable; it was false.[124] This view assumes that whoever made the charge did not accept that Jewish Christians, before their coming to faith in Jesus, were sinners on a par with Gentiles.

Another suggestion is that those from James would regard as sinners both non-circumcised Gentiles and those who had fellowship with them, and that the implication of the behavior of the latter was that they were turning Christ who, it was claimed, accepted Gentile sinners by faith, into a "minister of sin."[125] The opponents of Paul in Galatia, in a similar way, expected a true member of God's people not only to believe in Jesus as Messiah and in his atoning death for sins, but also to obey the Law. If Paul only concentrated on the former and if he ignored the latter and encouraged his converts not to follow all the Law's requirements, then, in their eyes, he would be guilty in effect of making Christ into someone who promoted sin by ignoring the Law, someone who made sin easy rather than opposing it.[126]

Of these two suggestions, the first might seem to fit better with "seeking to be justified in Christ," whereas on the second interpretation the conduct criticized is subsequent to the initial commitment of seeking to be justified, unless this be deemed to drive too much of a wedge between initial commitment and the life which flows from it. However, and this seems more decisive, the second explanation fits the situation at Antioch and the situation created by the message from James.

Paul repudiated the suggestion that Christ was an agent of sin with μη γενοιτο. Verse 18 gives the reason (γαρ) for this emphatic rejection of the imputation. "If I build up again those things which I have torn down, I prove myself to be a transgressor." We note that Paul has now moved to using the first person singular. Is he referring to himself specifically, or does the "I" stand for

---

123. Klein, *Rekonstruktion*, 191; Barrett, *Freedom*, 19.

124. This view, broadly speaking, is found in Klein, *Rekonstruktion*, 190–192 (as mentioned in n116. Klein suggested that here, in distinction to verse 16, the identity of Jewish and Gentile Christians is worked out as the equality of sinners, 191); Bruce, *Galatians*, 140–41; Wilckens, "Was heisst bei Paulus," 93.

125. Dunn, *New Perspective*, 233; Hansen, *Abraham*, 105; Gombis, *Arguing with Scripture in Galatia*, 84–85. This view assumes a more hostile approach within James's message than the suggestion which we made above (12–13).

126. Martyn, *Galatians*, 255; cf. Barclay, *Gift*, 384, "This sentence reflects not a general discovery that all humanity is sinful (cf. 3:22), but those specific occasions (such as at Antioch) when living 'in a Gentile fashion' out of loyalty to the good news causes believers to be labelled 'sinners' (as defined by the Torah)."

any Jewish Christian (the "we" of verses 15–17)? Furthermore, what is envisaged as being reinstated after having been taken down, and who is envisaged as doing the "building up" after having taken them away?

The building up again of those things which had been torn down refers to the reinstatement of the need to fulfill the Law as a requirement for salvation,[127] which Paul and other Jewish Christians had abandoned (cf. v. 16). If, after preaching salvation apart from keeping the Law through God's action in Christ in delivering us from this present evil age (1:4), he or anyone then reinstated the need to keep the Law—either by direct teaching or by practical conduct, then they would show themselves to be a transgressor of either God's purposes[128] or the Law (v. 18).[129] God had shown that the way of salvation was through Christ; while, on the other hand, to reinstate the Law as a necessary component of salvation would be to go back from the conviction stated in 2:16 and to admit that accepting Gentiles on the basis of faith and having table fellowship with them was a breaking of the Law, whereas Scripture in fact condemned all as sinners (Gal 3:22) and foresaw that God would justify the Gentiles on the basis of faith (Gal 3:8). The mention of "Law" in verse 19a may favor the latter interpretation, but no great difference of sense exists between the two in the end.

Do then verses 17–18 refer to *Paul* (with the "I" having a specifically personal reference) or to *Peter's* behavior at Antioch (with the "I" representing a group)? Since Paul did not seek to reinstate keeping the provisions of the Law as a means of justification,[130] we must assume that if he was speaking here solely of himself, then he was speaking hypothetically.[131] On the other hand, initially, Peter had participated in table fellowship with Gentile Christians at Antioch, disregarding the food laws. For this he and

---

127. So Schlier, *Galaterbrief*, 97; Bruce, *Galatians*, 142; Witherington, *Grace*, 187. Others limit it to the food laws, including Dunn, *Galatians*, 142; Martyn, *Galatians*, 265; Glombis, *Arguing*, 84–85. Mussner, *Galaterbrief*, 178, lists either the food laws or the law as a protective wall for Israel. Gaston, *Paul*, 71, suggests that Paul is thinking of the church, on the grounds that elsewhere Paul uses the language of building (οικοδομεω and οικοδομη) of the church, but the context does not support such an interpretation.

128. Witherington, *Grace*, 185.

129. Klein, *Rekonstruktion*, 199; Dunn, *Galatians*, 143.

130. Galatians 5:11 can hardly be invoked to support such a position (see Dunn, *Galatians*, 278–80, for a lengthy discussion of the various interpretations of this puzzling reference).

131. Dunn, *Galatians*, 142–43, expounds this verse in terms of Paul and his ministry: to ask him to accept that his ministry of outreach to the Gentiles was one long act of transgression, which put him beyond the pale of God's acceptance, would be an impossible contradiction of what the gospel meant (143). Martyn, *Galatians*, 255, believes that Paul was arguing here from a (hypothetical) position if he had followed Peter at Antioch. Barclay, *Gift*, 385, argues that Paul was using himself as a paradigm.

others had been criticized or were open to criticism (regarded as sinners because ignoring those food laws), as pointed out by those who came from James. Their conduct in eating with Gentiles was in effect to make Christ one who encouraged sinning, which is for Paul a preposterous suggestion. But if verse 17 did have specifically Peter in mind, the "I" could be taken as a generalizing "I," and refer to anyone whose conduct matched what was being said.[132] There is much to be said for the view that verses 17-18 had Peter and other Jewish Christians in mind, as at verses 11-14.[133]

Another γαρ clause follows in verse 19; this verse explains verse 18. The new sentence continued in the "I" form, but it is reasonably clear that Paul was here speaking personally.[134] Mussner has commented that "We have here before us also a compact performance, within which a rhetorically impressive transition from you to we and from this to I takes place. Paul's linguistic competence generates sentences, in which the I can be related differently without any difficulty."[135] That Paul has died to the Law amounts to much the same as what is involved in the phrase α κατελυσα. He had died to the Law as the way of salvation parallels in sense that Paul had pulled down the Law as the way of salvation. (Jewish Christians had accepted that the Law was not the way of salvation, verse 16.)[136] Living to God (ινα Θεω ζησω) is obviously the opposite of being a transgressor. But how has Paul died to the Law? By being crucified with Christ (v. 19b). Union with the Christ who was crucified and raised to life by God is the way of salvation.[137] If union with Christ crucified was the way of salvation,

---

132. So Bonnard, *Galates*, 55; Kümmel, *Individualgeschichte*, 166-67, 169; Mussner, *Galaterbrief*, 178-79; Bruce, *Galatians*, 142; Witherington, *Grace*, 188. Burton, *Galatians*, 132, thinks that Paul tactfully applied the statement to himself.

133. Burton, *Galatians*, 130-31; Bonnard, *Galates*, 55; Mussner, *Galaterbrief*, 177-78; Lührmann, *Galatians*, 47-48; Longenecker, *Galatians*, 90; Watson, *PJG*, 127; Morland, *Curse*, 188-89; Glombis, *Arguing*, 84-85.

134. Cf. Burton, *Galatians*, 132. Witherington, *Grace*, 188, comments: "Things appear to become more personal with Paul giving something of a testimony about his own experience." Bonnard, *Galates*, 55, denies this—for him, the εγω is still literary.

135. Mussner, *Galaterbrief*, 178.

136. Cf. Klein, *Rekonstruktion*, 199.

137. Union with Christ in his death and resurrection takes place through the believer's response in faith to Christ and through baptism (e.g., Rom 6:1-11). For Paul, faith and baptism go together theologically, and probably timewise as well. Barrett, *Freedom*, 20, rightly emphasizes faith here. Dunn, *Galatians*, 144-45, reflects on how Christ's own death was an identification with the outcasts and Paul felt commissioned to go to the Gentiles, regarded as outcasts by so many Jews.

if this led to living for God, then it would be absolutely absurd to suggest that Christ was a minister of sin.[138]

But what of the phrase διὰ νομου? How can Paul have died to the Law "through the Law"? There may be two reasons. In his own case, it was his zeal for the Law (1:13-14) which had paradoxically led him into outright opposition to the purposes of God, so that he ended up in fact under God's judgment.[139] Like others who did not obey the Law (3:10), he was in fact under the curse pronounced on sinners by the Law.[140]

Secondly, as will become clear later in the letter, Christ ended up on the cross because he there bore the curse on sinners pronounced by the Law (3:13-14). In other words, the Law had a part to play in the death of Christ—hence Paul's phrase "through the Law."[141]

The idea that Christians through union with Christ were taken out of the sphere of the Law and obligation to it *in order that* they might live for God would, of course, be horrifying to those who had appeared in Galatia.[142]

The believer had been incorporated into the crucifixion of Christ and was, therefore, a dead person as far as the Law was concerned.[143] "I have been crucified with Christ" (v. 19b). As a result of this union with Christ crucified, Paul can go on to say in verse 20 that he no longer lived, but Christ lived in him and the life he now lived he lived by faith in the Son of God (εν πιστει τη του υιου του Θεου). The εγω in one sense had been replaced by Christ, yet, in another sense, it was still Paul of course, but Paul transformed by this union with the Christ who was crucified and now lived. Paul lived out this new life in the flesh. To be justified was not being taken out of this world, out of bodily existence, but rather a new life with the risen Jesus at its center in this present life. The presence of the indwelling Jesus was the

---

138. Cf. Klein, *Rekonstruktion*, 201.

139. Dunn, *Galatians*, 143.

140. Lightfoot, *Galatians*, 118; Mussner, *Galaterbrief*, 180; Thielman, *Law*, 129-31. Betz, *Galatians*, 122, refers for an explanation to the thought of the Law's confining all under sin until the promise was realized in Christ in Galatians 3:22.

141. Schlier, *Galater*, 101; Bruce, *Galatians*, 143; Martyn, *Galatians*, 257; Witherington, *Grace*, 189; Harvey, *Jesus and the Constraints of History*, 22; Hooker, "Paul and Covenantal Nomism," 55. Morland, *Curse*, 190, assumes that in verse 19 Paul is using νομος in different ways in the one sentence—"I through what is written in the Pentateuch/Scripture died to the claims of the Mosaic commandments." He suggests that this would be in accordance with the topic "intention of the framer of the law," and Paul's full argument on this topic would emerge at 3:8-14.

142. See Barrett, *Freedom*, 20; Martyn, *Galatians*, 257. For Barclay, *Gift*, 386, the phrase "signals a profound dislocation: like all other Jews, he desires to 'live to God,' but the Torah no longer defines what this entails."

143. Schlier, *Galater*, 98-100, stresses this strongly.

essential characteristic of life before God, and not the Mosaic Law. If the living Christ who was raised by God the Father from the dead (1:1) lived in Christians like Paul, they could hardly be accounted sinners.[144] Christ living in his followers was not going to encourage them to sin.

To the title Son of God Paul attached two participial constructions, "who loved me and gave himself for me" (2:19-20). They have a creed-like flavor and could be traditional expressions. Together they focus attention on the death of Christ, which is motivated by love for Paul (and all others). Though it was not overtly stated, no one could hear these words without remembering that at one point Paul had been a virulent opponent of the cause of Jesus and had persecuted his followers (as Paul himself had already mentioned earlier [1:13] in the letter). Yet Christ's love and saving death embraced even the persecutor! This was grace indeed! Far from nullifying God's grace (the sudden mention of such a possibility might be due to the fact that this accusation had been hurled at him),[145] Paul's own experience and message were the reverse. But the crucial importance of Christ's saving death would be undermined if right standing with God depended on keeping the Law So Paul asserted: "If right standing before God comes through the Law, then Christ has died in vain"[146] (2:21). Strictly speaking, as far as Paul was concerned, both clauses were contrary to fact, and so we ought really to translate: "If right standing were through the Law, then Christ would have died in vain." Paul denied that righteousness could be gained by doing the Law, while the idea that Christ had died to no purpose was clearly an absurd statement in Paul's eyes.[147]

---

144. Morland, *Curse*, 191.

145. Paul might have been accused by the opponents of nullifying God's grace to the Jewish nation in the gift of the Law—so Longenecker, *Galatians*, 94; Martyn, *Galatians*, 259; Morland, *Curse*, 191. Burton, *Galatians*, 140; Schlier, *Galater*, 104; Betz, *Galatians*, 126, consider that Paul is rebutting a charge made against him, but Bonnard, *Galates*, 57-58, denies that anyone accused Paul of denying the grace of God. Bruce, *Galatians*, 146, thinks that perhaps Paul was accused of misusing the grace of God. Dunn, *Galatians*, 148, while not believing that any such charge was levelled at Paul, thinks that this is Paul's own formulation: he does not nullify the grace of God by setting aside the Law and insisting that all including Gentiles are justified by faith and not by works of the Law.

146. Bauer, *Lexicon*, 209, gives "in vain, to no purpose" for δωρεαν in Galatians 2:21 (so also *LSJ*, 464, listing Gal 2:21 as the sole example). Burton, *Galatians*, 140-41, prefers "without cause" or "needlessly" as in John 15:25. Gaston, *Paul*, 67, argues for "as a free gift," as at Romans 3:24. He shows that the LXX uses δωρεαν in both senses—freely, without payment, and undeserved, without cause. But is it convincing to say that the natural meaning of 2:21 *in its context* is that no one had any grounds for killing him (however true that may be)?

147. See Lightfoot, *Galatians*, 119; Burton, *Galatians*, 140-41; Bruce, *Galatians*,

Paul now turned specifically to the Galatians. So amazed was he that they should contemplate turning away from complete reliance on Christ and his redeeming death that he suggested that someone might have bewitched them. They must have been beguiled by some form of magic (3:1). Paul's first line of argument was an appeal to experience. Did the Galatians first receive the Spirit as a result of doing what the Law required or as result of the message (about Christ crucified)[148] which evoked faith in them (v. 2)?

Indeed, this question applied not only to the past and their initial Christian experience, but also to their present experience and the fact that God was still giving them the Spirit and working miracles among them (v. 5). It is for Paul astonishing that the Galatians, having started their Christian experience by the Spirit, should contemplate trying to attain perfection through the "flesh," by which term Paul probably has in mind the actual act of circumcision in the flesh, an act which for him now belongs to the realm of "flesh" in a theological sense, i.e., reliance on human effort as opposed to reliance entirely on divine grace and help. Having begun in the Spirit, the Galatians should have continued in the Spirit (cf. 5:25). It was foolish indeed to change courses. Doing the works demanded by the Law had played no part in the Galatians' experience of the Spirit. The Galatians should remember that they were uncircumcised Gentiles when they received the Holy Spirit (this would have been difficult for the opponents to explain within the boundaries of Jewish theology).[149]

It is at this point that Paul mentioned Abraham for the first time in the letter. So we now turn to the way in which Paul used the figure of Abraham in this letter to the Galatians.

147; Bonnard, *Galates*, 58; Betz, *Galatians*, 126; Martyn, *Galatians*, 260; Witherington, *Galatians*, 192; Barrett, *Freedom*, 21; Smith, *Saved*, 88. In his Damascus Road experience, Paul had learned that the once crucified now risen and glorified Jesus was God's Son, and so the Law could not be the way to salvation. It would be absurd to assert that Jesus had died in vain; rather, his death was necessary for the salvation of all; cf. Blaschke, *Beschneidung*, 375–76.

148. Taking ακοη as indicating what is heard rather than the act of hearing. Thus, that they received the Spirit εξ ακοης πιστεως means on the basis of the gospel message which evoked faith in them. So Betz, *Galatians*, 133; Martyn, *Galatians*, 284, 286–89; Hays, *Faith of Jesus Christ*, 146–48.

149. Morland, *Curse*, 193. For the view that within Jewish theology the gift of the Spirit was reserved for the Jewish people in the eschatological era, see Philip, *Origins of Pauline Pneumatology*, 32–120, who considers the idea of the Spirit's being given to Gentiles to be almost non-existent both in the Hebrew Scriptures and post-Biblical literature. Morales, *Spirit and the Restoration of Israel*, 76, virtually agrees with this verdict.

1.3. Paul's Use of Abraham in the Letter to the Galatians

The references to Abraham (3:6-8, 14, 16, 18, 29) are an indication that we should see the whole of chapter 3 as a unit, even if we may subdivide it into, e.g., 3:1-5, 6-14, 15-29. As Wright has stressed, Paul had Genesis 15 in mind throughout. Not only did Paul quote Genesis 15:6 (Gal 3:6), but in verses 15-29 we encounter key terms from Genesis 15:7-21, viz. διαθηκη, κληρονομια, and σπερμα.[150]

1.3.1. Galatians 3:1-5

Paul began a new section of the letter with several rhetorical questions addressed very pointedly to the Galatians (3:1, 2, 5). Paul asked firstly who had bewitched them, to whom Christ crucified had been clearly presented? Secondly, he asked (3:2) whether they received the Spirit by doing the works required by the Law (εξ εργων νομου) or by faith evoked by his preaching of Christ crucified (εξ ακοης πιστεως)? Finally, he asked on which of these two bases was God supplying the Spirit and working miracles in the ongoing life of the congregations (3:5)? (He seems to take up the matter of faith in verses 6-9,[151] especially in relation to Abraham, while verses 10-14[152] elaborate on what the phrase "works required by the Law" involved in contrast to faith.)

With his rhetorical questions Paul clearly expected that the Galatians could only answer that it was indeed the message about Christ crucified which had evoked their faith and resulted in the experience of the Spirit.[153] Why did Paul so phrase the question as to focus on receiving the Spirit? Is it not because receiving the Spirit is for Paul an essential aspect of our union with Christ, or, to phrase the matter in a different way, of the experience of salvation? He has gone back to the initial experience (cf. εναρξαμενοι πνευματι

---

150. Wright, *Pauline Perspectives*, 526, 574. Wright (565) argues that Paul read Genesis 15:7-21 as epexegetic of 15:6.

151. In verses 6-9, the noun πιστις occurs three times, the verb πιστευειν occurs one time, and the adjective πιστος appears one time. The noun πιστις occurs in antithesis to νομος three times in verses 10-14.

152. In verses 10-14, the phrase εργα νομου occurs one time, and αυτα referring to them two times, while we meet νομος on its own four times. For this suggested division of verses 6-14, see Sanger, *Verkündigung*, 260-61.

153. Lee, *Blessing of Abraham*, 24, refers to Pelser's description of this as the technique which "forces the reader to choose between mutually exclusive alternatives."

[3:3b]).¹⁵⁴ On the basis of their experience, Paul sought to show that the gift of the Spirit was not linked to doing what the Law required.¹⁵⁵

Wright constantly in his contributions emphasizes table fellowship as the problem behind the writing of Galatians.¹⁵⁶ In other words, he seems to make the episode of 2:11-14 determine the issue at stake in Galatians.¹⁵⁷ But if table fellowship were the burning issue in Galatia, would we not expect to see a direct reference to that, and a further reference back to the Antioch incident? As it is, Paul does not mention it specifically. Wright is correct to the extent that ultimately if some of Paul's converts acceded to the pressure to be circumcised while others did not, then the issue of table fellowship would arise because a separation between the circumcised and non-circumcised would have been created. As it is, we do not seem to have reached that stage.

1.3.2. Galatians 3:6-14

Paul backed up this antithesis of faith and works required by the Law by referring to what the Scripture had said about Abraham: "Just as (καθως) Abraham believed God and this was reckoned to him for righteousness" (Gen 15:6). The καθως clause is probably to be taken with the preceding paragraph, verses

---

154. Cf. Dunn, *Baptism in the Holy Spirit*, 108: "Becoming a Christian is essentially a matter of receiving the Spirit."

155. Barclay, *Gift*, 390, points out that the appeal to experience establishes a logic similar to the passage 2:15-21. The Christ-gift is not located within the framework of "living Jewishly" (2:14).

156. Wright, *Pauline Perspectives*, 89, 213-14, 259, 375, 538-39, 541, 545. Here we may quote two passages from these references: "Paul's initial introduction of the topic [justification] is embedded within and seems to be the sharp edge of, the question at issue between himself and Peter at Antioch and, we may assume, bears some close relation to the dispute between himself and the 'agitators' in Galatia. . . . It was the question of whether Christian Jews ought or ought not eat with Christian gentiles" (213-14) and "Justification, in its first Pauline exposition in Galatians, is all about the question of who belongs at the Messiah's table" (545). It is precisely about this assumption that we are raising questions.

157. Thus, e.g., he criticizes Wischmeyer for moving in what he considers the wrong direction. Wischmeyer, "Wie kommt Abraham in den Galaterbrief?," 132, had said that the theme of Galatians is *"how or by what means the Galatians have come into the state of salvation or life?"* It is worth noting that in the same volume as Wischmeyer's contribution, Soding, "Glaube, der durch Liebe wirke," 173, who fully recognizes the function of circumcision, food laws, etc., as boundary markers, made the comment: "That the wall separating Jew and Gentile has been torn down is the point of the letter to the Ephesians. In Galatians, however, ecclesiology stands in the shadow of soteriology; works of the Law will be excluded because they cannot contribute anything to justification."

1-5,[158] while also functioning as a means of moving on to further stages in Paul's argument. At this point, it is not what one might call another argument, a second point, after that about experience, though many have so taken it and spoken about two arguments, experience and the case of Abraham. Rather, it *backs up* the point about experience by drawing a parallel between the experience of the Galatians and that of Abraham.[159]

We need to note that Paul here quoted Genesis 15:6 according to the LXX, which translated the Hebrew *wh'mn* by the Greek aorist indicative active επιστευσεν, which carries a punctiliar sense. Paul has thus interpreted Abraham's believing as a specific act of trust in the word or promises made by God to him.[160]

The way in which in fact Paul turned from their experience to Scripture, specifically the example of Abraham, was somewhat abrupt.[161] This makes one ask whether there was something in the situation in Galatia which renders this transition intelligible? It could suggest that he expected the Galatians to be acquainted with this portion of Scripture. Did Paul himself make use of Abraham during the time when he preached and taught among them? Or had his opponents emphasized the figure of Abraham, in their argument for the continuity of the people of God in the present with the past story beginning with the patriarch of Israel?[162]

Probably it was not a case of either/or, but both/and.[163] Paul could hardly have spoken about Jesus without indicating his place in the history of God's saving activity and without making, therefore, some reference to Israel and the ancestor of Israel, Abraham.[164] On the other hand, it is equally a reasonable

158. So Bruce, *Galatians*, 147–53; Wakefield, *Where to Live*, 160–61. Konradt, *Die aus Glauben*, 38, takes the καθως Αβρααμ clause as elliptical: "With you it is exactly as with Abraham."

159. Note the verbal link between the mention of the noun πιστις at the end of verse 5 and the appearance of the verb επιστευσεν in the quotation in verse 6.

160. What Dobbeler, *Glaube als Teilhabe*, 134, calls his "conversion" faith. Since Paul understands Abraham's faith as the conversion of a sinner, he reduced Abraham's faith to the moment of conversion.

161. Koch, *Die Schrift*, 106, points out that here (Gal 3:6) Paul moves Αβρααμ to the beginning of the quotation for emphasis (unlike Rom 4:3).

162. For this view, see Barrett, *Allegory of Abraham*, 154–70; Martyn, *Law-Observant Mission*, 307–324; Moxnes, *Theology*, 211; Donaldson, *Remapping*, 120, 125–26; Watson, *PJG*, 131–32.

163. E.g., Das, *Paul*, 164.

164. Cf. Hays, *Faith*, xxxiv, who writes: "Paul writes as a preacher engaged in a lively intertextual interplay with an audience that knows well the story of Jesus' crucifixion (as Paul reminds them in Gal 3:1) *and the broad framework of the story of Israel*" (my italics). See also Hays, *Faith*, xxxv–xxxviii, though on 285 he seems to support Barrett, Martyn, et al. (see note 162 above). Seifrid, *Christ Our Righteousness*, 79, doubts

assumption that those who had arrived in Galatia introduced the Galatians to a different interpretation of Abraham: they stressed Genesis 17 and the place of circumcision in his life and the divine command that circumcision should be a characteristic mark of his descendants forever.[165]

On this assumption, we may be certain that Paul is endeavoring to undermine this stress by appealing to Genesis 15. That Paul was silent on Genesis 17 may have been deliberate on his part. Alternatively, Genesis 15 may equally have been used by his opponents, and Paul is asserting that his is the correct interpretation.[166] Both Paul and those with whom he disagreed recognized the importance of Abraham; they differed in how they interpreted that importance.

It is important to remember that the passage from which Paul quoted initially—the story of Genesis 15—preceded the story recorded in Genesis 17.[167] In other words, in the Biblical narrative, long before God asked Abraham to be circumcised as a sign of His eternal covenant (Gen 17), He had made a promise to Abraham of descendants. To this promise, Abraham, though childless and advanced in years, had responded in trusting faith, and God had counted that response of faith for a right standing with Himself (δικαιοσυνη [Gen 15:6]). This divine promise is the basis of the covenant which God made with Abraham according to Genesis 15:7-19 (together with the further promise of land [v. 19]). It is no doubt this feature of the covenant

---

whether Paul was forced to appeal to Abraham because his opponents appealed to him as a model of circumcision. Scroggs, *Salvation History*, 220-21, wryly comments, "Are we to suppose that Paul had not thought about Abraham before Galatians?" and believes that the burden of proof lies on those who think that Paul created this topic de novo due to the situation. Wright's repeated stress on Paul's assumption of a narrative, a story of God's dealings with Israel, must be endorsed as fundamentally correct (*Pauline Perspectives*, 211-12, 244, 303-316, 358, 479-80, 516-17, 519, 548-49, 551-53). Thiessen, *Paul and the Gentile Problem*, 75, also believes that the Abrahamic narrative was already a significant part of Paul's preaching before the Galatian controversy.

165. Cf. Zeller, *Juden und Heiden*, 93-94. Martyn, *Galatians*, 289-94, suggests that the Jewish Teachers had probably expounded Genesis 17 with its mention of covenant and circumcision, and taught that circumcision was the initial step of observing the Law which was the way to overcome the Evil Inclination of the flesh.

166. So Barrett, *Allegory*, 159; *Freedom*, 22-25; Stanton, *Law of Moses*, 107.

167. The issue of whether Genesis 15 and 17 constitute variant traditions of God's making a covenant with Abraham does not, of course, arise as far as we are concerned, since Paul like his contemporaries would have read Genesis as a continuous story. At the same time, their sequence—faith followed by circumcision—could have been used by those who were seeking to persuade the Galatian Christians to be circumcised and keep the provisions of the law (a point made by Barclay, *Obeying*, 53). Paul does not in fact address this potential problem for his case.

in Genesis 15 which enabled Paul in the course of his argument to insist on the priority of God's promise over Law (3:17; cf. Rom 4:9-10).[168]

So, Genesis 15 had priority over Genesis 17! For Paul, the Genesis 15 passage was a vital clue in discerning what was the basis on which God intended to deal with Abraham and his descendants, and, ultimately, through them, with all human beings: viz. God's promise and our response in trusting acceptance, or, to put the matter in another way, God's saving action implementing His promise and our response in trusting acceptance. Thus, for Paul the Genesis 15 passage indicated that what God was looking for was faith. So he can say that faith is what should characterize the "sons of Abraham." (We might have expected Paul to have referred to οι δικαιοι, but clearly the issue was incorporation into the Abrahamic covenant and family, and so sonship fitted better.)

A crucial question must now be faced. What exactly was it that Abraham believed? In Genesis 15, as mentioned above, God promised the aged and childless Abraham an heir begotten by himself and descendants ("seed") as innumerable as the stars in the heavens (15:4-5). From what Paul said in Galatians 3:8, he had interpreted these descendants who should be as innumerable as the stars in the heavens *as inclusive of non-Jews*. He refers to the statement in Scripture (viz. Gen 12:3/18:18) that in Abraham all the nations (εθνη) would be blessed. God made Abraham a promise of a world-wide family. How would this come about? Clearly, to anticipate, the relationship of non-Jews to God must be set on a right footing and their relationship to Jews must be clarified.

We return to the quotation from Genesis 15:6. It had really given the answer to the two questions with which Paul started this section of the letter in 3:2 and 5. The verb in the quotation επιστευσεν picked up the noun πιστις in verses 2 and 5. This text, then, highlighted the importance of faith. By drawing a parallel between Abraham's faith and the Galatians's faith, Paul clearly intended to emphasize to the Galatians that faith, the faith which they had initially exercised, was what God was looking for, for a right relationship with Himself and for belonging to His people.[169] In other words, if one was going to talk about being a member of the people of God in terms

---

168. This is something which Martyn constantly emphasizes throughout his individual studies on Galatians and in his commentary. Cf. Vogel, *Heil*, 66, who states that for the opponents to correlate the Abrahamic covenant and the Law was for Paul destructive of the former whose essence was promise.

169. Clearly, there are *implications* to be drawn from this, and one of these is that faith, and not circumcision and other aspects of keeping the Law (e.g., the food laws, the observance of the Sabbath, etc.), is what matters before God; and ultimately, that there should be table fellowship between Jew and Gentile within the community of believers.

of being a son or descendant of Abraham, then to be a true son or descendant of Abraham was to be a person of faith like him.[170]

This is precisely what Paul in fact goes on to say in verse 7:

> Therefore, learn [from this][171] that it is people of faith who are sons of Abraham. Now Scripture foresaw that God would justify the Gentiles on the basis of faith and it announced the good news to Abraham in advance. "In you shall all the nations be blessed." So then, it is people of faith who are blessed with faithful[172] Abraham. (3:6–9)

Scripture, here personified, speaks the word of God. Scripture is a source of revelation of what was God's will in the future. It had a prophetic role—it foresaw God's action in the future. From this we may deduce two things. In the first place, we may say that the word of Scripture long ago in connection with Abraham pointed ahead to Jesus Christ. Paul looked back from the standpoint of having come to this realization, and saw the promise to Abraham as an anticipation of the gospel about Jesus Christ.[173]

In the second place, the word of Scripture also had the effect of underlining the authority of what Paul was preaching.[174] What Paul had earlier claimed as revelation given to him personally (1:11–12, 15–16) accorded completely with what God had already disclosed in Scripture (προευαγγελίζεσθαι–Scripture preached the gospel/good news *beforehand*).[175] The very gospel which Paul had preached to the Galatians (1:6–7), which he

---

170. Even though Genesis 15 does not explicitly say that faith should characterize the descendants of Abraham, nonetheless, a son was expected to be like his father, and a Jewish exegete like Paul could legitimately claim that faith should be a characteristic of Abraham's offspring, as Siker, *Disinheriting the Jews*, 36, rightly points out. Zeller, *Juden und Heiden*, 98, states that Paul was arguing that access to being an heir was not through a chain of many heirs, a human continuum, but only via Jesus Christ and faith in him.

171. For this possible nuance of γινωσκετε, see Bauer, *Lexicon*, 160; Betz, *Galatians*, 141; Donaldson, *Remapping*, 332n29. The verb may, of course, be an indicative—"You know"—and appeal to what the Galatians know already, or should know.

172. As Dunn, *Galatians*, 167, points out, this is the natural translation. It would not be wrong to translate the Greek as "believing Abraham," even if this is not exactly euphonic in English, or indeed "Abraham who believed." Clearly, for Paul, Abraham's faith was the basis for his continuing faithfulness.

173. Barclay, *Gift*, 415, 418, calls this "the hermeneutical priority of the Christ-event" and asserts that Paul "finds *echoes of the gospel in the Scriptures of Israel*."

174. Cf. Hansen, *Abraham*, 80–82, 89.

175. It is worth reminding ourselves that Paul was not concerned to state some new Christian truth but that which was already attested in Scripture. Cf. the comment on Romans 3:31 of Frankemölle, "Völker-Verheissung," 289.

had laid before the Jerusalem leaders (2:2), for whose integrity he had not yielded an inch (2:5), which had been recognized by those leaders (2:7), and for departing from which he had publicly rebuked Peter at Antioch (2:14), this gospel was in line with what God had said long ago to Abraham. It was not any human invention.

Faith figures in verses 7-8a and 9, though not actually in the quotation from Genesis 12:3/18:18, which Paul calls upon in verse 8b, but Paul had already quoted Genesis 15:6 at verse 6, with its reference to the fact that Abraham had believed God's promise.

While the introduction to the quotation in verse 7a says, "Scripture, because it foresaw that God would *justify* the Gentiles on the basis of faith, preached the gospel beforehand to Abraham," the actual quotation says, "All the nations[176] will be *blessed* in you." Two things call for comment. In the first place, being justified and being blessed seem to be set in parallel. Then, secondly, the Scripture actually quoted moved from God's dealings with Abraham himself to the indication that God had a universal purpose in calling Abraham and making a nation from him. God intended to use Israel, Abraham's descendants, to bring blessing to the nations.[177] It never was His intention from the beginning to restrict His blessing only to one nation.[178]

Paul in his introduction to the quotation from Scripture conjoined gospel and justification. What God said to Abraham was a preaching of the gospel in advance, and its message spoke about justification (δικαιοι τα εθνη ο Θεος). The Gospel was adumbrated clearly in the Genesis story about Abraham. Paul drew a connection between that promise to Abraham and the Gospel: the promise is the content of the gospel proclaimed to Abraham. That is to say, Paul saw justification as an integral part of God's dealings with Abraham and, therefore, of all humanity in the future. The same God who made promises to Abraham and declared him in the right with Himself

---

176. Paul has altered Genesis 12:3, which read πασαι αι φυλαι της γης into παντα τα εθνη from Genesis 18:18, in order to gain a correspondence between his assertion in verse 8a that the blessing promised to Abraham concerned the Gentiles and the scriptural quotation in verse 8b. See Koch, *Schrift*, 162-63.

177. Blessing is a key term a little later in this section in verse 14, where it is equated with receiving the Spirit. Paul was clearly preparing the way for this climactic point already at this earlier stage in his argument. Wakefield, *Where to Live*, 133-34, sees a chiastic structure in the OT quotations, especially in verses 8-14, and, indeed, in verses 6-14.

178. Wright, *Pauline Perspectives*, 33, 91, 122, 217, 432, 434, 505, constantly stresses this theme. Wisdom, *Blessing*, 137-42, 85-86, has shown that the promise of blessing for the nations was taken up only relatively rarely in the Old Testament outside the patriarchal narratives and that in post-biblical Judaism it is ignored by the Qumran writings and by Josephus, while elsewhere it is interpreted as the positive influence received by Gentile communities through the presence of righteous Israelites in their midst.

is the God who has acted in Jesus to set those who believe in Jesus in the right with Himself. For Paul, God's word of promise to Abraham had been realized eschatologically in the justification of those who like Abraham exercised faith.[179] Justification, it would seem, was not an innovation produced under the pressure of the opposition faced in Galatia. Justification was characteristic of how God acted from the beginning. The gospel, what it promised, viz. blessing, and justification, go together.[180]

The actual quotation at verse 8—"In you shall all the nations be blessed"—is, strictly speaking, an amalgam of Genesis 12:3 and 18:18. The promise to Abraham at the time when God called him to go out from Ur of the Chaldees did include a universal note, but Genesis 12:3 LXX actually has πασαι αι φυλαι της γης. It is Genesis 18:18 LXX which included the phrase το εθνη της γης, and was thus ideal for Paul's purposes. There is, of course, no basic difference in sense between all the tribes of the earth and all the nations, but "nations" was better suited to Paul's argument from a verbal point of view.

Though Paul described Scripture as preaching the Gospel beforehand to Abraham because it foresaw that God would justify the Gentiles by faith, the actual key word in the quotation is "blessed." The Gospel is all about blessing coming to the Gentiles. At this stage in his argument, there is, as mentioned above, an implicit equation of blessing and justification. Genesis 15:1-6 is being used to interpret Genesis 12:1-3.[181]

The point being made is this: If blessing was promised to the Gentiles in and through Abraham, the one whose faith was reckoned as righteousness, this in turn showed that Scripture had foreseen that God would justify the Gentiles also on the basis of faith (v. 8).[182] And this justification is reckoned to Gentiles qua Gentiles,[183] not on Gentiles who have undergone circumcision and would count as proselytes

---

179. Sänger, *Verkündigung*, 86–87

180. Sänger, *Verkündigung*, esp. 82–151, stresses this entwining (Verschränkung) of the two in Paul. He criticizes Käsemann's interpretation, in which he feels there is a danger that in the end Israel's election becomes submerged in the faithfulness of the Creator to the whole of creation and the promise is subsumed into justification (102–6). Esler, *Galatians*, 176, thinks that Paul claimed "righteousness" as part of the social identity of his congregations (the ingroup), seeking to wrest it from the advocates of circumcision (the outgroup).

181. See Sänger, *Verkündigung*, 265; Wisdom, *Blessing*, 140–43.

182. Cf. Hansen, *Abraham*, 114. Scripture itself extends the principle of righteousness by faith attested for Abraham to the Gentiles.

183. Konradt, *Die aus Glauben*, 40.

Paul's conclusion runs: "So then, it is people of faith who are being blessed with Abraham who exercised faith"[184] (3:9). He gathered up the two key terms of the previous sentences, "faith" and "blessing." Basically, what Paul had done was to redefine what being a son/daughter of Abraham was. It was not a case of race or ethnicity; it was not a case of a biological factor of physical descent within the people of Israel, the descendants of Abraham, the ancestor of the nation. Nor was it a case that circumcision was an essential mark of being a son/child of Abraham. To be a child of Abraham meant being like him in the exercise of trusting faith in the God who called Abraham and made promises of blessing to him.

If we have discerned the flow of Paul's thought correctly, there was an intertwining of soteriological and ecclesiological concerns. Soteriology was involved but so also was the issue who was a member of Abraham's family.

Paul did not immediately explain what he envisaged this blessing for the Gentiles to be (the answer comes at the end of the very next paragraph of the letter).[185] Instead, having argued that faith was the distinguishing mark of those who were (true) sons/ daughters of Abraham (vv. 7-9), Paul continued by contrasting this with those who relied on doing the works of the law (v. 10), since this was the issue at stake in the controversy.

To whom does this phrase οσοι εξ εργων νομου (v. 10) refer? Do we have here a general reference, i.e., was Paul referring to his fellow country men and women who regarded the doing what the law required to be the basis of getting in to the Age to Come,[186] or is it a specific reference, i.e., had Paul in mind the opponents in Galatia, on whom he had already called an anathema in 1:8-9?[187]

---

184. The words "who exercised faith" is an attempt to render the adjective πιστος, on the grounds that Paul is here adopting an interpretation of Abraham which differed from his Jewish background (cf. Schlier, *Galater*, 127, "mit dem gläubigen Abraham"; Mussner, *Galaterbrief*, 211, 216 (like Schlier); Bruce, *Galatians*, 153, 157, "the man of faith"; Betz, *Galatians*, 137, 143, "with Abraham the believer"; Longenecker, *Galatians*, 115-16, "the man of faith"; Ulrichs, *Christusglaube*, 98 [like Schlier and Mussner]). Dunn, *Galatians*, 166-67, retains "faithful," maintaining that Paul saw no danger in speaking of Abraham's faithfulness.

185. From within 3:8, as suggested above, one could deduce that justification on the basis of faith was the blessing that God had in mind. But for Paul, receiving the Spirit (so verse 14 interpreted the promised blessing) was an integral part of the process of being set right with God.

186. Critics of the New Perspective have argued that Sanders, Dunn, and others have not paid enough attention to the issue of who would be acceptable to God at the Last Judgment and so enter the Age to Come.

187. Hansen, *Abraham*, 116-20; Wisdom, *Blessing*, 160-64, 223; Morland, *Curse*, 202-3, 211; Lee, *Blessing*, 43; Gombis, *Arguing*, 82-83, 90. Morland, *Curse*, 206-211, goes further and believes that Paul was here claiming that the Law, i.e., the Pentateuch,

We shall first examine the general interpretation. Here the question of what Paul had in mind with the phrase "works of the law" must be answered. Did he have in mind the particular laws which served to mark out the distinctive character of the Jewish nation over against other nations—circumcision, food laws, sabbath observance, or was he thinking of the Law in its entirety? It should be observed that Paul's remarks are phrased in general terms, as earlier at 2:16 and 3:2: it was not a question of some particular laws nor was the issue of ethnicity at stake,[188] even if the approach of those who sought to do what the Law required had, as its corollary and consequence, the fact that the blessing promised by God in the Law (the passages in Genesis 12 and 18!) was confined to those who belonged to ethnic Israel and who observed the requirements of the Law.

For Paul, then, those who sought to be justified before God by doing what the Law required were, in fact, contrary to their intention, under the curse pronounced by the Law (v. 10). To support his assertion, Paul quoted Deuteronomy 27:26: "Cursed is everyone who does not continue in all that is written in the book of the Law, to do them."[189] There is, however, a puzzle here, because this quotation seems to play into the hands of Paul's opponents.[190] This quotation appears to be exactly the kind of thing that they were saying.[191]

Over a long period of time, many scholars have seen in the way Paul's argument proceeded an indication of how he sought to circumvent the

---

taught the need for faith, and that the opponents in Galatia were, therefore, guilty of not fulfilling the Law in playing down the importance of faith alone. But 3:11–12 seems to tell against this suggestion: not only did Paul quote Habakkuk 2:4 there as the key text but also actually said that the Law was not based on faith.

188. So Das, *Paul*, 157; Westerholm, *Perspectives*, 302, 315.

189. Deuteronomy 27:26 is the conclusion to a whole series of curses, set on Mount Ebal (vv. 15–25). See Koch, *Schrift*, 163–65, for discussion of the details of what alteration of Deuteronomy 27:26 Paul made. It had the effect of emphasizing the written character of the Law. Koch, *Schrift*, 165, also points to Paul's use of γραμμα (2 Cor 6) to show that the Law leads to death.

190. This has been noted by many—e.g., Dunn, *Galatians*, 171, who comments that Paul's claim was exactly the opposite from what it should have been; the text from Deuteronomy simply contradicted the claim it was supposed to support. See also Wakefield, *Where to Live*, 66, 158; Lee, *Blessing*, 41–42.

191. Martyn, *Galatians*, 309, in fact assumes that this was one of the texts which they quoted on the grounds that Paul neither uses Deuteronomy 27:16 nor does he develop the curse/cursed theme elsewhere. Sanders, *Paul, the Law, and the Jewish People* (hereafter PLJP), 21, believes that Paul chose Deuteronomy 27:26 simply because it was the only text which linked Law and curse, but Paul seems to have had a deeper reason than just a verbal link up in referring to this passage from Deuteronomy. Furthermore (pace Sanders), only if in fact the stress is on πασιν (cf. 5:3), does Paul's argument about doing the Law in verses 11–12 hold up (cf. Smith, *Saved*, 76–77n16).

exploitation of passages like Deuteronomy 27:26; namely, that he seems to presuppose that no one in fact did keep the whole Law.[192] This has been called the "missing premise" argument and may be set out as follows:

- Cursed is everyone who does not obey all of the Law (v. 10b).
- No one is in fact capable of obeying the whole Law (unexpressed).
- Therefore, whoever seeks to obey the whole Law must be under a curse (v. 10a).[193]

This approach has come in for some criticism on the grounds that if this were what Paul was really getting at, it was not what he actually said.[194] While this seems at first glance to expose a considerable weakness in the view which it criticizes, it may not, on reflection, be a compelling point. Paul had already stated earlier that he and Jewish believers like Peter knew that no one could in fact be justified before God by doing the works of the Law (2:15, supported by a quotation from Psalm 143:2),[195] while at 3:11[196] he

---

192. So, e.g., Mussner, *Galaterbrief*, 224-26; Longenecker, *Galatians*, 118; Luz, *Geschichtesverständnis*, 149; Thielman, *Paul*, 126; Westerholm, *Perspectives*, 375n66; Kim, *Paul*, 129, 141-43; Das, *Paul*, 145-70; Donaldson, *Remapping*, 336n83; Thurén, *Derhetorizing*, 87, 114; Smith, *Saved*, 76-85 (for a list of those who have adopted this approach, see 81n29); Konradt, *Die aus Glauben*, 41; Barclay, *Gift*, 405 (pointing to Pseudo-Philo, *4 Ezra*, and the Hodayot as examples of Jewish writers with a pessimistic view of Israel's capacity to keep the Law. Barclay does not refer to the missing premise terminology, but simply states that Paul's logic presupposes a lack of ability to remain faithful to the Law).

193. Cf. Smith, *Saved*, 82.

194. E.g., Wakefield, *Where to Live*, 67. Cosgrove, *Cross*, 53-54, also rejects the missing premise approach.

195. In seeking to work out how they might have reached this conclusion, the point made by Das (see note 70), originally made in connection with Paul, should be borne in mind: the history of Israel would amply demonstrate that the idea of life through obeying the Law was illusory, while sectarian Judaism clearly believed that a majority of their fellow country men and women had strayed from the way of obedience to the Law. Indeed, Jesus regarded Israel collectively as "lost sheep" (Matt 10:6, taking οἴκου Ἰσραηλ as an epexegetic genitive).

196. See Westerholm, *Perspectives*, 303-4, for a full discussion of the various ways of taking 3:11. There is a dispute as to how 3:11 should be translated. Should δῆλον be taken with the first ὅτι clause, producing, "It is clear that no one is justified before God by doing the Law, because," followed by the Habakkuk 2:4 quotation (so Mussner, *Galaterbrief*, 228; Sanger, *Verkündigung*, 269n439); or should δῆλον go with the second ὅτι, producing, "Because no one is justified before God by doing the Law, it is clear that" followed by the Habakkuk quotation? (For a defense of this translation, see Wright, *Climax*, 149n42; Thielman, *Paul*, 127 [Thielman sees in the progression of thought in 3:11 the movement from plight to solution—in opposition to the suggestion of Sanders that Paul moves from solution to plight; cf. *Plight to Solution*, 69]; Martyn *Galatians*,

asserted that "no one is justified before God εν νομου"—this phrase being a stylistic variation on the earlier εξ εργων νομου.

There is another argument brought against the view that Paul was assuming that no one can keep the Law, namely, that no one in Judaism believed that the Law could be perfectly obeyed and that repentance and the sacrificial system were available for the forgiveness of sins and so for the maintenance of one's position within the Covenant.[197] Against this position, it may be argued that Paul before his Damascus Road experience did believe that he had kept the Law blamelessly (Phil 3:6b).[198] Furthermore, the use of the sacrificial system to atone for sins could easily be regarded by some as performing what the Law required, with the danger that the element of divine grace in that system could tend to be submerged.[199]

Wright believes that Paul was talking about the nation of Israel and what happened when the nation as a whole failed to keep the Law.[200] But the context does not seem to be concerned with the nation of Israel as a whole.

Recently, Chee-Chiew Lee has pointed to the prophetic tradition, which, she claims, will have influenced Paul. In the proclamation of prophets like First Isaiah, Jeremiah, and Ezekiel, Israel was roundly condemned for its failure to keep the Law, a failure which was due to their *refusal* to keep the Law rather than any *inability* to do so. Indeed, the book of Deuteronomy asserted that the Law was not all that difficult to keep (Deut 30:11–14). In the end, this refusal to obey the Law of God had led to a hardening of the heart. She suggests that this prophetic tradition should

---

311; and especially Wakefield, *Where to Live*, 162–67, 207–214, who complains that the issue has hardly been discussed by commentators.) From our point of view, it does not greatly matter whether the Habakkuk grounds the assertion or the Habakkuk quotation is the conclusion drawn from the previous statement. Either way, it is of key importance.

197. Sanders, *PPJ*, 93–94, 135, 137, 143, 147, 157, 168, 203–5, has stressed that the rabbis did not expect people to fulfill the Law perfectly. The intention to remain within the covenant and keep God's commandments was the all-important thing. Criticizing this view, Esler, *Galatians*, 187, points out that non-compliance does not mean that compliance was impossible, appealing to Deuteronomy 30:11–14.

198. Whether he meant absolute obedience to everything that the Law required or whether a great deal of obedience plus use of repentance and the sacrificial system to atone for his transgressions (i.e., habitual obedience) may be left on one side here. Jesus' parable of the Pharisee and the Tax Collector (Luke 18:9–14) suggests that Jesus had met some Pharisees who shared Paul's confidence. This piece of evidence may not be summarily dismissed.

199. Again, the Pharisee in Jesus' parable, referred to in the previous note, springs to mind.

200. Wright, *Climax of the Covenant*, 137–56. Accordingly, in verses 13–14, he sees "Christ" as the Messiah representing Israel, who takes on himself the curse of Israel's exile and inaugurates the return from exile (*Climax*, 151, 153–55).

also be taken into account when we are considering Paul's argument at Galatians 3:10.[201] Certainly, the history of Israel could be said to support Paul's contention, for the Scriptures afforded amply witness of Israel's failure to be an obedient and faithful people of God.

Accordingly, the so-called "missing premise" argument may not be dismissed. It still has a cogency, notwithstanding the criticism levelled against it. Paul maintained that those who sought to rely on doing the Law, whether to ensure their status in the covenant and so inherit life in the Age to Come or for non-Jewish believers in Jesus to ensure that they were properly in the covenant which God made with Abraham/Israel, both were in fact under the curse pronounced by that very Law which they sought unsuccessfully to keep: "Cursed is everyone who does not remain in all that is written in the book of the Law, to do them" (v. 10b; quoting Deut 27:26).

Although we do not wish to fall into the trap of interpreting Galatians by Romans, nevertheless it is difficult to imagine that Paul's criticism in Romans of the human race, whether Jew or Gentile, that all were guilty before God and stood condemned by the Law (Rom 1:18-30, 23; 5:12, 14, 20), was not his view when he wrote Galatians. If it is reasonable to suppose that he believed that all were sinful and unable to keep the Law, then it is reasonable to assume that that view stood behind Paul's argument in Galatians 3:10-12.[202]

Wakefield has proposed a variant of the interpretation just criticized.[203] He follows Martyn's apocalyptic approach—that Paul was working with the contrast between the two ages, the present (old) age and the new age already penetrating the present age through what God had done in Christ for us humans. Wakefield suggests that the Law belongs to the old age, which stands under God's condemnation. He takes the phrase in verse 10 οι εχ εργων νομου to mean those who were living in the sphere

---

201. Lee, *Blessing*, 198–200. She also points out that the LXX adds "all" to the statements of Leviticus 18:5 and Deuteronomy 27:26, and that this might also have influenced Paul in the idea that God required the carrying out of all the Law (200–201). Esler, *Galatians*, 184–88, discusses Galatians 3:10–12 only very briefly, but assumes that Paul is here engaging in negative stereotyping of those with whom he disagrees in order to promote the identity of his own group. Paul, therefore, accused Israelites of a factual failure to keep the Law. This comes close to the missing premise position from a different angle.

202. Sanger, *Verkündigung*, 268, argues that from the standpoint of the cross, Paul saw all people as godless and not in a position to keep the Law. Berger, *Abraham*, 51, states that non-fulfillment of the Law was a fact for Paul, and that he combined law and curse without hesitation.

203. Wakefield, *Where to Live*, 179–80. This is part of Wakefield's overall thesis that the key issue in Galatians is "Where to Live"—in the Law or in the Spirit.

of the Law (irrespective of whether they fulfilled the Law's demands or not—which Wakefield sees as irrelevant to Paul's argument): they were automatically under a curse (v. 10a).

But is it convincing to interpret the phrase in this way? We may ask why did not Paul simply write οι υπο νομον?[204] He could have achieved a chiastic type balance between υπο νομον and υπο καταραν thereby. Furthermore, Paul's previous use of the phrase εξ εργα νομου at 2:16; 3:2, 5 suggests that he had in mind the actual doing of what was required by the Law, rather than just living within its sphere. When later on he said that if the Galatians had had themselves circumcised, they were under an obligation to do the whole Law (5:3), deeds are clearly and inescapably in mind. Accordingly, we do not feel that Wakefield has made out his case at this point.

We turn now to the second interpretation of 3:10 mentioned above, which, it is claimed, would do justice to Paul's capacity to argue his case and at the same time avoid the "missing premise" argument. Wisdom has argued that the phrase οι εξ εργων νομου referred in fact to the trouble makers in Galatia.[205] They were the ones under a curse![206] Why? Because, by insisting that Gentile converts accepted circumcision and the prescriptions of the Law, they were in fact resisting God's promise to Abraham to bless the nations through his descendants, the promise which had been brought into effect in Jesus and his cross, to be received on the basis of faith in Jesus crucified and raised.[207] Their version of the gospel was in fact not a gospel and Paul called down a curse on them for preaching such a travesty of the true gospel; for him it was equivalent to apostasy and idolatry (1:6-9),[208] for this other gospel functioned as another god which enticed the people of God away from

---

204. As he does, e.g., Gal 4:5, 21; Rom 6:14-15; 1 Cor 9:20 (three times).

205. Wisdom, Blessing, 160-64, 223. We shall interact with Wisdom rather than Hansen (see note 183), who argues from Galatians 6:13 (where Paul accused his opponents of not in fact keeping the Law) that they are in mind at 3:10. Hansen adheres to the missing link approach as a result.

206. Wisdom, Blessing, 17, 19, 153, 182, 221, argues that Paul was operating with the Deuteronomic framework of blessing for obedience and curse for disobedience to the Covenant with the God of Israel. (Wisdom, Blessing, 155n6, maintains that this is the "missing link" behind Galatians 3:10-14, i.e., Paul's conceptual assumptions.)

207. Wisdom, Blessing, 145, 153, 160, 167, 179-81, 223-24.

208. Wisdom, Blessing, 181, 191-200. Equally, for the Galatians to follow the opponents' teaching would be to repeat Israel's sin in the wilderness (202-3, assuming an allusion to Exodus 32:8; Deuteronomy 9:6, at Galatians 1:6) and they would fall under the curse themselves (162).

loyalty and obedience to God.[209] Its proponents ignored the fact that the Law was intended to be temporary until Christ and Faith came.[210]

Wisdom's approach could claim to ease the problem over the flow of Paul's argument in Galatians 3:10-14. It still bears on the issue of what characterizes those who were members of the people of God and the issue of how Gentiles were to be incorporated into the people of God. It also fits in with Paul's insistence on God's dealings with Abraham as the clue to how He wished to deal with all peoples, rather than the Law given on Sinai through Moses. There would be no difficulty in fitting Wisdom's approach concerning the specific reference to the trouble makers at 3:10 into the general approach which sees the reference to "works of the Law" as more than just those signs of Israel's national distinctiveness (circumcision, sabbath observance, food and ritual purity laws), though of course including them.

Despite all this, it must be pointed out that a reference to the trouble makers as Paul saw them would be somewhat abrupt (even if they can never have been far from his thoughts).[211] Paul had really been concentrating on the Galatians themselves since 3:1. He had asked them whether they received the Spirit because of doing the works required by the Law or through believing the message which Paul had proclaimed (3:2)? He had asked them whether God was performing miracles among them because they performed the works required by the Law or because they had believed the message (3:5)? The *Galatians* were his major concern at this point: it was their spiritual well-being which was at stake and he was filled with concern lest they became spiritual casualties. This makes us hesitant to endorse Wisdom's suggestion.

Thirdly, mention should also be made of the position put forward by Bachmann.[212] He believed that Paul has linked two syllogisms.[213] In this intertwining, the minor premise of the first syllogism became the proposition of the second syllogism. In both syllogisms, sentences from the Scriptures functioned as the premises to confirm the correctness of the proposition. Since the Scriptures were accepted as authoritative, the use of sentences from Scripture substantiated the truth of the proposition.

His reconstruction may be set out as indicated by his own table:

---

209. Wisdom, *Blessing*, 174, 181, 206-7.

210. Wisdom, *Blessing*, 147 50, 181.

211. Nowhere else in the letter when Paul refers to his opponents does he describe them simply by the phrase οσοι/οι εξ εργων νομου.

212. Bachmann, *Argumentation*, 524-44.

213. "Um die Verkettung zweier Syllogismen bemuht" (Bachmann, *Argumentation*, 537).

Syllogism 1: Proposition 3:10a
Major Premise 3:10b = Deuteronomy 27:26
Minor Premise 3:11a
Syllogism 2 Proposition 3:11a
Major Premise 3:11b = Habakkuk 2:4
Minor Premise 3:12ab = Leviticus 18:5[214]

Bachmann does not simply translate Paul's actual words, but offers his own paraphrases, which will need to be examined closely.

What strikes one about this suggestion is that it is rather complicated and makes considerable demands on the recipients (who would in the majority of cases presumably *hear* Galatians read to them rather than read it themselves and be able to reflect on it), and this in a letter where absolute clarity was needed in order to carry the addressees with the author because of the critical nature of the situation.[215]

Bachmann's paraphrases of the premises need to be examined, particularly in his syllogism 1. He paraphrases the major premise of the first syllogism as follows: "Every transgressor of (at least one of the) individual regulations of the Law is an accursed person [see Deut 27:16]." We may accept this as a reasonable paraphrase in view of the stress on "all that is written in the book of the law," together with Paul's own assertion that if a person accepted circumcision, they were indebted to keep the whole Law (5:3). Then Bachmann paraphrases the minor premise with "Every one who is in the Law/of works/individual regulations of the Law, is a transgressor of (at least one of the) individual regulations of the Law [see Gal 3:11b–12]." Here one suspects that his paraphrase depends more on his previous paraphrase of the major premise rather than on what Paul actually says in 3:11a.[216] What Paul actually said was that no one is counted in the right (righteous) before God through the Law.

---

214. Bachmann, *Argumentation*, 539.

215. I am not competent to say whether this intertwining of two syllogisms was widely used by Greek authors, and, as far as I can see, Bachmann himself does not indicate this in his article. What he says (537) is that the use of pre-given material to support the correctness of the proposition was common to Jewish and Greek writers. This is, of course, not the same as saying that the intertwining of two sets of syllogisms was common to both spheres of literature. Bachmann refers to Siegert, *Argumentation bei Paulus*, 157–64, but this is an excursus on Paul's use of Scripture, which Siegert prefers to describe as the use of Scripture in argument rather than Scriptural proof.

216. To use an analogy from the game of snooker, he is like a player trying to build a break who gets somewhat out of position with a shot, as a result of which the subsequent shot is made all the more difficult because he has landed out of position.

Furthermore, does not what Bachmann say in his paraphrase virtually amount to saying that no one in fact keeps the Law—the so-called implied premise which we discussed earlier-although he rejects this?[217]

When it comes to his syllogism 2, Bachmann paraphrases the proposition (still 3:11a) as: "Every one who is in the Law/of works/individual regulations of the Law, is not a righteous person," which is different from his paraphrase of verse 11a as the minor premise of syllogism 1. Then he paraphrases the major premise (3:11b) as: "Every righteous person will live/ is of faith [see Hab 2:4]," and the minor premise (3:2a–12b), "Every one who is in the Law/of works/individual regulations of the Law is not of faith (but will live in/is of individual regulations of the Law) [cf. Lev 18:5]." While this captures the sense of being in a sphere which can be described as the Law, one might have expected Bachmann to reproduce a reference to actual performance or doing what the Law required.

All in all, we do not feel that Bachmann's argument is convincing.

To return to Paul's argument. Paul, then, found confirmation of the fact that no one was justified before God by doing the Law in the words of the prophet Habakkuk: "The one who is in the right with God on the basis of faith shall live."[218] (Paul here was following the LXX text of Habakkuk, but he omitted μου after εκ πιστεως and, exploiting the ambiguity of the position and relationship of εκ πιστεως in the sentence, referred it to the believer, ο δικαιος.)[219]

By contrast, the Law was based on a different principle: "But the Law is not based on the principle of faith (ουκ εστιν εκ πιστεως),[220] but the person who does these things shall live by them" (v. 12). Clearly, in this section of his argument, Paul was setting out Law (deeds) and faith as alternatives,[221] on the basis of which a person would live[222] (we shall come back to the

---

217. "This thesis on the argument of 3:10–12 emerges also without accepting the implicit premise and is in this respect to be clearly differentiated from P. Lampe's attempt at reconstruction" (Bachmann, *Argumentation*, 53).

218. The alternative translation is: "The one who is in the right shall live on the basis of their faith."

219. See Koch, *Schrift*, 127–29, for discussion of the details of Paul's alterations (the Habakkuk quotation was only usable if μου was omitted) and whether there was a text like Paul's which existed before him.

220. Sprinkle, *Law*, 138, sees Paul drawing εκ πιστεως from the Habakkuk quotation in order to provide a contrast with the "doing" of the Leviticus quotation which follows in verse 12b.

221. For a similar contrast between Law and faith, see Romans 4:13–16.

222. Sprinkle, *Law*, 138, says that for Paul, Habakkuk and Leviticus are making two mutually exclusive soteriological statements. He adds later that they depicted two ways of escaping the covenant curses and attaining the blessing of life (140), and that

meaning of live). He accorded a priority to Habakkuk 2:4 over against Leviticus 18:5, and thus we have a sharp contrast. On the one hand, the Law, which was based on the principle of doing, insisted that it was the person who did what it required who would live by these actions (v. 12, quoting Lev 18:5); on the other hand, the person who had faith, a trust in Christ who was God's Son sent to effect our deliverance from this evil age (1:4), would live. Watson puts it well: Paul sought to establish on the basis of Habakkuk 2:4, "The radical priority of divine saving action even over the human action enjoined in the law itself."[223]

As to how Paul argued in 3:11-12, his argument appears to rest on a syllogism. However, instead of proceeding to state two arguments and then to draw a conclusion, he begins by stating his conclusion[224] in verse 11a: "No one is justified before God through the Law." The support for this is then given, firstly, by means of the Habakkuk quotation in verse 11b, "The person who is in the right with God by faith (εκ πιστεως) shall live," and then, in verse 12a, by the assertion "But the Law is not characterized by faith (ουκ εστιν εκ πιστεως), rather 'The one who does them [the Law's regulations] will live by them.'"

The syllogism may be set out as follows:

> Premise: The one who is just/righteous by faith will live (3:11b).
> Premise: But the Law does not enjoin faith (3:12a).
> Conclusion: Therefore, no one is justified by the Law (3:11a).[225]

"Leviticus promotes a Deuteronomic 'if . . . then' pathway to life, and Habbabuk anticipates God's intervention as the solution to the failure of the Deuteronomic paradigm" (163). Both passages offer life. Westerholm, *Perspectives*, 237, puts it sharply: "Hence the law's promise that 'the one who does the commandments will live by them' (3:12, quoting Lev 18:5) is false, in flat contradiction of the divine promise that 'the one who is rectified by faith will live' (Gal 3:11, quoting Hab 2:4)." See also Westerholm, *Perspectives*, 377. Thielman, *Paul*, 126, sees here a movement from plight to solution. Deuteronomy had predicted Israel's failure to keep the Law and that the curse of the Law would come upon her; Habakkuk 2:4 points to the solution: God grants life to those who trust in His saving deliverance.

223. Watson, *Hermeneutics*, 162; cf. 162-63: "There is a deep fault line within Scripture itself. If Habakkuk 2:4 represents one side of this fault line, Leviticus 18:5 represents the other" (although equally Watson maintains that faith and law are ultimately in harmony with one another, alluding to Romans 3:31). Sanger, *Verkündigung*, 272, states that the alternatives of ποιειν and πιστις reflect, on the anthropological and soteriological level, the antithesis of Torah and the Gospel of Christ.

224. Cf. Betz, *Galatians*, 146; Das, *Paul*, 165-66n59; Morland, *Curse*, 204-5. This view can call on 6:13, where Paul alleged that the opponents do not in fact keep the Law.

225. See Das, *Paul*, 165n59.

It is well at this point to recall our earlier discussion of what Paul learned on the Damascus Road, namely that his zeal for the Law had brought him to the point where he was in fact under the curse pronounced by that very Law! It was only the grace of God responded to in faith that brought him out of that sphere of the curse and into the sphere of blessing. It was through that same grace that God had called Abraham and promised through him to bless the nations. Some of what Paul learned through his Damascus Road experience was what he enunciated in 3:10-12.

If we take what Paul said in 3:10-12 as a whole, we see that he made certain assertions. As stated, it is quite likely that he took up a text used by his opponents, viz. Deuteronomy 27:26, but proceeded to nullify this by quoting Habakkuk 2:4. He assumed that in practice no one could claim to be justified before God at the Last Judgment on the basis of doing the Law.[226] Paul had thereby implied that those devout Jews of his day who had assumed that a verdict of acquittal before God depended on keeping the Law within the covenant people of God, are in fact under that very curse pronounced by the Law in Deuteronomy 27:26. (The same would apply to Gentiles who accepted the teaching of those who maintained that Gentiles wishing to become part of God's people and to have any chance of acquittal before God must keep the Law's commandments.) On the contrary, the way to right standing before God was that of faith (as response to what God had promised/done), as the prophet Habakkuk demonstrated. Paul has here set doing the Law and responding to what God has done with faith, over against each other.

In other words, Paul had to neutralise his opponents' use of Deuteronomy 27:26 and Leviticus 18:5, and did so by bringing in Habakkuk 2:4. In addition, Paul had in effect by means of the keyword πιστις and words with the root δικ- (δικαιοσυνη and δικαιος) linked Genesis 15:6 and Habakkuk 2:4 (quoted at 3:6 and 11 respectively). It is faith which brings Israelites/anyone into a right relationship with God, on the basis of which they will live.

In what sense is ζησεται used in both the Habakkuk and the Leviticus quotations in 3:11-12? There are two possibilities: either Paul was referring to life in the Age to Come as a result of final justification before the judgment seat of God (an eschatological, soteriological sense),[227] or he was referring to the

---

226. So, e.g., Berger, *Abraham*, 51; Kim, *Paul and the New Perspective*, 141-42 (Kim refers to the "implicit premise" behind 3:10a, that no one can keep the law perfectly); Westerholm, *Perspectives*, 375n66. Watson, *Hermeneutics*, 163n61, is critical; he thinks that this point is actually being read into the passage (specifically referring to Matera, *Galatians*, 124), while Paul is content to leave the two scriptural texts in stark juxtaposition.

227. Lee, *Blessing*, 46, in arguing for the sense of receiving future life, maintains

ongoing life in the present age, based either on a continuing exercise of faith or on keeping what the Law required[228] (the lifestyle of the people of God), or is it possible that Paul wished to insinuate both senses? It is not impossible that the apostle hoped that the recipients would draw both senses from the verb. If we take Galatians as a whole, Paul was concerned both with identity and behavior. He dealt with the question of who was a true son/daughter of Abraham, who was therefore a member of the people of God (identity); but he was also concerned with how believers in Christ should conduct themselves, and especially in the new communities being formed through the Gospel (behavior). The identity factor was the basis for the behavior aspect; conduct springs out of one's identity. Accordingly, we are inclined to leave open the possibility that both senses are to be held together.

The reason why faith was crucial in the process of salvation was because of what God had done for us in His Son, Jesus Christ, which is what Paul went on to describe in verses 13-14. He now gave an interpretation of the death of Jesus, precisely in terms of the curse and blessing, terms previously mentioned at verses 10 and 8-9 respectively. He wrote:

> Christ has redeemed[229] us[230] from the curse of the law, having become a curse for us, because it is written, "Cursed is everyone who hangs on a tree," in order that on the Gentiles the blessing promised to Abraham might come in Christ, in order that we might receive the promised Spirit through faith.[231] (3:13-14)

---

that Paul's interpretation is latent in the context of Habakkuk, where the faithful will look to God for deliverance so that they might survive the invasion and live by faith/faithfulness.

228. Wakefield, *Where to Live*, 169-70, 174-77, 183-84. Wakefield reports that both Ebeling and Lührmann refer to the possibility of taking ζησεται in this way, but that neither elaborated on the suggestion.

229. Paul used εξηγορασεν here and the same verb in the aorist subjunctive active εξαγοραση at 4:5.

230. The meaning is surely Jew and Gentile (so Dunn, *Galatians*, 176; Martyn, *Galatians*, 317; Hansen, *Abraham*, 122-23, against Betz, *Galatians*, 148, who limits it to Jewish Christians).

231. Deuteronomy 21:23c: Paul has substituted the adjective επικαταρατος for the perfect participle passive κεκατηραμενος, thus enabling him to link up with the quotation from Deuteronomy 27:26 at verse 10 (cf. Koch, *Schrift*, 165-66); he has omitted υπο Θεου after the adjective επικαταρατος (the idea that God cursed Jesus would be impossible for him *as a believer in Jesus as the Christ and the Lord*, though before his conversion it is quite probable that Paul had used this Deuteronomic passage to argue that Jesus of Nazareth could not possibly be the messiah of God because he had been cursed by God) and added the article ο between πας and the participle κρεμαμενος.

The death of Jesus on the cross was a representative enduring of the curse pronounced by the Law on all who did not keep the Law. In him the power of that curse was exhausted. God in fact raised him from the dead. Those united to him by faith, those who share in his death-to-sin, also share in the new life which he lives by the power of God.[232] There is an interchange:[233] the curse came upon Christ, but the blessing came to us. As a result of Christ's redemptive death, the nations/Gentiles had received the blessing promised to Abraham: ινα εις τα εθνη η ευλογια του Αβρααμ γενηται εν Χριστω. If Paul had finished his sentence at that point, the implication would be that the blessing promised to Abraham would consist of redemption from the curse, or justification before God. However, Paul proceeded to add another ινα clause: ινα την επαγγελιαν του Πνευματος λαβωμεν δια της πιστεως. God had poured out His Spirit on those who believed in His Son. Syntactically, is this second clause dependent on the first, and so explains the first one,[234] which would suggest that Paul interpreted the blessing promised to Abraham for the nations to be the gift of the Spirit? Or, is it co-ordinate with the first and dependent on the main verb, and so added a further purpose behind the death of Christ, which would suggest that Paul saw the gift of the Spirit as related to but distinguishable from justification/redemption, both coming about through the curse-bearing death of Jesus?[235]

A little later in his argument, at 4:4–7, Paul distinguished two aspects of Christian experience, though of course they are closely related. He said that Christians had received adoption (which we may accept as another image to describe the result of God's saving intervention through His Son), and then he added, "Because you are sons,[236] God has sent the Spirit of His Son into our hearts, crying Abba, Father. So then, you are no longer slaves but you are sons, and if sons, then also heirs through God" (4:6–7).[237] This supports

232. Hansen, *Abraham*, 126, suggests that the εν Χριστω Ιησου echoes the εν σοι of verse 8, because Paul already has in mind his assertion in verse 16 that Christ is Abraham's seed.

233. See Hooker, "Interchange in Christ," 349–61.

234. Schlier, *Galater*, 140–42; Dunn, *Galatians*, 179–80; Esler, *Galatians*, 175; Berger, *Abraham*, 54. Although Lee, *Blessing*, 53–59, accepts this syntactical explanation, she differs from Dunn in distinguishing between justification and the gift of the Spirit: "The content of the two clauses is related but not equated."

235. Lightfoot, *Galatians*, 139; Mussner, *Galaterbrief*, 235; Bruce, *Galatians*, 167–68; Longenecker, *Galatians*, 123–24; Martyn, *Galatians*, 321–24, 324–28; Witherington, *Grace*, 239–40 (who, however, takes the "we" to refer to Jewish Christians—which hardly seems right after 3:1–5).

236. The use of inclusive language (e.g., NRSV) rather destroys the link with His Son.

237. See Lee, *Blessing*, 55, for a table setting out the parallels between 3:13–14 and

taking 3:14b as indicating a related but not equated thought, with verse 14a. The weakness of this position is that Paul used the word "promise" which in the section which follows was certainly the promise made to Abraham (see vv. 18–19). This, however, may be met by expanding Hays's observation that "the material content of the promise to Abraham is subsumed entirely into categories supplied by the Church's experience [of the redemptive death of Christ and] of the Spirit."[238]

Paul had begun his argument by referring to the Galatians' experience of the Spirit (3:1–5);[239] now the reference to the Spirit in verse 14b is a reminder to the Galatians that they have already experienced what God promised.

By the phrase "through faith" at the end of verse 14 Paul once more emphasized that it was faith which God was looking for as the response to His redemptive act in Jesus. It also reminded the Galatians that it was nothing that we do or contribute which produces this gift—they had received the Spirit by faith (3:2). Through this phrase "by faith," Paul had created another link-up with his starting point in this section of the letter. "Faith" also linked up with verse 8, and verses 8 and 14 indicate that justification and receiving the Spirit are two sides of the same coin, the initial Christian experience.[240]

1.3.3. Galatians 3:15–20

Paul had not yet finished with the use which he wished to make of the story of Abraham. Paul made two further points in his next paragraph (vv. 15–20). Firstly, he played on the singular seed (σπερμα). The word of Scripture recorded God's promises to Abraham himself "and to your seed" (3:16; so Gen 12:7; 13:15; 17:7; 24:7). The term is a collective noun, meaning descendants. Paul knew that perfectly well. Most scholars assume that, in a way not out of keeping with the way Scripture was handled by Jewish exegetes of his own day and later,[241] Paul chose to take it in a

---

4:4-5.

238. Hays, *Echoes*, 110.

239. Many scholars have observed that "Spirit" in verses 2, 5, 14, acts as a clamp binding verses 1–14 together.

240. Whichever interpretation of the two ἵνα clauses we adopt, we may agree with this way of putting the matter. See especially, Dunn, *Baptism*, 108; *Galatians*, 179.

241. On this point, see the remarks in Bruce, *Galatians*, 172–73; Hansen, *Abraham*, 129, 207–8, 250n186; Dunn, *Galatians*, 183–84. Bassler, *Impartiality*, 75, 229n98, makes the comment that the possibility of a singular meaning of this equivocal word was always present. Daube, *NT and Rabbinic Judaism*, 438–44, has shown that in midrashic teaching the generic singular can be interpreted as a specific one. In one

strictly singular sense and to claim that in fact the promise referred to Christ himself (v. 16g).[242] God had in mind the person of Jesus the Christ when He made His original promise to Abraham. Paul has interpreted the promise in a Christological manner.[243] He has appropriated the promise of the Genesis passage for Jesus Christ. Jesus Christ was the seed of Abraham (and those united by faith with Christ will share in this status as well, but Paul did not say that yet, but he would do later; see 3:29), and he was the channel of the blessing promised to Abraham.

Hays has suggested that what inspired Paul to this exegesis was the famous promise to David in 2 Samuel 7:12-14, where the singular noun "seed" is not a collective noun but a reference to a specific royal successor to David.[244]

Does this mean that the Promise was, as it were, inapplicable between Abraham and Jesus Christ? Luz[245] argues in this way. He believes that in Galatians 3 promise marks the freedom and contingency of God's action in history. Promise shows that God's past historical activity can never be taken up into a mere visible continuity (Sukzession), but can be heard only as gracious favor (gnadiger Zuspruch). He goes on to say that the time before the Law was not characterized in a different way than the time after the Law: the promise was in force, but clearly not active in this period before the giving of the Law (immer in Kraft, aber offenbar . . . nicht wirksam). He maintains that history after Abraham is withdrawn directly from the visible effectiveness of the previously given promise. Paul does not mention Isaac or Jacob or God's action in Egypt. Paul does not reflect on justification by faith after Abraham. Earlier Luz had raised the question whether Paul's statement that people were imprisoned by the Law meant that there was no possibility of

---

interpretation of Genesis 15:13, "your seed" was taken to refer specifically to Isaac, and Daube sees this as a source of Paul's argument. In another interpretation, that of "man" in "God created man," a generic singular was given the force of a specific one, viz. the original, ideal Adam alone. Brewer, *Techniques and Assumptions*, 14-15, has argued that in scribal traditions there was a distinction between *peshat*, which sought the plain meaning of the text, and *derash*, which tried to find a hidden meaning, unrelated to the primary meaning of the text and was rare among the scribes. As to the former, one form was an ultra-literal interpretation, which was put forward even when the context and the plain meaning of the idioms used denied such an understanding. This could correspond to Paul's use here.

242. Grässer, *Alte Bund*, 60, believes that Paul's logic behind his equation of seed – Christ flows from his exegesis of Genesis 15:6 developed in 3:6-14.

243. Cf. Martyn, *Galatians*, 340: "Paul hears in Gen 17:8 a messianic prophecy, showing that the point of departure for his exegesis is the advent of Christ."

244. Hays, *Echoes*, 85; Luz *Geschichtsverständnis*, 182-85.

245. Luz, *Geschichtsverständnis*, 182-85.

salvation for people living in the period of the Law?[246] Paul would have conceded exceptions—otherwise he could not have spoken about David and the prophets as he does, but it was not his intention to make objective statements on the issue of the possibility of salvation for individuals.

Luz's theological exegesis is stimulating and thought provoking. Judging by Galatians 3:10, 21b, 23–25, salvation would in principle be ruled out before Jesus (cf. Rom 3:9–20, 23; 5:12, 21; 10:21), but even Luz himself notes that Paul's references to David and the prophets, together with that to the remnant in Romans 11:4–5, suggests that Paul would have made exceptions (those retrospectively saved by Christ's death). But it is questionable whether this concession goes far enough. Currently, with the emphasis on narrative theology, there would be many voices who would argue that Paul had in mind a continuous story of Israel, beginning with Abraham, then taking in the Exodus and the giving of the Law under Moses, David, the prophets including Elijah and Isaiah, the remnant idea, and on to Jesus.[247]

Wright has put forward a different interpretation of "seed."[248] He believes that Paul intended a collective meaning rather than an individual, purely Christological sense. Wright bases his case on two grounds. In the first place, precisely because for Paul Jesus was Israel's messiah, he in fact incorporated the people of God; Χριστός carried for Paul an incorporative sense. We may agree that in Hebraic-Jewish thinking there would be a natural tendency to think of the Messiah not just as an individual but also as the Messiah plus the people of Israel or the elect. However, while the risen Jesus is an inclusive figure in Paul's thought, it is surely best to take the corporate connotation to be revealed in this passage first at verses 26–29, especially verse 29: "So then you are Abraham's seed."

Secondly, Wright takes "seed" to mean family, and so assumes a contrast between the many families created by the Torah (in dividing Gentiles from Jews) and the single family incorporated in Christ. He relied on Burton,[249] for the sense of "family," but Burton pointed out that the examples he mentions are from late Hebrew usage and he did not himself favor assuming the sense of "family" here.

---

246. Luz, *Geschichtsverständnis*, 154.

247. Probably it was Hays, *Faith*, esp. 1–117, who started the approach of narrative theology in Pauline studies. It has been strongly taken up and argued by Wright (e.g., *Pauline Perspectives*, 129, 205, 245, 277, 298–99, 397–99, 401, 516, 519, 523) and others.

248. Originally in Wright, *Climax*, 157–74, and repeated in *Pauline Perspectives*, 531–32, 575.

249. Burton, *Galatians*, 505–510.

It should be pointed out that a number of scholars are inclined to combine the individual plus the incorporative sense here.[250]

The second point which Paul made in verses 15-20 was that the covenant sworn to Abraham by God could not be abrogated by anything that came later, not even by the Law promulgated on Sinai. He played on the double meaning of the word διαθηκη:[251] it can mean a covenant or a last will and testament. Bammel[252] has argued that Paul's statements here have in mind the Jewish institution of an irrevocable gift of a living person (*mattenat bari*). Under this, property could be transferred to someone else (though the donor might retain the right to usufruct during his own life). This did not allow any kind of cancellation once it had been made.[253]

Another possible explanation of Paul's statement at 3:15b is that ουδεις meant a person other than the testator: such a person cannot alter the will or add a codicil to it.[254] But might we not have expected Paul to have used αλλος or ετερος if he was thinking of another person?

Either interpretation could explain Paul's statement at 3:15b that "Once a person's διαθηκη has been ratified, no one can set it aside or add a codicil," and his insistence that the Law, given 430 years after the promise made by God to Abraham, could not in effect alter the terms of the promise. Therefore, the promise to Abraham had priority in disclosing God's intentions and purposes.[255] Irrespective of which interpretation is preferred,

---

250. See Burton, *Galatians*, 181-82; Longenecker, *Galatians*, 131-32; Witherington, *Grace*, 244-45. Dunn, *Galatians*, 191, however, is dismissive, and describes Wright's exegesis as tortuous. Hays, *Echoes*, 121, has reminded us that Paul's ecclesiocentric hermeneutic and his christological convictions are complementary, not contradictory.

251. As Paul stressed at 3:15, this is a human illustration. Greek and Roman law, just as we today, envisaged the possibility of someone changing their mind, either for personal reasons or because events required it, and altering their will.

252. Bammel, *Gottes ΔΙΑΘΗΚΗ*, 313-19. This view is accepted by Mussner, *Galaterbrief*, 236-37; Betz, *Galatians*, 155; Luz, *Geschichtsverständnis*, 164n184; Gaston, *Paul*, 58; Vogel, *Heil*, 65; Bachmann, *Anti-Judaism*, 47.

253. A weakness of Bammel's suggestion must be whether Paul's hearers/readers in Galatia would know about this Jewish institution. Betz, *Galatians*, 155, quotes from a personal letter to him from Professor R. Yaron (author of *Gifts in Contemplation of Death in Jewish and Roman Law*) in which he stated that he had little doubt that the arrangements akin to mattenat bari' were widespread in the Near East in NT times.

254. So Longenecker, *Galatians*, 130; Dunn, *Galatians*, 182; Martyn, *Galatians*, 338. Paul's argument that the Promise had both temporal and theological priority over against the Law is still clear, whichever interpretation of verse 15 is accepted.

255. Cf. Siker, *Disinheriting*, 38, "Thus one should not evaluate God's covenant with Abraham from the perspective of the Mosaic Law . . . rather, one should evaluate the Mosaic Law from the perspective of God's prior covenant with Abraham." Hansen, *Abraham*, 128, suggests that Paul has preferred to use the concept of promise rather than covenant, because the latter was loaded with nationalistic over-tones (cf. the

the thrust of Paul's argument was the unbreakable nature of what God promised to Abraham.[256]

Paul insisted that God dealt with Abraham on the basis of promise, and that this ruled out any idea that the inheritance (newly introduced at verse 18) promised to Abraham was to be enacted on the basis of the Law (3:18a). On the contrary, God graciously gave (κεχαρισται)[257] this inheritance to Abraham on the basis of His promise (v. 18b).[258]

Paul's approach has thus reached a point where the promise had been exalted (as it were) above the Law. This inevitably led to the question "What, then, was the purpose behind the giving of the Law?" and so, Paul was drawn into a brief discussion on why the Law was promulgated (vv. 19-25). He said three things about it at this point. Firstly, it was added των παραβασεων χαριν. The main interpretations of this phrase have been: either that it gave the reason "because of transgressions,"[259] or, that it gave the goal or purpose, with the sense that it aimed at actually encouraging transgressions.[260] Of these two, the subsequent statements of Paul about the Law acting as a jailor would seem to favor taking the meaning here as the Law's providing a check or break on sin. However, Dunn has queried whether there was negative nuance to the Law's role as custodian here: he believes that the role of the Law is that of protective custody.[261]

---

approach of Grässer, *Alte Bund*, 77, 130). Lategan, *Argumentative Situation of Galatians*, 388, thinks that Paul was here countering the stress on the Law by pointing out that Abraham, their spiritual father and model, was "uncircumcised, without the formalized law—in fact, a Gentile," when God called him. Later, in Romans 4, Paul made this point explicitly, of course.

256. As Grässer, *Alte Bund*, 58-59, rightly points out.

257. Berger, *Abraham*, 55, sees in the use of this word the exclusion of the way of works in the context of the promise.

258. Esler, *Galatians*, 175, 233, points out that a group's sense of destiny was part of their social identity; where they were heading was important to a sense of who the group was.

259. I.e., either to reveal or show up sin for what it is—transgression—and so, in that sense, produce transgressions (so Bruce, *Galatians*, 175), or with the implication that such would be punishable (so Mussner, *Galaterbrief*, 245-46; Esler, *Galatians*, 195-97; Luz, *Geschichtsverständnis*, 189-93; Hansen, *Abraham*, 130; Thurén, *Derhetorizing*, 84), or to provide some sort of break upon transgressions (so Betz, *Galatians*, 164). Of course, by providing some sort of break on sin, the Law also would have the effect of showing up sin for what it was.

260. Schlier, *Galater*, 152; Martyn, *Galatians*, 354-55. Many scholars take Romans 5:20 in this sense, but for a challenge to this view, see Esler, *Galatians*, 240-43. He takes το παραπτωμα—and not νομος—as the subject of the verb πλεοναση, which he understands in a transitive sense, and takes the ινα as consecutive: "So that transgression increased."

261. Dunn, *Galatians*, 190; *New Perspective*, 183, 269-70, 273-75, 282, 451-52,

Secondly, the Law was only intended to be in force until the seed should come (in Paul's interpretation, Jesus Christ, as we have seen). There is thus an era between the promulgation of the Law at Sinai and the coming of Christ. The limits of this era are clearly defined—until the Christ should come. The Law has a role limited in time.

Finally, the Law was promulgated at Sinai by angels by means of a mediator. Whom did Paul have in mind in using the passive διαταγείς? The Jewish idea that the Law was mediated through angels was probably based on Deuteronomy 33:2,[262] and was in no way whatsoever designed to detract from the absolute importance of the Law. It is another matter as to how Paul took the idea. By his phraseology, it is just possible that Paul might be preparing for his later assertion that when/if the Galatians endeavor to keep the commandments of the Law and, in particular, observe certain times and seasons as laid down by the Law, they were in fact returning under the power and sway of the elements of the universe (4:8–10).[263]

---

favors providing some sort of remedy for transgressions, i.e., the sacrificial system, and so sees this as a positive role in the sense of actually protecting Israel, which he sees confirmed by the use of the verbs φρουρεω and συγκλειω at verse 23 and the imagery of the παιδαγωγος at verse 24. Esler, *Galatians*, 200–201, also takes this verb in the sense of to protect/preserve from attack.

262. See Gaston, *Paul*, 35–37, for a denial of any Jewish tradition that the Law was given by angels and not by God directly. He suggests that the idea that the Law was given through angels was an exclusively Pauline concept. He does not state whether he thinks that Paul was the source of the idea for Hebrews 2:2 and Acts 7:53.

263. It is impossible to go fully into the debate about the meaning of τα στοιχεια του κοσμου (4:3) and τα στοιχεια (4:9). Lexical studies have shown that the most common meaning of this phrase at that time was the elemental substances from which the cosmos was made, while the lexical evidence for this phrase, meaning "elemental spirits," is actually later than Paul. Two points need to be borne in mind. Firstly, at 4:9, Paul implied that the Galatian Christians used to worship τα στοιχεια. Since in Hellenistic Judaism it was assumed that Gentiles worshipped as gods such parts of creation as fire, wind, stars, the luminaries of heaven, etc. (e.g., Wis 13:1–5), we may suppose that Paul, with this phrase, was picking up on this idea. Secondly, the Jewish calendar itself was aligned with the movement of the sun and moon: "Precise computation of their movements was vitally important for the construction of the Jewish calendar. In Judaism the exact calculation of the dates of the various festivals was a matter central to religion" (Rowland, *Open Heaven*, 120). There was lively debate and disagreement over whether a solar or lunar calendar should be observed.

When we put these two factors together, we can see that Paul thought both Jews and Gentiles were under the power of the elemental forces of the universe. Paul has placed the Law alongside of these alleged forces. Barclay, *Gift*, 409, puts it thus: "Paul represents both Torah—observance and pagan religious practice—hugely different though they were—as beholden to the natural order of the cosmos through the alignment to the elemental, physical components."

Martyn believes that the rival teachers in Galatia encouraged the congregations there to move from revering the elements to worshipping the Creator of these elements,

Paul in talking about a mediator seems to be saying that where a party involved in an agreement consists of a group, that group needs a mediator, but an individual does not need a mediator. God, being one (an allusion to Judaism's firm adherence to the oneness of God), did not need a mediator (although, strictly speaking, one person may employ a mediator) (v. 20). The angels as promulgators of the Law needed a mediator. But Moses could hardly function as their mediator, but he could and did function as the mediator on behalf of the people. It is possible that Paul was thinking of one of the archangels, or the Angel whom God promised would accompany the Israelites on their way to the promised land, as in Exodus 14:19; 23:20-21; 32:34; Acts 7:38.[264] Certainly, Paul sees this need of a mediator in the Sinai event as a sign of the inferior nature of the Law, compared with the direct way in which God Himself gave the promise to Abraham.

---

just as indeed Abraham had moved in this way to knowledge of the true God, and had observed the holy feasts at the correct times. See comment 41, entitled "Christ and the Elements of the Cosmos" (Martyn, *Galatians*, 393-406). Martyn (404-6) goes on to suggest that Paul had specifically in mind as enslaving forces the religious, socio-economic, and gender distinctions so powerful in the ancient world, which Paul had mentioned as being overcome in Christ. This is certainly a helpful pointer to a contemporary application of Paul's thought, but whether this is exactly what Paul had in mind is another matter.

264. So Vanhoye, *Un médiateur*, 403-411, followed by Bruce, *Galatians*, 179.

While Paul almost seems to be distancing God from the promulgation of the Law,[265] he did not actually say so,[266] and there are two reasons for doubting whether that was what he was suggesting. In the first place, it was hardly likely that Paul personally held that sort of view (e.g., Gal 5:13c–14 from within the letter itself), and, secondly, his opponents could easily quote Scripture in support of the divine origin and promulgation of the Law.[267]

There is an interesting contrast to the way ὁ Θεός is emphasized in verse 18c in connection with the Promise given to Abraham and the non-mention of Him directly in connection with the giving of the Law in verse 19d.[268]

That God is one was, of course, standard Jewish belief, and would have been a conviction which was shared by Paul and his opponents. The one God could be seen as behind the promise to Abraham and the Law.[269] There seems to be here also a suggestion, not fully developed, that since God is one, He must be God of Gentiles as well as Jews.[270]

265. Stanton, *Law*, 113, accepts that it was "a subtle distancing of God from the giving of the law" (cf. Esler, *Galatians*, 199), while Koch, *Schrift*, 125, speaks of a tendency in Galatians 3:19–20 to distance the Law from God. Barclay thinks that Paul has distanced the Torah, somewhat obliquely, from God, and says that "Paul's argument requires a *distance* between God and the Torah, not a *complete dissociation*" (Barclay, *Gift*, 403n35). It is important to distinguish in the scholarly debate between those who see Paul's statements as indicating the inferiority of the Law (Burton, *Galatians*, 189; Bruce, *Galatians*, 177; Longenecker, *Galatians*, 140), and those who assert outright that he has actually dissociated God from the giving of the Law (O'Neill, *Recovery of Paul's Letter*, 52 [though treating it as a gloss]; Drane, *Paul*, 34, 113; Hübner, *Law in Paul's Thought*, 26–29; Grässer, *Alte Bund*, 64–66; Martyn, *Galatians*, 364–70). Martyn *Galatians*, 367, states that "the covenantal God played no role in the genesis of that [Sinaitic] Law." Sanders, *Law*, 68, sees Galatians 3:19 as "a thrust against the law in the heat of debate. It does not represent an actual change of mind which is systematically carried through." Räisänen, *Paul and the Law*, 128–33, sees this passage as one of Paul's contradictions: Paul has expressed himself very radically in the heat of the debate, but he did not intend to exclude God altogether from the giving of the Law. Note the comments of Luz, *Geschichtsverständnis*, 189, that Paul's statements in 3:19b–20 stand on the boundary of dualism [an der Grenze des Dualismus], and Schlier, *Galater*, 158, that Paul was on the way to a Gnostic understanding of the Law, but that unlike the Gnostics, he did not go beyond the idea of the inferiority of the law; he did not proclaim its anti-God origin or nature.

266. E.g., Betz, *Galatians*, 169; Lührmann, *Galatians*, 72; Dunn, *Galatians*, 190–91.

267. As Sprinkle, *Law*, 144, points out. That it is highly unlikely that Paul saw the Law as an evil power is also rightly maintained by Wright, *Pauline Perspectives*, 572, 575; Bachmann, *Anti-Judaism*, 51, 83; Thurén, *Derhetorizing*, 80–83; Wisdom, *Blessing*, 149.

268. Cf. Stanton, *Law*, 113; Barclay, *Gift*, 404.

269. Bachmann, *Anti-Judaism*, 52, 54, 81.

270. "That God is one, was no longer an argument for the uniqueness of Israel,

1.3.4. Galatians 3:21–4:6

It would seem that Paul's argument has set up an antithesis between the promise and the Law, but he recoiled sharply from such a suggestion: μη γενοιτο (v. 21a). He denied that God ever gave the Law with the intention of setting matters right and providing the way of life (v. 21b).[271] In verse 22 Paul still operated with a Law/Promise antithesis—sin seems to be the characteristic of the Law's regime,[272] while on the other hand, faith is characteristic of the promise. But he now also spoke of Scripture in relation to Law and Promise. "Scripture συνεκλεισεν all things[273] under sin in order that the promise might be given on the basis of faith in Jesus Christ to those who believe." The Scripture is presumably the curse pronounced by Deuteronomy 27:26, quoted by Paul at 3:10,[274] while the Promise is Genesis 12:3/18:18 and 15:6, quoted by Paul earlier at 3:8 and 6, respectively. But how is the verb to be translated? The verb may mean to hem in, confine, enclose, to hold confined, to imprison. Is the sense a restrictive guarding, or a protective one? Probably, we should take account of what Paul went on to say at verse 23. Here the verb συγκλειειν is repeated and linked with φρουρειν. It is unlikely that Paul would alter his view of what Scripture had done in so short a space.[275] The use of the παιδαγωγος illustration (3:24-25) and the trustees illustration in 4:1-2 can also assist.

The verb φρουρεω can be used of guarding in a negative sense, where there is a curtailment of a person's freedom and they are imprisoned,[276] or a positive sense of protecting or guarding someone, a protective custody,

---

but rather for the inclusion of Jews and non-Jews into one community of all who had received the Spirit" (Moxnes, *Theology,* 214; cf. Hansen, *Abraham,* 133). Paul actually asserted this link between the oneness of God and His being the God of both Jews and Gentiles in Romans 3:27-31.

271. As Jewish thought insisted (e.g., Lev 18:5; Deut 6:24; Ps 119:93; Prov 6:23; Sir 17:11; 45:5; Bar 3:9; 4:1; *Pss. Sol.* 14:2; *4 Ezra* 7:17, 21; 14:30; *Pirque Aboth* 2:7).

272. Barclay, *Gift,* 407, maintains that the assumption of 3:22 is the same as 3:10 and 2:16, viz. that sin rules over everything, reducing it to a condition which requires not only release but also the creation of new life.

273. τα παντα (accusative plural neuter) suggests the whole of the cosmos, though probably the human race is primarily in Paul's mind.

274. So Lightfoot, *Galatians,* 147-48; Burton, *Galatians,* 195-96; Bruce, *Galatians,* 180; Longenecker, *Galatians,* 144. Mussner, *Galaterbrief,* 252; Dunn, *Galatians,* 194, think of the catena of passages later quoted in Romans 3:10-18.

275. So rightly, Burton, *Galatians,* 199.

276. The majority of commentators opt for this sense (e.g., Burton, Bonnard, Schlier, Betz, Bruce, Longenecker, Lührmann, Martyn). See also Sanders, *PLJP,* 144; Räisänen, *Law,* 20, 131.

as we might say.²⁷⁷ Which sense would cohere with the παιδαγωγος and trustees illustrations? There were various tasks assigned to a *paidagogos*: he would accompany the son of the family to school, see that he behaved himself, and train him in social etiquette and cultural norms, i.e., his role was not a purely negative one. Thus, it could be said that the Law gave Israel "the protection it needed from idolatry and the lower moral standards prevalent in the Gentile world."²⁷⁸ Equally, in 4:1-2, trustees were appointed to look after the interests of the heir, and this would include seeing that he did not jeopardize his inheritance. Both pictures, therefore, could include positive and negative aspects.

At the same time, it should be observed that later in the letter, at 4:21-31, Paul quite clearly stated that the living under the Law was a form of slavery and he used the verb δουλευειν (v. 25) and noun δουλεια (v. 24), and then in the imperative at 5:1 he urged the Galatians to stand fast in the freedom given them by Christ and not to submit to the slavery which the Law brings about. Has Paul here "stepped up a gear"? Was he here intensifying the thrust of his argument? Is the use of the δουλ- group of words rhetorically conditioned, because Paul was aiming to denigrate the position of his opponents and their supporters? If we do interpret συγκλειειν and φρουρειν more in terms of "protective custody," we are compelled to such a view. Interestingly, Dunn²⁷⁹ states that what Paul asserted here was not a new claim, but was implicit in the words of 3:23 and explicit in the illustration of 4:1-3, but he does not go further into defining the relation of the statements of 3:23-25 and 4:21-31.

Thus, returning to συνεκλεισεν of 3:22, Paul would be suggesting that Scripture taught that the Law was given with a view to confining Israel under its jurisdiction. What happened in actual fact was that Israel disobeyed the ordinances of the Law and so ended up "under sin," under the divine condemnation of its sin. But God intended that this jurisdiction was to be temporary and last until what He had promised might be given on the basis of faith in Jesus Christ, His Son. What He had promised referred to the Genesis passages containing God's promise to Abraham. That promise was blessing which in effect means justification on the basis of faith and, as a result, reception of the Spirit, as explained in 3:14. Though the Law could

---

277. Both Dunn, *Galatians*, 197-98, and Esler, *Galatians*, 200-203, have advocated this idea of protective custody, and play down the idea of a jailor imprisoning someone. Before them, Mussner, *Galaterbrief*, 255, maintained that a positive role was being assigned to the Law ("It had to watch that sin remained sin!")

278. Dunn, *Galatians*, 199; Esler, *Galatians*, 200-201. Both rely on Lull, *Law Was Our Pedagogue*, 481-98; Young, *Paidagogos*, 150-76.

279. Dunn, *Galatians*, 250.

not give life, but, by operating until faith should come (cf. vv. 23, 25), it is thus seen to enforce the original terms of the promise.[280]

In the paragraph verses 21–25, while the Law is certainly not against the Promise, its role has some negative aspects.[281] It cannot give life (v. 21); it acted as a kind of guardian keeping watch on[282] until the era of faith should dawn with the coming of Jesus Christ (vv. 22–23); it is like the household slave who looked after the master's children and kept them in order[283] (v. 24). The Law's regime lasted until Christ came "in order that we might be justified by faith." (v. 24). When the era of faith had come, believers were no longer under the supervision of a "household slave" (v. 25). It is implied that in the purposes of God this negative role of the Law excluded any thought or any possibility of a way of salvation other than what God had done in sending His Son and in that Son's atoning death.[284]

Excursus on the Apparent Negative View of the Law in Galatians

We may pause here and reflect on the rather negative color in which Paul painted the Law in Galatians, mindful that there are those who believe that Paul changed his mind during the interval between Galatians and Romans, or at any rate "rowed back" from some of his more extreme statements in Galatians either for tactical reasons in addressing the church at Rome, or on more sober, calmer, less angry reflection. There is, it would seem, an Achilles heel to this idea. The majority prevailing opinion of the order in

---

280. Matlock, *Saving Faith*, 83. Berger, *Abraham*, 57, believes that the Law indirectly made possible the fulfillment of the promise through the coming of Jesus Christ.

281. Dunn, *Galatians*, 197–98, also comments on the positive and negative sides of the Law's role, though with somewhat different emphasis than set out here.

282. The "guarding" idea at the heart of this image, together with the charge that contemporary Judaism was in bondage (4:25), in effect put Jews on the same level as Gentiles whom Paul described as in bondage to those who by nature were no gods (4:8). Cf. Westerholm, *Perspectives*, 378; Sanders, *PLJP*, 69, who says that the common denominator between the Law and the *stoicheia* was bondage.

283. The REB corrected NEB's surprising reversion to the older translation of παιδαγωγος as tutor, with the rather bland: "The law was thus put in charge of us." The NRSV has "disciplinarian," which gets the nuance of the word better.

284. Cf. Martyn, *Galatians*, 373. Sanders, *PLJP*, 47, puts it thus: "What is wrong with the Law, and thus with Judaism, is that it does not provide for God's ultimate purpose, that of saving the entire world through faith in Christ and without the privileges accorded to the Jews through the promises, covenants and the law."

which Paul wrote his letters would be 1 Corinthians, 2 Corinthians (either as a whole or parts), Galatians, and Romans.[285]

Now, while the Law does not figure in the Corinthian correspondence to anything like the degree it does in Galatians and Romans, there is some highly significant material in it nonetheless.[286]

In 1 Corinthians, in the section of the letter devoted to considering the general resurrection and the nature of the resurrection of the body, Paul remarked: "The sting of death is sin, and the power of sin is the Law" (1 Cor 15:56). Although this sentence to some extent comes as a surprise in the midst of the theme of resurrection, there is no need to regard it as an interpolation (for which there is no textual evidence).[287]

What this terse, epigrammatic sentence reveals is that for Paul there was an association between Law and sin, and that he had reached this conclusion before the Galatian crisis. Somehow, in a manner not explained at this point, the Law gives sin its driving force, its power to operate. Given what we have said above about Paul's experience on the Damascus Road and its repurcussions on his understanding of the Law, this should not really occasion surprise.

In addition, while handling the issue of whether one should remain in the situation in which a person was when they were called, Paul said, "Neither circumcision nor uncircumcision counts for anything, but (only) keeping the commandments of God" (1 Cor 7:19). This statement, as has been pointed out by several scholars, would be absurd to Jewish ears, since circumcision is firmly laid down as a requirement for God's people in the written Law. Clearly, Paul was taking "the commandments of God" to mean what Jesus had revealed of God's will, and this is "far more radical than the observance of any code, whether ceremonial or moral, could be."[288]

---

285. Kummel, *Introduction to the New Testament*, 197; Robinson, *Redating the New Testament*, 57; Schnelle, *History and Theology*, 94–95; Lightfoot, *Galatians*, 36–56, esp. 55; Bonnard, *Galates*, 14; Mussner, *Galaterbrief*, 10; Westerholm, *Perspectives*, 366 (apparently). Martyn, *Galatians*, 20, while accepting the north Galatian provenance of the congregations, believes that Galatians antedated all the Corinthian correspondence. If, however, we were to date the letter before the Jerusalem Conference, the usual preference of advocates of the south Galatian hypothesis (so Bruce, *Galatians*, 55–56; Longenecker, *Galatians*, lxxii–lxxxviii; Drane, *Paul*, 140–43), we would have to rephrase what we have written as follows: what the Corinthian correspondence would then show is that even where the Law was not a burning issue, Paul could still draw a link between the Law and sin.

286. It is to the credit of Thielman, *Paul*, to have stressed this.

287. It actually has its appropriate place in a discussion of death. The theory of an interpolation is firmly rejected in Barrett, *First Epistle*, 384.

288. Barrett, *First Epistle*, 169; cf. Fee, *1 Corinthians*, 312–14; Thielman, *Paul*, 103.

On the other side, Paul quoted rules from the Law of Moses and applied them to the Christian community and its workers: there is the rule about casting out an offender from the ranks of Israel and applied to the man at Corinth who was cohabiting with his step-mother (1 Cor 5:13) and the rule about oxen and applied to preachers of the Gospel (1 Cor 9:9).

In 2 Corinthians, Paul contrasts the Sinai ministry under Moses ("written on stone tablets" [3:7; cf. earlier, in v. 3]) and that of the ministry of the Gospel as preached by himself (3:6). While he concedes that the Sinai ministry was attended by glory (he said this no less than three times, at 3:7, 9, 11), how much more can that be said of the ministry inspired by the Spirit? (3:8; cf. 3:3, 6, where the influence of Ezekiel 36:26; 11:19-20 is clear. Paul saw the new age envisaged by the prophet Ezekiel, when God by His Spirit would rectify the "plight" of Israel by removing its heart of stone and giving it a new heart filled by His Spirit, already being fulfilled in his ministry.) In spite of the fact that it was attended by glory, the Sinai ministry brought only condemnation and death (vv. 7, 9), whereas the ministry inspired by the Spirit mediated righteousness (i.e., acquittal and right standing before God, as opposed to condemnation [v. 9]). The Sinai ministry is impermanent, whereas the Gospel ministry is permanent (v. 11). The greater glory of the Gospel ministry casts the Sinai ministry into the shade (v. 10). Because the Sinai ministry brings condemnation and death, it does nothing to rectify the position of human beings. As Westerholm remarks,[289] "With or without the Sinaitic covenant, 'in Adam all die.'" There is no life-giving capacity in the Law. It does not and cannot save men and women.

If we place the Corinthian correspondence before that of Galatians and Romans, it is clear that the negative view of the Law expressed by Paul in Galatians was not the result of the Galatian crisis, but had been part of his theological convictions for some time before he wrote Galatians.[290] If, however, we consider that Galatians was Paul's earliest extant letter and to be placed before the Jerusalem Conference, the Corinthian correspondence shows that even in a situation where the Law was not really a burning issue as such, Paul could still link the Law and sin, and see it as bringing condemnation and death.

Either way, may it not be time to bid farewell to the picture of Paul in a blazing temper rolling out extreme, unbalanced, ill-judged, and erroneous statements about the Law?[291] Controlled anger might be a better way of describing the passion behind Galatians.

---

289. Westerholm, *Perspectives*, 363.

290. Cf. Fee, *1 Corinthians*, 806.

291. See Thurén, *Derhetorizing,* 59-64, 73, for a similar conclusion but reached

We may briefly point out also that much the same might be said about justification. Paul can use terms associated with what we call justification by faith in 1 Corinthians, even though he is not handling a dispute about this topic nor how men and women arrive at such a state before God. Thus, at 1:30, Paul asserts that God was the originator of the fact that believers were in Christ, the Christ who had become (εγενηθη) for us wisdom from God, δικαιοσυνη και αγιασμος και απολυτρωσις. Here righteousness means "right standing with God" and does not carry an ethical meaning. Likewise, in 1 Corinthians 6:11, after stating that some of the Corinthians before their conversion had lived the kind of morally evil lives which would have excluded them from the Kingdom of God, but they have received cleansing,[292] they have been consecrated to God, and they "have been justified (εδικαιωθητε) in the name of the Lord Jesus Christ and by the Spirit of our God."[293]

1.3.4. Continued

Returning to the flow of Paul's argument in Galatians 3: he declared that in union with Christ Jesus "you are all sons of God through faith" (3:26). He proceeded to back up this statement with the assertion (γαρ):

> For you who have been baptised into Christ, have put on Christ. There is neither Jew nor Greek, there is neither slave nor free, there is neither male nor female, for you are all one in Christ Jesus. (3:27–28)[294]

from a different perspective—Paul had not lost control but was using effective contemporary rhetorical means. See the many articles in Nanos, *Galatians Debate*, 1–113, 157–96, for a stress on Paul's use of rhetorical strategies throughout the letter, together with Mitternacht, *Foolish Galatians*, 408–433.

292. The middle voice reading aopelou/sasqe suggests that active participation of the individual in the process of faith-baptism. They submitted in faith in Jesus Christ to baptism and received cleansing of their sins. See Beasley-Murray, *Baptism in the New Testament*, 162–64. Barrett, *First Epistle*, 141–42, thinks that the middle voice was used with a passive sense and allows that baptism is in mind, but in its inward meaning rather than outward circumstances; Fee, *1 Corinthians*, 245–47, thinks that Paul was more concerned with the spiritual transformation in their conversion experience than specifically thinking of baptism. Whether or not baptism was specifically in Paul's mind does not in fact affect the point which I am making.

293. The points made here about justification can be used against the idea that justification was not at the heart of Paul's theology, and was only used in certain situations where Paul had to defend the right of his Gentile converts to be part of God's people without first becoming Jews.

294. There is no need for us to discuss the question whether Paul himself composed this formula ad hoc or whether he took over an existing formula (it is certainly true that he did not need, strictly speaking, to mention the slave-free and male-female pairs,

The union with Christ Jesus was not a purely individual matter: believers were bonded together. They were like a single organism in this union with Christ. The old racial, socio-economic, and sexual barriers have been surmounted. They were no longer of relevance in this new community. Those old cultural norms should be a thing of the past.[295] Believers should take their system of values from Jesus Christ.

Now comes the conclusion to which Paul had been heading since his introduction of the figure of Abraham. "Now (δε is not here adversative) if you belong to Christ, then you are Abraham's seed, heirs according to the promise" (3:29). Union with Christ who was the true seed of Abraham (so 3:16) meant that believers were incorporated into the descendants of Abraham. They were, therefore, heirs of what Paul understood by "inheritance."

Basically, Paul had arrived at a similar position to that which he stated at 3:7: "Know, therefore, that it is people of faith who are the sons of Abraham." The promise of God that all the nations would be blessed in and through Abraham (3:8) had come true, through the agency of God's Son, Jesus Christ, and our incorporation into him who himself was the true seed of Abraham. Given that God had willed that Jesus and faith in him was now the basis for belonging to the people of God, the children of Abraham, it would be entirely wrong to insist the Gentile believers should observe the works of the Law.[296]

The next paragraph (4:1–7) explains what Paul meant by "heirs" (κληρονομοι) mentioned in 3:29. He points out that someone who is an heir but under age has to be under guardians appointed by his father (vv. 1–2).

Scott has proposed a different interpretation from the usual assumption that Paul is here using an illustration from what happens when a father died leaving an underage son. He points to incongruity between illustration and application (e.g., God the Father in verses 4–7 is very much alive and active), and puts forward linguistic arguments (e.g., that νηπιος was not a technical term for a minor; that κυριος παντων was a phrase denoting universal sovereignty; that επιτροποι και οικονομοι do not fit the picture of Roman guardianship but refer to subordinate state officials; and that προθεσμια was

---

because the topic under consideration was whether non-Jews needed to become Jews and obey the Law's requirements in order to belong to or continue to belong to the people of God).

295. Barclay, *Gift*, 397, puts it thus: "The *evaluative freight* carried by these labels, the encoded distinctions of superiority and inferiority" have been altered. "All forms of symbolic capital not derived from 'belonging to Christ' now lose their ultimacy."

296. Wisdom, *Blessing*, 153, maintains that to make such a demand was to frustrate God's plan and so to come under the curse. Hansen, *Abraham*, 138, sees Paul's arguments substantiating his rebuke of the Galatians for their foolishness in thinking to gain better status or blessing by works of the Law.

not a technical term for a date set by a father to terminate guardianship, but meant a set date or pre-determined time limit). He suggests that Paul was referring back to 3:17 and that he had in mind Israel during the 430 years of enslavement in Egypt, the time set by Yahweh when making a promise to Abraham according to Genesis 15:13. Israel was no better than a slave even though she had been promised ultimate universal sovereignty (Sirach 44:21 had so interpreted that promise to Abraham and Romans 4:13 referred to this type of interpretation). The Second Exodus typology of Galatians 4:3-7 fits this approach as antitype to type.[297]

What may be said about Scott's proposed new interpretation?[298] The following observations may be made. Firstly, the discrepancy between an illustration and its application is not unknown elsewhere in Paul's writings, as, e.g., Romans 7:1-6 shows.[299] Martyn's comment on Galatians 4:1-7 is not unreasonable: "Paul paints the picture solely for the sake of the use he will make of it, thus allowing himself both freedom in shaping the picture itself and freedom to close with a development that goes beyond it."[300]

Secondly, Scott takes the article in ο κληρονομος as anaphoric, i.e., referring to what had been previously mentioned, and maintains that Israel is in mind. In 3:29 the phrase κατ'επαγγελιαν κληρονομοι occurs. This refers to those who had believed in Jesus and been baptized into him (3:26-27). It would be a rather harsh switch if Paul suddenly without warning spoke of Israel in 4:1. Thus, the usual interpretation of ο κληρονομος as generic is to be preferred.

In the third place, while it is true that in both Jewish and Christian thinking, the righteous/the saved will share in the reign of the Messiah (for Paul, see 1 Cor 6:2; cf. Rev 20:4), to apply the phrase κυριος παντων ων to Israel again seems demanding a lot from the addressees. Given that the early Christian confession was "Jesus is Lord," one might have expected Paul to have chosen an alternative phrase if he were referring to Israel's anticipated eschatological destiny.

Fourthly, the same could be said about taking του πατρος to refer to God the Father. Why did not Paul write Θεου, as he does at 4:7 (δια Θεου)?

---

297. Scott, *Adoption as Sons of God*, 121-48.

298. Dunn, *Galatians*, mentions it en passant but without discussion, while Witherington and Martyn do not mention it at all in their commentaries, though they are aware of Scott's book.

299. Dunn, *Romans*, 2:673. As to the appositeness of the olive tree illustration (Rom 11:17-24), note Dunn's comments: "Whether or not Paul was aware of the possibility of grafting a wild shoot into a cultivated tree is no more relevant than the identity of the tree as an olive tree in the first place. What matters is the point being clearly made."

300. Martyn, *Galatians*, 386.

Finally, perhaps the most serious objection which can be raised against Scott's proposal, however, is his suggestion that the time allegedly set by God mentioned in 4:2 (προθεσμια) refers back to 3:17 and the 430 years between the Abrahamic promise and the giving of the Law on Sinai. Not only is 3:17 a long way off, but even more damaging is Scott's suggestion that the period of 430 years was one of enslavement followed by freedom. But 3:17 refers to the giving the Law, and the Law, according to Paul, does not give freedom but acts as a custodian (Gal 3:23–24). It is only with the coming of Christ and the possibility of faith in him that we come out of this custody and enjoy true freedom (3:24; 5:1, 13).

Accordingly, we do not feel that Scott has made out his case. However, rejecting his interpretation of verses 1–2 does not preclude accepting that Second Exodus motifs were used by Paul in 4:3–7.

Paul said that we were at a stage of spiritual immaturity (νηπιοι [v. 3]) until, in the fullness of time, God sent forth His Son in human form[301] within the Jewish people, with a redemptive mission (vv. 4–5). The purpose was to redeem those confined under the Law which was powerless to give life (cf. 3:23–24; 4:3) "in order that we might receive adoption." On the basis of this relationship to God of father and children,[302] God had sent the Spirit of His Son into our hearts. In focussing on the Spirit, Paul could be said both to pick up his starting point once again (3:2, 5), and also to remind the Galatians of his earlier statement that the gift of the Spirit was the blessing promised to Abraham for the nations (3:14).

The conclusion is that the believers were no longer slaves, but sons/daughters, and, therefore, heirs through God. The concluding phrase δια Θεου served to remind the Galatians that God was the source of redemption/adoption. We do not contribute to the new relationship with God. The initiative lies with Him, not us.

Does Paul's argument end up by denying the election and story of Israel, if Christ is the one and only seed of Abraham? For the moment, the point must be discussed in respect of *the evidence of Galatians*. What Paul said in Romans cannot control the exegesis of Galatians, for, as some have

---

301. This is the force of "born of woman," an idiomatic phrase meaning a human being—all of us are born of woman. "Born under the Law" indicated that Jesus was a member of the Jewish nation.

302. For the OT conviction that God had adopted Israel, see Exodus 4:22; Hosea 11:1. For the eschatological hope of Yahweh's re-gathering His children scattered because of their disobedience, see Hosea 1:10 (2:1 LXX); Jeremiah 31:9.

maintained,³⁰³ Paul could have changed his mind during the interval between writing the two letters.³⁰⁴

One must be careful at this point to bear in mind the rhetorical strategy of Paul. He was not writing a Church Dogmatics, carefully and systematically setting out a doctrinal system. He was in Galatians responding to a crisis situation, the urgency of which was the driving force in his approach. Rhetorical strategies were bound to enter into his presentation, consciously and unconsciously. We ought to bear in mind the possibility that Paul might have expressed himself ultra-forcefully to make a point.³⁰⁵ So then, has Paul then ended up in Galatians by denying in fact the election and story of Israel? Here we make the following points very briefly, deferring more detailed discussion to later.³⁰⁶

Paul operated with a Two Ages viewpoint, a very Jewish approach, which assumed a divine plan in which God would intervene to vindicate His people and initiate the glorious Age to Come (1:4). He asserted that God sent His son in the fullness of time and that Jesus was born "under the law." This assertion surely presupposed the election of Israel, to whom it was "natural" (so to speak) that God should send His Son in the first place. The divine plan involved that Jesus was born within the Jewish people and that his ministry was, in part at any rate, aimed at redeeming the Jewish people (4:4–5a).

The Law was given at a particular point and its recipients were Israel at Mount Sinai (3:19). It had a role, albeit a limited and temporary one in God's purpose. When Paul referred to "us who are Jews by birth and not Gentile sinners" (2:15), it is clear that he presupposed a Jew/Gentile divide and the assumption that Jews were in a different position than Gentiles, i.e., he pre-supposed their election and story.

Paul assumed that Jerusalem held a significant place. While, after his "call," he did not go straightaway to Jerusalem, as one might have expected (1:17), later he did pay two visits there (i.e., before writing Galatians), the second of which was due to a revelation with the purpose of putting before the Jerusalem church leaders the gospel which he had been preaching

---

303. See the works of Drane, *Paul*; Räisänen, *Paul*; Hübner, *Law*.

304. Perhaps a less likely event the closer the composition of Galatians and that of Romans is deemed to be.

305. In general, too, we need also to bear in mind that often in respect to the Christian gospel there are paradoxes, both sides of which have to be held together in tension in order to capture the whole truth of the gospel. Thus, e.g., it is not unreasonable that from one angle, Paul might want to say that the Law was no longer a controlling factor in the life of Christians while also wanting to say that Christians were fulfilling the Law.

306. See the Excursus at the end of this chapter (141–51) for a full discussion.

(2:1–2). Behind the fact that former Galileans had made Jerusalem the "headquarters" of the Jesus' movement and the fact that Paul felt obligated to get the approval of the Jerusalem church and its leaders, lay the convictions about the centrality of Jerusalem or Zion in the eschatological expectations of Israel. Paul cannot have been unaware of these expectations. What we see in Galatians was a small tip of the iceberg, so to speak.

We might also mention the fact that Paul used the phrase "Israel of God" (6:16). Irrespective of whether Paul meant the people of Israel "after the flesh"[307] or whether it was a case of a transfer of a title of honor from "old Israel" to the followers of Jesus (Jewish and Gentile believers together), regarded now as the people of God,[308] the title itself presupposed the story of Israel, with the genitive του Θεου indicating the elective purposes of God.

None of these points taken in isolation would necessarily prove conclusive, though some are quite impressive even on their own, but, taken cumulatively, they make out a strong case against Martyn's thesis. We believe that he has pushed what was an exegetical tour de force to an unwarranted extreme. Or, to put the matter another way, he has not at this point done justice to the rhetorical polemic of the apostle and he has ended up attributing an extreme position to Paul.[309]

How Paul handled the issue of Israel after the flesh in Romans, especially chapters 9–11, could now be adduced as some corroboration of a conclusion reached on the basis of Galatians itself. We might add a further,

---

307. Mussner, *Galaterbrief*, 417; Bruce, *Galatians*, 275; Richardson, *Israel in the Apostolic Church*, 74–84. Dunn, *Galatians*, 346, suggests, "Israel not excluding Jews as a whole, but as including Gentile believers," but then says that the Israel of God "is the seed of Abraham understood in terms of the argument of chs iii–iv," which seems to put him in the other category of interpretation.

308. Lightfoot, *Galatians*, 221; Schlier, *Galater*, 283; Bonnard, *Galates*, 131; Betz, *Galatians*, 323; Longenecker, *Galatians*, 298–99; Martyn, *Galatians*, 574–77 (a proclamation of the gospel to the Galatians); Barrett, *Freedom*, 89; Barclay, *Obeying*, 98; Thielman, *Paul*, 138; Longenecker, "Defining the Faithful," 94; Horrell, *Paul's Narratives*, 161.

309. Wright, *Pauline Perspectives*, 573, criticizes Martyn for wrongly deducing "that Paul must also be opposed to the idea of a continuing narrative, stretching back to Abraham, within which he and his converts would find themselves now at the leading edge. Indeed, it sometimes appears that Martyn, along with his mentor Käsemann, was determined to see all things Jewish, including the idea of that single great narrative going back to Abraham, as the classic case of *homo religiosus;* and that was the special target of Paul's polemic." Barclay, *Gift*, 412–14, in responding to Martyn, draws a distinction between the narrative of human history and the narrative of God's promise. While acknowledging that Martyn's stress on the invasive character of the Christ-event rightly stresses the incongruity of God's promise with the human condition, Barclay does not think that his stress fits the narrative arc projected by the divine promise from Abraham to Christ. On that narrative line, Israel's history is an undifferentiated era of unfulfilled anticipation.

if small, point from Romans. It is unlikely that Paul's concern for, and anguish over, his fellow country men and women (Rom 9:1–5; 10:1–2) was something which would have surfaced only suddenly as he was writing that letter, but would have been with him for a long time (1 Thess 2:14–16 not withstanding).

1.3.5. Galatians 4:21–5:1: The Hagar-Sarah Allegory

Although Abraham is not the figure of main interest in 4:21–5:1 of the letter, nonetheless he is mentioned at 4:22 as having had two sons.[310] The two women are related to him as wife and slave, and he is in the background elsewhere (for example, the command to cast out Hagar and Ishmael [4:30] was actually directed to him).[311] So, a brief consideration of this passage seems appropriate.

While we cannot be certain, it is quite probable that Paul's opponents had talked about the birth of Isaac and how God had determined that Abraham's line of descent should run through Isaac, the child promised to him and Sarah in their old age, and that Gentiles who wished to be part of God's purposes must be adopted into the family of Abraham by being circumcised and keeping the Law.[312] (Whether they went further and themselves equated Isaac with freedom and Ishmael with bondage, cannot be said with certainty.) This could explain why Paul took up the story of Abraham's two sons and argued in a manner atypical of him, though not outside some of the methods of exegesis current in his day.[313] Paul specifically described his

310. Paul does not bother to mention that Abraham actually had more sons, by a woman called Kenturah, according to Genesis 25.

311. Later, of course, at Genesis 21:12, God endorsed Sarah's injunction, and overcame Abraham's reluctance (v. 11).

312. See Barrett, *Allegory*, 154–70, esp. 158, 161, 165; Esler, *Galatians*, 210; Martyn, *Galatians*, 433–66; Thiessen, *Paul and the Gentile Problem*, 75–80 (who sees their "gospel" as universalistic, since they believed that the boundary between Jew and non-Jew was permeable and that Gentiles could share in the promises made by God to Abraham by accepting circumcision and the demands of the Law).

313. See Betz, *Galatians*, 243; Barrett, *Allegory*, 163–64. Esler, *Galatians*, 210–13, describes the exegetical method as *derash*, in reliance on Brewer, *Techniques*, 14–15 (see note 244). Hays, *Echoes*, 111, points out that before Paul, the author of Jubilees had taken up and interpreted the reference to the fact that, though God would make of Ishmael a nation, Abraham's true seed would be traced through Isaac (Gen 21:12–13). In Jubilees 16:16–18, the author says that Abraham would have six more sons after Isaac (cf. Gen 25:2). These sons would become nations, but they would be counted with the nations, whereas that would not be the case with Isaac, whose descendants would be a holy seed ruled by the Most High, the portion and special possession of the Most High. The discussion was advanced by Mattei, *Paul's Allegory*, 102–122 (cf. Longenecker,

exposition as an allegorization of the Genesis story about the two sons of Abraham and their respective mothers (v. 24a).³¹⁴

Paul opened with a direct address to the Galatians: "Tell me, you who want to be under the Law, do you not listen to the Law?" (v. 21). The story of Isaac and Ishmael occurs, of course, within the Torah!³¹⁵—hence Paul's connecting link, "For it is written, Abraham had two sons" (v. 22a). Paul contrasted the two boys, Ishmael and Isaac, in two ways. Firstly, they were born of a slave girl and the free-born, legal wife respectively (v. 22b), and, secondly, they were born κατα σαρκα and δι'επαγγελιας respectively (v. 23). Though the first contrast is in one sense a factual one about the socio-legal status of the two women, Paul exploited the theological and spiritual significance of the slavery-freedom contrast.³¹⁶ The second contrast is clearly a theological interpretation. Ishmael was born as a result of the natural human desire for an heir and by an arrangement in accordance with custom of the time (κατα σαρκα).³¹⁷ Isaac, however, was born when Sarah was beyond the normal age of child-bearing as a result of divine promise (δι'επαγγελιας). His birth was the result of divine intervention in fulfillment of God's own promise.³¹⁸

Galatians, 209), who is followed by Thiessen, *Gentile Problem*, 84–87. Mattei points out that in Hellenistic rhetorical treatises the verb αλληγορεω means predominantly to speak allegorically rather than to interpret allegorically, and he points out that in the Hagar-Sarah allegory Paul's method is the pesher type of exegesis, applying prophetic texts to one's own present, and that his use of Isaiah 54:1 is akin to the Jewish use of the haftarah reading (the prophetic passage) in order to read the Torah eschatologically. He concludes that there is nothing un-Jewish about Paul's exegetical method in Galatians 4:21–31. For the fact that Jewish exegetes were familiar with allegorical interpretation and believed that the Scriptures spoke allegorically, see the full discussion in Niehoff, *Jewish Exegesis*. Barclay, *Gift*, 416, stresses that Paul related the figures in the story to their equivalents in his own time (see the contrast between τοτε . . . νυν at 4:29); but that he did not dissolve the characters from their historical particularity into signifiers of a timeless truth.

314. Esler, *Galatians*, 211–15, sees Paul seeking to achieve a stereotypical differentiation of the in-group and the out-group. Sarah is aligned with the in-group (Paul's congregations), while Hagar with the out-group (those who advocated circumcision for Gentile converts and those who supported them). In this way, Paul achieved a very positive identity for his congregations.

315. Cf. Martyn, *Galatians*, 434.

316. As Hays, *Echoes*, 113, points out, the text of Genesis does not specifically refer to Sarah as free. It is Paul who has introduced this description of her, and this plays an important role in his argument.

317. Von Rad, *Genesis*, 186.

318. It may be true, as Christiansen, *Covenant*, 243–44, asserts, that Paul is here working on two simultaneously existing identities built on opposed principles (rather than on an historical development of old and new covenants), but it would be unwise

The two mothers were given a deeper meaning. Firstly, they were equated with two covenants (v. 24b).[319] Paul dealt with Hagar first.[320] She was equated with the covenant made at Sinai (v. 24c). Then Paul said: "Now (δε) this (το) Hagar is mount Sinai in Arabia," or "Now this Hagar is Sinai, a mountain in Arabia."[321] How did Paul reach this equation? Some scholars think that there was a play on words here between Hagar and Hagra, the name of a mountain in the vicinity of Petra, Arabia. In the Targumic tradition, there is evidence of such a word play for the first century among Jewish communities.[322] Attractive as this is, one does wonder whether the Galatian Christians with a pagan background would have been able to follow this line of argument? Another possibility is that put forward by P. Borgen.[323] He prefers the similarity expressed in the theme of slavery: Hagar was a slave and the Sinai covenant bore children for slavery. Paul did stress this point of slavery in connection with the Sinai covenant in verse 24. Mount Sinai was obviously associated with the giving of the Law to Moses, and Paul now continued to maintain the idea (as he had done just previously at 3:22-25; 4:1-7) that the Sinai covenant enslaved its adherents: εις δουλευειν γεννωσα (v. 24d).

The next step was the equation of Sinai and contemporary Jerusalem: Sinai, though situated in Arabia, corresponded to[324] Jerusalem (v. 25b). Paul explained this equation "for she is in slavery with her children" (v. 25c). Jerusalem was the spiritual center of Judaism and the Law was at the center of Judaism. Thus, contemporary Judaism was enslaved under the Law.[325] Since

---

to deduce from this particular instance that Paul had no concept of salvation history.

319. For the unusual nature of this idea of two covenants in Paul, see Martyn, *Covenants of Hagar and Sarah*, 184-87.

320. The με\ν clause never actually receives a corresponding δε\ clause.

321. One solution to the question why Paul did this is that he presupposed the geographical link of Hagar and Arabia and the location of Sinai in Arabia, the land of Ishmael. See the commentaries, e.g., Koch, *Schrift*, 207-8. Vogel, *Heil*, 69, leaves it open whether Paul assumed the location of Mount Sinai in Arabia or an etymological link between Αγαρ and Σινα. Hays, *Echoes*, 115, calls this equation "a puff of rhetorical smoke" to distract the audience from the equation of Law and slavery!

322. For a strong advocacy of this view, see Mattei, *Paul's Allegory*, 110-11n37-40.

323. The equation is "based on the similar nature of Hagar's identification with the covenant/law and Mount Sinai's identification with the Law of Moses" (Borgen, *Some Hebrew and Pagan Features*, 159).

324. The verb συστοιχει means to stand in line with or on the same rank as.

325. It is difficult to agree with Mattei, *Paul's Allegory*, 110n30, when he maintains that there is nothing offensive or heretical in what Paul says here, since Judaism believed that the Sinai Covenant demanded submissiveness to the Law. While the latter point is absolutely true, the contrast with freedom in this passage seems to demand a stronger connotation than submissiveness (in fact, Mattei himself uses servitude in the same paragraph).

in the letter Paul was counteracting the influence of a Jewish Christian mission, what he said would include them alongside non-believing Jews.[326]

Thus, there is a triple chain in respect of Hagar: Hagar—the Sinai Covenant—contemporary Judaism (plus Judaizing Jewish Christians) and the characteristic of this chain is spiritual slavery.

Whether the rival missioners had appealed to the Abraham-Sarah stories or not, they would certainly have regarded Paul's inversion of the sense of the Genesis narrative as completely unacceptable.[327] This much may be said on Paul's behalf: he saw that the fundamental issue in God's purpose in connection with Isaac rather than Ishmael was to do with the people of God. To that extent we can at least understand the aim behind his exegesis, even if the details of that exegesis seem to be forced. Earlier, Paul had wrested Abrahamic sonship away from physical descent from the patriarch (3:7, 16, 29); here he went on to claim Sarah as "our mother" because his converts had become children on the basis of God's gracious promise (4:28; cf. 3:29), Christ's atoning work (3:13), and the gift of the Spirit (3:2, 14).[328]

Then Paul comes to the second woman. Sarah is never specified by her personal name, nor, actually, did Paul explicitly equate Sarah with a specific covenant. He simply proceeded to say "'The Jerusalem above is free, who is our mother" (v. 26).

Before considering the concept of the heavenly Jerusalem, let us ask what covenant might be connected with Sarah in Paul's mind? Is it the

---

326. Mussner, *Galaterbrief*, 325; Longenecker, *Galatians*, 219; Dunn, *Galatians*, 250; Martyn, *Covenants*, 160-92; *Galatians*, 439, 457-66; Vogel, *Heil*, 69-70, 72, hold that Paul's attack is in fact directed against the other teachers in Galatia or Jewish Christianity in Jerusalem. But it seems difficult to evacuate the phrase "Jerusalem which now is" (or "contemporary Jerusalem") of all reference to Judaism of Paul's day. Betz, *Galatians*, 246; Bruce, *Galatians*, 220; Witherington, *Grace*, 334; Lincoln, *Paradise Now*, 27; Tobin, *Paul's Rhetoric*, 66, accept that Judaism as well as the Judaizers in Galatia is in mind, while Barclay, *Obeying*, 250, believes that there is "an implicit attack on law-observant Judaism for its cultural imperialism." See also Barclay, *Gift*, 417n64. Konradt, *Die aus Glauben*, 47, also believes that ultimately what Paul said excluded non-believing Jews from being true children of Abraham.

327. "To Jews his exegesis must have seemed preposterous" (Bruce, *Galatians*, 219). Hays, *Echoes*, 112, refers to Paul's "hermeneutical jujitsu," which would leave his audience agape, with its outrageous claim that the Torah rightly understood warrants the rejection of keeping the law.

328. "Christology is the foundation on which his ecclesiocentric counterreadings are constructed" (Hays, *Echoes*, 120). The whole of his discussion on 120-21 is extremely helpful. See the comment of Aageson quoted in note 348 below, that Paul has grasped the function of the story about Isaac's priority over Ishmael, even if he has given a new content to it.

covenant made with Abraham[329] or has Paul in mind the new covenant?[330] Certainly in the context of the letter, the covenant which God made with Abraham had been to the fore since 3:7. That covenant could not be annulled by the promulgation of the Law at Sinai 430 years later (3:17), though Paul preferred to use the term "promise" when contrasting God's dealings with Abraham and what happened on Sinai (3:15-22). Nonetheless, as Paul made clear, he was speaking allegorically. Would not this lead the addressees to expect a referent different than the covenant with Abraham? If Hagar stood for Sinai, would we not expect Sarah to stand for something outside the Genesis narratives? Certainly for Paul the covenant which God made with Abraham and the promises which He gave him had been fulfilled in Jesus and the new covenant established in his atoning death.[331] Perhaps it was precisely this which explains the fact that Paul did not in fact complete his allegorical interpretation when he came to Sarah. It would be difficult to find an exact correspondence to balance Sinai geographically, as the new covenant was not geographically localized in the way the Sinai covenant was. It seems reasonable to think that Paul might have had in mind the covenant made with Abraham as fulfilled in Jesus the messiah and Son of God.[332]

Sarah, then, represented the Jerusalem above (v. 26b), who, Paul claimed, is "our mother." Here Paul was making use of a concept of an already existing heavenly Jerusalem (destined to be realized on earth at the End) which is to be found in some Jewish apocalyptic writings.[333] The characteristic of this heavenly Jerusalem was freedom (v. 26). So the implication was that the children of this heavenly Jerusalem were born to enjoy that freedom. For Paul, this Jerusalem from above was connected to the Christians—she is "our mother" (v. 26).

Paul will return to the theme of (spiritual) freedom at the climax of this section of the letter (5:1), but for the moment, in order to ground his

---

329. Bruce, *Galatians*, 218; Mussner, *Galaterbrief*, 321; Dunn, *Galatians*, 249-50; Martyn, *Galatians*, 454-57; Witherington, *Grace*, 331-32; Hays, *Echoes*, 114-15.

330. Burton, *Galatians*, 258, 262; Betz, *Galatians*, 243, 245; Longenecker, *Galatians*, 211; Behm, "διαθηκη," *TDNT* 2:130; Lincoln, *Paradise*, 16; *Stories*, 183.

331. Apart from the account of the Last Supper/Lord's Supper in 1 Corinthians 11:23-26, Paul only uses "new covenant" in the phrase "ministers of the new covenant" (2 Cor 3:6), while "old covenant" figures in the same passage, when he refers to "the reading of the old covenant" (2 Cor 3:14). It would be tempting to fill in the missing link as follows: Sarah—Golgotha—Jerusalem above, but see Susan Eastman, *Recovering Paul's Mother Tongue*, 138-39, for a warning not to fill in the gaps which Paul has left unfilled.

332. Witherington *Grace*, 332, is inclined to favor this both-and approach.

333. See especially *1 En.* 90:28-38; *4 Ezra* 7:26; 8:52-53; 9:38-10:57; *2 Bar.* 4:1-7. In the NT, see Heb 12:22-24; Rev 21:2, 10.

assumption that Sarah represents the Jerusalem which is above, he quoted Isaiah 54:1 LXX:

> Rejoice, you barren woman who has never given birth to a child,
> Break forth into song and cry aloud, you who have never been in labor,
> Because the children of the deserted woman will be more numerous than those of the one who has a husband.

This verse originally was the promise that Zion-Jerusalem, likened to a barren and divorced woman, would be taken again as wife by Yahweh and would have numerous progeny and a glorious future. How apposite is the use of this passage for Paul's purposes? After all, Sarah is not specifically mentioned in it, while she did have a husband (unlike the woman in the quotation who is described as "abandoned"—της ερημου). The word "barren" (στειρα) in the quotation is one point of contact which enabled Paul to link the quotation with Sarah, since in Genesis 11:30 LXX she was described as "barren."[334] But it is reasonable to suppose that Paul had in mind the whole of Isaiah 54 and its context, and that this is another example of inter-textual exegesis. Indeed, Susan Eastman has claimed that Paul "refracts the birth narratives of Isaac and Ishmael through the lens of Isaiah 54:1."[335]

Second Isaiah addressed not only the exiles in Babylon but he also had a message for Zion-Jerusalem. Indeed, his work started with a message of comfort for God's people *and for Jerusalem* (40:1–2). Zion felt that she had been abandoned by God (49:14). God acknowledged that He had punished her by divorcing her, but His action was justified by Israel's past sins. At the same time, He indicated that as Creator He had the power to transform and change situations (50:1–3). Zion was assured that, despite her fears, God had not forgotten her. Rather, He had engravened her on the palms of His hands (49:14–16). She was promised an overflowing population, so large in fact that she would be utterly amazed (49:17–21, 22–26). Zion was promised that her present waste places would become like Eden (51:3). God's ransomed people would return (51:11). Zion was exhorted to arise and put on beautiful garments and to break forth into joyful praise (52:1–2, 7–10).

In 51:1–3, those who seek the LORD were told:

> Look to Abraham your father and to Sarah who bore you;[336]

---

334. Susan Eastman, *Mother Tongue*, 142, sees "barren" as the textual link between Isaiah 54:1 and Sarah's story, and she refers to Sarah as the quintessential example of the barren matriarch.

335. Eastman, *Mother Tongue*, 128; cf. 146.

336. LXX: τη\ν ωδινουσαν υ9μας.

for when he was one I called him, and I blessed him and made him many.

The way God dealt with Abraham and Sarah was an indication of how He could deal with Zion-Jerusalem in the present. God overcame the barrenness of Sarah and she conceived a son, and over the years descendants increased in fulfillment of the promise to multiply them. So also, God was able to restore Zion's fortunes and make her a fully populated city once more.[337]

With all this, it comes as no surprise that in chapter 54 Zion is likened to a barren divorcée who would be married again and would have numerous children. Yahweh was her creator, redeemer and husband (v. 5). She would forget the shame of her past (v. 4). Her children would "possess the nations and make cities at present laid waste to be inhabited" (v. 3bc). God's wrath had been only temporary; His compassion and kindness would be everlasting, and He would make a "covenant of peace" with her which should stand forever (vv. 7-8, 10).

Hays sees "an internal echo hinting at the correspondence between the city in its exilic desolation and the condition of Sarah before Isaac's birth, a correspondence that also implies the promise of subsequent blessing."[338] This link by Second Isaiah between Abraham and Sarah on the one hand and the eschatologically restored Jerusalem on the other was significant for Paul's use of Isaiah 54:1 in his letter to the Galatians.

For Paul, the passage had a double referent. Firstly, the barren woman referred to Sarah, who had been told that she would be the mother of many nations (Gen 17:16), while the second referent was the very fact that the promise

---

337. The story of Abraham and Sarah was a witness to God's power to deliver and multiply and to transform desolation into abundance. See Eastman, *Mother Tongue*, 143. Eastman, *Mother Tongue*, 152, claims that Isaiah's story of transformation from barrenness to fecundity came to its climax in 66:7-14, where God's redemptive power brought to pass what was humanly impossible—miraculous birth without labor pains. She then (155-60) imports this into Isaiah 54:1, quoted in Galatians 4:27b, and takes η9 ουοκ ωδινουσα to refer to miraculous birth without labor pains, viz. the eschatological fulfillment of Paul's apostolic labor mentioned in Galatians 4:19. A grammatical question arises: to what point in time do the participles refer? Robertson, *Grammar*, 891, points out that the present participle is timeless and durative, and one of his categories is "past action still in progress" (892). If that is the case here, in Galatians 4:27, then the barren woman was thought of as in a state of never having brought forth children/ suffered labor pains. Moulton, *Grammar*, 127, mentions that η9 τικουσα was common in Greek tragedy as a practical synonym of η9 μη/τηρ and refers to Galatians 4:27. It would seem that the sense is that the woman apostrophised was not and had never been in the past a mother. The idea of an inter-textual link with Isaiah 66:7-9, however, does not seem to be soundly based.

338. Hays, *Echoes*, 119-20. Burton, *Galatians*, 264, had raised this possibility, but felt that there was no clear indication.

of many children made to the former barren one was being fulfilled in the Law-free mission of Paul and his co-workers, i.e., the Christian communities coming into existence as a result of the Christian mission and including Gentile believers.[339] The quotation substantiated Paul's claim that Christians have Sarah, meaning heavenly Jerusalem, as their mother.[340]

This second referent of Isaiah 54:1 explains why Paul in verse 28 claimed that Christian believers were "children of the promise" just as Isaac was (v. 28).[341] He added that just as Ishmael had persecuted Isaac,[342] so in the present those enslaved under the Sinai covenant were persecuting those who believed in Jesus Christ (v. 29).[343] This persecution was in fact proof that they were sons of the free woman.[344]

At this point, Paul quoted what in Genesis was Sarah's demand, but was here simply introduced by "Scripture says," i.e., God says: "Cast out the slave woman and her son, because the son of the slave woman shall certainly not inherit along with the son of the free woman."[345] In the context of the

---

339. Cf. Barrett, *Allegory*, 164: "The future . . . is with the church of justified sinners rather than law-keeping Judaism." See also Hays, *Echoes*, 120.

340. Mussner, *Galaterbrief*, 328; Longenecker, *Galatians*, 215; Eastmann, *Mother Tongue*, 141 (the passage grounded Paul's affirmation of the Galatians' new identity as the children of the free woman made in verse 26), 143, 153.

341. Koch, *Schrift*, 209, has remarked that there are no children κατα\ σαρκα either for Sarah or the Jerusalem above: hence the conclusion of verse 28. Barclay, *Gift*, 417n64, comments that the birthing of the "free" has nothing to do with ethnicity. As Paul says, it is κατα\ πνευμα and is based on God's promise (4:28–29).

342. Paul is making use of a Rabbinic interpretation of Genesis 21:9, which was taken to mean Ishmael's hostility and enmity towards Isaac. In the antithesis κατα\ σαρκα/κατα\ πνευμα, Paul took up the antithesis κατα\ σα/ρκα/δι' επαγγελιας from verse 23 (see 3:14 for the link between promise and Spirit).

343. Paul himself had experienced the hostility of his own countrymen and women (as the catalogue of hardships in 2 Corinthians 11:24–29, esp. 11:24, reveals; see also 1 Thess 2:14–16). At the same time, it could be that he was thinking of the Judaizing campaign within the Galatian congregations, their hostility, and their smear tactics directed against himself, and the unsettling effects on the new Galatian converts themselves. Burton, *Galatians*, 266; Martyn, 445; Vogel, *Heil*, 72, take "persecute" in a metaphorical sense of the propaganda of the opponents' mission.

344. Berger, *Abraham*, 62.

345. Paul changed Sarah's μου in the phrase "my son" (Gen 21:10), and replaced it with της ελευθερας, which fitted his context and picked up his previous interpretation (Gal 4:32) (cf. Koch, *Schrift*, 150). The demand (which could be said to be based, in a sense, on the promises of Genesis 17:21) was confirmed by God at Genesis 21:12. Aageson, *Written for Our Sake*, 84–85, maintains that while Paul gave the Scriptural text a new content, he has not disregarded the basic function of the story, which was to help to establish the "identity" of the true people of God—they should be traced through Isaac, not through Ishmael. The identity of the people of God since Jesus was now based on faith in Jesus as the fulfillment of the promise to Abraham.

Letter, it could be an appeal to the Galatians to dissociate themselves from the Judaizing invaders and, indeed, to expel them.[346] Then comes the conclusion: "Therefore, brothers and sisters, we are not the children of the slave woman but the children of the free woman," and the consequence is drawn for the situation in Galatia: "Christ has set us free for freedom. Stand firm, therefore, and do not be subject to the yoke of bondage again" (5:1). The two verses (4:31; 5:1) must be taken closely together. Together they form the climax of Paul's argument (rather than just 4:30).[347] They illustrate the close link of the indicative and imperative in Paul's thinking.

In Hansen's structural analysis of the letter, which he sees as a rebuke-request type of letter, he made out a strong case for seeing a new section, viz. the request section, starting at 4:12.[348] He believes that the allegory of Hagar and Sarah furnished the basis for the ethical demands of the rebuke section. The allegory works with two pairs of opposites: slavery-freedom (vv. 22-26, 30-31) and flesh-spirit (vv. 23, 29), and these two opposites are prominent in the section which follows: there is the demand to preserve the freedom given in Christ with his gospel (5:1, 13; cf. 6:12-15) and there is the contrast between the works of the flesh/Law and the fruit and leading of the Spirit (5:13-6:2).[349]

While there is a Christological foundation for how Paul interpreted and argued, Hays is right in stressing the fundamental ecclesiocentric thrust of Paul's argument.[350] *Gentile believers were members of the people of God stretching back to Abraham-Sarah on the basis of being born of the Spirit through God's promise, and were not under any compulsion to be under the Law.* The promise of God was linked with freedom from the Law.[351]

---

346. So Mussner, *Galaterbrief*, 332; Longenecker, *Galatians*, 217; Martyn, *Galatians*, 446; Witherington, *Grace*, 338-39; Vogel, *Heil*, 72-73; Wisdom, *Blessing*, 161n30, 166n50, 217-18; Wilson, *Curse of the Law*, 26-27, 43. This tells against the view of Hardin, *Galatians and the Imperial Cult*, 93-94, 114, 152, that the "agitators" had withdrawn from the congregation(s) at the time of the writing of the letter.

347. Eastmann, *Mother Tongue*, 132-33, maintains that 5:1, and not 4:30, is the climax of this section of the letter.

348. Hansen, *Abraham*, 44, 46-51, 141-45. Eastmann, *Mother Tongue*, 30, 130-34, 182, also sees a new section beginning at 4:12. She maintains that 4:12-5:1 sets the ground for the outworking in practical behavior of its assertions about the identity of the Galatians, in what follows in the letter.

349. Hansen, *Abraham*, 48, 151-54.

350. Hays, *Echoes*, 113, 117, 120-21.

351. Berger, *Abraham*, 63.

1.4. Summary

Firstly, we may mention that Paul showed himself to be a theologian of the Scriptures. He engaged with the story of Abraham because it was a vital part of the Scriptures of Israel, the people of God. He exegeted in accordance with the kind of techniques which Jewish teachers of the period utilized. He drew in Habakkuk 2:4 to his discussion of Genesis 15:6 because both contain πιστις and words of the δικ- root. He saw significance in the singular σπερμα of Genesis. He explored what was the meaning of the blessing for all the nations in God's promise to Abraham. He wrestled with what significance the Law could have in God's purposes if Genesis 15 was the clue to how God wished to deal with human beings. Paul brought the insights, given to him in God's revelation of His Son, to his understanding of the Scriptures, and now read them in a new way compared with his previous Rabbinic training.[352]

Secondly, for Paul what was indicated in the promise to Abraham found its fulfillment in the coming, death, and resurrection of Jesus and the outpouring of the Spirit. He saw in the promise of God to Abraham, that all the nations of the world would be blessed in and through him and his descendants, a crucial indication of God's intention to bless all humanity. God had a world wide purpose when He chose and called Abraham. Now God had put that purpose into effect through the mission of His Son. Paul had come to see this through God's own call to him personally (1:16). In his own ministry he had seen how, through the preaching of the gospel of His Son Jesus Christ, God was calling Jew and Greek, slave and free, male and female, into one body in Christ. The outpouring of the Spirit of God on all believers was the fulfillment of the universal blessing contained in the promise to Abraham (3:14-15).

Thus, Abraham might be regarded as a prototype of how God intended to deal with human beings. Yet, on the other hand, he was the start of a family who were destined to play a role in God's purposes. This leads us on to the next point.

Thirdly, Paul redefined who was a descendant of Abraham. He replaced the physical criterion of biological descent from the nation's ancestor. To be a child (son) of Abraham was to share in the characteristics of the father. That meant for Paul supremely a trust, a confidence, in God's word and promise. It was οι εκ πιστεως who were the children of Abraham (3:7). Just as Abraham believed God's promise, so believers have trusted in the

---

352. "For Paul, Christ relativizes the law and puts the law in proper perspective, whereas for the Teachers in Galatia, the law seems to relativize Christ and place Christ in proper perspective" (Siker, *Disinheriting*, 48).

same God, who had promised that those who believe in His Son, crucified and raised, were in the right with Him and would enjoy life. It was the union with Christ which meant that believers become children of Abraham and heirs of the inheritance promised by God (3:29).

It should be observed that the place of the Jews was not a theme in Galatians.[353]

Fourthly, faith was obviously important. It determined whether one was really a child of Abraham (3:6-9); the quotation from Habakkuk 2:4 "trumps" Deuteronomy 27:26 and Leviticus 18:5 (3:10-12); a person received the gift of the Spirit as the blessing promised to Abraham (3:14); faith operated in the era of the fulfillment of the Promise which superseded the Law (3:22-25); and through faith, one was baptized into Christ and put on Christ (3:26-28). Prior to chapters 3-4, Paul had unequivocally stated that faith was directed to Jesus, the Son of God (2:16, 20).

Fifthly, we observe that in Galatians Paul seems to draw a fairly sharp division between Promise and Law. Law was described in rather negative terms—the pictures of the custodian and that of the *paedagogos* underline this (compare the analogy of the guardians controlling an heir until he comes of age in 4:1-3). The era of the Law was one in which people were basically immature and in need of constant supervision and control. The era of the Law was for a specific period of time—until the Christ, Jesus, came. The Law brought condemnation and curse, and was unable to give life. Its mediation by angels was a sign of its inferiority (3:19). For the Galatian converts to submit to the requirements of the Law was the equivalent of going back under those elemental forces which had dominated them in their pagan past (4:8-11).

Excursus: Did Paul Use the Concept of Justification under the Pressure of the Galatian Controversy?

There is a body of scholarly opinion which believes that Paul's teaching on justification by grace through faith was developed under the pressure of the dispute in Galatia and the need to defend the inclusion of Gentiles in the people of God without circumcision and adherence to other demands of the Law. It is claimed that the true center of his teaching was the idea of "being in Christ," a participatory soteriology.

Can this view be substantiated? We shall assume that Galatians was certainly written after 1 Corinthians, quite possibly before 2 Corinthians (or parts of our present 2 Corinthians), and not overly long before Romans. The

---

353. Noted in Berger, *Abraham*, 51, 58.

evidence of the Corinthian correspondence becomes of special importance to answer the question which concerns us.

Paul indicated to the Corinthians that among the gifts flowing to those in Christ Jesus from God were wisdom, δικαιοσυνη, holiness, and redemption (1 Cor 1:30). That these were gifts from God through Christ means that δικαιοσυνη must mean "right standing with God."[354] This had come about through the cross of Jesus, which had dominated the discussion since 1:17.

Paul asserted (1 Cor 6:11) that some of the Corinthians had in the past been among those whose behavior excluded them from the Kingdom of God, but he went on to say "but you were washed, consecrated,[355] justified in the name of our Lord Jesus Christ and by the Spirit of our God." Justification is one of three descriptions of the conversion of the Corinthians, conversion involving faith, baptism, and belonging to the Body of Christ. The sequence of the verbs was not intended in a temporal sense. They are "coincident facets of the believer's one experience of union with Christ."[356]

In 2 Corinthians, Paul described his ministry as one of δικαιοσυνη as opposed to the Sinai ministry which is one of κατακρισις (2 Cor 3:9). The opposite of condemnation is acquittal, the declaration of being in the right, justification.[357]

The phrase "the righteousness of God" occurs at 2 Corinthians 5:21. Paul had talked about the representative death of Christ: "One died for all; therefore, all died." The aim of this representative death for all was that those who have benefited (described as οι ζωντες because they have shared in the resurrection of Christ) should no longer live for themselves "but for the sake of him who died and was raised for them" (5:14-15). Then Paul spoke of what had thus happened as "new creation" (v. 17) and of reconciliation as a gift of God through Christ (vv. 18-19). This process of reconciliation involved not counting our transgressions against us (v. 19). Not counting or reckoning our transgressions is equivalent (in negative terms) to declaring in the right (cf. Rom 4:6). The act of reconciliation must be announced, and so there is a ministry of reconciliation, which had been entrusted to Paul (and others, vv. 19b-20). Verse 21 comes near to an "explanation" of how the not counting

---

354. Barrett, *First Epistle*, 60-61; Fee, *First Epistle*, 86; Hill, *Greek Words and Hebrew Meanings*, 147; Fung, *Justification by Faith*, 248. Fee deduces that "righteousness" (justification) "was already a common metaphor for Paul to express the saving work of Christ."

355. Hill, *Greek Words*, 147, translates as "sanctified" but adds, "that is, *separated to a life of holiness*" (my italics).

356. Fung, *Justification*, 251.

357. Hill, *Greek Words*, 147. Fung, *Justification*, 252-53, combines forensic and ethical righteousness here.

our transgressions and the reconciliation with God had occurred. "God made him who knew no sin [viz. Jesus] (to be) sin on our behalf in order that we might become the righteousness of God in him" (v. 21).

This is one of Paul's famous "interchange in Christ" passages.[358] Jesus, the perfectly obedient one ("knew no sin"), had entered into our situation (characterized by transgressions, and locked into the sphere dominated by sin) even to the extent of dying for us. Now the risen Lord, he can confer life on those who have died and been raised with him. In what sense do believers become the righteousness of God? We might have expected that Paul would say δικαιοι ενωπιον Θεου. One possible explanation is that Paul used δικαιοσυνη to create a literary symmetry with αμαρτια in the first part of the sentence.[359] Whatever the explanation, we may understand the genitive Θεου as a genitive of origin, and so δικαιοσυνη is something which passes from God to men and women, and the phrase as a whole means right standing conferred by God.[360] It is in effect the equivalent of "justified."[361]

Wright has proposed a very different interpretation of "righteousness of God" in 2 Corinthians 5:21.[362] He believes that the phrase "the righteousness of God" in Romans means God's faithfulness to the covenant made with Abraham, though not in the nationalistic way that Israel imagined. He points out that in context of 2 Corinthians 5:21, Paul claimed that he had been entrusted with the ministry of announcing God's action to reconcile us to Himself in Jesus Christ, and that as a result he was an ambassador for Christ through whom God was making His appeal to men and women. In this preaching Paul became a living embodiment of the voice of God. In the power of the Spirit, Paul was the means through whom the divine "covenant faithfulness" (δικαιοσυνη Θεου) could become effective for any and all. The reminder of the larger context of Paul's ministry as the suffering apostle of the new covenant is timely, as is the idea that Paul, as the ambassador of Christ on God's behalf, is the living voice and embodiment of the One whom he serves. However, Wright's interpretation seems to involve a change in the referent of the first person pronoun between

---

358. On this idea in Paul, see Hooker, *From Adam to Christ*, 13-69.

359. See Hill, *Greek Words*, 142; Thrall, *2 Corinthians*, 1:443. Thrall quotes Allo, *Saint Paul*, 172; Bruce *1 and 2 Corinthians*, 211, as also holding this explanation.

360. Hill, *Greek Words*, 142; Fung, *Justification*, 255-57. Kasemann, *NT Questions of Today*, 168-82, Stuhlmacher, *Gerechtigkeit Gottes bei Paulus*, 75-77, interpret the phrase as God's eschatological act setting the whole cosmos right with Himself. It is not easy, however, to see how the verb γενωμεθα fits nicely with this sense of the phrase.

361. Hughes, *2 Corinthians*, 214; Barrett, *Second Epistle*, 180; Thrall, *2 Corinthians*, 1:439, 442-44; Hill, *Greek Words*, 142.

362. Wright, *Pauline Perspectives*, 68-75.

the two halves of the verse. The first occurrence (υπερ ημων) refers to the addressees and anyone and everyone, including Paul himself, while the second (ημεις) would refer to Paul himself. That is quite a sharp change, perhaps not impossible, but avoidable if Paul had said in verse 21a υπερ παντων, as he did twice previously (vv. 14–15).

Summary

The evidence of the Corinthian correspondence suggests that Paul's use of the δικ-group of words was already part of his vocabulary to present the saving work of God in Jesus and was not just the product of the controversy reflected in the Galatian Letter.[363] He could use this terminology when writing to what appears to have been a predominantly Gentile church, and he did not need to explain himself.

It is true that the Corinthian correspondence appears to originate after the Antioch incident and that Jewish Christian missionaries of some sort had arrived at Corinth and their preaching had created trouble for Paul. However, circumcision, food laws, sabbath observance, and calendrical issues play no part in the controversy between Paul and them as revealed in 2 Corinthians. It beggars belief that Paul made no reference to these issues had they been playing a part in the controversy.

---

363. See the view of Fee, *First Corinthians*, 86, already quoted in note 322 above. Fung, *Justification*, 257, has expressed himself thus: "The fact that Paul freely employs the concept of justification even in contexts where the legalistic point of view is not discussed at all . . . strongly argues that it cannot fairly be regarded as a purely polemical doctrine born of, and intended for use in, the debate with Jews and Jewish Christian legalists only."

2

Paul's Letter to the Romans

2.1. Introduction

THE LETTER TO THE Romans was written sometime later than Galatians. Paul was on the point of visiting Jerusalem for the purpose of taking the collection of money, contributed by his mission churches, to help the poor among the mother church (15:25–27). He was clearly somewhat apprehensive about his reception not only by unbelieving Jews in the city but also by the church there, and he asked the Christians at Rome to pray for him that he might be delivered from the former and that the gift which he was taking might be acceptable to the church. Once the collection had been delivered, Paul then proposed to make a long-hoped for visit to Rome, a church which had not been founded by him (1:8–15; 15:22–23). Paul had planned to visit Rome for a considerable while, but these hopes had been hindered, though he does not say by what he had been hindered (1:13; 15:22). He expressed the hope that the church there would provide some support for a mission to Spain and the western Mediterranean (15:24, 28).[1]

Paul may have had a number of reasons for writing Romans. Among these at least could have been the desire to sum up the presentation of his gospel as an introduction of himself to a church which he had not founded

---

1. Such is the implications of προπεμφθῆναι (15:24). See Bauer, *Lexicon*, 716: "Help on one's journey with food, money, by arranging for companions, means of travel, etc." This, however, can hardly have been the major reason for writing Romans.

or visited (1:5; cf. 15:20).² Although he had to proceed delicately in view of this, Paul presented himself as one who had received an apostleship to bring about "the obedience of faith among the all the Gentiles" (1:5) and described himself as apostle to the Gentiles (11:13) and minister of Christ Jesus to the Gentiles (15:16).³ Precisely because he felt under an obligation to Greeks and barbarians, wise and ignorant, he wished to preach the gospel to people in Rome (1:14–15). In addition, by setting out his gospel message, he could hope both to succeed in dispelling any unease or suspicion as a result of hearing about Paul and his mission,⁴ and gain the support of the Roman Christians for his proposed mission to Spain (15:24).⁵ On the other hand, he seems to have been informed about certain issues which were troubling the church⁶ and he dealt at length with them in 14:1–15:13, while in chapter 11 he reprimanded Gentile Christians for an attitude of boastful pride towards those of Jewish descent (vv. 13–32, esp. 17–19). This lends weight to the idea that there were tensions between Gentile Christians and those Jewish Christians who had returned to Rome after the death of Claudius and the end of

---

2. See 1:9–12; 15:14–21, for the delicate balance which Paul had to observe between approaching a church which he had not founded and his sense of being the apostle to the Gentiles and, therefore, of wanting some "fruit" among the people of Rome, the capital of the Empire.

3. Barclay, *Gift*, 457–58, 523, suggests that Paul wanted the Roman Christians to accept him, in his capacity as the apostle to the Gentiles, as *their* apostle.

4. In this way we can integrate the main body of the letter (1:16–11:36) with the framework chapters (1:1–15; 12:1–16:25).

5. But, as Theobald, "Warum schrieb Paulus den Römerbrief?," 4, points out, this comes only at the end and in a brief reference.

6. Stuhlmacher, *Purpose of Romans*, 237–38, points out that, under favorable sailing conditions, mail could be taken from Corinth to Rome in only seven or eight days, so that Paul could have known about the Roman Church quite easily. (The same applies in the reverse direction, so that the Roman Christians could have known about something of the Christian community in Corinth, a knowledge which Tobin, *Paul's Rhetoric in Context*, assumes on the part of the Roman Christians and which, he thinks, was one of the reasons for the suspicion and distrust which they had towards Paul and his views and which Paul seeks in the letter to allay.) Barclay, *Gift*, 456, is among those who believe that the references to the issues behind chapters 14–15 are not very specific.

the validity of his decree expelling Jews from Rome,[7] and/or that Paul had to counter suspicions about his gospel among Jewish Christians.[8]

Judging by chapter 16,[9] he had over the years met and worked with many people who were now in the various house churches in Rome. He clearly hoped to enlist their encouragement and support.

There is fairly widespread agreement that Paul has given us a heading to the letter: "I am not ashamed of the gospel, for it is the power of God leading to salvation for every one who believes, to the Jew first and to the Greek; for in it God's way of setting us in the right with Himself is revealed on the basis of faith from start to finish, as it stands written, The person who by faith is righteous shall live" (1:16–17).[10]

Paul then proceeded to argue in differing ways that the entire human race, Gentiles and Jews alike, were in fact sinful before God (1:18–3:20). Most scholars assume that the Gentile world was condemned in 1:18–32 for its gross idolatry and immorality, springing from a worship of the creature and a refusal to honor the Creator. Here Paul's critique agrees with similar criticisms about Gentile religion and morality, expressed by Hellenistic Jewish writers like the author of the Wisdom of Solomon. However, echoes of Israel's archetypal sin at Horeb/Sinai, as mentioned in Psalm 106:20, have been noted at Romans 1:23,[11] so the view that only the Gentile world is in mind in 1:18–32 may not be as straightforward as has been assumed.[12] On the other

---

7. See a number of the contributors (with differing emphases) in Donfried, *Romans Debate*; "False Presuppositions," 103; Wiefel, *Jewish Community in Ancient Rome*, 96; Jewett, *Following the Argument of Romans*, 276–77; Beker, *Faithfulness of God*, 331–32. The dissenting scholars are Karris, *Romans 14:1–15:13*, 65–84, 125–27; Aune, *Romans as a Logos Protreptikos*, 278–96. Sanger, *Verkündigung*, 93, adds a word of caution about overstressing the virulence of anti-Jewish sentiment among the Gentile Christians at Rome. Barclay, *Gift*, 456, believes that too much weight has been placed on what he describes as "the opaque notice" of Suetonius, *Claudius* 25.4 (*impulsore Chresto*).

8. Watson, "Two Roman Congregations," 206, 212; Stuhlmacher, "Purposes," 236, 239–40, both in Donfried, *Romans Debate*.

9. Assuming the integrity of chapter 16. See Gamble, *Textual History*. Both Meeks, *Urban Christians*, 56; Watson, *PJG*, 183–87, have expressed the view that Paul did not necessarily know personally all the individuals mentioned in chapter 16.

10. I have paraphrased δικαιοσυνη in order to try and get the sense of God's activity involved and the phrase εκ πιστεως εις πιστιν, which is far from easy to unravel—it *may* include a certain play on words, "from God's faithfulness to man's faith." In the Habakkuk quotation, I have taken εκ πιστεως with ο δικαιος, rather than with ζησεται, on the grounds that that seems to be the way in which Paul's argument runs (it is possible, however, that Paul deliberately left the position ambiguous to suggest both possibilities, as Dunn, *Romans*, 1:45–46, maintains). For a very thorough discussion of Romans 1:16–17, see Theobald, "Der strittige Punkt," 278–323.

11. Hooker, "Further Note on Romans," 87.

12. Barclay, *Gift*, 462, is one the latest scholars to query whether only the Gentile

hand, in Romans 10:2-3 Paul acknowledged that contemporary Israelites had a zeal for God, even if it was not according to knowledge.[13]

Certainly, in 2:1-5 Paul accused anyone who voiced such criticisms of being guilty of doing the same things.[14] Undoubtedly, Israel's history after the entry into the land of Canaan was constantly marred by idolatry and immorality as the prophets amply testify. As Paul's argument progresses, it is clear that he did not think that the Jew was in any better position and could not hide behind the mere possession of the Law and circumcision. The OT conviction that God shows no partiality was used by Paul as an argument against any claim by the Jew to "favored status" (2:11).[15] Likewise, the traditional motif of judgment according to one's deeds was also used to undermine any idea of preferential treatment for the Jew.[16] Any claim by the Jew that Jews would be treated differently from Gentiles at God's judgment was simply untenable.[17] It would be the doers of the Law, not mere hearers of it, who would be declared in the right at the Last Judgment (v. 13).

The Jew had not in fact kept what the Law commanded (2:21-23). Because some immorality existed within Israel, his boast of being "a guide to the blind" and "a light to those in darkness" was proven to be false (2:17-24).[18] Certainly, in Romans 2, Paul attacked what he considered a misplaced confidence in the possession of the Law, which was the embodiment of knowledge and truth and which opened up knowledge of God. But possession of the Law was not enough. Paul indicted the Jew of *actually*

---

world was in mind in 1:18-32. Likewise, Linebaugh, *God*, 101-15, who suggests that Romans 1:18-32 tells the diverse stories of Adam, Israel, and the Gentiles: it is the story of the ανθρωπος. Paul has created a common human history. Unlike the Wisdom of Solomon, Paul included Israel in the charge of idolatry and ungodliness.

13. A point made by Thiessen, *Gentile Problem*, 47.

14. Linebaugh, *God*, 100-104, argues that at 2:1 the "judge" was included in the pattern of idolatry and immorality just described in 1:18-32 ("do the same things"). The "judge" "is a Jew in the theological tradition of the *Wisdom of Solomon*." For the suggestion that the "judge" of 2:1 is a Gentile who condemns the immoral behavior of his contemporaries, see Stowers, *Re-Reading Romans*, 97-107; Thorsteinsson, *Paul's Interlocutor in Romans 2*; Thiessen, *Gentile Problem*, 53-54.

15. See Bassler, *Impartiality*.

16. See the treatment of this motif in the OT, Second Temple Judaism, and Paul by Yinger, *Judgment*.

17. See Dunn, *Romans*, 1:88; Chae, *Paul as Apostle*, 106-7; Wilckens, *Römer*, 1:126; Barclay, *Gift*, 463, who says that Paul will not allow any exceptionalism nor any appeal to God's kindness, even one based on Exodus 34:6-7.

18. Wright, *Pauline Perspectives*, 98. Thiessen, *Gentile Problem*, 60-61 points out that the three vices mentioned in 2:21 were a common *topos* in Hellenistic moral philosophy and also were encountered in Hellenistic Jewish writers like Philo and the author of Wisdom of Solomon.

transgressing the Law (2:21-23), and so dishonoring God (vv. 23-24). He upbraided the Jew with a glaring contradiction between his claim and his actual conduct.[19] One might almost say that the criticism implied a lack of a true sense of the seriousness of breaking the Law.

Paul even said that there were Gentiles who actually kept the Law despite not having received it as part of their cultural inheritance.[20] They will condemn (i.e., in the sense that their lives will provide evidence which will secure the condemnation of)[21] the Jew who for all his possession of the Law and circumcision,[22] was a transgressor of the Law (v. 27). Paul then proceeded to define the true Jew as one who was a Jew inwardly, and true circumcision was of the heart through the Spirit (vv. 28-29).[23]

Paul's conclusion runs: "We have previously made the charge that Jews and Greeks are all under sin," followed by a long catena of OT quotations.[24] These quotations (3:10-18) back up Paul's contention that his fellow countrymen and women stood condemned of sinfulness before the bar of divine justice. The final indictment runs: "We know that whatever the Law says it says to those who live under its jurisdiction, in order that every mouth may be stopped and the whole world be held accountable

---

19. Wilckens, *Römer*, 1:147, 149-50; Smith, *Saved*, 91-92.

20. Who were these Gentiles who did keep the Law? After the indictment of the whole world in 1:18–3:20, we would not expect to hear of any who do what the Law required. The contrast between 2:14-15 and the whole of 1:18–3:20; plus the allusion to Jeremiah 31:33 and Ezekiel 36:26-27 in the phrase about what the Law required being written on their hearts; plus the later reference in Romans 8:4 to those who live by the Spirit fulfilling the Law's demands, all combine to make a good case for seeing a reference to Christian Gentiles here, people whose lives Paul had helped to change in the work of his mission. Barclay, *Gift*, 466-68, is one of the recent scholars to defend this view. He also maintains that in 2:14 φυσει should be taken as meaning "by birth" and linked with "who do not have the Law."

21. For this sense of κρινει, compare the use of κατακρινει in Luke 11:31//Mathew 12:42 (NEB/REB translation).

22. This assumes that δια\ γραμματος και\ περιτομης is a genitive of attendant circumstances. (Thiessen, *Gentile Problem*, 64-67, denies this and maintains an instrumental sense in accordance with his view that Paul believed that only eighth day circumcision was valid circumcision and that Paul's interlocutor in chapter 2 was a Judaizing Gentile convert.)

23. In these verses Paul is following in the wake of Jeremiah 31:31, 34 and Ezekiel 11:29-30; 36:26-27. Barclay, *Gift*, 469, points out that God's transformative power reconstitutes Jewish identity as well. The Jew's value before God is no longer calculable in terms of circumcision. Circumcision of the heart is the only essential definition of a Jew. Jewish identity is created not by birth or custom, but by God. See Berger, *Abraham*, 63, for the suggestion that 2:25-29 is the decisive premise for Romans 4.

24. See Koch, *Schrift*, 94, 179-84, for arguments in favor of this as a planned composition by Paul.

to God, because no one will be declared in the right before God on the basis of doing the Law" (3:9, 10-18, 19-20).[25] The whole world, and that included the Jew! The Law in fact put the Jew on the same guilty footing as the Gentiles self-evidently were.[26]

But Paul maintained that this sorry state of affairs had been rectified by God Himself. He had set those who believe in Jesus Christ in the right relationship with Him as a free gift based solely on His grace, expressed in the redemptive, atoning death of His Son[27] and not in any way related to doing what the Law required (3:21-26).[28]

For Paul, this gracious gift of God excluded any human boasting (3:27a). What did he have in mind in referring to "boasting"? Was it a confidence in one's own righteousness before God or a sense of national superiority over against other races? But it was not just pride in one's national standing which was condemned in passages like 2:21-22 and 3:10-18, but actual specific deeds, or rather *lack* of them.[29] The Jews no less than the Gentiles needed to be restored to a right relationship to God.

Boasting was excluded, because a person was in fact justified before God on a basis which stood entirely apart from doing what the Law required, viz. on the basis of faith (3:28; as stressed at vv. 22, 25, 26). So, Paul set a sharp contrast between works of the Law and faith. If in fact this were not true, it would make God the God of the Jews only (v. 29a).[30] That would be absurd, and, in fact, would contradict monotheism, the cardinal doctrine of Judaism.

25. The logic behind Paul's case that *the whole world* was guilty before God was that God had set an order in creation and that this order was a revelation of the will of God akin to the revelation of God's will in the Law, a thought to be found in many early Jewish writings (as Reinmuth, Geist und Gesetz, 41-47, esp. 43, has shown). Reinmuth points out that Paul (Rom 1:19-21) said that God can be known through His works in the created order, and this meant a knowledge of τo δικαιωμα του Θεου according to verse 31. This interpretation is to be preferred to that put forward by Barrett, *Romans*, 70, and Ziesler, *Romans*, 104, who assume that Paul's thought is that if the Law (all the quotations are put under its rubric) finds the Jew guilty before God, how much more will the Gentile world be found guilty before God? Watson, *PJG*, 222, sees a different emphasis: though the Law is speaking *to* Jews, it is speaking *of* Jews and Greeks. Its verdict is in fact universal. The primary addressees are not exempt from the scope of this verdict.

26. Cf. Dunn, *Romans*, 1:152; Watson, *PJG*, 221-22.

27. Apart from the commentaries including his own, Theobald, *Studien zum Römerbrief*, 21-23, 30-67, deals with the crucial importance of 3:21-26 in several of his essays.

28. It is χωρις νομου, although it is witnessed-to by the law and the prophets (3:21). As Wright, *Pauline Perspectives*, 31, has put it, it needed to be apart from the Law, since the Gentiles did not have the Law, while the Law condemned the Jews.

29. Gathercole, *Boasting*, 205-215, 223; cf. Smith, *Saved*, 91-92.

30. Paul is assuming the belief in God's impartiality, which he mentioned in 2:11.

There was only one God, the God of the whole world and all creation. God had chosen to set Jews and Gentiles alike in the right with Himself on the basis of His free gift, to be received by faith (vv. 29-30).[31]

Does this emphasis on faith nullify the Law? To Jewish opponents and some Jewish Christians, Paul's approach to the Law seemed to call in question the uniqueness of Israel, whose identity to them was bound up with the Law received from God. Paul strongly denied that his emphasis on faith did nullify the Law; on the contrary, his emphasis on faith established the Law (v. 31).[32] Earlier, Paul had said that the fact that God had set us in the right with Himself had been revealed apart from the Law, yet, nevertheless, the Law and the prophets bore witness to it (3:21).[33] Paul had quoted from the prophet Habakkuk at 1:17, and he intended shortly to quote a passage from the Law in Genesis 15:6.

At this point, it is appropriate to mention that the above discussion dissents from the proposal put forward by Stowers in his work on the Diatribe and Romans. Stowers[34] believes that Paul is engaging with an imaginary interlocutor and that the latter, who is the kind of Jew imagined in 2:17-24, speaks in 3:27a, 27cd, 29c, 31a; 4:1-2a with Paul responding in 3:27b, 27ef-29b, 30, 31bc; 4:2b. Stowers thinks that this imaginary interlocutor showed himself persuaded by Paul's argument about justification by grace through faith, but then raised the question whether justification by faith abrogated the Law and whether Abraham constituted an exception. Without in any way wishing to deny that Paul has made use of the style of the diatribe at places in Romans (in a way that he does not do elsewhere in his surviving correspondence, especially in connection with objections and false conclusions drawn from teaching/preaching),[35] it is doubtful that Stowers has made out a convincing case for his rather elaborate reconstruction, but his view that a Jewish interlocutor speaks at 4:1-2a is on the right

---

31. There is no distinction intended between εκ πιστεως and δια πιστεως. The difference is no doubt purely stylistic or rhetorical, as Michel, *Römer*, 112; Leenhardt, *Romans*, 112; Barrett, *Romans*, 84; Cranfield, *Romans* 1:222; Käsemann, *Romans*, 104; Ziesler, *Romans*, 119; Wilckens, *Römer*, 1:248; Dunn, *Romans*, 1:189, all affirm. Flebbe, *Solus Deus*, 151, while agreeing that the usage is rhetorical, suggests that the difference is not without its significance, since differences have been overcome and relativized in the solidarity of faith.

32. Cf. Kaylor, *Paul's Covenant Community*, 84: "For in the Torah itself Abraham is said to be right with God through faith."

33. Theobald, "Verantwortung vor der Vergangheit," 24, aptly and succinctly comments: "The Law in the service of grace!"

34. Stowers, *Diatribe*, 164-67.

35. A point to which Stowers, *Diatribe*, 179, has drawn attention.

lines.³⁶ Paul had come under attack for seeming to undermine the Law by teaching justification by faith. His Letter to the Galatians shows that he had been confronted by others with the need to explain what was the purpose of the Law given on Sinai in God's plan.³⁷

It is probable too that Stowers places too much emphasis on the idea of Paul as a teacher, derived from the setting of the diatribe in the philosophical schools of Greece and Rome. It seems better to assume that Paul was here working out his arguments in the light of discussions which he had had with Jews and Jewish Christians in the past, and using a style drawn from the diatribe, especially in connection with dealing with objections and false conclusions.³⁸

At this point in the letter, while there is a case for saying that Paul felt the need to defend the argument of 3:27-31 or 3:21-31,³⁹ the argument of Romans 4 ought not to be treated as if it were merely an appendix to 3:21-31 or 3:27-31. While the theme of God's reckoning righteousness on the basis of faith does figure in Romans 4 (especially the opening section of vv. 1-8), the scope of Romans 4 is wider than illustrating justification by faith through the example of Abraham. A number of scholars have pointed this out. Thus, Zeller stressed that the universality of salvation and the justification of the Gentiles were equally concerns alongside justification by faith.⁴⁰ Neubrand has also stressed the theme of the equality of God's action towards Jews and

---

36. "The claim is that Abraham has a right to boast . . . the interlocutor accepts the interpretation of Abraham as one who was justified by his righteous acts as an assumed truth which is problematic for the argument in 3:27-29 that boasting is excluded" (Stowers, *Diatribe*, 172).

37. Irrespective of the fact that Paul faced this issue personally as a result of his Damascus Road experience (as we mention on pages 10-11).

38. This assumption differs considerably from the approach of Gaston, *Paul*, e.g., 7-8, 146-49, who assumes that all Paul's converts were Gentiles and suggests that what Paul saw amiss in his fellow Jews was not so much their rejection of Jesus as rejection of their God-destined missionary role of being a light to the Gentiles. See further the discussion on pages 95-97.

39. Wilckens, *Römer*, 1:258. Luz, *Geschichtsverständnis*, 173, 175, while he denied that the theme of Romans 4 was set by 3:31 (which he describes as a Zwischengedanke), believes that the theme of 3:21-31 is taken up in chapter 4, as does Tobin, *Paul's Rhetoric*, 145. Moxnes, *Theology*, 228, pointed to the links between 3:27-31 and chapter 4. See Stowers, *Diatribe*, 155-58, 168-74, for strong arguments for dealing with 3:27-4:25 as a unit. Sanger, *Verkündigung*, 107, maintains that chapter 4 serves to demonstrate what has been asserted at 3:21-22, viz. that the righteousness of God was in accordance with Scripture. Barclay, *Gift*, 482, also accepts that 4:1-8, 9-12, unpack and ground the claims of 3:27-30.

40. Zeller, *Juden und Heiden*, 100.

Gentiles, an issue which itself raises the question of the Law.[41] Flebbe has argued that Paul's discussion in Romans 4 is dominated more by the question of God than other issues.[42] Barclay sees the mode of Abraham's relationship with God (faith), the breadth of the promise to Abraham, and the means by which Abraham's seed had come into being as central concerns, with the incongruity between divine action and human status being the unifying theme of Paul's argument.[43] Other questions than just justification by faith are, then, dealt with in Romans 4, issues which were significant for Paul and his mission, and for the aim of the letter as a whole.

Thus, we may surmise that having enunciated his conviction that God had acted in Jesus Christ to set sinners in the right with Himself, a gift to be received by faith, a gift open to both Jews and Gentiles alike, Paul dealt with a probable objection from the Jewish side which, it is likely, he had had to deal with in the past: "What about Abraham?"[44]

2.2. Paul's Use of Abraham in the Letter to the Romans[45]

2.2.1. Romans 4:1–5[46]

Much Jewish interpretation of Abraham accorded to the patriarch an exalted status and magnified his righteous behavior, and had used Genesis 15:6

---

41. Neubrand, *Abraham Vater*, 2, 15–17, 26, 97, 125. Neubrand believes that scholars have neglected 3:29–30 in defining the theme of Romans 4.

42. Flebbe, *Solus Deus*, 163–267.

43. Barclay, *Gift*, 481.

44. We may legitimately assume that much of Paul's argument in Romans reflected discussions which he had had with his contemporary non-Christian fellow country men and also Christian Jews of a conservative persuasion. Cf. Luz, *Geschichtsverstndnis*, 179; Moxnes, *Theology*, 34, 69. Donfried, *Romans Debate*, 123, rightly asks why Romans cannot be both a sharing and repeating of insights gained in prior situations *and* addressing a real situation? Likewise, Niebuhr, *Heidenapostel*, 139, believes that actual past disputes have fed into Paul's expositions in Romans.

45. The most thorough treatments of Paul's handling of Abraham in Romans 4 are the monographs by Neubrand, *Abraham*; Schliesser, *Abraham's Faith in Romans 4*; Flebbe, *Solus Deus*, 163–267. There is a substantial treatment of Romans 4 in Jewett's massive commentary on Romans in the Hermeneia series (see bibliography). The treatment of Barclay, *Gift*, 479–90, under the sub-title "'The Abrahamic Family Trait,'" though brief, is most helpful.

46. The division of the chapter 4 into sub-units is not to be pressed too sharply (thus, e.g., Dunn in his commentary treats the whole of chapter 4 en bloc, while Jewett in his commentary divides into two large sections, verses 1–12 and 13–25), but has been undertaken in the hope of helping the reader follow the flow of Paul's thought.

in their exposition of his significance. Paul now takes this view "head on," as it were. "What shall we say that Abraham our forefather in terms of natural descent found?[47] For if Abraham were declared in the right with God on the basis of works, he would have (grounds for) boasting" (4:1-2a).[48]

This translation has been challenged, initially by R.B. Hays. Hays argued for a double question in verse 1 and that Abraham was the object of ευρηκεναι and not its subject, producing the translation that headed his article: "Have we found Abraham to be our forefather according to the flesh?"[49] He believed that this referred to a Jewish standpoint which Paul proceeded to criticize.[50] Hays has been followed by Gaston (who suggests translating, "Have we obtained Abraham as our forefather according to the flesh?"), Neubrand, and Wright.[51] Wright, however, modified Hays's suggestion, proposing that the "we" referred not to Jews but to *Christians*, whether Jews or Gentiles. He argued that the "subject"—ημας—was implied in the verb of the first question ερουμεν plus the ημων, and for Paul to have specified the ημας would have been otiose. Wright believes that the question was implying that Gentile Christians should become circumcised (cf. the issue behind Galatians). He believes that the question of the fatherhood of Abraham is the dominant issue behind the whole of Romans 4, and maintains that, therefore, his translation coheres with the way its thought flows.

---

47. There is a textual problem in verse 1, since ευρηκεναι is absent from B 1739 Origen and Chrysostom, and its position is not uniform in the manuscript tradition. See Wilckens, *Römer*, 1:260-61, for a discussion. On the whole it seems best to accept ευρηκεναι as original.

48. As Cranfield, *Romans*, 1:228 remarks, Paul regarded the statement of the protasis as totally untrue. See also de Roo, *Works of the Law*, 63, for a similar view to that espoused above (she rightly criticizes the assumption that Paul was saying that Abraham did have good works and could boast of them before other people, but could not do so before God, maintained by Klein, *Sündenverstandnis*, 249-82). Note that the αν in the apodosis of unreal or contrary to fact conditional sentences was no longer obligatory—see BDF para. 360 (pace Gaston, *Paul*, 66). Neubrand, *Abraham*, 192, takes both clauses of verse 2 as contemplating a theoretical possibility, which Paul rejected in verse 3. Flebbe, *Solus Deus*, 172, says that 4:2 is not entirely contrary to fact, since it represented a broad section of Jewish opinion.

49. Hays, "Have We Found Abraham," 76-98.

50. He appealed to BDF 396 for support for his syntactical argument, but Romans 4:1 is discussed actually under an entirely different category by BDF 480(5), viz. ellipsis. BDF 480(5), which accepted that the B text was correct in not having the ευρηκεναι, suggested that "has done" or "has experienced" should be supplied.

51. Gaston, *Paul*, 124-25; Neubrand, *Abraham*, 174-88; Wright, *Pauline Perspectives*, 101-2, 505, 579-84.

There are three issues here: grammar, flow of the argument, and who or what lies behind the question of what Abraham found out (v. 1) and might, therefore, have been the basis for boasting (v. 2)?

Despite Wright's assertions, the grammatical objections seem to remain significant. Dunn,[52] has objected, surely rightly, that to begin a sentence with an accusative and infinitive construction where the accusative was unstated "would be rather odd."[53] We may also point out that Paul never elsewhere follows τι ουν ερουμεν with the accusation and infinitive construction (he usually employs questions expecting the answer "no" [3:5; 6:1; 7:7; 8:31; 9:14] or once a statement at 9:30). Thus, 4:1 would be unique if it were a case of an accusative and infinitive construction.

Wright has contended that the fatherhood of Abraham is the key theme of Romans 4. But the flow of the thought could still be that the apostle first set out Abraham as the justified sinner (vv. 1-8), and then, on that basis, proceeded to consider him as the spiritual progenitor of all who believe (vv. 9-25). The analysis of Romans 4[54] fits the traditional translation just as well as the suggestion of Hays-Wright.

On the assumption that Paul did write ευρηκεναι, we may ask what might have prompted him to use that particular verb? A number of scholars detect here an echo of Genesis 18:3 where Abraham approached the three strangers/God humbly: "If then I have found favor in your sight" (ει αρα ευρον χαριν εναντιον σου). On the other hand, the verb ευρισκειν can connote the idea of learning something through experience, and Paul used it in that sense at Romans 7:21,[55] and possibly also at 7:10.[56] If that were the sense here, we would have a natural transition to verse 2. Some might think that Abraham did have grounds for boasting.

Is then Paul at 4:1-2 picking up an objection or assertion which he had encountered in his presentation of the gospel? Since Hays has now accepted Wright's proposal, we may concentrate on what Wright has maintained. In an essay from 1995, Wright paraphrased 4:1 as follows: "Does this mean that we Christians, Jews and Gentiles alike, now discover that we are to be members of the fleshly family of Abraham?" Presumably he meant by this that Jewish Christians believed that they were right in demanding that Gentile converts should be circumcised and that Gentile Christians had come to realize and accept this. This would be comparable

---

52. Dunn, *Romans*, 1:199.
53. See also Tobin, *Paul's Rhetoric*, 146n52.
54. See, e.g., Dunn, *Romans*, 1:199.
55. See Bauer, *Lexicon*, 325(2); Michel, *Römer* 178; NEB.
56. So Abbot-Smith, *Lexicon*, 189.

to the situation in Galatia where there was pressure on Gentile Christians to be circumcised, in order to become full members of Abraham's family. And this is what Wright points out in his essay of 2013,[57] stated in terms from a Jewish Christian standpoint.

In a slightly earlier essay of 2012 Wright had suggested that the opening question of 4:1 could be construed as based on a Jewish assertion that "if Abraham himself was marked out as God's covenant partner, as the starting point of the family who were the appointed means of the world's salvation, by or in relation to his possession of or adherence to Torah, as in 2:17–20, then the kauchēma begins right there."[58] Here boasting akin to Romans 2:17–20 is postulated. This would seem to imply that a Jewish interlocutor was behind Paul's question in 4:1. That a Jewish interlocutor is behind 4:1 would certainly fit in with the idea of boasting mentioned not only in 2:17–20 but also 3:27–31.[59] In actual fact, Abraham was eulogized in much early Jewish writings. Jewish writers certainly did boast about Abraham and his obedience! This affords a smooth transition to verse 2.

In verse 2, Paul said that if Abraham were justified on the basis of anything that he had done, he would have grounds for boasting.[60] But, alleged Paul, Abraham did not in fact have such grounds *before God* (v. 2c). This is the crucial point. As Flebbe points out, God is the framework within which the ensuing argument takes place.[61]

Why can Paul make this categorical statement? He appealed to Scripture, the accepted authority. "For, what does Scripture say? "But[62]

---

57. Wright, *Pauline Perspectives*, 582.

58. Wright, *Pauline Perspectives*, 505–6.

59. Stowers, *Diatribe*, 165, believes that Paul was "discussing with a student: a fellow believer, or at least an open-minded fellow Jew."

60. Several commentators are agreed that there was no implied contrast between a right to boast before fellow human beings and the right to boast before God. Rather, Paul raised the possibility that Abraham might have been justified on the grounds of what he had done, only to deny this strongly in the αλλ'ου προς Θεον. Jewett, *Romans*, 309, points to Jubilees 21:1–3, where Abraham is portrayed as claiming that throughout the 175 years of his life he had remembered the Lord and sought to do His will and walk in His ways uprightly. It is precisely this kind of assumption in Jewish tradition that Paul counters.

61. Flebbe, *Solus Deus*, 174.

62. See Koch, *Schrift*, 132–33, for arguments that δε is not merely a stylistic variation to και, but introduces a deliberate counter to the interpretation of the Abraham story assumed in the protasis of 4:2.

Abraham believed[63] God, and (this) was reckoned[64] to him for righteousness."" (v. 3). This is a quotation from the story recorded in Genesis 15:6, i.e., before God required circumcision from Abraham as part of the Covenant made with him recorded in Genesis 17. At the same time, we should bear in mind that Paul here is not just quoting an isolated sentence, but he is thinking of Genesis 15 as a whole. Terms like μισθος, σπερμα, and κληρονομειν, which occur in Genesis 15, were used in the course of Paul's discussion in Romans 4.[65]

Paul assumed that the trust which the aged and childless Abraham placed in God's promise, that he would beget a son and heir, was the response for which God was looking for to be the basis of a right relationship with Himself from the human side. From God's side, there was a promise; from the human side, there came the trusting acceptance of that promise. This seems to be the nuance of "believe" in the story of Genesis 15:5-6. Later in the chapter, Paul would say that Abraham believed that God was able to do what He had promised. Jewish interpreters took Genesis 15:6 in conjunction with especially Genesis 22, and believed that Abraham was justified by his works, his faithfulness in all his testings.[66]

If it is correct that Paul had in mind the whole of Genesis 15, we need to ask what precisely was it that Abraham believed? God made him a promise that he would beget an heir (and so his heir would not be his steward, Eliezer) and that his descendants ("seed") would be as numerous as the stars in the heavens. How did Paul understand these descendants promised by God? Since later Paul argued that Abraham would be the father of both Jews and non-Jews who believe and quoted God's promise that Abraham would be the father of many nations, it is clear that Paul had in mind a multi-racial

63. The Hebrew wh'mn suggests a basic attitude, while the LXX translation by means of the aorist indicative active, επιστευσεν, points to a particular completed past action.

64. Wieser, *Abrahamvorstellungen*, 60, sees a creative sense behind ελογισθη: God restored the relationship because Abraham was a godless idolater. The flow of the argument in Romans 4 seems to favor this suggestion. On the other hand, Yahweh called Abraham (Gen 12:1-3) and Abraham responded in obedience (Gen 12:4), while in response to Yahweh's appearing to him (Gen 12:7), Abraham built an altar to Yahweh (cf. verse 8, where it is also said that Abraham built another altar to Yahweh and called on the name of Yahweh). The flow of the Genesis story does not suggest that Abraham was regarded as a godless idolater any longer after his call in Genesis 12. However, since Paul could ignore the story of the sacrifice of Isaac and (in Romans) the story of Hagar and Ishmael, he could equally well have chosen to ignore the implications of Genesis 12-13.

65. This point is made by both Wright, *Pauline Perspectives*, 31, 505, 550, 556-57, 592, and Neubrand, *Abraham*, 198.

66. Dunn, *New Perspective*, 205n47, 224, 297-98, 308-9, 371n12, 387-88, doubts that here Paul is criticizing his fellow Jews for believing that they could achieve or earn acceptance by God by means of their own efforts and hard work.

family, people drawn from all nations. Wright is, therefore, surely correct when he speaks in terms of a world wide family, and that not just in terms of Jews spread throughout the nations of the world, but a family consisting of both Jews and Gentiles.[67]

Here is a convenient point to mention and evaluate the thesis of Gaston, viz. that Genesis 15:1–6 should be taken in the sense that God promised to act righteously with Abraham's descendants,[68] and he paraphrases God's promise in this way: "You have some righteousness coming to you, which I shall exercise on a later occasion."[69] In other words, the passage is not about Abraham's personal standing with God so much as God's action for the Israel of the future. Gaston claims that in Jewish tradition there are some instances where God's action on behalf of Israel was due to God's regard for Abraham.[70]

Likewise, Gaston argues, Paul's concern in Galatians 3–4 and Romans 4 is not with the justification of individuals by their faith but with the descendants of Abraham and the inclusion of Gentiles among the elect people of God. His quarrel with his fellow Jews was not about Judaism as such but about their attitude to the Gentiles.[71]

In response there is, firstly, some general points to be made: Gaston makes the assumption that Paul's converts were all (sic) Gentiles.[72] That is surely too sweeping an assumption. It ignores passages like 1 Corinthian 9:19–23; 2 Corinthians 11:24 (Paul presumably did not sit quietly in a Synagogue service—it must have been something in his missionary approach which evoked such punishment, and that on five occasions); and Romans 11:13–14; possibly Romans 16, if some of the Jewish names there were Paul's converts as well as people whom he had met and with whom he worked in the Christian mission; quite apart from the evidence of Acts, whose account of Paul's mission approach, while clearly schematic, cannot be entirely discounted.

Another statement which seems surprising to say the least is that for Paul Jesus is "neither a new Moses nor the messiah, he is not the climax of

---

67. Wright, *Pauline Perspectives*, 432, 505, 569–70, 591–92; on Galatians 3:16, see 212, 215, 530, 532, 575.

68. Gaston, *Paul*, 54.

69. Gaston, *Paul*, 55.

70. Gaston, *Paul*, 55–56, mentions the episode at the Sea of Reeds (Mekilta of R. Ishmael on Exod 4:31); the birth of Isaac (Philo, *Abr.* 262–73; Heb 11:11); the sparing of Isaac (Jas 2:22; perhaps 1 Macc 2:52); whenever God was gracious to Israel (Isa 41; Neh 9); the blessing of the nations (Isa 51:1–8; Sir 44:19–21).

71. Gaston, Paul, 13–14, 33–34.

72. Gaston, *Paul*, 8.

the history of God's dealing with Israel, but he is the fulfillment of God's promises concerning the Gentiles, and this is what he accused the Jews of not recognizing."[73] This completely ignores evidence to the contrary: to mention a few examples, the formula quoted in Romans 1:3-4; the use of Isaiah 11:1 in Romans 15:12; while in the Corinthian correspondence Paul's statement that he preached "Christ crucified," a message which was a stumbling block to Jews (1 Cor 1:22-24) and later his interpretation of the rock which in Jewish tradition followed the Israelites in the wilderness as Christ (1 Cor 10:4), and his claim that Jesus was the "Yes" to *all* God's promises (2 Cor 1:20).[74]

Gaston also asserts that the phrase to be under the Law refers to Gentiles. But, outside of Galatians and Romans, it would be difficult to take the phrase and its opposite (not under the Law) in 1 Corinthians 9:20 as referring to anyone else other than Jews and Gentiles respectively.[75] In Galatians 3:23-25, when Paul spoke of the time before the coming of faith (vv. 23a, 25a) or the coming of Christ (v. 24a), and said that this era was one of being under the jurisdiction of the Law,[76] it makes far better sense to assume that he is speaking of Jews and the Sinai Law. Then again, in 4:4, Paul says of Jesus that he was born "under the Law," which can only mean that he was born a Jew and so lived under the directions of the Law. Gaston is unconvincing in his assertion.

Specifically, if we examine the flow of Paul's argument in Romans 4, there is clearly an emphasis on *Abraham himself*, as Jewett has rightly pointed out in criticism of Gaston.[77] Thus, in 4:9-10 Paul was keen to establish the point at which "righteousness" was reckoned to *Abraham*: it was not when he had been circumcised but when he was uncircumcised. He received circumcision as a sign of the faith which *he exercised* while still uncircumcised. At 4:13 Paul said that God did indeed make Abraham, and adds "and his seed," a promise that *he* (αυτον) should inherit the world. A little later (v. 17), Paul recalled the promise that *Abraham* should be the father of many nations, and this was for Paul an indication that Gentile believers were to share in God's salvation and be included in His people. At the end of chapter 4, Paul maintained that the phrase ελογισθη αυτω εις δικαιοσυνην

---

73. Gaston, Paul, 33.

74. See Novenson, *Christ among the Messiahs*, for more detail on this point.

75. Dunn, *Galatians*, 9n3 (cf. *New Perspective*, 53n209) regards it as implausible and, in the context of the argument from 3:17 onwards, "virtually impossible."

76. See the earlier discussion of this passage in chapter 1.

77. See Jewett, *Romans*, 311n51; 339n190.

"was not written *for his sake alone* but for the sake of us to whom it should be reckoned," viz. Christian believers.

It is wise not to set up an antithesis—either justification freely offered by God in His grace to be received by faith, or the inclusion of the Gentiles in God's people, the true descendants of Abraham. We should hold both together. It is because God declared Abraham to be in a right relationship with Himself because of his response in trust in God's promise that God also constituted him as the beginning of God's purposes which ultimately included non-Jews as well as Jews.

We come now to Romans 4:4–5. We shall begin by setting out the usual interpretation of these verses and then we shall consider an alternative approach. Paul now drew on an analogy from daily business life. When a workman was paid wages, this would not be a matter of graciousness on the part of his employer, but an obligation. The worker has done the work required; he has earned his wages; and, therefore, he should be paid (v. 4).[78] Paul did not, however, complete an antithetical statement about some one being paid when they had not in fact worked, but he hastened on to the "spiritual" application:[79] "but to the person who does not work but believes *the One who justifies the ungodly*, that person's faith is reckoned for righteousness" (v. 5). The italicized phrase contains the heart of the gospel—God justifies the ungodly![80] We are probably meant to interpret this as an act of grace, Paul having mentioned in the first part of verse 4 that to pay a workman wages for work done is not κατα χαριν (according to grace).[81]

Without in any way wishing to deny that Paul was here stating something that is fundamentally true, we need also to ask whether he had Abraham specifically in mind as well as the general truth. The answer to this must be in the affirmative. It would not agree with the flow of the argument if Abraham were not also in mind. Adams has seen this when he commented, "As ασεβης, Abraham's initial status before God, prior to

---

78. Cranford, *Abraham in Romans 4*, argues that Paul is explaining λογιζεσθαι, and not εργα in verses 4–5. But this drives too sharp a wedge between "reckon" and the basis on which the reckoning takes place. If an employer pays a workman wages, it is precisely because the workman has done work and payment is his due. He "merits" payment.

79. Westerholm, *Perspectives*, 280n45, points out that Paul's argument is elliptical.

80. Käsemann, *Perspectives on Paul*, 84, calls the formulation that God justifies the ungodly as "the indispensable key to Paul's doctrine of justification."

81. Dobbeler, *Glaube als Teilhabe*, 134, goes so far as to say that χαρις receives a key position.

his being reckoned as righteous, was exactly that of the ungodly Gentiles portrayed in 1:18–32."[82]

He, the Divine Judge, does what a human judge should not do (Deut 25:1). Indeed, more than that, He has done what He Himself had said that He would not do (Exod 23:7; 34:7; cf. Job 10:14; Nah 1:3)—acquit the wicked: God declared the sinner in the right with Himself!

The implication[83] that Paul regarded Abraham as a sinner is confirmed by three further reasons. In the first place, Paul has proved that all have sinned (Rom 3:9, 19–20, 23), and Scripture has itself asserted that there is no one who is righteous, not even one (Ps 14:1 [13:1 LXX],[84] quoted at Rom 3:10a). There can be no exceptions. Secondly, Paul stated that Abraham had no grounds for boasting before God (4:2). Thirdly, in some parts of Jewish tradition Abraham was regarded as the first proselyte: he was a Gentile who had come to faith in the one, true, living God from an idolatrous background.[85]

Kreuzer has pointed to evidence that some Jewish interpreters took the event of Genesis 15 as *preceding* even that of Genesis 12 and to be located in Gentile territory and in God's first contact with him.[86] This tradition arose out of an attempt to reconcile the four hundred years of Genesis 15:13 and the four hundred and thirty years of Exodus 12:40. The solution arrived at was based on the reference to descendants in Genesis 15:13 and on counting the four hundred years from the birth of Isaac. Because the age of Abraham was seventy five when he entered Canaan (Gen 12:4) and a hundred when Isaac was born (Gen 21:5), it was assumed, therefore, that Abraham was seventy when God spoke to him in Ur and that he had spent five years in Haran.

---

82. Adams, *Abraham's Faith*, 52. This is part of Adams's case that there are textual links between chapter 4 about Abraham and the indictment of the Gentile world in 1:18–32.

83. Adams, *Abraham's Faith*, 59, rightly says that Paul asserts rather than argues for Abraham's prior ungodliness.

84. Watson, *PJG*, 221, says that it is the material from Psalm 14 (13 LXX) which bears the greatest weight in Paul's catena, because this passage alone asserts the universality of sin. This is the Law's negative verdict on humankind in general and the Jewish people in particular.

85. See Jub 11:15–17; *Apoc. Abr.* 8:1–5; Philo, *Abr.* 69–72; *Virt.* 212–16; Josephus, *Ant.* 1.154.

86. Kreuzer, *Der den Gottlosen rechtfertigt?*, 208–219. In putting Genesis 15 before Genesis 12, reconciling the numbers took precedence over the narrative sequence!

If this were accepted,[87] then Abraham would be regarded as godless, not in a moral sense, but as a Gentile, when God gave him the promise of Genesis 15:5-6 and made the covenant with him (15:7-21).[88]

Thirdly, verse 6 (introduced by καθαπερ και) suggests that Abraham received the blessing mentioned by David, namely, the forgiveness of sins.

So, the implication is clear: Abraham was, therefore, a justified sinner![89]

Paul had fastened on Genesis 15:6 and used it as a backup for his gospel—the Law witnessed to the free gift of salvation offered by God (cf. 3:21). Or, to put it in another way, the justification of sinners proclaimed in the gospel (1:16-17) was in harmony with Scripture, and, therefore, with God's revealed will and purpose.[90] Paul had here handled Genesis 15:6 in a way different from many Jewish exegetes who linked Genesis 15:6 with the story of the offering of Isaac (Genesis 22) and saw Genesis 15:6 really fulfilled in that episode. Paul, in effect, saw Genesis 15:6 as the "lens" through which the story of Abraham was to be viewed. Genesis 15:6 seems to dominate

---

87. The evidence includes LXX (possibly its Hebrew Vorlage); the Samaritan Pentateuch; Jub 11:18-21; 4Q252.2.8-10; Philo, *Abr.* 66-67; *Migr. Abr.* 177; Josephus, *Ant.* 1.154; Acts 7:2; Genesis Rabbah 39.8. Of these, Kreuzer is assuming that Jubilees is a similar tradition to driving off the birds mentioned in Genesis 15:11, though in Jubilees Abraham is only fourteen years old; Philo mentions two migrations without specifying Abraham's age or how long he stayed in Haran; while Josephus has Abraham leaving Chaldea in his seventy-fifth year and moving directly to Canaan. The strongest evidence is, therefore, really 4Q252; Acts 7:2; Genesis Rabbah 39.

88. Flebbe, *Solus Deus*, 201-3, while acknowledging that the evidence adduced by Kreuzer falls short of complete proof, is inclined to accept the position outlined by him.

89. Cf. Leenhardt, *Romans*, 115; Käsemann, *Perspectives*, 85; Hahn, *Genesis 15:6 im Neuen Testament*, 102; Hanson, *Abraham the Justified Sinner*, 52-56; Hübner, *Law in Paul's Thought*, 118-21; Wilckens, *Römer*, 1:263 (cf. earlier in Wilckens, *Rechtfertigung*, 96); Cranfield, *Romans* 1:232; Dunn, *Romans*, 1:229; Dobbeler, *Glaube*, 134; Flebbe, *Solus Deus*, 194-213; Gathercole, *Justified by Faith*, 156; O'Brien, *Was Paul Converted?*, 379; Blocher, *Justification of the Ungodly*, 490; Horn, *Juden und Heiden*, 35, 37; Penna, *Meaning of* παρεσις, 269; De Roo, *Works of the Law*, 69, 144, 150, 153, 165, 169, 174, 203, 221, 222, 226; Watson, *PJG*, 265, 269; Barclay, *Paul's Story*, 151; *Gift*, 484-85 (where he states that nothing Abraham did made him worthy of the favor of God; nothing in Abraham's conduct made God's crediting of righteousness a matter of congruous reward); Lincoln, *Stories of Predecessors*, 184; Bergmeier, *Gerechtigkeit*, 106. Cranfield, *Abraham*, 82, argues that Paul sees Abraham as ungodly—not in a moral sense but rather as an uncircumcised Gentile—while Neubrand, *Abraham*, 210, denies that Paul sees Abraham as a sinner and believes that Paul is seeking rather to align Abraham with the one who does not work in verse 5. The arguments mentioned above, however, seem compelling.

90. Cf. Sanger, *Verkündigung*, 87.

Paul's discussion in verses 1-12, and is combined with Genesis 17:5 in verses 13-22, at the end of which Genesis 15:6 is partially quoted.[91]

By establishing that Abraham was justified by faith, Paul had also established who could legitimately claim the promise made to him, the promise now in its End-Time fullness.[92] Above, we pointed out that what Paul said about God's justifying the ungodly stands in tension with OT passages like Exodus 23:17 and Deuteronomy 25:1. At the same time, of course, it must be said that there is plenty of evidence in the OT for God's willingness to forgive guilty Israel. We might mention (without seeking to be exhaustive) the promise made in Hosea that God could not give Israel/Ephraim (the northern kingdom) up and would not execute His fierce anger (11:8-9); in Ezekiel the promise of a new heart and of God's Spirit within His people in a renewed land (36:16-36); the promise in Second Isaiah that God had blotted out Israel's sins and would cause His righteousness/salvation to come near (44:22; 46:12-13); the promise of a new covenant in Jeremiah 31:31-34 based on God's free forgiveness; and the promise that God would bring His dispersed people back from exile to their homeland in Deuteronomy 30:1-10. *In general terms*, therefore, it would not be right to say that Paul in Romans 4:5 was enunciating an entirely new teaching.[93] *In particular*, it is understandable that those Jews who magnified the virtues of Abraham would find it "the most provocative and polemical argument in [Paul's] controversy with Jews" (as Moxnes asserts).[94] But, even here, as we have seen, Paul could claim that God had forgiven freely the Abraham who had been involved with idolatry in his past, so that Paul was arguing from a base within Jewish tradition.[95]

Wright has put forward a different interpretation. He rejects the view that Paul was purely using an analogy from business life. Instead, Wright suggests that Paul was interpreting Genesis 15 and had in mind the very opening verse of Genesis 15, in which God said to Abraham in a vision: "Do not be afraid, Abram. I will defend you. Your reward will be very great."[96] What is the reward which God promises? That is revealed in the

---

91. Cf. Hahn, *Genesis 15:6*, 103 (whereas Chae, *Paul*, 182-83, thinks that Genesis 15:6 controls the discussion in verses 2-12 and Genesis 15:5 dominates the discussion in verses 13-25).

92. Cf. Zeller, *Juden und Heiden*, 100. Adams, *Abraham's Faith*, 63, puts it this way: that Paul used Abraham to make the Gentile route to God the standard and the rule.

93. See, e.g., Hofius, "Rechtfertigung des Gottlosen," 121-47

94. Moxnes, *Theology*, 110.

95. As Flebbe, *Solus Deus*, 199, emphasizes on Romans 4:5, and continually in his study of various other passages in Romans.

96. So LXX. The MT runs, "Do not be afraid, Abram. I am your shield. Your reward

combination of the statement that Abraham will beget an heir (v. 4) and the illustration or sign of the stars in the heavens with the accompanying word that Abraham's seed (descendants) would be as innumerable as the stars (v. 5). If the reward was to be descendants as innumerable as the stars, this suggests a world-wide family. Wright proposes that Paul had this in mind when he said that "to the one who does not work but believes in Him who justifies the ungodly" (4:5). Only if God somehow sets the ungodly in the right with Himself can Abraham have a family of such innumerable proportions. Since Paul had just accused both the non-Jewish world and the Jewish people of being guilty before God, God would have to justify both Jews and non-Jews. But this is precisely what God had done according to Paul's argument in 3:22-31! He had justified the Jews and non-Jews on the basis of the atoning death of Jesus the Messiah and the response of faith (cf. "everyone who believes" [3:22]; "will justify the circumcised on the basis of faith and the uncircumcised through faith" [3:30]).[97]

Once we accept that Romans 4 is very much an exposition which has in mind the story of Abraham, especially in Genesis 15 and also elsewhere in Genesis 17-18, Wright's suggestion becomes very attractive and has much to commend it. In Romans 4, Paul was particularly concerned with Abraham's fatherhood: thus, in verses 11-12 he mentioned Abraham's fatherhood of Gentile believers and Jews or Jewish believers,[98] while in verse 17 he quoted the promise that Abraham should become the father of many nations. Paul had already laid the foundations for his conviction that God had set humanity in the right with Himself through the atoning work of Jesus the messiah; Romans 3:22-26 had already shown that God justifies the ungodly. On this interpretation, Paul believed that Abraham grasped that truth, as well as the truth that God gives life to the dead and calls into being that which does not exist, as mentioned in 4:17. It is precisely this trusting acceptance of God's promissory word, grounded in the nature of God, that God was looking for. Hence, "it was reckoned to him for righteousness" (Gen 15:6).

---

will be very great." The JB, REB, NRSV all have "your reward will be very great," with the RV mg "thy reward shall be exceeding great." The RV has "*and* thy exceeding great reward," and the NIV "your very great reward." The suggestion of a link via μισθος with Genesis 15:1 had also been noticed by Wilchens, *Was heisst bei Paulus*, 95; Neubrand, *Abraham*, 198, 207; Schliesser, *Abraham's Faith*, 344, but none of them had pursued this in the way Wright has done.

97. For Wright's exposition, see *Pauline Perspectives*, 434, 505, 532, 550, 556-63, 578.

98. See below for the discussion whether Paul has in mind one or two groups in verse 12.

Is Wright correct in this interpretation? It should be pointed out that Wright's interpretation of 4:5 is linked with his interpretation of 4:1 (discussed above), though actually it need not depend on it. It should also be pointed out that his interpretation does not involve a weakening of the fundamental statement that God justifies the ungodly. What his interpretation does do is to remove Abraham personally from the referent of this statement.[99] Those in mind are a much wider circle, viz. Gentiles (possibly Jewish unbelievers).

It will be worthwhile to quote Wright's actual words: "Romans 4 is not about Abraham as example of a soteriological scheme; it is about Abraham as the father of the worldwide covenant family" and he continues "Who are the ungodly [Rom 4:5] for whose justification Abraham is trusting God? The normal answer, I take it, is to say that it is Abraham himself who is 'ungodly,' so that in this passage Abraham is trusting God to justify *him*. No doubt that is an element in it. . . . But the emphasis, exactly as in Galatians 3, is on the gentiles who are to come into the family. That is what Abraham believed: not that God would justify him, but that God would give him a worldwide family, *which could only come about if God were to bring the 'ungodly,' that is, the gentiles, into the family by an act of sheer grace.*"[100]

We may wonder whether Wright has drawn up too sharp an either/or here. His grudging concession that there is an element of Abraham as the ungodly person whom God justifies may be significant. After all, Paul had just proved that all without exception, Jews as well as Gentiles, were sinners before God, and, in Romans 4, he went on to point out that Abraham received the assurance of being justified before he was circumcised and would, therefore, strictly speaking, be an uncircumcised Gentile (just as some Jewish writers regarded him as the first proselyte). We may pose the question: could Paul have envisaged Abraham other than a justified sinner? Does not the idea of Abraham as the start of something imply that the pattern of the future family will be set in its head and origin?[101] May then Paul have wanted to get *both* truths across: Abraham as sinner justified by

---

99. Wright, *Pauline Perspectives*, 432-34; cf. Gaston, *Paul*, 125-26, who also sees the "godless" of verse 5 as the Gentiles.

100. Wright, *Pauline Perspectives*, 433, 434.

101. Barclay, *Gift*, 483, made a significant remark: "The Abrahamic story is fulfilled *as it began*: in faith—dependence upon a divine decision irrespective of inherent human worth" (my italics). Later, on 4:18-21, he says: "By tracing God's *creatio ex nihilo* in the story of Abraham, *the starting point of election,* Paul can place Israel, believers, and the world, on a common trajectory, since nothing is impossible for the mercy of God (11:28-30)" (489, my italics).

faith and the world-wide family looking to him as its spiritual head to be constituted on exactly the same basis?[102]

We believe that Wright is correct in what he affirms, but not in what he wants to deny.

2.2.2. Romans 4:6–8

The next stage of Paul's argument is to bring in another OT quotation, this time from the Writings, on the principle that linking two texts with a word or phrase in common and letting them mutually interpret on another, was a legitimate exegetical procedure among Jewish scholars.[103]

The key word is λογιζεσθαι ("reckoned"), which occurs both in Genesis 15:6 and in Psalm 32:1–2 (31 LXX). Paul assumed it in verse 8 and used it in verses 9,10, and 11. The wording of Genesis 15:6 has also influenced the way in which Paul has introduced the quotation from Psalm 32 in verse 6. Paul said that David speaks of the blessedness of the person to whom God *reckons righteousness* apart from works (of the Law):[104]

> Blessed are those whose wrong doings have been forgiven,
> and those whose sins have been covered;
> Blessed is the man whose sin the Lord will not reckon. (4:6–8)

By means of the quotation from Psalm 32:1–2 Paul interpreted the reckoning of a right relationship (δικαιοσυνη) as equivalent to the forgiveness of sins.[105] Both ideas are part of the "blessing," which God confers in His graciousness on those who respond to Him. The emphasis is solely on

---

102. Barclay, *Gift*, 481, states his aim in discussing the Abraham chapter of Romans as integrating Paul's dual portrayal of Abraham as both *believer* in God and *father* of a multinational family.

103. Known as gezerah shawa. See Barrett, *Interpretation*, 383–84, for a list of rabbinical exegetical principles, ascribed to Hillel.

104. Χωρις εργων picks up and makes more precise τω μη εργαζομενω of verse 5, as Wilckens, *Römer*, 1:263, points out. It also may be said to pick up the χωρις εργων νομου of 3:28 (cf. Neubrand, *Abraham*, 213).

105. Paul does not use the concept of forgiveness a great deal in his writings, but this passage suggests that he may not have held such an impoverished concept of forgiveness as is sometimes suggested in order to account for its non-use in his letters. Note also Romans 11:26–27, where Paul quotes Isaiah 59:20–21, which speaks of the deliverer coming from Zion to turn away wickedness from Jacob. "And this is my Covenant for them, when I shall take away their sins," which is the idea of forgiveness expressed in different words. Schliesser, *Abraham*, 351–52n955, rightly points out that faith, forgiveness, salvation, and justification all belong to the same complex of ideas.

what God has done.[106] But the use of Psalm 32:1–2 also shows that forgiveness was part of the Jewish experience.[107]

Some scholars have pointed out that David was a member of the people of God but a sinner (his affair with Bathsheba and his arranging for Uriah to meet an almost certain death in battle). So, the examples of Abraham and David were really those of a Gentile, an ungodly idolater (the first proselyte), and an Israelite sinner within the covenant. Both experienced God's freely granted justification/forgiveness/restoration.[108] In so arguing, Paul was going against contemporary Jewish understanding of both Abraham and David!

If this reckoning of righteousness to a person by God was "apart from works" (and works of the Law are clearly what were in Paul's mind), then there was the potential for God to give forgiveness to those outside the Sinai covenant. It may be significant that Paul in fact used the term ανθρωπος in verse 6 (as he did in 3:28), while ανηρ occurs in the quotation from Psalm 31:2. He was probably insinuating that God deals with humanity equally and not on the basis of whether one is a Jew or a non-Jew.

It needs to be pointed out and emphasized that up to now Paul's argument in relation to Abraham, and David, has been his/their relationship with God. God sets the ungodly and the sinner in the right with Himself. Circumcision, to name but one of Israel's ethnic and nationalistic identity markers, has not been an issue.[109]

2.2.3. Romans 4:9–12

Paul then raised the question whether this blessing in the case of Abraham was related to a state of circumcision or uncircumcision?[110] We should note that Paul did so only *after* he had dealt with the issue of blessedness freely granted by God and without working to earn it. He pointed out that the

---

106. As Flebbe, *Solus Deus*, 221, remarks, human action is neither primary nor plays any role. David is an illustration of God's undeserved saving action for the sinner.

107. Tobin, *Paul's Rhetoric*, 147.

108. Hofius, *Paulusstudien*, 129; Sanger, *Verkündigung*, 118n247; Gathercole, *Boasting*, 246; Schliesser, *Abraham*, 352, 355. Dunn, *Romans*, 1:205, feels, however, that "David is cited merely as author, not as a second example alongside Abraham."

109. Emphasized strongly by Westerholm, *Perspectives*, 280–81n46.

110. Neubrand, *Abraham*, 217, points to the prior occurrence of περιτομη and ακροβυστια at 3:30. Dunn, *Romans*, 1:208, believes that Paul's interest lies in whether the blessing comes to Gentiles as well as Jews. Jewett, *Romans*, 317, points out that it is likely that most Jews would have understood the blessing to be available to themselves but not to Gentiles.

statement of Genesis 15:6 was spoken about Abraham while he was still not circumcised (vv. 9b–10), a point so clearly important to Paul that he repeated it again in verse 11 and at the end of verse 12.[111] The moment of *when* God reckoned Abraham in the right with Himself (v. 9a) is important, but this in turn is related to the issue of *to whom* righteousness was reckoned—was it only to those circumcised, or was it a possibility for those who were uncircumcised and not under the Law? The particular case of Abraham has general ramifications. If the great patriarch was justified when he was uncircumcised, then such would be a possibility for others who were not circumcised. That is the conclusion which Paul drew in verse 11d.

In the case of Abraham, circumcision[112] was given him as a sign of the status of being right with God which God had pronounced on the faith exercised while Abraham was still uncircumcised (v. 11ab). For Paul, circumcision is not (as it were) an end in itself; it points to the saving relationship established by God. Paul saw a divine purpose in this: it was "in order that he might be the father of all who believe though uncircumcised [δι' ακροβυστιας is a δια of attendant circumstances], in order that[113] righteousness might be reckoned also to them" (v. 11cd). This assertion within verse 11 may form something of an inclusio with verse 9 and be the answer to the question raised there.[114] Since God set the uncircumcised Gentile, Abraham, in a right relationship with Himself, the possibility of His doing so to Gentiles in Paul's day was thereby opened up. God willed to be their God.[115]

Paul then continued with the original purpose clause and indicated that Abraham was also a "father of circumcision." To what or whom, then, does this other fatherhood refer? The phrase πατηρ περιτομης, though it is unusual and probably a Pauline construction, was meant to stand in contrast to the "father of all who believe even though uncircumcised" of verse 11c. Abraham was father of the Jews, circumcision standing by metonymy for the Jewish people, for whom circumcision was very much a sign of their national and cultural identity. This phrase "father of circumcision" is

---

111. Wieser, *Abrahamvorstellungen*, 61, comments that the temporal priority is an actual priority.

112. The genitive περιτομης is to be taken as an explanatory (or epexegetic) genitive: a sign which consisted of circumcision.

113. Grammatically, this articular infinitive of purpose is dependent on the earlier articular infinitive construction introduced by εις το ειναι. It is a parenthesis within the first articular infinitive construction.

114. So Neubrand, *Abraham*, 228.

115. Flebbe, *Solus Deus*, 228. Jewett, *Romans*, 319, comments: "Abraham's example legitimates the acceptability of Gentiles who have responded to the message of unconditional grace in Christ."

followed by two datives of advantage. How we are to understand these datives of advantage is a matter of considerable dispute:

τοις ουκ εκ περιτομης μονον αλλα και τοις στοιχουσιν τοις ιχνεσιν
of the faith which Abraham our father had when he was uncircumcised. (v. 12)

Did Paul have in mind one group (Jewish Christians, who were Jewish [circumcised] and who believed)[116] or two groups (all Jews, that is, those who were circumcised, and Jewish Christians who, unlike the majority of their fellow countrymen and women at that moment, believed)?[117] In other words, was Paul in effect confining Abraham's fatherhood of the Jew to Jewish Christians (the corollary of the one group interpretation) or was he holding on to the election of Israel on grounds of physical descent through Abraham, while seeing Jewish Christians as realizing the full implications of God's elective purpose because they had believed in Jesus, God's messiah for Israel (the corollary of the two groups view)?

What are the arguments which must be considered in coming to a decision? Firstly, there is a grammatical issue. There is a twofold τοις, and this might suggest that Paul had in mind two groups.[118] Secondly, there is a syntactical point. Paul uses "not only . . . but also." While Wilckens[119] believes that to postulate two groups would basically destroy the sense of the "not only/but also" (i.e., he assumes that this introduces a contrast between the two halves), Maria Neubrand has shown that Paul never elsewhere uses this construction to correct the first member, but rather an equivalent expansion (eine gleichwertige Erweiterung).[120] This means that the group to whom Abraham is related as father of circumcision is itself divided into

---

116. e.g., Sanday and Headlam, *Romans*, 108; Michel, *Römer*, 120; Barrett, *Romans*, 91 (apparently); Käsemann, *Romans*, 116 (while he stated that an ongoing relation of the patriarch to Judaism was now acknowledged, he went on to say that Abraham was called the father of the circumcision only as the father of Jewish-Christians); Black, *Romans*, 77; Wilckens, *Römer*, 1:265-66; Cranfield, *Romans*, 1:237 (though Cranfield followed this [238] by saying that we must not conclude that Paul intended to deny the reality of the kinship κατα σαρκα); Morris, *Romans*, 204; Dunn, *Romans*, 1:210-11 (while recognizing grammatical difficulties and asserting that Paul did not intend to deny the Abrahamic fatherhood of the Jewish people—see note 97); Ziesler, *Romans*, 128-29; Donaldson, *Remapping*, 333n43; Flebbe, *Solus Deus*, 231; Barclay, *Gift*, 487n103.

117. See the detailed discussion in defence of this in Neubrand, *Abraham*, 234-43.

118. Along with several others, Cranfield, *Romans*, 1:237, argues that the τοις is a grammatical mistake, with the idea of two groups contrary to the sense of the passage, and so is a mistake of either Paul or Tertius or a very early copyist.

119. Wilckens, *Römer*, 1:265-66.

120. Neubrand, *Abraham*, 235-36.

two.¹²¹ Thirdly, there are theological issues involved. In chapter 3 Paul argued that Jewish unfaithfulness could not nullify God's faithfulness (v. 3). He elaborated on this in chapter 11, where he repudiated strongly the notion that God had cast off His people (11:1-2a, 11a) and maintained that God's gifts and calling were irrevocable (11:29) and envisaged the salvation of all Israel (11:26a). At the same time he had argued that there is in sinfulness no distinction between Jew and Gentiles, and since there is no partiality with God, the Jew will be condemned equally with the Gentile (see especially 3:9, 19-20, 23). Paul seems to resolve this dilemna by means of the idea of the remnant (see 11:1-7 and the olive tree illustration in 11:17-24) and the hope of the ultimate salvation of Israel because, though temporarily enemies of God, they were still beloved because of God's election in and through the patriarchs (11:28).¹²²

In the light of especially Romans 11, we are inclined to think that Paul envisaged two groups in 4:12. Abraham is the father of unbelieving Jews (described as those "of the circumcision") and those Jews who have confessed Jesus as Messiah (i.e., they have followed in the footsteps of the faith which Abraham exercised before his circumcision).¹²³ In the light of the

---

121. Jewett, *Romans*, 320.

122. It is by no means certain that Chae, *Paul*, 192-93, who thinks that in verse 12 Paul was referring to Jewish and Gentile believers, is right in arguing that it is unlikely that Paul would stress that Abraham was the father of unbelieving Jews in the light of 9:6b-8 and 2:25-29. But in the light of Paul's emphasis on faith, it is unlikely that he envisaged that his vision that all Israel would be saved (11:26a) would come about by any other means than by faith in Jesus, Messiah, Son of God (against those who argue for Paul's holding a two route salvation — one for Jews and the other for Gentiles. Dunn, *Romans*, 2:683, dismisses such a view as posing a false and quite unnecessary antithesis).

123. Among those who hold that there are two groups of circumcised in verse 12 and only the second group are qualified as believers, see Moxnes, *Theology*, 81, 112, 250-51; Neubrand, *Abraham*, 233-44 (she quotes Luz, *Geschichtsverständnis*, 175, as holding this view, but this does not seem to be correct). Jewett, *Romans*, 320-21, accepts two groups but takes the second group as Gentile believers. Schliesser, *Abraham*, 363-64, maintains that the initial και at the beginning of verse 12 is explanatory and that Paul had used the first περιτομη in a figurative sense, akin to 2:25-29 and Philippians 3:3, and the second περιτομη in a literal sense; this produces a reference to Jewish believers in the phrase τοις ουκ εκ περιτομης μονον and to Gentile believers in the "but also" phrase (τοις στοιχουσιν κτλ). This is ingenious, but it must be said that the double sense of περιτομη in such a short space is unquestionably harsh, especially as the reference to circumcision/uncircumcision previously had always been literal, and while Paul was certainly stressing in context that justification was open to Gentiles on the basis of faith, Schliesser's interpretation does produce a certain imbalance between Jewish and Gentile believers in verses 11-12, while the lack of any specific reference to the faith of οι εκ περιτομης in Schliesser's interpretation seems a weakness of it. (Schliesser can claim the support of Käsemann, *Romans*, 116, for this interpretation of περιτομη,

whole letter, we could say that while the election of Abraham's descendants remains in the purposes of God, only those Jews who have believed in Jesus as Messiah have entered fully into God's elective purpose:[124] they are the ones through whom the divine purposes were being carried forward and into whose fellowship Gentile believers were being incorporated. Their compatriots who did not believe needed to acquire the faith of Abraham for them to enter truly into the fatherhood of Abraham.[125]

Why did Paul coin the phrase father of circumcision? It was probably with a view to indicating that God's purposes still included the Jewish people. Even if God all along had the inclusion of Gentiles in His saving purpose, this did not mean that the Jews were now neglected or left out of consideration.[126]

Does this interpretation of verse 12 threaten the importance of faith? With Paul, we might respond with μη γενοιτο! Clearly, the important thing is faith, not being circumcised. Abraham can be the father of those who are not even proselytes, those who, in order to become proselytes, would have had to have been circumcised. It is faith which determines the essential kinship with Abraham.[127] If God's dealings with Abraham are paradigmatic, then circumcision is not essential but faith is.[128] Faith is soteriologically sufficient

---

though Käsemann did not provide detailed exegesis. In his *Perspectives*, 88, Käsemann stated that justification does not set aside salvation history, but it removes its barriers by tearing down the fence of the Law.) Furthermore, how could Abraham be the father of circumcision to Gentiles, since the not only/but also clauses both relate to the phrase father of circumcision? Tobin, *Paul's Rhetoric*, 148–50, argues for an abb/a/ structure in verses 11-12, so that Abraham is the father of Gentile believers in verse 11c, father of Jews in verse 12a and verse 12aα, and father of Gentile believers in verse 12b. Similar objections to those against Schliesser's proposal may be raised against this suggestion. The phrase referring to Abraham's faith while he was uncircumcised (της εν ακροβυστια πιστεως) is probably added to emphasize the point made earlier in verse 10.

124. Cf. Dunn, *Romans*, 1:233.

125. Berger, *Abraham*, 68, seems to be saying this: "Those who possess circumcision must obtain the faith of his [Abraham's] uncircumcised state, then Abraham is also the father of their circumcision." According to 11:23, if the presently unbelieving Jews did not remain in their unbelief, they could be grafted back into the olive tree.

126. Cf. Dunn, *Romans*, 1:211: "Paul does not deny or wholly set aside Abraham's fatherhood of the Jewish people as such (cf. 4:1)." Flebbe, *Solus Deus*, 230–32, 263.

127. Wieser, *Abrahamvostellungen*, 60, states that Paul assumed that the events involving Abraham have constitutive character for the entire people of God and he goes on to say (62) that these events have an inclusive character for Gentile and Jewish Christians.

128. Cf. Kaylor, *Covenant Community*, 85: "Since it was Abraham's faith and not his circumcision that was decisive, those circumcised should not rely on the confirming sign but rather follow the real example of Abraham, his faith, further, they should recognize their kinship with all who share Abraham's faith, whether circumcised or

for uncircumcised Gentiles.[129] Believing Gentiles were not obliged to adopt circumcision, and with it, the other demands of the Law.

This was a revolutionary statement for a Jew to make!—even if Paul remained a loyal Jew and retained a belief in the election of the Jews in God's ultimate purposes.

2.2.4. Romans 4:13–16d

Paul now proceeded to take on another question. What about the Law[130] given to Israel through Moses on Mount Sinai? The word "promise" will become a *Leitmotiv* in this next section (vv. 13–16).[131] Paul sets promise off against Law. In 4:13 he asserted that God's promise to Abraham, that he should be heir of the world—a promise which included his descendants—was not made through the Law but was based on the fact that he had been reckoned in a right relationship with God on the basis of faith.[132] The antithesis "not through the Law . . . but through the righteousness by faith" would not be acceptable to Jews. The Law, God's gift accompanying election and covenant, was paramount in the God-Israel relationship. Now Paul was putting Promise + Faith as the basis of our relationship with God.

According to Paul, God's promise was that Abraham or his seed would be heirs of the world. Actually, God's promise as recorded in Genesis 12:7; 13:15–16; and 15:7 embraced the land of Canaan but said nothing about the world. However, in inter-testamental Judaism, that promise of the land of Canaan was enlarged to embrace the whole world. Thus we read in Sirach 44:21: "Therefore, the Lord swore an oath to him . . . that their [his descendants'] possessions should reach from sea to sea, from the Great River [Euphrates] to the ends of the earth," while we read in *4 Ezra* 6:55, 59 that the seer asks "You

---

not." Jewett, *Romans,* 320, suggests that Paul's intention in adding the αλλα και clause was to direct attention of Jewish Christians away from the primacy of circumcision and toward the primacy of faith as the basis for group identity and as a means of lessening conflicts between them and Gentile Christians.

129. Chae, *Paul,* 189. Dobbeler, *Glaube,* 136, also sees πιστις as significant for the community's quest for identity. Faith is the decisive characteristic of the similarity with the founding father, Abraham ("our father").

130. This is the first time that νομος occurs since 3:31.

131. Moxnes, *Theology,* 257, sees Romans 4:13–16 as the same in summary form as Galatians 3:15–22. Neubrand, *Abraham,* 246, points out that επαγγελια, σπειρα, and κληρονομος appear for the first time in chapter 4. Jewett, *Romans,* 322, stresses that these are key ideas in the whole of verses 13–25.

132. The language αλλα δια δικαιοσυνης . . . πιστεως is a further indication that Genesis 15:6 is very much in Paul's mind.

made this first world for our sake.... Why, then, may we not take possession of our world? How much longer shall it be so?"¹³³ Paul is clearly keying into this tradition in his phrasing of 4:13.¹³⁴ At the same time, the concept of the world prepares the way for his use of the quotation from Genesis about Abraham's being the father of *many nations* (see vv. 17-18).

The crucial question is then: Who are the seed/descendants who will be Abraham's heirs? Who will be the beneficiaries of the promise made by God to Abraham? If those of the Law were heirs (which would be the Jewish view and which would be, in Paul's view, contrary to fact), then there would be two consequences. In the first place, η πιστις would have been emptied of its significance. How is πιστις used here? Is it used in a general sense, or is the faith that of Abraham in mind? Although verse 14 has been taken as stating a general truth,¹³⁵ Maria Neubrand has argued that Paul had Genesis 15:6 in mind, on the grounds that the article with faith and with promise in verse 14 points back to Abraham's faith and God's promise to him.¹³⁶ That is, she has taken the article η used with both nouns as the so-called anaphoric usage here: viz. the reference back to something previously mentioned,¹³⁷ in this instance the faith of Abraham and God's promise to him. The verb κεκενωται (perfect indicative passive) could equally fit this context: Abraham's faith would be evacuated of its significance, but this would conflict with Genesis 15:6, whose importance had been pointed out from verse 3 onwards.

In the second place, the promise would be abrogated, again, in conflict with Genesis 15:5. The promise-faith nexus of Genesis 15:5-6 would be set aside (v. 14). To ask more than the faith which is mentioned in Genesis 15:6 would be to nullify the promise of Genesis 15:5.¹³⁸ The net result would be to

---

133. See also Jubilees 32:18-19, where God appeared to Jacob and promised to increase his descendants: "And there will be kings from you; they will rule everywhere that the tracks of mankind have been trod. And I shall give to your seed all of the land under heaven and they will rule in all nations as they have desired. And after this all of the earth will be gathered together and they will inherit it forever" (cf. 22:11b, 13-14). Someone taking literally the promise of descendants like the stars in the heavens or like the sand on the seashore, might well assume that Canaan would be too small!

134. Wright, *Pauline Perspectives*, 569, neatly puts it: "The whole *kosmos* . . . would now be the extended 'promised land.'"

135. Verse 14 "makes a general, basic statement in the form of a thesis and a type of formulation of his teaching [thetisch und lehrsatzartig]" (Luz, *Geschichtsverständnis*, 183).

136. Neubrand, *Abraham*, 256-59.

137. For this usage, see *BD* para. 252.

138. While Moxnes, *Theology*, 255, points out that Paul has split Jewish tradition about Abraham and Sinai and set one part against the other, Neubrand, *Abraham*, 251,

confine the promise to Jews and exclude everyone else. But since the promise was not given on the basis of the Law, it is not in principle confined to the Jewish people (equally, obviously, it does not exclude them either).

In addition, whereas the promise was to do with good things like descendants, land, and blessing, the Law (so Paul alleged) aroused and produced God's wrath (v. 15a), because it defined transgression. This is the implication of verse 15b, where Paul stated, "Where there is no law, there is no transgression."[139] The idea that the Law produced God's wrath as its primary effect stands in opposition to Jewish assertion that the Law was the source of life.[140]

Paul's next statement is incredibly terse:

16a δια τουτο εκ πιστεως

16b ινα κατα χαριν

16c εις το ειναι βεβαιαν την επαγγελιαν παντι τω σπερματι

Both the main clause (v. 16a) and the purpose clause with ινα (v. 16b) lack a subject and a verb! Is the subject "promise?" This could claim support from the fact that promise was the subject of verse 14b and promise occurs in verse 16c as being "confirmed." On the other hand, a general term like righteousness (which means the gift of a right standing with God) or salvation or plan of salvation could fit equally well.[141]

A paraphrase is clearly needed: "God's promise of salvation is offered on the basis of its being received in faith. God's purpose in proceeding like this was to ensure that the promised salvation rested solely on His grace, and this in turn would render secure the promise made to all Abraham's descendants,

---

denies an antithesis and prefers to see that Paul is concerned with what mediates the promise, viz. the free and undeserved promise from God's side and faith from the human side.

139. And of the later 5:13, "Sin is not reckoned in the absence of the Law," and 5:20, "The Law entered in alongside (of the promise) in order that the transgression might increase."

140. See, e.g., Lev 18:5; Sir 17:11; Bar 4:1; *Ps. Sol.* 14:2; *4 Ezra* 14:30; *2 Bar.* 38:2; *Aboth* 2:8. On the other hand, *4 Ezra* 7:116-26 is evidence of a very pessimistic view about the possibility of living righteously. For Paul, sin had got hold of the Law and thus produced the situation where people were unable to keep the Law's commands (see, e.g., Rom 7:7-11; 8:3).

141. Barrett, *Romans*, 95-96, believes that a broader term than promise is needed, and he prefers "God's plan," as does Black, *Romans*, 78; Cranfield, *Romans*, 1:242. On the other hand, Dodd, *Romans*, 69; Michel, *Römer*, 123; Leenhardt, *Romans*, 67; Wright, *Climax*, 168; Dunn, *Romans*, 1:215, 235; Watson, *Hermeneutics*, 243, assume "promise"; with Käsemann, *Romans*, 121, "the promised inheritance," basically in agreement. Wilkens, *Römer*, 1:271; Jewett, *Romans*, 328, prefer the fulfillment of the promise to Abraham.

not just Jewish believers but also Gentiles who believe. God's procedure means that salvation rests entirely on Himself, on His promise, and not on us. It is this which makes salvation reliable and certain."[142]

What is the reference in "the whole seed"? The argument links faith and grace in verse 16ab, i.e., faith from the human side and grace from God's side. He promises; we accept His promise. This acceptance, this trusting receiving what God promises, is open to all who believe. This would seem to limit the "seed" to believers. Does this produce a tension[143] with verse 12, where we have suggested that Paul did not exclude even unbelieving Jews from belonging within Abraham's fatherhood? We should not be surprised that Paul wished to hold on to two aspects: that God's promises were irrevocable and, therefore, He would bring the Jews to salvation in Christ (a point he made forcibly in chapter 11) and that God looks for faith as the way to receive His gracious gift of right standing before Him and membership of the family which He promised to Abraham. So, here, Paul was concerned to stress that the promise is open to "the whole seed of Abraham" (v. 16c). That means not only those who possess the Law (and belonged to the Jewish nation) but those who share in the faith of Abraham, whom Paul described as "the father of us all" (v. 16e), which clearly includes Gentile believers as well as Jewish ones.[144]

The importance of grace for Paul comes across in the ινα κατα χαριν clause. God's promise of salvation and membership of Abraham's offspring depend utterly on God's grace (cf. the phrase κατα χαριν at verse 4, and also at 3:24 where God's grace and the redemptive death of Christ are linked).

2.2.5. Romans 4:16e–22[145]

Paul then interjected something of a parenthesis (vv. 16e–17a):

> Who is the father of us all, as Scripture says, "I have appointed you father of many nations" [Gen 17:5].

---

142. Wieser, *Abrahamvorstellungen*, 63, remarks that only if the promise rests on God, and not on human ability, will it be trustworthy (βεβαια). More recently, Flebbe, *Solus Deus*, 227, has stressed that Paul's emphasis in these verses is on God.

143. Sänger, *Verkündigung*, 110, uses the term "unevenness" (Unebnigkeit).

144. The comment of Käsemann, *Perspectives*, 89, is worth quoting: he maintains that the promise bursts apart the circle of receivers so that to be a child of Abraham is no longer the privilege of Judaism but Gentiles believers too are his children.

145. The point made in note 413, about not drawing too sharp a division between the sections, is especially to be borne in mind.

The idea of Abraham as the father of many nations[146] supplies scriptural backing for Paul's concept of Abraham as having both Jews and Gentiles as his seed. He is the father of all believers, whether circumcised or uncircumcised. Scripture had foreseen that in God's purposes Gentiles would be incorporated into the descendants of Abraham.

After this parenthesis, Paul returned to reflect on the nature of Abraham's faith. As a result of the parenthesis, the Greek is awkward but not difficult to disentangle. Verse 16d had spoken of Abraham's faith. This was exercised "before" or "in the presence of" God in whom he believed:

κατεναντι ου επιστευσεν Θεου

= κατεναντι Θεου ω [or εις ον] επιστευσεν.[147]

Then, what Paul said about God was highly important: "Who gives life to the dead and calls into being things which do not exist" (v. 17bc).

It is important for two reasons. Firstly, because the description of God as giving life to the dead accords fully with OT-Jewish belief in God as possessing creative, sustaining, resurrecting, and converting power. God is the source of life, and all life depends upon Him, and He will at the end of history raise the dead. Käsemann has stressed the link between justification of the ungodly on the one hand and resurrection from the dead and creation ex nihilo on the other. He maintains that justification is the creation ex nihilo which occurs in the eschatological era and that it anticipates the resurrection of the dead. The same power of God is at work in creation and new creation/salvation/justification: both depend completely on Him.[148] On the other hand, Flebbe has drawn attention to the fact that in the work *Joseph and Asenath*, ζωοποιειν is used of God's work in converting the Egyptian woman, Asenath: her conversion is a passage from death to life and to the community of salvation.[149] He prefers this illustration of the turning of

---

146. Von Rad, *Genesis*, 194–95, says that we should not think of Ishmaelites, Edomites, and the sons of Keturah, but of proselytes. Williamson, *Abraham*, 154–62, argues for a non-biological nuance of 'b: it is not used in a physical sense but a metaphorical sense. As their spiritual benefactor, Abraham is the mediator of God's blessing to them. Moxnes, *Theology*, 275, stresses that Paul's own missionary work was helping to bring about the realization of this promise to Abraham.

147. Cf. BD 294 (2); Bauer, *Lexicon*, 422. The Θεου has been pulled away from κατεναντι because Paul wanted to attach two articular participles (του ζωοποιουντος . . . καλουντος) to it.

148. Käseman, *Perspectives*, 92, 95. Barclay, *Gift*, 489, says much the same thing in different language: that Paul traces a deep agreement between the incongruity of grace and the incongruity of divine power.

149. Flebbe, *Solus Deus*, 238–40. See *Joseph and Asenath* 8:10–11; 12:1; 20:6. Flebbe also points out that at 4 Kings 5:7 LXX, the king of Israel asks whether he is God του

the God of Israel to Gentiles and bringing them into the sphere of salvation as the background to Paul's statements rather than relating creation and justification. We need not set these as alternatives, but rather hold both emphases together. Both come from the rich OT-Jewish tradition, which Paul is utilizing in his argumentation.

The concept of God's calling that which did not exist into being is yet again a thoroughly Jewish belief.[150] The LXX uses καλειν in the account of Creation (Gen 1:5[bis], 8, 10[bis]). That God names what He creates is a sign of His creatorship. In Genesis 2:19 (bis), 20, 23, He delegated that task to Adam. In Isaiah 40:26 LXX God calls all the stars individually, which is a sign of His lordship over creation. The verb καλειν is also used of God's calling Israel into existence in Isaiah 41:9; 48:12; Jeremiah 11:16.[151] It is also used of God's calling Cyrus to be His instrument at Isaiah 41:9. So, God's calling activity is manifest in creation and in history. He is absolute lord and sovereign over both.

Secondly, what is said about God in verse 17 is important because it fits the context of which Paul is thinking, viz. the childlessness and advanced years of Abraham and Sarah and the birth of Isaac[152] (just as Paul, with the reference to the birth of Isaac, was working towards mention of God's raising Jesus from the dead). It was in this life-giving God that the aged and childless Abraham believed, hoping against hope.[153] (There is thus what we might call a strong element of hope in Abraham's faith).[154] Paul linked this believing with his becoming "the father of many nations" (the phraseology of Genesis 17:5, previously quoted at verse 17), and this time Paul backed

---

θανατου θανατωσαι και ζωοποιησαι in connection with the healing from leprosy of the non-Israelite, Naaman, the general of the king of the Arameans.

150. See Flebbe, *Solus Deus*, 242.

151. At Hosea 11:1, the verb μετακαλειν is used of God's calling Israel out of Egypt to be His son.

152. Note that the reference to Abraham's body as good as dead (νενεκρωμενον) in verse 19 links back to the assertion that God gives life to the dead (τους νεκρους) in verse 17 and forwards to the statement that God raised Jesus from the dead (εκ νεκρων); cf. Neubrand, *Abraham*, 282; Theobald, "Abraham sah hin," 410.

153. παρ' ελπιδα επ' ελπιδι. The επ' ελπιδι should be taken modally with the verb. Clearly the sense is not that Abraham believed in hope. See NRSV, NIV, REB, and JB for various ways of rendering it.

154. Theobald, "Abraham sah hin," 406, maintains that "in hope against hope" is the key to the entire section (vv. 18-22), with verse 19 explaining "against hope" and verses 20-21 explaining "in hope." Barclay, *Gift*, 489, puts it thus: "Abraham's hope against all reasonable expectations (4:18) is a mirror of his faith in the absence of works (4:4-5)."

up this idea with a quotation from Genesis 15:5: "According as it was said, So shall your seed[155] be" (v. 18).

In that promise[156] Abraham in hope believed. But how are we to understand Paul's statement which runs: επιστευσεν εις το γενεσθαι αυτον κτλ? There are three possible ways of taking the articular infinitive construction:[157] expressing purpose,[158] result,[159] or the content of what Abraham believed.[160] In the majority of instances when Paul used this construction, he expressed purpose;[161] however, there are a number of cases where the idea of result is being conveyed,[162] while arguably in one instance only, the content of what has been taught seems to be in mind.[163] This makes the third suggestion precarious grammatically, and even the second suggestion less secure than the first. In the end, there does not seem to be anything objectionable in seeing the sense as Abraham believed the promise of God which said that his descendants would be as numerous as the stars and the sand on the seashore and that part of that faith was directed to accepting that the promise would mean that he would become the father of many nations.[164]

---

155. "Seed" had been prominent in the earlier section (vv. 13-16).

156. As Berger, *Abraham*, 73, notes with regard to the differences between verses 13 and 17-18, the content of the promise may vary in how it is phrased according to the function demanded by the argument.

157. They are listed by Michel, *Römer*, 125.

158. So, e.g., Dunn, *Romans*, 1:219; Neubrand, *Abraham*, 280; Tobin, *Paul's Rhetoric*, 152; Schliesser, *Abraham's Faith*, 393.

159. So, e.g., Käsemann, *Romans*, 124; Cranfield, *Romans*, 1:246; Morris, *Romans*, 210; Harrisville, *Abraham*, 223n162; NIV, NEB/REB.

160. So, e.g., NRSV; Michel, *Römer*, 125; Bultmann, "πιστευω κτλ" *TWNT* 6:206 (without discussion); Jewett, *Romans*, 335-36 (who lists previous scholars holding this view, but whose appeal to *BD* 406.2 does not seem correct). See Cranfield, *Romans*, 1:246; Morris, *Romans*, 210, for hesitations about this use of the articular infinitive.

161. Confining ourselves to the undisputed Pauline letters, there appear to be thirty-six instances of the εις το construction, of which I would judge twenty-six to express purpose: Rom 1:11; 3:26; 4:11(bis), 16, 18; 7:4, 5; 8:29; 11:11; 12:2; 15:8, 13, 16; 1 Cor 9:18; 10:6; 11:22, 33; 2 Cor 1:4; 4:4; Phil 1:10; 1 Thess 2:12; 3:2, 5, 10, 13.

162. I judge there to be eight instances: Rom 1:20; 6:12; 12:3; 1 Cor 8:10; 2 Cor 7:3; 8:6; Gal 3:17; 1 Thess 2:16.

163. Phil 1:23 (while 1 Thess 4:9 could also come into this category). To love one another is the content of what they have been taught by God (though Rigaux, *Les Épîtres aux Thessaloniciens*, 517, thinks that both goal and consequence are intended).

164. The consecutive interpretation sees "believed" used absolutely, but with the sense "believed God." The result of this faith was that he did in fact become the father of many nations.

He believed, then, in order to be the father of many nations. Fatherhood is once more underlined, as at verses 1, 11–12, and 16.[165]

The focus is on Abraham, though it is not unreasonable that what is said about Abraham's faith has reverberations on what should characterize his seed.[166] God had His sights on the Gentiles from the beginning.

Verse 19 explained the "against hope" aspect of Abraham's faith. A textual variant in verse 19 partially complicates interpretation, but perhaps, in the long run, the sense is not too drastically altered whichever variant we opt for. Paul began by saying that Abraham without weakening in his faith either κατενοησεν το εαυτου σωμα (א A B 1739)

Or ου κατενοησεν το εαυτου σωμα (D G 33 it).

On the first reading, Abraham did consider the facts about himself and Sarah, but he did not weaken in his faith. On the second reading (the so-called Western reading), he ignored the facts about himself and Sarah; he did not take these adverse facts into consideration. As Metzger says, "Curiously enough, each of the two readings gives good sense."[167] Apart from the support of א A B, there is this, perhaps, in favor of the first reading that Paul had Abraham not just ignoring the facts but facing up to them squarely and not wavering.[168]

Paul had Abraham facing up to the fact that he was very old (νενεκρωμενον, usually translated as "as good as dead") and the fact that Sarah was past child bearing age (την νεκρωσιν της μητρας Σαρρας).[169] He looked these facts squarely "in the face," as it were. Theobald sees here a rational aspect. This was not blind trust, but a critical assessment and observation of the facts; he had no illusion about the hopelessness of the human situation and all that spoke against the reality of God's promise.[170]

---

165. Neubrand, *Abraham*, 283–84, 287, stresses that Abraham is not being considered as an example to follow but in relation to his fatherhood.

166. Zeller, *Juden und Heiden*, 105, wants to stress this aspect.

167. Metzger, *Textual Commentary*, 510; cf. Cranfield, *Romans*, 1:247.

168. Cf. Wilckens, *Römer*, 1:276; Dunn, *Romans*, 1:196, 220; Käsemann, *Romans*, 124 (and *Perspectives*, 92); Theobald, "Abraham sah hin," 412–13; Schliesser, *Abraham*, 381–82. See Schmitt, *Gottesgerechtigkeit-Heilsgeschichte-Israel*, 35, for justified criticism of Klein's attempt to claim that Abraham is a timeless example of faith: Abraham and Sarah are characterized by their precise physical state when God made His promise to them.

169. Theobald, "Abraham sah hin," 410, draws attention to the fact that, independently of Romans, Hebrews 11:12 uses νενεκρωμενου of Abraham, and he wonders whether this phraseology had been used before Paul in the Greek language Abraham tradition.

170. Theobald, "Abraham sah hin," 402–3.

In verses 20–21 Paul explains what believing with/in hope meant for Abraham. On the contrary (δε of verse 20 is fully adversative), he did not waver in his faith/trust in God's promise. Abraham did not doubt God's promise through unbelief, but he ενεδυναμωθη τη πιστει. Should this be translated as a genuine passive "was strengthened in respect to his faith,"[171] or is it "grew strong in faith"?[172] The context favors the first interpretation. Morris finely puts it: "Paul is not saying that faith, so to speak, took a weak Abraham and put strength into him. He is saying that God took a weak Abraham and put strength into him."[173] Through God's help, Abraham's reliance on God became stronger. As a result, he gave glory to God (he did what everyone should do but which humanity by and large had refused to do according to Romans 1:21).[174] He was fully convinced that God was able to do what He had promised.[175] The conviction that God is able (δυνατος) to do what He has promised or said is asserted in Israel's faith[176] and, in the New Testament, by Jesus (Mark 10:27; 14:36); Paul (here and Rom 11:23); the author of the Pastorals (2 Tim 1:12); and Hebrews (11:19—also of Abraham's conviction). In this recognition of God's power and in his giving God glory, Abraham once again does what Gentiles should have done (according to Romans 1:20–21), and which at the end of his letter Paul hoped that Jewish and Gentiles believers would do in unity together (15:5–6).

2.2.6. Romans 4:23–25

Finally, Paul turned to apply what he had said about Abraham to the Christian community (vv. 23–25). He returned to Genesis 15:6 once more.[177]

---

171. So Sanday-Headlam, *Romans*, 115; Leenhardt, *Romans*, 125; Morris, *Romans*, 212; Cranfield, *Romans*, 1:248–49; Dunn, *Romans*, 1:220–21; Dobbeler, *Glaube,* 139.

172. So Michel, *Römer*, 125–26; Barrett, *Romans*, 97–98; Bauer, *Lexicon*, 263.

173. Morris, *Romans*, 212.

174. Ουχ ως Θεον εδοξασαν η ηυχαριστησαν.

175. Perhaps an echo of Genesis 18:15: "The LORD said to Abraham . . . is anything too hard for the LORD?"

176. Moxnes, *Theology*, 43, stresses that while traditional, Paul has used this traditional affirmation to support an untraditional thesis, that the promise is for both Jews and non-Jews. Flebbe*, Solus Deus*, 251, believes that Paul is aiming at his own actual mission situation with the existence of mixed congregations of believing Jews and Gentiles

177. Neubrand, *Abraham*, 287, describes God's action in the death and resurrection of Jesus mentioned in verses 23–25 as the theological basis for understanding Paul's *relecture* of the Abraham saga in Genesis, and she quotes Minde, *Schrift und Tradition bei Paulus*, 100, who sees these verses as the hermeneutical key to Romans 4. Hahn, *Genesis 15:6*, 105, describes verses 23–25 as formally an appendix but actually the

The trust of Abraham, the reliance on God's promise, the confidence in God's ability to do what He had promised, this faith directed to God, "was reckoned to him for righteousness." God was looking for just this faith, this trust, this dependence, for a right relationship with Himself. Abraham did not do anything. He simply trusted in God and relied on God's character and His ability to fulfill His word.[178]

Now this word of Genesis 15:6 had a twofold aim according to the apostle. It did set down something about Abraham, but not only for his sake.[179] It had a message for us, for believers of Paul's own day. There is an application not only for the past, but also for all believers, both Gentiles and Jews, in the present. The object of our belief is the same God in whom Abraham believed, now known as the God who raised Jesus our Lord from the dead. We move then from the promise of the birth of a son, Isaac, to Abraham and Sarah (the birth being an example of quickening the dead [the deadness of Sarah's womb] and calling what did not exist into being), to the event of the resurrection of Jesus, an even more profound act of quickening the dead and calling what did not exist into being. God raised our Lord Jesus from the dead (vv. 23-24).

Abraham's faith is, then, the archetype of Christian belief which should rely wholly and solely on God and His life-giving power.[180] Faith in both cases, Abraham and ours, looks for no support but God's own action. (There is no suggestion that Abraham's faith had soteriological consequences for his descendants. Here again Paul departs from much contemporary Jewish exegesis of the figure of Abraham.)[181] This faith opens up the possibility for believing Gentiles to belong to Abraham's descendants. Believing Jews and believing Gentiles share equally in the justifying grace of God.

---

cardinal point of the chapter.

178. Jewett, *Romans*, 339, has commented: "Abraham had no virtue to display, and had not conformed to the law. Even his faith was evoked and sustained by God's power rather than his own. . . . He receives the status of righteousness not as an achievement but as a gift."

179. It is not easy to see how the writing down of the story of Genesis 15 could be said to be for the sake of Abraham himself. However, Jewett, *Romans*, 340, suggests that here διά with the accusative means "for the honor of." The ascription of righteousness to him by God was the ultimate honor which one could receive, and the written record meant that Abraham should receive that recognition by future generations.

180. Cf. Wieser, *Abrahamvorstellungen*, 65.

181. Against Hays, *Abraham*, 95; Cranford, *Abraham*, 83, 86, 88. See, e.g., Schliesser, *Abraham*, 388, for a strong denial of such an interpretation (he quotes the apt comment of Heckel, *Der Segel im Neuen Testament*, 125, that Abraham receives the blessing, but is not the originator of it). See the excursus at the end of this chapter.

Verse 25 is usually held to be a formula utilized by Paul:[182]

> He was handed over because of our transgressions, and raised because of our justification.

The παρεδοθη is a divine passive and is probably intended to recall Isaiah 53:12[183] and to suggest that Jesus was the Suffering Servant of the Lord.

We should not press the distinctions between the effects of the death and resurrection of Jesus; rather, we should make allowances for some rhetorical parallelism. Jesus' resurrection was proof that the same life-giving power of God which worked in the case of Abraham and Sarah was still at work in this new era of God's dealings with humanity, this new era of His creation of congregations of believing Jews and Gentiles.[184]

Excursus: Was Paul Attacking the View That Abraham Was a Source of Salvation for Jews?

In her monograph, Jacqueline Roo has suggested that in Romans Paul was attacking the view held by many Jews that Abraham was a source of salvation for Jews. Due to his extraordinary obedient life, culminating in his willingness to offer Isaac as a sacrifice to God, he was elevated into a virtually perfect human being and was deemed to have obeyed the Law fully even before it was promulgated at Sinai. On the basis of Abraham's good deeds, others would be blessed, forgiven, and saved. She believes that the idea of the atonement effected by the sacrifice of Isaac (usually referred to as the Akedah) was around in the first century.

Roo suggests that to counter this viewpoint, Paul stressed that Abraham was sinful and that the blessing which Abraham received from God was not earned but was given by grace (Rom 4). Paul's critique of circumcision was aimed at the belief that that was a sign of God's eternal covenant with

---

182. If this is correct, it has relevance for trying to work out the contours of belief of those who were in Christ before Paul, but in terms of the argument of Romans, the important thing is that Paul has integrated it into what he was trying to say (as Flebbe, *Solus Deus*, 257–58, rightly maintains).

183. The LXX reads at verse 12: ανθ'ω παρεδοθη εις θανατον η ψυχη αυτου . . . και δια τας αμαρτιας αυτων παρεδοθη. At 53:5 the LXX reads that αυτος δε ετραυματισθη δια τας ανομιας ημων και μεμαλακισται δια τας αμαρτιας ημων, and then at verse 6 και δια τας αμαρτιας αυτων παρεδοθη. The Targum rewrote verse 12 substantially and at verse 5 said that the Holy Place had been delivered to the enemy for our iniquities.

184. Flebbe, *Solus Deus*, 260, sees this goal of Paul's argument in Romans 1:18–4:25 as confirmation that 4:1–25 is to be related to 3:27–31 rather than 3:21–26.

Abraham and his descendants, possession of which was a guarantee that the Jews would escape the eschatological wrath of God and receive final salvation. Over against any exaltation of Abraham, Paul stressed that Jesus alone is the one who has accomplished redemption/atonement. It is by the one man, Jesus Christ's obedience that believers will be established as in the right with God; Jesus alone reversed the consequences of Adam's sin (Rom 5:12-21).

The case is ably made and much of it is absolutely right. In much early Jewish literature there are not a few appeals to God to remember His covenant with Abraham and so come to the rescue of a persecuted Israel.

But, quite apart from the uncertainty as to how far the Aqedah was widespread in the first century AD, was not the descent from Abraham and the belonging to the covenant made with the nation at Sinai and the possession of the Law given there, the vital foundation of their privileged position rather than that Abraham by his alleged perfect obedience was an actual source of salvation?

In much early Jewish literature Abraham's role as an example of steadfast adherence to the will of God is stressed as an encouragement to Jews faced with a choice of loyalties, rather than that he was an actual source of salvation. If Paul was attacking a belief that Abraham was the actual source of salvation, might we not have expected a specific reference to this in chapter 4 and also in the Adam-Christ comparison and contrast in Romans 5?

2.2.7. Romans 9–11

By the time he had reached the end of Romans 8, Paul was in a position to tackle certain questions which he had raised but left unanswered earlier in the letter, at 3:1-8.[185] Thus, if Israel had failed to respond to the gospel, did this mean that God's purposes had failed? Were the promises which He had made to Israel now worthless? In addition, if God's promises to Israel were no longer applicable, what about His promises in the gospel? Were they any more reliable?[186] The reliability of salvation for the Gentiles, the trustworthiness of Paul's own message, and his own self-understanding as the apostle to the Gentiles, were all called in question.[187] In other words,

---

185. E.g., Dunn, *Romans*, 2:519-20. Quite apart from the commentaries, there have been a huge number of monographs or studies of Romans 9–11. For a few of these, see those in the bibliography by Munck, Müller, Zeller, Siegert, Lübking, Hofius, E. Johnson, Piper, and Sanger. See also Wright, *Climax*, 231-51; Dunn, *Theology*, 499-532; Watson, *PJG*, 301-343; Kim, *God, Israel, and the Gentiles*; Wilk and Wagner, *Between Gospel and Election*.

186. Cf. Sanger, *Verkündigung*, 100-101.

187. This is stressed by Niebuhr, *Heidenapostel*, 148, 173, 183.

the whole issue of the trustworthiness of God was raised in an acute form by events surrounding Jesus of Nazareth and the mission of his disciples. There seemed a sharp discrepancy between the promises made to Israel as recorded in Scripture (e.g., 9:4–5a) and the actual position outside salvation of contemporary Israel (implicit in 9:1–3 and explicit at 10:1, where Paul's prayers are for the salvation of his fellow countrymen and women).

Paul confronted the problem head on with the assertion in 9:6a: "It is not as though the Word of God has failed."[188]

He grounds this statement with a γαρ clause in verses 6b–7:

ου γαρ παντες οι εξ Ισραηλ ουτοι Ισραηλ
ου δ' οτι εισιν σπερμα Αβρααμ παντες τεκνα.
Αλλ' Εν Ισαακ κληθησεται σοι σπερμα.

One translation would run something like:

> 6b Not all who are descended from Israel [εξ Ισραηλ] are Israel,
>
>   7a nor, because they are Abraham's seed, are all (his) children,
>
>   7b but (Scripture says [Gen 21:12]) "In Isaac shall your seed be called."[189]
>
>   8 that is, it is not the children of Abraham who are the children of God, but the children of the promise are reckoned to (his) seed.
>
>   9 For this is the word of the promise [Gen 18:10, 14]: "At this time I will come and Sarah shall give birth to a son" (vv. 8–9).

This translation assumes that at verses 6b–7a, Paul was both drawing a division within empirical Israel (not all those who are physically counted as being members of the Israelite nation really belong to the true Israel, the true people of God), and also distinguishing between the biological descendants of Abraham (only those descended through Isaac count as his true children). In this, Paul is arguing against what would be a fundamental assumption within much of contemporary Judaism that those descended from Abraham through Isaac were children of Abraham and belonged to Israel. So, Berger maintains that the phrase "seed of Abraham" is the

---

188. This is the key theme to be dealt with in Romans 9–11 (cf. Siegert, *Argumentation*, 124; Piper, *Justification*, 50; Flebbe, *Solus Deus*, 275; Barclay, *Gift*, 526). Paul's expression of grief at the attitude and position of the majority of his fellow countrymen and women could be construed as implying the failure of God's word and promise. So Lübking, *Paulus und Israel*, 61–62; Cranfield, *Romans*, 2:472; Jewett, *Romans*, 573.

189. With variations, this represents the sense of the RSV, NIV, NEB/REB, GN, JB/NJB, Moffatt, and Phillips.

comprehensive term, while τεκνα is the choice from within that.[190] But even he has to acknowledge that in the quotation of Genesis 21:12 which follows in verse 7b, it is Abraham's *seed* which is to be traced through Isaac, but seeks to circumvent the difficulty by saying that the emphasis falls on κληθησεται (some translations offer "will be traced." Although this conveys the sense in modern English, it loses the richness of the biblical notion of the "call" of God and its importance later on in 9:11, 24-26, and indeed previously at 4:17; 8:30).

Even in verses 8-9, where Paul first uses τεκνα of both Abraham's physical descendants and children of God, he then speaks of the children born as the result of God's promise being reckoned as Abraham's *seed*.

In view of the difficulties just mentioned, a number of scholars dissent from the kind of translation offered previously. They suggest that because of the OT quotation "In Isaac your seed shall be called" in verse 7b, "seed" in verse 7a should be taken as the key phrase. That is: verse 7a says that it is not all his children (physical descendants) who are Abraham's seed. Grammatically speaking, on this view, in verse 7a τεκνα is the subject and σπερμα is the predicate.[191]

If this is correct, then it has implications for how we understand both ου γαρ in verse 6b and ουδ' οτι in verse 7a. Instead of translating verse 6a in the way mentioned above, we could render it by supplying a verb between γαρ and παντες as follows: "For it is not as if all who are descended from Israel are Israel." As to ουδ' οτι in verse 7a, we can hardly ignore it,[192] while the phrase can hardly be rendered "nor because." We may take it as parallel to the ουχ οιον οτι in verse 6a (as Dunn and Flebbe suggest).[193] This would mean that it introduces something which Paul denies, just as he denied that the word of God had failed in verse 6a. This produces a translation as follows:

> 6b For it is not as if all who are descended from[194] Israel are Israel,

---

190. Berger, *Abraham*, 80-81; cf. Jewett, *Romans*, 575.

191. So Barrett, *Romans*, 180-81; Jewett, *Romans*, 575. Both Dunn, *Romans*, 2:540, and Flebbe, *Solus Deus*, 280, take "seed" as the narrower, more restrictive term and "children" as the broader concept (Cranfield, *Romans*, 2:473, assumes the very opposite for verse 7a, but then accepts the reverse for verse 8).

192. As Barrett, *Romans*, 179-80, does (in fairness to Barrett, his commentary is on the English text).

193. Dunn, *Romans*, 2:538, 540, 547; Flebbe, *Solus Deus*, 281. Jewett, *Romans* 570, translates verse 7a as "nor [is it] that . . ."

194. Barclay, *Gift*, 530n23, points out that the preposition εκ in the context of ethnicity means descent and points to 9:5, 10; 11:1; Phil 3:5.

7a nor is it the case that all his children are Abraham's seed but "In Isaac[195] your seed shall be called."[196]

As if to counter objections, Paul followed this up by an explanatory "that is": "It is not the children born as a result of the flesh who are children of God, but it is the children born as a result of God's promise who are reckoned as (Abraham's true) seed" (v. 8). This assertion is also grounded in Scripture with another γαρ clause: "For the word of promise is this: 'At this time I will come[197] and Sarah will have a son'" (v. 9). This is a quotation from Genesis 18:10, 14. What Paul is here contrasting is the line of descent from Abraham as a result of Abraham's own physical efforts (his intercourse with Hagar) and the line of descent from Isaac who was born not as a result of human action, but as a result of divine promise and action when all hope of natural procreation had ceased. God made a promise based on His choice and intervened — one might say, against the course of nature — and determined who should constitute the true line of Abraham, as His word recorded in Genesis 21:12 indicated.[198]

The divine initiative and role receive emphasis in these few verses: there is reference to the "word of the promise" together with the fact that we have two divine passives — κληθησεται and λογιζεται (vv. 7b, 8b) and then the verb ελευσομαι, a deponent future middle with an active sense, in the quotation from Genesis 18 at verse 9. God calls, reckons, and will come. His word and action are determinative. To be a child of God is determined by God's promise (vv. 8-9); one does not belong to the children/people of God through mere physical descent.[199]

---

195. As, e.g., Wilckens, *Römer*, 2:192; Jewett, *Romans*, 576, rightly point out, the meaning is *only* in Isaac.

196. This is the position of Dunn, *Romans*, 2:540; Flebbe, *Solus Deus,* 281; Jewett, *Romans*, 575; Reinbold, *Zur Bedeutung des Begriffes*, 414. The NRSV comes close to this.

197. Paul replaces either the αναστρεψω of Genesis 18:14 LXX or ηξω of Genesis 18:10 LXX (apart from the quotation of Isaiah 59:26 in Romans 11:26, Paul does not use ηκω), with ελευσομαι as better suited to his own context. See Koch, *Schrift*, 141-42, for details.

198. Jewett, *Romans*, 576, rightly objects to the view that Paul has Christians in mind at this point.

199. Lübking, *Paulus und Israel*, 61-68, strenuously and consistently denies that Paul is introducing a division within empirical Israel here or throughout the chapter; likewise, Flebbe, *Solus Deus*; Barclay, *Gift*, 528. Jewett, *Romans*, 575, comments: "What Paul denies here is that the covenantal promise extended to all Abraham's children. It was the child of Sarah (Gen 21:1-3), not the children of Hagar and Keturah (Gen 16:15; 25:2), who would bear the promise of becoming the people of Israel (cf. Gal 4:22-31)."

Paul looked at the stories about Abraham and Sarah in Genesis 12–25. These stories showed that Abraham had, in addition to Isaac by Sarah, another son, Ishmael, by Hagar, Sarah's slave girl, and also sons by Keturah whom he married after Sarah's death. But God had made it abundantly clear that Abraham's true descendants were to be traced through Isaac (Gen 25).[200]

In other words, God made a choice.[201] He elected a son born of the union of Abraham and Sarah, not any of the other sons whom Abraham fathered. This election was determined long before Isaac was born, as the promises of Genesis 15:4; 17:16–19; 18:10–14, amply showed. The principle of divine election operated at the very beginning of Israel's story. Human activity or influence played no part; all depended on God.

Before moving on, we should mention another suggestion which has been made concerning verse 6b. Some scholars take the first Ισραηλ of verse 6b as a reference to Jacob[202] and assume the meaning to be "Not all Jacob's descendants are Israel," i.e., the community who enjoy salvation.[203] How are we to judge this suggestion? The introduction of Jacob is rather abrupt and unexpected. Jacob has not figured in Paul's discussion hitherto. Of course, Paul was perfectly well aware of the equation Jacob = Israel, as the quotation of Isaiah 59:20–21 in 11:26 shows, but never elsewhere in his writings does he use Israel = Jacob. There is also the fact that in Romans 4:1 he referred to Abraham as our ancestor, plus the fact that the historical order is reversed if the first "Israel" = Jacob, whereas there seems to be a careful following of the historical sequence in Romans 9:6–18: Abraham, Isaac and Rebekkah, Jacob and Esau, Moses and Pharaoh and then the prophets like Isaiah.[204] These facts must count as a weakness of this suggestion, attractive as it is in some ways.[205]

The same kind of circumstance, viz. God making a choice, was true in the next generation (vv. 10–13). Of Isaac's two sons by Rebekah,[206] God

---

200. See especially Genesis 17:19–21, where it was said that God's covenant would be with Isaac, and Genesis 21:12, where God ordered Abraham to dismiss Hagar and Ishmael from his household, "for in Isaac shall your seed be called" (cf. Gen 22:16–18).

201. Wilckens, *Römer*, 2:191, neatly heads 9:6–13, "Erwählung als Auswahl" (which we might render in English by "Election as Selection").

202. Schlatter (according to Käsemann, *Romans*, 262); Michel, *Römer*, 231; Flebbe, *Solus Deus*, 279; Haacker, *Römer*, 191 (according to Flebbe, *Solus Deus*, 279n49); Reinbold, *Bedeutung*, 408–414.

203. Flebbe consistently uses the term Heilsgruppe (literally the group of salvation).

204. Mentioned by Michel, *Römer*, 230.

205. Jewett, *Romans*, 574, rejects this suggestion, though without argument.

206. Whereas different mothers were involved in Abraham's various children, in

chose Jacob the younger son. God declared His choice while the two boys were not yet born but still in their mother's womb, and before, therefore, they had done either good or evil. In other words, God's choice was not determined by the moral behavior of the two sons, but solely by His own decision.[207] The pre-birth declaration ("The elder will serve the younger" [Gen 25:23]) took place, according to Paul, "in order that God's elective choice (η κατ' εκλογην προθεσις του Θεου) might continue, not on the basis of works but based on Him who calls" (vv. 10-12).

The phrase "not on the basis of works" (v. 12a) is intended to suggest to his addressees a parallel between God's electing action at the beginning of Israel's story and His justifying action on behalf of both Jews and Gentiles in His Son, Jesus Christ, earlier set forth in the letter. The description of God as the One who calls (ο καλων) picks up the earlier reference to the fact that God had said that Abraham's seed should be "called" (κληθησεται) in and through Isaac (v. 7), and it prepares the way for the later assertion in verse 24 to "us whom He also called [εκαλεσεν ημας] not only from the Jews but also from the Gentiles."

Paul then added a further scriptural quotation: "I have loved Jacob, but I have hated Esau" (Mal 1:2-3).[208] The sharpness of the Hebrew idiom reinforces the idea of divine election.[209]

We note that Isaac is described as "*our* father" in verse 10, which is very significant in view of the fact that in verse 8 Scripture had been quoted which said that Abraham's seed should be "called" in Isaac. Paul had in mind the communities of believers, both Jewish and Gentile, which had been formed as a result of his mission.

Thus, in the very first two generations of Israel's story, in the story of the fathers, Paul saw God electing some, through whom His purposes would continue to operate. This election was grounded in the mystery of

---

the case of Esau and Jacob they had the same father (hence the reference in verse 10 to Rebekkah's conceiving by one man, εξ ενος).

207. "The divine word rather than physical lineage determines the heir of the promise" (Jewett, *Romans*, 577).

208. Paul has put τον Ιακωβ before the verb, thus destroying the chiasmus of Malachi 1:2-3 LXX. Koch, *Schrift*, 107, thinks that thereby Paul sharpens the antithetical statement of the Scriptural word, but this seems to claim too much. Siegert, *Argumentation*, 126, points out that Paul has demonstrated his case with quotations from the Law and the Prophets.

209. Transposed into modern English, the idiom would be "I have loved Jacob more than Esau." See Caird, *Language*, 111-12, for what he calls Hebrew absoluteness in expression. In Luke 14:27, there is a comparable use of love and hate, with the sense that disciples must love Jesus more than any member of their family.

God's own being and decision, not on human achievement or personality.[210] The implication was this: if God wished in the first century AD to choose those who believe in Jesus, Israel cannot object.[211] The principle of God's elective choice had already been discerned in Israel's history (Isaac, not Ishmael; Jacob, not Esau). If Israel's own Scriptures were properly understood, it would be clear that the Word of God had not failed (v. 6)![212]

This, of course, raised a question about God's fairness and justice, and Paul handled this immediately in verse 14: "What then shall we say? Is there unfairness (αδικια) with God? Certainly not!" We need not pursue this issue here, as it does not concern our theme.

At the end of chapter 9 there are echoes of the promise to Abraham in the quotation from Isaiah 10:22-23 at verse 27.[213] Isaiah had referred to the (incalculable) number of the sons of Israel being like the sand on the seashore, and this reminds one of the promise made to Abraham in Genesis 22:17 (to a lesser extent of Genesis 15:5). The fact that of these a remnant would be saved (v. 27b, 29b) would no doubt be in Paul's mind scriptural confirmation of what he had asserted at 9:6-7 about the difference between Abraham's children and his seed (to be traced only through Isaac),[214] and pointed forward to his use of the remnant idea in 11:4-5.

We sum up: in Romans 9, Paul is arguing the case that God in His sovereign freedom chose some and did not choose others, *to carry out His purposes* (he is *not* dealing with the eternal destiny of Ishmael or Esau, or indeed the Pharaoh of the oppression, vv. 17-18).[215] Israel is constituted by God's sovereign election and call. Right at the beginning, in the time of the creation of Israel, the determining factor was God's choice. No other criterion was operative.[216]

---

210. As Lübking, *Paulus und Israel*, 67, says, promise and election are the sole ground for participating in Israel. God's electing word is the mode of His working from time immemorial.

211. See Barrett, *Romans*, 183, for a helpful comment on the implications of Paul's argument for Christians and the church today.

212. Dunn, *Romans*, 2:549-50, aptly comments that the word of God has not failed; it has simply been misunderstood by the people whose Scriptures they are. "The word of God has not failed. . . . It is Israel according to the flesh who have failed."

213. Noted by Watson, *PJG*, 321.

214. Käsemann, *Romans*, 276, suggests that here we have "a backward glance at what was said about the genuine seed of Abraham in verses 7ff, and the term "seed" in the quotation [presumably a reference to Isaiah 1:9 quoted at verse 29] is reminiscent of that."

215. For an opposite view, see Piper, *Justification*, 56-73, 151-216.

216. Barclay, *Grace and Agency*, 140-57, draws attention to the different ways in which Philo and Paul dealt with this theme. Philo sought to absolve God's choice from

This stress on God's sovereign freedom as a way in which Paul handled the problem of Israel continued to some extent in the section beginning at 9:30. In a quotation which combined Isaiah 28:16 and 8:14 at 9:32,[217] Paul showed that God was going to establish in Zion (the heart of Israel) "a stone of stumbling and a rock of offence," i.e., a stone which would cause people to trip over it and stumble and a rock at which people would take offence, though, if people believed on it, they would not be put to shame. The implication of this is quite clearly that God did intend some to stumble, while also implying that He intended some to believe and so to be saved (cf. 10:5-13). Later, in chapter 11, Paul will point to the fact that God had hardened the majority of Israelites.[218] Watson has rightly protested against the rigid separation of the themes of 9:1-29 and 9:30-10:21 into God's sovereign freedom and Israel's personal responsibility respectively.[219] While there is an element of the fact that Israel could not plead ignorance of the message which had gone out into all the world (10:18-21), God remains very much the One who acts behind the statements of 9:30-10:21.

In Romans 11, Paul discussed the question whether God had definitively repudiated His people (as a result of their rejection of Jesus and the preaching of the Gospel). Initially he spoke about the remnant, i.e., Jewish Christians like Paul himself, who was an example of how God could transform someone hardened in opposition, into a "vessel of grace." This remnant had provided continuity with the past history of salvation. Paul saw himself and other Jewish Christians as a sign that God had not rejected His people. There was a remnant which was the recipient of the fulfillment of God's past promises, even if God had hardened the rest (v. 7). Paul repeated his earlier question in a different way by asking whether Israel stumbled (over Jesus described as "the rock of stumbling" in 9:33) in order that she

being arbitrary by speaking of God's foreknowledge of the character and behavior of those whom He chooses.

217. Lübking, *Paulus und Israel*, 79, sees this mixed quotation as the center of Paul's argument in 9:30-10:21.

218. Sänger, *Verkündung*, 159-60, has rightly pointed out that in 11:7 Paul stated that while the election (abstract for concrete, i.e., specifically Jewish Christian believers) obtained the righteousness of God, "the rest were hardened," i.e., *by God*, and that he went on to quote Scripture [Deut 29:4; Isa 29:10] to the effect that God gave them a spirit of stupor, eyes so that they should not see, and ears that they should not hear, to this very day. This hardening, which resulted in the "fall" of the majority of Israelites, had the aim in the purposes of God, however, of enabling the message of salvation to go to the Gentiles.

219. Watson, *PJG*, 322-23. Later, he comments: "According to Paul's reading of Scripture in Romans 9-11, Israel's failure to attain God's righteousness is actually decreed by God" (325n41). Behind this lies an ultimately saving purpose, as Paul indicated in 11:11, 12, 25-32.

might fall from salvation? This is once again dismissed, and explained as part of the divine strategy to enable Gentiles to hear and receive salvation. Paul clearly implied that Israel's present position would not be a permanent one (11:12), and went on to say "If their rejection (has meant) reconciliation for the world, what will be their reception but life from the dead? If the first fruits are holy, so also is the lump; and if the root is holy, so also the branches" (vv. 15-16). To whom or what was Paul referring when he spoke of the first fruits and the root? While it is possible that Paul had different referents in mind with first fruits and root,[220] it seems best to take the two together. Either Paul was here referring back to the origins of the people of God, i.e., the patriarchs and perhaps, specifically, Abraham,[221] or he was thinking of the remnant, the Jewish Christians,[222] while some scholars suggest that he might have had both in mind.[223] The overwhelming number of commentators assume that Paul was thinking of the patriarchs in general, perhaps Abraham specifically, and point to what Paul said at 11:28. On the other hand, in the recent context (11:1-7), he had been speaking about Jewish Christians as a remnant, and it is possible that they were in mind. But in the light of the importance of Abraham in chapter 4 and the reference to the fathers in 9:5, the former option seems more likely to be in Paul's mind. That would mean the same referent when Paul went on to say to Gentile Christians at Rome that they should not boast over the Jews who appear to have been rejected by God, because they do not bear the root but the root bears them (11:18).[224] But is the reference to Abraham/the patriarchs personally? Would not this set up a contradiction with how Paul has argued in 9:6-29? To avoid this difficulty, Barclay has suggested a refinement of the view that Abraham/the patriarchs were in mind. He has argued that Paul was thinking of the calling or election of God (which began with Abraham and the patriarchs). The root is the unconditional favor of God on which Israel's existence depended from the very start. God called Abraham and gave His promises as an act of unconditional grace. This was the very basis

220. Leenhardt, *Romans*, 286; Cranfield, *Romans*, 2:564, take the first fruits to mean Jewish Christians, but the root to be the patriarchs.

221. Michel, *Römer*, 274; Luz, *Geschichtsverständnis*, 275-76; Black, *Romans*, 144; Käsemann, *Romans*, 308; Wilckens, *Römer*, 2:246; Hofius, *Paulusstudien*, 186-87; Cranfield, *Romans*, 2:565; Morris, *Romans*, 411; Dunn, *Romans*, 2:672

222. Barrett, *Romans*, 216.

223. Dodd, *Romans*, 178-79; Ziesler, *Romans*, 277-78; Dahl, *Studies in Paul*, 151 (quoted by Ziesler, *Romans*, 277).

224. Jewett, *Romans*, 682-83, denies any allegorical significance to verse 16. He believes that the verse provides the essential premise for the allegory of the wild olive tree (viz. extended holiness from the first batch of dough or the first fruits of the harvest to the whole of the bread or harvest).

of Israel as a nation. On this unconditional grace, Gentile Christians also depend, a fact which they must never forget (11:18–22).[225]

Siegert has detected what he thinks is another allusion to Abraham in the midst of the olive tree analogy in Romans 11.[226] He believes that there is a reference to the faith of Abraham when Paul says that the Gentiles have become partakers of the rich root of the olive tree. The literal phrase is "the root of richness" (της ριζης της πιοτητος [v. 17]), which Siegert takes as the sap which bears fruit. This stands for faith according to the example of Abraham. For Siegert, this interpretation is confirmed by the reference to faith which occurs in verse 20, where Paul says that the Jews have been lopped off because of their unbelief, whereas the Gentiles stand (in their present position within the olive tree which stands for God's people) because of their faith (τη πιστει). While this is not impossible, it must be said that it is not immediately obvious and it may well press a point of the allegory too far.[227]

While we could say that Romans 9–11 is like a rope which is made up of many strands: divine predestination or election; human responsibility to believe or not; the remnant; the divine will to show mercy, *the fundamental issue is one of God's faithfulness, His trustworthiness, God's ability to fulfill His sovereign purpose.* All these were bound up with the question of Israel because God in the mystery of His purposes elected Israel in the beginning, but His purpose embraced His whole creation and included non-Jews as well.

From our point of view, Paul used part of Abraham's story to back up his argument about the mystery of God's choice. As a result, we see that Paul was reading the term Israel in a non-racial or non-ethnic sense. He is getting away from a purely physical or biological interpretation of the word. Israel was constituted by God's choice, God's promise, with faith and trust the fitting human response. Being a child of God was not inherited.

There is still more on our theme in Romans 9–11, and to that we now turn. As Siker points out,[228] references to the fathers frame the section 9:1–11:32. At the beginning of chapter 9, Paul expressed what inner pain and sorrow the refusal of his fellow countrymen and women to believe in Jesus

---

225. "What matters about the patriarchs is that they were rendered significant by a grace which bore no relation to their intrinsic worth. In other words, the 'root of fatness' that sustains the olive tree is not *the patriarchs themselves*, but *the calling or election of God* that constituted them as patriarchs, and thereby constituted Israel as a whole" (Barclay, *Gift*, 550). Cranfield, *Romans*, 2:565, comes very close to this position too, as does Walter, *Zur Interpretation von Römer 9–11*, 180.

226. Siegert, *Argumentation*, 168–70.

227. Neither Dunn, *Romans*, 2:673, nor Ziesler, *Romans*, 280, discuss Siegert's suggestion, though they know and use his work elsewhere in their commentary.

228. Siker, *Disinheriting the Jews*, 65.

caused him. That inner anguish was exacerbated when he considered who they were and what they had been given. The fathers were included in what might be regarded as the advantages of the Jew (to use a phrase from 3:1), or, alternatively, as one of the factors central to Jewish identity (9:4-5).[229] He could even wish himself accursed and separated from Christ if only they would come to belief (v. 3).

Towards the end of his discussion, Paul said that a partial hardening had befallen Israel, which would last until the full number of the Gentiles had come in, and then all Israel would be saved (vv. 25b-26). Paul backed this up by a quotation from Isaiah 59:20-21: "The redeemer will come from Zion, to turn ungodliness away from Jacob. And this will be my covenant with them when I forgive their sins."[230] Then comes a carefully constructed, antithetical sentence[231] which reflected on unbelieving Israel's position now and in the future:

> As regards the (preaching of) the Gospel, (they are) enemies, for your benefit, but as regards (God's) election they are beloved because of the fathers. (v. 28)[232]

Paul meant that through the combination of divine hardening and Israel's refusal to believe in Jesus, the gospel had been proclaimed to the Gentiles, and so they were being included in the people of God on the basis

---

229. Watson, *PJG*, 303-5, believes that in 9:1-5 Paul was anticipating a charge that he had turned his back on his own people and was indifferent to their fate. He was blamed for preaching a form of the Gospel to the Gentiles which made it unacceptable to most Jews, while his claim that God had turned from the Jews to the Gentiles seemed to invalidate the scriptural doctrine of election.

230. For a criticism of views which tone down the "all" of Paul's statement, see Jewett, *Romans*, 701-2.

231. Technically, known as paaromoiosis. Note the κατα μεν ... κατα δε; δι' ... δια + accusative; and assonance at the end of each clause: εχθοι ... υμας and αγαπητοι/ ... πατερας. See Siegert, *Argumentation*, 174.

232. Some assume that "enemies" is to be taken in an active sense, i.e., Jews are hostile to God (so Leenhardt, *Romans*, 294-95; Jewett, *Romans*, 707; Flebbe, *Solus Deus*, 373), others prefer a passive sense, i.e., regarded as enemies by God, in the sense of under His wrath and judgment (so Michel, *Römer*, 282; Käsemann, *Romans*, 315; Barrett, *Romans*, 224-25; Cranfield, *Romans*, 2:580; Morris, *Romans*, 422; Dunn, *Romans*, 2:693). Ziesler, *Romans*, 286, while saying that it is impossible to distinguish between the two possibilities, in the end says that some element of God's opposition to the Jews is impossible to avoid. The carefully constructed, antithetical sentence might suggest the latter, to be balanced by "beloved" in verse 28a. That elsewhere Paul and the New Testament in general uses "enemy/enemies" in an active sense does not necessarily preclude Paul's using it here in a passive sense to sharpen the paradox expressed in verse 28.

of faith.²³³ In God's purposes, Israel's refusal to believe had worked out for the spread of the gospel and the universalizing of the people of God. But side by side with this aspect of being enemies, Paul placed another aspect: "as regards (God's) election, they are beloved because of the fathers" (v. 28b). Here Paul utilized a thought often expressed in the OT. He meant that God made certain promises to Abraham, Isaac, and Jacob. These were promises which were still valid in Paul's opinion, "for the gifts and calling of God are irrevocable" (11:29). The period of Israel's disobedience would give way to a time when she would receive God's mercy again. "For God has shut up all to disobedience [Gentiles and Jews at different periods], that He might have mercy on all" (v. 32).²³⁴

Paul did not say how exactly he envisaged this actually happening. We may be confident that Israel's salvation would not be apart from Christ and faith in him. If God could save a hardened sinner like Paul, it would not be beyond His ability to save others hardened in opposition to Him at the moment.²³⁵

It is indicative of how important God's promises to Abraham,²³⁶ repeated to Isaac²³⁷ and Jacob,²³⁸ were to Paul that he can express himself as he does in 11:28b. God gave His word; He made promises; He will not go back on them. He remains faithful and He can be trusted.²³⁹ His word will not fail!

2.2.8. Romans 15:7–13

The same thought of God's faithfulness to His promises occurs at 15:8. Paul had just called on the Roman Christians to receive one another to the glory of God. Where Christians accept one another as brothers and sisters (just as Christ had accepted them), that redounds to the praise of God, because it shows that God has the power to bring together people of different races,

---

233. Jewett, *Romans*, 707, sees an additional meaning behind δι' ὑμας, viz. "Zealous resistance against the gospel was directed against Gentiles and all who would accept their polluting presence in the realm of God."

234. Wieser, *Abrahamvorstellungen*, 82, comments: "The grace of God based on His sovereign freedom alone remains."

235. Cf. the remark of Hofius, "Evangelium und Israel," 198; "*Israel comes to faith in the same way as Paul himself!*" As Paul was overcome by an encounter with the risen Lord, so will all Israel.

236. Gen 12:1–3; 15:5, 18; 17:1–21; 22:16–18.

237. Gen 26:2–5, 24.

238. Gen 26:2–5, 24.

239. Cf. Rom 3:3–4.

sexes, and socio-economic backgrounds. Paul then went on to say that Christ became, and continues to be,[240] a servant of the Jewish people (the circumcision)[241] for the sake of the trustworthiness of God, "in order to confirm the promises made to the fathers"[242] and also in order that the Gentiles might receive God's mercy and might glorify God for it, together with the Jews.[243] This second purpose idea (introduced simply by δε) is probably dependent on the εις το construction in verse 8b. Thus Jesus is the embodiment both of God's faithfulness to His promises to Israel through the fathers and of God's mercy to the Gentiles.[244] In the work of Jesus the messiah (now risen), the promises of God to the patriarchs were being fulfilled (cf. 2 Cor 1:19-20), including of course that through Abraham's descendants all the nations would be blessed.[245]

The result is that both the Gentiles and the Jews do what previously Paul had indicted them for not doing:[246] they glorify God (15:5-6, 8).

In the catena of scriptural quotations which follows, the first three ground the idea of both Jews and Gentiles glorifying God. In the first (Ps 18:49), the speaker[247] said that he would praise God among the Gentiles; the second (Deut 32:43) summoned all Gentiles to rejoice with God's people; and the third (Ps 117:1) summoned all peoples (Israel being included)

---

240. This is the nuance of the perfect infinitive middle, γεγενησθαι.

241. Jewett, *Romans*, 891, points out both that this is the group stereotyped as weak in Rome and that circumcision was often used as a term of abuse by Gentile writers against Jews.

242. Υπερ αληθειας Θεου. Jewett, *Romans*, 801-2, argues for the meaning "the truthfulness of God," on the grounds that the translation "faithfulness" undercuts the link with the earlier argument of Romans. On the other hand, Romans 9-11 has been about the reliability of God's word and promise.

243. Flebbe, *Solus Deus*, 413-15 has pointed out that to glorify with the grounds for praise is expressed in the LXX and the NT by δοξασαι επι plus the dative, whereas δοξασαι υπερ means "to have an opinion about someone/something." While acknowledging the difficulties of interpreting Paul's statement, his preferred solution is to take τα εθνη as an accusative of respect and relate it to διακονον γεγενεσθαι; to put a comma after υπερ ελεους (syntaktisch ein Einschnitt zu machen); and interpret δοξασαι as an infinitive of purpose, thus producing "to confirm the promises made to the fathers and for mercy in respect to the Gentiles, so that they might glorify God," which Gentiles had failed to do according to Romans 1:21 (Flebbe, *Solus Deus*, 416). Might we not have expected Paul to have written εις το before δοξασαι in that case?

244. Cf. Dunn, *Romans*, 2:852-53; Watson, *PJG*, 339.

245. See the brief but very helpful remarks in Theobald, "Dem Juden zuerst," 114-15, who compares Romans 1:3-4 and 15:8-9.

246. See 1:21 for the Gentiles; 2:24 for the Jews; and 3:9-20 for both.

247. We need not here go into the question of whether the speaker is Christ, the psalmist, or Paul.

to sing God's praise. The final quotation (Isa 11:10)[248] announced that the Davidic descendant (a root from Jesse) would rule over the Gentiles who would hope in him. The idea that the Gentiles would set their hope on him suggests that this vision was different from that of the subjugation of the non-Jewish world under Israel which occurs in many descriptions of the age to come.[249]

Thus, God's faithfulness and His mercy are the reason and basis for what Flebbe has called a "doxological universalism."[250]

God's purposes embrace both Israel and the Gentiles. The birth and ministry, death and resurrection of Jesus of Nazareth among the Jewish people was in fulfillment of promises made ages ago to the patriarchs and demonstrated God's faithfulness to His word. It also fulfilled the promise made to the patriarchs that the nations would be blessed through their descendants. There is a double prong, as it were: Israel and the Gentiles, to be one people of the one God.[251]

Thus, 15:8 reinforces the impression gained from 11:28b of how significant for Paul were the promises made to Abraham and his successors.

2.3. A Comparison of the Use of Abraham in Galatians and Romans

In both letters, we see Paul as a scriptural theologian, who stood within the Jewish tradition and carried on his argument within it. As in Galatians, so in both passages in Romans where Abraham is specifically mentioned (chapters 4 and 9), Paul argued his case from Scripture. He interacted with the story of Abraham in order to make it relevant for his own day in the aftermath of what God had done for human beings in Jesus Christ and in the light of the mission to the Gentiles. But it is important to note that Paul was not really bringing something totally new which was discordant with the biblical story. Jewish tradition was not monolithic and Paul can be placed within the trajectory of Jewish interpretation, not in total opposition to it

---

248. Thus, the quotations come from the Law, the Prophets, and the Writings; cf. the assertion of 3:21 that the Law and the Prophets bear witness to the saving righteousness of God, and the reference to the encouragement supplied by the Scriptures in 15:4.

249. So Dunn, *Romans*, 2:853; Jewett, *Romans*, 895–96.

250. Flebbe, *Solus Deus*, 429.

251. See Barclay, *Gift*, 551n75, for a critique of Christine Johnson-Hodge's view that the Gentiles are aggregated to Israel as distinct peoples of the God of Israel.

but highlighting aspects already present in that tradition and drawing them out still further and more sharply perhaps than hitherto.[252]

Secondly, Genesis 15:6 and Habakkuk 2:4 are once again key texts. Both occur in Galatians 3, at verses 6 and 11 respectively. In Romans, the Habakkuk quotation figures in the prothesis or heading of Romans at 1:16-17, but not in chapter 4, where Paul specifically used Abraham. In addition in Romans, Paul links Genesis 15:6 with Psalm 32:1-2 (via the word λογιζεσθαι). As to the actual use of Genesis 15:6, in Galatians 3 Paul concentrated more on "believed"[253] from Genesis 15:6 rather than λογιζεσθαι.[254] In Romans 4 both ideas are given good coverage. Thus, in verses 4-12, 23-25, Paul focused more on λογιζεσθαι (eleven times in all), while the verb to believe occurs six times (three times in vv. 1-12; three times in vv. 13-25) and the noun πιστις occurs 10 times (four times in vv. 1-12; six times in vv. 13-25).

Paul used the promise which God made to Abraham in Genesis that in him all the nations would be blessed. This occurred at Galatians 3:8 and is a blend of Genesis 12:3 and 18:18. This indicated the universal implications of God's purposes. This text is not used in Romans 4, but there, at verses 17-18, Genesis 17:5 is utilized: "I have appointed you the father of many nations." In 4:18 Paul used the phrase from Genesis 15:5: "So shall your seed be." Galatians uses neither Genesis 17:5 nor 15:5. Koch has pointed to the fact that in Romans 4 Paul supported his argument by reference to Genesis 15-17 in such a way that the flow of his argument as a whole is closer to the text than in Galatians 3.[255]

Paul did not replicate the seed = Christ interpretation found at Galatians 3:16. The seed of Abraham in Romans 4 comprises both Jewish and Gentile believers (4:11, 16).

Thirdly, there is in Romans 4 far more detail about Abraham himself. Whereas in Galatians Paul assumed a fair degree of knowledge about the patriarch, in Romans Paul was far more explicit that Abraham exercised faith in God's promise while he was uncircumcised and went into what function circumcision had (4:8-10). We learn explicitly that Abraham was old, that his body was as good as dead, he being a hundred years old, and that Sarah was barren (4:19). We learn that Abraham believed that God was able to

---

252. As Flebbe, *Solus Deus* (e.g., 316, 329, 353-54, 380), never tires of stressing. See also Barclay, *Gift*, 491, where he says that there is nothing inherently "un-Jewish" about Paul's theology in the matter of grace: "He is part of a contemporary Jewish debate about the operation of divine mercy and gift."

253. With, for him, its opposite principle ποιειν.

254. The statistics for Galatians 3 are: the verb πιστευειν occurs one time and the noun πιστις fourteen times, while λογιζεσθαι occurs only once.

255. Koch, *Schrift*, 97.

quicken the dead and call into being what did not exist, and so he hoped against hope that he would be the father of many nations, as God promised (4:17). He did not waver in unbelief but his faith grew stronger, because he was fully convinced that God was able to do what He had promised (4:21). This leads on naturally to the next point.

In the fourth place, faith is crucial in drawing out the implications of the story of Abraham. According to Galatians, faith was the criterion for being a child of Abraham: "Those of faith are the sons of Abraham . . . so then those of faith are blessed with believing Abraham" (3:7, 9). In Romans, the focus is on Abraham's fatherhood and the example of faith which he had set. He is the father of all who believe, whether circumcised or uncircumcised, Jew or Gentile (4:11c–12, 16cd). Following in the footsteps of his faith is crucial.

The flow of the argument in Romans 4 is somewhat more theocentric than in Galatians 3.[256] Beker maintains that in Galatians the object of faith is Christ (2:16, 19; 3:8, 14, 22, 23–24), while God is the object of faith in Romans 4.[257] Indeed, Christ is not mentioned in Romans 4 until at the end of the discussion, and then the emphasis is on God's having raised him from the dead. Nonetheless, the hearer/reader of Romans would be well aware of the Christological reference of faith from 3:21–26.

Fifthly, the promise-Law contrast observed in Galatians also occurs in Romans. In Romans 4:13–16b, the promise was that Abraham and his descendants should inherit the world, and it came about in conjunction with the declaration that Abraham was in a right relationship with God on the basis of his faith, and not linked with the law (4:13). Paul then set forth what would be the consequences if οι εκ νομου were designated the heirs of the promise: it would empty faith of any significance and nullify the promise (v. 14), and would remove God's grace as the cause of our receiving the promise (v. 16). Later, Paul said that Abraham did not waver in his faith and doubt God's promise despite his age and Sarah's barrenness, because he was convinced that God was able to do what He had promised (vv. 20–21). There is a more elaborated argument in Galatians concerning the promise(s). Paul is concerned to deny that the giving of the Law at a later date altered the character of the promise in any way (Gal 3:16–22). In Galatians he mentioned receiving the promised Spirit by faith (3:14).

The negative aspect of the Law is not so elaborated upon in Romans as in Galatians,[258] but Paul did say that it "works wrath" because it estab-

---

256. Stressed very much by Flebbe, *Solus Deus*, 165n9, 183, 215, 267.
257. Beker, *Paul*, 103.
258. Though even in Galatians Paul was keen to affirm that the Law is not against

lished transgressions (4:15). Later he said that the Law came in alongside the promise to increase sin (5:20; cf. 7:5), and in chapter 7 he depicted sin as using the Law as a bridgehead to attack us and stimulate us to sin (7:7–11). The imagery of the Law as a jailor which is present in Galatians is latent in the phrase εν ω κατειχομεθα ("by which we were held bound")[259] in Romans 7:6, while according to 8:2 it brings about sin and death.

Over against this, Paul affirms in Romans that the Law is holy and the commandment is holy, righteous, and good (7:12). The Law is spiritual (7:14). It witnesses to justification by grace through faith (3:21; cf. 3:31). The Law is summed up in "Love your neighbor as yourself." Love is the fulfillment of the Law (13:8–10), as in Galatians 5:14. The negative side is balanced by the positive aspects of the Law.[260] And we must never forget that Genesis 12–25 is part of the Law!

Before we leave this point, we need to look more closely at what precisely is the content of the promise in the two letters. In Galatians, the plural "promises" occurs at 3:16, 21, and the singular at verses 17, 18 (twice), and 22. According to 3:21, 23, and 25, Paul said that if a Law which conveyed life could have been given, truly righteousness would have been (given) on the basis of the Law. The parallelism between "making alive" and "righteousness" suggests that Paul was thinking of that right relationship which depends on the life-giving power of God, i.e., justification and the gift of the Spirit. This is confirmed by the fact that in verses 23–25 Paul went on to say that the realisation of the promise had to wait till Christ (faith) arrived.

In Romans 4:16 Paul said that the promise to Abraham and his seed was that he should be heir of the world. Cranfield[261] and Dunn[262] suggested that Paul was thinking of the restoration of man's inheritance lost through sin, i.e., restoration of man to his Adamic status as steward of God's creation over against a more nationalistic understanding of the promise. Käsemann[263] thinks that the world to come is in mind, and Ziesler[264] mentions this possibility. However, a little later in chapter 4, Paul referred to Abraham's believing that God had promised that he should be the father of many nations (vv. 17–18). Here the thought was that Abraham's descendants

---

the promise (3:21) and stated that love was the fulfillment of the Law (5:14).

259. The JB renders "freed by death from our imprisonment."

260. Rather than saying that Paul changed his mind between Galatians and Romans (so, e.g., Drane; Hubner), it is better to say that his view of the Law in Romans is more differentiated—so, e.g., Theobald, "Verantwortung vor der Vergangenheit," 22–23.

261. Cranfield, *Romans*, 1:240.

262. Dunn, *Romans*, 1:213.

263. Käsemann, *Romans*, 120.

264. Ziesler, *Romans*, 129.

should include many nations and thus the way was open to relating it to the fact that on the contemporary scene the gospel was making converts from all nations of the world.

Sixthly, we may mention that whereas in Galatians Paul ignored any reference to the circumcision of Abraham (Gen 17), in Romans 4:9-12, he raised the question of the time of "the reckoning of righteousness" to Abraham, and pointed out that it occurred before he was circumcised. Circumcision is interpreted positively as a confirmatory seal of the righteousness already granted to him when he was uncircumcised.

Seventhly, the redemptive death of Jesus on the cross/tree is mentioned in Galatians 3 as the basis on which the blessing for the Gentiles promised to Abraham could materialize (3:13–14). The recipients of Romans would come to the passage about Abraham after having heard/read the exposition of the death of Jesus in 3:21–26, while at the end of the chapter there is a reference to the fact that Jesus was delivered up for our transgressions (4:25a) and in chapter 5 there are references to the death of Christ as an illustration of God's love and the means of reconciliation with God, followed by the contrast between Adam and Christ in which Christ's act of obedience (on the cross) completely reversed the consequences of Adam's sin.

In Romans 4, there is a major stress on God's power to give life and to raise from the dead and this provides the analogy between the gift of a son to Abraham and Sarah on the one hand and the resurrection of Jesus from the dead on the other (4:17b–25). In the Galatians passage, Paul went on to speak of the gift of the Spirit as a result of Jesus' curse-bearing death. There is no such allusion in Romans 4, though the Spirit dominates the discussion in Romans 8, and 8:4 speaks of God's condemning sin in the flesh of Jesus.

Eighthly, the use of Abraham in Romans 9 offers some points of contact with the Hagar-Sarah allegory in Galatians 4:21–5:1. In Romans 9, Paul also used the expression "children of promise." At 9:7, he said that not all Abraham's children were his seed. He then quoted Genesis 21:12: "In Isaac shall your seed be called." This then enabled him, without fear of misunderstanding, to go on to say that it was not the children born as a result of the flesh/physical effort (τα τεκνης της σαρκος) who were the children of God, but it was children born as a result of the promise (τα τεκνα της επαγγελιας) who were reckoned as Abraham's seed (9:8). God's elective purpose worked through Isaac at the beginning of Israel's history. Paul used Isaac to establish the principle that God's elective purpose was present from the start in Israel's story, for God chose Isaac, not Ishmael, though both were sons of Abraham.

In Galatians 4, Paul contrasted Hagar's son, Ishmael, born κατα σαρκα, and Isaac, Sarah's son, born δι'επαγγελιας. Paul's equation of non-believing Jews with Ishmael, as children κατα σαρκα, would have been very offensive to Jewish ears. Isaac, on the other hand, became a representative of Christians who live by the promise, which had now been fulfilled in Christ in Paul's day.[265]

There are, then, differing emphases in the use of "children of promise" in the two letters.

The theme of freedom runs through Galatians 4. Thus, Sarah is the free woman; the Jerusalem above is free; Christians are children of Sarah the free woman; with the culmination in the appeal, based on Christ's liberating work, to stand fast in the freedom of Christ. But it does not figure in Romans 4 and 9. It does figure in the theme of being set free from sin and death in Romans 8:2, "For the law of the Spirit of life in Christ Jesus has set you free [ηλευθερωσεν] from the Law of sin and death" (cf. 6:18, 21: "set free from sin and become slaves of God"), and indeed in the cosmic thought that at the End the whole of creation would be set free from its bondage to decay and enjoy the glorious liberty of the children of God (8:18-23).

Finally, in Galatians the Gentiles are so prominent in the discussion that the question and problem of Israel is not really handled. In Romans, while the issue of whether the Gentiles can be members of the one people of salvation is a key topic, so also is the position of Israel, who had received such great promises in the past from God but who in Paul's view were now in a position of being under the wrath and judgment of God and, therefore, salvation-less. Paul handled this question in great detail in Romans 9-11. The problem of Israel is, of course, a problem about God, His purposes, His consistency.[266]

The difference of emphasis which scholars have argued for between the two letters may be accounted for by observing the purpose behind them.[267] In Galatians Paul is overtly polemical and combative. The Letter may rightly be classified as a "polemical letter." By contrast, Paul in Romans is seeking to persuade the Christians at Rome to stand with him, both now and in the immediate future with their prayers of intercession, and, in the long term, with support for his proposed mission to Spain and the western end of the Mediterranean (15:23-32). Paul set out his gospel, and sought to meet the objections raised against it by his critics, in order that the Roman Christians might be "on his side." In this way, the main body of Romans coheres with

---

265. See Schmitt, *Gerechtigkeit*, 82-83, for a discussion of the different emphases in the use of Isaac in Galatians 4 and Romans 9.

266. Rightly stressed throughout his work by Flebbe, *Solus Deus*.

267. Thus, e.g., Beker, *Paul*, 97, 99-100, thinks that Galatians emphasizes the discontinuity, while Romans stresses the continuity in salvation-history. Lincoln, *Predecessors*, 191, concurs.

the announcement of his plans made at the end of the letter, as Wilckens has argued. He suggests that Romans is a repetition of Galatians with new reflection demanded by the need to justify himself over against his Jewish Christian critics during his imminent visit to Jerusalem, lest the unity of Jewish and Gentile Christians (of which the Collection stood as a potent symbol for Paul) should break apart through disagreement in Jerusalem.[268]

If Paul wished to persuade his own people that Jesus was the promised redeemer from Zion, he would have to do so on the basis of Scripture. Abraham, as the father of the nation and a figure highly respected and revered on many accounts, was going to be a crucial "battle ground." If Paul could not square faith in Jesus with Abraham, he could not hope to succeed in his heart-felt desire to convince his fellow countrymen and women of the truth of the gospel.

The story of Abraham provided Paul with the raw materials, but it was his experience of God in and through the risen Jesus which provided what we call "the hermeneutical key" by which to approach the "raw material" of tradition. Tradition took on a new meaning in light of Jesus, crucified and risen. This assertion needs to be explained further. Flebbe has stressed that Paul argued in Romans 4 on the basis of Scripture and Tradition, and not on the basis of Christology. This tradition was not monolithic but diverse, and Paul can accentuate or sharpen particular aspects of that rich and varied tradition. But we still have to ask why Paul chose to accentuate and sharpen what he did. What impelled him to exegete the story of Abraham the way in which he did? Was it not his own experience of the grace of God to him, a persecutor of the church of God and a rebel against God's purposes in Jesus? His own experience chimed in with particular strands in the Scriptures and traditions of his people. May we not say that Christology and soteriology are the sub-structure of what he says about Abraham and his paradigmatic value for understanding God's ways from time immemorial?

The story of Abraham became the paradigm of how God wished to deal with the human race. Paul discerned a pattern: first, God's grace (in the case of Abraham a word of promise or words of promises), then the human response of accepting in trust what God had said in His promise(s) and, without wavering from that trust, living in the light of that promise.

---

268. Wilckens, *Rechtfertigung*, 110–66, esp. 138–39, 142–43. Cf. the way Luz, *Geschichtsverständnis*, 285–86, explains the difference between Galatians 3–4 and Romans 9:1-5; 11:16-32 concerning the position of Israel and the idea of the people of God. In Galatians Judaism is repudiated because grace is the sole means of access to God, not through the Law, the way which Israel has chosen; whereas in Romans Paul must, against Gentiles' taking their standing in grace as self-evident, assert the radical nature of God's grace and the continuity of God's activity in His dealings with Israel. Luz puts it epigrammatically: Paul can say contradictory things in order to say the same thing.

Abraham's position was such that he could not contribute (as it were) to the implementation of the promise. The realization of the promise depended on God and on Him alone. Just so, humanity, guilty before the bar of divine judgment and in bondage to the sway of sin/Sin, Jew no less than Gentile, is unable to rectify its parlous position before God. Only God in His grace can so act to overcome the guilt, the alienation, the captivity, of human beings. That is precisely what He has done in Jesus of Nazareth, His Son and Messiah, in his death on the cross and in raising him from the dead. God has acquitted human beings and set us free to love and serve Him, Gentiles as much as Jews. What so many of Paul's contemporaries expected at the End had already occurred in advance of that End.

The text "Abraham believed God and it was reckoned to him for righteousness" of Genesis 15:6 became a crucial text for the apostle. He could use its temporal priority in the biblical narrative to affirm the priority of faith over circumcision and the Law. It encapsulated the pattern of which we have just spoken: the grace of God in His promises and the trusting acceptance of that from Abraham's side.

Men and women in Paul's day confronted with the gospel were faced with the declaration that God had already acted to put men and women in the right with Himself. The gospel promised them forgiveness and reconciliation with God and incorporation into the people of God. They were faced with the decision whether to believe that this message was the power of God leading to salvation and to membership of a people which embraced erstwhile enemies, Jews and Gentiles, into one body, a message which indeed had implications for the whole cosmos (Rom 8). This gospel message was offered to all. Once again, the story of Abraham afforded crucial "evidence" for Paul. God had declared to Abraham that in and through him and his descendants all the peoples of the world would be blessed and that Abraham would be the father of many nations. For Paul these promises were being fulfilled as the gospel went out into the world: offered to the Jew first and then to the Gentiles. The gospel was the vehicle of divine blessing to all who would believe. Whether it was the blessing of justification/forgiveness, the gift of the Spirit, spiritual freedom, membership of God's people, God had fulfilled and was fulfilling His ancient promises, and had proved Himself the reliable and trustworthy God. What He had promised to Abraham and the other patriarchs had been confirmed and Gentiles were being brought in to join His ancient people in worship, praise, and service (Rom 15:7-12).[269]

---

269. Wieser, *Abrahamvorstellungen*, 82, observes that it is the divine word of justification which is the divine word which begets the promised descendants of Abraham.

Not only did Paul use the Abraham story to defend his gospel of God's grace to all, irrespective of race, independent of keeping the Law, but he also used the Abraham story to defend the faithfulness of God to the people of Israel. The divine purpose of mercy, mercy for all, would in the end triumph even over Israel's obduracy of heart and disobedience. God corralled the Gentiles into disobedience while Israel received the blessing of His election; now Israel was undergoing a period of disobedience while the Gentiles were receiving the gospel. But in the end God's purpose would win out and all Israel too would be saved. God's purposes had not failed and they would not.[270]

Excursus: *The Meaning of* πιστις Ιησου Χριστου *in Galatians and Romans*

The debate over the meaning of this Greek phrase has recently flared up again.[271] Is the genitive a subjective or objective one? That is, is the faith that of Jesus himself (subjective genitive), or is it the faith of believers in Jesus (objective genitive)? We shall review the arguments and seek to assess their weight.

Firstly, there is a general point. It is maintained that Paul could have expressed himself more clearly if he intended the believer's faith in Jesus. Thus, some scholars point to Romans 4:12 where the phrase της πιστεως του πατρος ημων Αβρααμ quite clearly refers to Abraham's own faith (cf. 4:16, too); so, why should not πιστις χριστου refer to Jesus' own faith? In response, it is pointed out that in Mark 11:22 the command of Jesus runs: εχετε πιστιν Θεου, where the meaning is clearly to have faith in God, not imitate His faithfulness. This, of course, may indicate that context is all important in deciding the meaning of the genitive in this phrase, as in everything. Then again, Jesus Christ is never found in Paul as the subject of the verb πιστευειν,

---

270. Wieser, *Abrahamvorstellungen*, 75, has maintained that Gospel and Election are according to form and content the same. God's faithfulness to His word in electing Israel guarantees also the trustworthiness of the Gospel; the goal of God's gracious activity is a saved people greater than Israel, in which the election of Israel finds its culmination.

271. There is a helpful setting out of the arguments on both sides in the exchange of views between Hays and Dunn in Hays, *Faith of Jesus Christ*, 19–62, 249–97, and the useful collection of essays in Bird and Sprinkle, *Faith of Jesus Christ*. Ulrichs, *Christusglaube*, deals with the issue in a highly competent manner, as one could expect from someone trained in classical philology and philosophy in addition to theology, and decides for an objective understanding. It is a pity that the contributors to the volume edited by Bird and Sprinkle did not engage with Ulrichs's treatment of the subject.

nor is the adjective πιστος applied to him.²⁷² It has also been pointed out that the connotations and associations of the titles which Paul uses for Jesus do not make us think of the faith of Jesus. Thus, for example, Χριστος is used particularly in association with the death and resurrection of Jesus.²⁷³ Rather striking is the fact that early Christian writers like Origen and John Chrysostom assume that the phrase is an objective genitive without any discussion.²⁷⁴ Due weight should be given to this, since Greek was the native language of such men. In addition, the Arians based their idea of the personal faith of Jesus on Hebrews 3:2, not on any Pauline text.²⁷⁵

Secondly, some scholars have argued that Paul interpreted the phrase ο δικαιος εκ πιστεως in Habakkuk 2:4 LXX messianically,²⁷⁶ and from that go on to assert that when Paul used the phrase πιστις Ιησου Χριστου he was referring to the personal faith of Jesus.²⁷⁷ On the other side, it is pointed out that "it was reckoned to him for righteousness" was not applied to Jesus. Furthermore, it is suggested that Paul has formulated the phrase under discussion to balance εξ εργων νομου (e.g., Gal 2:16; Rom 3:20, 22),²⁷⁸ or, alternatively, that the influence of the Habakkuk 2:4 quotation has generated the instrumental use of either εκ or δια with πιστις.²⁷⁹

Thirdly, on a syntactical level, Porter and Pitts have maintained that while oblique cases [here, the genitive case] restrict the meaning of the head term [here, faith], they do not determine it. They maintain that a preposition with an anarthous πιστις [head term] with the genitive carries an abstract sense unrelated to the explicit participant in the discourse [here, Jesus]: that is, Jesus Christ is the proper object of faith, and "faithfulness" is not the meaning.²⁸⁰

---

272. Ulrichs, *Christusglaube*, 100, 144, 165, has pointed to instances where, if the faith of Jesus personally were in Paul's mind, it is strange that he did not use αυτου, since Jesus Christ is mentioned in the near context (Gal 3:14, 24; Rom 3:25a).

273. Ulrichs, *Christusglaube*, 36-37, 54. Paul does speak of the obedience of Jesus (Rom 5:19; Phil 2:8), but while obedience is linked with faith by Paul when speaking of believers, it would be unwise, to say the least, to claim that he had in mind the personal faith of Jesus when he did refer to his obedience.

274. E.g., Matlock, *Saving Faith*, 86-88.

275. Cf. Matlock, *Saving Faith*, 87.

276. Before Hays, *Faith of Jesus Christ*, 134-38, Hanson, *Studies*, 42-45, had advocated this interpretation.

277. E.g., Hays, *Faith of Jesus Christ*, 134-38; *Apocalyptic Hermeneutics*, 119-42.

278. Dunn, *Once More*.

279. Watson, *PJG*, 233-41.

280. Porter and Pitts in Bird and Sprinkle, *Faith of Jesus Christ*, 33-53.

The issue of the non-use of the article has played a part in the discussion. It has been claimed that since the article regularly appears with the subjective genitive, its absence points to an objective genitive. But this has been shown to be inaccurate, and Ulrichs has demonstrated that certain nouns in Paul are followed both by objective and subjective genitives.[281]

Fourthly, many scholars argue that the contexts in which the formula πιστις with Ιησου or Ιησου Χριστου appear to favor the objective sense. That is to say, when Paul is talking about human sin, God's promise, and the way of justification through God's grace offered to men and women, he used the formula to give weight to his justification statements. This is the case with Galatians 2:16, 20; 3:22; Romans 3:22, 26; and Philippians 3:9–10.[282] We may add that if one of the reasons for Paul's turning to Abraham in Romans 4 was to support his arguments in 3:21–31 (even if not the whole reason), then the fact that the faith spoken of throughout chapter 4 is the faith exercised by Abraham, does not this lend support to the fact that faith exercised by believers is of vital significance in the discussion of 3:21–31? And, however we interpret the phrase "the law of faith" in 3:27, it can hardly be taken as a personal reference to Jesus himself.

Fifthly, scholars in favor of the subjective genitive argue that at both Galatians 3:22 and Romans 3:22 to take the phrase as an objective genitive would simply be a case of unnecessary redundancy, since in both these texts Paul refers to (all) those who believe (using the articular participle construction).[283] Against this it is pointed out that "Paul did not share our aversion to repetition,"[284] and/or that Paul has included both the phrase under consideration and a further reference to (all) those who believe for the sake of emphasis. The term "maximal redundancy," drawn from literary criticism, is used to cover this sense of a reasonable repetition which should not be branded as tautology.

Matlock has pointed to what he maintains is the equivalence of πιστις and πιστευειν in Paul's arguments. Thus, in Romans 4, Paul can use the verb "Abraham believed" in quoting Genesis 15:6 in verse 3, while he speaks of the faith which was reckoned as righteousness to Abraham when quoting the same verse from Genesis in verse 9.[285] Then Matlock turns to

281. Ulrichs, *Christusglaube*, 25–29: examples are grace, revelation, Christ. At Philippians 1:27, there is an objective genitive with the article: the faith of the gospel.

282. Ulrichs, *Christusglaube*, 41–42.

283. E.g., Hays, *Faith of Jesus Christ*, 158.

284. Hunn, *Debating the Faithfulness*, 23. Watson, *PJG*, 243–44n55, points to the adjacent rhetorical redundancy of εις ενδειξιν της δικαιοσθνης αυτου and προς την ενδειξιν της δικαιοσυνης αυτου in Romans 3:25–26!

285. Watson, *PJG*, 242–43, 324, agrees with this argument, and also points to

the passages where others claim that there would be redundancy if the objective sense of πιστις Ιησου Χριστου is read, and asks what semantic force do these additional phrases employing the verb πιστευειν exert on the phrase πιστις Ιησου Χριστου? He believes that given the equivalence of meaning between verb and noun, an objective genitive sense to our phrase becomes very likely. Ulrichs has, however, maintained a different position on why Paul used the verb and noun in close proximity. He suggests that Paul felt that the verb πιστευειν was not sufficiently precise in everyday Greek to convey what he wanted to say.[286] Paul, therefore, employed the noun πιστις to ensure what he intended to say.

Sixthly, those who argue for a subjective genitive maintain strongly that it does not make sense to say that the Righteousness of God is revealed through our faith (in reference to Paul's argument at 3:22). It is far more satisfactory to believe that Paul was saying that the Righteousness of God was revealed through the faith/faithfulness of Jesus Christ.[287] It is interesting to read the comments of scholars who favor an objective genitive on a text like Romans 3:22. Many speak about God's activity in setting us in the right with Himself and this becomes effective[288] or active through faith; it reaches its goal in the faith of men and women; it imparts itself by means of faith in Jesus Christ to all, for all are called to believe. Or if the Righteousness of God is taken in the sense of a gift from God, then this is given to or received by means of, faith. What emerges is that when commentating on Romans 3:22, most commentators do not feel compelled to carry over πεφανερωται from verse 21 into the verbless appositional clause of verse 22, and feel that they can paraphrase to get what they assume to be the sense of verse 22. These paraphrases in no way make faith the means of revealing the Righteousness of God but rather the means of appropriating or receiving

---

similar phenomena in Romans 9:32-33, where the ο πιστευων in the quotation from Isaiah 28:16 and the πιστις of Paul's comment in verse 32 carry the same sense, and Romans 10:16-17, where the verb and noun are both elicited by the message. In neither case is the faithfulness of Jesus in mind.

286. Ulrichs, *Christusglaube*, 76, 96, 105, 112, 150, 178. Galatians 2:16 is the first occurrence of the phrase πιστις Ιησου Χριστου. Before that, the verb had been used only once, at 2:7, where Paul said that he had been entrusted (πεπιστευμαι) with the gospel to the non-Jew (the uncircumcised). For a similar type of statement, see the earlier letter, 1 Thess 2:4. For other non-theological uses, Ulrichs lists 1 Cor 9.17, 13.7, Rom 3:2; 14:2; John 9:18.

287. Ulrichs, *Christusglaube*, 169, has in response asked how the righteousness of God is revealed by Jesus' faith/faithfulness?

288. Cf. the NEB/NRB translation. The NRSV translates literally without supplying any verb.

it. While the initiative always lies with God, faith is the channel by which access to what God has done and given us is opened up.

Finally, we may mention the question raised by some of the supporters of the objective genitive interpretation: how is sin dealt with on the subjective interpretation? They argue that the cross seems to be less important than Jesus' relationship with God which reveals itself in the cross.

The above review of the arguments seems to me on balance to leave the scales still tilting in favor of the objective genitive position, and Ulrichs's closely argued monograph has put this case on an extremely sound footing.

Excursus: Has Paul Paganized the History of Israel?

1. Overview of Contrasting Approaches

During many years of the twentieth century, there was disagreement between those on the one hand who espoused the existentialist approach to the study of the NT, with a deep suspicion of the idea that revelation takes place within history and is, therefore, exposed to the vagaries of historical criticism, and those on the other hand who argued for the Salvation-History approach, which maintains that God's revealing and saving action is rooted in history, beginning with the election of Israel in the call of Abraham, through the story of Israel, culminating in the ministry of Jesus of Nazareth, his death and resurrection, and the gift of the Holy Spirit, and then widening out to include the Gentile world, until the Parousia and the ultimate triumph of God's rule.

In the immediate post second world war years, Cullmann represented the Salvation History approach over against Bultmann's and others' distrust of history and stress on the Kerygma and faith. Then in the early 1960s there was a contre-temps between Ulrich Wilckens (representing the Pannenburg School) and Gunter Klein (whose stance can be described as influenced by the existentialist approach).[289] It was Klein who used the language contained

---

289. The sequence of articles was as follows. Wilckens wrote "Die Rechtfertigung Abrahams nach Römer 4" in 1961. Klein wrote "Römer 4 und die Idee der Heilsgeschichte" in 1963 (in which he referred to Wilckens's article) and he also wrote "Individualgeschichte und Weltgeschichte bei Paulus" early in 1964. Wilckens replied with "Zu Römer 3:22–4:25: Antwort an G. Klein." This elicited "Exegetische Probleme in Römer 3:21–4:25: Antwort an U. Wilckens" in the same year by Klein. Klein published a summary in the form of his main theses in a short article entitled "Heil und Geschichte nach Römer iv" (1967). The two articles by Wilckens were reprinted in his *Rechtfertigung als Freiheit*, and all Klein's articles, except the short NTS contribution, in his *Rekonstruktion und Interpretation*. Other scholars joined in, e.g., Kümmel, "'Individualgeschichte' und 'Weltgeschichte'" (1973); Goppelt, "Paulus und Heilsgeschichte"

in the heading of this excursus that Paul had desacralized the history of Israel. He also used "paganized" and "brutalized," language which Wilckens, not surprisingly, considered very inappropriate.[290]

This "spat" might seem to have been confined to the German university faculties, for it does not seem to have influenced English speaking scholarship.[291] Yet in a sense the issue has had a recrudescence in the work of J. L. Martin, who denied that Paul worked with a linear approach and emphasized that the apostle held to an unprecedented "apocalyptic" divine invasion in saving grace in the ministry of Jesus of Nazareth. In addition, two volumes of essays by British and American scholars have appeared, many of which have been devoted to whether or not Paul held a Salvation-History approach, or, to use different terminology, whether a story or narrative undergirded the apostle's theological statements: viz. volume 1 of *Pauline Theology*, edited by Jouette M. Bassler,[292] and *Narrative Dynamics in Paul*, edited by B. W. Longenecker.[293]

2. General Considerations

We may begin with some general comments. Firstly, we need to bear in mind the rhetorical aims of a particular writing in the NT. These are different in the case of Galatians and Romans, and this has bearing on how we might assess, for example, the assertion that Christ is the sole seed of Abraham in Galatians 3:16, or that Hagar represents contemporary Judaism/Jerusalem in Galatians 4:21-31.

Secondly, the use of analogy and typology calls for comment. Analogy works from something known either from the personal experience of the readers or auditors or knowledge of events from past history, in order to illuminate for them something else which the author feels needs explaining. Usually, the thing known is known from past experience, whereas the thing which needs explaining is something new/unusual in the present or immediate past. Context alone can indicate whether the writer is assuming a line between the illustration and the event or situation which is being illustrated

---

(1966-67).

290. Wilckens, *Rechtfertigung*, 59-60n10.

291. E.g., Neither Dunn nor Witherington discuss Klein's thesis in their commentaries on Galatians, and while Cranfield mentioned it in a footnote in his commentary on Romans, he made no attempt to engage with Klein's viewpoint, though it is clear that he would have certainly rejected it.

292. For contributions by Martyn, Scroggs, and Lull, see bibliography.

293. For contributions by Hooker, Dunn, Barclay, Horrell, Lincoln, and Marshall, see bibliography.

by the analogy. We may assume that in 1 Corinthians 10 Paul did have in mind the fact that the Israelites in the desert were the people of God, and that they provided a negative example of what ought to be avoided by Christians of Paul's day who had been made members of God's people by God's gracious redemptive action in Jesus Christ and the gift of the Spirit.[294] But in the case of the illustration of labor pains coming upon a pregnant woman (1 Thess 5:3) or the boxing athletic analogy (1 Cor 9:26), there is obviously no historical linkage. The actual literary form of analogy is not intended, of itself, to indicate a historical line between the analogy and the situation of the addressees. Context must do that.

As regards typology, once again this does not of itself indicate a line between the events in the past and the present.[295] In the case of the Adam-Christ passage in Romans, the context is significant.[296] Paul said that sin and death entered the world through the transgression of Adam, and then stated that death came upon everyone because[297] all had sinned (Rom 5:12). Thus, Paul left the two statements side by side. Adam sinned, and, as a result, death gained entry; every one sins and suffers death. Human beings have endorsed by their own choices the pattern of behavior of their primeval ancestor: all have sinned (Rom 3:23). But he went on to postulate some connection between Adam and all his subsequent descendants. There is a corporate aspect of sin:[298] Adam's sin implicates us all (5:15b, 17). The larger context indicates the subsequent history. Paul, however, is not saying that God's grace was totally absent in the period between Adam and Christ.

Thirdly, we may ask whether in general Paul's criticism of Israel was any more harsh, abrasive, and insulting than when Isaiah called the Jerusalem authorities of his day rulers of Sodom and Gomorrah, or when the Qumran writers branded their contemporaries as sons of Belial or sons of darkness? The language of polemical confrontation in antiquity was far more forthright and robust than would be regarded as permissible in today's society.[299]

294. See the use made of this story in Hebrews 3.

295. Cullmann, *Salvation in History*, 132, made a similar point: "In typology, however, the connection is limited to the two points being dealt with. Those parts and members of the salvation history which fall in between the two points *are either passed over or are not considered in this manner of confrontation*" (my italics).

296. Luz, *Geschichtsverständnis*, 204-5, describes Romans 5:12-21 as the only time that history as a whole is in mind. It is a sketch of Unheil, yet also the place of divine grace. The Unheil serves to offset the certainty of salvation.

297. See Bauer, *Lexicon*, 287. Dunn, *Romans*, 1:290, however, urges caution and prefers the imprecise "in that."

298. Dunn, *Romans*, 1:274, speaks of the constraints of hereditary, educational, and other social conditioning factors.

299. One may wonder whether today we have gone too far in the opposite direction

3. Klein and Martyn

We may now briefly summarize the case put forward by Klein and Martyn as those who have been the major proponents of the case against a Salvation-History approach.[300]

Klein held to the view that the flow of time meant nothing to Paul. He sees a difference of assessment of history in Galatians 3:15 and 3:23.[301] In 3:15, there is a direct link between Abraham and Christians, whereas in 3:23 Paul envisaged successive historical eras, the Law and Faith eras. The indifference of historical distinctions in pre-believing humanity is illustrated by Galatians 4:3, where all, Jews and Gentiles, are said to have been slaves of τα στοιχεια. Klein deduces from all this that the flow of time as such presents no theological factor for Paul.[302]

Abrahamic sonship was based on faith in Jesus Christ. This concept of belonging to the descendants of Abraham through faith undermined the concept of the election of Israel based on descent from Abraham. In Romans 4 Abraham as a figure of past history plays no role. He is an illustration of a structural element of justification.[303] He is a model of faith, a timeless example.[304] There is no historical continuity between Abraham and Christians,[305] and there is no need for empirical Judaism or Jewish Christianity as a mediation between Abraham and believers.[306] The continuum between Abraham and believers rests on faith, not history.[307] This means the theological irrelevance of the course of history and any notion of salvation-history. Klein also fastened on to the words of the quotation from Isaiah 54:1 at Galatians 4:27, and took this to mean that the barren woman had not borne any children in the pre-Christian era, which for Klein confirms his argument that there is no Abrahamic sonship before Christ.[308]

---

and whether some people can be somewhat too quick to take offense and cry "foul"!

300. Some others in varying degrees include, e.g., Kümmel, Goppelt, Luz, B. W. Longenecker, Barclay, and Watson (see bibliography for details). Those who support the view that Paul espoused a salvation history perspective include Käsemann, Scroggs, Lull, Hooker, Dunn, Horrell, Lincoln, and Marshall (details in the bibliography)

301. Klein, *Rekonstruktion*, 213.
302. Klein, *Rekonstruktion*, 214.
303. Klein, *Rekonstruktion*, 153.
304. Klein, *Rekonstruktion*, 163.
305. Klein, *Rekonstruktion*, 157.
306. Klein, *Rekonstruktion*, 155
307. Klein, *Rekonstruktion*, 163.
308. Klein, *Rekonstruktion*, 216.

Similarly, since the righteousness of God was identical with the death of Jesus on the cross, how could there be any salvation before this event and how can Abraham be introduced as Scriptural proof for that righteousness of God when he lived at a time when the righteousness of God was not experienced?[309]

The Law constituted the essence of Israel's existence, yet Paul disputed the divine origin of the law in Galatians 3:19 and 4:9-10. Even the Law is said to be the sphere of power of τα στοιχεια (Gal 4:9-10), according to Klein's exegesis of these passages. Klein maintained that Paul had reduced the significance of circumcision to something purely ethnological and secular, according to his exegesis of Rom 4:9-12.

In conclusion, we may mention that for Klein the sole continuum between Abraham and the present event of salvation is the Word, and the Word become Scripture. He believes that at Galatians 3:9 the receiving of the blessing by Abraham and believers is treated by Paul like a contemporary event.[310] When he says that the now (νυνι) of Romans 3:21 will never become a past thing,[311] he presumably means that, in the ongoing preaching of the gospel, the righteousness of God in Jesus Christ continually faces the hearer and demands a decision from him/her (cf. Rom 1:16-17). We may affirm what Klein asserts, while rejecting what he denies. Paul holds together past and present. The righteousness of God revealed in the death and resurrection of Jesus Christ can never lose its quality as a past event, but equally, because of God's vindication of Jesus in the resurrection, the cross becomes at the same time something which confronts every hearer of the message of Christ crucified (it is the power of God which leads to salvation, as Rom 1:16-17; 1 Cor 1:18-25; 2:1-5 affirm).

Martyn characteristically lays all the emphasis on the apocalyptic divine incursion into this world in Jesus Christ. He maintained that Abraham is a distinctly punctiliar figure rather than a linear one in Galatians. The singularity of the seed in Galatians 3:16 is "anti-linear" as well as anti-plural: it spells the end of salvation history. There is "no linear preparatio evangelica, no saving linearity prior to Christ." There is "no indication of a covenant-created people of God during the time of the Law." In his

---

309. Klein, *Rekonstruktion*, 150-51. (In view of Paul's clear acquaintance with Isaiah 40-55, it seems strange that Klein assumes that for Paul the righteousness of God first appeared with Christ.) Cf. the position of Luz, *Geschichtsverständnis*, 182-85, who maintains that history after Abraham is withdrawn directly from the visible effectiveness of the previously given promise, though even he admits the unity of God's saving action (*Geschichtsverständnis*, 82).

310. Klein, *Rekonstruktion*, 205.

311. Klein, *Rekonstruktion*, 147.

comments on 4:21–5:1, Martyn reiterates his previous assertions. Continuity is to be found only in God and His saving deed, not in the creation of a historical linearity. He speaks of Paul's by-passing the history of Israel in order to speak of the eschatological purpose of God. Paul is anti-salvation history. For Martyn, covenantal nomism and salvation history are characteristic of the message of the "Teachers" (which is Martyn's term for those whom Paul opposed in Galatians).[312]

4. Critique of Klein and Martyn

The first question to discuss is the assertion that Paul has desacralized or paganized Israel and debased the meaning of circumcision and whether this agrees with what Paul says.

In response, we begin, firstly, with the way Paul lists the *advantages* of Israel—twice in Romans, at 3:1-2 and 9:4-5. Then again, Paul asserts that the prophets announced beforehand the Gospel—Galatians 3:8 and Romans 1:3. That announcement, now enshrined in Scripture, offered the key to understanding what took place in the ministry of Jesus of Nazareth. Furthermore, Paul by his use of language drawn from Jeremiah 1:5 and Isaiah 49:1 to describe his call placed himself in the prophetic succession.

Then, secondly, Paul insisted that God had not rejected His people (Rom 11:1) and that God's calling and gifts were irrevocable (Rom 11:29).

In the third place, Paul asserted that God had exercised forbearance (ανοχη) towards sins previously committed, which would include Israel's sins, as a result of which God's name was blasphemed among non-Jews (Rom 2:17–24; 3:9, 25–26a).

Fourthly, when Paul said that Jesus was born under the Law to redeem those under the Law or that Jesus was a descendant of David (Gal 4:4–5; Rom 1:3, 9:5, 15:12), this implied that his ministry was, in part at any rate, aimed at redeeming the Jewish people, and also surely presupposed the election of Israel, to whom it was "natural" (so to speak) that God should send His Son in the first place. This does not suggest that God had written off His people; rather, it suggests continuing concern for and engagement with His people for their good.[313] This is confirmed by Romans 15:8 where Paul said that Christ became a διακονος of the Jewish people for the sake of the reliability of God and His promises (as well as ultimately that the Gentiles might join in praising God for His mercy). Also Paul recognized

---

312. Martyn, *Events in Galatia*, 60–79.

313. Bachmann, *Anti-Judaism*, 95, 105, 114, sees the fact that Paul refers to Jesus' being born under the Law as an indicator of God's positive dealings with Israel.

that God had given the ministry to the Jews to the apostle Peter (Gal 2:7–8), and expressed the hope that, even now in spite of the refusal of the majority of Jews to believe, there was the possibility that Israel might be grafted back into the olive tree (Rom 11:23).

Fifthly, here we might also mention the fact that Paul had a deep respect for Jerusalem, not just the mother church there, though that was important,[314] but Jerusalem as the spiritual center of the people of Israel. It is possible that one of the reasons for the Collection was that it aimed to move Israel to jealousy (cf. Rom 11:11) and bring her back into the family of God.[315] For Paul, at the end of all things, the Redeemer would come from Zion in order to turn ungodliness from Israel ("Jacob"). God's covenant with them remained: "This is my covenant with them when I take away their sins"[316] (Rom 11:26–27).

Sixthly, we may point out that Klein's exegesis leading to his assertions about Paul's attitude to the Law & circumcision is by no means convincing.[317]

Finally, we might add a further, if small, point from Romans. It is unlikely that Paul's concern for, and anguish over, his fellow country men and women (Rom 9:1–5; 10:1–2) was something which would have surfaced only suddenly as he was writing that letter, but would have been with him for a long time (1 Thess 2:14–16 not withstanding).

Cumulatively, these points tell decisively against Klein's suggestion that Paul had paganized the history of Israel. The evidence points to Paul's holding something like what we are accustomed to call the history of

---

314. Although he did not immediately visit Jerusalem after his experience on the Damascus Road (probably because he knew that his former associates would have regarded him as a renegade and apostate and as a consequence his life would be in danger), nevertheless it was important for him to be recognized by the Jerusalem Church leaders. The way in which Paul reported how the agreement with the Mother Church leaders was sealed is probably significant: he said that when the three pillar apostles (James, Cephas, and John) had recognized the grace of God given to him, they "gave the right hand of fellowship to me and Barnabas" (2:9). As Bachmann, *Anti-Judaism*, 106, has pointed out: "It was not the other way round (nor could it have been)."

315. There is the sheer amount of time and energy which he expended on the Collection (to which he had committed himself at Jerusalem, 2:10). Why did he bother, especially when we may legitimately surmise that it must have seemed at times to have been a distraction from his burning passion to preach the gospel of Jesus Christ? He clearly saw it as important in cementing relations between the churches of his mission and the mother church at Jerusalem; and he also saw it as something of an obligation for Gentile Christians to repay the Mother Church for having received the spiritual benefits of the Gospel (Rom 15:27).

316. Quotation from Isaiah 59:20–21. The reference to the taking away of sins could be something of an echo of Jeremiah 31:34.

317. See our discussion of the passages Galatians 3:19; 4:9–10; Romans 4:9–12.

salvation. Of course, we may agree wholeheartedly that this concept must not be taken in the sense of some evolutionary development within history or in some deterministic sense. Paul believed both that God had remained faithful to His promises through the story of Israel[318] and that room had to be left for God's sovereign intervention as and when He saw fit. These sovereign interventions, whether in judgment or salvation, created what we might call a crisis of decision for the people of Israel as a whole or individuals within it, to which they were required to respond with believing trust as Abraham had done.

We might argue that there is a dialectic in Paul's relationship to the traditions of Israel. On the one side, because the views of the Galatian agitators seemed to him to imperil the very heart of the gospel, he was compelled to attack their position with arguments which seem to denigrate the Law and, possibly, empirical Judaism; on the other hand, he knew full well that God had been at work in the history of Israel, beginning with Abraham, and that the coming of Jesus was not like some strange meteor invading our world, but rather "in the fullness of time" (Gal 4:4), at the moment for which God had planned and prepared and of which Scripture had already testified (3:8, 11). We may well feel that Klein has "homed in" on one side of this dialectic and not done justice to the other side.[319]

The second major question to be faced is *whether Paul did in fact see Abraham as a timeless example?*

We may say that Abraham is both an example and very much a historical figure. Paul does give some information about him and Sarah, in Galatians. He mentioned that he had two sons, one by a slave woman, Hagar (he does not use the name Ishmael for this son in either Galatians or Romans), another one by the "free woman" (he described Sarah in this way because he wished to develop the theme of slavery/freedom). We learn that her name was Sarah from Romans 4:19. We learn that Sarah had been childless and was past the normal age of child bearing before giving birth to Isaac (Rom 4:19). Paul noted Sarah's command to cast out Hagar and her son (Gal 4:30), with which God had concurred and emphasized that "for in Isaac your seed shall be called" (Gen 21:12), which Paul actually quoted at Romans 9:7.

---

318. One could speak of "a continuum of the faithfulness of God as the One who has brought the promises which He gave to Abraham into play in Christ eschatologically" (Schmitt, *Gottesgerectigkeit*, 33).

319. Cf. the statement of Luz, *Geschichtsverständnis*, 153, that Klein's concept of "profanisation" describes only one side of what happens with OT salvation history in the conversation with Judaism, viz. the destruction of a claimed sacred history, but does not take into consideration the "holiness" of this history and its claim. See also Schmitt, *Gottesgerechtigkeit*, 22, 31.

We learn that Abraham was not circumcised when he believed God's promise of a son and that he received circumcision as a seal of God's approval of his faith in believing God's promise (Rom 4:9-10). Abraham received the promise from God of numerous descendants and the assurance that he would be the father of many nations (Rom 4:18).

All this presupposes a knowledge of Genesis 12-24 on the part of those to whom Paul was writing in Galatia and Rome.

A comparison with Philo's portrait of Abraham is revealing. While clearly Philo accepted that Abraham was a real, historical person, the weight of Philo's emphasis in his picture is on Abraham as a paradigm of the journey of the soul in the quest for the knowledge of God's existence and of His divine providence. Paul does not let us forget that Abraham was a flesh and blood character, even though his story helps Christians to understand the meaning of righteousness and of faith (Rom 4:23-25).

A third major issue is *whether Paul leapt from Abraham to Jesus Christ (Gal 3:15) and thereby indicated that the intervening period possessed no significance?*

There are a number of passages where Paul indicated that God acted and intervened in this lengthy period. We begin, firstly, by noting that the righteousness of God had a "history" *before* Jesus and the cross. For example, in Second Isaiah God said that He was going to cause His righteousness to draw near, and His righteousness is set in parallel to His salvation (in context the liberation from exile and captivity in Babylon and the return home): 46:13; 51:5-6; cf. 45:21; and see also 56:1. Some of the Psalms mention the righteousness of God in the sense of His mighty acts (e.g., 85:9-13; 145:4-9).[320]

We may note, secondly, the implications of the promise to Abraham that he would have descendants as numerous as the stars in the heavens and that he would be the father of many nations (Gen 15:5; 17:5, respectively; both alluded to at Rom 4:17-18). This clearly envisages an extended future period under God's blessing.

Thirdly, Paul in Romans 9:6-18 mentioned that God chose Isaac, not Ishmael, and Jacob, not Esau, and that He brought Pharaoh on the historical scene to act as a foil to His deliverance of the Israelites from slavery and so demonstrate His power and cause His name to be proclaimed abroad in the earth.

In the fourth place, Paul maintained that the preexistent Christ accompanied the Israelites in their journey through the wilderness ("The

---

320. We do not need to discuss whether Second Isaiah was innovating and this influenced some psalmists, or whether he was influenced by a concept already present in Israel's worship.

Rock was Christ") and that the Israelites had in the passage through the Reed Sea and in the manna and water from the rock smitten by Moses a form of sacraments analogous to baptism and the Lord's Supper in the era of the Gospel (1 Cor 10:1-11).

Following on from the Wilderness experience, we may mention, fifthly, that Paul said that the covenant at Sinai and the giving of the Law, mediated through Moses, came "with glory," albeit a glory not comparable to the glory of the Gospel (2 Cor 3:9-11). Paul here asserts that God was present in His power at the giving of the covenant and law at Sinai. God gave the Law. Even the seemingly negative remarks about the Law's being a jailor to keep people in custody (Gal 3:22-24) show that God had not in fact abandoned Israel but was concerned for it and wished to keep it from going totally "off the rails," as we might say.[321]

Sixthly, in Romans 4:6-8, Paul stated that David enjoyed the blessing of forgiveness of sins, which is set in parallel to justification by faith without works (4:6-8). In other words, David enjoyed what Abraham had experienced, viz. being counted in the right with God through an act of divine forgiveness.

In the seventh place, in Isaiah's day, God executed a punitive judgment on His people Israel, but did leave a remnant (Rom 9:27-29). Indeed, Paul quoted God's word through Isaiah concerning His attempts to win Israel back to obedience: "I have stretched out My hands all day long to a disobedient and rebellious people" (Rom 10:21). Long after the initial foundational period, God was actively seeking to engage with His errant people. Since Paul picked up the references to God's laying "a stone of stumbling" and "a foundation stone" from Isaiah 8:14 and 28:16 respectively in Romans 9:32-33, he was obviously acquainted with the crises through which Isaiah had lived.[322]

Finally, we may refer to the fact that Paul mentioned Elijah's complaint about Israel's opposition to Yahwism in general and to himself in particular, only to receive a rebuke that Yahweh had kept for[323] Himself[324] 7,000 loyal supporters.

---

321. See the comment in Beker, *Paul*, 253: "Paul presses the distinction in Scripture between 'the promise' and 'the law' in order to assign the law its proper function in Scripture, that is, as the negative but necessary component of salvation-history (Gal 3:8-22)" (cf. 213-15).

322. Hays, *Echoes*, 203n23, suggests that Paul saw "Isaiah and his followers as figurations of Paul's own community of Christians."

323. For this translation of κατελιπεν, see Bauer, *Lexicon*, 414.

324. Paul has added εμαυτω to the LXX version. This adds a little emphasis to God's action.

Cumulatively, these references show that for Paul God was active in the period between Abraham and the coming of Jesus Christ. God was not "an absentee landlord." In addition, they also supply a convincing answer to the next question.

The fourth question to be addressed is *whether Paul had a connected view of history*? Paul was not in either Galatians or Romans giving a review of Israel's history (a possible genre to be found in many parts of the OT and traces in the NT).[325] He selected episodes as they were illustrative of the points which he was making, especially God's sovereign freedom to act in accordance with His own nature and to fulfill His purpose.[326]

Martyn seems to operate on the assumption that God's action in His Son Jesus Christ was so special that it sundered any connection with the past (he asserts that Paul did not operate with a linear approach). While we may affirm the positive in what Martyn has said, we may legitimately query what he denies. For example, Israel's theologians took the events of the Exodus, Wilderness Wanderings, and Conquest as sui generis, but they also asserted continuity. It was the God who had appeared to Abraham and the fathers who called Moses and commissioned him to lead the Israelites out of slavery (e.g., Exod 3; 6). Deutero-Isaiah asserted that God was going to do something new, but it would be a second Exodus! There is both discontinuity and continuity, uniqueness and the familiar, newness and sameness. For Paul, too, God had done something new, unexpected, surprising, through the cross, but He is the same God who created the universe (2 Cor 4:6) and who bore witness to His righteousness through the Law and the prophets (Rom 3:21). But equally God, when in His grace He acted in Jesus Christ, far exceeded expectations (Rom 3:21; 5:20b). Amid this combination of continuity and discontinuity, we, nonetheless, receive from Paul the impression of a unity and consistency in God's action in history.[327] God indeed acts to punish (Rom 11:7b-8, 22); He indeed acts to promote His glory (e.g., Rom 9:17); but ultimately all His activity is to the end that He might have mercy on both Jew and non-Jew alike (Rom 11:30-32) and that both might praise

---

325. See Jeska, *Die Geschichte Israels*, 44-118, who gives a comprehensive survey of Summaries of Israel's History to be found in the OT and in early Jewish literature. The issue of whether the speech at Pisidian Antioch in Acts 13 represents Paul's preaching is too large an issue to go into here. No appeal will therefore be made to it.

326. So also, e.g., Schmitt, *Gottesgerechtigkeit*, 206n336; Hooker, "Heirs of Abraham," 85-96.

327. Cf. Luz, *Geschichtsverstandnis*, 82, stressing the unity of God's saving action. Horrell, "Paul's Narratives or Narrative Substructure?," 157-71 (esp. 167n18), puts it in this way: the Christ event (as the generative beginning of the Gospel) "gives meaning to a temporal narrative of God's creative and saving purposes and then gains meaning from that narrative."

Him in unison (Rom 15:5–13). No wonder Paul broke out in praise "O the depths of God's riches and wisdom and knowledge! How unsearchable are His decisions and (how) unfathomable His ways!" (Rom 11:33).

Our conclusion after this rather long excursus is that to say that Paul desacralized Israel and its story is a misconstrual of his intentions. The evidence as a whole from within even Galatians, where it might seem that Klein has a case, in fact does not support such a conclusion. We may conclude with a paraphrase of Paul's paradoxical words in Romans 11:28: "As regards the preaching of the Gospel, Israel is in the position of enemies so that you Gentiles might receive God's mercy; but as regards God's election, they are still beloved because of the promises which He made to the fathers."

3

Abraham in the Letter to the Hebrews

3.1. Introduction

THE AUTHOR WROTE A word of παράκλησις (13:22), which is probably best translated "exhortation." He certainly does a fair amount of exhortation, which is blended with extended exposition of certain OT texts. It is incorrect to describe Hebrews as *a* sermon, equipped with a letter-like conclusion (13:22-25). It would be better to describe it as a *series of mini-sermons*, each expounding an OT text, backed up by a second text or passage (often linked to the first by a catch-word),[1] provided that we recognize that probably the work was conceived as a written work from the start.[2]

Without attempting a complete analysis of the structure of the work, it may be said that while many scholars divide the work into three major parts: 1:1–4:13; 4:14–10:18 (or 10:31); 10:19 (or 10:32)–13:17/25,[3] within

---

1. There is far too much material in Hebrews as we have it for it to constitute one sermon. What could be offered in epistolary form and which could be read at various sessions of worship is very different from what might be preached on one occasion.

2. A collection of many teaching addresses and a unified work conceived in written form are not mutually exclusive.

3. E.g., Nauck, *Zur Aufbau des Hebräerbriefes*, 199–206; Michel, *Hebräer*, v; Weiss, *Hebräerbrief*, 8–9; Kümmel, *Introduction to the New Testament*, 274; Zimmermann, *Das Bekenntnis der Hoffnung*, ix; Soding, *Die Antwort des Glaubens*, 396; Schnelle, *New Testament Writings*, 370; cf. Backhaus, *Hebräerbrief*, 10–11 (with 1:1–4; 13:1–25

this overarching structure we could say that Psalm 8:5-7 is expounded in chapter 2, with a string of other texts used in chapter 1, on the theme of the relation of Jesus to angels; Psalm 95:7-11 is the key text in chapters 3-4, with Genesis 2:2 in support (key words are rest/to rest); Psalm 110:4 is the basis for chapters 5-7, with the story of Genesis 14 used as back-up (Melchizedek is the word which links the Psalm and the Genesis passage). It is less easy to decide about chapter 8:1-10:18 since Jeremiah 31:31-34 is exegeted in chapter 8 and is also quoted at 10:16-17, while Psalm 40:6-8 comes into consideration in chapter 10:1-18. Jeremiah 31 might be regarded as the dominant passage in 8:1-10:18 with Psalm 40 in a supportive role; alternatively, we might regard the theme of chapter 8 as the new covenant, while that of 9:1-10:18 as dealing with sacrifice.[4] As to 10:19-12:3, Habakkuk 2:3-4 is vitally important, while a roll-call of heroes of the faith in the story of Israel illustrates what living by faith involves and costs. Proverbs 3:11-12 is prominent in 12:4-13, while Haggai 2:6 is expounded in 12:25-29.[5] This "word of exhortation" is not *one* sermon!

The readers/hearers had been Christians long enough really to be teachers by now (5:12). In the past they had suffered persecution. This involved abuse and confiscation of property, while some had been imprisoned (10:32-34). But this persecution did not involve martyrdom (12:4). They had served God's people, and indeed were still doing so (6:10). But they had become "sluggish" in the Christian life, and there was a danger of spiritual drift and backsliding (2:1-3; 3:12; 6:11-12; 12:1-3). Some had become lax in meeting together (10:25). They needed to hold firmly and unswervingly to what they had committed themselves (3:6, 14; 10:23), in the midst of some unspecified unpleasant experience which God was using to discipline them like sons and daughters (12:7-11). They must pay close attention to what they had heard in the beginning (2:1; cf. 13:7).

---

as exordium and conclusion), though Grässer, *Brief an die Hebräer*, 1:29, has a different tripartite division (viz. 1:1-6:20; 7:1-10:18; 10:19-13:21). But there is certainly no general agreement among scholars on how the author has structured his work, as Lane has pointed out (*Hebrews*, lxxxviii-xc). Some scholars divide according to content and may have as many as thirteen (Montefiore, *Epistle to the Hebrews*), eight (Bruce, *Epistle to the Hebrews*), or ten sections (DeSilva, *Perseverance in Gratitude*).

4. Note how the quotation of Jeremiah 31:33 in 10:16-17a is framed by reference to προσφορα at verses 14 and 18b.

5. Stolz, *Der Höhepunkt des Hebräerbriefs*, has argued that the section 12:12-29 is the climax of the letter. This differentiation between the tripartite division and division according to interpretations based on OT passages corresponds to what Backhaus calls the macro-structural level and the micro-structural level. See his comments in Backhaus, *Der neue Bund*, 47-64.

The message which the writer drives home constantly is this. Firstly, the OT was incomplete, knew this, admitted it, and looked for something more perfect yet to come.[6] Secondly, that perfection had come in the person of Jesus Christ, the Son of God. He had fulfilled the destiny for humanity which God had in mind (Ps 8); he inaugurated the rest for God's people (Ps 95); he is the priest forever after the order of Melchizedek (Ps 110:4); he inaugurated the new covenant (Jer 31:31–34); he came and perfectly did God's will, offering himself as the one true perfect sacrifice for sins which does not need to be repeated (Ps 40:6–8); he is the one who should come to usher in eternal salvation (Habb 2:3); he is the perfecter and finisher of faith (12:2). He is far superior to Moses and Joshua (3:3; 4:8), indeed far superior to angels (1:4–14), being the radiance of God's glory and the exact representation of God's being (1:3).[7] Thirdly, the implication was: therefore, why slip away from him and back to the old securities of Judaism?[8] Let them nail their colors firmly to the mast and align themselves fully and wholeheartedly with Jesus (13:10–14).

As to where the writer was and where the recipients of his "word of exhortation" were, we do not know.[9] Nor do we know when he wrote.[10] But these are issues which do not need to be settled before embarking on our theme. The author has a powerful intellect, and yet has also a deeply pastoral heart. He writes as a "scholarly pastor." He ranks as one of the great theologians in the NT, but his pastoral concern must never be forgotten.[11]

---

6. See especially Caird, *Exegetical Method*, 44–51; *New Testament Theology*, 64.

7. Hays, *New Covenantalism*, 163, argues that the author of Hebrews believed that "the events narrated in Scripture actually happened and that they nonetheless point forward to a christological meaning beyond themselves." See also page 167.

8. Loader, *Sohn und Hohenprieste*, 111, 239; cf. 89, 145. Most recently, Morrison, *Who Needs a New Covenant?*, 16, 58, maintains that the argument of Hebrews presupposes that the only other viable option for the readers was the old covenant, viz. Judaism.

9. 13:24b *may* favor seeing the author as away from Italy and writing to Italy-Rome. For the view that anonymity was part of the author's literary strategy, see Kampling, *Fragen*, 34.

10. That he did not mention the destruction of the Temple/Jerusalem seems to me still a convincing reason for a date before 70 AD, but this by no means universally agreed.

11. Increasingly recognized: e.g., Kuss, *Der Brief an die Hebräer*; *Der Verfasser des Hebräerbriefes*, 329–58; Grässer, *Brief an die Hebräer*, 1:viii, 26. And frequently: Weiss, *Der Brief an die Hebräer*; Laub, *Bekenntnis und Auslegung*; Loader, *Sohn*, 111, 239; Wider, *Theozentrik und Bekenntnis*, 161, 196; März, *Studien zum Hebräerbrief*; Kampling, *Ausharren*, 31; McKelvey, *Priest and Pioneer*.

3.2. Abraham in the Letter to the Hebrews

3.2.1. Hebrews 2:5-18

The first passage which mentions Abraham is in the author's reflections on the humanity of Jesus, prompted by his application of Psalm 8 to him. Jesus was not ashamed to call us his brothers and sisters (2:11). He shared the same blood and flesh (2:14). He experienced death (2:9, 14), as a result of which he destroyed the devil, who is credited with having the power of death, and thus Jesus was able to liberate those men and women who suffered from a bondage to fear of death throughout their lives (vv. 14b-15). This last assertion is backed up by a "for" sentence (v. 16): "For of course he does not take hold of angels but he takes hold of the seed of Abraham." The phraseology used here is in line with the theme which has been so prominent since 1:4. Whereas earlier the author sought to prove the vast superiority of the Son over the angels and whereas he acknowledged through Psalm 8 that for a little while, in his incarnate life, the Son had been made a little lower than the angels, here the issue is the recipients of the benefits of the work of the Son. The contrast is between the angels and the "seed of Abraham." The verb used in both halves of the verse, επιλαμβανεται, means basically to take hold of, in the sense of rescue or protect. "The picture of Christ, the αρχηγος, taking hold of his followers on the way to glory is in perfect conformity with the imagery of the whole passage."[12]

Who, then, is in mind with the phrase "seed of Abraham"? It seems as if the author presumed that the phrase was familiar to the addressees, as he made no effort to explain it. In context, he had referred to the "many sons" whom God wants to lead to glory (v. 10); to Jesus' brothers and sisters; and to the children whom God had given Jesus (vv. 11, 13). In the light of this,[13] it seems reasonable to assume that the author has in mind the

---

12. Attridge, *Hebrews*, 94; cf. DeSilva, *Peverserance*, 120: "'Laying hold' here speaks of Jesus' role as rescuer, deliverer, and protector of his clients in the new exodus from the shakable realm and entrance into the "rest" of God." Delling, "λαμβανω," *TWNT* 4:9, suggests that the sense here is "to draw someone to oneself to help and thus to take him into the fellowship of one's own destiny." Ellingworth, *Hebrews*, 177, also relying on context, sees the nuance of the verb as marking a point in the argument half way between μετεσχεν of verse 14 and βοηθηναι of verse 18. To see a reference to the incarnation is to run the risk of importing the two natures idea into the text, and also not to do justice to the present tense of the verb. There is an interesting parallel with Sirach 4:11, without wishing to suggest dependence on Sirach: "Wisdom exalts her sons and takes hold of (επιλαμβανεται) those who seek her."

13. There is a possible use of the language of Isaiah 41:8 LXX, where Israel, God's servant, is described as "seed of Abraham"—so Michel, *Hebräer*, 86; Spicq, *Hébreux* 2:46; Lane, *Hebrews*, 1:63-64; Ellingworth, *Hebrews*, 176; DeSilva, *Perseverance*, 119;

Christian community.¹⁴ This need not mean that Hebrews was indebted to the apostle Paul, who regarded believers as the seed of Abraham (Gal 3:29; Rom 4), but he could be picking up a designation for Christians current in early Christianity. In the verse which follows, there is a further reference to "brothers" (v. 18). The author could well have in mind also those who would in the future hear the gospel and respond positively, and possibly those who trusted in God under the old covenant.¹⁵

On the basis of the fact that at 2:11, where the author said that "he who sanctifies and those who are being sanctified are all ἐξ ἑνός," Rissi has argued that "he intends a reference to Abraham,¹⁶ and not God¹⁷ or Adam.¹⁸ God as creator of all things has been mentioned in 2:10, as has His purpose to bring many sons and daughters to glory through the Son. This seems to favor God, especially as Adam is not mentioned at all anywhere in the Letter, while Abraham is first mentioned at verse 16. Would one in context naturally think of Abraham in verse 11? It does not seem likely.¹⁹

Backhaus, *Hebräerbrief*, 130. Isaiah 41:13 refers to God's taking His servant by the right hand, though the verb used is κρατειν, and of reassuring His servant of His help.

14. So Michel, *Hebräer*, 86–87; Spicq, *Hébreux*, 2:46; Bruce, *Hebrews*, 51–52; Montefiore, *Hebrews*, 67; Attridge, *Hebrews*, 94; Weiss, *Hebräer*, 221; Lane, *Hebrews*, 1:3; Ellingworth, *Hebrews*, 178–79; DeSilva, *Perseverance*, 119; Koester, *Hebrews*, 232; Backhaus, *Hebräerbrief*, 129–30; Moxnes, *Theology in Conflict*, 185; Loader, *Sohn*, 130.

15. Grässer, *Brief an die Hebräer*, 1:150, prefers to interpret the phrase as "those to be redeemed as imitators of those who inherit the promise through faith and patience." Söding, *Die Antwort des Glaubens*, 396, takes the phrase to mean the fellowship established before time by God of all those who need redemption and enter the rest of the eternal sabbath thanks to Jesus our High Priest.

16. Rissi, *Die Theologie des Hebräerbriefs*, 60; Richardson, *Pioneer and Perfecter of Faith*, 15. Ellingworth, *Hebrews*, 164–65, believes that the evidence in favor of Abraham is stronger than for any other candidate, but that Hebrews deliberately did not limit the reference to Abraham at this stage.

17. So Westcott, *Hebrews*, 50; Michel, *Hebräer*, 80; Spicq, *Hébreux*, 2:41; Bruce, *Hebrews*, 44; Montefiore, *Hebrews*, 62; Attridge, *Hebrews*, 89; Lane, *Hebrews*, 1:58; Koester, *Hebrews*, 229–30; DeSilva, Perseverance, 114. Weiss, *Hebräer*, 212–13, thinks that the theological explanation does not exclude an anthropological one, and either God or Adam is intended.

18. So Héring, *Hébreux*, 34. But Adam is never mentioned in the letter elsewhere.

19. Backhaus, *Hebräerbrief*, 123–24, favors taking ἑνός as neuter, with the sense of creaturely origin; cf. Vanhoye, *La Structure Littéraire de l'Épitre aux Hébreux*, 235; see NEB/REB "of one stock" and NIV "of one family."

3.2.2. Hebrews 6:13-20

The next passage which mentions Abraham is the paragraph 6:13-20. It is *primarily* about God and the reliability of what God had promised. It follows a section in which there are juxtaposed a terrifying warning against apostasy and the inevitable loss of salvation which results from it on the one hand (6:1-8), and a reassurance that the writer had every confidence in the recipients,[20] on the basis of both past and present service to God's people, on the other hand (6:9-10). Then comes the pastoral appeal to show the same eagerness as in the past; to maintain the assurance of their hope (v. 11); and not to become sluggish in their pilgrimage; but rather to be imitators of those who inherit God's promise διὰ πίστεως καὶ μακροθυμίας (v. 12). This phrase is probably a hendiadys, where one thing is expressed by two words. Assuming this, the second word μακροθυμία meaning patience, endurance, steadfastness, pulls πίστις over into the sense of faithfulness.[21] This sense of faith as patient faithfulness, steadfastness, receives confirmation from the occurrence of hope in the context. The writer encouraged those addressed to demonstrate the same enthusiasm now as in the past, with a view to maintain "the assurance of hope" (6:11). Hope and steadfastness in moving towards its realization naturally go together.[22]

All this is an interesting pointer to the different way in which Hebrews envisages faith over against the apostle Paul. One cannot really imitate faith in the Pauline sense of trusting commitment and abandonment to Christ as God's appointed redeemer. One either has it or one does not have it; but one can imitate faithfulness!

The author then refers to an incident involving Abraham, viz. the sequel to his willingness to offer up Isaac as a sacrifice. "When God made a promise to Abraham, since He could swear by no one greater, He swore by Himself, saying, "I will certainly bless you and multiply you" " (vv. 13-14, quoting Gen 22:17). Here the author concentrated on the aspect of descendants contained in God's promise, which He backed up with an oath. The author continued: "And so after he had continued steadfast (μακροθυμήσας) Abraham obtained the promise."[23] Abraham had been stopped from actually sacrificing Isaac,

---

20. DeSilva, *Perseverance*, 244-45, quotes Aristotle's advice to follow frank speech by reaffirming a favorable estimate of the hearers.

21. Cf. Grässer, *Glaube*, 28; Michel, *Hebräer*, 243.

22. Grässer, *Glaube*, 115, points to the occurrence of πληροφορία πίστεως (10:22) as indicating the closeness of faith and hope in Hebrews: "Pistis and elpis are identical." Cf. Dautzenberg, *Der Glaube im Hebraerbrief*, 163-64, who agrees that the two concepts are almost interchangeable.

23. There might seem a contradiction between this and 11:13, 39, where it is said

so he still had the "son of promise," the son through whom the promise of God would be fulfilled.[24] In this sense, it could be said that he obtained the promise, or, as one might say, the first installment of it.[25]

To what was the author referring when he mentioned Abraham's steadfastness? A number of possibilities could be suggested. The author might have in mind the interval after the original promise of Genesis 12:1-3; or the test of offering up of Isaac; or the further interval after the offering of Isaac (Abraham's death is recorded in Genesis 25:7-8); or the tradition that over his lifetime Abraham was tested ten times by God and came through all of them. Of these, the test of offering up Isaac seems the most likely.

So then, Abraham in his steadfastness is himself an example of those who through steadfast endurance inherit the promises of God (v. 12).[26]

It looks as if Hebrews was aware that the statement that God swore an oath had caused problems to some people, because he now made certain comments about oaths.[27] He assumes two things about oaths, as verse 16 shows. Humans swear by someone greater than themselves to give credibility to what they say, and an oath is accepted to establish the veracity of something and so to put an end to a dispute. God wanted to demonstrate the unchangeable nature of His purpose to those who would inherit the promise, and so He used an oath. Since God could not swear by anyone greater than Himself, He swore by Himself (v. 17). Thus, two immutable things were involved: God's promise to Abraham and His oath (v. 18; which

---

that Abraham, and indeed the OT heroes of the faith generally, did not obtain the promise of God. However, whereas 11:13, 39, have in mind the "city which is to come," prepared by God for those faithful to Him (cf. 11:10; 13:14), the promise in 6:15 refers to descendants.

24. It is not expressly said in Genesis that Abraham saw his grandsons, but on the basis of Genesis 21:5; 25:20, 26, this might be inferred. Certainly, the book of Jubilees assumes that Abraham and Jacob were very close to each other (19:15-29; 22:10-23:3).

25. Michel, *Hebräer*, 156. Hebrews is moving towards the use of God's promise with an oath to the Son (Psalm 110:4 [109:4 LXX]), while there was also the promise of eschatological rest in God's Kingdom for believers (4:9), which the Son had opened up through his atoning sacrifice and exaltation to God's right hand. By showing that God's promise to Abraham was reliable, our author shows by implication that God's promises to the Son and to the Son's followers were reliable. See Furman, *Vergeben und Vergessen*, 117.

26. See Backhaus, *Hebräerbrief*, 246-47: Abraham is characterized by that attitude which Hebrews wished to strengthen in his hearers, viz. persistent waiting in hope for the invisible.

27. It is significant that Philo discusses the appropriateness of speaking of God uttering an oath in a number of passages. He maintains that God did so to accommodate Himself to human understanding. See *Abr.* 273; *Sacr.* 93-94; *All. Leg.* 3.203-8; *QG* 4.180 (Köster, *Die Auslegung*, 98-102, lists nine points of contact between Philo and Hebrews and deduces a tradition from which both drew).

oath the author has in mind will be considered in a moment). It is impossible, therefore, that God should be lying when He spoke thus. This double confirmation should be an enormous encouragement to believers.

Two inter-related questions pose themselves. The first is whether Abraham had disappeared from the author's train of thought after verse 15 or not? This depends in turn on how we interpret the reference in verse 17 to God's intervening with an oath in order to demonstrate the unchangeable nature of His purpose or will (βουλη). So, secondly, which oath has the author in mind? Does the author still have Genesis 22:16-18 in mind?[28] Or has he moved on (as it were) and is he thinking of the promise in Genesis plus the oath of Psalm 110:4, which will be so important in chapter 7, towards which the author is working, as 6:20 indicates with its reference to Jesus' having become a high priest forever after the order of Melchizedek?[29]

To answer this question of which oath is in mind, two factors must be weighed against one another. Firstly, actually, Psalm 110:4 is not formally quoted till 7:17 and 21, though alluded to in 6:20. We might have expected a clearer indication if Psalm 110:4 were in mind at 6:17-18. Furthermore, Abraham does figure in the discussion at the opening of chapter 7 (vv. 1-10). Finally, the promise backed by God's oath in Genesis 22 referred very emphatically to Abraham's heirs. So, these points might suggest that the story involving Abraham was still in mind in verses 17-20.

Secondly, whereas it is stated in verse 15 that Abraham obtained the promise, at verses 17-18 the author spoke of the fact that God wanted to demonstrate to *"the heirs of the promise"* the absolute reliability of His purpose. Who are the heirs? Our earlier discussion of the statement in 2:16 that Jesus took hold not of angels but the seed of Abraham can assist us. As mentioned there, this phrase indicates Christian believers. So here "the heirs of the promise" are those who have confessed Jesus as God's Son (4:14). Later,

---

28. Those who think that Genesis 22:16-18 is still in mind include Westcott, *Hebrews*, 159-64; Michel, *Hebräer*, 157; Spicq, *Hébreux*, 2:162; Bruce, *Hebrews*, 131; Montefiore, *Hebrews*, 115; Lane, *Hebrews*, 1:152; Weiss, *Hebräer*, 364; Ellingworth, *Hebrews*, 342; Koester, *Hebrews*, 328; Köster, *Abraham-Verheissung*, 100 (though he goes on to say later [107] that it would not be false to say that the two irrevocable things are the Melchizedek-oath of Psalm 110:4 and Jesus as Son).

29. Those who favor Psalm 110:4 include Hofius, *Vorhang*, 85n207; Attridge, *Hebrews*, 181-82; DeSilva, *Perseverance*, 250; Fuhrmann, *Vergeben*, 119; Mackie, *Eschatology and Exhortation*, 202. Variations include the promise plus the oath of Psalms 2:7 and 110:4, quoted at Hebrews 5:5-6 (Backhaus, *Hebräerbrief*, 249-50); the Melchizedek-oath and the interpretation of Jesus' sonship as a high priesthood after the order of Melchizedek (Laub, *Bekenntnis*, 245); the promise to Christians and the Melchizedek-oath to Jesus (Grässer, *Brief an die Hebräer*, 1:377-79, 381); or the entrance of Jesus the Son of God within the veil and his eternal priestly status as guaranteed by divine oath (Fuhrmann, *Vergeben*, 121).

in 11:40, the author indicated the unity between the faithful under the old and new covenants. The household of faith, the family of God, includes the faithful of both OT and NT eras.

So, some have argued that there does seem to be a difference between what is being referred to in verse 15 and verses 17-18.[30] The words of the oath recorded in Psalm 110:4, taken to be addressed in fact to the Son and constituting his appointment as eternal high priest (see 5:6; cf. 7:17, 21), are clearly of importance to Christians since they guarantee to them one who will act as intercessor on their behalf (which will be implied at 6:20, where the images of forerunner and high priest occur and merge,[31] and stated at 7:25). For some scholars, this suggests that at verses 17-18 the author is thinking of Psalm 110:4 and God's purpose involving His Son and, through him, believers who confess him.

But is such a differentiation absolutely necessary, particularly as there do not appear to be any indications in verses 17-19 which point unmistakably to Psalm 110:4? On balance, it seems that the story of Abraham continued to be in the author's mind through-out the whole of 6:13-20. Yet, on the other hand, we could say that probably the reflections on the divine oath help to *prepare the way* to appreciate the importance of the oath in connection with Psalm 110:4,[32] when the author mentions it in 7:20-21, 28.

God, then, wished to show to the future heirs of the promise the immutable character of His purpose and so He intervened with an oath which He gave to Abraham after the patriarch demonstrated his willingness to offer up Isaac. This meant for the author that two immutable items were involved: God's promise in the first place and then the oath accompanying it, it thus being impossible for God to be untruthful. This in turn gives Christians strong encouragement to lay hold of the hope set before them. The author uses εχωμεν ("*we* might have"). In other words, "we" is set in parallel to "heirs of the promise." This confirms the earlier observation that Christians of the author's day are heirs of the promise, of which that made to Abraham and his response to it provide a paradigm.[33] Thus,

30. Cf. Köster, *Auslegung*, 105-6; Furman, *Vergeben*, 119.

31. Stressed by McKelvey, *Pioneer*, 49-50, in line with his thesis that pioneer and high priest go together and form the main components of the author's Christology.

32. Vanhoye, *Structure*, 123; Bruce, *Hebrews*, 130.

33. So Grässer, *Brief an die Hebräer*, 1:373; Weiss, *Hebräerbrief*, 364, who speaks of God's promise confirmed by His oath to Abraham as the Urbild for what is in mind in verses 17-18; Furman, *Vergeben*, 122, who refers to the formal correspondence (*formeliter* italicized); Backhaus, *Hebräerbrief*, 250, who describes the episode with Abraham as prototype of divine faithfulness for Christians.

Those who see the promise as still the promise of God to Abraham include Westcott, *Hebrews*, 160; Spicq, *Hébreux*, 2:162; Bruce, *Hebrews*, 131; Montefiore, *Hebrews*, 115;

there is one people of God down the ages right up to the present.[34] For this people God has a land ready, or, more specifically, a city prepared (11:16). Entry into this city is still in the future, but our hope is sure and reliable. It is like an anchor. Our hope is in fact Jesus who has already entered heaven as a forerunner (6:19-20).

In verse 18, the "we" are described as οι καταφυγοντες (aorist participle active) which lacks an accompanying phrase (e.g., with εις or προς).[35] Is this to be translated "we who have fled"[36] or "we who have taken refuge"[37]? On the former, Christians have fled from the eschatological catastrophe soon to take place (10:25; 12:25-29); on the latter, Christians have taken refuge in the Christian community, the present household of Christ on earth (rather like in the OT some might take refuge in a town to save themselves from arrest and trial).[38] Either meaning could fit the context.

The main purpose of this paragraph, as already mentioned, is to emphasize the *reliability of God's word and promise*. For this purpose, the concept of God's oath to Abraham is of considerable importance, both in its own right (vv. 13-15) and as a paradigm of the promise-cum-oath made by God to His Son. Given this divine assurance, it means that the Christian faith rests on a sure foundation. This is a further help to the writer in his purpose of giving those addressed confidence in the utter reliability of the salvation given through Jesus,[39] and, correspondingly, encouragement to prove themselves reliable in their pilgrimage of faith.[40]

Just as God gave to Abraham a promise backed by an oath, so His promise to believers now is based on His oath to the eternal Son as mentioned in Psalm 110:4, which has been referred to at 1:13, will be alluded to at 6:20,

---

Lane, *Hebrews*, 1:152; Ellingworth, *Hebrews*, 334 (his claim that this is the usual interpretation may be correct for English-speaking scholarship, but does not seem correct for recent German scholarship); Koester, *Hebrews*, 328.

34. The oneness of the people of God under old and new covenants is also stressed by Scholtissek, *Den Unsichtbaren vor Augen*, 140, 143, 160, 162-64.

35. Westcott, *Hebrews*, 162, describes the absolute use as harsh.

36. So Bruce, *Hebrews*, 131; Attridge, *Hebrews*, 182; Weiss, *Hebräer*, 365; Grässer, *Brief an die Hebräer*, 1:382.

37. Ellingworth, *Hebrews*, 344; cf. Bauer, *Lexicon*, 421. Montefiore, *Hebrews*, 116, insists that both meanings are present for the author; cf. Lane, *Hebrews*, 1:153.

38. See Gen 19:20; Deut 4.42, 19.5, Num 35.25-26, cf. Isa 10.3. See Spicq, *Hébreux*, 2:163, for a full discussion of the use of καταφευγειν in the LXX.

39. Note the description of the Christian hope as a sure and reliable anchor of the soul, which is bound to the heavenly sphere whither Jesus has gone as our forerunner (6:19-20).

40. Cf. Köster, *Abraham-Verheissung*, 106.

and will be quoted at 7:20–21, 28.[41] Therefore, just as Abraham was steadfast and endured, so Christians should behave likewise. As Abraham held firmly to the promise which God gave him, so Christians should hold firmly to the hope set before them. Like Abraham, they will then obtain the promise.[42] Abraham is certainly a paradigm of how Christians should behave.[43]

3.2.3. Hebrews 7:1–3

Reference to Jesus' entry into heaven and to his having become (γενομενος) a high priest forever after the order of Melchizedek (6:20), prepares the way for a long reflection on the high priesthood of Jesus after the order of Melchizedek in chapter 7.

Melchizedek is mentioned twice in the OT, and both passages are used by the author of Hebrews. The first reference is Genesis 14, an "erratic boulder" in the Pentateuch.[44] It portrays Abraham as a warlike sheik who, with allies, engaged in war with Chedorlaomer, King of Elam, and his allies (who had seized Lot). Abraham defeated them, and released Lot. Melchizedek, King of Salem, came out to meet the victorious Abraham.[45] Melchizedek blessed Abraham and his God, and "he gave him a tenth of all" (Gen 14:18–19).

All this the author briefly summarized in 7:1–3, and also explained etymologically the meaning of Melchizedek and Salem, of which he was king, and mentioned certain qualities of Melchizedek.[46] Finally, he says

41. "But the oath, which was uttered after the Law, appointed the Son who has been perfected forever" (Heb 7:28b).

42. See Laub, *Bekenntnis*, 244, for the correspondence between Abraham as a paradigm and the addressees. See also Köster, *Abraham-Verheissung*, 103, 106; Fuhrmann, *Vergehen*, 121.

43. Even if Fuhrmann, *Vergeben*, 121, is in the end correct that the addressees know that Jesus himself is the real model of persistence in faith.

44. So in the view of many OT scholars. See the remarks of von Rad, *Genesis*, 170.

45. "With bread and wine" is a point which the author of Hebrews does not mention!

46. Often explained as due to the silence of Scripture (e.g., Bruce, *Hebrews*, 137; Montefiore, *Hebrews*, 119; Attridge, *Hebrews*, 190; Lane, *Hebrews*, 1:166; DeSilva, *Perseverance*, 266), but the discovery of 11 Q Melch at Qumran might suggest that a tradition, in which Melchidezedek was a heavenly figure destined to be a key person in the eschatological drama, existed among at least some circles within Judaism. That this kind of tradition might be known to the author of Hebrews is affirmed by Jonge and Woude, *11Q Melchizedek*, 301–326; Fitzmyer, "Further Light on Melchizedek," 25–41, but denied by Attridge, *Hebrews*, 192–93; Lane, *Hebrews*, 1:160–61; Laub, *Bekenntnis*, 240. Even if we reject Hebrews' direct acquaintance with 11 Q Melch, some acquaintance on his part with the post-Biblical traditions about Melchizedek seems likely (so, e.g., Attridge, *Hebrews*, 191; McKelvey, *Pioneer*, 61–68).

that Melchizedek was made like[47] the Son of God (v. 3c). This has consequences for when the author said that Abraham honored Melchizedek by giving him a tenth of the spoils.

The author then drew certain conclusions from the encounter of Abraham with Melchizedek. Two aspects of the story suggest that Melchizedek was regarded as superior to Abraham. In the first place, since Melchizedek blessed Abraham, this is a clear sign of his superiority over the patriarch (v. 7). Secondly, if Abraham voluntarily gave Melchizedek a tenth of the spoils, he must be greater than Abraham.[48]

In accordance with Hebrew ways of thinking, Abraham's descendants (who were "in his loins," so to speak) are involved in the act of acknowledging the superiority of Melchizedek. As his descendants included the priestly tribe of Levi, in effect in Abraham the Israelite priesthood acknowledged the superiority of the priest Melchizedek (7:5-10).

This is one stage in the author's argument that a priesthood after the order of Melchizedek was superior to the Levitical priesthood, i.e., Jesus as a priest in that order was superior to the Levitical priesthood. Abraham only figures in 7:1-10, where Genesis 14 is interpreted. Thereafter, in chapter 7, Psalm 110:4 furnished the basis for the argument that the priesthood of Jesus, a priesthood after the order of Melchizedek, was superior to that of the Levitical priesthood.[49]

3.2.4. Hebrews 10:32–12:3

Finally, we turn to 10:32-12:3.[50] After referring to previous sufferings following their conversion (they endured [υπεμεινατε] a great struggle with sufferings), the author appealed to them not to throw away their confidence, which would have a great reward, for they continued to need endurance [υπομονη] in order to do God's will and obtain what He had promised. As

---

47. The perfect participle passive, αφωμοιωμενος, indicates the continuing relevance of the Melchizedek incident for the recipients of Hebrews. It stands recorded in the authoritative Scriptures. Moule, *Idiom Book*, 14, has called this "the perfect of allegory," which appears several times in the NT when the OT is being expounded.

48. Söding, *Antwort*, 396, puts it that Abraham gave honor to the Son of God in the figure of Melchizedek.

49. Cf. Zimmerman, *Bekenntnis*, 81.

50. Our chapter divisions at 11:1 and 12:1 are unfortunate. There is no break either between 10:39 and 11:1 or between 11:40 and 12:1. See most recently, the work of Richardson, *Pioneer*, 111-66, for arguments for taking 10:19-12:29 as a unit, within which 10:32-12:17 comprises a division, and for taking 12:1-3 as the climax of the discussion on faith.

they had endured in the past, so they needed to exercise the same endurance in the present. The author backed this appeal up (γαρ [v. 37]) with a quotation primarily from Habakkuk 2:3-4,[51] but also with a phrase taken from Isaiah 26:20 LXX (μικρον οσον οσον: "in a very little while," i.e., soon) to begin the quotation.

37 a In yet a very little while,
37b ο ερχομενος ηξει και ου χρονισει;
38a ο δε δικαιος μου εκ πιστεως ζησεται
38b και εαν υποστειληται
38c ουκ ευδοκει η ψυχη μου εν αυτω.

The author has altered the LXX text in several ways. In verse 37b, he has added the masculine article ο to the anarthous participle ερχομενος. Thus, he transformed the messianic potential of the Habakkuk text into an unambiguously personal reference, "he who comes," and, indeed, we might say, into a messianic reference. The "he who comes" is none other than Jesus who was destined to come a second time (9:28). Secondly, he has altered an ου μη plus the aorist subjunctive into the straight future indicative (ου χρονισει), but this is not a particularly significant change. Thirdly, in verse 38, he has reversed the order of the clauses in the LXX. The LXX runs, "If he draws back, I will not delight in him, but the righteous one will live by my faithfulness." The reason for this is not hard to see. Having made the previous line to refer to the returning Christ ("he who comes"), it would be inconceivable that *he* should draw back and not come.[52] Now, with the reversal of the order in 10:38, there is an effective contrast between the righteous person (v. 38a) and the person who apostasizes (shrinks or draws back) in verse 38b. Finally, the author has removed the personal pronoun μου after πιστεως and inserted it after δικαιος, producing "My righteous one will live by (his) faithfulness." Thus the emphasis falls on the believer and his or her faithfulness (rather than on God's faithfulness as in the LXX).[53]

The result of these changes may be briefly summed up. The author made the Habakkuk text refer to Jesus' second coming (v. 37b). Faced with

51. See Gheorghita, *Septuagint*, 147–224, for a very technical discussion of the Hebrew and Septuagint traditions and the text of Hebrews 10:37–38.

52. Thus preserving the LXX's different referents for the subjects of the two occurrences of the verb υποστελλειν. See Gheorghita, *Septuagint*, 216–17.

53. For details, apart from the commentaries, see Gheorghita, *Septuagint*, 211–24, who shows that the author of Hebrews has addressed and wrestled with the syntactical and logical inconsistencies of the Septuagint text in order to convey a coherent meaning and to apply the text to a new situation. The author of Hebrews developed the potential inherent in the Septuagint text.

this, the righteous person will hold on, in whatever time remains. He/she will continue faithful to the end. If, however, someone chooses to backslide, there is the warning that God will have no pleasure in such a person.

The author followed up this warning with an encouraging note: "But we do not belong to those who shrink back [ουκ εσμεν υποστολης] and go to destruction; but we belong to those who exercise faithfulness [αλλα πιστεως] and obtain life [εις περιποιησιν ψυχης]" (v. 39).

We have translated πιστις in verse 39b as "faithfulness," both because this agrees with the sense of πιστις in verse 38a in the Habakkuk quotation; and because this secures the contrast intended in verse 39 between "shrinking back" (υποστολη) and "holding on," "enduring steadfastly."[54]

If we are on the right lines, this section has prepared us for how to take the famous definition of πιστις in 11:1:

Εστιν δε πιστις ελπιζομενων υποστασις.

Etymologically speaking, υποστασις is υπο plus στασις, which means, literally, standing under. Of course, what a word originally might have meant is no guarantee that it remained so in the course of time. υποστασις had been used in philosophical discussions to mean the actuality of a substance. Hence the rendering "faith is the substance of things hoped for," but this labors under the difficulty that faith can hardly be what gives substance to things hoped-for.[55] An alternative "faith is the assurance of things hoped-for" has become very popular,[56] but its weaknesses lie in the fact that such a meaning of υποστασις is regarded as in itself doubtful,[57] and especially in the fact that it gives a different nuance to πιστις in 11:1 than in 10:37-39. While that is not impossible, it demands much of a hearer/reader. A third possibility is "faith is the title deeds of things hoped-for,"[58] i.e., faith is like holding the title deeds of a property which one hopes to inherit. While Spicq is favorably disposed and assumes that the sense is "anticipated possession" or "guarantee of future possession,"[59] Bruce pointed out that this sense, found

---

54. Wider, *Theozentrik*, 181, says that there is a specific combination of lifestyle and self understanding behind either πιστις or υποστολη (whether one is related to God as Creator or not).

55. Despite NEB/REB and JB "can guarantee" and Köster, "υποστασις," *TWNT* 8:587. See Wider, *Theozentrik*, 183, for the point that the context tells strongly against the view that faith is somehow power which confers that for which it hopes (in agreement with Brawley, *Discoursive Structure*, 81). Rose, *Die Wolke der Zeugen*, 101-3, also rejects the translation "substance."

56. RV, NEB margin, NIV (being sure of), NRSV.

57. See Koester, υποστασις, 586; Attridge, *Hebrews*, 308 (relying on Koester); Söding, *Zuversicht*, 234; Rose, *Wolke*, 99.

58. Moulton and Milligan, *Vocabulary of the New Testament*, 659-60.

59. Spicq, *Hébreux*, 2:337. DeSilva, *Perseverance*, 383, also follows this interpretation,

in several papyri, relates to property transactions, whereas such a context is not that of our Letter, while Attridge drew attention to the fact that the papyri examples with this meaning are later than Hebrews.[60]

That which agrees with 10:35–39 best is, however, faith as remaining firmly committed to, holding fast to, persisting in, or adhering to, taking one's stand under.[61] It is the very opposite of shrinking back, which was mentioned in 10:39 (υποστολη).

The second half of the definition runs:

Πραγματων ελεγχος ου βλεπομενων.

ελεγχος is primarily the testing or proving of someone or something, with the sense of conviction ensuing from this process. Faithfulness involves the certainty of the eschatological events not as yet seen.[62]

The two lines are not identical in sense but come to close to each other.[63]

Among others, Michel argued that chapter 11 as whole reads like an excursus on 10:39.[64] While there is something to be said for this view, insofar as the section 10:32–39 calls for a clarification of what the author means by πιστις,[65] it must not be held in such a way as to lessen the vital

---

while Weiss, *Hebräerbrief*, 562, believes that the sense stands close to that in the papyri.

60. Bruce, *Hebrews*, 278; Attridge, *Hebrews*, 309. This interpretation is also rejected by Montefiore, *Hebrews*, 186.

61. Among those who argue for this are Grässer, *Glaube*, 45–53; *Brief an die Hebräer*, 3:92, 95–97; Laub, *Bekenntnis*, 260n257; Weiss, *Hebräerbrief*, 127; Ellingworth, *Hebrews*, 563; Rose, *Wolke*, 99–107; Söding, *Zuversicht*, 225; *Antwort*, 403; Scholtissek, *Den Unsichtbaren*, 151. Probably we should include Caird, *New Testament Theology*, 326n89, who translated this half of the verse as "a secure grasp of the objects of hope." On the other hand, Richardson, *Pioneer*, 121–22, maintains the sense of "steadfast confidence," without engaging with the view of Grässer, et al. He seems to have tried to combine the two senses of steadfastness and confidence. Koester, *Hebrews*, 479, while opting for "assurance," says that the author has allied it with "perseverance" and "endurance."

62. Rose, *Wolke*, 123–33, stresses the objective side of this being convinced.

63. Rose, *Wolke*, 132, suggests synthetic parallelism and that verse 1a stresses the active aspect of faith, while verse 1b stresses the passive aspect.

64. Michel, *Hebräer*, 243. He did not mean by this that the chapter was less than important. He would have agreed with the comment of Attridge, *Hebrews*, 305–6, that its connection to its context is intimate. Crosby, *Rhetorical Composition*, 29, says that, functionally, the definition is formulated to validate the exhortation delivered in 10:19–29. Cf. Mosser, *Rahab Outside the Camp*, 392: "Chapter 11 elaborates on the πιστις mentioned in the quotation from Hab 2:4." Backhaus, *Hebräerbrief*, 378, follows Michel and heads his section on 11:1–40, "Exkursus: Der tragfähige Realismus des Glaubens (11:1–40)," which may be broadly translated as, "Excursus: The Supportive Realism of Faith."

65. Richardson, *Pioneer*, 128, states that the definition of 11:1 presupposes and

significance of chapter 11 for the author's overall pastoral aim. In the end, it is perhaps best to avoid the term excursus, since it runs the risk of not doing full justice to the way in which 10:32–12:3 form a coherent and well-constructed whole.

Michel's other conviction (following Windisch before him) that Hebrews had taken over an existing "document" and used it for his own purposes[66] is more debatable, and it is by no means certain that we should look for anyone else but the author of Hebrews himself as the composer of this section, and Grässer and subsequently Rose and others have mounted a robust defence of this position.[67]

What is clear is that the sections within chapter 11 on Abraham (vv. 8–12, 13–16, 17–19) and then on Moses (vv. 23–28) are far larger than those devoted to other characters. This is an indication that Abraham is one of the foci of attention in this list of heroes of faith.

The section on Abraham began with the call of God to go out from where he lived, to another place (τοπος, replacing the LXX γη at Gen 12:1). Abraham obeyed this command (11:8). Faith involves obedience. Abraham is represented as a pilgrim,[68] but one who sets out on a journey without

---

summarizes 10:19–39 and prepares for the discussion of faith in Israel's history in chapter 11.

66. Michel, *Hebräer*, 244–45, 284, argued that the author may have added at points πιστει, which occurs no less than seventeen times and which, at times, Michel alleged, has a decidedly artificial ring about it, but Rose, *Wolke*, 78–333, has shown that in fact the examples fit the definition of 11:1 and that the phrase πιστει is not used haphazardly. Michel complained that only Windisch, *Der Hebräerbrief*, had taken the question of a source seriously, though Stauffer, *Theology of the New Testament*, 240, had indicated briefly his acceptance of such an idea. Subsequently, Attridge, *Hebrews*, 306–7, 339; Laub, *Bekenntnis*, 258n233; Söding, *Zuversicht*, 226, have also adhered to the view that Hebrews used a source; cf. Wieser, *Abrahamvorstellungen*, 39–35; Weiss, *Hebräerbrief*, 556–58

67. Grässer, *Brief an die Hebräer*, 3:88–90, while Rose, *Wolke*, 82–84, equally is convinced that, though making use of traditions from early Judaism and early Christianity, the author of Hebrews is himself responsible for the composition of chapter 11. Rose (e.g., *Wolke*, 180) also believes that Hebrews works on the analogy principle or Gezera schawa. Where the OT or Jewish traditions said that a person was righteous, then such a person must have faith (on the principle of Heb 11:6; Habb 2:4 quoted at 10:37–38). Among others who see chapter 11 as Hebrews' own composition are Thompson, *Beginnings of Christian Philosophy*, 69n73; Crosby, *Composition*, 57–91; Scholtissek, *Den Unsichbaren vor Augen*, 146; Eisenbaum, *Jewish Heroes*, 84–85; Ellingworth, *Hebrews*, 558–59; Koester, *Hebrews*, 470–71; McKelvey, *Pioneer*, 51. Richardson, *Pioneer*, 15, 142–64, sees the author combining a typological approach characteristic of Jewish-Christian tradition and the genre of an encomium from Graeco-Roman rhetoric, with the strategy of comparison characteristic of both.

68. Here we might assume that the author is picking up passages from Genesis which describe Abraham either as living in tents (Gen 12:8; 13:18) or as a sojourner in Canaan (Gen 17:8; 23:4; also Gen 24:37 LXX). As DeSilva, *Hebrews*, 395, 399–400,

knowing where he was going (11:8). The quality of his faith is thus underlined by the fact that he obeyed even though he was uncertain of where his journey would immediately lead him. He thus illustrated the fact that, as stated at 11:1, faith is the conviction of things not seen.

It is probably significant that Abraham was described as going out (εξελθειν), in view of the fact that the readers will be encouraged to go outside the camp to Jesus in 13:13 (εξερχωμεθα προς αυτον). Abraham abandoned security; believers in Jesus are called to be ready to do the same.[69]

In the light of verse 10 and the whole of the paragraph verses 13-16, it is reasonable to suppose that by τοπος Hebrews was not thinking of Canaan, but the heavenly fatherland or city (or the eschatological rest, as mentioned in 3:7-4:11).[70]

Abraham's obedience and faithfulness were tested by the fact that he lived like a stranger in the γη της επαγγελιας (v. 9). With him are bracketed his son Isaac and grandson, Jacob, who were fellow heirs of the promise made by God to Abraham. Their rootlessness is indicated by the two verbs used (παροικειν and κατοικειν) and by the reference to their "dwelling in tents" (v. 9). But how are we to take γη της επαγγελιας. Literally, the land of promise, does it mean "the promised land" (which would seem to imply the land of Canaan, which could call on Gen 12:7; 13:14-17; 15:18)? But this seems to run counter to verse 10 and the later verses 13-16. How could Canaan be described as the "promised land" if Abraham was looking for the city created by God, viz. the heavenly Jerusalem? Rose has suggested that we should translate the phrase as "the land to which the promise directed him."[71] Presumably, Rose means that the promise was about the heavenly homeland but that it included a direction to go to Canaan, which was really a station on the way to the heavenly fatherland/city,[72] and it would be this heavenly land which he would inherit. That Canaan is actually a symbol of a greater reality will be made clear by verse 10.

Rose's suggestion is attractive from the point of view of eliminating tension between verses 9 and 10 (13-16). But can the Greek bear this sense

---

says, Hebrews uses these statements with a different intention from that of the author of Genesis.

69. Backhaus, *Das Land der Verheissung*, 174; Morrison, *New Covenant*, 71; McKelvey, *Pioneer*, 53. See DeSilva, *Perseverance*, 394-95, for a helpful review of the evidence from Dio, Lucian, Plutarch, and Ben Sirach, relating "both to the importance of one's native land for one's sense of identity and to the trials that attended the foreigner and sojourner" in antiquity.

70. Rose, *Wolke*, 210, 217, 220. Cf. Backhaus, *Land*, 173.

71. Rose, Wolke, 217 ("das Land, in den ihn die Verheitzung wies").

72. Cf. Käsemann, *Wandering People*, 68 (*Gottesvolk*, 41); Rose, *Wolke*, 217, 222.

(a point Rose does not discuss)? If Rose is right, then the author has expressed himself in an extremely compressed manner. He could easily have written "the land where he received the promise . . . and because of this he was looking for etc.," or even not used the genitival phrase της επαγγελιας but written "in the land of Canaan . . . for he was looking for the city . . . which God had promised him."

The genitive is certainly an "immensely versatile and hard-working" case.[73] Backhaus has suggested that the genitive is one of direction:[74] "The land which leads to the promise." This seems an excellent suggestion, and it fits the precise context, and the need to have verse 10 really supporting the assertion of verse 9.

The author then explained Abraham's faithfulness to a promise never realized as follows: "For he was looking forward to the city which has foundations, whose designer and maker is God" (11:10). Abraham was convinced of the reality of the city of God, which is an apocalyptic concept.[75] This idea that Abraham was in reality more interested in the Heavenly City than the land of Canaan fits in with the notion that Christ is coming again (10:37b) and with the idea of persistent adherence to what is hoped for, to things not seen (11:1). And more than that: this forward-looking characteristic is anticipatory of the way Jesus endured the cross "for the sake of the joy set before him" (12:2b). Richardson has put it this way: "just as Abraham looked forward to the eschatological hope and inheritance of the heavenly homeland, Jesus fixed his eyes on what was before him . . . the future, unseen hope of entering into God's presence and the heavenly city of Jerusalem."[76]

A number of English translations make Sarah the subject of verse 11,[77] but there is a serious objection to this, viz. the Greek phrase εις καταβολην σπερματος refers to the male sexual act. Furthermore, the context both before (vv. 8-10) and after (v. 12) concerns Abraham. The reading και αυτη

---

73. Moule, *Idiom Book*, 37. BDR devotes paragraphs 162–186 to describing it.

74. Backhaus, *Land*, 174, refers to BDR 166, which gives a few examples of such a classification of the genitive, though not listing any passages from Hebrews. Backhaus also points to Hebrews 9:11-15; 10:19 as further examples of this kind of genitive within Hebrews itself. In his commentary, he does not state this as clearly. His comment runs: "The land of promise is also no longer the promised land, but the land, in which the promise was issued and it is what matters. It is not exhausted in the possession of earthly land, but aims at the perfect fellowship with God in eternity" (Backhaus, *Hebräerbrief*, 390).

75. E.g., *4 Ezra* 10:25; *2 Bar.* 4:2; cf. *1 En.* 90:29; Rev 21:2. Backhaus, *Land*, 175, sees the author as leaving his biblical source and entwining the vertical orientation with the horizontal future eschatology.

76. Richardson, *Pioneer*, 193

77. RV; JB; NEB/REB.

Σαρρα στειρα [ουσα] of P46 D* may be the original and may represent the Biblical Greek circumstantial clause, here meaning "although Sarah herself was barren."[78] The στειρα may have been omitted due to homoiteleuton, thus producing the text now offered by P13 vid ℵ A Dc.[79]

The author gave the reason why Abraham was able to beget a child: "since he considered Him who promised to be faithful" (v. 11b). This clause evokes God's promise to Abraham in Genesis 15:1-6 (a promise renewed at 17:2-6; 18:10), that he would have as many descendants as the stars in the heaven, and Abraham believed God. The human response of continuing and faithful trust in the promises of God is the only fitting response to divine faithfulness.[80]

The greatness of what God promised is underlined by the descriptions of Abraham: he was past the normal age (of being a father) (v. 11) and was as good as[81] dead in respect of begetting children (v. 12). What God promised was against all the laws of nature. Thus, it is clear that for Hebrews Abraham was convinced of things not yet seen and so was able to hold on firmly to God's promise.

Then comes an interpretative paragraph (vv. 13-16). Whatever our decision on whether the author of Hebrews used a source or not, we may be confident that verses 13-16 come from the author himself. To some extent,

---

78. See the discussion in Black, *Aramaic Approach*, 83-89. Translations which make Abraham the subject are GN; NIV; NRSV. Those who accept this approach include Lane, *Hebrews*, 2:353-54; Weiss, *Hebräer*, 587-88; Grässer, *Brief an die Hebräer*, 3:132; DeSilva, *Perseverance*, 398; Koester, *Hebrews*, 484, 487; Rose, *Wolke*, 228-29; Söding, *Antwort*, 398n27; Richardson, *Pioneer*, 188n58.

79. An alternative textual solution which would keep Abraham as the subject is to accept the reading of P13 ℵ A Dc [και αυτη Σαρρα δυναμιν] and translate "and with Sarah herself he received strength to beget a child and that when he was past the age." The στειρα may have arisen through dittography of Σαρρα, while αυτη Σαρρα would be taken as an associative dative (So Michel, *Hebräer*, 257, 262; Bruce, *Hebrews*, 302; Attridge, *Hebrews*, 325-26; Ellingworth, *Hebrews*, 586-88).

80. Cf. 10:23: "Let us hold fast unswervingly the confession of our hope, for (God) who has made promises is faithful." Grässer, *Brief an die Hebräer*, 3:133, emphasizes strongly that faith as unswerving adherence to the promise of God is the fitting human response to the faithfulness of the God who promises. As to a possible tension with Genesis 17:16-17 (the mention of Abraham's laughter at the news that Sarah would have a son), Rose, *Wolke*, 232-33, points out that Targum Onkelos translated Genesis 17:17b to the effect that Abraham received the news with joy, while other Targums weaken the Hebrew text, and that Jubilees 14:21 stressed Abraham's faith at the news. Hebrews may have known of this development of the Genesis story.

81. DeSilva, *Hebrews*, 398-99, objects to the importing of "as good as" in translation, since, he believes, this weakens the full force and starkness of the Greek: the author is concerned to stress God's power in the face of the "deadness" both of Sarah's womb and Abraham's procreative parts.

on first impression, it might seem to break up the narrative sequence of events connected with Abraham (vv. 8–12, 17–19).[82] We are told that all mentioned previously (or specifically the patriarchs?) died without having received the promises, but they died κατα πιστιν: they were living faithfully when they died. In this attitude of faithfulness, they saw from afar and greeted what was promised.

This mention of the "seeing" on the part of the patriarchs picks up a theme which has already occurred at 11:3 and in the example of Noah (11:7), and which will be mentioned again in the story of Moses (11:25–27) and the exhortation to his addressees to look to Jesus (12:2). Scholtissek has highlighted what he believes is this dialectic between seeing and not seeing as constitutive for Hebrews' understanding of faith.[83] Thus, faith "sees" beyond earthly circumstances to the invisible God[84] and the hoped-for blessings which God had promised, and lets this influence and direct daily living, specifically, to stand firm amidst pressures and temptations and to maintain their journey on the pilgrim way.[85]

Bracketed with their seeing from afar what God had promised and springing from it, is the fact that the patriarchs confessed that they were strangers and pilgrims on earth (v. 13cd). Here the author takes people like the patriarchs as pilgrims on the way to the heavenly City of apocalyptic hope. He sees them as looking beyond a geographical entity like Canaan. They were seeking in reality another country, a better one, a heavenly one. While they were on earth, this remained afar off. They glimpsed the heavenly city and set their sights on it. It motivated their attitude to life. Here on earth they were but strangers and pilgrims.[86] The author remarked that had they been mindful of that country which they had left, they would have had opportunity to return (v. 15). But for them there was no turning back. Because they had their sights set on a better, a heavenly, country, God was not ashamed to be called their God, "for He has prepared a city for them" (v.

---

82. Hays, *New Covenantalism*, 163, comments: "Precisely because these verses digress from the listing of specific examples, they flag the theme that is the hermeneutical key to the whole chapter." Rose, *Wolke*, 247, believes that a vitally important consideration for Hebrews, sufficient to explain his breaking up the flow of examples, is to stress that perfection still awaits these examples of faith, as verse 39 stresses.

83. Scholtissek, *Den Unsichtbaren*, 150–51. Söding, *Zuversicht*, 220, had earlier remarked that Hebrews teaches the need both for right hearing of the Word of God and the right looking at Jesus (2:9; 3:1; 12:2).

84. And in Christian terms, to our high Priest Jesus Christ the Son of God who is now with the Father.

85. For this paragraph, see Scholtissek, *Den Unsichbaren*, 150–57.

86. Cf. Genesis 23:4: Abraham's comment to the Hittites of Hebron—παροικος και παρεπιδημος εγω ειμι μεθ' υμων ("I am an alien and stranger among you").

16). As God's faithfulness to His promises evoked their faithfulness to Him in response, so their faithfulness in turn evoked from Him pride in them and a willingness to be associated with them and to be called their God.

At 11:1 the author had pointed us to the future by the phrases "things hoped for" and "things not seen." This future orientation comes out strongly in verses 13–16. Whether these verses are an insertion into a source used by Hebrews or not, they almost read like a commentary, a pause to take stock, and to draw some preliminary observations which will be relevant and helpful when reflecting on other members of this roll call. It is clear that for the author the situation of the patriarchs is analogous to the Christian addressees.[87] Thus, we may say that the first impression of an interruption (mentioned above) is incorrect.

At verse 17 the author resumed his items of people and actions which illustrate his theme of πιστις. He began again with Abraham and his willingness, when put to the test, to offer up Isaac (Gen 22). The second half of the verse basically repeats the first half, but with fine pathos: "He who had received the promises offered up[88] his only son, concerning whom it had been said, 'Your descendants will be traced through Isaac' " (v. 18; quoting Gen 21:12; 15:4).[89] The quotation is a parenthesis, for verse 19 gives the reason why Abraham was prepared to obey God's command when that command seemed to fly in the face of the very promise that God had previously made. Isaac was the son through whom the promise would be realized, yet here was God demanding that he be sacrificed! The aorist participle middle (λογισαμενος) carries a causal sense: "Because he reckoned that God was able to raise up even from the dead."

The usual approach to verse 19 is to assume that Abraham was actually stopped before he had carried out the sacrifice of Isaac: the verb προσενηνοχεν is taken as indicating an action permanently recorded in Scripture,[90] and the verb προσεφερεν in verse 17 is taken as a conative imperfect.[91] However, some scholars have dissented from this view and have suggested that within Judaism some did believe that Isaac was actually

---

87. Lane, *Hebrews*, 2:219-21, 355-57; Attridge, *Hebrews*, 329; Salevao, *Legitimation*, 135.

88. προσενηνοχεν is the perfect indicative active of προσφερω. See next paragraph for discussion.

89. Lane, *Hebrews*, 2:360, has commented, "When Abraham obeyed God's mandate to leave Ur, he simply gave up his past. But when he was summoned to Mount Moriah to deliver his own son to God, he was asked to surrender his future as well."

90. See Moulton, *Grammar of New Testament Greek*, 1:129.

91. E.g., Attridge, *Hebrews*, 334.

sacrificed. Among some recent examples, we might mention Rose,[92] who argues that Hebrews believed that Abraham did sacrifice Isaac. He argues as follows. On the linguistic level, Rose emphasizes the perfect tense of προσενήνοχεν, and quotes the work of Weiss who, in his study of φερω and its derivatives, concluded that in Hebrews the verb προσφερειν "always means "to accomplish the sacrifice" and not just to bring the offerings to the altar or the priest," though Weiss does not discuss the question whether Hebrews believed that Isaac was actually sacrificed.[93] Rose takes προσφερεν as indicating the manner of the action.[94] He understands the verb κομίζεσθαι to indicate the receiving back of something which one owned but had lost, and points to its use for the hope of resurrection in 2 Maccabees and Josephus.[95] He takes the phrase εν παραβολη| to mean that Abraham received Isaac back from the dead as a symbol of the resurrection still to come.[96]

Furthermore, Rose believes that there is some evidence for this interpretation in Jewish writings and points to LAB 18:5 (and possibly 40:2) and some rabbinical evidence for this view.[97] If Rose is right, then Abraham becomes an even more impressive witness of faith, who is convinced of things not seen (here, resurrection from the dead and the subsequent eschatological rest), and so holds firmly to what is hoped for. Would such a view endanger the uniqueness of Jesus' resurrection? Perhaps not, since Isaac eventually did die.

A year before Rose, Levenson,[98] had also discussed the evidence for the view that some Jewish thinkers believed that Isaac was sacrificed.[99] He is more cautious than Rose, because of the extreme precariousness of dating rabbinic sources. He suggests that a possible terminus a quo for this transformation of the Aqeda may have been the lethal persecution by Hadrian (132–35), but its underlying exegetical moves may go further back. He points out that efforts were made to blunt this new idea. Levenson's concern is to trace the way in which Jewish tradition treated the incident of Genesis 22; he is not concerned to discuss the views of the author of Hebrews. He has been mentioned because, independently of Rose, he has suggested a

---

92. Rose, *Wolke*, 235–45.

93. Weiss, "Φερω, κτλ," *TDNT* 9:67.

94. BDF 327. The comment on Hebrews 11:17 runs "a supplementary descriptive characterization of what was peculiar in this case."

95. Rose, *Wolke*, 238, referring to 2 Macc 7:39 and Josephus, *BJ* 2.153.

96. Rose, *Wolke*, 237.

97. Rose, *Wolke*, 239–42.

98. Levenson, *Death and Resurrection*, 192–99.

99. Levenson, *Death and Resurrection*, 194–98. The rabbinical texts to which he draws attention differ from those produced by Rose.

strand of Jewish tradition in which it was believed that Isaac had actually been sacrificed, and then raised to life by God.

What, then, are we to make of this suggested interpretation put forward by Rose?[100] While linguistically he has much on his side in respect to προσενήνοχεν, the use of the imperfect προσέφερεν tells against him. The conative sense helps to interpret the previous perfect.[101] Furthermore, dating the traditions in rabbinic sources remains problematical. Finally, if the idea was current in Hebrews' day, would he have linked on to what appears to have been a minority view amongst Jewish scholars? It seems safest to adhere to the traditional interpretation which agrees with the Genesis text: that Abraham was prepared to offer Isaac and his intention was accepted as equivalent to an actual carrying out of the command.

We were told at verse 12 that Abraham was as good as dead and yet God had enabled him to beget a child, to create life. Now, at the moment of testing, Abraham goes on faithfully trusting God, convinced of God's power to effect resurrection from the dead. According to verse 19b, the stay of execution is parabolic of God's mysterious power to raise up from the dead, to bring life out of death.

Clearly, the author of Hebrews is crediting Abraham not only with a conviction that God had the power to raise the dead, but also with a belief in the resurrection of the dead.[102] Here the author goes beyond Genesis, but he shares the conviction of some Jews of his day that at the end of history God would raise the dead for judgment either for life or punishment, while in the meantime the righteous were in some form of paradise and the unrighteous in a place of torments.[103]

With that, the author moved on from Abraham's story to mention other characters from the OT and later. Before we sum up the author's treatment of Abraham, it will be useful to look at the conclusion at 11:39–40 and

---

100. It is perhaps disappointing that neither Koester, *Hebrews*, nor Backhaus, *Hebräerbrief*, discuss Rose's interpretation, though they are aware of his book and refer to it. DeSilva, *Perseverance*, does not list Rose's work in his bibliography.

101. Cf. Söding, *Antwort*, 402.

102. Söding, *Antwort*, 402, has suggested that the author believed that Abraham derived his conviction about resurrection of the dead from the fact that Isaac was given to him when he was "already dead" (ταυτα νενεκρωμενου, 11:12).

103. Luke 16:19–31 illustrates this kind of belief. The Testament of Levi 18:10–11 and Luke 23:43 illustrate the idea of paradise post-mortem. Both the Wisdom of Solomon 2–5 and 4 Maccabees 7:18–19; 16:25; 17:12; 18:23 have the concept of immortality of the soul, so that death is followed by being in God's eternal rest. Bruce, *Hebrews*, 311–12, suggests that Hebrews deduced from Abraham's comment that he would return with Isaac (Gen 22:5) that Abraham was convinced that God would raise Isaac from the dead.

also 12:1-3 which is really the climax of the roll-call of the heroes of faith. The author indicated that there was not enough time to go into detail with people after the entry into Canaan (v. 32), but he did give a general survey, the details of which in many respects recall the Maccabean martyrs without specifying them (vv. 33-38).

He then gave a brief reflection before mentioning Jesus:

> All these, though well attested by their πιστις did not obtain the promise, because God had foreseen something better for us, that they should not be made perfect without us. (vv. 39-40)

This shows that there is a strongly corporate connotation to the concept of perfection/being made perfect.[104] God has, as it were, held back the OT heroes of faith in order that Christians might enter this perfection with them. The two groups, the faithful before Jesus and those after him, will comprise the one people of God and enter together the Heavenly City which God has in store for them. In the divine plan and through the divine action, all will be brought to perfection and share in it together.[105]

The imagery switches from the journey or the pilgrimage to a race. With the example of those in the past who have lived a life of faithfulness to God in mind, the addressees should lay aside everything that hinders the running of the race, and especially sin which clings so closely. They should run the race set before them δι'υπομονης (12:1-2). Once more, we encounter this idea of steadfastness, endurance, stickability. The author had urged the addressees to exhibit this quality at 10:36, and now he emphasized this exhortation again. In this race their gaze must be fixed on Jesus, εις τον της πιστεως αρχηγον και τελειωτης. Someone who is an αρχηγος is a pioneer, one who blazes a trail, who opens up a way, goes "where no man has trodden before." A τελειωτης (a rare word)[106] is one who completes or finishes or perfects something or a commission or task. Here the idea is that Jesus not only pioneered but completed the race of πιστις.

It is astonishing how many ancient and modern translations render "our faith." Not only does ημων not occur (granted that sometimes it is legitimate to introduce it in an English translation), not only is the Greek definite article used with abstract nouns as here, but "our faith" basically introduces a new understanding of πιστις over against the whole of chapter

---

104. Cf. Caird, *Just Men Made Perfect*, 89-98.

105. This passage itself is a strong argument against the charge of supersessionism sometimes levelled against Hebrews. For a full discussion and rebuttal of the charge, see Hays, *New Covenantalism*, 151-72.

106. See Delling, "τελος κτλ," *TWNT* 8:86.

11.[107] The phrase should surely be rendered "the pioneer and perfecter of faith," i.e., Jesus himself started and finished the race; he began it and ended it in the Heavenly City.[108] He was entered for the race of faith like the rest of us, but he ran it perfectly. He did not stumble or give up or veer off the track. He started and completed the race perfectly (cf. 2:10; 5:9; 7:28).[109]

In running this race, Jesus faced the cross. But he despised the shame associated with such a death, and because of[110] the joy set before him, he endured (υπεμεινεν) the cross. The Son of God displayed endurance and steadfastness when faced with the cross. As a result, he has now sat down, and remains seated, at the right hand of God's throne.

It is because of this twofold aspect—endurance of the cross and reward in heaven—that the writer can urge the addressees: "Consider him who υπομεμενηκοτα (endured) such hostility directed against himself by sinners." (v. 3). This is the second use of υπομενειν in respect of Jesus himself in 12:2–3, and illustrates how important this whole idea is for the author.

Of course, Jesus is more than just an example or model, but he is that. The addressees should be inspired by his example, while at the same time they know that their salvation depends on him (he is "the pioneer of our salvation" [2:10]; he is the cause of eternal salvation [5:9]; he is the forerunner who has opened up the way to God's presence for us [6:20]; by his sacrifice he has obtained the cleansing and forgiveness of our sins. [1:3c; 2:17; 9:24–26; 10:12]).[111]

---

107. McKelvey, *Pioneer*, 136, expresses similar surprise at the English translations, and points out that happily the REB and TNIV have "pioneer and perfecter of faith."

108. Cf. Bruce, *Hebrews*, 351; Attridge, *Hebrews*, 356; Lane, *Hebrews*, 2:411–12; DeSilva, *Perseverance*, 431–32; Hamm, *Faith*, 280; Söding, *Zuversicht*, 229–30; Rose, *Wolke*, 338–43; Still, *Christos*, 752; Marshall, *Soteriology in Hebrews*, 212; Richardson, *Pioneer*, 96–105, 162, 222–28. Delling, "τελος," *TDNT* 8:86–87, acknowledges that "one cannot rule out" this interpretation.

109. In these three texts, the author either said that God made Jesus perfect (2:10) or he used the aorist or perfect participle passive at 5:9 and 7:28 respectively, indicating divine action upon Jesus.

110. Αντι normally means "instead of." Montefiore, *Hebrews*, 215; Lane, *Hebrews*, 2:399, adhere to this meaning, as does Schneider, "σταυρος," *TWNT* 7:577, while acknowledging that αντι can mean "for the sake of." But the meaning "for the sake of" is preferred by Spicq, *Hébreux*, 2:387; Bruce, *Hebrews*, 353; Attridge, *Hebrews*, 357; DeSilva, *Perseverance*, 435–38; Rose, *Wolke*, 340–41; Richardson, *Pioneer*, 101. In context, the joy set before him seems to be the sitting at the right hand of God mentioned at verse 2c.

111. Rose, *Wolke*, 342, aptly says that Jesus is both an *exemplum fidei* and also the *fundamentum fidei*. For similar emphasis, see Hamm, *Faith*, 270–91; Söding, *Zuversicht*, 231–32; Still, *Christos*, 746–55; Richardson, *Pioneer*, 162, 164, 226, where he describes Jesus as the *model* to follow and the *means* by which salvation has been accomplished. More recently, Whitlark, *Enabling Fidelity to God*, esp. 146–80, has argued that the

Excursus: Some reflections on πιστις in Hebrews

Lest there be any misunderstanding from what has been said about faith, as if the implication of the discussion is that the author of Hebrews has emptied faith of any Christological reference, it will be as well if we look at this issue here.

In 1965, Erik Grässer published a monograph on faith in Hebrews,[112] which became highly influential.[113] Grässer goes through the letter and exegetes passages to determine the sense of "faith." He pointed out that the noun πιστις is used with God, not Christ as the object (6:1), and similarly with the verb πιστευειν (11:6). The adjective πιστος is used of God (10:23; 11:11) and of Jesus (2:17; 3:2). God's promises are absolutely sure, reliable, and unbreakable. Faith is the virtue which corresponds to this faithfulness of God and the reliability of His promises and the faithfulness of Jesus. Faith is a standing firm, a holding fast, a persistence, an unwavering stability towards what one hopes for, a στασις; it is the mode of conduct which is directed to a future goal, to what is invisible which alone has reality. The idea of πιστις has shaded over into faithfulness, endurance, holding fast to. It has a number of synonyms such as υπομονη, υποστασις, υπακοη, ελπις, παρρησια, and μακροθυμια. Its antonym is απιστια which also has a number of correlates such as υποστολη, υποστελλεσθαι, απειθεια, παρακοη, αποστηναι, and παραπιπτειν. The power to stand fast diminishes as the intensity of hope diminishes. Jesus himself is the crowning example of this faith (12:2), and from his destiny, which was the joy that was set before him, that is, to be in the presence of God (12:3), the addressees can deduce what continuing steadfastness will lead to.

His case is an impressive one. But more recently, there have been several voices raised in criticism of this one-sided approach and to defend the

---

author of Hebrews rejects the concept of reciprocity between a benefactor and beneficiary, with its exchange of favors on the one hand and gratitude and support on the other, as a way of understanding the relationship between God and believers. Rather, there is need for God to transform the human condition, and He has done this through the atoning work of His Son on the cross, which has secured the forgiveness of sins and the establishment of the new covenant, as 8:1–10:18 sets forth (through Jeremiah 31:31–34, God has proclaimed that He would not remember our sins—cleansing from sins has an abiding transformative benefit—and would write His laws on the human heart). This, plus the certainty of the promised future salvation in the Heavenly City, motivates ongoing faithfulness.

112. Grässer, *Der Glaube im Hebräerbrief.*

113. E.g., he was to a large extent followed by Dautzenberg, *Der Glaube im Hebräerbrief*, 161–77, though Dautzenberg did disagree with Grässer's view that the Christological emphasis in faith was being displaced by a theological emphasis in the post-apostolic period (174).

view that there are Christological and soteriological aspects to faith in the letter as well as the faithfulness nuance.[114]

Two general remarks may be made by way of introduction. The first was made by Schunack. He posed the question whether such a stylishly, rhetorically, and theologically careful writer as the author of Hebrews would simply merge πιστις into any number of synonyms and did not distinguish between faith, hope, patience, confidence, which Grässer alleged?[115] The second is to point out that over against the lack of the use of Jesus/Jesus Christ as the object of the verb to believe or the noun faith, attention must be directed to the way that the author insisted on the need to hold firm to the confession of Jesus as the Son of God (4:14; cf. 3:1; 10:23)[116] and his insistence that the addressees "have" a great high priest in Jesus (4:14-15; 8:1; 10:21). The author stressed the fact that Jesus by the atoning sacrifice of himself had obtained eternal redemption for us and had opened up the way to God and access to Him. We should note also the way in which attributes of the God of Israel are transferred to Jesus as the Son (e.g., creative power via the quotation of Psalm 102:5-7 at 1:10-12, and the concept of sameness at 1:12 together with 13:8). To this may be added the use, as elsewhere in the NT, of the Son's sitting down at the right of the Father in the heavenly places (e.g., 1:3, 13, etc.).[117] We might say that Hebrews has an overall theocentric emphasis within which there is also a Christological stress, which is captured right at the beginning, in the prologue (1:1-4) and indeed in the thrust of 1:5-13.[118]

---

114. Among those who are critical of Grässer and maintain that the concept has a soteriological and Christological aspect are Thompson, *Christian Philosophy*, 69; Rissi, *Theologie*, 105; Rose, *Wolke*, 349-50; Scholtissek, *Den Unsichtbaren*, 150-64 (who stresses the seeing/not seeing aspect of Hebrews' exposition in relation to faith); Söding, *Zuversicht*, 221, 234-35 (who argued that there is a Christological aspect in faith in God in Hebrews: faith is theocentric and Christocentric).

115. Schunack, *Exegetische Beobachtungen*, 208.

116. Schunack, *Exegetische Beobachtungen*, 212, has put this in a sharply pointed manner when he said, "Christian existence is existence in confession."

117. Rhee, *Faith in Hebrews*, has gone carefully through the letter and has argued that for the author Jesus Christ is the object and the content of faith and that faith has an eschatological orientation (primarily futuristic, but not neglecting the present aspect), as well as involving moral qualities like faithfulness, steadfastness, and confidence in God's promise. Surprisingly, Rhee does not actually examine the occurrences of πιστις throughout the letter.

118. Grässer, *Glaube*, 3, himself recognized and stated the paradox that Hebrews has Christ at the center of salvation, and yet his concept of faith is rather primitive and rooted in the Old Testament and early [Grässer actually used the term "late," which was then current among scholars] Judaism, especially Hellenistic-Alexandrine Judaism (Philo offers illuminating analogies). Grässer (184) placed Hebrews on the threshold

We may illustrate the theocentric emphasis by looking at two sentences in chapter 11. The first is verse 3: "By faith we perceive (νουμεν) that the worlds were created by the word of God so that the seen has come into being (γεγονεναι) from what is not seen (μη εκ φαινομενων)." The phrase "from what is not seen" could refer to the heavenly realm of God and intend God Himself, just as in the main clause the subject is "the word of God."[119] The idea of steadfastness or endurance is not appropriate here. Faith sees the hand of God behind the created universe, or, as Hebrews puts it, that the word of God is the creative power which brought the universe into being. Reference to the word of God recalls the fact that for the author God is the God who speaks (1:1-2; 4:12-13; 12:28) and the God who has made promises (4:1; 6:12, 15, 17; 7:6; 8:6; 9:15; 10:36; 11:9, 13, 17, 33, 39). This aspect of faith as penetrating beyond the visible to lay hold of God who cannot be seen comes out elsewhere in chapter 11 to which we shall return shortly.

The second verse is 11:6. Here the author says that it is impossible to please God, for whoever approaches God must believe that He is/exists or is the one true, living God[120] (πιστευσαι ... δει ... οτι εστιν) and that He is a rewarder of those who seek Him. This belief is not a purely cerebral matter, an intellectual adherence to a theological proposition about the existence of God, but is a conviction that God is the living God, the God who speaks and acts, to fall into whose hands is a fearful thing (10:31). Faith orientates the whole being of the person on God, not earthly matters. But there is also a future aspect. God is the One who rewards those who seek Him. The reward is to receive the promises (cf. 6:17-18), to inherit the unshakeable kingdom not as yet seen (12:28).

These two convictions about God are the foundation of existence for the one who believes.[121]

The Christocentric emphasis within "faith" can be seen in the fact that through his death (his blood), Jesus has opened up a new and living way into the presence of God and that he is the great priest over the sanctuary of God. On this basis, the author exhorts "Let us draw near with a true heart in

---

between early Christianity and the post-apostolic time. He links the shift in what he perceives as Hebrews' understanding of faith with the delay of the parousia (195-96), and sees Hebrews' interpretation as a new and legitimate interpretation of the original kerygma in the second generation of Christianity (219).

119. For this interpretation, see Schunack, *Exegetische Beobachtungen*, 229.

120. See Morgan, *Roman Faith and Christian Faith*, 334, who argues that since atheism was extremely rare in the ancient Mediterranean world, it is unlikely that εστιν simply means "exists."

121. See Schunack, *Exegetische Beobachtungen*, 226-27. Cf. Scholtissek, *Den Unsichtbaren*, 151, 164: faith has vividly before it Him who is invisible and the hoped-for blessings.

the full assurance of πιστις" (10:22a) The idea of steadfastness or endurance is hardly appropriate here. What is entailed in this "faith" is developed by two participial phrases:

> Having got our hearts sprinkled clean from an evil conscience
> and our bodies washed with pure water.[122]

The two phrases are set in a parallelism. "Heart" and "body" express the whole person, while the language of "sprinkled" and "washed" seem indebted to OT language of purification.[123] The reference to "water" probably evokes the act of baptism.[124]

The full assurance of faith rests on the finished, once-for-all work of Jesus as our High Priest, mediated and appropriated in believer's baptism. Faith has a soteriological reference here.

We now turn to instances where faith is conjoined with the idea of patience, endurance, steadfastness, "stickability." We begin with 6:12. The addressees are called on to imitate those who through πιστις and μακροθυμια inherit the promises. At the very least one can say that these two concepts are so conjoined and so related that "patience" arises out of faith and is a natural expression of true faith. Secondly, there is 12:1b-2. "Let us run the race set before us with υπομονη." The race is the race of *faith*, Jesus being the only one who has started and finished the race of faith perfectly. In the race of faith, the quality of endurance, steadfastness, perseverance, is absolutely essential.

In 6:12; 13:7, and, by implication, 12:2, Hebrews summons the addressees to imitate the faith of others, those of the past like Abraham and their former leaders now dead, together with the others named and unnamed in the roll call of faith in chapter 11, including Jesus himself in 12:1-2. As we have already pointed out, it is impossible to imitate the personal trust/commitment involved in the Pauline and Johannine understanding of faith in Jesus, but one can imitate someone's endurance.

The third passage is 11:1. We have already discussed this passage, and argued that the sense of πιστις is akin to faithfulness, to steadfastness, sticking to, persistence in. There is no need to repeat the discussion.

At this point it is appropriate to mention that a number of scholars have pointed to the way Hebrews depicts Jesus not only as an example to be

---

122. The translation seeks to reflect the fact that the two participles, ρεραντισμενοι and λελουσμενοι are the perfect *middle* (nominative masculine plural, agreeing with the subject of the hortatory subjunctive προσερχωμεθα), not passive.

123. See Lev 16; 18; Ezek 36:25.

124. For details, see the discussion in Beasley-Murray, *Baptism in the New Testament*, 247-50.

imitated, but also as supplying motivating power to resist the temptations and withstand the testings and the pressures of this world and to maintain their Christian stance firm to the end.[125] Thus, for example, in the light of the sacrifice of Jesus believers may confidently draw near to God (4:14-16; 10:19, 22; cf. 7:19). In the light of the fact that Jesus not only started but perfectly finished his race of faith, they may draw strength to follow in his footsteps (12:2-4, 12-13). Jesus, though the Son of God, is able, because of his incarnation ("made like us in every respect, yet without sin" [4:15]), to sympathize with our weakness and *help* those undergoing testing and temptation (2:18; cf. 4:16). As one who is the same yesterday, today, and forever (13:8), he intercedes for us (7:25). As the exalted one in the presence of God, he is the objective basis of that hope which is described as the anchor of the soul[126] (6:19-20). We should also not ignore the concluding prayer-doxology where God is asked to equip the addressees with everything good to do His will, working in us what is pleasing to Him (13:21).[127]

Earlier, we mentioned that faith penetrates beyond the visible to the unseen realities, to Him who is invisible (this would include the exalted Jesus who now sits at God's right hand in the heavens). Chapter 11 contains a number of examples of this "seeing" of faith. At 11:7, the author says that Noah was warned about *things not yet seen* (i.e., the Flood). He proceeded on the basis of faith in God and the reliability of the warning given him and with godly fear to construct an ark with the purpose of saving his family. A little later (11:13) it is said of the patriarchs that they *saw from afar* and greeted what God had promised: for Hebrews, this is not so much the land of Canaan, but a heavenly country, a city whose maker and builder is God (11:10, 14-16). Under the rubric of faith, Moses is said to have preferred to be maltreated with the people of God rather than enjoy the temporary pleasures of sin. He considered the reproach of the Messiah better riches than the treasures of Egypt, for he *was looking to* the reward. By faith he left Egypt, not afraid of the king's anger, for he persevered, as *seeing* Him who is invisible (11:25-27). Finally, at 12:2, the recipients of the letter are told to run with perseverance the race set before them, *looking to* Jesus pioneer and

---

125. See note 111 above, with reference to the views of Rose, Hamm, Still, Söding, Richardson, and Whitlark.

126. See not dissimilar statements to this way of putting the matter in Bruce, *Hebrews*, 131; Grässer, *Glaube*, 34; Attridge, *Hebrews*, 184. I have so phrased the matter because, grammatically speaking, the relative pronoun ἣν refers to hope (ἐλπίδος [v. 18]). This way of phrasing the matter answers the objections of Hofius (*Vorhang*, 85-86) to identifying the anchor with Jesus and his preference for taking hope as Hoffnungsgut promised to the community. Hofius (*Vorhang*, 85n263) lists those scholars who interpret Jesus himself as the anchor.

127. See Whitlark, *Enabling*, 147.

perfecter of faith. Jesus is at the right hand of God in the heavens and cannot be literally seen. Faith, however, *sees* him, who for our sake became lower than the angels for a little while, now crowned with glory and honor (2:9).

In all these instances, the various verbs to see[128] are used in a metaphorical sense of spiritual perception and insight.[129]

We may mention briefly how the stress on hope in Hebrews has much in common with the stress on faith. It is likely that hope includes the objective and the subjective nuances: objective in the sense that God has promised certain blessings[130] and these are what are hoped for; subjective, in the sense that the believer exercises hope to receive what God has promised.

Four times the author urges the recipients to hold fast to or maintain hope: they should hold fast (κατασχωμεν) to both their boldness and the hope of which they are proud (3:6); they should demonstrate the same zest as in the past to maintain the full assurance of hope to the end (6:11); they should hold fast (κρατησαι) to the hope which lies before them (6:18); and they should hold fast (κατεχωμεν) without wavering to the confession of hope (10:23). These exhortations are similar to the exhortations to hold fast the confessions of what they believe about Jesus (4:14) and the need to draw near to God in the full assurance of faith (10:22).

It is not that hope and faith are identical, but that they do come close together, since faith is directed to what God has promised to those who are faithful to the end.

Further light can be shed on our theme by looking briefly at the fact that the author saw his addressees facing an analogous situation to the generation which came out of Egypt and wandered in the wilderness (never actually to see the promised land). He stated that, as with his addressees, the wilderness generation had had good news preached to them. God had promised them "rest" but they were not found worthy to enter the promised rest. Hebrews explained why this was so. They had "an evil heart of unbelief" (απιστια [3:12, 19]); they were guilty of disobedience (απειθεια [4:6]). In echoes of the account of the rebellion of the Israelites in the wilderness in reaction to the report of the spies about the land and its inhabitants in Numbers 14:1–24, the author asks

---

128. Των μηδεπω βλεπομενων (v. 7); ιδοντες (v. 13); απεβλεπεν (v. 26); ορων (v. 27); αφορωντες (12:2); βλεπομεν (2:9).

129. Cf. the comment of Scholtissek, *Den Unsichtbaren*, 164, at the conclusion of his article: "Faith develops the power of resistance because it has vividly before it the One who is invisible and the hoped for blessings."

130. In German, *Hoffungsgut*, which, in the context of the NT, could be freely paraphrased "the blessings for which we hope." See Grässer, *Glaube*, 33–34.

Who rebelled when they heard? Was it not all those who came out of Egypt under the leadership of Moses? With whom was God angry for forty years? Was it not with those who sinned, whose bodies fell in the desert? To whom did God swear that they should not enter His rest if not to those who were disobedient? So we see that they were not able to enter because of their unbelief. (3:16-19)

We note the close association of lack of faith and disobedience: hence the warning "See to it, brothers and sisters, lest there should be among any of you an evil heart of unbelief in falling away from the living God" (3:12). The corollary is that faith and obedience go together (as illustrated in the case of Abraham, who "by faith, when called, obeyed by going out to a place which he was going to receive for an inheritance and he went out, not knowing where he was going" [11:8]).

Why was it that the majority of the Israelites turned against Yahweh? The answer comes at 4:2: ουκ ωφελησεν ο λογος της ακοης εκεινους, μη συγκεκασμενους τη πιστει τοις ακουσασιν.[131] The author asserted that the word from God which they heard did not benefit them, because they were not united by faith with those who listened. The phrase "those who listened" presumably refers to Joshua and Caleb and perhaps also Moses.[132] The author meant that those who rebelled did not share the same faith in God, in His word, and in His power to do what He had promised, as Joshua and Caleb had. Faith is here directed to the word.[133]

In conclusion, we may say that Hebrews reveals a rich use of πιστις. There is a range of nuances contained in his usage,[134] and context is all-important. It is wrong to suggest that faith has become a virtue displayed by humans. It has a theocentric, Christological, and soteriological nuance in

---

131. This assumes that συγκεκερασμενους is the correct reading (P13 P45 A B C D, some it mss) as against συγκεκερασμενος (supported by ℵ, some it mss, Ephraem, with Cyril quoting it once out of two references to it), on the grounds that it is the more difficult reading and more likely to have been altered by copyists.

132. Spicq *Hébreux*, 2:81; Lane, *Hebrews*, 1:98; DeSilva, *Perseverance*, 164; Backhaus, *Hebräerbrief*, 160; Koster, *Hebrews*, 270. Westcott, *Hebrews*, 93; Michel, *Hebräerbrief*, 111; Montefiore *Hebrews*, 82, agree that this is so if one accepts the reading συγκεκερασμενους, though preferring συγκεκερασ-μενος themselves. Attridge, *Hebrews*, 126, interprets the εκεινους of Christians contemporary with the author, but this seems somewhat strained.

133. Grässer, *Glaube*, 14, himself speaks of a union of hearing, word, and faith, and of a coordination of faith and word.

134. Morgan, *Roman Faith*, 335, commented that it is clear from chapter 11 that Hebrews' understanding of πιστις is "complex, making use of a wide range of meanings, including trust, faithfulness, belief, confidence, obedience, and hope," to which we would wish to add endurance.

some passages, while in others the focus is on the steadfastness/faithfulness which is the appropriate response to the divine faithfulness and the reliability of what God promises. It comes close to υπομονη and to ελπις without being identical with them, and is the opposite of υποστολη or falling away from the living God.

Excursus on Pamela M. Eisenbaum's Interpretation of Hebrews 11

In her monograph, *The Jewish Heroes of Christian History: Hebrews 11 in Literary Context*, Pamela Eisenbaum has argued that Hebrews has put forward a new interpretation of Biblical history. He has de-nationalized Biblical history and made it supra-national. He has concentrated on the personal odyssey of the heroes, with the aim of making it possible for Gentile Christians to appropriate the Biblical story as their history. These Jewish heroes become the ancestral heritage of Christians.

She stresses that these heroes are marginalized individuals who are portrayed as standing outside the nation of Israel (She stresses, e.g., that there is no mention of any of the covenants with God in chapter 11). They have the ability to see into the future and to discern something better in the midst of adverse conditions. She goes further and argues that these heroes have undergone a "transvaluation." The author diminishes their national status, and Eisenbaum stresses that they did not receive honor, reward, or recognition in their lifetime. They could not, a priori, have been perfect before the ministry of Jesus, and so can only be partial models.[135]

How sound is this case? There is considerable validity in the idea of denationalization. In general, this was a concomitant of the admission of non-Jews into the company of believers. Paul himself had said that "there is neither Jew nor Greek, slave nor free, male nor female, but you are all one in Christ" (Gal 3:28). If he is quoting a tradition here, this obviously widens the spectrum within early Christianity which espoused this supra-national perspective. Later, the author of 1 Peter was to point out to the addressees of his letter that fellow Christians throughout the world were undergoing similar sufferings.[136]

Still on a general level, the detailed comments on individual heroes finished with Rahab, i.e., before the Israelites had settled in the land and had developed national institutions. It could be argued that this actually

---

135. These two paragraphs draw on statements made by Eisenbaum throughout her book, *Jewish Heroes*, 3, 81, 87, 142, 161, 165–66, 173, 178, 179–88, 192, 218–20, 225–26.

136. The author uses the term αδελφοτης in the κοσμος (5:9).

shows that Hebrews was not interested in national institutions. On the other hand, the author had spent a considerable amount of space and time discussing worship, priesthood, sacrifice, tabernacle, and covenant already (7:1–10:18), and had argued on typological grounds that they prefigured the greater priesthood, worship, sacrifice, and sanctuary, in connection with Jesus, his death, and exaltation to heaven. There was no need to labor the points already made so forcibly. He operated with the approach of "Correspondence-Difference-Superiority," and this inevitably involves a degree of de-nationalization. A further important point on a general level, is the fact that Hebrews emphasized the transcendental goal of the pilgrimage of faith: it is a matter of looking towards the city which is to come, of entering God's everlasting rest (13:14; cf. 4:1, 6–11; 12:22–24). There was bound to be a corresponding diminution of the idea of the inheritance of an earthly country. Again, this idea was inherent in Christian conviction from early on (e.g., Phil 3:20–21).

Then again, towards the end of his list of heroes, the author comments that the world was not worthy of them (v. 38), just as earlier he had said of the pre-deluvian hero, Noah, that by his action of building an ark, in obedience to God's instructions, he "condemned the world" (v. 7). In both passages, we have as it were a trans-national perspective.

However, there is a danger of pushing this idea of trans-nationalization too far. We may ask, firstly, whether the nation of Israel is as absent as Eisenbaum makes out. She believes that Hebrews portrays the heroes as isolated from the nation. The following observations may be made. In the first place, this does not seem to fit Abraham. After all, he was the start and origin of the Hebrew people. How can it be said that he stood apart from the nation? The assertion does not seem meaningful in his case. Then again, there is a reference to the descendants of Abraham: Hebrews quoted the promise "Your descendants [σπερμα] will be traced through Isaac" (v. 19). It does not seem accurate to say that Abraham is unconnected to national promises.[137]

Then, secondly, as to Moses, the author says that he preferred to suffer maltreatment with *"the people of God"* rather than be counted as son of Pharaoh's daughter and enjoy the temporary pleasures of sin (vv. 24–25). He is also said to have celebrated the Passover (v. 28). Eisenbaum's statement "Like Abraham, Moses leaves his nation of origin, only neither hero does so in order to become part of Israel" is puzzling, and seems to say the exact opposite of what the text is saying. That Moses was an Egyptian by origin is nowhere stated in verses 23–26, and, if the author assumes some knowledge

---

137. Eisenbaum, *Jewish Heroes*, 159. She also stresses how little Abraham received from God during his lifetime, which actually helps to enhance Abraham as a person of faith!

of the Biblical story on the part of the addressees (the meager reference to the fact that Moses was "hidden for three months by his parents" suggests this), would contradict the statements of the book of Exodus.

Thirdly, in verse 29, the reference to the crossing of the Reed Sea, the verb διεβησαν does not formally have a subject. The subject refers back to the αυτων of the previous verse, but it may be reasonably claimed that ad sensum "the people of God" of verse 25 is very much still in the author's mind.

Then, fourthly, verses 33–38 are universally accepted as making allusion both to Daniel and his three colleagues and to the Maccabean struggle. Now in one sense Daniel and his three colleagues were isolated from the nation by their position in the Persian court, but in another sense they felt the bond with their nation and its traditions (e.g., Dan 2:23; 5:13; 6:3; 7, etc.). The Maccabean struggle was not only a struggle against a foreign king, Antiochus Epiphanes, but also a struggle against those regarded as traitors, the enemy within, the hated collaborators with Antiochus, the Hellenizing party. Now clearly details indicating that that struggle centered on covenant and law (circumcision and food laws) are not given; nevertheless, it was a struggle for what was deemed the heart and soul of the nation and its heritage. The author of Hebrews seems to be assuming knowledge of all this on the part of his addressees. May we not invoke the principle of inter-textuality, so much stressed nowadays? The author of Hebrews is not arguing in a vacuum.

Finally, we might also mention the concluding remark by Hebrews to the effect that all these heroes of faith did not receive what God had promised. In the purpose of God, they were held back (as it were). God did not intend that they should be made perfect *without us*: that is, until after Christ had opened up the new and living way into the presence of God (10:19–20). For Hebrews, there is one people of God embracing past and present.[138]

What of Eisenbaum's stress on marginalization? Obviously, there is considerable truth in this.[139] If we take the case of Abraham, he was marginalized in the sense that at God's call he left his country of origin and became a stranger in Canaan. Eisenbaum stresses that Hebrews does not specifically mention Abraham's wealth. But, on the principle of inter-textuality, this may be an item that he assumed would be known by his addressees.

---

138. Scholtissek, *Den Unsichtbaren*, 159–60, 163–64, is also critical of Eisenbaum. In Hebrews there is no conflict with the mother religion and no attempt to disinherit the Jewish community.

139. It is also true that this may make a greater appeal to people today aware of the plight of the poor and marginalized the world over, than what might seem the otherworldly piety of "the pilgrim's progress."

To the modern ear, living in tents conjures up pictures of the poverty and misery of overcrowded refugee camps, but in Hebrews 11 it is both a way of saying that he and Isaac and Jacob were nomads and of indicating that their lifestyle corresponded with their convictions that here they had no permanent abode, but were looking for an heavenly country (vv. 9-10, 13-16).[140] In other words, our author emphasized Abraham's choice. Of course, that choice was in response to God's call. The same element of choice comes out in the story of Moses: "he refused . . . he chose" (ηρνησατο λεγεσθαι . . . ελομενος [vv. 24-25]). He chose a course of action and a life-style commensurate with it (one aspect of this was his refusal to be afraid of Pharaoh [v. 27]) because of his faith in God.

While marginalization suggests a position imposed by society on some of its members or residents, what Hebrews is depicting is a *deliberate choice* on the part of Abraham and Moses. This choice had certain social consequences which they put up with because of their conviction about God and what God was promising to those who obey Him (vv. 10, 13-16, 26-27).

Furthermore, there are parts of chapter 11 where it would be difficult to maintain that marginalization is dominant. In verses 33-34, the author says that there were those who "through faith conquered kingdoms . . . shut the mouths of lions, quenched the power of fire . . . grew powerful from weakness, became mighty in warfare, put to flight foreign armies." These generalizing remarks drew on stories from the book of Judges, the exploits of David, Daniel and his friends, and the Maccabean warriors, and celebrate their *achievements*, which ultimately were due to God's power. It is, of course, in verses 35-38 that the marginalization of the past people of faith is most powerfully present.

Attridge has a helpful comment: "The encomium on faith had indicated the many dimensions of that virtue."[141] Briefly, we may mention that these heroes of the faith looked beyond the present to the future, to things unseen, and to God who is invisible (so Noah [v. 7]; Abraham [vv. 10, 13-16]; Isaac [v. 20]; Jacob [v. 21]; Joseph [v. 22]; and Moses [vv. 26-27]); they trusted in God as the One who kept His promises (Abraham and Sarah [v. 11]) and who was able to raise the dead (v. 19); they were liberated from fear and enabled to endure even the severest difficulties (Moses [v. 27]).

---

140. "The tent is the dwelling of the nomad and the traveller" (Michel, *Hebraer*, 259). Attridge, *Hebrews*, 323, says that the tent as the image of nomadic existence makes for a vivid contrast with the city, which is an image of permanence and stability that is the ultimate goal (vv. 10, 16).

141. Attridge, *Hebrews*, 354, in describing faith as a "virtue," is obviously influenced by Grässer.

Eisenbraum mentions these (as we have indicated), but they seem to be submerged under the marginalization motif.

This brings us to the place within Hebrews 11 of the anaphoric πιστει/κατα πιστιν. By his constant repetition of this, has not the author guided our attention to where *he* wished to place the emphasis. Some may feel that occasionally he has not chosen particularly apt illustrations and has passed over better examples.[142] But that is not the point. The more we stress that Hebrews 11 is the author's own work and that it is crafted in a linguistically and rhetorically skilful manner, the more we ought to follow him in his stress on πιστις.

Pamela Eisenbaum has put us in her debt by her stimulating treatment of Hebrews 11, but in the end we believe that she has not made out all aspects of her case.

3.3. Summary

How then does the author use the person and story of Abraham?[143]

He referred to the following events in the story of Abraham: the call of Abraham (11:8); the wanderings of Abraham (11:9); the battle with the Canaanite kings and the meeting with Melchizedek (7:1–10); the begetting of Isaac when Abraham and Sarah were old (11:11); and his willingness to sacrifice Isaac (11:17–19). In addition, he referred to Abraham as the recipient of a promise from God that God would bless him and multiply him (6:13–14) and that he would inherit land (11:8–9). In the first of these passages, he used God's promise to Abraham, reinforced by the divine oath, to indicate the utter reliability of that promise. God could not play false with what He had said. This assists the author's pastoral purpose of giving assurance to the addressees and, thus, of strengthening them in their confidence and of encouraging them to press forward in their pilgrimage.

The story of Melchizedek's encounter with Abraham helps towards the conclusion that God intended an order of priesthood to appear which would be different from the Levitical one, and one superior to it, namely a priesthood after the order of Melchizedek. Abraham's acknowledgement of

---

142. See Eisenbaum, *Jewish Heroes*, 140–41, for this viewpoint. Cf. Attridge, *Hebrews*, 306, 348.

143. For a brief but excellent summary of Hebrews' use of Abraham, see Backhaus, *Bund*, 249. Backhaus also points out how, unlike in Paul, the promise of a son and of land play no determinative part nor is there any mention of the covenant with Abraham. The two covenants mentioned are the Sinai covenant and the new one established by Jesus Christ (248, 250).

Melchizedek's superiority is a pointer to the superiority of a future priesthood. The story helps to illustrate the point made by Psalm 110:4.

He described Abraham along with Isaac and Jacob as *strangers and pilgrims* on earth, in search of an another country, the Heavenly City (11:10, 13-16).

The following *qualities* of Abraham are highlighted. In the first place there is the stress on the steadfast, patient endurance of Abraham (μακροθυμησας [6:15]). Then, secondly, there is his obedience to God's call. Abraham went out, even though he did not know the ultimate destination of his journey (11:8). Once committed to going forth, he did not think of turning back (11:15). In the third place, there is Abraham's conviction about God's faithfulness to His promises (11:11) and about God's power to raise even from the dead (11:19).

As regards these points about Abraham's qualities, it could be said that the idea of Abraham's obedience to God's call springs naturally from Genesis 12:1-3, which is followed by the terse statement "So Abram went as the LORD had spoken to him" (v. 4). The reference to Abraham's ignorance of his destination could be based on the vagueness of God's directions in Genesis 12:1, while the reference to Abraham's trust in God's faithfulness to His promises is an entirely natural assumption based on Genesis 15:5-6, even if the language about God's faithfulness is a more broadly based OT concept taken up into early Christian faith.[144]

The concept of Abraham's steadfast endurance gives a particular slant to the life of Abraham, though it could be argued that it is a theme which is the product of reflection and meditation on the Genesis narrative. It exploits the potential of the story, so to speak.

It is, however, with the concept of Abraham as a pilgrim, journeying through this present life towards that Heavenly City which God has established and which He has prepared for those who faithfully stick to the journey, and trusting in this God who calls and makes promises, who is invisible but real,[145] that we see the clearest reinterpretation of the Abraham saga. Hebrews here stands in an exegetical tradition of which Philo of Alexandria is our best illustration.[146] For Philo, Abraham's earthly journeys are allegorized or spiritualized as the journey of the soul in the quest for God.

---

144. See 1 Thess 5:24; 2 Thess 3:3; 1 Cor 1:9; 10:13; 2 Cor 1:18; 1 John 1:9.

145. 11:1, 6; compare what is said of Moses at 11:27: "He did not fear the anger of the king [of Egypt], for he persevered (εκαρτερησεν) as seeing Him who is invisible."

146. I have discussed Philo's use of Abraham in *Abraham in the OT and Early Judaism*, a companion volume to this one. While Spicq, *Hébreux*, 1:79-83, argued for a singular affinity between Hebrews and Philo on the subject of faith, Williamson, *Philo*, 331-72, minimized the links. Rather than literary dependence, it is probably best to

The author of Hebrews has utilized this tradition in his own way. Abraham's earthly journeys are allegorized or spiritualized as the pilgrimage to the world beyond this one, to the Heavenly Country or City. He has actualized it in order to encourage his hearers to cease drifting and to press forward on their journey. Abraham is par excellence one of the cloud of witnesses which surround us and whose example of faithful, steadfast endurance they and all who seek to journey on the pilgrim way are called to imitate (cf. 6:12). He is an example to be followed.

---

see Hebrews standing in a similar tradition, as, e.g., Grässer, *Glaube*, 145–46; Söding, *Zuversicht*, 237, maintain.

4

Abraham in the Letter of James

4.1. Introduction

THIS LETTER STARTS BY giving the sender's name as James, servant of God and of the Lord Jesus Christ (1:1). Debate over whether this is the James who was Jesus' brother and who became leader of the church at Jerusalem, or somebody writing in the name of this James continues.[1] It would go far

---

1. Among modern scholars, the following positions on the authorship may be mentioned:
    (a) By James the brother of Jesus: so Mussner, *Der Jakobusbrief*, 1–8, 237–40; Johnson, *Letter of James*, 121; Bauckham, *James*, 25; Hartin, *James and the Q Sayings of Jesus*, 239–40 (but see in 2 below for a change of view); Maynard-Reid, *Poverty and Wealth in James*, 5–9; Thomson, *Transformation of Post-70 Judaism*, 121. Penner, *Epistle of James and Eschatology*, 277, without specifying James the brother of Jesus as the author, regards its composition "about the mid portion of the first century in Palestine" as "highly plausible."
    (b) James's teaching was edited by his disciples or one of them: so Davids, *Epistle of James*, 12–13, 22, 34; Martin, *James*, lxxvi–lxxvii; Hartin, *James*, 16–25; *Ethics in the Letter of James*, 289.
    (c) The letter is pseudonymous: so Dibelius, *James*, 11–21; Laws, *James*, 38–42; Frankemölle, *Jakobus*, 1:45–54; Tsuji, *Glaube zwischen Vollkommenheit und Verweltlichung*, 50; Popkes, *Jakobus*, 59, 64–69; Burchard, *Jakobusbrief*, 1–2; Pratscher, *Der Herrenbruder Jakobus*, 209–213; Painter, *Just James*, 242–43; Wachob, *Voice of Jesus*, 200–201; Edgar, *Has God not Chosen the Poor?*, 223–24; Schnelle, *New Testament Writings*, 384–88; Theobald, "Der Kanon von der Rechtfertigung," 214n208; Nienhuis, *Not by Paul Alone*, 215–16. Walls, *Community of the Wise*, 10, suggests that the name "James" is a metaphor of a theological tradition.

beyond the limits of this work to enter into this debate in any detail. Suffice to say that we accept the view that this Letter is a pseudonymous composition. It is a letter, which addressed those known to the author (e.g., my brothers [1:3, 16; 2:1, 14; 3:1; 5:12, 19]; my beloved brothers [1:19; 2:5]). It sees the recipients who believe in Jesus as Lord (2:1), as the people of God in continuity with the twelve tribes of Israel (1:1). The author seeks to change some of their thinking and their behavior (e.g., 1:13; 2:14-17, etc.).

The Letter may be classified as a circular letter. Indeed, one might describe it as a "diaspora letter" on the analogy of Jeremiah 29; 2 Maccabees 1:1-9; 1:10-2:18; *2 Baruch* 78-86; and in the NT, 1 Peter; Acts 15:23-29.[2]

The writer drew on traditions from the Wisdom Literature both of the Jewish people and of the Christian tradition, together with Greek philosophical ethical teaching, but never slavishly.[3] He appears to have been able to draw on sayings of Jesus; and he believed in the not too distant coming in glory of the Lord Jesus.

It is impossible to say with any degree of assurance exactly when it was written. Clearly, those who see the author as James the brother of Jesus date the Letter before his martyrdom in 62 AD. Those who think that it was edited by his disciples suggest either an early date or after his death.[4] Those who accept the work as pseudonymous usually content themselves with the last decades of the first century.[5]

The issue of the date is of some significance for our theme, since, if it was written before 62 AD or shortly afterwards, then it would be possible to argue that James was in some way relating to Paul's teaching or a form of Paul's teaching while Paul was still alive. We shall discuss this issue when we have considered what the letter actually says on the theme of Abraham.

---

2. Cf. the description of "encyclical letter to the diaspora" put forward by Bauckham, *James*, 25-28, and argued in more detail by Tsuji, *Glaube*, 18-37; Hartin, *Spirituality*, 45-56. But later, in his commentary on James, Hartin argues for classifying the letter as "protreptic Discourse," which aims to provide moral exhortation in the form of a focused, sustained argument and demonstration.

3. Frankemölle, *Jakobus*, 85, 87, 91, sees the work as a piece of wisdom writing in the form of a letter, which grounds its practical advice theologically. The wisdom which he teaches is very much practically orientated. Specifically Frankemölle would argue for a considerable influence from Sirach (in particular, Sir 2:1-18; 15:11-20; 18:30-31).

4. Davids, *James*, 22, suggests either 55-65 or possibly 75-85. Martin, *James*, lxxvi-lxxvii, offers no suggestion about the date, but we might infer that he thought of James's disciples moving to Antioch around the outbreak of the Jewish War.

5. So Burchard, *Jakobusbrief*, 7; Frankemölle, *Jakobus*, 60; Schnelle, *New Testament Writings*, 388.

4.2. Abraham in the Letter to James

4.2.1. James 2:1–13

As our interest is in how the story of Abraham is used in the Letter of James, naturally our attention will be directed especially to 2:14–26. However, while in one sense this section could be extrapolated and discussed on its own, there are strong grounds for not only seeing a link between it and 2:1–13,[6] but also accepting that James has prepared the way for both 2:1–13 and 2:14–26 in the opening chapter, especially, 1:2–18, which has been likened to a table of contents (an elaborated one!) for what follows.[7] We shall begin by looking at the links between 2:14–26 and the immediately preceding section.

The section 2:1–13 begins with a warning against partiality in the treatment of people, since such partiality is incompatible with the Christian faith.[8] A contrast is drawn between the treatment given to a rich person and that meted out to a poor person, both of whom enter a meeting of the congregation.[9] The former is given a good seat, whereas the poor person is made to stand or given an inferior place (2:2-3). The writer protested against such discrimination and accused those who behaved in such a way of elevating themselves into being judges and of giving corrupt decisions (2:4).[10]

The reasons given for this protest are threefold. Firstly, God has chosen the poor (who are assumed to be those who trust in God, for they have no one else, and nothing else, to trust in) to be rich in faith and heirs of the

---

6. Johnson, *James*, 219; Burchard, *Jakobusbrief*, 28–30; Flüchter, *Die Anrechnung*, 148; Nienhuis, *Not by Paul Alone*, 21–16. Popkes, *Jakobus*, 152–214, deals with 2:11–26 as one section.

7. See Heilgenthal, *Werke als Zeichen*, 27–33, and especially Frankemölle, *Jakobus*, 135, 152–80, 210, 470, 480–81; Burchard, *Jakobusbrief*, 51; Popkes, *Jakobus*, 49; Bauckham, *James*, 71; Hartin, *Q Sayings*, 23–34; *Spirituality*, 9 (who follows D. J. Moo in comparing chapter 1 with the overture to a symphony). The suggestion of Johnson, *James*, 174–75, that chapter 1 is "something of an epitome of the work as a whole" is severely criticized by Bauckham, *James*, 72–73, as a wrong use of the term.

8. Whether Ιησου Χριστου is an objective genitive (the faith about our Lord Jesus Christ) or a subjective genitive (the faith exercised by our Lord Jesus Christ) need not detain us. See the commentaries for a full discussion, and also for the problems concerning the meaning of the genitive της δοξης.

9. Again, we need not decide here whether the meeting is one for worship (Laws, *James*, 101; Mussner, *Jakobusbrief*, 116) or a judicial assembly (Ward, *Partiality in the Assembly*, 87–97; Davids, *James*, 108–9; Martin, *James*, 57–59, 61, 64–69, 73; Johnson, *James*, 223, 227; Walls, *James*, 105, 111).

10. For the translation "corrupt decisions," see Bauer, *Lexicon*, 185; Laws, *James*, 102; Martin, *James*, 64; Wall, *James*, 113. Those who prefer "evil thoughts" include Mussner, *Jakobusbrief*, 119; Davids, *James*, 110; Popkes, *Jakobus*, 164; Burchard, *Jakobusbrief*, 95.

coming Kingdom (2:5). Secondly, the rich in general oppress Christians, drag them before the courts, and blaspheme the name of Jesus (2:6). Thirdly, discrimination of the sort mentioned conflicts with the Love Command of Leviticus 19:18, which is regarded as summarizing the Law (2:8–9).

James began verse 10 with γαρ, which indicates that what he was going to say grounds the previous assertion about committing partiality and being a transgressor of the Law. He stated that even if one keeps the whole Law but breaks one of the Law's commands,[11] this means that one stands condemned as a breaker of the whole Law (v. 10).[12] This was then backed up by another γαρ sentence: "For He[13] who said, "Do not commit adultery," also said, "Do not commit murder"; but if you do not commit adultery but commit murder, you have become a transgressor of the Law" (v. 11). But, how can one keep the whole Law and yet also break one of its commands? Jackson-McCabe suggests that the Love Command, though having a summarizing function, in the end remains only one among the commands; James does not regard it as simply equivalent to keeping the whole Law. He is concerned lest Christians develop an eschatological confidence based on attention to the general principles and neglect other elements of the Law which are ultimately of equal importance.[14]

The advice is, therefore: "So speak and act as those who will be judged by the law of freedom.[15] For judgment will be without mercy on those who do not show mercy. Mercy exults[16] in expectation of the judgment" (2:12–13).

Thus, in this section, there is a sustained emphasis on behavior which is consistent with the Christian faith and on the Law as interpreted by the Love Command. James is concerned for deeds which are in harmony with the Lord Jesus Christ and the Love Command (which Jesus himself had seen as the key to the Law along with the Shema—Mark 12:28–34; Luke 10:25–37). He draws a discernible link between a confession of Jesus

---

11. Presumably, the Love Command is especially in James's mind. Cf. Sir 34:21–22, where it is said that whoever denies support to his neighbor murders him.

12. Cf. Deut 27:26; Gal 5:3.

13. Presumably God, as the giver of the Law (4:12).

14. Jackson-McCabe, *Logos and Letter*, 172–74.

15. The law of freedom is the same as the royal law of 2:8. Johnson, *James*, 236, maintains that verse 12 anticipates verses 14–26. Cf. Wall, *James*, 130, 133. Jackson-McCabe, *Logos*, 157, also accepts the overarching unity of chapter 2.

16. For this translation rather than "triumph over" (advocated by Bauer, *Lexicon*, 412), see Wenger, *Der wesenhaft gute Kyrios*, 252n1529.

as Lord and as the revelation (of the Glory) of God on the one hand and conduct on the other.[17]

This is, as we shall shortly see, precisely the position emphasized in 2:14-26. Not faith on its own, not deeds on their own, but faith-with-works.

What of the opening chapter which gives a foretaste of many of the themes to come? We mention the following points. Firstly, James is concerned for a faith which develops in maturity to completeness, wholeness, and perfection,[18] a faith which trusts God fully (1:2-4, 6). Secondly, James was concerned about the poverty-wealth issue as it affects Christians especially. He advised the lowly to boast of their exaltation—i.e., by God at the End, while the rich (presumably as a Christian their eyes have been opened to the impermanence of wealth and of those who put their trust in riches) should boast in their being brought low (1:9-11).[19] In the third place, James was concerned that his hearers be not just hearers but doers of the word, for blessing awaits the doers (1:22-25). This follows a statement that Christians have been given birth[20] by the word of truth (1:18) and the exhortation to receive "the implanted word which can save you" (1:21). The experience of conversion (if we may so describe it) must express itself in actions, deeds, the doing of the word. Fourthly, James gave a highly practical definition of true religion: "to care for orphans and widows [OT types of the defenseless and needy] in their distress and to keep oneself unspotted from the world" (1:27). We could say that this definition confirms the point that the coming to Christian faith results in a life of doing the word. Finally, at 1:12 James alluded to the Last Judgment and the eschatological reward awaiting those who endure testing (cf. the implication of the reference to "save" in 1:21).[21]

---

17. Cf. Johnson, *James*, 219-35, who comments on the demand for consistency in practice. Cf. Wall, *James*, 130.

18. For the idea of perfection, see, apart from discussions in the commentaries, Delling, "Τελος κτλ," *TDNT* 8:49-87, esp. 74-75, 82; Hartin, *Spirituality*, 60-92, who offers a good, non-technical discussion (acknowledging his debt to P. J. du Plessis, ΤΕΛΕΙΟΣ [not available to me]). Hartin maintains that for James perfection is the goal of a life wholly and undividedly devoted to God, expressing itself and demonstrating itself in practical action in following the will of God as expressed in the Torah and aided by the gift of divine wisdom implanted in the souls of those who have experienced rebirth. James is indebted to the Old Testament and Jewish tradition (there being an overlap with the idea in the classical world of perfect/perfection being completeness, the attaining of that for which one was striving).

19. Johnson, *James*, 228, says that this points forward to 2:5-6.

20. Απεκυησεν ημας: "He [God] has given birth to us."

21. Frankmölle, *Jakobus*, 422, argues that the issue of justification stands behind verse 12, even if the terminology as such is not used.

Of these five points, how many are taken up in 2:14–26? In our section, verse 22 speaks about faith being completed (ετελειωθη) by works, so that there is something of an echo of 1:4 (εργον τελειον . . . τελειοι). Secondly, the poverty-wealth theme issue surfaces in the example of 2:15–16, where those who have more than enough do not help the destitute. Thirdly, though the language hearers-doers of the word does not actually occur in 2:14–26, one could argue that the gist of it does in the person who says "I have faith" but lacks works (v. 14) and the affirmation that faith must demonstrate itself in deeds (v. 18). Fourthly, the definition of true religion has alongside moral uprightness an emphasis on practical caring for the needy, and that too is present in 2:15–17. Finally, the outcome of the Last Judgment is in mind when at 2:14 James posed the question, expecting a negative answer, whether a faith without accompanying deeds can save a person, while the immediate preceding verses (vv. 12–13) have spoken about the Judgment.

So, all-in-all, chapter 1 has, like the prelude to a symphony, insinuated certain themes which will be taken up and developed later more fully in the letter.[22] We are now ready to turn to the section 2:14–26.

4.2.2. James 2:14–26

In seeking to discern the flow of the argument in 2:14–26, we notice that on three occasions, in similar or not too dissimilar wording, James passed a verdict on a faith which is not accompanied by deeds. At verse 17 he said that such a faith, by itself, was dead (νεκρα); at verse 20 faith apart from deeds was useless (αργη); and, finally, at verse 26, in the conclusion to the whole, faith apart from deeds was dead (νεκρα). The change from νεκρα to αργα in verse 20 was probably due to a certain play on words with εργα. These three statements could well be indicators of subdivisions within the whole section. Each acts as a kind of conclusion to the argument preceding it. They also help us to see that the theme of the section is faith and its relation to deeds.[23]

James posed a question at verse 14: "What good does it do if someone claims to have faith but does not have deeds? Can their faith save them?"[24] "Save" here refers to the verdict at the Last Judgment, which has just been mentioned at 2:12–13.

---

22. Cf. Wall, *James*, 127, who, commenting on 2:12–13, says that the passage is "expanded in what follows in 2:14–15."

23. Correctly emphasized by Popkes, *Jakobus*, 211.

24. Some scholars treat it as a hypothetical one, but there is no reason why it could not arise from concrete situations which James had encountered.

What is the meaning of εργα here? Earlier, James had said that the person was blessed who not only looked into but also continued to do the perfect law which gives freedom (1:25). For James, the Law had been summed up in the command "Love your neighbor" (2:8). In the light of this, and of what follows in our paragraph, we may take deeds here in verse 14 as basically deeds of kindness. Verses 15-16 confirm this assumption, in their clear ethical teaching: "If a brother or sister is naked[25] and lacks daily food, and a member of your congregation [τις εξ υμων] says to them, Go in peace; be warmed and fed, but does not give them what the body needs, what good does it do?" There was a failure to respond to the actual needs of people, who were their fellow Christians, on the part of those to whom James was writing.[26]

Deeds, then, are deeds of kindness, expressing love of the neighbor. These are what the Law demands. In view of this, the fact that James did not use the phrase εργα του νομου may not necessarily be significant.[27] Certainly, ritual acts like circumcision, food laws, sabbath observance, etc. (which were integral parts of the Law for the devout Jew and which in addition functioned as boundary markers to distinguish the Jew, as a member of God's chosen people standing within His covenant, from the Gentile, who was outside that covenant) do not seem to be in mind at all.[28] The controversy in which Paul was embroiled in Galatians is not at stake in the Letter of James.

Though we believe that it is correct to say that deeds of kindness are very much to the fore in the section which we have been discussing, they are not always the sense of εργα. At 2:21 James posed the question, "Was not our father Abraham justified on the basis of works when he offered Isaac his son on the altar?" What Abraham was prepared to do was in obedience to a

---

25. I.e., inadequately clothed: so Laws, *James*, 118, 120; Davids, *James*, 121; Martin, *James*, 84.

26. James addresses his hearers directly in the words τις . . . εξ υμων . . . μη δωτε, as Garleff, *Urchristliche Identität*, 292, points out.

27. Tsuji, *Glaube*, 196, does not think so. The absence of εργα του νομου has been used by some to support the view that James was not attacking Paul.

28. Tsuji, *Glaube*, 112-13, 201, believes that James accepts that the ritual laws no longer have validity, a position which he shares with his Gentile addressees, and that James stood in a line of tradition with Antiochene Christianity. On the other hand, could James have said that to keep the whole law but break one of the commandments means that one is guilty of transgressing the whole Law (2:10), if he believed that the ritual laws were no longer relevant? Hartin, *Spirituality*, 84, comments: "The command to love one's neighbor operates as the embodiment of the Torah. It does not replace the Torah, but gives expression to the pulsating heart and direction of the Torah as God's will for God's people."

command of God; it was not a charitable deed nor something done to obey one of the ritual laws, as Crompton pointed out.[29]

The second question concerning salvation, posed by James in verse 14, presumably refers to the Last Judgment, to which there was a reference in verses 12–13: "So speak and act as those who will be judged by the law of freedom. For judgment will be without mercy for the person who does not practice mercy. Mercy exults over judgment." Phrased by James, it expects the answer "No," but it could well be that the "someone" (possibly the leader of a group) referred to in verse 14 actually did think that a person could be saved solely by their faith.[30] The "What good is it?" (τι το οφειλος) at the end of verse 16 picks up the similar phrase at the beginning of verse 14. Then James rounded off his first brief treatment of his theme with: "So also faith, if it does not have deeds, is by itself [καθ' εαυτην] dead" (v. 17). For him, deeds are inseparable from faith. Belief and practice go together. "Faith alone" is insufficient.[31]

A new subsection begins with verse 18, a verse which bristles with problems.[32] The τις suggests that a third speaker is being introduced, different from the τις of verse 14: "But someone will say . . ." This phrase in the diatribe literature usually introduces someone who is hostile or in error.[33] We would, then, expect that this third speaker represents a view different from James, rather than a supporter of James, and indeed different from the "someone" of verse 14.[34] But, if that is so, where does his contribution end and James's response begin? To assist clarity, let us set out verse 18:

18a αλλ' ερει τις, Συ πιστιν εχεις But someone will say, You have faith
18b καγω εργα εχω and/but I have deeds
18c δειξον μοι την πιστιν Show me this[35] faith

29. Crompton, *James 2:21–24, 25–26.*

30. So, e.g., Popkes, *Jakobus*, 184. Popkes also thinks that verse 19 contains the implicit link between faith and salvation (185).

31. Frankemölle, *Jakobus*, constantly stresses that James is attacking "Faith on its own" (Glaube allein), and that the opposition "Faith on its own/Faith with deeds" thoroughly influences his treatment (e.g., 422, 431).

32. See Burchard, *Jakobusbrief*, 118–21, for a listing and discussion of the various suggestions which have been made to explain this difficult verse.

33. So Dibelius, *James*, 150; Davids, *James*, 129; Wall, *James*, 135, 140; Burchard, *Jakobus*, 117; Cargal, *Restoring the Diaspora*, 123.

34. E.g., Wenger, *Kyrios*, 36, suggests that the τις is not a theological opponent but a church member who lacks understanding and who could have been unsettled by the kind of things that have been said in verses 14–17; Garleff, *Identität*, 295, thinks of someone who is struggling for the right understanding and who outlines a view after what has been said in verses 14–17.

35. It seems preferable to take the article as equivalent to a demonstrative (the

χωρις των εργων κτλ apart from deeds etc.

Modern translations tend to accept that the opening of verse 18 represents a third speaker.³⁶ The NIV, TNIV, and NRSV put verse 18ab in inverted commas, with NIV/TNIV then beginning a new paragraph, presumably to indicate that James responded with verse 18c. The NEB/REB boldly insert "to which I reply" before "show me this faith [etc.]," to indicate that James was responding to what had just been said.

If verse 18ab represents what the third speaker says, then the meaning could be as follows. This third speaker addresses the τις of verse 14. If the "someone" of verse 14 took the position "I have faith," the speaker of verse 18a seems to accept this, at any rate partially,³⁷ but adds "And/but I have works." Verse 18ab runs: "*You* have faith and *I* have deeds." This could suggest that there are, as it were, complementary forms of the Christian faith.³⁸ This speaker's viewpoint seems to rest on the kind of belief that the Spirit has given different gifts to various people in the Christian congregations: thus, at 1 Corinthians 12:4-11, Paul listed πιστις among the gifts distributed by the Spirit, alongside the practical gifts of healing and miracles, while Romans 12:6-8 mentioned both giving and the showing of compassion as gifts.³⁹ This speaker accepts "I have faith" of verse 14 as valid, but sets alongside of it "I have deeds." This speaker has joined in the debate, as it were, and has addressed the τις of verse 14.⁴⁰

On this view, James responded with verse 18c. While there is no formal indication that someone else, i.e., James, had started speaking at verse 18c, nevertheless the implication of the demand for demonstration in verse 18c is that James had responded to the third speaker.

---

so-called anaphoric use [see *BDR* para. 252], rather than supplying a "your," as do NIV and NRSV, since verse 18c asks for a demonstration of faith apart from works, whereas the "I" of verse 18b has said, "I have works."

36. So also in their translations Laws, *James*, 118; Johnson, *James*, 237; Burchard, *Jakobus*, 109.

37. Cf. Walls, *James* 140; Cargill, *Restorung*, 124, "Thus, a person may choose *either* faith *or* deeds."

38. Laws, *James*, 123-24; Davids, *James*, 123; Johnson, *James*, 240; Walls, *James*, 136-37, 141 (though on different grounds); Burchard, *Jakobus*, 121; Verseput, *Reworking the Puzzle*, 109; Nienhuis, *Not by Paul Alone*, 219-20.

39. So Laws, *James*, 123-24; Davids, *James*, 123-24; Heiligenthal, *Werke*, 35; Nienhuis, *Not by Paul Alone*, 220. Rejected by Martin, *James*, 87.

40. Martin, *James*, 87, suggests that James has restated the argument of his opponent, so that "You have faith" represents the opponent, while "I have works" is his own standpoint. But would we not expect verse 18 to open with something like "So you say that you have faith" rather than the adversative αλλα? Furthermore, James does not set faith and works over against each other antithetically. For him, faith and works go together.

We ought to mention another possible approach, viz. the view which assumes an ellipsis at verse 18b: καγω [ερω], Εργα εχω.[41] On this approach, the third speaker addressed James in verse 18a, "You have faith," and James responded with verse 18b, "And I will say, I have deeds." While attractive, there is perhaps a weakness here that one has to assume an "also" in James's reply,[42] in addition to the ellipsis of an ερω. In addition, this seems to attribute to James a view of salvation "only by deeds,"[43] whereas in fact James does not minimise the importance of faith; on the contrary, it is faith active in producing deeds which James passionately defended. To avoid this difficulty, Frankemölle takes the εργα as "deeds of kindness," with verse 18c elaborating εργα as deeds of kindness which demonstrate faith from which they have naturally developed.[44]

Another alternative approach is to assume that verses 18ab represent a rhetorical device which enabled James to pursue the discussion on the relation of faith and deeds,[45] while verse 18c is the key point in the argument:[46] "Show to me your faith apart from works and I will demonstrate to you my faith by my deeds." For James there was no such thing as genuine faith which does not express itself in deeds of practical caring and mercy. In other words, in verse 18c he assumed that it would be impossible to show faith without deeds springing from it. Verse 18c shows that genuine faith works out in practical deeds. James thus rejected the idea of a separation of faith and deeds as if in the purpose of God each, separately, on their own, was valid.

So, according to verse 18c, one importance of deeds is their demonstrative value.[47] They help to differentiate a faith apart from deeds and a faith visible in deeds.

---

41. This is the approach of Neitzel, *Eine alte crux interpretum*, (who takes it as a question); Jackson-McCabe, *Logos*, 218n104 (who assumes a question. He also quotes Klein, *Ein vollkommenes Werk*, 70-72, as supporting this view); Flüchter, *Anrechnung*, 158-59 (taking it as a statement, as reproduced here).

42. See the translation of Flüchter, *Anrechnung*, 159: "*Ich* habe aber (auch) *Taten*."

43. Frankemölle, *Jakobus*, 438

44. Frankemölle, *Jakobus*, 439-40.

45. This would be the position of Dibelius, *James*, 154-58; Laws, *James*, 124; Frankemölle, *Jakobus*, 425-26, 440-41; Wall, *James*, 136; Popkes, *Jakobus*, 198-99; Bauckham, *James*, 58-59. The position of Nienhuis, *Not by Paul Alone*, 217, is that the diatribe technique enabled James to focus on the issue rather than the person of Paul. He thinks that James wanted his readers to *hear* Paul somewhere in the background, but did not want to appear to be disagreeing with him.

46. Popkes, *Jakobus*, 198.

47. Popkes, *Jakobus*, 199.

Verse 19 is part of the argument against separating faith and deeds. "You believe that God is one [this is the standard Jewish monotheistic belief, as seen in the Shema (Deut 6:4)]. You do well. But [or Even][48] the demons believe and tremble." Here πιστις begins to have an element of the intellectual assent to a doctrinal or credal proposition or formulation ("believing that . . ."), though it need not be solely that. While it includes "believing that,"[49] we should remember that the Schema itself in fact did call for love which expressed a total commitment.[50] But demons were certainly not offering this in any way, shape, or form! They remained wedded both to their opposition to this one God and to a commitment to an evil way of life which aimed to destroy the good creation of God.

James, then, pointed out that even though demons also subscribe to monotheistic belief, it had not changed their behavior or saved them. Theirs was a "faith" without appropriate deeds.[51] Such a faith cannot save anyone.

In view of the subsequent reference to Abraham, it is worth reminding ourselves that the book of Jubilees described Abraham as discovering that there was one God, rejecting idols and idolatry, and seeking to persuade his father, Terah, to follow him in this.[52] In other words, Abraham's monotheism did have practical consequences in his life. It indeed changed the course of his way of life.

The author rounded on the interlocutor: "O foolish man, do you want to know that faith apart from deeds is useless?" (v. 20). What the latter had been prepared apparently to hold apart, James held inextricably together. In verse 20 he described a faith without accompanying deeds as useless. This is a conclusion comparable with verse 17, where it was described as dead. Thus, a similar conclusion was put before the two dialogue partners of verses 14 and 18. The latter verse reinforced and underlined the former.

The conclusion of the second subsection was also a launching pad for the argument involving Abraham (and Rahab) in verse 21-26; it set up the

---

48. The και in the Greek could bear either sense.

49. Though occasionally, "believing that" occurs in Paul (e.g., Rom 10:9), predominantly he uses πιστις as trust in God or Christ, commitment in love, acceptance of what God offers or has promised in Christ.

50. As Popkes, *Jakobus*, 201, rightly points out: "Deut 6:4 presses forward to verse 5." Frankemölle, *Jakobus*, 444, also denies that faith has declined into something purely intellectualistic. Wengst, *Kyrios*, 37-38, likewise stresses that this OT-Early Jewish belief has ethical consequences, as illustrated in the Decalogue.

51. Frankemölle, *Jakobus*, 447, points out that for James the faith of demons stands as the opposite of an integrated faith, in which confession and behavior which expresses practical solidarity with one's fellow believers (solidarische Praxis) form a unity.

52. Jub 11:16-17; 12:1-8, 17-21.

situation for James to bring in the revered figure of Abraham as an illustration of the need to combine faith and deeds.

At this point, it is important that we pause and consider verse 19 in relation to the whole letter. It is true that at 2:19 πιστις bears the sense of what is believed, and that James endorsed the content. It was, after all, standard Jewish and Christian belief![53] This remains true whether we take καλως ποιεις as intended ironically or not. What James was rejecting and attacking is the approach which remained content with this understanding of faith (both at verse 14 and 18) without any bearing of what one believes on the way in which one behaves.

It ought not to be thought that James's own faith only embraced an intellectual assent to doctrine; on the contrary, the rest of the letter reveals a very different picture.[54] A brief review is in order.[55]

Faith is in the first place linked to Jesus Christ (2:1), who is the Lord and the Glory. While this is not expanded upon, James pointed out that a certain type of behavior (viz. discrimination against the poor and partiality towards the rich) was incompatible with this faith. In giving an example of partiality towards the rich and discrimination against the poor (2:2–4), James offered, as one reason for his criticism, that God had chosen the poor of the world to be rich in faith and heirs of the Kingdom, which He had promised to those who love Him (2:5). The use of "rich" in respect of faith is chosen to make a rhetorical contrast between the materially rich person mentioned in 2:2–4, and thereby the importance of faith to James was indicated. Faith is true wealth! "There is a promise for the poor, but inasmuch as their poverty is accompanied by faith and the love of God, and as they are chosen in order that it should be so."[56] That God was "on the side of the poor" has OT roots. The poor are rich in respect to faith. Faith is used here in the sense of trust, of a hopeful turning to God.[57] Clearly this is not faith as subscription to a body of belief, however much certain convictions about God and Christ may underlie it.

53. Verseput, *Reworking*, 110–11, suggested that the monotheistic confession may refer to a central act of worship in the Christian community. Lindemann, *Paulus in altesten Christentum*, 245, probably somewhat overstated matters when he asserted that while Paul agreed that God is one (Rom 3:30; 1 Cor 8:6; Gal 3:20; cf. Eph 4:6; 1 Tim 2:5), "this statement is never for him a sentence of πιστις." We may add 1 Thessalonians 1:9 to the texts which Lindemann mentions.

54. The statistics are: πιστις occurs sixteen times in James, eleven of which occur in 2:14–26; πιστευειν occurs three times, all in 2:14–26.

55. Both Mussner, *Jakobusbrief*, 133–36, and Frankemölle, *Jakobus*, 222–31, have an excellent excursus on faith in James. See also Flüchter, *Anrechnung*, 186–87.

56. Laws, *James*, 103.

57. As Popkes, *Jakobus*, 166, rightly maintained.

Secondly, when faith is tested and comes through the testing(s), then the result is steadfastness or endurance. A refining process takes place. Clearly, faith matures and develops on the way to perfection (1:2-4, esp. 3). This is not just a cerebral notion of faith.

In the third place, faith is linked to prayer (1:6), which should be offered without doubting but in the wholehearted trust in God as a generous and consistent giver (1:5, 17; 4:6). This confident trust is contrasted with the "double-minded" person, whose vacillation between faith and doubt will not lead to the hearing of their prayer (1:7-8). The wholeheartedness of true faith is contrasted with divided loyalties. A particular instance in relation to prayer is when the elders of the church are called to a sick person to pray for them and anoint them with oil with a view to their healing. "The prayer of faith will save the ill person and the Lord will raise them up" (5:15).

In addition to these occurrences of πιστις, we should note that James believed that we may enjoy the friendship of God, provided that we do not wish to have at the same time friendship with the world (4:4).[58] This imagery in its suggestion of the accessibility of God is akin to the concept of God as Father and believers as His children. James also used language drawn from the sphere of worship in the OT: "Draw near to God and He will draw near to you" (4:8). The significance of this language is similar to that of friendship with God.[59]

This brief survey has been necessary to prevent a wrong conclusion being drawn from 2:19 as to how James himself understood faith. Though he endorsed the traditional monotheism, James's understanding of faith went far beyond this and embraced the whole of life and its activities, as, of course, would be true for genuine faith in Judaism.[60]

We turn now to the third subsection in 2:14-26, viz. verses 21-26. To illustrate his contention that faith without deeds is useless (and dead) and to follow up his promise to show his faith from his works (v. 18),[61] James referred to an acknowledged authority, Scripture, and to the story of Abraham (and Rahab).

> Was not Abraham our father justified by his deeds[62] when he offered Isaac his son on the altar? You see that faith worked

---

58. Cf. 2:23, where Abraham is called the friend of God.
59. Cf. Laws, *James*, 183.
60. As Frankemölle, *Jakobus*, 44, rightly points out.
61. Wenger, *Kyrios*, 259 (see also next note).
62. The phrase εξ εργων picks up the phrase εκ των εργων at verse 18b, as Wenger, *Kyrios*, 259, points out. He follows Hamann, *Faith and Works*, 36, in taking the phrase εξ εργων as an abbreviated formula for something like "a faith demonstrated as perfect

together with his deeds and his faith was perfected by his deeds, and the Scripture was fulfilled which says, "And Abraham believed God, and this was reckoned to him for righteousness," and he was called the friend of God. (vv. 21-23)

This is exactly the position of a number of Jewish authors. For example, the author of 1 Maccabees had Mattathias interpreting Genesis 15:6 as a reference to the test of sacrificing Isaac: "Was not Abraham found faithful when tested [εν πειρασμω ευρεθη πιστος], and it was reckoned to him as righteousness?" (1 Macc 2:52).[63] The promise of Genesis 15 became a reality after Abraham had stood the testing imposed by God.

What sense does "justified" (the first occurrence of the verb in James) have in this context? There are scholars who do not think that this refers to a declaration of God at the Last Judgment, but to a declaration by God that Abraham was righteous, in the right, in a right relationship with Him.[64] God recognized this quality of Abraham when he had bound Isaac and placed him on the altar. God recognized that Abraham was acting within the Covenant relationship. "His deed is a proof of his faithfulness to God's word and God's response establishes that Abraham corresponded to the ethos of the Covenant."[65] However, James has been concerned with being "saved" (v. 14).[66] While "justification" and "salvation" are not identical, the former draws the latter with it,[67] so that it is probably best not to drive too sharp a wedge between the covenantal and the eschatological connotations of "justify."[68]

Then verse 22 draws an insight (βλεπεις) from this story of the offering of Isaac. "You see that his faith worked together with[69] his deeds and his

---

by works" (Wenger, *Kyrios*, 259n1567).

63. Cf. Sir 44:19-21. Sirach has exactly the same phrase as 1 Maccabees—εν πειρασμω ευρεθη πιστος—but does not quote Genesis 15:6 specifically, referring to God's oath promising to multiply his offspring and to cause them to inherit the earth generally. Jubilees refers to the ten testings of Abraham, the climax being the offering of Isaac, in all of which Abraham proved faithful (chapter 17). In addition to the commentaries, Penner *James and Eschatology*, 64; Wenger, *Kyrios*, 259, may be mentioned as among many who think that James was in line with Jewish traditions prior to Paul.

64. E.g., Jeremias, *Paul*, 368-71; Laws, *James*, 133; Davids, *James*, 127-28

65. Popkes, *Jakobus*, 203, 208.

66. E.g., Cargill, *Restoring*, 132.

67. As Burchard, *Jakobus*, 124, has remarked.

68. Cf. Martin, *James*, 91-92, who refers to "God's eschatological pronouncement" on one whose faith is authentic, and goes on to say that this line of interpretation takes up the Jewish interpretation of "justification" because righteousness is there seen as the covenant fidelity or obedience expected of those who are to survive the judgment.

69. The imperfect συνηργει has iterative sense. Wenger, *Kyrios*, 259n1568, criticizes Bauer, *Lexicon*, 795, for offering as a translation "faith worked with (and thereby aided)

faith was completed⁷⁰ by his deeds." For James, Abraham's conduct showed the relationship of faith and deeds;⁷¹ it showed that his faith was involved in the offering of Isaac.⁷² Mussner pointed out that in verse 22 faith is primary for James: James does not say that deeds work together with faith, but he says the opposite.⁷³ This is an important observation, though obvious when one considers that πιστις is the subject of the sentence!⁷⁴ It is faith together with its deeds which will issue in salvation at the Last Judgment (cf. the question at verse 14b). Faith becomes perfect through deeds. The deeds produced by faith made Abraham's faith into perfect faith. Faith is incomplete unless it is expressed in works. The two go together; they are a unity, indissolubly linked together.⁷⁵ It rules out any attempt to draw a sharp antithesis between the two (as was done in the approach and opinions expressed in verses 14 and 18). Faith then received its completion through its deeds.⁷⁶ It moved to its maturity and perfection through deeds (cf. 1:2-4). "Faith has a goal."⁷⁷

In turn, this fulfilled Scripture. "Abraham believed God and it was reckoned to him for righteousness,⁷⁸ and he was called the friend of God" (v. 23).

---

his good deeds." For Wenger this makes faith and works into two entities which, though working together, are independent and which give a mutual hand to each other (see note 73 for a similar view held by Lodge of the relationship of faith and works).

70. The aorist indicative ετελειωθη has a complexive sense.

71. Frankemölle, *Jakobus*, 452-53; Popkes, *Jakobus*, 205.

72. Crompton, *Justification*, 38

73. Mussner, *Jakobusbrief*, 142. Cf. Lodge, *James and Paul at Cross-Purposes?*, 199: "Instead of faith and works as two subjects acting upon one another, faith *acts* (συνηργει) and *receives* its wholeness or completion through works"; Crompton, *Justification*, 39; Hartin, *Spirituality*, 87; Wenger, *Kyrios*, 259.

74. It needs to be borne in mind when we consider the relation of James and Paul.

75. Frankemolle, *Jakobus*, 453, rightly stresses that for James faith is always Werk-Glaube [which we may paraphrase as "faith which produces works"] and that he is fighting against "faith without works" or "only faith" (2:17, 20).

76. It might be best, therefore, to avoid the use of the term "synergistic" (see, e.g., Nienhuis, *Not by Paul Alone*, 221, who says that for James faith and works are synergistic, requiring each other to function properly. Faith enables someone to do works, but is in turn completed by works 2:22). Schnelle, *New Testament Writings*, 396, voices reluctance: "This cooperation of faith and works in James need not be conceived as synergistic, for in James 2:22 faith consistently remains the subject, having the primacy over works."

77. Popkes, *Jakobus*, 205.

78. Επιστευσεν δε Αβρααμ τω Θεω και ελογισθη αυτω εις δικαιοσυνην differs from the LXX only in having δε where the LXX has και at the beginning. Paul has exactly the same form as James in Romans 4:3, but is the substitution of δε or και sufficient to claim this as further indication that James was criticizing Paul's teaching of justification apart from works (as Lindemann, *Paulus*, 246, does)? Such a stylistic alteration could be something undertaken by two authors entirely independent of each other. As to the

James understood Genesis 15:6 as a prophecy[79] which Abraham fulfilled by his action in offering up Isaac. Abraham confirmed its correctness.[80] Genesis 15:6 proleptically anticipated the event on mount Moriah.

The designation φιλος Θεου (friend of God) expresses the close friendship between God and Abraham. This friendship which Abraham enjoyed with God flowed out of his belief in God which expressed itself in deeds. For this designation, James drew on biblical and Jewish tradition about Abraham.[81] Jacobs has drawn attention to the fact that there is evidence that Jewish tradition interpreted the designation of Abraham as one who feared God (see Gen 22:12) as due to his love of God and/or his obedience.[82]

In verse 24, James reverted to the plural (ορατε), having used the singular at verses 19-20, 22, and proceeded to point out to his addressees an inference to be drawn from what had just been said. In the light of what he had been arguing, "deeds" in verse 24 must be taken as deeds produced by or developed out of faith.[83] They will be done in obedience to God's will, and that includes actions which carry out the love command (2:8), but in context are not to be limited to them.

The sentence has been formulated sharply in view of the opinion mentioned in verse 14 (which says "I have faith" and is unconcerned about deeds) and that mentioned in verse 18 (which accepts "faith" and "deeds" as two separate, entirely valid expressions of Christianity). It is perhaps this sentence especially which has led so many interpreters to conclude that James is attacking Paul, or, if not Paul himself, then a distorted Paulinism. "You see that a person (ανθρωπος) is justified by deeds (εξ εργων δικαιουται) and not by faith alone (ουκ εκ πιστεως μονον)." Paul's words in Romans 3:28

---

second half of the quotation, 1 Maccabees 2:52 also has και ελογισθη εις δικαιοσυνην.

79. This interpretation is challenged by Davids, *James*, 129; Martin, *James*, 93, who see this more as the confirmation of what James had been saying. However, James was here standing within an early Jewish tradition of exegeting Genesis 15:6 (some scholars see this use of Genesis 15:6 as an indication that James knew Paul's argument in Romans and Galatians, e.g., Tjusi, *Glaube*, 189-91).

80. Mussner, *Jakobusbrief*, 143, maintains that his action was the expression and result of his faith and his faith led to this action. Faith and works worked together in exemplary fashion in the case of Abraham.

81. See Isa 41:8; 2 Chr 20:7; Jub 19:9; 30:20; CD 3:2; *4 Ezra* 3:14; *T. Ab.* 13:1, 6; *Apoc. Ab.* 9:6; 10:6; frequently in Philo; and also in 1 Clem 10.1; 17.2. In Daniel 3:35 LXX Abraham is referred to as ο ηγαπημενος by God.

82. Jacobs, *Midrashic Background*, 457-64, refers to R. Meir; Philo, *Abr.* 170; a Baraitha about the seven types of Pharisees; and the Zadokite Document. That Jewish writers linked Genesis 15 and 22, as James does, can be seen at Sirach 44:20-21; 1 Maccabees 2:52; the Targum on Genesis; Philo; Pseudo-Philo; and later rabbinic midrashim.

83. So rightly, e.g., Mussner, *Jakobusbrief*, 145; Frankemolle, *Jakobus*, 460; Theobald, "Der Kanon von der Rechtfertigung," 216.

are usually quoted: "For we reckon that a person (ανθρωπος) is justified (δικαιουσθαι) by faith (πιστει) apart from works of the law (χωρις εργων νομου)."[84] It will be noticed straightaway that Paul uses the phrase "works of the law," whereas James has been talking about deeds as deeds of love and kindness (e.g., 2:15-16; cf. 2:8). Furthermore, Paul does not appear to use the phrase "by faith alone" (εκ πιστεως μονον), even if that be held to be the essence of what he was saying.[85] We shall come back to the relation between Paul and James later. The use of "alone" here by James is conditioned by his argument hitherto, not by reference to Paul or a Paulinist.[86]

A second OT example is given in verse 25 to illustrate James's insistence that faith must express itself in deeds: Rahab. She discerned that the God of Israel was so powerful that He would deliver the city of Jericho into the hands of the Israelites (Josh 2:11). She "received"[87] Joshua's spies and protected them and ensured their safe escape. This was a form of faith which expressed itself in deeds.[88] As a result, she and her family were spared when the Israelites captured the city (Josh 6:22-25). Rahab came to be seen as a model example of a proselyte (as was Abraham).[89]

That we are justified in interpreting verse 25 as a faith-deeds combination is seen by the way in which at verse 26 James drew his discussion

---

84. Davids, *James*, 131, lists the variety of verses quoted by those who think that James was attacking Paul. These include Romans 4:16, but μονον here is part of the construction ου μονον . . . αλλα και, and one would never translate it "descendants of the Law alone"! Tjusia, *Glaube*, 189-91, concentrates on three linguistic agreements (viz. James 2:21/Rom 4:2; 2:23/Rom 4:3; and 2:24/Gal 2:16 + Rom 3:28) and the example of Abraham's offering of Isaac. (Here Tjusi does not think the example is suitable to combat justification by faith alone, and feels that the antithesis of faith and works has been read into the example.)

85. Nienhuis, *Not by Paul Alone*, 222, while accepting that Paul never uses "by faith alone," maintains that he did separate faith and works. In view of Galatians 5:6 in particular and the general way Paul holds together the indicative of salvation and the imperative of ethical action, this does not seem to be fair to Paul. It runs the risk of ignoring the rhetorical context of his remarks on faith and works of the Law.

86. Cf. the comment by Heiligenthal, *Werke*, 41, that "not by faith alone" is for James a hypothetical idea which is in itself absurd. See Theobald, "Der Kanon von der Rechtfertigung," 214-17, for the view that James had access to a form of what Theobald calls the "canon" of Justification, which he sees as originating in the Antioch Christian community and which was deepened by Paul in Galatians 2:16; Romans 3:28. For James, writing in the post 70 period, the canon no longer concerned entry into the community of salvation but rather is directed to baptized Christians who are called upon to prove the authenticity of their faith by deeds of compassion and neighborly love.

87. To read the hospitality motif into υποδεξαμενη as some do (e.g., Wall, *James*, 152-54) goes too far (in agreement with the criticism of Popkes, *Jakobus*, 209).

88. Laws, *James*, 138.

89. Laws, *James*, 138; cf. Davids, *James*, 132.

to a close. "For as the body apart from the spirit is dead, so also faith apart from deeds is dead." With this conclusion that faith-apart-from-deeds is dead, James picked up his assertion of verse 17. Deeds show that faith is present; deeds show the reality of faith.[90] Mussner comments: "A dead faith is like a corpse. . . . Deeds of love make faith into a saving fides viva according to James."[91]

James does not mention justification in this conclusion, but reiterated his previous assertion in verse 17 that faith without deeds was dead, a point which offers some confirmation that the subject which dominated his thoughts was the relation of faith to deeds,[92] and, specifically, the alternatives "faith for itself alone" (without works) and "faith with works."[93]

We are now in a position to sum up James's position. James had encountered people who claimed to "have faith" and that this was sufficient to receive salvation at the Last Judgment before God. They appear not to have drawn ethical consequences from this belief, and, for example, were negligent of their responsibilities as believers towards those in need.[94] He also postulated another outlook which appears to accept that some "have faith" and some "have deeds": each was a valid expression of Christianity, since God through His Spirit apportions different "gifts" to different people.

James did not agree with either position. With respect to the first position, he argued that a faith which did not express itself especially in deeds of compassion and caring (as laid down in the Love Command [Lev 19:18], a command endorsed by Jesus himself) was dead. Against the second position, he continued to maintain that faith could only be demonstrated by the deeds to which it leads; otherwise, it is useless. He pointed out that the confession "God is one," the standard expression of Jewish orthodoxy based on Deuteronomy 6:4 and taken over into Christianity, was admitted by demons, but their reaction was to shudder. Their confession did not lead them to behavior pleasing to God.

---

90. Cf. Johnson, *James*, 245.
91. Mussner, *Jakobus*, 151.
92. Popkes, *Jakobus*, 210.
93. Frankemölle, *Jakobus*, 477. On the same page, Frankemölle uses the phrase "eine leibhaftige und tat-kräftige Glaube" [a faith which powerfully expresses itself in concrete deeds in the physical realm]. Garleff puts it in a slightly different way. James 2:14-26 "is related to 2:12f and can be understood as an excursus on the theme of judgment. The author here once again presents in detail what was only mentioned briefly in 1:18-25: Christian faith is the integration of hearing and doing the word" (Garleff, *Identität*, 302).
94. Perhaps 1 John 3:17 might offer an analogous situation.

Earlier in the letter, when pleading for his hearers to be doers of the word and not just hearers (1:22), James likened the person who is merely a hearer of the word to someone who sees themselves in a mirror, but then goes off and promptly forgets what they look like. In the "perfect law of freedom," everyone has a chance to see what God wants us to do in our lives. But to forget that divine demand on us is wrong and unacceptable. One must never forget what the perfect law of freedom demands from us. One must build (as it were) on the initial experience of salvation; hence, the combination of the statement that God has given the hearers birth by His word of truth in 1:16 and the demand in verse 21 to receive the implanted word.[95]

Thus, faith which has no deeds is dead and useless. James's position is then neither to belittle faith nor over-exalt deeds, but to hold them together: it is a case of faith-with-deeds. Faith is completed or perfected in deeds; the two are really inseparable in a true Christianity.

Though he did not in 2:14–26 explain what he meant by faith, and though the mention of faith in 2:14–26 tends to carry the connotation of an intellectual subscription to a credal confession *because that is the kind of faith with which James disagrees,* a look at the other references to faith in the letter suggests that faith for James has a dynamic character. It includes trust in a generous and consistent God; it is refined by testing circumstances, and through these it grows and develops towards perfection; and it should express itself in conduct compatible with the Lord Jesus Christ who is the embodiment of the glory of God.

Thus, faith is part of the process by which people are justified before God.[96] But this faith must demonstrate itself in deeds of compassion and obedience to any command of God. Faith-with-deeds is the pattern according to the will of God. Faith on its own without deeds is dead and useless.

---

95. Popkes, *Jakobus*, 136, comments that the special danger of the pious person is to remain with the initial spiritual experience and to think that what is the essential has been attained (this is their self-deception). But the initial spiritual experience is the beginning of a way, on which one should remain and mature. Later (214) he says in a general comment on 2:14–26 as a whole that the problem of the erroneous theological connection (theologischen Fehlschaltungen) of faith and works is rooted in the self-deception of the pious person who imagines that they are "religious" while ignoring the Love Command. See Frankemolle, *Jakobus*, 1:42, 44, 90–91, 163–64, 168, 171, etc., for a vigorous defense of James and his conviction that God can supply the wisdom and all that is necessary for Christians to progress towards a perfect life.

96. Cf. Popkes, *Jakobus*, 187: Faith has a place in justification. Flüchter, *Anrechnung*, 186, expresses the point negatively: "It is not a case for the author of justification by deeds to the exclusion of faith."

4.3. The Relation of James and Paul and Their Respective Use of Abraham

We are now in a position to discuss whether James was attacking Paul or an extreme form of Paul's teaching which ends up by, if not denigrating works, at least relegating them to an insignificant role in the Christian life.

It is worth reminding ourselves that twice in Romans Paul indicated that he had been accused of indifference to ethics. At 3:8, he said that some smeared him with the accusation that he taught "Let us do wrong that good may occur." He raised the question later at 6:1, when he was ready to answer the charge: "Shall we continue sinning that grace might abound?" Earlier, in 1 Corinthians, within a congregation founded by him, some were touting the slogan "All things are lawful" (6:12; 10:23) and saw nothing wrong with consorting with prostitutes (6:12–20) or attending pagan temples (8:7–13). These passages are mentioned to show that some misinterpreted Paul in his lifetime, and indeed among his own converts, but such a possibility could obviously have arisen after his lifetime as well.

But is it necessary to invoke Paul or Paulinism as the background for 2:14–26? An increasing number of scholars have recently challenged what had in effect become critical orthodoxy, viz. that James was attacking Paul or Paulinism.[97] What then are the arguments to be considered on this issue?

In the first place, James used εργα, but never "works of the law," whereas Paul attacked reliance on these. That said, however, it is probably wisest not to draw too hasty conclusions from this linguistic point. In James 2:8–12, the Law is part of the discussion. On the other hand, in James there is no mention of circumcision, food laws, sabbath observance, etc, and no discussion of the basis on which Gentiles might be admitted as members of the people of God. Though "works" include obedience to any expression of God's will (e.g., the prohibition of adultery and murder [2:11] and sins of speech [3:1–12]), James does stress εργα as deeds of compassion towards the needy and destitute, in accordance with the Love Command of Leviticus 19:18 (in 2:8, the "the royal law," "the perfect law of freedom," is encapsulated by them). The importance of the Love Command is also, however, recognized by Paul. Twice he quoted it and said that love was the fulfillment of the Law (Gal 5:14; Rom 13:8–10). Both James and Paul affirm the vital significance of deeds of love and compassion, no doubt influenced by the teaching of Jesus (as it appears now in Mark 12:28–34; Luke 10:25–37).

---

97. Among those who think that James was attacking Paul or (an extreme form of or a misunderstood form of) Paulinism, we may mention the following as examples: Dibelius, *James*, 174–80; Laws, *James*, 128–39; Dunn, *Unity and Diversity*, 251; Koch, *Schrift*, 243.

Secondly, James attacked both a view which said that faith on its own was sufficient and a view which saw faith on its own as one possible valid expression of Christianity. James chose to illustrate the position by taking faith to be subscription to a doctrinal proposition (e.g., God is one). To carry weight in the discussion, what James said must have had relevance or it could simply be dismissed easily as lacking in cogency. Accordingly, we may assume that there were some who placed all emphasis on adherence to "orthodox" doctrines.

His own personal concept of faith was very different and included the elements of trust and confidence in God who is generous and who answers prayer. Paul's understanding of faith is also itself predominantly trust, trust in the promises of God in Jesus, a total commitment of oneself to the one who was crucified for us and is now, as raised from the dead, the living Lord. If James was attacking Paul, then he has seriously misunderstood him! And even if a Paulinism is postulated as the target of James, one has to say that neither Colossians and Ephesians on the one hand nor the Pastorals on the other suggest that "Paulinists" espoused anything like the disregard of deeds of compassion which James was attacking.[98]

In the third place, such similarities as exist—both appeal to Abraham, and both quote Genesis 15:6, both with a slight difference over against the LXX[99]—could be explained by the fact that both stood within a Jewish Christian tradition, in which the figure of Abraham was reflected upon and his significance for God's covenant people was pondered upon, elaborated, and recycled.

Fourthly, the same could be said of the use which James makes of Rahab. He could be dependent on Jewish tradition, which had elaborated her story, while Abraham and she also figure in Hebrews 11:8-19, 31, and 1 Clement 10-12, which could suggest that Christian tradition made use of Jewish traditions. (The author of Hebrews uses the key word πιστις to link all the characters in chapter 11, while hospitality is the theme in 1 Clement.) This reinforces the suggestion of point three.

---

98. There is of course in the Pastorals evidence from the "faithful sayings" and the emphasis on "sound teaching" of the fixation of Christian belief (what has been called the formalization of faith, e.g., Dunn, *Jesus and the Spirit*, 349), but we should not forget that the Pastorals know the danger of "holding a form of godliness but denying its power" (2 Tim 3:5). Even Lindemann, *Paulus*, 250, who thinks that James was attacking Paul, agrees that the evidence of Acts, Ephesians, the Pastorals, and 1 Clement show that there was an area of the church which had not the slightest to do with a "degenerate hyperPaulinism."

99. Both have δε instead of an initial και, and spell Αβρααμ with two alphas in the second syllable, whereas the LXX has only one, but at 1 Maccabees 2:52, the LXX has Αβρααμ.

In the fifth place, some scholars have detected a different nuance in the use of δικαιουν in James and Paul. It is claimed that Paul used the verb in a judicial sense of God's verdict at the Last Judgment,[100] whereas in James God declared Abraham to be (morally) righteous. If we cast the net a little wider than the verb δικαιουν, we observe that James used "save" at 2:14 with reference to the Last Judgment (cf. the context of 2:12-13).[101] At 2:21 he asked, "Was not Abraham justified by his deeds," referring to the binding of Isaac, and followed this up by quoting Genesis 15:6, "Abraham believed God and it was reckoned to him for righteousness," at verse 23. This seems to carry the meaning "declared to be righteous."[102] Then he says at verse 24, generalizing, "You see that a person is justified on the basis of deeds and not by faith alone." (δικαιουται is the present indicative!). Here the verb seems to be referring to God's verdict at the Last Judgment, whether one is righteous or not. (It is not the justification of the ungodly/sinners, of which Paul speaks in Romans 3:24; 4:5.)

Thus, James can speak of God's past declarations concerning Abraham and Rahab—of their being righteous, and of the future declaration at the Last Judgment (2:24). Paul used the verb "to justify" of past, present, and future, and has in mind the forensic declaration which sets the sinner in the right with God (forgiveness and restored covenant relationship expressed in a judicial metaphor). James emphasized the inseparable link between faith and deeds, while Paul spoke of faith working itself out in love (Gal 5:6) and of judgment according to deeds (Rom 2:1-11, 13).

All these reasons show that the previous consensus is by no means assured. Are there any alternatives? Can we supply a different but cogent background against which to place 2:14-26? Penner trenchantly remarks that the human tendency to rest on conviction without translating this into deeds is widely attested.[103] He has been countered by Popkes who asserts that the contrast in Jewish tradition is more between merely studying the law and actually doing it.[104] We need to go into this issue.

The evidence which Popkes adduced is *Aboth* 1:15, 17; Philo, *Praem.* 79ff.[105] In *Aboth* 1:15, Shammai is reported as having said that the Torah

---

100. Actually, Paul uses δικαιουν of a past event (Rom 5:1, 9; 8:30; 1 Cor 6:11; cf. Gal 3:24), a present experience (Rom 3:24, 26, 28; 4:5; Gal 2:16), and a future hope (Rom 2:13; 3:20).

101. Cf. Mussner, *Jakobusbrief*, 147; Davids, *James*, 120.

102. So Davids, *James*, 127-28.

103. Penner, *Eschatology*, 73.

104. Popkes, *Jakobus*, 115.

105. Popkes, *Jakobus*, 115n41, 42. He also refers the reader to the commentaries on Matthew 7:26; Romans 2:13, and specifically to Luz, *Commentary on Matthew* 1:412-13; Wilckens, *Römer*, 1:113-14.

should be made the foundation of one's life. "Say little and do much." Here the contrast appears to be between talking about the Torah and actually doing it.[106] In 1:17, Simon, son of R. Gamaliel,[107] is reported as having said, "Not study is the chief thing but action." Thus, of the two sayings from *Aboth*, only 1:17 contrasts the actual study and doing of the Torah mentioned by Popkes. As to Philo, the relevant passage runs: "If, He says, you keep the divine commandments in obedience to his ordinances and accept his precepts, not merely to hear them but to carry them out by your life and conduct, the first boon you will have is victory over your enemies."[108] But this does not contrast study of the Law and the doing of it, but the mere hearing of it and the doing of it, which is similar to what James says in 1:22. It must be confessed that the evidence that Popkes had adduced to support his contention is not impressive.

One of the sources for James's teaching is that of the sayings of Jesus. At the conclusion of the great sermon[109] Jesus is recorded as telling the Parable of the Wise and Foolish Builders, who built on secure and insecure foundations respectively. Each half of the parable is furnished by an introduction: "Every one who hears these words of mine and does them will be compared to a wise man. . . . Every one who hears these words of mine but does not do them will be compared to a foolish man" (Matt 7:24, 26).[110] Luke recorded a saying of Jesus "Why do you call me Lord, Lord, but do not do what I say?" (6:46). The Matthean parallel is probably an expansion, but retains the essence of the saying: "Not everyone who says Lord, Lord, will enter the kingdom of heaven, but the one who does my heavenly Father's will" (7:21). In the Parable of the Two Sons (Matthean special material, 21:28-32), the concern for doing again surfaces. One son said that he would go and work in the vineyard but did not do so; the other at first refused, but then changed his mind and went and worked. Jesus contrasted the positive response by tax collectors and prostitutes to the preaching of John the Baptist with the

---

106. Cf. Dibelius, *James*, 114n38.

107. Herford, *Pirke Aboth*, 694, believes that this Simon was actually the son of Hillel and the father of Gamaliel, not his son. If this conjecture were correct, then he would be roughly a contemporary of James, the brother of Jesus.

108. Dibelius, *James*, 114n38, gives the Greek and a translation.

109. The Sermon on the Mount in Matthew's Gospel (chapters 5-7) and the Sermon on the Plain in Luke (6:20-49). Probably a majority of scholars accept that the hypothetical source Q contained a sermon, which probably Matthew considerably expanded.

110. Luke's version runs slightly differently: "Why do you call me, Lord, Lord, but do not do what I say? Every one who comes to me and hears my words and does them I will show you to what he is like: he is like a man. . . . But the one who hears but does not do them is like a man" (6:46-48a, 49a).

lack of response by the religious authorities. The former heard his message and did something about it; but the religious authorities heard what he had to say, but it did not affect them.

Jesus issued some pungent criticism of Pharisees and scribes, some of whom in his eyes were guilty of appearing righteous but not putting into practice all their teaching (e.g., Luke 11:39-47, 52. The Matthean parallel in 23:1-33 has been heavily edited by Matthew under the *Leitmotiv* of hypocrisy).

Working back from Jesus to the Old Testament, there is a text from Ezekiel which used the contrast between hearing and not doing. The evening before he heard of the fall of Jerusalem, Ezekiel was commissioned by God to speak a word of judgment to those who remained in the land and who were making the assumption that the land belonged to them and not the exiles (33:23-29). Then God warned him that people would come to his house to listen to his words (now that his prediction of the fall of Jerusalem had been vindicated), but in fact they would not act upon his words, with the implication that they too would incur divine judgment instead of salvation. The LXX of 33:31 runs:

Ακουουσιν τα ρηματα σου και αυτα ου μη ποιησουσιν.[111]

In the LXX, they are compared to people who listen to the sound of a sweet-sounding, well-tuned harp (the Hebrew has singer of love songs), and then the charge was repeated that they would listen to Ezekiel's words but would not do them (v. 32).

In the preaching of the prophets before Ezekiel, we can say that the substance of this charge was present, even if not formulated in this precise way. It was widely assumed by the eighth and seventh century prophets that the leaders and the people knew what the Law required. They had heard it read to them at the great festivals, but they had refused to obey it. Amos assumed that people frequented the sanctuaries at Bethel and Gilgal (e.g., 4:4), but the demands of the Law were consistently flouted (e.g., 2:6-8). Isaiah passed on the charges of God: the people honored Him with their lips but their hearts were far from Him (29:13). Despite the prophet's pleas not to entangle the country in an alliance with Egypt, "they refused to listen" (28:12). They refused to listen means that *they heard but they did not respond positively and obey what God demanded of them.*[112] The unwillingness

---

111. In the Hebrew, the reason given is that their hearts are set on their ill-gotten gains; the LXX states that "falsehood is in their mouth and their heart (goes) after (their) defilements."

112. Cf. the comment of Kittel: "[Biblical religion] is a religion of the Word, because it is a religion of action, of obedience to the Word" (*TDNT* 1:218).

to hear was basically an unwillingness to put into practice what had been heard (cf. Jer 7:13; Hos 9:17a).

The book of Deuteronomy may also be said to emphasise both the hearing of the words of the Law and the doing of them. Moses is depicted as saying: "Hear now, O Israel, the statutes and laws which I am about to teach you, and obey them. . . . I have taught you statutes and laws, as the Lord my God commanded me; these you must duly keep when you enter the land and occupy it. You must observe them carefully, for this will show your wisdom and understanding to the nations" (4:1, 5).[113] In chapter 5, Moses summoned the people and bade them to hear God's statutes and laws; they must learn them and be careful to observe them (v. 1).[114] Later, at 31:9-13, Moses was reported as having told the priests and elders to assemble the people every seven years at the Feast of Tabernacles to read the Law to the people so that they might hear it and learn to fear the LORD and observe all these laws with care (και ακουσονται ποιειν παντας τους λογους του νομου τουτου [v. 12 LXX]). Hearing and doing go together.

The emphasis in the Wisdom literature is basically the same. The teacher passed on instruction: the pupil/son was expected to take the teaching to heart and put it into practice. "My son, do not forget my teaching, but guard my commands in your heart; for they will bring you long life and years in plenty and prosperity as well" (3:1) is typical. The advice and teaching was to be heard, assimilated, and lived out in daily life and the result would be "favor and success in the sight of God and man" (3:4). The opposite of this way can be seen in the words of Wisdom herself. "Because they hate knowledge, and have not chosen to fear the LORD, because they have not accepted my counsel and spurned all my reproof, they shall eat the fruits of their behavior and have a surfeit of their own devices" (1:29-31).

Even this meagre survey has been sufficient to show the truth of the assertion that Israel was expected to hear the word/Law of God and to do it. God's people must obey what God commands. Hearing and doing are inextricably linked together.

Paul's argument in Romans 2 picked up this. God judges all according to their deeds (v. 6).

> He will give eternal life to those who by persistence in doing good seek glory, honor, and immortality, but He will inflict

---

113. LXX has ακουε . . . ποιειν (v. 1) . . . ποιησαι (v. 5) . . . φυλαξεσθε και ποιησετε (v. 6).

114. LXX has ακουε . . . και φυλαξεσθε ποιειν αυτα (v. 1). See also verse 27, where the people promise και ακουσομεθα και ποιησομεν what Moses passed on of what God had said to him. Cf. also 6:1.

(His) wrath and anger on those who are motivated by party spirit, disobey the truth, and obey what is wicked. (vv. 7–8)

Paul was critical of Jews who claimed to be able to instruct others in the ways of God and the demands of His Law, but in fact did not themselves keep the Law and, thereby, dishonored the name of God (see 2:17–29).

Finally, we might mention that in the Fourth Gospel Jesus maintained that, though his opponents claimed to be the children of Abraham, their claim was belied by their deeds, for they were seeking to kill him. So, they were not doing the deeds of Abraham, despite their claim, and the result was that they were not his true children. Deeds reveal one's parentage. This was similar to the stress that Israel as God's son and people must obey Him and so reveal His will and character in their own national life.

To sum up, the evidence adduced to support the claim that the background of James's command not to be hearers of the word only but doers of it is the rabbinic contrast between just studying the Law and actually doing it in practice, is not particularly impressive. On the other hand, there is much more convincing evidence in the teaching of Jesus, now recorded in the Synoptic Gospels, of the link between hearing his word/teaching and doing it. His teaching in turn could be claimed to have its roots in the expectation that Israel as a whole and the individual Israelite in particular was expected to hear instruction in the revealed will of God and the teaching of the wise person and carry that out in daily living. Thus, a credible background other than a direct attack on Paul or Paulinism has been put forward.[115]

The figure Abraham was and had become in Jewish thinking extremely important. The story of Abraham had been pored over, reflected upon, retold, recycled, reapplied to new situations of the people of Israel to make it freshly relevant for the people, as they grappled with new problems in their national life. James stood within this interpretative tradition.

James quoted Genesis 15:6 about Abraham's faith and referred to the willingness of Abraham to sacrifice Isaac in Genesis 22. In this move, James in no way wished to exclude any reference or stress on Abraham's faith. James's comment in 2:22, "You see that (his) faith worked together with his deeds and (his) faith was perfected by (his) deeds," rules that out of court immediately. Abraham's faith was a vitally important component of his story, and James fully recognized that. What Abraham illustrated for James was a faith which expressed itself in deeds. Abraham's faith alone was not the whole story. That faith was producing or flowing out in

---

115. Johnson, *James*, 247, has reminded us that "the issue of the authenticity of faith which is professed but is not demonstrated in deed" is "one typical for moralists both in Greco-Roman and Jewish cultures."

deeds, and in that sense could be said to be working together with deeds and to be completed by his deeds. Faith cannot remain by itself. As such, it would be useless and unprofitable; it would, in fact, be a dead faith. Abraham's faith showed itself in his willingness to offer Isaac, even though Isaac was the heir through whom God's promise was to be realized. James interpreted Genesis 15:6 as justification on the basis of faith-working-out-its-meaning-in-practical-deeds. This became apparent in the incident involving Isaac in Genesis 22.

Thus, when James said that "a person is justified by deeds and not by faith alone," he was assuming that faith does have a significant role to play in justification, but not faith alone. Faith is demonstrated by deeds, as verse 18 shows. Faith cannot prove its genuineness without deeds. Deeds demonstrate its authenticity.

Abraham is thus for James not just an example but the supremely important example of what we may call faith-with-deeds. Only in this way can a believer be confident of pleasing God. The reference to "our father Abraham" fits in with a good deal of early Christian belief that followers of Jesus were part of God's people stretching back to Abraham. For James, those who are characterized by faith-with-deeds are Abraham's children. Faith-with-deeds is the true mark of those who have the faith of our Lord Jesus Christ.

5

Abraham in Luke-Acts

5.1. Introduction

THE HEARERS/READERS OF LA first encounter the name of Abraham in the opening two chapters of Luke's Gospel, in which the evangelist introduces the hearers/readers to John the Baptist and Jesus by way of narratives about the events surrounding their birth.

Abraham is referred-to in the two songs or psalms, the Magnificat and Benedictus, which, together with the message of the Angelic chorus to the shepherds and the Nunc Dimittis of the aged Simeon, could be said to act as theological commentaries on the events being described in Luke 1–2. One would expect these references to be formative for our understanding of how Luke interpreted the figure of Abraham.

One approach would be to take Luke 1–2 as they stand and to summarize what emerges from these chapters in respect of the figure of Abraham and his significance for Luke's story (the synchronic approach). But the matter is not as straightforward as one might expect, and we cannot discuss the references to Abraham without considering wider issues concerning the way these two chapters as a whole have been put together and their relationship to the rest of LA (the diachronic approach). This latter kind of approach may well reveal significant aspects for our theme before Luke as well as for Luke himself. After initially considering the literary structure of Luke 1–2, we will first adopt the synchronic approach, and then afterwards use the diachronic approach.

5.2. The Birth Stories

5.2.1. John and Jesus: Comparison and Contrast

As has often been noted, the first two chapters of Luke are built on a comparison and contrast between John the Baptist and Jesus, the superiority of the latter being clearly established.

Firstly, there is an annunciation to John's father, Zechariah, and to Jesus' mother, Mary. Within these two scenes, we are told that John the Baptist will carry out a highly significant task as prophet of the Most High, to turn the people of Israel back to the Lord their God in the spirit and power of Elijah (1:16-17), whereas Jesus is the Son of the Most High, who will give him the throne of his ancestor, David (1:32).

Secondly, there is an account of their birth. While the circumstances surrounding the birth of John the Baptist caused a stir among the neighbors (1:57-66), the birth of Jesus was heralded by the appearance of an angel of the Lord accompanied by a host of angels who announced the birth and its significance to shepherds near Bethlehem (2:8-14).

Thirdly, the circumcision and naming of the two on the eighth day after birth[1] are narrated, but again the superiority of Jesus is maintained. Two characters of outstanding piety, Simeon and Anna, declare the significance of the child Jesus for both Israel and the Gentiles (2:25-32, 36-38).

Fourthly, there is a general note about the growth and development of the two (1:80; 2:40, respectively).

But, finally, unparalleled in the case of John the Baptist, we are given an incident from the youth of Jesus when he was twelve years old and had gone up to Jerusalem with his parents for the Jewish festival of the Passover. In this story, Jesus revealed his sense of closeness to God as his Father (v. 49, confirming what had been said earlier in the annunciation scene to Mary at 1:32).

The two stories are linked by an encounter of the two mothers, Elizabeth and Mary (1:39-45). It is in this meeting of the two mothers that we have the first of the two songs mentioned above, the Magnificat, the song of Mary (1:46b-55), whereas the Benedictus is Zechariah's praise to God (1:67-79) when his son had been born and he had been liberated from the temporary dumbness, the punishment for his unbelief towards the announcement of the birth of a son to Elizabeth and himself (1:20).

---

1. Thiessen, *Contesting Conversion*, 114-16, 122, 140, sees in the fact that both John the Baptist and Jesus were circumcised on the eighth day one indication, together with others, that Luke believed that Jewish Christians should circumcise their baby sons on the eighth day in accordance with Genesis 17:9-14.

5.2.2. Abraham in Luke 1

We turn now to consider Luke 1, where the references to Abraham occur, in its present form, i.e., the form in which the final author wished the intended audience to hear/read it (the synchronic approach).

In the characters whom Luke set before us in chapters 1–2, we meet people—Zechariah and Elizabeth, Mary and Joseph, Simeon and Anna—who were the pious, the devout, the saints in the land. Priest and lay, men and women, they are God-fearing and Law-keeping members of the Chosen People. They look to God and hope for the fulfillment of His ancient promises.

Luke's story opens with a description of the priest Zechariah and Elizabeth, a godly but childless couple. Zechariah was chosen by lot to offer incense on the altar of incense within the Holy Place of the Temple building. While there, he received a visit from the angel Gabriel, who announced that Elizabeth would conceive and have a son, whom Zechariah is to name John. This John will be filled with the Holy Spirit from birth. His future work will be carried out in the spirit of Elijah. It will consist of turning many Israelites back to God by restoring harmony within family relationships, and by causing the disobedient to return to righteous ways. In short, he will go before the Lord to prepare a people equipped to serve the Lord. Zechariah's reference to his and Elizabeth's age was interpreted as a sign of unbelief, and Gabriel announced that Zechariah would be struck dumb until the birth of their son (1:5–20).

The reference to the work of John is reminiscent of the predictions in the last book of the collection of prophetic writings, Malachi 3:1–5; 4:5–6. In response to an assertion that God approves those who do wrong rather than those who do good and a question "Where is the God of justice?" (2:17), God, through Malachi, announced that He would send His messenger before Him to prepare for His coming. When He does come, it will be for judgment. He will punish evil doers (3:1a, 5). It looks as if a redactor has added 3:1b–4.[2] These verses seem to give information about God's messenger, now described as "the messenger of the covenant." But the question of verse 2, "But who can endure the day of his coming, and who can stand when he appears?" seems to point to God. Not surprisingly, therefore, there has been discussion as to whether these verses are about God or His messenger. The solution of the difficulty may well lie in the way in which Hebrew thinkers could identify God's messenger and God, and apply God-language (as in

---

2. As a result, in Malachi 3:1–5, there is a somewhat confusing mention of "my messenger," the Lord, "the messenger of the covenant," the LORD of Hosts (v. 1), the LORD (vv. 3, 4), and I (v. 5).

verse 2) to His messenger. If that is the correct approach, it is the messenger who will purify the sons of Levi (the priests). His activity is compared to one who refines metal or a launderer who washes dirty linen and makes them clean. *Moral renewal is how he prepares the way of the LORD.* The result of 2:17–3:5 would be that a messenger would precede God's coming and prepare the way for God's coming by purifying the priests, and then God Himself would come and judge evil-doers.[3]

This announcement of a messenger to precede the coming of God is taken up in what is widely regarded as an addition by a later redactor at the end of the book.[4] "Lo, I will send you the prophet Elijah before the great and terrible day of the LORD comes. He will turn the hearts of the parents to their children and the hearts of children to their parents, so that I will not come and strike the land with a curse" (4:5–6). Elijah had been translated directly to heaven (2 Kgs 2:11), and this verse in Malachi is evidence that some in Israel speculated on his future role. As he had successfully withstood the inroads of Baalism in his day, so in the future he would help to prepare Israel to meet its God. This Malachi passage is clearly in mind in the annunciation by Gabriel to Zechariah in Luke 1:13–17, where the predicted son to be born to Zechariah and Elizabeth will minister in the spirit of Elijah and will turn many Israelites to the Lord their God. He will turn the hearts of fathers to their children and the disobedient to the wisdom of the righteous and to make ready a people prepared for the Lord.

The way in which these passages in the last book of the Hebrew Scriptures are taken up in the identification of John the Baptist with the coming Elijah has led to the suggestion that Luke saw his work as a continuation of the Scriptures of the Old Covenant.[5]

A second annunciation scene follows. This time, the same angel meets a woman called Mary, engaged to a man called Joseph, a descendant of David. Gabriel promised Mary that she would have a son and call his name Jesus. He will be Son of the Most High who will give him the throne of his father David and he will reign forever (vv. 26–33). In response to Mary's reaction that she has not "known" a man, the angel said that the Holy Spirit, the power of the Most High, would overshadow her and she

---

3. See the discussions in Mason, *Haggai*, 151–54; Petersen, *Zechariah 9–14*, 207–212; Redditt, *Haggai*, 175–78.

4. So Mason, *Haggai*, 136, 159–62; Petersen, *Zechariah 9–14*, 252–53; Redditt, *Haggai*, 155, 185.

5. This is an intriguing suggestion! Luke seems to be aware of the threefold division of the Hebrew canon when he has the risen Lord reminding the disciples that he had told them that the things concerning himself in the Law, Prophets, and Psalms had to be fulfilled (Luke 24:44).

would conceive. This meant that the son to be born would be holy, the Son of God. Gabriel concluded by mentioning that her relative, Elizabeth, was also expecting a baby, and this was an indication that nothing was impossible for God (1:34–38).

The message of Gabriel to Mary recalls a number of Scripture passages: the promises made to David as recorded in 2 Samuel 7 and as they found a place in Israel's psalms (esp. Ps 89; 132), together with the predictions found in Isaiah (Isa 9; 11). It is possible that the LXX version of Isaiah 7:14, with the statement that a virgin would conceive and bear a son who would be called Immanuel, was also in Luke's mind (a covert allusion rather than an explicit one).

These two annunciation scenes set the drama going, as it were. After the scene between Gabriel and Mary, Mary visited Elizabeth, an episode which links the two stories of John and Jesus. The older woman, filled with the Holy Spirit, greeted her with a twofold blessing: "Blessed are you among women, and blessed is the fruit of your womb" (1:41–42). She expressed surprise that the mother of her Lord should visit her, and reported that the child in her womb had leapt for joy at the sound of Mary's greeting. A third beatitude follows: "Blessed is she who believed that there would be a fulfillment of what the Lord had spoken to her" (1:43–45). Mary responded with the psalm of praise which we call the Magnificat (1:46–55).

The first part of this psalm is certainly personal to the speaker, even if there is nothing specific in it concerning a woman about to have her first child. Mary used "my" and "to me" and referred to herself as God's handmaiden (δουλη). Many phrases used are reminiscent of the Song of Hannah in 1 Samuel 2, but Mary's ταπεινωσις is not, as in Hannah's case, childlessness, but her lowly station in life. In context, "the great things" which God has done for her (v. 49) is the choice of her to be the mother of the Messiah. God had intervened to cause her to conceive and her son would be the holy Son of God.

With verse 50 the perspective seems to widen. God's mercy will be upon all succeeding generations of those who fear Him, and this seems both to round off the first section (vv. 47–50) and also provide a transition to the second half of the psalm (vv. 51–55). In verse 54, it is said that God had come to the aid of His servant, *Israel*. In context, Mary seems to speak from verse 51 as representative of Israel, i.e., the true Israel, those who are the lowly and the hungry (both economically and those who hunger for righteousness). The tenses used in this second half of the psalm are the aorist indicative.[6] They express a series of future actions which are sure to take place.[7]

If God is to establish His will, His reign, then all obstacles and forms of opposition will need to be removed. Hence, the proud, the mighty, the rich—all these terms in verses 51b-53 are loaded with the nuance of ungodly—must be humbled, brought low, and dispossessed of their capacity to thwart the purpose of God and to harm those devoted to doing His will. A reversal of existing socio-economic, political, and religious structures will take place.[8] God will exalt those who have trusted Him (the humble and the hungry). This is summed up in the phrase—"He has come to the aid of His servant, Israel" (v. 54a).[9]

These actions of God are held to be in fulfillment of what God had said to "our fathers." God has come to the aid of Israel by remembering[10] His intention to show mercy. His mercy means what God had promised to Abraham, Isaac, and Jacob ("as He spoke to our fathers" [v. 55a]). "Mercy" thus encapsulates God's faithfulness to His covenant relationship with Abraham and his descendants. The promises to the fathers are clearly constitutive for the people of God, the descendants of Abraham.

How that divine rescue of Israel might play out receives some hints. The son of Zechariah and Elizabeth will be a new Elijah: his role is to prepare God's people by reconciling family differences and promoting righteous conduct. His work will cause much rejoicing for many. The picking up of Malachi 3:1; 4:5-6 might suggest that a transcendental intervention by God, during or after John's ministry is in mind, on "the great and terrible Day of the LORD."

We may pause here to consider what Luke's purpose thus far might be. He has used the promise and gift of a child to Hannah and her Song, as a model for God's intervention to help the despised and lowly, and to

---

6. εποιησεν, διεσκορπισεν, καθειλεν, υψωσεν, and αντελαβετο.

7. They are akin to the Hebrew prophetic perfect. By this statement, we make no implied statement on whether the Magnificat was originally composed in Hebrew or not.

8. Cf. Schürmann, *Lukasevangelium*, 1:76.

9. This kind of hope will be later explained and expanded upon in the utterances of the godly Simeon (the Nunc Dimittis and his prophecy to Mary, 2:28-35) and the statement that the devout Anna spoke about Jesus to those who were waiting for the redemption of Jerusalem (2:38).

10. Taking μνησθηναι as an explanatory infinitive with Plummer, *Luke*, 34; Grundmann, *Das Evangelium nach Lukas*, 66; Marshall, *Gospel of Luke*, 85; Evans, *Saint Luke*, 176; Nolland, *Luke*, 1:73; Moule, *Idiom Book*, 127, in preference to an infinitive of result maintained by Schürmann, *Lukasevangelium*, 1:1, or infinitive of purpose with Fitzmeyer, *Luke*, 368.

indicate the appropriate human response. Luke has captured the ethos of the godly of the land on the brink of the time when God was going to fulfill His promises and deliver Israel His servant, who is oppressed and despised. God acts out of His own nature: He made promises to the founding fathers of Israel and He will keep to His word. The waiting period of the faithful is over. The era of salvation has dawned.

The narrative turns back, after the annunciation to Mary, to Elizabeth, to the birth of her son, the naming of the child as John (despite objections from relatives, but confirmed by the father who wrote the name on a tablet), and a note about the way people reacted with astonishment at the events surrounding the birth of John. They wondered how his life would turn out (1:57–66).

Luke says that Zechariah was filled with the Holy Spirit and he prophesied (1:67–79). In context, his prophecy answers the astonished question of those who heard about John's birth and the naming of the child. "What will this child turn out to be?" for, as Luke added, "the hand of the Lord was with him" (vv. 65–66).

The Benedictus falls into two main parts. There are grammatical reasons as well as the difference of content for this judgment. In verses 69–73, the tenses of the verbs seem to be aorist indicative, and the theme is the Saviour from the house of David.[11] However, in verses 76–79, attention shifts to John himself, with the tenses in the future indicative, though verses 78–79 could be said to veer over into the appearance of the one described as Lord.

The psalm begins with praise to God who has redeemed Israel and has raised up a saviour ("a horn of salvation") for "us" in the house of David. Obviously, this could not be referring to Zechariah's son, but refers to Mary's son who was described as a descendant of David (1:32).

This conviction about redemption is set forth in this-worldly terms. The negative side is the deliverance from the hands of their enemies and those who hate them (vv. 71, 74a), while the positive aspect is that conditions will be created in which the faithful Israelites will be able to serve God in righteousness all their days (v. 74b).

If God's purposes are to be realized, if Israel is to be redeemed, all that stands in the way must be removed—hence deliverance from their enemies (mentioned twice, vv. 71, 73ab). This prepares the way for the unhindered devotion to God in worship and holy living according to God's covenant Law. However the enemies are eliminated from the scene, life on earth will continue and God's people will be holy.

---

11. As John was a Levite, he is not the subject of the reference to the house of David.

All this intervention and its results are dependent on the fact that God has acted

> to show mercy to our fathers,
> and to remember His holy covenant,
> the oath which He swore to Abraham our father. (vv. 72-73)

The cluster of ideas—mercy, our fathers, covenant, oath, Abraham—are rather similar to the essence of what the Magnificat said (even if it did not specifically mention covenant and oath). Clearly Luke intended to emphasize that the events surrounding the birth of John and of Jesus fulfilled the Scriptures and, specifically, what God had promised to the founding fathers, especially Abraham.

In this reference to Abraham and what God had said to him and to Isaac and Jacob after him, Luke has tapped into themes which the sources for early Judaism amply reveal. For example, there is an appeal to "the fathers" in the additions to the books of Daniel and Esther; the Damascus Document; 1 Maccabees; Philo the epic poet; Ezekiel the Tragedian; and the Psalms of Solomon. There are references to the covenant with "the fathers" and/or the oath accompanying it in the Wisdom of Solomon; Pseudo-Philo's LAB; *4 Ezra*; and *2 Baruch*. Motives for the use of the Abrahamic story may vary: he may be referred to as a ground of hope of deliverance from present distressing circumstances which conflict with what the promises held out to Abraham's descendants, or as a means to remind God that He should do something on behalf of Abraham's descendants; or he may be held up as model to be imitated in his faithfulness under testing and so a ground for the appeal not to abandon faith in the God of Israel.

The references in the Magnificat and the Benedictus to God's covenant, oath, and promises to Abraham and the fathers thus fit in with what the literary sources of early Judaism enable us to see was a living tradition at the time of the birth and ministry of Jesus of Nazareth.

5.2.3. Is Luke 1 Primarily Tradition or Lucan Composition?

The diachronic approach to which we now turn asks certain questions: How have these chapters come about? Are they the result of Luke's welding together different traditions which he had received from various sources? To give one example, a number of scholars have suggested that Luke took over material emanating from the circle of John the Baptist's disciples.[12]

---

12. E.g., Dibelius, *Jungfraunsohn und Krippenkind*, 8 (though Dibelius did not include the Benedictus); Bultmann, *History of the Synoptic Tradition*, 294-95; Vielhauer,

To this source they would assign, broadly speaking, the annunciation to Zechariah, the birth of John the Baptist, and his naming and circumcision, together with the Benedictus.[13] Alternatively, has Luke composed the birth stories himself, using as his inspiration Old Testament models such as the annunciation of a birth of a longed-for child to a hitherto childless couple and the rich tradition of the praise of God for His deeds contained in Israel's Psalter?[14] Or did Luke come across the hymns/psalms and move them into a narrative of his own composing?[15] Are there clues which can help us answer these questions?

5.2.4. The Benedictus

In now adopting the diachronic approach, we will commence by looking at the Benedictus,[16] which confronts us with a number of critical issues. We shall briefly mention some of these.

Firstly, there is a question of the mode of composition. Was it an originally unified piece, which was composed for its present position in the Gospel of Luke,[17] or which came to Luke and was used by him? Or are we possibly dealing with two pieces which have been combined? Various suggestions have been made along these lines, given that there is something of a suture between verses 75 and 76. Did verses (67) 76-79, which deal specifically with John the Baptist, form one piece of tradition, with another consisting of verses 68-75, which may have been a psalm circulating on its

---

Das Benedictus des Zacharias, 256; Winter, *Magnificat and Benedictus*, 328, 338, 340-41; Grässer, *Alte Bund*, 34-36 (at least 1:5-25, 57-66, with the Annunciation perhaps addressed to Elizabeth, while the Magnificat and Benedictus were originally independent Jewish eschatological hymns).

13. The annunciation scene demands a report of the birth of the son to Zechariah and Elizabeth and also the fulfillment of the sign given to Zechariah (see Kaut, *Befreier und befreites Volk*, 113), just as the question of their kinsfolk "What shall become of this child?" (v. 66) also calls out for some answer, which the Benedictus supplies (so Gnilka, *Der Hymnus des Zacharias*, 219). This material (vv. 5-25, 57-80) does not really need the meeting of the two mothers (vv. 26-56).

14. Von Harnack, *Das Magnifikat der Elisabeth*, 538-66; Cadbury, *Making of Luke-Acts*, 192-93; Creed, *Luke*, 306-7.

15. Farris, *Hymns of Luke's Infancy Narratives*, 14-30, 152, 154, 158-60.

16. The justification for starting with the Benedictus rather than the Magnificent is that the former has often been assigned to a John the Baptist source. It is, of course, true that since Harnack there have been some scholars who have attributed the Magnificat to Elizabeth and thus to a John the Baptist source, but this is not such a widely held view.

17. E.g., Turner, *Relation of Luke I and II*, 100-109; Minear, *Luke's Use of the Birth Stories*, 111-30; Marshall, *Luke*, 87.

own and which was inserted into verses 67, 76–79;[18] or were only verses 76–77 inserted into 68–75, 78–79 (like the previous view, this suggestion sees a suture between verses 75 and 76).[19]

Secondly, there is the question whether verses 69–70 were added at some stage. A grammatical question is involved, since "salvation" in verse 71, which is intended to explain the "salvation" mentioned in verse 69, does not agree with it in case.[20] As to this lack of agreement between σωτηριαν in verse 71 and σωτηριας in verse 69, it must be pointed out that we have the same phenomenon in verse 73 where ορκον is really in apposition to the genitive διαθηκης of verse 72.[21] As to verse 70, a very similar sentence appears in Acts 3:21. While it could be a Lucan insertion, equally Luke could have been influenced by what he had written in the Benedictus when he was composing Acts. If verse 70 does have the feel of a parenthesis in the Benedictus, that is by no means a conclusive argument against its originality here.

Thirdly, the change of tense from the aorist indicatives of verses 68–69 to that of the future indicative in verse 78b needs clarification.[22] In verses 68–69 God is praised for having already acted to redeem His people and for having raised up a savior for them in the house of David, whereas in verse 78b this savior is to come. This may be a sign of the different origin of verses 76–79 or 78–79.

Fourthly, what of the reference to David in verse 69 and to Abraham and the fathers in verses 72–73? While some see a tension here, actually that is hardly the case, because the promise to David is seen as the fulfillment of the promise to Abraham that kings should arise from him and Sarah (Gen 17:16). God's covenant promise proceeds from Abraham through the fathers to David. There is absolutely no need to import the critical knife here!

Fifthly, it has been suggested that there is a tension between the first part of the Benedictus (vv. 68–75) and what is said about Zechariah's future

---

18. So Schürmann, *Lukas*, 1:88–89; Hahn, *Titles of Jesus in Christology*, 366; Gnilka, *Hymnus*, 219–20, 231; Kaut, *Befreier*, 178–83; Vogel, *Heil*, 38.

19. Benoit, *L'Enfance de Jean-Baptiste selon Luc 1*, 182, 184, 188, 190, who rejects the theory of an origin of the material in Luke 1 in the circle of John the Baptist's disciples and believes that Luke is responsible for composing the infancy story with the aid of oral tradition and an old Jewish Christian hymn. He sees verses 76–77 as a Lucan composition skilfully inserted into this hymn. See also Brown, *Birth of the Messiah*, 381; Farris, *Hymns*, 27; Mittmann-Richert, *Magnifikat und Benedictus*, 37–38, 42, 44, 49.

20. In verse 69 σωτηριας is in the genitive singular case, whereas σωτηριαν in verse 71 is in the accusative singular case.

21. See *BDF* 295.

22. This assumes that επισκεψεται is to be accepted, with the aorist επεσκεψατο an alteration to agree with verses 68–69 (Metzger, *Textual Commentary*, 132).

son (vv. 14-17, 76-77, 79). Grässer believes that vv. 14-17, 76-79, are indebted to the concept of an eschatological prophet who will precede the coming of Yahweh at the Last Day, as, e.g., in Malachi, whereas vv. 68-75 assumes the national hope of a Messiah from the House of David.[23] On the other hand, the coming of Yahweh in salvation and judgment and the activity of a messianic figure like a descendant of David need not be mutually exclusive, but rather complementary. Thus, the prophet Ezekiel in chapter 34 can report what Yahweh said that *He* would do on behalf of His sheep whom the leaders of Israel have badly treated (vv. 10-16, 25-31), while at the same time it would appear that Yahweh will use a Davidic descendant as His instrument to feed His flock (vv. 23-24; cf. 37:24).[24] The person responsible for the final shape of Luke 1 clearly did not feel that the material contained irreconcilable motifs in this particular case.

This quick run-through the points where some scholars have seen the evidence of different sources suggests that it is chiefly the difference of tenses between verses 68-69 and 78[25] and the specific turning to the newly born child at verse 76 which are the main pointers to the possible differences of provenance of the material.

There are, however, other factors still to be taken into consideration. The study of the Benedictus cannot be divorced from the immediate context of the Lucan Birth Stories and, indeed, from the wider context of Luke-Acts. That may be opened up specifically by examining the picture of John the Baptist which emerges in the Birth Stories compared with that in Luke 3:1-Acts 28:31. In his treatment of the birth stories, Kaut, while defending the hypothesis of an origin of material from the circle of John the Baptist's disciples, maintains that there are different emphases in the picture of John the Baptist in chapter 1 and in the rest of Luke-Acts.[26] His case rests on the following points. In very close agreement with Conzelmann,[27] Kaut points to Luke's attempt to separate Jesus and John the Baptist geographically in the main body of his gospel. He also believes that in the main body of the gospel Luke portrays John the Baptist as belonging to the time of promise reaching right up to the coming of Jesus, but not actually part of the era of fulfillment of salvation. Kaut claims that Luke attributes forgiveness of

---

23. Grässer, *Alte Bund*, 35.

24. Eichrodt, *Ezekiel*, 478, comments: "All the things previously stated about the help and deliverance by Yahweh are now carried out by his servant as his earthly plenipotentiary and representative. One can see Yahweh himself at work in this servant . . . [He] exercises his own office of shepherd through his servant."

25. See point 3 above.

26. Kaut, *Befreier*, 32-82.

27. Conzelmann, *Theology of Saint Luke*, 18-27.

sins to Jesus, not John the Baptist. He asserts that Luke in Luke 3–Acts 28 portrays John the Baptist as one who prepares for the coming of Jesus; and that he has emphasized the theme of imminent judgment in John the Baptist's preaching, together with its socio-economic dimension relevant for the interim period before the coming judgment. By contrast, in the birth story, John the Baptist's ministry is portrayed in very positive terms: through it comes the knowledge of salvation, the forgiveness of sins, light for darkness, and peace. Kaut, working on the assumption that Luke 1:76-79 was an originally separate piece of tradition, argues that there is an equation of John the Baptist as "prophet of the Most High" (1:76) and the imagery of the arising of the ανατολη εξ υψους (1:78). In other words, John the Baptist was being seen as a messianic figure himself.

While not all these points carry equal conviction,[28] there is certainly at first impression a noticeable difference between the terrifying prospect of judgment at the hands of the coming one who is greater than John the Baptist (Luke 3:7-9), on the one hand, and the positive aspect of the saving mercy of God mediating salvation through John the Baptist in 1:77 on the other hand. Furthermore, Luke 1:76-79 do not give the impression of the imminent end of the age and arguably envisage history carrying on so that Israel can enjoy peace. But, even if the picture of Luke 3:7-9 seems to assume the final reckoning of the Last Judgment with no further opportunity for amendment of life and salvation ("the chaff" will be burned with unquenchable fire), nevertheless it assumes that the new age, though not mentioned, will commence after the judgment: "the wheat" will be gathered into the barn, and this would be decoded as indicative of the enjoyment of the new age by the saved. So, while the stress in Luke 1 seems to be on John the Baptist's preparing a people for God and in Luke 3 on the Coming One's execution of judgment and the separation of the righteous from the wicked, the differences to which Kaurt has drawn attention are differences of emphases and are not necessarily incompatible, but could be said to stress different points in the series of events leading up to the End Time.[29]

Like several scholars before him, Kaut draws the conclusion that Luke was not himself responsible for the composition of the stories about John the Baptist in Luke 1. He argued that Luke inherited this material, which

---

28. As to whether Kaut's reliance on Conzelmann is justified, we may mention the criticisms of Conzelmann (e.g., Robinson, *Der Weg des Herrn*; Minear, *Note on Luke*, 128-34; *Birth Stories*, 111-30; Kümmel, *Das Gesetz*, 89-102).

29. We might compare the primary stress on the offer of salvation in the preaching of Jesus, combined with some fearsome pictures of the fire of judgment, a duality which the Fourth Gospel has captured in the combination of salvation and judgment in, e.g., John 3:16-21.

originated from within the circle of disciples of John the Baptist and which had come into Christian circles (possibly from some of those disciples of John who had become followers of Jesus), and from there, from a pre-Lucan Christian author, to Luke.

The thesis that material in Luke 1 originated from a John the Baptist circle has to face certain criticisms. If "the prophet of the Most High" and the ανατολη εξ υψους are being equated, then how does this square with the Synoptic picture of John the Baptist insisting on the coming of one mightier than himself?

Now Vielhauer[30] also interpreted verse 78 of John the Baptist, but he then went on to draw the conclusion that John the Baptist's disciples honored him after his death as the messiah, i.e., they had a different messianology than John the Baptist himself who expected someone greater than himself. This alleged step seems improbable. That a martyr might be honored is understandable (e.g., 2 and 4 Maccabees), but it seems a huge leap to make an assumption that after his death John the Baptist was believed to be the messiah (despite Vielhauer's attempt to justify this from the evidence of the Pseudo-Clementines to the effect that John was "hidden" until his eschatological return).[31] Paul's statement in 1 Corinthians 1:22–23 seems to tell decisively against such a step (cf. John 12:34), quite apart from the fact that it seems to erect one hypothesis (John the Baptist's disciples coming to conviction against their own master's views) on top of another (a putative source emanating from John the Baptist circles).

The situation is altered if we do not equate "prophet of the Most High" and the ανατολη εξ υψους. This dissociation would tally with the Synoptic picture that John the Baptist was expecting one greater than himself. But would this of necessity demand an ultimate origin of the material from John the Baptist circles, albeit via Jewish Christian circles? Not necessarily. We could envisage that Jewish Christian circles composed a prediction that John the Baptist was the one ordained of God to prepare the way of the Lord, now seen as the Lord Jesus, just as later the fourth evangelist accepted that John the Baptist was a man sent by God but inferior in status to Jesus, the incarnate Word.

Continuing the study of the Benedictus, we note how closely it is related to its setting. In the first place, we are told that, when Zechariah recovered his power of speech, he spoke praising God: και ελαλει ευλογων τον Θεον (v. 64). This is picked up by the opening of the Benedictus with its ευλογητος

---

30. Vielhauer, *Benedictus*, 255–72, esp. 265–68.

31. Enoch and Elijah were both according to the OT translated *before* their death, so that it would be natural to describe them as "hidden" or "waiting" to return. But John the Baptist would have to wait for the resurrection of the dead before he could return.

κυριος ο Θεος του Ισραηλ (v. 67). The content of the psalm which follows gives *reasons why God is praised and blessed*. The language of verses 68-75 is certainly redolent of the Old Testament and Jewish prayer literature and some parts of the Qumran literature.[32] This psalm begins by celebrating the fact that God had visited and redeemed His people. The concept of God's "visiting" His people is rooted in the Old Testament. God may visit with saving or judging-punitive purpose. He may deliver Israel from oppression by her enemies or from likely defeat in battle, or He may use foreign armies to chastise His people for their ingratitude and disobedience manifest in the worship of foreign gods and social injustice. Here, in verses 68-75, God has brought about redemption and salvation for His people. This consists of deliverance from Israel's enemies, from those who hate her (v. 71).[33] This deliverance from her enemies will enable Israel to live without fear and worship and serve God in holiness and righteousness all their days (vv. 74-75). This is very much a this-worldly concept of salvation.

Why has Israel's God intervened to redeem His people? It is related to "the fathers." The redemption/salvation is described as

"to show mercy to[34] our fathers[35]
and to remember His holy covenant,
the oath which He swore to Abraham our father." (vv. 72-73)

God's intervention is due to the fact that He remembered the oath which He swore to Abraham.[36] Probably Genesis 15:18-19 and 22:15-18 are in mind, both of which mention the covenant made with Abraham and the oath sworn to him, while Micah 7:20 is also comparable: "You will show faithfulness to Jacob and mercy to Abraham, as You swore to our fathers in days long ago."[37] What was said by God was the gift of a covenant, backed up by an oath, first to Abraham, and then renewed to the fathers.

---

32. See the commentaries, together with Gnilka, *Hymnus*, 222-27.

33. On this analysis, σωτηριαν in verse 71 is in apposition to λυτρωσιν in verse 68 and explains it.

34. BD 206(3) suggests that the Greek μετα is equivalent to the Hebrew (*'m*), with the resultant sense here of "to show mercy *to*."

35. Marshall, *Luke*, 92, wishes to take the Greek in the sense of "to keep faith with our fathers," on analogy of OT phraseology. If verse 72a does carry the sense of "to keep faith with our fathers," then there is a synonymous parallelism in verse 72: "to keep faith with our fathers" and "to remember His covenant [made with them]."

36. Taking ορκον in apposition to διαθηκης, even though not in the same case (so Evans, *Luke*, 184).

37. The MT has *'mt* to Jacob and *hsd* to Abraham, with the LXX rendering αληθειαν τω Ιακωβ, ελεος τω Αβρααμ.

In other words, God's intervention is not due to any particular merit of Israel, but is due entirely to God's own promises made to Abraham and renewed to Isaac and Jacob. There is a link between what God had done in the present and what He promised to Abraham and the fathers in the past. The merciful intervention of God on behalf of the Israel of this psalmist's day is equivalent to mercy shown to their "fathers" (v. 73a). They were present in their descendants.[38] What God had done fulfills what He had promised of old to the fathers.[39]

If verse 69 is deemed to have been a later insertion (see the second point above), then there is nothing specifically Christian about this putative psalm. What precisely might have been its Sitz im Leben is impossible to say. It could have been treasured among Jewish Christians as part of their spiritual heritage, while they discerned and exploited the possibility of its reapplication to the situation brought about by God's acting in Jesus. If, however, verse 69 is preserved as part of the original, then it is difficult to see how the psalm could have originated anywhere else but in Jewish Christian circles.

The phrase "all our days," at the end of verse 75, is similar to one which does in fact bring some Old Testament psalms to a close, and could be a suitable ending to verses 68–75.[40]

We turn now to consider verses 76–79, both as regards content and whether they in their entirety or just verses 76–77 were combined with the psalm praising God for His redemption. Clearly, there is a change in the Benedictus at verse 76. Here Zechariah turns to address directly his infant son. The verbs change from being in the aorist to the future (κληθήση and προπορεύση [v. 76]). Now we were told at verse 67 that Zechariah was filled with the Holy Spirit and *prophesied*. Verses 76–77 could be described precisely as a *prophecy* of what the baby's destiny is going to be and could also be seen as the answer to the question raised by Zechariah's and Elizabeth's relatives and friends when they heard about the events surrounding John's birth. They had asked concerning the future of the child "What will this child be?" Luke adds "For the hand of the Lord was with him" (v. 66).[41]

---

38. Grundmann, *Lukas*, 72.

39. Cf. Nolland, *Luke*, 1:87. Grundmann, *Lukas*, 72; Marshall, *Luke*, 92, think that perhaps the fathers were thought of as alive.

40. For this or a similar type of phrase ending a psalm, see Psalms 16:11; 18:51; 28:9; 29:10; 30:13; 35:28; 41:13; 45:17; 61:8; 72:19, etc.

41. Gnilka, *Hymnus*, 219, makes these two points. Fitzmyer, *Luke*, 1:376, while himself making these two points, takes an opposite view and maintains that the Benedictus is separable from its context.

The conclusion is that the Benedictus has been well integrated into its context by the careful wording of verses 64, 66, and 67.

What interpretation of John the Baptist is offered in verses 76–77? In the first place, the role attributed to John is that of one who goes before the Lord to prepare for His coming. Taken in isolation the "Lord" could refer to God, rather as the returning Elijah's ministry in Malachi 3:1; 4:5–6 is to prepare Israel so that she might be spiritually ready to meet her God. This coheres with what was predicted of John by the angel Gabriel to Zechariah (1:16–17):

> He will turn many of the sons of Israel to the Lord their God. And he will go before Him in the spirit and power of Elijah, to turn the hearts of the fathers to their children and the disobedient to the wisdom of the righteous, to make ready a people prepared for the Lord.[42]

The task of John is to give knowledge of salvation with the message of forgiveness of sins (v. 77). Early Christian tradition recorded that John the Baptist preached a baptism based on repentance leading to the forgiveness of sins (Mark 1:4//Luke 3:3), which, coupled with subsequent obedience in the short interim period, would mean salvation when God held men and women to account in a judgment before the new age of God's perfect rule. The speech at Pisidian Antioch in Acts 13 can give us an illuminating insight into the way in which Luke could integrate a positive view of John the Baptist (he preached a baptism of repentance for all the people of Israel) into a picture which sets forth Jesus as the saviour promised by God. But the Paul of this speech indicated that John the Baptist disclaimed being worthy even to untie the thongs of the sandals of the one coming after him, viz. Jesus, whom God had raised from the Davidic house to be the saviour of Israel (Acts 13:23–25).

The role of the infant son of Zechariah was set forth in verses 76–77. What, however, of verses 78–79? They do not in fact refer to the role of John, but to the Davidic Messiah as the allusion to Isaiah 9:2 in verse 79 makes clear.[43] So do they belong to the psalm or to verses 76–77? The following points need to be weighed.

---

42. Obviously, in its present context in Luke's Gospel, "Lord" clearly refers to Jesus. Similarly, at 1:43, Elizabeth acknowledges Mary as the mother of her Lord when she asks, "Why has this happened to me that the mother of my Lord should come to me?"

43. Isaiah 9:2 runs: "The people who walked in darkness have seen a great light. Upon those who lived in the land of the shadow of death the light has shined." Luke 1:7 runs: "To shine on those who sit in darkness and the shadow of death."

Some argue for the Lucan nature of the vocabulary of verses 76–77. Thus, Benoit claimed υψιστος, ενωπιον, and αφεσις αμαρτιων as Lucan,[44] but even Farris discounts ενωπιον,[45] and, while υψιστος does occur more often in Luke than Mark and Matthew, it appears in the triple tradition and is frequent in the LXX. Mittmann-Richert stresses that in Luke's writings the removal of spiritual blindness is necessary to obtain salvation and so she sees verse 77a as Lucan,[46] while she also points to the lack of Old Testament allusions, apart from Malachi 3:1/Isaiah 40:3, worked into verses 76–77 in contrast to the earlier part of the Benedictus.[47] On these points, it may be said that while in general it is correct that for Luke spiritual blindness must be removed to obtain salvation, the actual word γνωσις only occurs here and at Luke 11:52 (probably a Q saying) in Luke-Acts. Then, while it is true, of course, that these two passages from the OT are found in Synoptic material and were known to Luke from this tradition and were used by him at 3:4 and 7:27, the force of the argument may be weakened by the observation that these two OT passages do occupy most of verse 76b (if we leave out the connective particle γαρ, there are seventeen words in verse 76b, of which the allusion to Malachi 3:1/Isaiah 40:3 comprises five words—almost a third!) and that in any case there is hardly much material about the activity of one who will prepare the way of the Lord in the OT.

There are a number of questions regarding connections, which Benoit especially has raised. He thinks that verses 78–79 fit awkwardly syntactically onto verses 76–77,[48] but do they fit smoothly on to verse 75? Farris, in defending the view that verses 76–77 are Lucan, made the comment: "The connection of verse 78 to 75 may be somewhat awkward but no more so than the present connection to verse 77."[49] With this we agree, but would then argue that since the syntactical links of the Benedictus are notoriously difficult at times, too much weight ought not to be placed on this point. It would be possible for a Christian author to assume that the full knowledge of salvation and the forgiveness of sins came with Jesus but that John the Baptist had intimated this in his role as forerunner.

Benoit also maintained that the phrase "all our days" (v. 75) does not always figure at the end of a psalm.[50] Perhaps we may say on this point

---

44. Benoit, L'enfance, 182.
45. Farris, Hymns, 23.
46. Mittmann-Richert, Magnifikat, 39.
47. Mittmann-Richert, Magnifikat, 37; cf. Farris, Hymns, 27.
48. Benoit, L'enfance, 185.
49. Farris, Hymns, 28.
50. Benoit, L'enfance, 185; Brown, Birth, 381. See Psalm 90:14; 128:5.

that the final editor of the Benedictus clearly felt able to tolerate the phrase "all our days" at the end of verse 75, while continuing for a further section. Benoit argues that verses 78-79 gives precision to verse 68 in a kind of thought inclusio: the allusion to the Davidic figure of Isaiah 9:1-6 in verses 78-79 elaborates on what "the horn of salvation" raised up by God from the house of David does in redemptive activity.[51] This is an argument for seeing verses 78-79 as belonging with the whole of verses 68-75 (and rejecting the idea of verse 69 being a later addition).

Brown makes a telling point that verse 77 refers to God's people and their sins in the third person, whereas verses 78-79 revert to the first person ("our God," "us," and "our feet"), which has characterized verses 69 and 71-75.[52]

While absolute certainty in a matter such as this is hardly ever attainable, there is certainly a case for seeing only verses 76-77 as the material combined with an existing psalm, with verses 78-79 belonging to that psalm and originally forming the continuation of verse 75.

If a pre-Lucan writer composed verses 68-75 and 78-79 of the Benedictus in praise of what God had done in the coming into this world of a Davidic messiah, why did Luke link the psalm with Zechariah, the father of John the Baptist? Mittmann-Richert has made the interesting suggestion that Luke, drawing on the fact that the prophet Zechariah at Zechariah 3:8; 6:12 announced the coming of the branch from David's line, saw the father of John the Baptist as a new Zechariah who announced that the branch from the Davidic house had come.[53] Hence, verses 76-77 was directly addressed to the infant son. At the same time, as Brown suggests, by placing verses 76-77 before verses 78-79, Luke has preserved (as it were) the preeminence of Jesus who actually brings salvation.[54]

We are now in a position to evaluate the fact that there is a change of tense from the beginning of the Benedictus, which praises God for having visited and redeemed His people (v. 68), and the future tenses of verses 76-77, which describe the role of John the Baptist as the forerunner of the one who will bring salvation. God has acted: the messiah from David's line has been conceived, as the readers/hearers know from what Elizabeth said to Mary when the two mothers met (Luke 1:39-45)—hence the aorists of verses

---

51. Benoit, *L'enfance*, 186. The textual variant at verse 78 complicates matters. Benoit, *L'enfance*, 185; Farris, *Hymns*, 28, opt for the aorist, while Mittmann-Richert, *Magnifikat*, 45-47, decides for the future.

52. Brown, *Birth*, 381.

53. Mittmann-Richert, *Magnifikat*, 236

54. Brown, *Birth*, 383.

68–69; but his ministry is yet to take place and his way is yet to be prepared by the son of Zechariah—hence the future tenses of verses 76–77.⁵⁵

Zechariah's son has a great role, but he is only a forerunner. Verses 78–79 bring us back to the one whom God has destined to be the messianic savior. On account of God's mercies, light will shine on those in darkness (either spiritual darkness or a metaphor for a this-worldly state of desolation and distress) and in the shadow of death (any lessening of life means that one is in the shadow of death) and to guide men and women into the ways of peace, peace with one another (cf. Sir 48:10).

This light is due to the appearance of ανατολη εξ υψους (v. 78b). What is the meaning of ανατολη here? The word can be used of either the sprouting of a plant or the shining of a star.⁵⁶ In determining the primary meaning here we need to take account of two factors. The first is linguistic usage. In the LXX, the word ανατολη is only used once of the rising of a heavenly body, viz. Isaiah 60:19.⁵⁷ Some scholars, on the other hand, see here an allusion to Numbers 24:17 where it is said that a star will arise out of Jacob, though here the LXX uses αστρον, not ανατολη, and the lack of εξ υψους further tells against a derivation from Numbers 24:17. On the other hand, the LXX translators used ανατολη for three occurrences of the Hebrew *smh* to indicate a Davidic descendant metaphorically described as a branch or shoot, viz. Jeremiah 23:5; Zechariah 3:8; 6:12. In some sections of Judaism, "branch" had become a messianic designation.⁵⁸ This background fits nicely here: there would be a reference to the Messiah whose coming is traced to God (εξ υψους).

The second factor is context. In the context of the Benedictus, it is said that the ανατολη from on high has come (or will come) in order to *shine* on those who sit in darkness and in the shadow of death and will *guide* people's feet into the ways of peace, and this, it has been claimed by some scholars,⁵⁹ tilts the balance in favor of star being the uppermost sense of ανατολη. Heavenly light is radiated forth to give illumination and guidance.

---

55. Cf. Brown, *Birth*, 379; Mittmann-Richert, *Magnifikat*, 237.

56. See Schlier, "ανατελλω, ανατολη," *TWNT* 1:351–53.

57. Pointed out by Mittmann-Richten, *Magnifikat*, 132. The word occurs in a phrase to indicate those who live in the east. In other words, the rising is conceived of as from the earth, not from the heavens! The cognate verb ανατελλω is used of the rising of the sun.

58. See, e.g., 4Q Flor 1:11; and the Jewish prayer, the fifteenth Benediction.

59. So Schlier, ανατελλω, 352–53; Plummer, *Luke*, 43; Creed, *Luke*, 276; Schmid, *Lukas*, 62; Schürmann, *Lukasevangelium*, 1:92–93; Marshall, *Luke*, 94–95; Evans, *Luke*, 187; Nolland, *Luke*, 1:90; Brown, *Birth*, 373–74, 390–91. Fitzmeyer, *Luke*, 1:387, prefers the messianic sense but retains "Dawn from on high" in translation.

However, whichever reading of επισκεπτεσθαι is adopted for the main verb of verse 78, the sense of "visit" fits a person better than a star. If the two infinitives of purpose in verse 79 speak of shining and guiding, such a mixing of metaphors—the visit of a person and light shining forth from that person to guide—can hardly be described as impossible or even inelegant.

Furthermore, in verse 79 there is a quite clear allusion to the passage about the Davidic Messiah in Isaiah 9:1–7, where it is said that the people who walked in darkness have seen a great light and that light has shone on those that dwell in the shadow of death. These words are clearly taken up in the closing verse of the Benedictus. The Davidic Messianic background of Luke 1:79 strengthens the case for seeing ανατολη as a messianic title, the Branch.[60]

In the light of this, and given that the infant John was a Levite and that his role was to be "prophet of the Most High," it is obvious that the description of heavenly light refers to a blessing which comes from the (Davidic) messiah whose way John the Baptist is to prepare rather than from John's activity itself.[61]

Benoit has argued that the lack of any reference to John the Baptist's future baptizing activity is inexplicable in a piece allegedly originating from a circle of disciples of John the Baptist.[62] "Inexplicable" is probably too strong a word to use, since the nature of the prophecy of Zechariah did not to lend itself to such a detailed reference like baptizing (after all, even a specific reference to preaching is absent), even though Benoit is right in rejecting an origin from the circle of John the Baptist's disciples.

Is it necessary to postulate two originally separate pieces of tradition, most of verses 68–75 and 76–79, as Kaut does?[63] Not necessarily. If the already mentioned links with verses 64 and 67 are allowed to carry weight, with the conclusion as suggested above that the Benedictus has been well integrated into its context, this leads us to believe that it was in its entirety

---

60. Ellis, *Gospel of Luke*, 79; Gnilka, *Hymnus*, 227–29 (while allowing the ambiguity in the term, in the end comes down on a messianic name for the Davidic messiah, who brings God's salvation); Mittmann-Richert, 121–27. A free translation would, therefore, be "the Messiah." Grundmann, *Lukas*, 74; Farris, *Hymns*, 140–41, combine both meanings in their expositions.

61. Just as in the present context of Luke's Gospel, the reference to the Lord whose way John the Baptist is to prepare (1:17) is to Jesus, who is "the Son of the Most High" (1.32).

62. Benoit, *L'Enfance*, 190; Gnilka, *Hymnus*, 232. Vielhauer, *Benedictus*, 267, countered this by saying that the lack of reference to baptizing activity was "due to the style of the infancy legend."

63. So, e.g., the analysis of Kaut, *Befreier*, 173–265, who calls verses 76–79 Benedictus II and verses 68, 71–75 Benedictus I, with verses 69–70 as Lucan additions.

planned by the author of verses 57-67.⁶⁴ The original author combined what may be termed a psalm of praise celebrating God's mighty deeds and a birth poem (technically called a genethliakon) predicting the destiny of the new born child, in one composition.

Although we have already touched a little on verses 69-70, we must consider the view that they represent a later insertion more fully. Some of the arguments put forward to defend this view are as follows. In the first place, it is argued that verses 69-70 break up the smooth flow between verses 68b and 71. If verses 69-70 are removed, it would have the advantage of removing the grammatical difficulty mentioned above in the present state of the Benedictus. At present, the word σωτηριαν at verse 71, which is in the accusative case, does not agree with its intended antecedent in verse 69—κερας σωτηριας, which is in the genitive case. If verses 69-70 are removed, however, the word σωτηριαν in verse 71 would be in apposition to λυτρωσιν in the accusative case in verse 68: the salvation from the enemies explains the redemption which God has obtained for His people. Yet, as we have already pointed out, a similar lack of grammatical agreement occurs in verses 72/73,⁶⁵ so that this point is not necessarily totally compelling. Then, secondly, it is claimed that there is a theocentric emphasis throughout the rest of 68-75 which the reference to the Davidic messiah to a certain extent breaks up. Several Jewish texts can describe God's saving intervention without reference to a messiah, and that is the impression created by verses 68 and 71-75. Yet there is no necessary conflict between asserting that God has done something and also that He has acted through a human agent,⁶⁶ as is the case, e.g., in Ezekiel 34 already mentioned, and also the Psalm of Solomon 17. Theocentricity and messianology were by no means incompatible. Again, this second argument is not necessarily convincing. A third argument suggests a certain difference between the clear reference to a Davidic representative in verse 69 (already the angel Gabriel had announced the Davidic ancestry of the child Jesus to be born [v. 32]) and the reference at verses 72-73 to God's remembering the covenant and the oath given to Abraham and the fathers. In other words, within the one hymn, we have two bases for God's activity: to fulfill the divinely-inspired prophetic announcement of a Davidic descendant (v. 70) and the oath/covenant with

---

64. Gnilka, *Hymnus*, 217-21, argues for its unity—the Benedictus never existed other than in its present combination of psalm and birth poem; it is a unit of composition created ad hoc. Gnilka, *Hymnus*, 220-21, attributes verse 70 to Luke himself and leaves open whether verse 69 is Lucan or was already in his source.

65. ορκον in verse 73 is supposed to be in apposition to διαθηκας αγιας of verse 72b, but is in a different case.

66. Cf. our earlier comments on pages 220-21 and note 985.

the fathers of Israel (vv. 72-73). The former would lead us to think of Isaiah 11:1-10; 30:9; Jeremiah 23:5-6; Ezekiel 34:23-24; 37:24. In none of these, however, is there any explicit reference to the Abrahamic covenant and the oath accompanying it. But we have already seen that there is no need to set up a tension between these two ideas, since David was a descendant of Abraham and his emergence as king of Israel was seen as a fulfillment of the promise of kings to be among Abraham's descendants.

A fourth point concerns the phrase in verse 70, "He spoke through the mouth of His holy prophets from of old." At Acts 3:21, there is a very similar phrase about God's speaking through the mouth of His holy prophets from the beginning.[67] Luke's interest in the theme of fulfillment of prophecy is well known.[68] On the other hand, the influence could go the other way, from Luke 1:70 on Acts 3:21, while the idea of the coming of Jesus and what he achieved as the fulfillment of prophecy was a theme common to all early Christians and not a special preserve of Luke (e.g., 1 Cor 15:3-4; the fulfillment quotations both in Matthew and John; the use of OT quotations in Hebrews, etc.).

Thus, although these arguments, which have led many to suggest that Luke himself may have been responsible for adding a reference both to the descendant of David who would be a "horn of salvation" and the fulfillment of prophecy,[69] have a certain persuasive value, they certainly fall short of being convincing.

From this albeit somewhat sketchy discussion of the various literary-critical questions, we could accept that we are dealing with a number of layers of tradition in the Benedictus. From the point of view of our interest in Abraham, we would need a three- (or possibly four-) fold probe:

what was the standpoint of the composition verses 68-75, 78-79?;

what were the aims of the pre-Lucan author responsible for the combination of 68-75, 78-79, and 76-77?;

what motivated the addition of verses 69-70?;

and, finally, what was Luke aiming at with the final product as we now have it?

67. Luke 1:70: καθως ελαλησεν δια στοματος των αγιων απ' αιωνιος προφητων αυτου
Acts 3:21: ελαλησεν ο Θεος δια στοματος των αγιων απ' αιωνος αυτου προφητων
Schürman, *Lukasevangelium*, 1:87; Marshall, *Luke*, 91; Fitzmyer, *Luke*, 1:384; Nolland, *Luke*, 1:83, 86-87; Evans, *Luke*, 184; Gnilka, *Hymnus*, 220-1, attribute verse 70 to Luke.

68. Vogel, *Heil*, 39, considers this motif "alien" to the context.

69. But Kaut, *Befreier*, 246-58, goes in an opposite direction and believes that a pre-Lucan editor had worked verses 69-70 into a Jewish psalm, which consisted of verses 68, 71-75, and that at Acts 3:21, Luke was dependent on the pre-Lucan editor's phraseology in what is now Luke 1:70 (see 249n220).

First, we can see the importance of the covenant and oath made by God with Abraham and the other patriarchs. This covenant had soteriological value, i.e., God had made such promises to Abraham that ultimately these would ensure a definitive salvation for the people of God descended from Abraham. This fits in with what early Judaism believed about Abraham.

Secondly, the pre-Lucan author believed that the God of the fathers had acted in the person of Jesus of Nazareth. The oath given to Abraham had been fulfilled: the "Branch" had come from on high. We are skeptical about attempts to give a precise Sitz im Leben to this composition of the pre-Lucan author, whether it be Winter's suggestion of Maccabean psalms, one sung before battle (most of our Benedictus) and the other afterwards (most of our Magnificat)[70] or Kaut's locating the work of this author in the period soon after the outbreak of the Jewish War after the initial successes against the Roman forces and before Vespasian took charge of the campaign against the Jews.[71] The language is too general to allow of such attempts at precision.

Thirdly, if we do assume that Luke was responsible for adding verses 69–70,[72] can we surmise what he was seeking to achieve? In the first place, the salvation brought about by God is unequivocally tied to the figure of a descendant of David, i.e., a messianic figure. God "has raised up a horn of salvation in the house of David His servant" (v. 69). In the setting of Luke's Gospel the figure of Jesus is here unmistakably referred to. The annunciation to Mary in 1:31–33 had prepared the way for this. Secondly, this divine action was seen as the fulfillment of what God "had spoken through the mouths of His holy prophets from of old."[73] Prophetic announcement had been fulfilled. The divine purpose, foretold ages ago, had come to fruition and completion.

Finally, comment on what was Luke's overall purpose might be is best deferred to the end of our study on the birth stories of Luke 1–2.

5.2.5. The Annunciation to Mary and the Magnificat

We turn now to consider the question of the non-John the Baptist material in Luke 1 (and 2). Clearly, the annunciation scene to Mary could not have originated from a circle of John the Baptist disciples. It magnifies the coming

---

70. Winter, *Maccabean Psalms*, 328-47. For a critique, see Kaut, *Befreier*, 237-39.

71. Kaut, *Befreier*, 239-46, 263, 316-17, 322.

72. See page 231 above.

73. For the idiom of God/Holy Spirit speaking through the mouth of His prophets, cf. Acts 1:16; 3:18, 21; 4:25.

son of Mary, announced by the angel Gabriel as Son of the Most High and as the future inheritor of the throne of his ancestor, David. The reader/hearer of the angel Gabriel's words is left in no doubt about the superiority of Jesus over John the Baptist.

The parallels between the two annunciation scenes have been often noticed. They may be briefly set out as follows:[74]

- The angel Gabriel appeared to both Zechariah and Mary;
- Both were disturbed by the angel's appearance;
- A son was promised to both and both were commanded to give the child a specific name;
- The significance of this son was revealed;
- Surprise was expressed that this event would happen;
- A sign was given to both. A punitive sign was given to Zechariah because his surprise was interpreted as lack of belief in God's promise; the positive sign given to Mary was Elizabeth's pregnancy.

The closeness of literary structure, not to mention a number of verbal links, seems to point to some sort of dependence, whether oral or literary.[75]

The meeting between the two women about to become mothers (1:39-45) is the link between the two stories about John the Baptist and about Jesus. Once again, this story could not have originated in a circle of John the Baptist's disciples, since the passage sets forth the superiority of the child to be born to Mary.

---

74. A more detailed table of the structure of the two annunciations is given in Brown, *Birth*, 297.

75. This seems preferable to supposing that independently of each other, two authors working on Old Testament models came up with two such closely related pieces. Kaut, *Befreier*, 116-18, argues for a dependence of the annunciation to Mary on the annunciation to Zechariah, which existed in the source emanating from John the Baptist circles. Given that Kaut believes that material about John the Baptist was in existence, his position is entirely logical. Brown, *Birth*, 283, 285, 293-98, however, believes that Luke composed the annunciation to Zechariah on the basis of a pre-Lucan and pre-Matthean story of an annunciation to Mary. In other words, both Brown and Kaut believe that Luke drew on pre-existing material: for Kaut, this came ultimately from John the Baptist's circle and was brought from there into Christian circles, and concerned Zechariah and his son John; while for Brown it came from Christian circles and concerned Mary and her son Jesus. If Luke did compose the annunciation to Zechariah, why did he not already introduce the motif of John's subordination to Jesus (as Dibelius, *Jungfrauensohn*, 8, pointed out)?

The Magnificat, in its context, is the response of Mary to what Elizabeth had said about her at 1:41-45.[76] Elizabeth had greeted her as one blessed among women and also pronounced the fruit of her womb blessed. Mary is indeed to be the mother of one who will be Elizabeth's Lord, and she is blessed as one who believed that what God had said to her would be fulfilled.[77]

The first part of the Magnificat is set forth in the first person. This part is the prayer of thanksgiving and praise of an individual person, and specifically an individual woman:[78] "*My* soul magnifies the Lord, and *my* spirit rejoiced in God *my* Saviour, because He has looked with favor on the ταπεινωσις of His *handmaiden* . . . because He who is mighty has done great things for *me*" (vv. 47, 49a). And yet there is in Mary's Song nothing specific about a child to be born and his destiny. There is nothing in the song itself which is specific to a woman expecting a baby, her first child, let alone that child to play the unique role of the future messiah from the house of David in the purposes of God, according to the annunciation to Mary by the angel Gabriel (1:28-38). But is there a hidden allusion? Ulrike Mittmann-Richert has suggested (in accordance with her conviction that the Magnificat and Benedictus were both originally composed in Hebrew)[79] that in the reference to God my Saviour there is an allusion to the name of Jesus. Even if she is correct about a Hebrew original and this allusion, this would be lost in Greek translation.

The phraseology of the Magnificat owes a great deal to the song of Hannah in thanksgiving to God for the gift of her son, Samuel, when she presented him to the Lord at the sanctuary at Shiloh (1 Sam 2:1-10). Exactly the same things could be said about Hannah's song as has been said about the Magnificat. There is this big difference between the situation of the two women, however. Hannah was childless after some years of marriage, whereas Mary is a young woman engaged to be married, with every prospect of bearing children once married. So, when there is a reference to

---

76. Kaut, *Befreier*, 308, 311, advances the suggestion that Luke 1:47-48a, 49-50a, originally belonged to a document emanating from the circle of adherents of John the Baptist and there was spoken by Elizabeth, with ταπεινωσις referring to Elizabeth's childlessness, earlier described as her disgrace (ονειδος). This is all rather speculative and an unnecessary multiplication of hypotheses.

77. There is a verbal link between Elizabeth's beatitude on Mary in verse 45 (και μακαρια) and the Magnificat itself, namely at verse 48b, "For behold, from now on all generations will call me blessed (μακαριουσιν)," though verse 48b enlarges the perspective to the future and to all generations.

78. E.g., Kaut, *Befreier*, 302, 310, 321.

79. The Hebrew word jeshuach means savior. No such play on words is possible in the Greek for savior and the name Jesus.

"the ταπεινωσις of His handmaiden" in the Magnificat at Luke 1:48a, that can hardly refer to her childlessness; rather, it suggests that a lowly station in life is in mind.[80]

Viewed in isolation, this first part of the Magnificat does not specify what are "the great things" which God has done for her. We might surmise that since the speaker is a woman, the role which God has assigned to her might have something to do with motherhood.[81] Obviously, in the total context of Luke's birth story, God's looking with favor on her lowly position can only refer to His choice of Mary to be the mother of the descendant of David who would be king of Israel as announced by the angel Gabriel (1:31-33).

Are there any other passages which might have been in the mind of the composer of the Magnificat besides Hannah's Song? It has long been acknowledged that the Magnificat is indebted to other Old Testament passages.[82] In respect to allusion, the crux is always to decide whether writers wished to evoke in their readers a deliberate "flashback" in the memory to a particular passage and its context, or whether they are steeped in the Scriptures and unconsciously draw on scriptural language to express themselves.[83]

---

80. Kaut, *Befreier*, 288-89, points out that ταπεινωσις does not refer to an attitude or character (i.e., humility) but rather to a status or state of being low, of being in distress or wretchedness. Nolland, *Luke*, 1:74, actually translates ταπεινωσις as "affliction," and says that Mary's "affliction is simply that of God's people awaiting his saving intervention on their behalf" (cf. Mittmann-Richert, *Magnifikat*, 197-98).

81. It is part of the methodology of Mittmann-Richert, *Magnifikat*, 102, 223, 225, that she assumes that the Magnificat and Benedictus were composed first and then were fixed narratively. She thinks that the annunciation to Mary may have been the second stage in the building up of the tradition.

82. See Plummer, *Luke*, 30-31; Creed, *Luke*, 303-4, for tables of the parallel phrases and sentences in the OT. Evans, *Luke*, 173, describes the Magnificat as "largely a cento of OT commonplaces" (a very similar expression is used by Fitzmyer, *Luke*, 1:359), and Nolland, *Luke*, 1:63, "indisputably a tissue of OT allusion." See, most recently, Mittmann-Richert, *Magnifikat*, 17-20, who expands the list fairly considerably. Her summary of the passages is given on page 21.

83. To take an example: In Luke 1:49 God is described as ο δυνατος, who has done great things for Mary. In Zephaniah 3:17 in the Hebrew there is a phrase in apposition to Yahweh your God which runs "a mighty one who will save"; the LXX translates δυνατος σωσει σε. Does this constitute an allusion or is the author using familiar language? Mittmann-Richert, *Magnifikat*, 11, claims that Zephaniah 3:17 is the closest comparative text even if not an exact parallel. Another instance is, "And holy is His name" (Luke 1:49b). Whereas 1 Samuel 2:2 runs "For there is none holy like Yahweh" (LXX 1 Regn 2:2: οτι ουκ εστιν αγιος ως κυριος), Psalm 111:9 (110:9c) has "Holy and awesome is His name" (αγιον και φοβερον το ονομα αυτου). Is it right to include the Psalm among the alleged parallels? Since holiness is so commonly attributed to God in the OT and since Hannah's Song contains a reference to this holiness, do we need to import the Psalm as

The interpreter needs to take into consideration motifs and their background alongside considerations of linguistic parallels.[84] Hannah's Song concludes with a confident prediction that God will destroy His foes and will judge the whole earth. The Hebrew runs: "And He shall give strength to His king, and exalt the horn of His anointed" (1 Sam 2:10de), while 1 Regn 2:1jk has: "And He will give strength to those who reign over us and He will exalt the horn of His anointed One." Hertzberg commented on the Hebrew sentences as follows: "It is uncertain whether the reference at the end is to the earthly king depicted in messianic colors or to the king of salvation of the last times; presumably the boundaries here are blurred."[85] Whether Hertzberg's conclusion is correct or not for the final redactor of the work, the reference to "His anointed One" was open later to a messianic interpretation. The author of the Magnificat was presumably not unaware of the potential of this reference to the Lord's anointed One. If that is a correct assumption, a field of motifs in passages messianically interpreted opens up before us: specifically, some of the royal psalms and the messianic passages in First Isaiah (chapters 7; 9; 11 plus 12).

Echoes of Psalm 89 (88) have long been noted at Luke 1:51. In this royal psalm, God is said to have scattered His enemies with the arm of His strength (v. 10; 88:11 LXX) and He is praised for having a mighty arm in verse 13. In the Magnificat, "He has shown strength with His arm; He has scattered the proud in the imagination of their heart" (v. 51). We have here resemblance in concepts, even if expressed somewhat differently, though with some similarity in vocabulary (βραχιων, διασκορπιζειν, υπερηφανος). Here the case for an allusion seems rather strong.

The motif of covenant, either the appeal to God to remember His covenant with Abraham or the grateful acknowledgment that God remembered His covenant with Abraham and took action on behalf of His people, is widespread in the OT and Early Judaism. Of these, Micah 7:20 LXX is particularly close to what is said in the Magnificat at 1:54–55: "You will show faithfulness to Jacob, and mercy to Abraham, as You have sworn to our fathers in former days."[86] Here we have God's showing mercy to Abraham

---

a further parallel? And why omit και φοβερον? Since the author of the Magnificat is not following Hannah's Song slavishly but using it creatively, the author may not have been consciously using the Psalm. There is thus room for difference of opinion concerning some of the alleged parallels.

84. Mittmann-Richert, *Magnifikat*, 17, complains about the lack of attention paid by exegetes to the question of *Motivhintergrund*.

85. Hertzberg, *I & II Samuel*, 31.

86. LXX runs: δωσεις αληθειαν τω Ιακωβ, ελεος τω Αβρααμ, καθοτι τοις πατρασιν ημων κατα τας ημερας τας εμπροσθεν. The sense of αληθεια veers over into faithfulness.

(ελεος τω Αβρααμ) and God's swearing an oath to our fathers (ωμοσας τοις πατρασιν ημων), which are quite close to what the Magnificat says. The mood of Micah 7 is the confident hope that God will intervene, forgive the sins of His people, chastise their enemies, and restore the people to their land and to an existence under His guiding, shepherding rule—not dissimilar to the spirit that pervades the Magnificat.

Two allusions to the story of Leah in Genesis have been noted and their occurrence may hint at a motif "old ancestress—new ancestress of God's people." The story teller informs us that when God saw that Leah was not loved as much as Rachel by Jacob, He enabled Leah to conceive and bear Jacob's first-born child, Reuben.[87] So then Leah bears the first of the twelve patriarchs of Israel. She is the mother of Israel. She thanks God "Because the Lord has looked on my affliction"—ειδεν μου κυριος την ταπεινωσιν (29:32 LXX). Mary says επεβλεψεν επι την ταπεινωσιν της δουλης αυτου. Later, when her own child bearing days had passed, Leah gave her maid servant, Zilpah, to Jacob and she bore a son who counted as Leah's, and Leah called his name Gad ("Good fortune"). Later Zilpah had another son, whom Leah called Asher (meaning "happiness/good fortune"). Leah said how happy she was and that the women would call her happy. The LXX runs μακαρια εγω οτι μακαριζουσιν με αι γυναικες (Gen 30:13). In Luke 1, Elizabeth calls Mary μακαρια (v. 45), and in the Magnificat itself Mary says that "From now on all generations μακαριουσιν με" (v. 48b). Mary is to be the mother of the messiah and, in a sense, mother of the (renewed) Israel. Of course, the scope of those who pronounce her blessed is widened considerably over against Leah. In Leah's case it is the women around her in Israel; those who acknowledge Mary's vital role will embrace all generations, as befits the mighty act which God is in the process of doing ("the great things" [v. 49a]).[88]

It is a curious fact, noted by Ulrike Mittmann-Richert,[89] that scholars have not considered Isaiah 7–12 as a possible source for reflection by the early Christians in relation to the birth of Jesus.[90] It is clear that the Benedictus refers to Isaiah 9:2 at Luke 1:79. We know that Matthew quoted Isaiah 7:14 LXX in his Gospel, and one could almost *a priori* suppose that Luke

---

87. Literally, "Behold a son," but, according to the author of Genesis, Leah is said to think of a related Hebrew phrase "looked upon my affliction."

88. Laurentin, *Structure et Théologie de Luc I–II*, 84, prefers an allusion to Malachi 3.10. In Malachi, however, as Laurentin acknowledges, all the nations declare Israel blessed.

89. Mittmann-Richert, *Magnifikat*, 20.

90. Actually, Dodd, *According to the Scriptures*, 61–110, did list Isaiah 6:1–9:7; 11:1–10, as among what he called primary sources of testimonies (he himself listed them among the "Scriptures of the New Israel").

was aware of this passage and, though he does not quote it, it might be in the background in the references to Mary as a virgin at 1:27; in the wording of the angel's message that she would conceive, bear a son, and name him Jesus at 1:31; and in Mary's reference to herself as a virgin in 1:34.[91] Ulrike Mittmann-Richert has pointed out that there are a number of words and motifs which the Magnificat shares with the hymn of thanksgiving at Isaiah 12 (which rounds off the first section of Isaiah [Isa 1–12]).[92] The hymn in Isaiah acknowledged Yahweh's judgment on His people and anticipated a time when He had acted to save His people, and they in turn must ensure that all peoples know about God's saving acts. It culminated in the confession "Great is the Holy One of Israel in the midst of you" (v. 6).

The lack of anything specific to a young woman expecting her first child plus the general likeness to the prayer literature of Israel in the Psalter has suggested that the Magnificat was originally an independent psalm only moderately adapted to fit its present position on the lips of Mary.[93] This suggestion might receive support not only from the general nature of the song but also from the fact that in the second half of the Magnificat, the thrust of the poem moves from Mary to Israel: God is praised because He had come to the aid of His servant, Israel (v. 54). From verse 51 to 55 we have, on form critical grounds, a psalm of praise of a *group* which regarded itself as among the lowly and the hungry, and which saw itself as (the true) Israel (v. 54).

This in turn raises the question whether, at whatever stage, two originally independent psalms—one, that of an individual (woman) who belonged within God's people, the other of a group which saw itself as representing

---

91. So Schürmann, *Lukasevangelium*, 1:62–63; Grundmann, *Lukas*, 60; Ellis, *Luke*, 73; Marshall, *Luke*, 64; Hahn, *Titles*, 296; Fuller, *Foundations of New Testament Christology*, 195–96, 202. On the other hand, Brown, *Birth*, 299–301; Fitzmeyer, *Luke*, 1:336; Evans, *Luke*, 155; Nolland, *Luke*, 1:51, all deny any influence of Isaiah 7:14 on Luke.

92. Mittmann-Richert, *Magnifikat*, 20. These are, in the order they occur in Isaiah 12: ηλεησας με (v. 1); σωτηρ μου and σωτηρια (v. 2); ονομα (v. 4); υψηλα εποιησεν (v. 5); and αγαλλιασθε and αγιος του Ισραηλ (v. 6). There does not appear to be any indication that there was as such "an Isaianic birth cycle" (a phrase Mittmann-Richert uses [*Magnifikat*, 147]), which the final redactor used, since other material breaks up any connection between chapters 7 and 9 and between chapters 9 and 11.

93. So Schmid, *Lukas*, 54; Grundmann, *Lukas*, 63; Schürmann, *Lukasevangelium* 1:78; Marshall, *Luke*, 79; Evans, *Luke*, 172–73; Fitzmyer, *Luke*, 1:309; Nolland, *Luke*, 1:63; Brown, *Birth Stories*, 350–55. Among those who are in favor of Lucan authorship are Von Harnack, *Das Magnifikat der Elisabeth*, 538–66 (quoted by Farris); Cadbury, *Making of Luke-Acts*, 192–93; Tannehill, "Magnificat as Poem," 263–75 (cf. Tannehill, *Gospel according to Luke*, 15–44, esp. 26–32); Drury, *Tradition and Design*, 49–50; Farris, *Hymns*, 108–126. Creed, *Luke*, 306, does not decide. If Luke had composed the Magnificat himself, might we not have expected that he would have related it more to what the angel Gabriel had said about Mary's future son in the annunciation? (cf. Evans, *Luke*, 172–73)?

Israel—have been welded together. Whereas verses 51-55, possibly with an introduction, could have circulated independently, the same cannot be said for verses 47-50, which requires either a narrative for it to be fully intelligible[94] or knowledge that Mary had given birth to the Messiah, on the part of the community within which the hymn was composed.[95] Something like the annunciation by Gabriel to Mary could have existed in oral form. This annunciation by Gabriel to Mary provides the intelligible background: Mary can rejoice that God had chosen her to be the mother of the messiah.[96]

Those who argue for two separate pieces of tradition probably overlook the fact that an individual could be a member of a group which saw itself as in some way representing or embodying Israel. The individual could lead off with praise and then the group took over because it was the beneficiary of God's intervention in using the individual in a special way—here of being mother of the messiah.

If Luke did receive from one of his sources a psalm which he adapted, then clearly the interpreter is faced with two levels: that of the pre-Lucan stage (which would be Jewish Christian) and that of Luke's own intention.

At the pre-Lucan stage, the singer and singers of this song represent Israel. God had acted so that an individual had been chosen to be the mother of the messiah. God was acting on behalf of His people. His mighty acts on behalf of the humble and the poor and against the proud, mighty and powerful were celebrated (1:51-53). He must overthrow the worldly conditions if His order was to come into being. "He has helped His servant, Israel." How had God done this? He had done so "by remembering

---

94. Some scholars wish to excise either the whole of verse 48 or, at any rate, verse 48b. In response one might argue that a double justification of the praise offered in verse 47, viz. in verses 48, 49, is no reason to eliminate one of these verses. The idea that future generations will recall the singer of the praise because God had done mighty things for her is not inconceivable in the light of a concern expressed not a few times in the Psalms that future generations might learn of God's mighty deeds (Ps 48:13; 78:4, 6; 79:13; 89:1; 102:12, 18; 135:13; and also the concern for the instruction of future generations about specific events in Exod 12:26-27; 13:8, 14; Deut 11:19; Josh 4:6-7; Joel 1:3) or about an individual (see Ps 45:17). Sirach 44-50 indicates that eulogy of the past ancestors found a place in Israel's faith, while books like Ruth, Esther, and Judith show that the exploits of women were remembered and celebrated. Mittmann-Richert, *Magnifikat*, 57, has pertinently asked what could have induced Luke to have added verse 48b, since he does not in the rest of Luke-Acts give to Mary a special role (Acts 1:14 could hardly be described as indicating Mary's prominence in the early community).

95. This is the view of Mittmann-Richert, *Magnifikat*, 144, 150-51, 192-93.

96. Mittmann-Richert, *Magnifikat*, 225, works in the opposite direction: first come the two hymns, the Magnifikat and the Benedictus, and then as a second stage of the building up of a narrative tradition comes the annunciation scene now at 1:26-38, but on her view the community who sang these two hymns must have reflected about the mother of the messiah to make Mary the spokesperson of the first half of the Magnificat.

His mercy; as He spoke to our fathers, to Abraham and his seed for ever" (vv. 54-55). The help given to Israel was in fulfillment of what God had promised to Abraham and his descendants. What God had spoken was first addressed to Abraham and subsequently renewed to Isaac and Jacob (as the Genesis narrative indicates).[97]

At the level of Lucan redaction, the song celebrated the intervention of God by making Mary conceive. The future child will not only be a descendant of David but he will be called the Son of the Most High. God had initiated His saving purpose adumbrated long ago in the promises which He made to Abraham, through whom He intended to bless the world. An arc is thus drawn from the beginning of Israel's story in Abraham to the imminent birth of Jesus.

5.2.6. Luke's View of Abraham

From the Magnificat and the Benedictus, we see basically two things about Luke's view of Abraham. Firstly, Abraham is described as "our father" (1:73) and he is foremost among "the fathers" (1:55, 72-73a).

Secondly, God made a covenant with Abraham, backed up by an oath (1:72-73a). He had now remembered what He promised then (1:54b-55, 77b), and had acted in the present to fulfill that promise: He had brought salvation and a saviour from the Davidic line (1:69). He had come to the aid of His people and servant, Israel (1:54a).

Irrespective of where Luke ultimately got his material from, the important thing is the use to which he put it. What is the overall impression which he has created with Luke 1-2 and, specifically, by recalling his readers/hearers to the covenant and oath given to Abraham by God? The link of Christian faith with its Israelite/Jewish roots is firmly set forth. The godliness and piety of the people mentioned in Luke 1-2 are those within whose circle the messiah was born and brought up (cf. Rom 9:5), and who ultimately will be made available for the world (2:32). To use Paul's analogy of the olive tree, they represent that cultivated olive into which the gentiles will be grafted, with the patriarchs representing the root which bears the tree.

In what sense did Luke understand the language of salvation which is set forth in this-worldly terms: liberation from their enemies enabling the rendering of service and worship without fear of being attacked and conquered and the living of holy and righteous lives (1:51-53, 74-77)?[98] The answer to

---

97. Genesis 15:18; 17:4-16; 22:16-17 (the oath); 26:3 (Isaac); 26:13-15 (Jacob).

98. Especially the Magnificat has become very popular not only amongst exponents of the so-called Liberation Theology emanating from South America, but also among

that could only come after someone had read the double volume. Then, any reader would understand that neither Jesus himself nor his followers were committed to the violent overthrow of existing power structures, specifically that of the Roman empire. The "enemies" of God's people are the forces of evil, the kingdom of Satan, all that opposes the holy will of God.[99] Though not a great deal is said about the living of the Christian life in Acts,[100] the gospel of Jesus and the word of God's grace proclaimed by preachers like Paul (Acts 20:32) are intended to give men and women an inheritance among all those who have been sanctified (εν τοις ηγιασμενοις πασιν). Holy and righteous lives should characterize those who follow Jesus.

5.3. Abraham Elsewhere in Luke-Acts

The concept of Abraham as the father of the nation appears throughout the whole of LA. John the Baptist is depicted as picking up an almost slogan-like claim and rebutting it. "Do not say[101] among yourselves 'We have Abraham as our father,' for I tell you that God is able from these stones to raise up children for Abraham" (3:8). In the parable of Lazarus and the Rich Man, Abraham is addressed by the latter as "Father Abraham" (16:24, 30), and is conceived of as existing in a post-mortem state of blessedness. Lazarus who has joined him is described as being in Abraham's bosom. Such close proximity to the great patriarch is an indication of the tremendous reversal of his fate as a beggar in his earthly life.

In Acts, Stephen's speech begins, "The God of glory appeared to our father Abraham while he was in Mesopotamia" (7:2). Israel's story starts with Abraham. Paul reports Ananias of Damascus as saying to him, "The God of our fathers has appointed you to know His will" (22:14), where the

---

those who favor a Christianity which emphasizes social involvement and a stress on God as "the God of the poor." How far, however, is the language of the Magnificat and of the Benedictus intended to be taken literally, and how far does it make use of traditional imagery from the Old Testament and Jewish tradition, in which the establishment of God's saving rule is accompanied by the overthrow of all forces hostile to God? Mittmann-Richert, *Magnifikat*, 205-9, comes down very strongly on the latter.

99. Grässer, *Alte Bund*, 37, suggests that freedom from foes is interpreted as the forgiveness of sins.

100. Wenk, *Community-Forming Power*, has sought to show some of the ethical dimensions of Lucan pneumatology. He highlights the Spirit's role in resolving interpersonal conflicts and in realizing the this-worldly dimension of salvation by bringing converts into community, which becomes a visible manifestation of God's kingdom in this world.

101. Possibly the full force of αρξησθε is intended, in which case we should translate, "Do not begin to say."

phrase includes Isaac and Jacob as well as Abraham. It is as if here, in a speech to fellow Jews near the Temple, the God of Abraham and the fathers is made to validate Paul as a witness to and for Jesus for all men and women (cf. 22:21, where the risen Jesus commanded Paul, "Go, because I will send you far away to the Gentiles").

The phrase with the plural also occurs in Peter's speech at the Beautiful Gate of the Tempe at 3:13, "The God of Abraham, Isaac, and Jacob, the God of our fathers." And later, before the Sanhedrin, Peter said, "The God of our fathers raised Jesus up" (5:30). Stephen reported God's words to Moses in the desert, "I am the God of your fathers, the God of Abraham and Isaac and Jacob" (7:32). Paul opened his speech at the Pisidian Antioch synagogue with, "The God of this people, Israel, chose our fathers" (13:17). Having specified Abraham at 7:2, Luke may have chosen a more abbreviated formula in this later speech.

5.4. Individuals as Children of Abraham

Individuals may be referred to as a son or daughter of Abraham (Luke 13:16; 19:9). There was something fitting and appropriate that the woman, bent double by Satan, should benefit from Jesus' healing *because* she was a daughter of Abraham. It was fitting too that she should be healed on a sabbath, which was the prototype and foretaste of the Age to Come when Satan himself would be annihilated (13:16). Equally, it was fitting that Zaccheus should return to God by changing his ways, in response to the friendship of Jesus, who, as Son of Man, had come seeking and saving the lost, *because* Zaccheus was a son of Abraham. "Today salvation has come to this house, for he also is a son of Abraham" (19:9). Zaccheus had been released from the bondage to Mammon and had received salvation. The lost had been found and saved. Those who are members of Israel should enjoy wholeness of life—salvation.

We might mention that Jesus himself is a descendant of Abraham according to the genealogical table set out by Luke (3:34), though Luke does not highlight this in the way that Matthew does (Matt 1:1).

5.5. The Fulfillment of God's Promise to Abraham/the Fathers

Although the word "promise" does not occur in the Magnificat and the Benedictus, we have seen that the idea does. God remembered what He said to the fathers, to Abraham and his seed (1:54-55); or God remembered the holy covenant, ratified with an oath, made with Abraham (1:72-73). The idea of God's fulfilling what had been said to Abraham occurs at a number of points in the speeches in Acts.

We turn first to Peter's speech in Acts 3. Peter linked the healing of the lame man, just effected, to faith in the name of Jesus who had recently been rejected and put to death in the city but raised from the dead by God. Peter urged the people to repent and return to God so that their sins might be forgiven and that they might enjoy seasons of refreshing from God who would send the appointed messiah, Jesus (vv. 19-20). Peter quoted the passage from Deuteronomy about a prophet like Moses whom God would raise up from among the people of Israel. They must listen to him (Deut 18:15); otherwise, they will be obliterated from the ranks of God's people (3:22-23). Then the speech continued: "You are the sons of the prophets and of the covenant which God made with your fathers, saying to Abraham, 'And all families of the earth will be blessed in your seed.' To you first God has raised up His servant and sent him to bless you in turning each of you from your wicked deeds" (3:25-26).

The addressees are described directly in a twofold way. They are "sons of the prophets and (sons) of the covenant"[102] which God concluded with the fathers. Of these two descriptions the first is unusual, though not difficult to see why Luke or his source may have used it. Peter had just referred to all the prophets twice (vv. 18, 21). The audience as Israelites are of the same nation as the prophets and inheritors of what they proclaimed and potentially, therefore, beneficiaries of their message and spiritually their "sons." The idea of Israelites as "sons of the covenant" is a natural description of descendants of Abraham, even if the phrase occurs only in Ezekiel 30:5 LXX (diff. from MT) and Psalm of Solomon 17:15.[103]

Then comes a reference to what God said to Abraham. The quotation appears to be closest to Genesis 22:18; 26:4, with a major difference being Luke's

---

102. οι υιοι governs the two attached genitives, των προφητων και της διαθηκης. Vogel, *Heil*, 341, thinks that Luke was responsible for των προφητων και, adding it into the traditional "sons of the covenant."

103. Ezekiel 30:5 LXX: Egypt, along with inhabitants of various countries παντες οι επιμικτοι [lit. mixed group of people; auxiliary and mercenary troops in the Egyptian army, according to Allen, *Ezekiel 20-48*, 115] και των υιων της διαθηκης [apparently Jewish mercenaries, so Allen, *Ezekiel 20-48*, 115. The MT has "sons of the land of the covenant," though the referent is the same] will fall by the sword in the Day of Yahweh's judgment.

Psalm of Solomon 17:15: "The sons of the covenant who live in the midst of the Gentiles surpassed them," i.e., in following Gentile customs (for the translation "surpassed," see Winninge, *Sinners and Righteous*, 91n390). In neither case, is the reference really complimentary.

use of πατριαι instead of εθνη (or even the φυλαι of Gen 12:3; 28:4). Grässer may be overinterpreting when he suggests that the change is significant. He believes that by it Luke includes Israel *and* the other peoples: the sending of Jesus from the beginning holds good for Israel and the other peoples.[104]

Peter recognized the prior claim of Israel, when he went on to say that God had sent His servant, Jesus, to the people of Israel *first*. Jesus is God's servant and the one through whom God fulfills His promise to the patriarchs, especially Abraham. Because of this promise, the descendants of Abraham, the "seed" of Abraham, the Israelites, had first claim on the blessings of his ministry. What is this blessing? Luke interpreted the blessing in terms of forgiveness of sins: the ministry of Jesus is intended to turn the people from their sins, with the implication that God will graciously forgive them. In the speech, Peter had mentioned forgiveness or blotting out of sins (vv. 19, 26); seasons of refreshing; the sending of the messiah already designated; and the restoration of all things.[105] Nevertheless, that "first" implies something beyond. All along God intended blessing for the whole world.

Diagrammatically this may be represented as follows:

Promise of Blessing > >>> Given to Abraham
|
Israel as recipient and agent
|
Jesus as God's servant
|
Jesus' followers—restored Israel,
|
Gentiles added
|
Restoration of All Things <<<<

Peter called on the people to repent (v. 19), just as he did when he preached on the day of Pentecost (2:38, 40), and referred to the threat in scripture of exclusion if people did not respond to Jesus, the messenger whom God had sent. This raises the question of the status of the people.

104. Grässer, *Alte Bund*, 40–41. Schrenk, "πατηρ κτλ," *TWNT* 5:1016, has shown that in the LXX πατρια is used in three ways: for the basic cell of the family with the father as head; the clans; and the nations. It is this last sense which is obviously intended in Acts 3:25. Schrenk briefly alludes to the possibility of liturgical influence, a point with which Holtz, *Untersuchungen*, 75, agrees.

105. In the speech on the Day of Pentecost, Peter promised to those near and those far off the forgiveness of sins, the gift of the Holy Spirit, and becoming part of the saved community (2:38–42).

They are "the sons of the prophets and of the covenant," but their position is parlous. Their position might be described as conditional. They face exclusion.

From Acts 3, we can discern two points relevant for our theme. Firstly, there is the concept of promise and fulfillment. The promise made to Abraham had been fulfilled in the ministry of Jesus and continued to be fulfilled in the ongoing work of the exalted Jesus, illustrated by the healing of the beggar at the Beautiful Gate of the temple and the preaching of the apostles in Jerusalem with their offer of repentance and forgiveness. Secondly, by implication there is a question of who constitutes the "seed of Abraham." If disobedience results in exclusion from the people (λαος), membership of God's people does not rest on the purely physical or biological factor of descent from Abraham. The true people of God was present when the word of Jesus the servant of God was heard and obeyed.[106]

Secondly, we turn to Stephen's speech. After having said that God appeared to Abraham in Mesopotamia, Stephen continued with God's instructions to go forth to the land which God would show him. Abraham went to Haran and from there, after the death of his father, God moved him "to this land in which you now live, though He did not give him even a foot of ground as an inheritance in it, yet He did promise it to him and his descendants after him to possess, although he had no child" (7:2–5). God's promise to Abraham is, then, that ultimately the land of Canaan should belong to him and his descendants. We note that apart from verse 4ab (Abraham left Mesopotamia and lived in Haran), the verse is mainly concerned with what God did and said. He is the main actor, and He made a promise (επηγγειλατο [v. 5]). Abraham is the recipient of that promise.

The phrase "in which you now live" (v. 4c) indicated that God had fulfilled the promise of occupying the land. God overcame the hindrance to the fulfillment of His promise: at the time of the promise Abraham had no child to be his heir. (Luke's addressees would know the problem of Abraham's and Sarah's childlessness.) We meet a second hindrance in the fact that Stephen then recalled that God had predicted[107] that Abraham's descendants would be enslaved in a foreign land for four hundred years, after which God would punish that country and enable Abraham's descendants to leave it and worship Him "in this place" (7:6–7). Here, instead of "this mountain" (Sinai) of Exodus 3:12, we have "this place," which refers to either Israel in general or the Temple in particular (7:6–7). Again, we may detect a note of fulfillment:

---

106. Cf. Grässer, *Alte Bund*, 41.
107. See Genesis 15:13–14, plus Exodus 3:12.

God promised deliverance and worship in Israel/the Temple. That had happened despite the slavery in Egypt.

At verse 8, in a terse statement, Stephen said, "And He gave him the covenant of circumcision," a reference to Genesis 17:10–14 where circumcision was to be a sign of God's covenant with the descendants of Abraham.[108] Abraham fathered Isaac and had him duly circumcised on the eighth day. The speech continued και Ισαακ τον Ιακωβ και Ιακωβ τους δωδεκα πατριαρχας.[109] A number of scholars accept that the predicate in connection with Abraham should be understood in the case of both Isaac and Jacob, or state that the emphasis falls on the act of circumcision rather than on the act of begetting, i.e., "Isaac fathered Jacob and had him circumcised on the eighth day, and Jacob fathered the twelve patriarchs and had them circumcised on the eighth day."[110] We notice that Luke has included the phrase "on the eighth day" with the verb to circumcise. He could have just used the verb on its own. That he included "on the eighth day" suggests that it was important for him, a point that Thiessen has emphasized.[111]

The sequence is first God's gift of the covenant of circumcision, and then Abraham fathered the heir who was to inherit God's promises, Isaac. This suggests that the latter was facilitated by God's gift of the covenant of circumcision.[112]

So, land, child, and circumcision plus the exodus from Egypt and worship in the promised land—the themes of promise and prediction—have all been fulfilled. Confirmation that promise-fulfillment is important to Luke can be seen at 7:17, where Stephen said, "As the time drew near for God to fulfill His promise to Abraham, the number of our people in Egypt greatly

---

108. Blashke, *Beschneidung*, 448, notes that this phrase became the most usual description of circumcision in late Judaism, and refers to the occurrence of the phrase in Tan *lk lk* 20 (c. 90 AD) and in M. Teh. 1:20 (before 135 AD).

109. Vogel, *Heil*, 259, suggests that the και is adversative, and that there is a contrast with verse 5 where it is said that God did not actually give him even so much as a foot of the land, but promised to give it to him and his seed after him as a possession. The covenant of circumcision is a substitute for the promise of the land. Blashke, *Beschneidung*, 449, agrees.

110. So many scholars translate or indicate that the stress falls on the act of circumcision: Bruce, *Acts*, 147–48; Schneider, *Die Apostelgeschichte*, 1:455; Pesch, *Die Apostelgeschichte*, 1:250; Roloff, *Die Apostelgeschichte*, 120; Barrett, *Acts*, 1:331; Johnson, *Acts of the Apostles* 116; Jervell, *Die Apostlegeschichte*, 234. Cf. Haenchen, *Acts of the Apostles*, 279; Thiessen, *Contesting Circumcision*, 117.

111. Thiessen, *Contesting Circumcision*, 117, who also points out that Luke's actual phrase is closer to the majority of LXX witnesses to Genesis 17:14 and Leviticus 12:3, than to Genesis 21:4.

112. Schneider, *Die Apostelgeschichte*, 1:455; Blashke, *Beschneidung*, 448–49 (in contrast to Sir 44:20–21, which stresses Abraham's obedience).

increased." This statement is an important clue to Luke's convictions. The connection with Abraham is emphasized. Jervell has rightly suggested that not only is the deliverance from Egypt going to fulfill the divine promise (cf. verse 7), but also the fact of the increase of the Hebrew population fulfills the promise to Abraham of descendants.[113]

Finally, we look at Paul's speech at Pisidian Antioch.[114] In the second of three direct addresses to his audience, Paul describes them as "Brothers, sons of the family of Abraham" (13:26). The first part of Paul's speech consisted of a brief and selective survey of the history of Israel. It began with the statement that God chose the fathers and it reached its climax in the raising up of David, described as a man after God's own heart, who would do God's will (v. 22). Paul then went on to say that from David's line God had, "according to (His) promise," brought on the scene a saviour for Israel, Jesus. The key points in this story of Israel are Abraham-David-Jesus. In this speech the stress is not on Sinai and the covenant and giving of the Law which took place there. The focus is on the election of Abraham, renewed in the election of David (who was, of course, a descendant of Abraham), and ultimately fulfilled in Jesus.

Later, Paul went on to claim that the *promise made to the fathers had been fulfilled*, and that was the good news which he had brought (13:32). God had indeed fulfilled this promise by raising Jesus from the dead in fulfillment of Psalm 2:7; Isaiah 55:3; and Psalm 16 (vv. 33–37). As a result of God's raising Jesus from the dead, Paul could proclaim forgiveness of sins and justification through Jesus (vv. 38–39).[115]

Twice, then, the theme of promise and fulfillment is emphasized in this speech.

5.6. The Post-Mortem Existence of the Patriarchs

A further sign of the importance of Abraham, Isaac, and Jacob is seen in the fact that Jesus assumed that the patriarchs were alive in a post-mortem existence. That there was a post-mortem existence and judgment of individuals was a belief which had been gaining ground in some sections

---

113. Jervell, *Apostlegeschichte*, 235–36.

114. See my *Paul's Pisidian Antioch Speech*.

115. The idea that the promise to the fathers has been fulfilled in Jesus, especially his resurrection, which led on to his exaltation and the outpouring of the Spirit (that resurrection being the guarantee of the general resurrection; cf. 26:23), seems to surface in Paul's speech before the Jewish king, Agrippa, in Acts 26. Paul said that he was on trial "for the hope of the promise made by God to our fathers" (vv. 6–7). He exclaimed, "Why should it be judged incredible by any of you that God should raise the dead?"

of early Judaism, particularly the western Diaspora.[116] In the Gospel, Jesus is reported as having used God's words to Moses ("I am the God of Abraham and the God of Isaac and the God of Jacob") as proof that the patriarchs must be alive, because God was the God of the living, not the dead (20:37–38). In the parable of Lazarus and the rich man, Abraham has a key role in Paradise. The beggar, Lazarus, was transported on his death "to Abraham's bosom" (16:23), and it was to Abraham that the rich man, now in torment, addressed his pleas and requests (16:23–31). It was Abraham who made a definitive pronouncement: "If they do not listen to Moses and the prophets, (they will not be persuaded) even if someone should rise from the dead" (16:31), which was a statement no doubt highly prophetic from Luke's perspective.

Jesus assumed that the patriarchs would be present at the messianic banquet and that people from all quarters of the world would sit down with them and all the prophets, whereas Israelites would be excluded (Luke 13:28–29).

5.7. Conclusion

In summary, we may say that Abraham is the one in whom the story of Israel began. He was the first Israelite, elected by God with descendants to come after him, but also with a universal programme of blessing in mind. He was, therefore, the father of the nation and the recipient of significant promises.

God had fulfilled that promise/those promises in Jesus of Nazareth, descendant of David and Abraham. Through Jesus, God's blessings were available for Israel if she responded to Jesus' ministry and yet these blessings were also intended for the whole world. For Luke, Gentiles who believe were incorporated into faithful believing Israel and so become part of God's people.

Abraham was envisaged as alive in a post-mortem existence and would share in the eschatological banquet of the Kingdom of God, when the story of the promise reached its final fulfillment.

Thus, we may say that God's promise "has a history." It began with Abraham, ran through David, and climaxed in Jesus. The promise thus realized made its way out into the world as the message of salvation taken to the ends of the earth. It will reach its climax in the Parousia of the risen, exalted Jesus, when at the eschatological banquet all believers will join with Abraham, Isaac, and Jacob and all the prophets in the joy of God's reign.

116. See Fischer, *Eschatologie und Jenseitserwartung*; Nickelsburg, *Resurrection*.

6

Abraham in the Gospel of John

6.1. Introduction

WE SHALL ASSUME, FIRSTLY, that the Fourth Gospel was written towards the end of the first century AD, perhaps in Greek-speaking Syria, perhaps in Ephesus.

Then, secondly, that Christians had separated from, or had been forced out of, the Synagogue. This is probably proved by three passages which mention that followers of Jesus would be excommunicated from the Synagogue (ἀποσυνάγος/οι [9:22; 12:42-43; 16:1-4]). Furthermore, while it was accepted that the Law was given by God through Moses (1:17), there are passages which suggest an attempt to distance the writer and his community from the centrality accorded to the Law in the Synagogue (there are references to "your Law" [8:17; 10:34] and "their Law" [15:25]). Nonetheless, the Law does bear witness to Jesus (e.g., 5:39, 45-47; cf. 6:30-35).

Although sometimes the evangelist does differentiate between various elements within the Jewish nation,[1] more frequently he refers to "the Jews" collectively. It would be odd for Jesus, for example, to refer to his own nation in this way. It would seem that the evangelist was conscious of a cleft between Christian Jews and those Jews who did not accept the claim that Jesus was the Messiah, the Son of God.

---

1. Thus, he mentions the Pharisees fifteen times; rulers four times; chief priests eight times (four of which are in the Passion Story); chief priests with the Pharisees four times; and the high priest in the singular eleven times.

It will be assumed that this separation of Christians from the Synagogue has left its mark on the way in which the evangelist has told the story.

In the third place, the evangelist has reflected on the stories and sayings of Jesus. The discourses (chiefly within a sign + discourse structure)[2] are meditative and apologetic reflections, seeking to draw out the significance of the life of Jesus of Nazareth, the incarnate Word of God, the Son of God come down from heaven, under the influence of the Paraclete-Spirit whose task it was to take what was Christ's and declare it in an interpretative way to the situation in which the evangelist and his community—and beyond this community, in other Christian congregations—found themselves. This Gospel draws out and makes explicit what is so often implicit or below the surface in the activity and teaching of Jesus in the Synoptic Gospels.

Fourthly, John 8, where Abraham is referred to in two parts of the dialogue, bears the imprint of a clash between Synagogue and Church, as do many other parts of the Gospel. That clash appears to have been bitter and ferocious and deeply wounding to both sides. The struggle had been, and continued to be, over who was the rightful heir to the legacy of the OT and the Jewish heritage. To use a phrase, this has been a clash between siblings over the family inheritance. Both non-Christian Jews and Christian Jews claim to be the true people of God. For example, in chapter 9, the Pharisees claim "We are Moses's disciples. We know that God has spoken to Moses, but as for this fellow, we do not know from where he comes" (9:29). By contrast, the Johannine Jesus warns:

> Do not think that I will accuse you to the Father. Your accuser is Moses, on whom you have set your hopes. For if you believed Moses, you would believe me, for he wrote about me. But if you do not believe what he wrote, how will you believe what I say? (5:45-47)

6.2. Abraham in the Gospel of John

6.2.1. The Problem of John 8:31

The section with which we shall be concerned begins at 8:31 with the words: "Then Jesus said to the Jews who had believed him," yet at verse 37 he accused them of trying to kill him, while further on in the conversation he called them children of the devil and they returned the compliment by

---

2. Sometimes, the claim in the form of an ἐγώ εἰμι saying precedes the sign, as at 8:12; 9:5, or the Farewell Discourse(s), which elucidate the significance of the sign of the cross.

calling him a Samaritan and demon-possessed (vv. 44, 48). This seems an utterly astonishing sequence, so much so that some scholars believe that πεπιστευκοτας αυτω at 8:31 is an interpolation by a later editor under the influence of verse 30.[3] There is, however, no textual support for this. In any case, would not an editor notice that he had created the tension with later statements in the dialogue by his insertion?

Another suggestion has been put forward by both Dietzfelbinger and Theobald.[4] Dietzfelbinger believes that the evangelist has drawn on and combined what were basically two different pieces of tradition, viz. verses 31-36 and 37-59 ("Abraham" is the catchword which has helped the evangelist to be able to weld the two pieces together), but he was not bothered by what Dietzfelbinger calls the absurdities of a sequence in which Jews who believed in Jesus are accused of wanting to kill Jesus (v. 37). Granted that there are some signs that the author did not, or was unable to, complete a final revision and polishing of his work, Dietzfelbinger's suggestion leaves us with the impression of a carelessness or indifference. As an explanation it does not seem convincing.

Theobald thinks that the reference to Jews who believed in Jesus has in mind the rulers in the synagogue who kept quiet about their faith for fear of being excommunicated (12:42).[5] It is because they wished to remain members of the synagogue that the evangelist lumps them together with Jews who want to kill Jesus.[6] In his comments on 8:37, Theobald says that here the evangelist is not referring to the Jews who believed in Jesus but has the Jerusalem authorities in mind.[7] As an explanation, this is more convincing than Dietzfelbinger's, but it still leaves the reader/hearer of the Gospel with the need to make a sharp transition from what verse 31 said about who were the addressees of Jesus.

The issue boils down to whether we can make sense of the text as it stands? Yes, if we take note of how the evangelist handles the theme of faith, which is of vital concern to him, as 20:30-31 amply testifies.

The coming of Jesus creates division. People are challenged by his words and deeds to believe in him, but many do not so respond. The works which he does are "signs" which to the believing eye show who Jesus is, yet they are also meant to evoke faith (20:30-31; 10:37-38; 14:10-11).

---

3. Brown, *Gospel of John*, 1:354-55; Lindars, *Gospel of John*, 323.

4. Dietzfelbringer, *Das Evangelium nach Johannes* 1:252, 264, 271; Theobald, *Johannes*, 587, 599, 609.

5. Theobald, *Johannes*, 590.

6. Theobald, *Joahnnes*, 597.

7. Theobald, *Johannes*, 599, 609.

A continual sifting process goes on, for a faith based solely on miracles is not adequate, as 2:23–25 suggests. The evangelist seems to explore this in the story of the healing of the nobleman's son in 4:46–54. The nobleman appears to be rebuffed by Jesus' sharp words in verse 48 (the verbs are, however, in the second person *plural*!). Despite this, the man believed the word which Jesus had said (v. 50), and this was confirmed later by the report that his boy was well (vv. 51–52). This produced faith in him and his household (v. 53). So, there is an interplay between sign-faith and faith-based-on-Jesus' word. After the discourse on the Bread of Life linked to the feeding of the five thousand, many of Jesus' followers turned away from following him (6:60–66). The sifting process continues in the section which is our concern. Faith is not something static. It must move onwards and forwards to deeper commitment, or else there is the danger that it will regress into opposition. That is the case with those Jews who had believed in Jesus, according to 8:31.[8]

6.2.2. John 8:31–47

We turn now to examine John 8:31–59, in which the figure of Abraham plays a significant part. It is a dialogue between Jesus on the one hand and Jews who had believed in him,[9] on the other hand. We shall assume that the sequence of 8:31–59 is what the evangelist wrote. The attempt of Bultmann to split up these verses[10] has not won acceptance, and reasonable sense can be made of the sequence as it now stands.[11]

---

8. For a fuller treatment of what is said in this paragraph, see my *Cross in the Johannine Writings*, 106–111. Dodd, *Behind a Johannine Dialogue*, 42–47, suggested that the reference was to Jewish Christians of the sort earlier condemned by Paul.

9. While some scholars delete the participial phrase "who believed him," others draw a distinction between the use of εἰς with πιστεύειν in verse 30 and with the dative in verse 31. Moloney, *Gospel of John*, 275, suggests that the believing Jews of verse 30 have departed and that the Jews mentioned in verse 31 only have partial faith. All these are attempts to ease the apparent tension between Jews who are said to have believed in Jesus and their hostile attitude to him which is revealed so quickly and which culminates in their wanting to kill Jesus.

10. Bultmann, *Gospel of John*, ix–x, xiii, 287–88, 314–15, 420, reconstructs a section entitled, "The Revealer's Struggle with the World," made up of parts of chapters 7–10. He places 8:48–50, 54–55, after 7:1–14, 25–52, under the title the hiddenness and contingency of the revelation. This sequence is followed by 7:30, 37–44, 31–36, 45–52, then comes 8:41–47, 51–53, 56–59, described as a fragment, the conclusion of which has been lost. Bultmann repositions 8:30–40 after 12:20–33 to be followed by 6:60–71.

11. E.g., "On the whole we have here a rather homogeneous discourse" (Brown, *John*, 1:361); "A single unit" (Schnackenburg, *John*, 2:204).

It may be that the evangelist wished to intimate something of a change in the dialogue partners at verse 48, since he says there that "the Jews said in response." We shall deal with that issue when we come to verse 48.

The theme of freedom, together with that of slavery, dominates the first section (vv. 30-36). The dialogue opens up with the claim made by Jesus:

> If you remain in my word, you will truly be my disciples and you will know the truth and the truth will set you free. (vv. 31b-32)

While truth is frequently used in John's Gospel, ελευθερουν (to set free) and ελευθερος (free) only occur in the Gospel in this section (each two times). The importance of the word (λογος) of Jesus is clear here, as elsewhere in this gospel.[12] Abiding in Jesus' word is an essential characteristic of being a true disciple of Jesus. Jesus' word conveys truth (indeed, he himself is the truth), because it is the word given to him by God and God's word is truth (17:11). This truth will liberate from false notions about God and false notions about ourselves, and from the power exerted by these false notions. Positively, truth reveals that God loves us and wills to draw us into union with Himself through the Son.[13] Truth in John is a *saving* concept.[14] This liberation enables movement from the sphere of the false to the sphere of the truth.[15] So it is absolutely necessary to remain in Jesus' word, and to maintain one's adherence to it and to him. Only so will those addressed become and truly be his disciples.

Why has John introduced the theme of freedom? Both Lona and Motyer have suggested that there is a link with the situation after the disastrous Jewish War of Independence which had ended in the destruction of Jerusalem and the Temple and the organs of government: freedom was a live issue within Judaism after this catastrophic defeat at the hands of the Romans.[16]

---

12. See 5:24; 12:48; 14:24; 15:3, as well as later in the dialogue, 8:37, 51-52, and also the reference to Jesus' ρηματα and their significance at 6:63, 68; 12:47-48; 14:10; 15:7.

13. This means eternal life (cf. 20:30-31).

14. Cf. Schnackenburg, *John*, 2:205.

15. Elsewhere, the terminology used may be from darkness to light; from below to above; from this world to being not of this world or being where the Son is.

16. Lona, *Abraham in Johannes 8*, 256-61; Motyer, *Your Father,* 74-104. See also the view of Thyen, *Das Johannesevangelium,* 436 (quoted by Theobald, *Johannes,* 589-90), who sees reflected in 8:31-58 "the distressing experience of the turning away from the messianic confession of Jesus by numerous Jewish Christians, who, after the catastrophe of the Jewish revolt against Rome and the debacle of messianism linked with it, had sought refuge in the relatively protected sphere of the synagogue."

The question had to be grappled with—why had the Jews suffered such a devastating blow?[17]

The response to Jesus' declaration mentions Abraham:

> We are the seed of Abraham, and have never been enslaved to anyone. How can you say, You will become free. (v. 33)[18]

The claim to be Abraham's seed reveals pride in descent from Abraham, the ancestor of the Jewish people. John the Baptist had attacked Jewish reliance on this fact of descent from Abraham when he said to the crowds "Do not say among yourselves, We have Abraham as our father" (Luke 3:8), and Paul attacked such reliance in Galatians and Romans, as we have seen. The claim to be the seed of Abraham takes descent from Abraham as conferring an inalienable possession, an unalterable right to this status,[19] which has soteriological consequences.[20] This reference to being Abraham's seed might suggest that these "believers" were not orientated exclusively to Jesus but placed Abraham alongside or above him.[21]

The assertion is probably another instance of misunderstanding by a conversation partner of Jesus, of which there are many examples in the Fourth Gospel. As a statement of political circumstances, the statement will obviously not stand up to scrutiny. As an assertion of spiritual realities, a case could be made out for its veracity. Israel was Yahweh's special possession; it lived within His covenant, originally made with its forefather, Abraham, and regarded as an everlasting covenant (Gen 17:7); and it lived under His Law, given on Sinai via Moses as the mediator of the national covenant made there (Exod 24). Certainly, the Pharisaic wing of Judaism would claim a spiritual

---

17. E.g., the works of *4 Ezra* and *2 Baruch* deal with this issue. See note 25 below.

18. See Theobald, *Herrenworte*, 478–506, for a discussion that this saying together with that of 8:51 were part of the Johannine community's tradition which the evangelist took up. Theobald assumes his results in his commentary.

19. As an illustration, we might refer to *T. Naph.* 1:10, where it was important to the writer to trace the ancestry of Bilhad (who gave birth to Naphtali on behalf of Rachel; see Gen 30:1–8) to Abraham as well, so that Naphtali might have his assured place among the descendants of Abraham, the people of Israel.

20. Cf. Heiligenthal, *Werke*, 84: "From 8:37 we may conclude that the fictitious conversational partners of John represent a position, which stressed the soteriological aspect of the tradition of the fathers"; Theobald, *Johannes*, 592, maintains that what Jesus had said in verses 31–32 conflicted with their self-understanding, since for them liberating truth was already contained in the Abrahamic covenant.

21. So Dietzfelbinger, *Johannes*, 252. He sees them as akin to Paul's opponents in Galatia.

freedom based on the study of the Law.[22] Heiligenthal[23] has drawn attention to the fact that Philo, in commenting on God's intention not to hide anything from Abraham because Abraham was dear to Him (Gen 18:7), said that Abraham was the only free man because, with God's opinion of him, he had been liberated from false illusion and opinion, which are like a proud mistress but which God had absolutely destroyed.[24]

The sudden switch from freedom to slavery to sin in Jesus' next statement confirms the correctness of our explanation of verse 33. The claim to spiritual freedom had been belied by the catastrophe of defeat. Why had Israel suffered disaster in 66-70 AD? Because of its sins—a verdict with which some Jewish writings, like *4 Ezra* and *2 Baruch*, composed around the same time as the Fourth Gospel, agreed.[25]

> Jesus said, "Truly, truly, I say to you that everyone who commits sin is the slave of sin" (v. 34). A close connection is drawn between the doing of a sinful act and the enslavement of the doer to Sin (personified as a power at work in the world).[26] How is one to escape from this bondage and secure true freedom? Verse 35 offers a mini-parable by way of illustration. "A slave does not remain in the house forever. A son remains forever. If, then, the Son makes you free, you really will be free."

While the parable draws a truth from every day life concerning the relative status of a slave and the son of the household (a slave may be sold or given away), it is also true that in the biblical story Ishmael did not have a permanent place in the household of Abraham,[27] whereas Isaac did. The implication is that the Jews, whose enslavement to sin had been proved by their defeat in the war against Rome, do not remain as part of God's family forever. Only the Son enjoys that privilege. For the evangelist the Son came from the Father and returned to the Father via the cross (e.g., 6:38; 7:33; 13:1, 3; 16:28) and he has prepared a place in his Father's house for those who believe (14:2). Because he is the Son who remains with the Father in His house, Jesus can confer

---

22. Schnackenburg, *John*, 2:207; Lona, *Abraham*, 254, 263; Carson, *Gospel according to John*, 349; Moloney, *John*, 275.

23. Heiligenthal, *Werke*, 84.

24. Philo, *Sobr.* 55–57, esp. 57.

25. See, e.g., 4 Ezra 3:25–27; 2 Bar. 77:8–10:79. For dating, see Stone, *Fourth Ezra*, 10; Klijn, 2 *(Syriac Apocalypse of) Baruch*, 615–17; Nickelsburg, *Jewish Literature*, 280, 287 (for 2 Bar.), 287–88 (for 4 Ezra).

26. Cf. Barrett, *John*, 346. For the idea of an evil power, cf. "prince of this world" 12:31; 14:30; 16:11.

27. Barrett, *John*, 346; Lona, *Abraham*, 250, 263–66; but denied by Theobald, *Johannes*, 594.

freedom from sin on any who believe in him. This claim is thus opposed to an attempt to place Jesus alongside Abraham and to any other claim like that which saw true freedom to exist in the study of the Law or to that hope still entertained by some for political independence.[28]

Jesus returned to the issue of the Jewish people as the seed of Abraham, and from verses 37–47 the issue is the respective origin of Jesus and his conversation partners:

> I know that you are Abraham's seed. But you seek to kill me, because you have no time[29] for my word. (v. 37)

The αλλα introduced the implication that there was a contradiction between the claim to be Abraham's seed and the desire to kill him. The evangelist had previously reported the attempts to kill Jesus at 5:18; 7:1, 25, 30; 8:20 (although, strictly speaking, Jews who believed in Jesus would not presumably have been involved in such attempts). Once more, the importance of the word of Jesus emerges at verse 37c, picking up the stress of verse 31. If they have no time for his word, if they will not listen to him, their opposition hardens into a desire to remove him from the scene. Rejection of his word leads to rejection of his person and his claims, deemed injurious to monotheism (cf. 5:17–18; 10:34–36).

The assertion that they have no time for his word is the start of undermining the claim to be Abraham's descendants. Verse 38 shows why it is so injurious not to make room for Jesus' word and insinuates that the Jews have a different "father" from the one whom they claim:

> I speak what I have seen from the (or my) Father, but[30] you do what you have heard from the (or your) father.[31] (v. 38)[32]

---

28. There was a revolt by Jews in the western Diaspora (117 AD), and then, a few years later, there was the second Jewish War of Independence (132–35 AD), which ended in a crushing defeat at the hands of the Romans.

29. Ου χωρει εν υμιν could be taken as "My word makes no headway with you" (Moffatt, REB) or "There is no place in you for my word" (NRSV; cf. NIV). Bauer, *Lexicon*, 898, offers both possibilities. However, the English idiom used in the translation offered above probably hits the sense correctly.

30. The και at the beginning of verse 38b seems adversative. So JB and GN. The REB and NRSV ignore it.

31. Although the sense is probably my and your father respectively (and many manuscripts do read παρα του πατρος υμων in the second half of the sentence), it is possible that the evangelist wished to be less precise at this point, in order to delay revealing the true parentage of the Jews until verse 44.

32. An alternative translation assumes that ποειτε is an imperative—"do what you have heard from the Father" (NIV margin; NRSV)—but since verse 39 follows better if "your father" is assumed for verse 38, whether it is translated as such or not, the

The Jews recognized that Jesus had denied their relationship to Abraham, and returned to their assertion of verse 33: "Our father is Abraham" (v. 39a). Jesus now seeks specifically to rebut this. The argument is based on the assumption that behavior gives a clue to one's paternal origin: *one behaves like one's father*. Conduct reveals one's origin.[33] Jesus said:

> If you were Abraham's seed, you would do the works of Abraham. But now you are aiming[34] to kill me, someone who has told you the truth which I heard from God. Abraham did not do this. You are doing the works of your father. (vv. 39b–41a)

The conditional sentence in verse 39 is contrary-to-fact in the present. The works of Abraham are either his obedience to God's commands in general (Gen 12:1–4; 15:1–6; 22:1–19), or, specifically, his receiving and showing hospitality to the three heavenly messengers, who somehow seem to embody Yahweh (Gen 18:1–8). In contrast to Abraham, Jesus' present interlocutors were trying to kill him, although he had passed on God's truth to them.[35]

The behavior of the Jews in seeking to kill Jesus belied their claim to be children of Abraham, and the earlier claim to be free;[36] rather, their designs showed that they were in bondage to sin. It is still not overtly said who their father was, but it is implied that it was not Abraham (v. 41a).

The response is: "We were not born as the result of adultery; we have one father, God" (v. 42b). This reply makes two assertions, one negative and one positive. It could be said that it denied the assertion made by Hosea (1:2; 2:6) and Ezekiel (16) that Israel was guilty of adultery against Yahweh. Then it contained the positive assertion of Israel's special relationship with God, as disclosed in Hosea 11:1 ("I called My son out of Egypt") and Exodus 4:22 ("Israel is My son, My firstborn").[37] Taken as a whole, this response reiterated the earlier claim not to have been in (spiritual) bondage by asserting that God was the father of Israel. The claim that God was their father pushed their claims beyond Abraham to the God who

---

indicative makes for a better flow of thought. Barrett, *John*, 347; Lindars, *John*, 327, opt for a statement.

33. Cf. Heiligenthal, *Werke*, 85: "εργα are the sole principle for recognition." Cf. Dietzfelbinger, *Johannes*, 1:256: doing is an expression of origin and being.

34. For this sense of ζητειτε, see Bauer, *Lexicon*, 339.

35. The mention of truth picks up that theme from the start of the dialogue in verse 32.

36. "Manifestly this murderous will is a particularly clear sign of their lack of freedom" (Bultmann, *John*, 443).

37. Also Deut 14:1–2; Jer 31:9; Mal 1:6.

chose and called him.³⁸ Through being sons of God, they were assured of being Abraham's children. There is an implied rejection of Jesus' claim to be God's spokesman (vv. 38, 40).

There may be an implied slur on Jesus' origins,³⁹ but it was not elaborated upon by the Jews and it was not picked up by Jesus.⁴⁰

Jesus now subjected this last claim of the Jews to scrutiny and rejection. He claimed that if God were their father, they would love him,⁴¹ because he had come from God. He had not come on his own authority; rather, he was sent (v. 42). Their failure to love him called in question their claim to love God as His children. This in turn explained why they did not understand what Jesus was saying—they were unable truly to hear his word (vv. 42-43).⁴²

Now, at verse 44, Jesus revealed their paternity:

> You are of your father, the devil⁴³ and you want to do your father's desires. He was a murderer from the beginning, and did not stand in the truth, because the truth is not in him. When he speaks what is false, he speaks from his own supply⁴⁴ because he is a liar and the father of lies.

---

38. Schnackenburg, *John*, 2:211, notes, against Bultmann, that there is a progression from the father (v. 38), through your father (v. 41a), to the father, the devil (v. 44), which binds the passage together.

39. Matthew 1:18-25; Luke 1:26-38 have a strong stress on conception by the Holy Spirit, while Isaiah 7:14 LXX is quoted in Matthew 1:23 and seems to underlie the Lucan narrative without actually being quoted. It is possible that the later Rabbinic charge that Mary was guilty of adultery was already being levelled at Christians in the first century AD, but it is another matter whether, even if it were, it originated independently of the Infancy Stories.

40. Schnackenburg, *John*, 2:212; Beasley-Murray, *John*, 135; Moloney, *John*, 281; Theobald, *Johannes*, 602, do not think that there was an insinuation that Jesus was born as a result of an adulterous liaison. Lincoln, *John*, 271-72, thinks that Jesus' interlocutors were more interested in defending their own perspective on their ancestry rather than attacking Jesus.

41. As in verse 39, this is a contrary-to-fact in the present conditional sentence. Lindars, *John*, 328, aptly comments that love "describes the conduct which would be appropriate to the claim to affiliation to God."

42. The evangelist distinguishes between what Jesus says (his λαλια) and his word (λογος), between speech and the content of what is uttered. In other words, faith is needed to understand what Jesus says. Cf. Bultmann, *John*, 316n7; Barrett, *John*, 348.

43. This assumes that του διαβολου is to be taken as a genitive of explanation (epexegetic genitive), even if not in accord with the strict application of the rules of Greek grammar according to *BDF* 268.2.

44. So Bauer, *Lexicon*, 370; cf. JB "He is drawing on his own store."

In attempting to kill him and in refusing the truth which he spoke from God, his interlocutors revealed only too clearly their kinship with the devil, who brought death on Adam and Eve, and their descendants, and told a lie to them (viz. that God had forbidden the fruit of the tree of knowledge of good and evil lest they should become like Him). The story of Genesis 3 is presupposed, and the serpent is equated with the devil.[45] The devil was using the human pair to achieve his own murderous ends. They were helping to translate his desires into action.[46] In the dualism of John's Gospel, if one rejects Jesus who brings truth and is the truth, one is ipso facto in the sphere of falsehood ruled over by the devil. We stress again that this is not, however, an ontological dualism, but is a dualism of decision. By their refusal to respond to the truth, by their failure to discern the truth in what Jesus was saying, they revealed their paternity. If one belonged to the father of falsehood, then one would not believe Jesus who speaks the truth (v. 45).

The refusal to accept that what Jesus said is from God was tantamount to declaring him to be a liar. Jesus responded to this implied accusation with "Which of you convicts me of sin?" Jesus spoke out of an awareness of always having done what pleases God (cf. 8:29). It followed that he can and does speak the truth. "If I speak the truth, why do you not believe me?" (v. 46) and he answered this question himself — because they do not belong to God.[47] Their unbelief conditioned their response to Jesus.[48] By contrast, whoever belongs to God hears God's words, as passed on by His representative (v. 47).

At this point, we have reached a stage in the argument where it is advisable to pause and take stock. For what purpose has the figure of Abraham been introduced? What are the two opposing views about Abraham which clash here?

On the one side, there is the view that a Jew ipso facto is a descendant of Abraham and belongs to "the seed of Abraham." This matter of descent from Abraham was considered to be a crucial factor in Jewish identity. There were other factors involved also (like circumcision, observance of the foods laws,

---

45. As 2 Cor 11:3; cf. 1 Tim 2:14. Cf. also Wis 2:24: "It was the devil's envy which brought death into the world." See *1 En.* 69:6, which is possibly earlier than these writings, if the Similitudes are pre-Christian; *2 En.* 31:6 (which may possibly be first century AD). On 1 Tim 2:14, see Hanson, *Studies in the Pastoral Epistles*, 64-77.

46. Theobald, *Johannes*, 604-5.

47. Lincoln, *John*, 274, appositely recalls Deutero-Isaiah's indictment of those "who are called by the name of Israel . . . and invoke the God of Israel but not in truth or right" (48:1).

48. "Their reaction results from a condition prior to the historic mission of Jesus" (Barrett, *John*, 350).

observance of the sabbath, etc), but descent from Abraham was fundamental. Both John the Baptist (Luke 3:8 par.) and Paul (e.g., Rom 2:28; 9:1, esp. 4–5) offer evidence of this pride in Jewish ancestry.

On the other side, we see a stress on works as indicative of a person's identity. We meet the phrase "the works of Abraham" (8:39) and "Abraham did not do this" (8:40). The Jews were doing two things, both of which called in question their dual claim to have Abraham and God as their father. They were seeking to kill Jesus and they were refusing to accept the truth which he was seeking to pass on from the Father (the two are linked). Such behavior was not in line with the conduct of Abraham. Self-evidently, if Jesus was sent by God and spoke what he heard from God, then to reject him was to reject God—to reject the Son was to reject the Father who sent him and was speaking through him. Those who reject Jesus cannot, therefore, claim to have God as their Father; otherwise, they would love Jesus.

In other words, deeds reflect one's paternal origin. Deeds reflect the father whose child a person truly is. In the dualistic framework of the Fourth Gospel, there were only two possibilities: either one is a child of God (being a child of Abraham is subsumed under this greater category), or a child of the devil. By refusing the truth from Jesus and trying to kill him, the interlocutors show their parenthood to be the devil, who was a murderer and a liar from the beginning. To "hear" Jesus truly, to love him, is a sign that one belongs to God, that He is one's Father.

Underlying the whole debate thus far is really the question "Who are the members of the People of God?" One answer is firmly rejected—one is a member of the people of God through physical descent from Abraham. One can, however, be a child of Abraham and of God judged by another criterion. The basic identity marker is whether one truly hears Jesus, accepts his word as God's truth, believes in him as sent by God, and loves him: put briefly, it is a *Christological issue*, related to a *theological* one. Whether one is truly a child of Abraham and a child of *God* depends on one's relationship to *Jesus*. This is now the "badge" of God's people. Precisely because Jesus was the Son sent by the Father and because he embodied the Truth from the Father, any attempt to put Abraham alongside of Jesus was inadequate and wrong. Those Jews who believed in Jesus according to verse 31 seemed to want to do this (v. 33), but the evangelist rejected that position.[49]

---

49. It will emerge later in the dialogue (8:56) that Abraham is basically a witness to Jesus. He points away from himself to one far greater than himself. The evangelist would answer the question posed at 8:53, "Are you greater than our father Abraham?" with a resounding, "Yes he is!" (cf. the question at 4:12, concerning Jacob).

6.2.3. John 8:48–59

Verse 48 opens, "The Jews replied and said to him." Since he no longer speaks of the Jews who had believed in Jesus, as at verse 31, but "the Jews," did the evangelist intend by this to signal a *different* set of interlocutors?[50] Or has he now *merged the former in the general category "the Jews"* on the assumption that they have now regressed from their earlier position?[51] We might have expected a slightly clearer indication if the former were the case. Accordingly, we assume that the latter interpretation is probably correct. The issue does not really affect the interpretation of what follows.

The Jews' response to the long speech of Jesus (vv. 42–47) was to accuse him of being a Samaritan and of being demon-possessed. Given Jewish attitudes to the Samaritans, the former could carry the connotation of being heretical and schismatic and no longer part of the true covenant with God;[52] in other words, of siding with the Samaritans who challenged the right of Jews to be the people of God. The latter term implied that he was part of the domain of Satan himself and dabbled in magic (v. 48). Jesus denied these charges, and contrasted his attitude to the Father and their attitude to him, the Father's representative: "But I honor my Father, whereas you dishonor me" (v. 49). Their dishonoring him, the Father's representative, amounted, in fact, to a dishonoring of the Father Himself (cf. 5:23). Coupled with the declaration that he was seeking the honor of the Father was the claim that he was not seek his own glory, i.e., he was acting as an envoy should act in seeking the honor and glory of his Sender. There was One, viz. God, who was his Sender, who would in fact see to his glory[53] and pass judgment on what he was doing—and on what they were doing (v. 50).[54]

Then comes the claim: "Truly, truly, if anyone keeps my word, they will never see death"[55] (v. 51). The dialogue had begun with a statement

---

50. This is the position of Siker, *Disinheriting*, 128.

51. Dodd, *Johannine Dialogue*, 46, believed that for the evangelist these Christians have emptied their faith of its contents and they are where they were before they made the act of faith recorded in verse 30. Having assumed this merging for earlier in the dialogue, Theobald does not discuss the issue at verse 48 in his commentary.

52. Schnackenburg, *John*, 2:218, suggests that heresy, blasphemous claims, and "adulterous" idolatry might all be embodied in the Jewish mind for being a Samaritan.

53. It is natural to supply "my glory" from the first part of verse 50.

54. Beasley-Murray, *John*, 136-37, says that "Jesus depicts a court scene in which he and his adversaries appear before God." Theobald, *Johannes*, 614: "God's court case with the unbelieving world is in full swing."

55. That is, "will die"; cf. the idiom "to taste death" in verse 52 and Mark 9:1. Cf. the statements made in 5:19–29.

that emphasized the importance of the word of Jesus. Here, yet again, that importance is stressed. The astonished Jews object:

> Now we know that you have a demon. Abraham died, as did the prophets. And you say, If someone keeps my word, they will never taste death. Are you greater than our father Abraham who died, as indeed the prophets. Whom are you making yourself out to be? (vv. 52–53)

Here Abraham and the prophets appear as great figures of Israel's history who died.[56] Jesus' claim seemed ridiculous when set against the fact of their mortality.

In reply, Jesus picked up the theme of glory mentioned earlier in verse 50:

> If I glorify myself, my glory will count for nothing.
> It is my Father who will glorify me, of Whom you say "He is our[57] God."
> You do not know Him, but I know Him.
> If I were to say that I do not know Him, I would be a liar like you.
> But I do know Him and I keep His word. (vv. 54–55)

Jesus began his answer by referring to his approach as the Father's Envoy. As such, his business was to bring glory, honor, and success to his Sender. If Jesus were to depart from this rule and seek his own glory, honor, and success, in actual fact such an attempt would be fruitless. Paradoxically, it is the Father who will glorify His Son and Envoy (in the cross, as 12:23 and 17:1 show. This is a case where more than one reading of the Gospel would be necessary for this allusion to the cross to become clear).[58] Although the Jews claimed that God was their and his God (as fellow Jews), they in fact did not really know Him, whereas Jesus can claim rightly to know Him (to deny this would make him a liar and put him alongside his interlocutors, whose claim was false—and again proved that they belonged to the father of lies). Because he knows God, Jesus can reveal Him. "The issue is that of how the one true God is known."[59]

---

56. Interestingly, Moses is not mentioned. Perhaps this was because one strand of Jewish tradition had elaborated the mysterious account of his death (Deut 34) into the idea that he was translated into heaven. See Jeremias, "Μωυσης," *TWNT* 4:854–55.

57. ημων is the more difficult reading and to be preferred on that ground to υμων, despite the fact that P66 has υμων.

58. For a discussion of this passage and a defence of this interpretation, see my *Cross*, 73–74.

59. Lincoln, *John*, 275. Cf. what Moloney, *John*, 276, said on 8:33: "The clash emerges

With verses 56-58 we come to the climax and key to the whole debate.

Abraham your father rejoiced to see my day.
He saw (it) and rejoiced.

The Jews object that Jesus was not even fifty years old. So how could he claim to have seen[60] Abraham (v. 57)? Jesus replied:

Truly, truly, I say to you,
Before Abraham was, I AM. (v. 58)

These verses contain the answer to the question from the Jews as to whether Jesus was greater than Abraham. To what is the phrase about Abraham's seeing the day of Jesus and rejoicing referring? A number of interpretations have been put forward. We may mention, firstly, the view that there may be a reference to the speculation which grew up around the episode of Genesis 15:9-21. Abraham prepared a sacrifice, as commanded. When dusk fell, he dropped off to sleep. Some Jewish interpreters said that God gave Abraham a vision of paradise, of the age to come, when he was asleep.[61] Then, secondly, some interpreters favor taking the reference to Abraham's rejoicing as his laughter (viewed in a positive light) at the news of Isaac's birth at Genesis 17:17: he saw beyond the birth of Isaac, the immediate bearer of God's promise, to the coming of the one who would be the fulfillment of God's saving purposes and promises.[62] Thirdly, some suggest that Abraham was alive in Paradise and so saw the day of Jesus.[63] Fourthly, Abraham's vision in the Apocalypse of Abraham (29:14-31; 30-31) has been suggested as a basis.[64] Finally, there is the view that there are two distinct actions in mind here: he "rejoiced" (Gen 17:17) and "he saw

---

between two differing understandings of the way in which God is made known."

60. εωρακας (read by P66 ac A Bc D and many others) is the harder reading, compared with εωρακεν σε (read by P75 and a*), and is to be preferred.

61. Strathmann, *Das Evangelium nach Johannes*, 153; Barrett, *John*, 351-52; Moloney, *John*, 294; Lincoln, *John*, 276, all follow this explanation. See *4 Ezra* 3:14 (which refers to God's love for and choice of Abraham, and then adds, "To him alone, secretly, at the dead of night, you showed how the world would end"); *2 Bar.* 4:4. LAB 23:6 refers to the night vision but does not relate it to the events of the age to come. According to Genesis Rabbah 44:25, R. Akiba said that God revealed both this world and the world to come to him. R. Eliezer deduced this idea from Genesis 24:1 ("he went into the days").

62. Supported by Wikenhauser, *Das Evangelium nach Johannes*, 185; Hoskyns, *John*, 348; Schnackenburg, *John*, 2:221-22; Dietzfelbinger, *Johannes*, 268-69; Theobald, *Johannes*, 619; and listed as a possibility by Wilckens, *Das Evangelium nach Johannes*, 152.

63. Bultmann, *John*, 326; Sanders and Mastin, *John*, 234.

64. See Esler, *Introverted Sectarianism*, 88-89.

(it)" (Abraham is alive in Paradise).⁶⁵ A few commentators are unwilling to affirm a specific background.

The following points should be borne in mind. Firstly, the words και ειδεν could be a way of emphasizing the fact rather than indicating a separate and distinct act from "he rejoiced to see." If this is correct, the fifth view above need not be considered. Secondly, John 5:28–29 suggests that the dead are regarded as in the tombs until the resurrection. In any case, "he saw and rejoiced" refer to the past. This would exclude the third view above. The parallel with "Isaiah saw his glory" (12:41) suggests a reference to the ministry (possibly the cross-exaltation) of Jesus. In other words, in the case of both Abraham and Isaiah, a prophetic vision of the future is in mind. This favors the first view above. Finally, there are enough references in Jewish literature roughly contemporary with the Fourth Gospel and a little later to the fact that God gave Abraham a vision of the age to come to suggest that the evangelist was taking over the idea for his own Christological purposes.⁶⁶ On the whole, the arguments favor the view that there is reference to the vision granted to Abraham on the occasion of the event mentioned in Genesis 15. It is clear that there is a complete gulf between Abraham and the Jews who are talking with Jesus.⁶⁷

Clearly, this claim was offensive to the Jews who point out that Jesus was not yet fifty years old; so, how could he claim that he had seen Abraham? (v. 57).⁶⁸ Jesus then enunciated his "I AM" claim: πριν Αβρααμ γενεθαι εγω ειμι. This is an example of the absolute use of εγω ειμι, i.e., without an accompanying predicate.⁶⁹ It is related to the divine self-revelatory formula given to Moses in Exodus 3:14 and to the form *ani hu*, taken as an equivalent of this formula, in Isaiah 41:4; 43:10; 46:4; 48:12;

---

65. Lindars, *John*, 334–35. The idea of two actions is firmly rejected by Hoskyns, *Fourth Gospel*, 347; Brown, *John*, 1:359; Schnackenburg, *John*, 2:222–23; Beasley-Murray, *John*, 139; Carson, *John*, 357.

66. Beasley-Murray, *John*, 138, quotes Schlatter as saying that to say that Abraham saw the Messiah was neither new nor offensive to Jewish teachers; it was its application to Jesus that was unbelievable. That the evangelist has *used the tradition for his own Christological purposes* counters the objection raised by Theobald, *Johannes*, 618, that in the Jewish tradition of the nocturnal vision of Genesis 15 there is no mention of the Messiah.

67. "What a contrast, not to say gulf, between Abraham and these descendants of his!" (Beasley-Murray, *John*, 138).

68. Yet another instance of misunderstanding used by the author to prepare for an important announcement.

69. In agreement with Barrett, *John*, 352; Carson, *John*, 358; Lincoln, *John*, 276, and against Bultmann, *John*, 3217n4; Lindars, *John*, 336; Beasley-Murray, *John*, 139; Moloney, *John*, 284.

52:6, which the LXX rendered as εγω ειμι. The Johannine Jesus takes upon himself the divine name of God in the OT. As the Son and Envoy, he is the representative of the Father to men and women. In that capacity, the use of the title is (as it were) permissible and appropriate. Presupposed, of course, is the utter and complete obedience of this Son and Envoy to the Father (e.g., 6:38). What he says is what the Father has given him to say; what he does are the works given him by the Father to accomplish. He always does what is pleasing to the Father. His food is to do the Father's will and accomplish His work. He does not seek his own glory or honor. He can do nothing except what he sees the Father doing.

The other side of the coin is "The Father loves the Son and has given all things into his hand" (3:35). Included in these "all things" are the power to give life and to execute judgment (5:21–23, 26–27). God has vested in the Son these supreme attributes and prerogatives of His, but always the Son's dependence on the Father is the basis (6:57).

The contrast between Abraham and Jesus is underlined by the different tenses used. The aorist middle infinitive γενεσθαι is used in respect of Abraham—he came to be at a certain point, but of Jesus, εγω ειμι. As the Word he existed before time with the Father, and he will return home to the Father via the cross.[70] Barrett states "The meaning here is; Before Abraham came into being, I eternally was, as now I am, and ever continue to be."[71] The saying "Before Abraham was, I AM," then, constitutes a statement of pre-existence. However the evangelist came to that conviction, here it is stated unambiguously. It fits in with the descent-ascent picture used throughout the Gospel, and of Jesus' coming from the Father/heaven and returning to Him, having accomplished His commission; or Jesus' going back to his Father's home.

As Schnackenburg rightly points out, however, this is not a statement about the metaphysical significance of Jesus, but a statement which provides "the basis of his promise of salvation to us . . . Christology is part of soteriology."[72]

---

70. Cf. Hoskyns, *Fourth Gospel*, 349: "The contrast is between an existence initiated by birth and an absolute existence."

71. Barrett, *John*, 352.

72. Schnackenburg, *John*, 2:223; cf. Beasley-Murray, *John*, 139; Theobald, *Johannes*, 620.

6.3. Summary

What then is the use to which the evangelist puts the figure of Abraham? Abraham is used as a witness to Jesus who, as God's Son and Envoy, far surpasses the patriarch, who is the revered head of Israel, God's people, and who is called "the friend of God." As Theobald has put it, Abraham is no longer a living figure of identification for the Johannine community.[73] The evangelist used the Jewish elaboration of the Biblical record for his own purposes. Some Jewish interpreters said that God gave Abraham a vision of that age to come. The evangelist said in effect that Jesus was the embodiment of the age to come. What Abraham rejoiced to see has come to pass; it has been realized and actualized. Jesus was in fact the fulfillment of Abraham's vision, of what God allowed the patriarch to see in advance.[74]

The claim of John 8:58 is firm and bold assertion, appeal, and defence, all rolled into one. It *asserts* that the divine presence is encountered in Jesus; in Jesus God is present in the flesh (cf. 1:14). It *appeals* to the Jews to see that Abraham was witnessing to something or someone greater than himself-the Scriptures bear witness to Jesus, if the Jews could only perceive this. It *defends* the claim of the Christian community to be the people of God. Like John the Baptist, Abraham must decrease and Jesus increase. Still respected, Abraham must, however, give way to one far greater than himself: Jesus the Messiah, the Son of God.

It is worth mentioning what John's Gospel does not mention in connection with the story of Abraham.[75] The evangelist does not take up the great promises of Genesis 12; 15; and 17. He does not mention Abraham's faith which resulted in his being justified before God, and becoming the father of believers; he does not pick up the idea that the nations will be blessed through the seed of Abraham. All is concentrated on Abraham as the witness to Jesus, Messiah, Son of God and Envoy of the Father.

---

73. Theobald, *Johannes*, 619.

74. Esler, *Introverted Sectarianism,* 89, is right to say that in John's view descent from Abraham is nothing in comparison with believing in Jesus, but goes too far with his sweeping assertion that Abraham is irrelevant to the Christian community. Even if John does not use the verb "to witness" of Abraham, in fact, Abraham is one of the many witnesses to Jesus (as was Isaiah, according to John 12:41). Theobald, *Johannes*, 619, suggested that being children of Abraham had lost its meaning for the Johannine community's self-understanding and that, rather, "children of God" was the decisive ecclesiological model (cf. Theobald, "Abraham—[Isaak]—Jakob," 180. He believes that it was the uncertainty of the identity of his community in face of the overpowerful synagogue which spoiled for the evangelist the awareness of the rooting of the church in Israel and its fathers [183]).

75. See the comments in Dietzfelbinger, *Johannes*, 264–65.

Excursus: Is John Anti-Semitic?

Before we conclude this chapter, it might be as well to examine the issue of whether the evangelist is anti-Semitic. Since that term as applied to the first century AD is probably anachronistic, it is better to use the term anti-Jewish. Our section of the Gospel is one of the major reasons why this accusation has been raised against this evangelist. He is accused of demonizing the Jews, of a blanket condemnation of the Jews for rejecting Jesus. To many Christians it is a matter of embarrassment that the Jews are branded as children of the devil in a Gospel within the canon of the authoritative sacred Scriptures of the Christian Church.

What may be said in response to this? In the first place, polemical speaking and writing was conducted then in a much more fierce, "no holds barred" manner than would be acceptable today.[76] One only has to think of Isaiah's calling the leaders and people of Judea and Jerusalem, "You rulers of Sodom . . . you people of Gomorrah" (1:10). Given the reputation of Sodom and Gomorrah in ancient times, one can hardly think of a greater insult to level at some one else. Also, in the eighth century BC, Hosea's comparison of Israel with an adulterous wife and from the next century Ezekiel's elaboration of this comparison in Ezekiel 16 are both devastating critiques of their own people's behavior.[77]

In the Qumran literature, non-members of the community (still fellow Israelites) are branded children of Belial, sons of darkness, who will suffer destruction at the End. John the Baptist can describe even the people[78] who came to hear him preach as "You offspring of vipers" (Luke 3:7). Jesus himself had some trenchant things to say about the Pharisees and teachers of the Law (Luke 11:39-48, 52)[79] and could collectively brand his generation as "evil" (Luke 11:29).

In the post-Easter church, Paul can wade into his opponents, Jews like himself, in no uncertain terms, branding them as "ministers of Satan" (2

---

76. Indeed this continued to be so for centuries. Consider the so-called saintly Thomas More's abuse of William Tyndale and Tyndale's equally harsh response in the early sixteenth century, or the Presbyterian Thomas Edwards's smear tactics against the early Baptists in his *Gangraena* during the 1640s, just to name but a very few examples of pamphlet warfare in England in the sixteenth and seventeenth centuries.

77. See Lincoln, *Gospel according to John*, 272-73, for passages in the OT and some from early Judaism where a similarly harsh polemic occurs against the nation.

78. Probably the original reading in Q. Less likely is "the Pharisees and Sadducees" according to Matthew 3:7 (probably Matthean editing).

79. The parallel Matthew 23 has undergone heavy editing in an anti-Pharisaic direction.

Cor 11:13–15) and workers of evil (Phil 3:2).[80] John of Patmos dubs the Synagogue at Smyrna and that at Philadelphia as "the Synagogue of Satan" (Rev 2:9; 3:9). Fierce attacks on those deemed "heretical" are also present in the Pastoral Epistles, Jude, and 2 Peter.

It should be noted, secondly, that in all these instances it is not a case of attacking the Jews as Jews, as Semites. Theological differences lie at the heart of the disagreement. The person of Jesus, the role of the Law and Jewish customs, the relation of Jew and Gentile to the purposes of God, the issue of who was the true people of God—all these issues were "provoked" by the ministry, death, resurrection, and exaltation of Jesus, and the coming of the Spirit. *These were the issues of the conflict—theological questions, not a racial antipathy.*[81]

Thirdly, would the evangelist have included on the lips of his Jesus "Salvation is of the Jews" (4:22b), if he had really been anti-Jewish? Would he virtually have constructed his Gospel in such a way as to show Jesus fulfilling what had been expressed in the OT, in the Temple, in the Jewish feasts[82] and symbols? Would the evangelist claim that Moses was a witness to Jesus, indeed that the Scriptures as a whole were, if he were anti-Jewish?

Fourthly, John's dualism must be borne in mind. This is not an ontological dualism, in which people's position is irrevocably fixed, but it is a "dualism of decision," to use Bultmann's famous phrase.[83] John sees two spheres of power, ruled over by God and the devil respectively. A person is either in the light or darkness, truth or falsehood, above or below, not of the world or of this world. All is black or white; there are no intermediate shades of grey. If one is not of God, then one must ipso facto be of the devil.[84]

---

80. "Concision" in Philippians 3:2 would be deemed highly offensive, as also "their god is their belly" at 3:19.

81. This is not to deny that theological convictions and sociological consequences may go hand in hand. On John 8:12–20, Grässer, "Die antijüdische Polemik," 144, has pointed out that Jewish issues are not discussed but rather solely Jesus' coming and going and what that means for the sake of the world. He maintains (151) that the *primary* motive for the anti-Jewish polemic lies "in John's theological reflection on Jesus" having come as the κρισις of the world.

82. Cf. the remark of Motyer, *Your Father the Devil?*, 124, "Each festival is hijacked for the Christian faith, as Jesus is portrayed as its true or real counterpart."

83. E.g., Bultmann, *Theology of the New Testament*, 2:21; Lincoln, *John*, 273, calls it an epistemological and ethical dualism.

84. Grässer, "Die antijüdische Polemik," 152–53, stresses this aspect: "But this polemic is a part of Johannine dualism in the service of the practical interests of the community." See also his "Die Juden als Teufelssöhne," 160, 163.

Finally, Stephen Motyer's description of John 8:31–59 as a prophetic appeal deserves serious consideration.[85] Motyer suggests that the prophet acted for Israel's good: he shocks to deter so that judgment might not happen. Here is Jew speaking to Jew (within the family).[86] He argues that the charge in 8:44 and 47 has ethical, not ontological force.[87] The passage functions as a warning against the power and influence of the devil.[88]

All in all, we believe that the charge that the fourth evangelist was anti-Jewish is seriously flawed. It rests on an inadequate reading of the text, and owes more to revulsion against the Holocaust in our own day than exegesis of John's Gospel itself.[89]

---

85. Motyer, *Your Father*, esp. 160–208

86. Motyer, *Your Father*, 212.

87. Motyer, *Your Father*, 185.

88. Motyer, *Your Father*, 198.

89. Nothing said in this paragraph should be construed as indicating that I do not share the dismay at the way Christians have treated the Jews down the centuries.

7

Abraham in the Gospel of Matthew

7.1. Introduction

THE GOSPEL OF MATTHEW was probably composed in approximately the same time span as the Gospel of John and, like it, also reflects the bitter conflict with the Synagogue from which the members of the Matthean congregation had been expelled or separated themselves.[1] While the evangelist directed his writing primarily to strengthen and challenge the faith of members of his congregation, at the same time the discernible apologetic interests serve that purpose too.

7.2. The Genealogy

The Gospel opens with a genealogy of Jesus,[2] which begins with the heading at 1:1:

---

1. The debate whether the Matthean community had actually separated from the main body of Judaism and had organized itself accordingly or whether it continued to be a part of but a deviant part of Judaism continues to be discussed. See the brief discussion in the Excursus at the end of this chapter.

2. It is not necessary for us to go into all the issues which Matthew's genealogy raises (e.g., the appearance of four women in the genealogy).

Βίβλος γενέσεως of Jesus (the) Christ, (the) Son of David, (the) Son of Abraham.[3]

The word γένεσις also occurs at 1:18, as the introduction to the pericope which follows the genealogy of Jesus. For this reason, many scholars assume that the word is used with the same meaning in both verses, and so translate 1:18 with the some such phrase as "the birth" or "birth record" of Jesus.[4] However, it is not impossible that the evangelist did use the word with different nuances because the word is part of the introduction of two different items, viz. a genealogy[5] and a story (1:18-25) designed to defend the inclusion of Jesus in the Davidic line, when Joseph was not the biological father[6] (see further below).

Some scholars suggest that the evangelist intended the phrase to carry more than one meaning, and so introduce the genealogy, the birth, and the whole book.[7]

The genealogy is rounded off with the comment:

> All the generations from Abraham to David are fourteen generations, and (those) from David to the deportation to Babylon are fourteen generations; and (those) from the deportation to Babylon until the Messiah are fourteen generations. (1:17)

Actually, this is not correct! Simplifying matters, one can mention that in the first section there are only fourteen if Abraham is counted twice (i.e., as someone begotten as well as someone who begat Isaac); three kings are omitted from the second section;[8] while in the third section there are only

---

3. This translation assumes that Χριστός, though anarthous, is actually used as a title, and that the same holds good of Son of David and Son of Abraham. Cf. the translation of the NRSV. Apart from the commentaries, Matthew 1:1 is the subject of a detailed study by Carter, *Matthean Christology*.

4. So the GN translation; Brown, *Birth*, 57. The RV put "birth" in the margin for both 1:1 and 18, preferring "generation" in the main text.

5. Gnilka, *Matthäusevangelium*, 1:2, 14, translates the two occurrences differently. He relates 1:1 to the genealogy (7) and verse 18 to the birth (16). Similarly, see Beare, *Gospel according to Matthew*, 61, 66.

6. For this function of 1:18-25, see Stendahl, "*Quis et Unde*," 94-105; Vögtle, *Die Genealogie*, 242-47; Frankemölle, *Jahwebund und Kirche Christi*, 13, 310. Also, the quotation of Isaiah 7:14 serves to underline that God caused Jesus to be miraculously conceived and indicated, by the name people (possibly the Matthean church) would give him, that God would be in the midst of His people to save it (Vögtle, *Genealogie*, 244). We need not here discuss the suggestion that Matthew 1:18-21, 24-25, were pre-Matthean material, into which the evangelist has inserted the quotation from Isaiah 7:14 (so, e.g., Davis, *Tradition and Redaction*, 404-421).

7. So Beare, *Matthew*, 64; Davies and Allison, *Matthew*, 1:149-55.

8. Namely, Ahaziah, Jehoash, and Amaziah between Jehoram and Uzziah at verse

thirteen (only by counting Jechoniah twice, i.e., in both the second and third sections, do fourteen generations appear in the third section). As to the omission of the kings, this could have arisen accidentally through the similarity of the names in the Greek[9] rather than due to a deliberate omission to secure the number fourteen.[10] As to the presence of only thirteen generations in the third section, it is not easy to explain this.[11]

Some scholars have suggested that fourteen by three is equivalent to seven by six, with, therefore, Jesus representing the seventh, i.e., perfection/ completion. But the weakness of this suggestion is that Matthew has not drawn attention to this notion.[12]

What we do know is that there were fourteen generations from Abraham to David according to the tradition recorded in 1 Chronicles 2:1-15 and Ruth 4:12, and this is the period which included the two important figures, Abraham and David, both recipients of vitally important promises from God.[13] We also know that many Jewish writings during the period ca. 200 BC to 200 AD did envisage the periodization of history under divine control. It is probable that Matthew "taps into" this approach in the genealogy of Jesus which he presented with his comment at 1:17. The genealogy has a kerygmatic purpose rather than a strictly historical one. It proclaims the conviction that the appearance of Jesus was due to the providential overruling of history by God, who led history to the goal which He intended.[14]

---

9. A fourth, Jehoiachim, the second son of Josiah and the father of Jechoniah and Zedekiah, is omitted at verse 11. See Davies and Allison, *Matthew*, 1:176-79, for details.

9. So Johnson, *Purpose of the Biblical Genealogies*, 181-82; Brown, *Birth*, 82.

10. Brown, *Birth*, 75, does not think that it is credible that the evangelist omitted the names deliberately and then drew attention to it as something marvelous and implicitly providential.

11. See the detailed but inconclusive discussion in Davies and Allison, *Matthew*, 1:178-79. Brown, *Birth*, 83-84, suggests that the last line of the second section should have read "Jehoiakim and his brothers" and the first line of the third section "Jehoiakim was the father of Jechoniah." Matthew recognized this and assumed it. But, one may ask, why did he not put matters right? Brown admits that it is only with such ingenuity that one can salvage Matthew's reputation as a mathematician! The suggestion that Matthew distinguishes between Jesus and his becoming Messiah (at the resurrection) is unconvincing and flounders on the fact that Matthew sees Jesus as the Messiah and Son of God from birth.

12. For skepticism about this suggestion, see Brown, *Birth*, 75.

13. Vögtle, *Genealogie*, 37, stresses this point.

14. Vögtle, *Genealogie*, 242, 48; Frankenmölle, *Jahwebund*, 309, 312; Gnilka, *Matthäusevangelium*, 1:11.

In Jesus, the story of Israel reached its God-intended climax.[15] Jesus was God's appointed Messiah, the Son of David, the Son of Abraham.[16]

Matthew, then, proclaimed Jesus as the Messiah, the Son of David and the Son of Abraham.[17] We shall make brief comments on Messiah and Son of David before examining Jesus as Son of Abraham.

7.3. Jesus as the Messiah and Son of David

When the wise men reached Jerusalem, they enquired where the King of the Jews was to be born (2:2). Herod sought information from the chief priests and the scribes of the people where the Messiah should be born. They replied:

> In Bethlehem of Judea, for thus it has been written by the prophet: "And you, Bethlehem (in) the land of Judah, are by no means least among the rulers of Judah, for from you a ruler shall arise, who will shepherd my people, Israel." (2:4-6, quoting Mic 5:2, with an addition from 2 Sam 5:2).

Those addressed by Matthew would presumably know that Bethlehem was the birthplace of David. The quotation of Micah 5:2 plus 2 Samuel 5:2 served to underline the link of Jesus with his ancestor, David, and act as some counterweight to the strong link of David with the city of Jerusalem which he had conquered and made the capital of the union of the ten northern tribes with Judah and Benjamin, and to which he had brought the ark.[18] Though

---

15. Cf. Davies and Allison, *Matthew*, 1:187.

16. Johnson, *Purpose*, 77-82, after listing nine different purposes of genealogies in the OT, concludes with the observation: "The genealogical form could be used as an alternative to narrative or poetic forms of expression, that is, as one of several methods of writing history and of expressing the theological and nationalistic concerns of a people." Brown, *Birth*, 85, refers to the 1972 Yale dissertation of R. R. Wilson (summarized in an article, "OT Genealogies in Recent Research," 168-89), who makes the point that it was possible to have conflicting genealogies of the same person if those genealogies had different purposes.

17. Carter, *Matthean Christology*, 143-65, after repeating a criticism, which he had made previously in several works, that Matthean scholarship has neglected the political and socio-economic aspects in the background of the addressees of Matthew's Gospel, examines each of the phrases or words in Matthew 1:1 He believes that each in its own way points to a social order which challenges Rome's imperial claims and oppressive rule. The reference to Jesus as Son of Abraham is meant to evoke Genesis 12:1-3 and point to the inclusion of Jew and Gentile in God's purpose in contrast to the abundant prejudices and social divisions which existed under Roman rule and which reflected and reinforced the exclusion of so many from a decent standard of living.

18. See Psalm 78:67-72 for the joint election of Zion/Jerusalem and David. Jewish

this is, from a formal point of view, not a "fulfillment quotation," it does fulfill exactly the same function. That Jesus was born in Bethlehem accords with what God had laid down in Scripture for the Messiah.[19]

Matthew edits his Q source about John the Baptist's question from prison to Jesus. Matthew said that it was when he heard about the works *of the Messiah* that John sent his enquiry to Jesus (11:2).[20] Matthew took over from Mark the Petrine confession at Caesarea Phillipi, but added "Son of the living God" to Messiah (16:16).[21] Then Matthew adds, over against his Marcan source, verses 17-19.[22] Within the beatitude pronounced on Peter Jesus refers to "my Father" which fits in with the confession that he is the Son of the living God. Then, in the secrecy command immediately following, Matthew recorded that Jesus told them not to tell anyone that he was the Messiah (16:20).[23] This removed any note of reserve towards the messianic confession which is discernible in the Marcan account. Jesus affirmed what Simon had just said, which had been revealed to him by God and had not sprung from his own insight or capability.

Of the remaining eight occurrences of Χριστός, most come from his Marcan source, including the two references to those who falsely claim to be the messiah (Matt 24:5, 23). In a series of conflict stories, one dispute concerned the idea that the Messiah would be a son (meaning descendant) of David (Matt 22:41-46//Mark 12:35-37).[24] Matthew rephrased Mark's

---

sources do not indicate that there was a belief that the coming messiah would be born at Bethlehem. See Davies and Allison, *Matthew*, 1:226.

19. Rochfuchs, *Die Erfüllungszitate*, 60-61, suggests that in addition to the interest in the question of the birthplace of Jesus, there is also an interest in the "my people" via 2 Sam 5:2. Jesus will save God's people and God appoints him as leader/shepherd of His people.

20. Luke 7:18 simply says that "John's disciples told him about all these things," i.e., what Jesus had been doing and saying as reported by Luke in his previous account.

21. See pages 301-2 below for what might be the doctrinal implications of this addition of "Son of the living God."

22. For detailed discussions of the history of the tradition of Matthew 16:13-23, see Vögtle, *Messiasbekenntnis und Petrusverheissung*, 1:252-72; 2:85-103; *Zur Problem der Herkunft*, 372-93; Gnilka, *Matthäusevangelium*, 2:46-80; Davies and Allison, *Matthew*, 2:602-647

23. Mark 8:30 has that they should tell no one about him. In Matthew 16:21, the evangelist has: "From then on, Jesus Christ began to show his disciples, etc."—the first hand of ℵ and B is strong support for this reading of Jesus Christ (the majority of manuscripts read ο Ιησους), though it is possible that the occurrence of Χριστός at 16:16 and 20 influenced the copyists.

24. See Schneider, "Die Davidssohnfrage," 65-90, for a thorough review of scholarly opinion on the Marcan passage from K. Schmidt to 1972, together with Schneider's own analysis. He believed that the pericope does not go back to Jesus; that 12:35b-37a

"How (is it that) the scribes say that the Messiah is David's son?" (Mark 12:35), so that the question now runs "What opinion do you hold about the Messiah? Whose son is he?" It is now his interlocutors who say "David's" (Matt 22:42). In what in Mark's version is a single utterance from Jesus now becomes a genuine discussion with both sides participating. In the end, there is, however, no difference of sense. Presumably early Christians like Matthew interpreted the pericope as indicating that, while Jesus did not deny the Davidic descent of the Messiah, there is much more to be said about the person of Jesus than descent from David. He is Lord.[25] Possibly, it is implied that he is Son of God.[26]

What Boobyer claimed to be true of Mark[27] could also apply to Matthew: viz. that it would be possible to take the Greek of Psalm 109:1 (MT 110:1) as indicating that the messianic Lord was existent in heaven at the time of the composition of the psalm. In other words, Psalm 109:1 LXX indicated that David knew his messianic Lord was then in heaven with God rather than that he foresaw something which only became true at the resurrection of Jesus.

While there are scholars who think that Jesus/pre-Marcan tradition/Mark in fact did deny that Davidic descent was in any way relevant as a criterion for discerning Messiahship,[28] that seems an unlikely suggestion in view

---

is pre-Marcan material, which asserted that David used "Lord" for the messiah, as Christians were doing; and that Mark was responsible for the framework of verses 35a and 37b, and saw Son of David as a legitimate title, but interpreted it in a way different from political nationalistic expectations.

25. E.g., Luz, *Thesen zur Christologie des Matthäus*, 225.

26. Hummel, *Auseindersetzung*, 121, follows Wrede, in suggesting that the introductory "Whose son is he [viz. the Messiah]?" (Matt 22:42) implies more than one sonship, that also of Son of God. Gnilka, *Matthäusevangelium*, 2:266, is of the same opinion. He believes that for Matthew this pericope is a resumé of his Christology and that the three most significant Christological predicates—Lord, Son of David, and Son of God—are to be observed within it; cf. Davies and Allison, *Matthew*, 3:256. Some commentators refer to Romans 1:3–4 with its confession of Jesus as Son of David according to the flesh, and Son of God on the basis of the resurrection (Beare, *Matthew*, 445). However, for Matthew, Jesus was Son of God from birth—as 2:15 shows.

27. Boobyer, *Mark 12:35–37*, 393–94.

28. See, e.g., Burger, *Jesus als Davidssohn*, 52–59, who believes that the material of Mark 12:35–37 is the creation of a church which knew that Jesus was not a descendant of David and which had to dispute the Jewish postulate of the Davidic origin of the messiah, and used Psalm 110. Mark has thus taken into his gospel traditions to which the thought of Jesus' Davidic sonship was strange, but he reinterprets them in the sense of Jesus' surpassing Davidic sonship. Jesus is more than the Son of David; he is the Son of God.

of the fact that in the whole of the NT Jesus' Davidic descent is accepted and proclaimed.[29] It may be confidently rejected in the case of Matthew.

The discourse directed against the scribes and Pharisees in Matthew 23 opens with some initial criticisms of them in verses 2-6, the final one mentioning their love of public greetings and their being called "Rabbi." Then Jesus suddenly turns to the disciples:

> But as for you, don't you be called Rabbi, for there is one who is your teacher and all of you are brothers. And don't call (anyone) on earth your father, for there is one who is your Heavenly Father. And don't be called Teacher, because the Messiah is your teacher. (vv. 7-10)

Whether that can be satisfactorily explained from a setting within the actual ministry[30] or whether it is a little section shaped by the pre-Matthean tradition or by the evangelist and directed from the very start to the Matthean church,[31] is a question that can be left on one side here. Suffice to say that it clearly does address the Matthean church and is intended as a direct message to leaders. It reveals a clear belief that Jesus is the Messiah.

Matthew edits Mark's report of the interrogation of Jesus by the high priest. After recording the statements of false witnesses against Jesus, the high priest asked why Jesus had made no effort to respond to what they had said. Jesus still continued to maintain his silence. So the high priest continued in an effort to force Jesus to say something. In Mark his words are a direct question "Are you the Messiah, the son of the Blessed One?" (14:62), while in Matthew he opens with "I adjure you by the living God"—which makes his words more solemn—"that you tell us whether you are the Messiah, the Son of God." There is a striking difference between what is Jesus' reply in Mark and that in Matthew:

---

29. It is of course true that there were a number of messianic claimants in the first century who were not Davidic descendants, and in the second century Bar Kochba was not a descendant of David but rather was recognized as the messiah by no less a person than R. Akiba. There might have been Christians who thought that Davidic descent was not essential for messiahship and that we do not have evidence for their viewpoint. The almost universally recognized pre-Pauline formula quoted in Romans 1:3-4 looks like evidence for a two stage Christology—Son of David in his earthly ministry; Son of God on the basis of the resurrection from the dead.

30. So apparently Morris, *Gospel according to Matthew*, 570, 577; France, *Matthew*, 325.

31. So most scholars, e.g., Haenchen, *Matthäus 23*, 43-45; Jeremias, *Prayers of Jesus*, 42. See Gnilka, *Matthäusevangelium*, 2:272n9, for a list of the different views of the literary-critical origin of verses 8-10.

Mark 14:62 runs: "I am; and you will see the Son of Man seated at the right hand of Power and coming on the clouds of heaven" (variant reading: συ ειπας οτι Θ f13 472 543 565 700 arm Orig).

Matthew 26:64 runs: "You have said so (συ ειπας); but I tell you, from now on (απ' αρτι) you will see the Son of Man seated at the right hand of Power and coming on the clouds of heaven"

A comparison of the two versions has raised a number of exceedingly difficult questions and we cannot here go into them in great detail. Even if συ ειπας does not indicate an outright denial but places the onus for having put the matter that way onto the interlocutor,[32] it remains striking that Mark has the unambiguous acceptance of the two titles mentioned by the high priest, whereas Matthew, apparently using Mark as his source and writing later, has the more ambiguous response, especially as in Matthew Jesus accepted with enthusiasm the two title confession from Peter at Caesarea Philippi. The evidence surveyed so far suggests that Matthew fully accepted that Jesus was the Messiah and Son of God; so, did he have access to another tradition which contained the more ambiguously phrased reply, a tradition somewhat akin to that used by Luke 22:66-68, 70, and perhaps used and remolded at John 10:24-38?[33] That would be an unnecessary hypothesis if the reading of Q f13 565.700.arm.Orig. at Mark 14:62 were to be accepted, as Streeter and others have done,[34] thus eliminating one of the so-called agreements of Matthew and Luke against Mark. Perhaps Matthew felt that Jesus did not want to accept the titles in the sense in which the high priest may have used them, but has Jesus continuing with πλην λεγω υμιν carrying a certain adversative sense, meaning but, nevertheless, however.

The less than direct acceptance of Messiah and Son of God here contrasts in one sense with the direct assertion about the Son of Man, especially given that Matthew's version opens with απ' αρτι, meaning from now on, which suggests *immediacy*.[35] But in what sense could Matthew

---

32. See Catchpole, *Answer of Jesus to Caiaphas*, 213-26. Gnilka, *Matthäusevangelium*, 2:428, maintains that the reply is intended in the affirmative and that Matthew has assimilated the high priest's question to Peter's confession. As to the latter point—this does not seem to be strictly accurate, as the phrase "living God" occurs in the oath formula and not with the title.

33. We would still be left with the question why Matthew preferred it.

34. Streeter, *Four Gospels*, 321-22; Taylor, *Gospel according to St. Mark*, 568. Cranfield, *Gospel according to St. Mark*, 444 ("intrinsically likely"). Robinson, *Jesus and His Coming*, 49, adopted a similar approach. Lohmeyer, *Das Evagelium des Markus*, 328, said that it could be original. It is strange that the UBS Greek NT does not mention this reading. More recent discussions of Mark 14:62 seem to be guided exclusively by theological rather than text-critical considerations.

35. Even Kruijf, *Der Sohn*, 98-99, who believes that the two phrases drawing on

envisage an immediate session of Jesus at God's right hand and a coming with the clouds?[36] Few scholars are prepared to consider that Matthew might have taken the two phrases "sitting at the right hand of Power" and "coming with the clouds of heaven" symbolically[37] and not literally. In a tantalizingly brief comment, Caird suggested that "the coming of the Son of Man was for [Matthew] not just an event at the end, but one which was to occur either continuously or repeatedly from the moment of the crucifixion."[38] If this possibility is rejected, one is left with the anomaly that an evangelist, who clearly edits his Marcan source quite freely at times, did not do so at a crucial point in the story and left an unfulfilled prophecy on the lips of Jesus, or preferred another tradition with its more reserved response on the part of Jesus.

The remaining two instances occur in the trial before Pilate, both on the lips of Pilate and add nothing for our purposes. Pilate is depicted as asking the crowd "Whom do you want me to release for you, Jesus the son of Barabbas, or Jesus who is called Messiah?"[39] (27:17). The chief priests incite the crowd to ask for Barabbas and Pilate in reply says "What shall I do with Jesus who is called Messiah?"(27:20-22).

On the basis of the evidence surveyed, we can say that the title Messiah is clearly of significance for Matthew. Equally, one could argue that the occurrence of "Son of God" is meant to deepen the significance of Messiah.[40] Thus its occurrence at 2:15 (in the form of "My Son"); at the baptism (also "My only [or beloved] Son" [3:17]); in the temptation story at 4:3 and 6,

---

Psalm 110:1 and Daniel 7:13 in 26:64 should be taken in parallel and interpreted together, says that the End Time, the kingdom of the Son of Man has already come *with the resurrection of Jesus*. Does not that weaken the απ' αρτι?

36. The same goes for Mark 14:62, "And you will see..." The explanation of Gnilka, *Matthäusevangelium*, 2:428-29, that the phrase marks the end of the work of Jesus in Israel and that, with this, the time of Israel has come to an end, does not seem very satisfactory.

37. The "sitting at the right hand of God" could be a static symbol of vindication (cf. Ps 110:1), while "coming on the clouds of heavens" would be a dynamic symbol of vindication (see the sense of the phrase in Daniel 7, where the human figure is brought to the Ancient of Days to be vindicated in the heavenly court).

38. Caird, *Language and Imagery of the Bible*, 252, 268.

39. Accepting Q fam1 700* syr(s) arm geo Orig, as the original reading, and assuming that scribes baulked at Barabbas having the name of Jesus.

40. Cf. Kingsbury, *Matthew*, 97-98. In this respect, one could say that Matthew is similar to the Fourth Evangelist, even though he does not develop any idea of the pre-existence of the Son of God. In 1:23, through the use of Isaiah 7:14, the evangelist indicated that Jesus would be called Immanuel, i.e., God is with us. Kingsbury, *Matthew*, 96, affirms: "In the person of Jesus Messiah, the Son of God, God has drawn near to dwell with his people, thus inaugurating the eschatological era of salvation."

together with the confession of the disciples at the time of the stilling of the storm ("Truly you are the Son of God" [14:33]); and the expansion of "the Messiah" of Mark 8:29 into "the Messiah, the Son of the living God" (16:16; cf. 26:64, the question of the high priest), all point in this direction. *But in what sense does it deepen Messiah?* The addressees of Matthew's Gospel know from the saying recorded in 11:27 that Jesus is the Son and has a unique relationship with the Father: "All things have been delivered to me by my Father, and no one knows the Son except the Father, and no one knows the Father except the Son and the person to whom the Son wills to reveal (Him)." Jesus, because of this relationship with the Father, carries out the role of exclusive revealer of the Father. A little later in the Gospel (14:22-33), Jesus is reported to come walking on the water to the disciples who are in difficulties in their boat on the Lake of Galilee. He rescues Peter who had stepped out of the boat to go to Jesus but had begun to sink. When the two had got into the boat, the wind dropped. The disciples in the boat worshipped him with the words "Truly you are the Son of God" (v. 33). The comment of Davies and Allison on this incident of Jesus walking on the water (14:22-33) is worth quoting: "Jesus exercises powers and displays attributes traditionally connected with God alone. . . . Jesus here exhibits an authority which the Jewish Scriptures associate exclusively with the deity . . . in Matthew's Gospel, God actively shares attributes characteristic of himself with another, his Son. The step towards the later ecumenical creeds, which affirm Christ's deity, appears undeniable."[41]

Thus, already by the time we have come to the Matthean Peter's confession of 16:16 we realize that the Matthean Jesus is somehow human and yet more than human.

Kruijf,[42] while accepting that Matthew would have thought less in metaphysical than in dynamic terms, was prepared to say that at 11:27 and 16:16 the thought of Jesus as the Son/Son of God goes beyond the functional and that Matthew was aware of the divinity of Jesus.[43] He thinks that the dynamic character rather than a static one predominates in Matthew's concept of Jesus as Son of God: that is, that Jesus shares in the authority and power of God. Davies and Allison on 16:16 commented: "The Messiah in Matthew is certainly a human figure. But he also stands in a special relation to God as God's Son. Unfortunately, we do not know how the First Evangelist conceptualized this, how exactly he thought of the person of Jesus. Did he conceive of him as transcending the traditional messianic categories

---

41. Davies and Allison, *Matthew*, 2:512.
42. See Kruijf, *Sohn*, 87, 138, 145-49.
43. Kruijf, *Sohn*, 147.

in such a way that Gundry's use of the term 'essential deity' is justified? Or would 'functional deity' be better. . . . Should one hazard that 'deity' is a significant implication of Matthew's Christology, as it was of John's? We only ask the question. We do not answer it."[44]

Many may think that Kruijf, Gundry, and Davies and Allison go too far. Nevertheless, that Jesus fulfills the Isaianic promise of one virgin-born who will be called Immanuel indicates clearly that for Matthew God was present in and through Jesus. Jesus was "the epiphany of God on earth"[45]; Jesus was Immanuel.

We turn now to the designation Son of David. We need to start with the pericope 1:18-25, which, as already mentioned, is a kind of appendix to the genealogy. Joseph was visited by an angel of the Lord who addressed him as Son of David and commanded him to do two things: he was to marry Mary his fiancée, whose pregnancy was due to the Holy Spirit; and to name the child to be born "Jesus," because he would save his people from their sins (vv. 20-21). Since he took Mary as his wife and named the child born of her as Jesus, in obedience to the command of the angel of the Lord, this meant that Joseph became the legal father of Jesus. So Jesus may be counted in the Davidic family tree, although the child was born of the action of the Holy Spirit on Mary. Thus, the way was prepared by this pericope for Jesus to be called Son of David.

The first such occurrence is at 9:27. The pericope as a whole (vv. 27-31) appears to be a Matthean creation, a doublet of his account of the healing of two blind men by Jesus at 20:29-34 (itself an edited version of Mark 10:46-52).[46] Two blind men followed Jesus and cried out, "Have mercy on us, Son of David." Jesus went into a house, and the blind men followed him. He asked them, "Do you believe that I am able to do this?" to which they replied, "Yes, Lord." Jesus responded by touching their eyes and saying: "Be it done to you according to your faith." Their eyes were opened, and Jesus charged them not to let anyone know, but they in fact noised the matter abroad (this secrecy command is reminiscent of Mark 1:44-45 which Matthew had not used at 8:1-4). Although Matthew's main concern was the theme of faith,[47] he showed that Jesus was recognized as

---

44. Davies and Allison, *Matthew*, 2:642. The reference to Gundry is to his *Matthew*, 330. Luz, *Thesen*, 235, ends his essay with the comment that Matthew's combination of what he calls the horizontal and vertical aspects in Matthean Christology contains "remarkable correspondences to later Church teaching on the two natures."

45. Frankemölle, *Jahwebund*, 19.

46. For details, see Held, *Matthew as Interpreter*, 219-22.

47. Held, *Interpreter*, 180.

the Son of David, i.e., Messiah, by those seeking healing like the blind.[48] A little later in the narrative, Matthew will record that Jesus answered John the Baptist's enquiry (prompted, the evangelist said, by hearing about the works of the Messiah [11:2]), by pointing to what he had been doing couched in scriptural phraseology mainly from Isaiah 35:4,[49] which was interpreted messianically in Judaism. Healing of the blind begins the list of what Jesus had been doing (11:5).

Matthew blended together both Marcan and Q material in his account of the Beelzebul controversy (Matt 12:22-30). In the introduction Jesus healed a blind and dumb person, to the amazement of the crowds, who commented "Can this be the Son of David?" (v. 23).[50] The Pharisees tried to quash this idea by the charge: "This fellow does not cast out demons except by Beelzebul, the prince of demons" (v. 24). We notice that for the second time the designation Son of David occurs in the context of the healing/exorcism work of Jesus.

The next occurrence is in the account of the healing of the Canaanite woman at 15:21-28 (in Mark she is a Syro-Phoenician woman). Matthew both abbreviated and expanded his Marcan source. After Jesus had left the district of Tyre and Sidon, a Canaanite woman came from that area, and on meeting Jesus called out "Have mercy on me, Lord, Son of David. My daughter is severely tormented by a demon" (15:22). Mark had reported the request in indirect speech with no title of respect ("She asked that he might cast the demon from her daughter" [Mark 7:26]). Once more, although Matthew's primary concern is the theme of faith and its significance for Gentiles (see 15:28),[51] he has brought the title Son of David into a healing miracle.

The Son of David title occurs twice in Mark 10:46-52 on the lips of blind Bartimaeus in his request that Jesus should heal him (10:47-48). Matthew at 20:29-34[52] made the one Bartimaeus into two blind men (cf. 9:27) and kept the Son of David in their two requests (20:30-31), adding κυριε to both

---

48. Davies and Allison, *Matthew*, 2:136, suggest that for Matthew Jesus is Son of David because he was known to be descended from David and because he, like Solomon, was recognized as a skilled healer.

49. Together with some phrases from Isaiah 61:1 (preaching good news to the poor) and 29:18. As to the latter, there is an overlap with 35:5 in the mention of the blind and deaf, but 29:18-19 specifically says that the deaf *shall hear* and that the eyes of the blind *shall see*, as in Matthew 11:5, though the LXX uses βλεψονται with the blind, whereas Matthew uses αναβλεπουσιν.

50. The question is phrased with a μητι and so must be a hesitant question (certainly not one expecting the answer no).

51. Held, *Interpreter*, 193, 195, 199-200.

52. For details, see Held, *Interpreter*, 220-23.

requests.[53] While the main theme appears to be "the mercy of Jesus towards the blind men, whose eyes he opens for his way and the following of it,"[54] once again we have the juxtaposition of Son of David and healing.

Matthew insinuates the title into the greetings shouted by the pilgrims on the way to Jerusalem. Where Mark has the crowds shouting:

> Hosanna.
> Blessed is he who comes in the name of the Lord.
> Blessed is the coming kingdom of our father David.
> Hosanna in the highest. (Mark 11:9)

Matthew's version runs:

> Hosanna to the Son of David.
> Blessed is he who comes in the name of the Lord.
> Hosanna in the highest. (Matt 21:9)

The stimulus to bring in the title Son of David may have been Mark's reference to the coming kingdom of our father David. This, however, refers to something still to come; Matthew has Jesus recognized as the Son of David there and then. In the light of the Old Testament quotation (mainly from Zech 9:9) formally introduced by Matthew at 21:5, Israel's King and Savior, the Son of David, is gentle and humbly rides on a donkey and not a horse prepared for war.

In Matthew Jesus, on entering Jerusalem, went straight to the temple[55] and proceeded to eject those who were selling and buying and to overturn the tables of the money changers and those who were selling doves (21:12–13). Only Matthew reports that the blind and lame came to Jesus and he healed them (21:14). This is in marked contrast to David himself, of whom 2 Samuel 5:8 LXX (Βασιλειων A) says that he barred the lame and blind from the house of the Lord.[56] Matthew also reported that children cried out "Hosanna to the Son of David," a shout of praise which picks up the similar praise voiced by the pilgrim crowds coming into Jerusalem at 21:9.[57] As

---

53. Gnilka, *Matthäusevaangelium*, 2:195, sees in this a combination of the confession of the Hellenistic-Christian and the Jewish-Christian congregations.

54. Held, *Interpreter*, 221n1. Duling, *Therapeutic Son of David*, 400, prefers to use the term "compassion," but in his comment that the blind men are healed not because of their faith but because of Jesus' compassion, he is really saying the same thing as Held.

55. Cf. Luke 19:45, an agreement of Matthew and Luke against Mark.

56. In Acts 3:1 the lame beggar was outside at the gate of the temple. It was when healed that he entered. John 9:1 gives no information about where the blind man was.

57. Gundry, *Use of the Old Testament*, 121, thinks that Matthew may have had in mind the rabbinic tradition that children sang praise at the crossing of the Re(e)d Sea.

Trilling pointed out, within Jerusalem only children offered praise, whereas the chief priests and scribes were indignant (vv. 15-16). He has also pointed out that after the wrathful act of cleansing the temple, Jesus shows himself as the βασιλευς πραυς and the king of the children.[58] It seems likely that 21:14-16 is a Matthean creation.[59] This short pericope contains an OT quotation from Psalm 8:3 LXX: "You have perfected praise out of the mouths of infants and sucklings" (v. 16). The Psalmist expressed the idea that even the very young have a sense of the greatness of God and His works, and their very recognition is an argument, so to speak, against those who are sceptical about God and His power. God works within the very young to elicit praise for Himself. Thus, the praise of the children in the temple in Matthew stands in marked contrast with the antagonism of the chief priests and scribes. It is appropriate that praise, properly directed to the God of Israel, should also be given to Jesus the Son of David, who is Immanuel.[60]

The final instance is in the pericope about the relation of the Messiah to David which occurs in Mark 12:35-37. Mark had Jesus asking "How is it that the scribes say that the Messiah is the Son of David?" and going on to quote Psalm 110:1 in order to pose the conundrum that there David appears to address the Messiah as his lord, so how can this lord be a descendent of his? (12:35b, 36-37). In Matthew, however, Jesus invited his interlocutors (the Pharisees) to express an opinion on whose descendant the Messiah would be (Matt 22:42a), and it is they who say "David's" (v. 42b). The rest of the pericope follows Mark with minor changes. Given that Matthew expected the immediate vindication of Jesus following his crucifixion (26:64; cf. 28:18, the fact that it is the risen, exalted Lord who met the disciples on the mountain in Galilee, as εδοθη makes clear), there is far more to be said about Jesus than Davidic descent, even if that is not of negligible significance. The implication is that he is God's Son[61] (who possibly is envisaged as seated at the right hand of God when the Psalm was spoken, and certainly for Matthew was there after his resurrection).

We may summarize this brief survey as follows:

1. Though virgin born of the Holy Spirit, Jesus is a descendent of David through the fact that Joseph was his legal father (1:20).

Davies and Allison, *Matthew*, 3:142, are favorably disposed to this suggestion.

58. Trilling, *Der Einzug im Jerusalem*, 307.

59. Stendahl, *School of St. Matthew*, 135; Gnilka, *Matthäusevangelium*, 2:207. For an opposite view, see Gundry, *Use*, 200.

60. Trilling, *Einzug*, 307

61. See our earlier discussion on pages 296-98 and note 26.

2. The majority of the occurrences of the title Son of David are due to Matthean editorial work (9:27; 12:23; 15:22; 21:9, 15). The other instances occurred already in his Marcan source and Matthew took them over (20:30-31; 22:45). Matthean redaction accounts for 5 out of 8 occurrences.

3. There is a link in four cases with Jesus' work of healing and exorcizing (9:27; 12:23; 15:22; 21:15).[62] His help in healing is given to the needy— the blind, the dumb, the lame,[63] and once even extended to a non-Jew, though this is exceptional (15:21-28).

4. In no instances does one of the twelve use the title. The title occurs on the lips of suppliants for healing (9:27; 15:22) or the crowds in response to such activity by Jesus (12:23) or the pilgrim crowds en route for Jerusalem (21:9) and by the children in the temple (21:15).

7.4. Jesus as Son of Abraham

After the comment on Jesus as Son of Abraham at 1:17, the reader/hearer of Matthew's Gospel might expect that Abraham would play a prominent role in the material to follow. But that is not the case.[64] However, there is a distinct possibility that in the story of the visit of the wise men Matthew is insinuating an allusion to the promise made to Abraham that all nations will be blessed in and through his seed. He would be hinting that here is a foreshadowing of a fulfillment of that promise.[65] Right at the beginning of his Gospel, Matthew has Gentiles paying homage to the new born baby. At the end of his Gospel, he has the risen Lord commanding his disciples to go and make all nations his disciples.[66] At the beginning the Gentiles seek out Jesus; at the end of the Gospel, the disciples of Jesus are to seek out

---

62. Cf. Dulling, *Therapeutic Son of David*, 392-410.

63. Kingsbury, *Matthew*, 100, 103, calls these the "no-accounts" of contemporary Jewish society, who perceive what Israel as a whole does not (13:13; 23:37).

64. Kingsbury, *Matthew*, 84-86, went so far as to classify "Son of Abraham" as a minor Christological term, whose function was to broaden and enrich selected facets of Matthew's Son-of-God Christology. But does not this ignore the fact that 1:17 is a key statement of the evangelist placed strategically so near the beginning of his Gospel?

65. Among those prepared to see an allusion to the promise to Abraham are Vögtle, *Genealogie*, 259-60; Frankmölle, *Jahwebund*, 217 (cf. 314); Brown, *Birth*, 68; Beare, *Matthew*, 65; Gnilka, *Matthäusevangelium*, 1:7; 2:536-37; Davies and Allison, *Matthew*, 1:158, 187; Carter, *Matthean Christology*, 163.

66. Frankmölle, *Jahwebund*, 326, says that Matthew has not ended his Gospel with the rejection of Israel but the story of Yahweh with the whole world intended in the promise to Abraham.

the nations and draw them into acknowledging the lordship of him who represented the presence of God in salvation and judgment in his earthly ministry and to whom now, as raised from the dead, the Father has given universal authority.[67]

In addition, there may also be an allusion to the Abrahamic promise of Genesis 12:3 in 1:21 if Matthew is thinking of the new people of God from all peoples in the phrase "his people," as Frankemölle believes.[68]

All other references to Abraham in Matthew's Gospel come from the tradition available to the evangelist. This is not to say that they are unimportant, merely taken over without much thought. The author of Matthew's Gospel is no mere editor, but an independent thinker and evangelist.

Firstly, Matthew reproduces the view of John the Baptist expressed in the double tradition material, Q, at 3:9 (// Luke 3:8). John the Baptist undercut the claim to special status and privilege before God for Israel. In the imminent judgment expected by John the Baptist, descent from Abraham would not avail—only repentance and amendment of life (described metaphorically as fruits which befit repentance [3:8]). God is not tied to the physical descendants of Abraham. He can raise up children to Abraham from the stones. We note that John the Baptist *kept* the link to Abraham. God can raise up others as "children to Abraham." They will still be children for him even if not physically descended from him.

Secondly, Matthew reproduces from the double tradition, Q, the story of the healing of the centurion's servant at 8:5–13 (// Luke 7:1–10). Almost certainly Matthew has inserted another Q saying at verses 11–12 (//Luke 13:28–29) because of the Jew-Gentile theme raised by the story itself. The centurion requested healing for his servant, but demurred at Jesus' willingness to go to his home. He believed that Jesus needed only to say the word and his servant would be healed (v. 8). He recognized an authority behind Jesus analogous to the authority (the Emperor's) behind himself when he gave commands (v. 9). This insight staggered Jesus who made the remarkable comment: "Truly I tell you, I have not found such faith in anyone in Israel" (v. 10).

Then Matthew added verses 11–12:

> I tell you that many will come from west and east and eat with Abraham and Isaac and Jacob in the Kingdom of Heaven. But the sons of the kingdom will be cast into the outer darkness

---

67. Gnilka, *Matthäusevangelium*, 1:7, sees an arc from verse 1 to 28:19-20. Cf. Frankemölle, *Jawhebund*, 321–24.

68. Frankemölle, *Jawhebund*, 16, 211–18. That Matthew is thinking of the new people of God would be widely accepted. Cf. Davies and Allison, *Matthew*, 1:210.

There, there will be weeping and gnashing of teeth (//Luke 13:28-29).

Those from East and West are non-Jews of devout and morally righteous lives, not Jews from the Diaspora since they would already be "sons of the Kingdom."

Clearly, Abraham, Isaac, and Jacob are expected to share in the banquet of the Kingdom in the Age to Come. From this logion by itself, it is not possible to say whether the three patriarchs would be raised to participate in the banquet, or whether they are alive in some form of post-mortem existence. Our next passage leaves no doubt that the latter is the case.

Thirdly, at Matthew 22:23-33, the evangelist reproduces the story of the incident when the Sadducees raised the question about the resurrection via an alleged story of seven brothers who in succession married the same women but left no offspring (cf. Mark 12:18-27; Luke 20:27-40).[69] Jesus quoted from the story of the burning bush when God described Himself to Moses as the God of Abraham, Isaac, and Jacob. As He is the God of the living and not of the dead, the inference was clearly[70] that the patriarchs were indeed alive in a post-mortem mode of existence (Matt 22:32//Mark 12:26-27; Luke 20:37-38).

The basic agreement between John the Baptist and Jesus on the fact that Israel cannot claim descent from Abraham as conferring on her a special status vis-a-vis the scrutiny of God's judgment raises the question of how Matthew regarded the Jewish nation. This problem is too large an issue to deal with in a short compass. What we can say is that Matthew's editing of the material at his disposal could well suggest that the Jewish nation had forfeited its position as God's chosen people because of its rejection of Jesus. A few illustrations of this may be offered.

In the Matthean edition of the Parable of the Wicked Tenants in the Vineyard, we read "I tell you that the Kingdom of God will be taken away from you and will be given to a people (ἔθνει) producing its fruits" (21:43).[71] While it could be argued that the parable is directed against the religious leadership, the concept of the Kingdom of God and the new people suggests that the view of Matthew goes wider than that.[72] The leadership is

---

69. Luke may have had access to a non-Marcan tradition as well as his Marcan source.

70. Not, it has to be said, to the modern mind.

71. See the detailed discussion of this passage in Trilling, *Das wahre Israel*, 55-65.

72. Frankmölle, *Jahwebund*, 249-50, 264-65, who states emphatically that here Matthew has asserted the replacement of Israel by the church.

representative of the Jewish nation/people as a whole.[73] Certainly, no doubt exists about our next passage.

The way in which Matthew tells the parable of the royal wedding feast and the way those originally invited refused to attend when the moment arrived (22:1–14), strongly suggests that he sees the fall of Jerusalem to the Romans as divine punishment for Jewish rejection of Jesus their own Messiah.[74]

Matthew edits the Passion Story received from Mark at several points. Especially noteworthy is his introduction of how, when the crowd demanded the crucifixion of Jesus and the release of Barabbas, Pilate washed his hands and declared "I am innocent of the blood of this man,"[75] whereupon the people (λαος, not οχλος which has been used hitherto in the passion story) cried out: "His blood be upon us and on our children" (27:24–25). In Matthew's eyes, the Jewish λαος accepted guilt for the death of their own messiah. This is the moment when the Kingdom of God was taken from them.[76]

Matthew edited the mockery at the foot of the cross. Three sets of people mocked Jesus, namely the passers-by (vv. 39–40), the chief priests with the scribes and elders who mocked the claim to be Son of God (vv. 41–43), and the rebel insurgents (v. 44). By contrast, the centurion and his men confessed Jesus as the Son of God (v. 52). The blood-guiltiness, accepted at verse 25, is illustrated in this mockery of Jesus.

It is reasonably certain that Matthew's copy of Mark ended at 16:8. Matthew added a story about the chief priests bribing the soldiers posted to guard the tomb (27:62–66) to say that his disciples had stolen the body while they were asleep. The evangelist commented that this report spread among *the Jews* until this day (28:15). The blanket term "the Jews," reminiscent of Johannine usage, speaks volumes: the Jewish nation has refused even the sign of Jonah (Matt 12:39)![77]

---

73. Cf. the assertion of Frankemölle, *Jahwebund*, 255–56, who states that in 21:41 Israel through its leaders recognized its own guilt and condemned itself in its condemnation of the tenants.

74. Cf. Trilling, *Israel*, 84–85.

75. Some manuscripts have "the blood of this *righteous* man," but this is almost certainly a post-Matthean addition, possibly under the influence of 27:19—where Pilate's wife sends a message to her husband, "Have nothing to do with this righteous man."

76. Cf. Trilling, *Israel*, 66–74. Frankemölle, *Jahwebund*, 210, describes the scene of verses 24–25 as giving the reason why Israel had squandered the privilege of being Yahweh's special people and so it furnishes an aetiology for the end of Israel.

77. Frankemölle, *Jahwebund*, 211n81. After 27:25, Matthew could no longer speak of the chosen people, Israel.

The embargo on any mission activity outside Israel to either Samaritans or Gentiles at 10:5–6 is lifted by the command of the risen, exalted Lord to whom all authority in heaven and on earth has been given by God: "Go and make all nations my disciples . . ." (28:18-20). The universal Lord authorized the universal mission, promising his universal presence. While "all nations" does not suggest that the Jewish people are excluded,[78] nevertheless the breadth of the extent of the mission suggests at the very least a diminution of the particularism of the election of Israel.

More evidence could be adduced to suggest that for the evangelist old Israel had forfeited its position due to its rejection of its own messiah.[79] Did the evangelist hold out any hope of a change of heart?

Some see a glimmer of hope in the saying which Matthew has placed at the end of his Woes on the Scribes and Pharisees chapter (23), to which Matthew has attached Jesus' lament over Jerusalem (which, it could be argued, stands for the nation as a whole). Despite all his efforts, Jerusalem/the nation has refused his overtures. He predicts "Look. Your house[80] will be abandoned to you," i.e., by God (23:38).[81] If οἶκος carries the sense of "temple," there would seem to be influence from Ezekiel's picture of the glory of God abandoning the temple in Ezekiel 10–11. The sad fate of Israel in 586 BC will be repeated once more. The logion concluded with the remark: "For I tell you, you will not see me from now on until you say, Blessed is he who comes in the name of the Lord" (v. 39). Scholars are divided as to whether this indicates a hope for a positive response from Israel at the Parousia,[82] or whether the acknowledgement comes too late.[83] While the cry of verse 39 does not seem like one of a terrified, awe-struck admission by those who realize that it is too late,[84] nevertheless the flow

---

78. Strongly maintained by Davies and Allison, *Matthew*, 3:557–58.

79. See the study of Trilling, *Israel*.

80. The word οἶκος may refer to the temple (see Bauer, *Lexicon*, 563, s.v. "οἶκος" 1.a.b, for examples) or, on occasions, it can refer to a city (the few instances of this listed in Bauer, *Lexicon*, 563, s.v. "οἶκος" 1.a.g, refer to Jerusalem).

81. The NEB paraphrases: "Look! There is your temple forsaken by God."

82. So, e.g., Schlatter, *Der Evangelist Matthäus*, 691; Morris, *Matthew*, 592; Davies and Allison, *Matthew*, 3:323–24; Schweizer, *Matthaus und seine Gemeinde*, 36–37; Stanton, *Gospel of Matthew and Judaism*, 276; *Gospel for a New People*, 159, 249–50.

83. So, e.g., Manson, *Sayings of Jesus*, 128; Trilling, *Israel*, 87; Strecker, *Der Weg der Gerechtigkeit*, 114–15; Hoffmann, *Studien zur Theologie der Logienquelle*, 177–78; Schulz, Q, 358; Gnilka, *Matthäusevangelium*, 2:305; France, *Matthew*, 332–33.

84. Hoffmann, *Studien*, 177–78, pointed to Enoch 62:5 as supporting the "too late" interpretation. But there, the response of kings and mighty ones is born of terror, dejection, shame, and anguished pain, and those concerned fall at the feet of the Lord of the Spirits and beg and plead for mercy. The cry of Matthew 23:39 is very different.

of the thought of the chapter (together with other evidence) seems to tell against a positive interpretation.[85]

6.5. Summary

Although Matthew seems to believe that Israel had forfeited its claim to a special position in the purpose of God, he also wished to maintain the link of the movement started by Jesus with its roots disclosed in the story of Israel recorded in the Old Testament Scriptures. Abraham was the founding father of Israel and his importance is revealed by the fact that Jesus mentioned that he together with Isaac and Jacob clearly have prominent places at the banquet of the Kingdom (Matt 8:11) and that John the Baptist had said that God could raise up children to Abraham from even the stones lying on the ground. Abraham together with Isaac and Jacob are regarded as alive in a post-mortem existence (22:32). Above all, the significance of Abraham is revealed in the genealogical table which Matthew has set at the beginning of his Gospel and which began with Abraham. The story of God's electing, saving activity began with Abraham. It is important that Jesus is the Son of Abraham, alongside being the Son of David (1:1). It seems likely that Matthew has hinted that the promise made to Abraham that in his descendants all the nations will be blessed was beginning to be fulfilled from the birth of Jesus on: the story of the visit of the magi from the east who seek and find and worship the Christ-Child and the climax of the Gospel in the command of the risen Lord for his disciples to make all nations his disciples (2:1-12; 28:18-20).

Excursus: Matthew's Congregation and Judaism[86]

In scholarly works of the post World War II era, one meets various descriptions of how the Matthean congregation related to Judaism: that it had separated (e.g., Kilpatrick, Trilling, Hare, Brooke); that it remained within Judaism (intra muros/within the walls, e.g., Bornkamm, Hummel, Celia Deutsch); or that the author of the Gospel was a Gentile and his interest was

---

85. See Trilling, *Israel*, 87, who commented that Matthew was not thinking of a conversion of Israel at the End, and he pointed also to 8:11-12 with its warning that the sons of the kingdom will be cast into outer darkness.

86. For details of the works of the scholars referred to in this excursus, see the Bibliography. This excursus does not attempt to be exhaustive in its coverage of all the issues involved in this contentious theme but rather seeks to highlight one major facet.

directed out to the Gentile world rather than to Judaism (e.g., K. W. Clark, Nepper-Christensen, Strecker, Tilborg, Gaston).

Some comments by Beare in the introduction to his commentary published in 1981 raise serious questions as to what meaning we read into phrases like "separation" or "intra muros" or "within the framework of Judaism."[87] Beare wrote that the Gospel "must have originated in an area where church and synagogue were in continual contact and conflict, and where Jewish influence was sufficiently strong to bring serious trouble to the communities of Christian believers . . . [Matthew] writes in and for a community in which the relationship with Judaism is of crucial importance." He later says that the community is served by scribes, prophets, and wise men, and that "the congregation itself is to act as a court for the discipline of recalcitrant members." This sounds very like separation! A few years previously, Hummel wrote that Matthew's congregation did not participate in Synagogue worship; that it was at the stage of consolidating itself, without however cutting itself off from the (recognized) Jewish body [Verband]; and that it possessed a strongly formed individual life, but yet still belonged to the Jewish Synagogue community. "Inner independence and external membership characterized its situation."[88]

If a group no longer worships in the Synagogue and has its own leaders and meetings, but engages in dispute with the members of the Synagogue, which is the more appropriate term to describe this state of affairs: separation or still in membership with the parent body? France has issued some wise warnings against applying too rigidly the concepts of insider/outsider in this respect, and he rightly points out that the process of separation did not happen "overnight" (as it were), but occurred at varying speeds and in varying ways in different areas.[89] Konradt also considers it advisable to give up entirely the use of the metaphor of walls,

---

87. The last mentioned term is that of Davies, *Setting of the Sermon on the Mount*, 290n3. Davies sees the Sermon on the Mount as "the Christian answer to Jamnia . . . a kind of Christian, mishnaic counterpart to the formulation taking place there. . . . Matthew's manifesto [was] a formulation of the way of the New Israel at a time when the rabbis were engaged in a parallel task for the Old Israel" (315).

88. Hummel, *Auseinandersetzung*, 29, 33, 159. He says that the sharpness of the dispute is "the proverbial sharpness of '*hostile brothers*'" (55, my italics). Cf. the use of the concept (derived from the sociologist Lewis Coser) in Stanton, *New People*, 98–107. The closer the relationship, the sharper the conflict evoked and the emnity generated, in Stanton's comparison of the Damascus Document and Matthew's Gospel.

89. France, *Matthew*, 100–102. He made the comment that Matthew's special blend of Jewishness and anti-Jewishness might appropriately be described as representing "Jewish Christianity" without this requiring our having to declare for or against an intra muros situation.

and simply conclude: "Judaism constitutes the primary context for the life of the Matthean community, and more specifically, the historical situation . . . is substantially characterized by the conflict between believers in Christ and the predominantly Pharisaic synagogue."[90]

We might think of the community at Qumran as a test case. It had organized itself separately from the parent body but regarded itself passionately as the truly elect people of God, the true Israel of God.[91] The document 4QMMT shows a desire to reach out to the representatives of official Judaism in the pre-70 era, even if later on attitudes hardened, hope of any rapprochement was abandoned, and the stance of outright rejection adopted.

Within the last thirty years or so, several studies have appeared which have used the results of sociological research and applied them to the study of Matthew: a composite volume edited by Balch, and works by Overman, Saldarini, Sim, Gale, Carter, and others.[92] The tendency has been to describe the Matthean community as a "sect" in a sharp and bitter dispute with the "parent body," often referred to as "Formative Judaism." While it shared the fundamental beliefs of Israel with the parent body, it differed to it in certain particulars, especially in respect of its interpretation of the Torah which, it claimed, should be normative. It had suffered persecution at the hands of the leadership of "formative Judaism."[93] These scholars eschew the term "separate," and strongly maintain that Matthew's Gospel must be understood as part of Judaism. Thus, e.g., to quote Sim, "Once we understand Matthew's community as a sectarian group in conflict with a Jewish body, it seems more appropriate to speak of a Jewish sect within Judaism than of a Christian sect outside Judaism."[94]

Without in any way denigrating the value of the application of sociological research to the situation of Matthew's community, one may legitimately ask whether it is necessary to set up such an either or model. It seems reasonable to hold together separation in terms of organisation and

---

90. Konradt, *Israel, Church, and the Gentiles*, 365.

91. Stanton uses the analogy of the Qumran community and the theological stance behind 5 Ezra. See Stanton, *New People*, 113–68, 256–72, as part of his case for believing that Matthew's community had separated and saw itself as the "New People" of God.

92. With Foster, *Community, Law, and Mission*, "bucking the trend" with his advocacy of a community separate from Judaism and looking to the Gentile world and the evangelist seeking to justify the complete break with Judaism and its new orientation to the Gentile world.

93. For this sort of description, see Overman, *Matthew's Gospel*, 8–34, 150–61; Saldarini, *Community*, 84–123; Sim, *Christian Judaism*, 109–163.

94. Sim, *Christian Judaism*, 5.

worship, and also an engagement with the parent body which has led to the experience of being persecuted.

We may conclude with what Konradt has said, while discussing the universalism to be found in Matthew's Gospel. He argued that the mission to the Gentiles and their inclusion in salvation was not a response to the alleged collective rejection of Jesus in Israel but emerged organically out of the ministry to Israel as the aim of the history of salvation begun with the election of Abraham.[95]

---

95. Konradt, *Israel, Church, and the Gentiles*, 374.

8

Summary and Concluding Reflections

1

WE MAY BRIEFLY SUMMARIZE our exegetical investigation of the use of Abraham in the New Testament. Several New Testament writers used Abraham as a model believer, but they mean different things by this. Each used Abraham with a peculiar nuance.

Paul used Abraham to defend his assertion that men and women, all of whom are sinners in God's sight, have been set right with God entirely on the basis of God's freely and graciously offered salvation through the life, death, and resurrection of His Son, Jesus Christ, and the human response of trusting faith, which receives gratefully what God freely offers. As a corollary of this, Paul can also use the figure of Abraham to vindicate the inclusion of the Gentiles within the people of God, on the basis of faith, that complete trust and dependence on God and His word/promise in the confidence that He is able to fulfill what He has promised. Promise on God's part responded to with this trust is the way in which God wishes to deal with us, not by means of doing what the Law requires. This had opened up the way of salvation apart from the Law to Gentiles.

The *author of Hebrews* used Abraham as a model of patient endurance, as one on a pilgrimage to the Heavenly City. In this author's view, a powerful component of the meaning of faith is faithfulness or steadfast endurance. Faith has shaded over into virtually an equivalent to υπομονη.

The author of the Letter of *James* used Abraham to argue for a Christianity in which faith leads on to works of love for the neighbor, thus fulfilling the Law, described as the royal law and the law of freedom. Faith is important, but it cannot exist by itself. To be genuine, it must issue in practical deeds.

Luke, in his double volume Luke-Acts, saw the promises made by God in His covenant with Abraham, backed up by a divine oath, fulfilled in the person of Jesus of Nazareth, the Messiah and Lord. The theme of promise-fulfillment was important for Luke. Christianity had its roots in God's purposes from the beginning, and could thus claim that it was not an innovation of recent times.

The *Fourth Evangelist* used Abraham both to argue that non-believing Jews were not true children of Abraham, and also as a witness to the messianic ministry of Jesus, the Son of God, who existed before Abraham with God in eternity.

Matthew's Gospel set forth Jesus in its opening Genealogy as both Son of David and Son of Abraham. The former figures prominently in the rest of the work, but there are indications that Matthew saw that the promise that through Abraham the nations would receive God's blessing and be brought into the people of God was in the process of being fulfilled through the ministry of Jesus and its consequences in the mission of his followers.

2

The variety of interpretations of the figure of Abraham is striking and raises a number of questions, pre-eminently this one: is it a question of each writer's manipulating the story and bending it to suit his own purposes? Did the writers bring their own presuppositions to the OT story and did this inevitably influence what they saw in that story? Did each writer look down the "well" of the Abraham traditions and see their own reflection?[1] (Exactly the same questions can, of course, be set to the interpretations of Abraham in the OT and early Judaism.)[2] Or are the traditions about Abraham so rich and varied

---

1. Pratscher, at the end of his careful study, comments on the different picture of James found in Jewish Christianity, Gnosis, and the Great Church: "Each group shapes its own James. Each preserves some few traits correctly; none, however, describes James in his total recognizable intention and activity even only to a certain extent correctly. Continually it is their own intentions for which James has been used and by which he has been seen and presented" (*Der Herrenbruder Jakobus*, 263). Has the same thing happened within the NT concerning the picture of Abraham?

2. Fretheim prefaces his consideration of "Abraham in Apocryphal/Deutero

that inevitably different aspects will appeal to or make a different impact on whosoever reads them? If the first of these two approaches were correct, then one would have to say that each writer used their own creative imagination and retold the story of Abraham with their own particular slant. On the second approach, while subjective influences inevitably play some part, there is more objectivity about what the writer produced, i.e., the tradition itself contained something within itself which has the potential to "speak" a fresh word of God in different circumstances and times.[3] On this approach, tradition is not a static thing, with (as it were) only one set meaning for all time, but it is a living and dynamic thing, or rather, perhaps one should say, that the Spirit of God is able to take the tradition and reinterpret it for a new situation (rather as the fourth evangelist said that the Paraclete-Spirit would take the things of Christ and interpretatively proclaim them to succeeding generations after the historical Jesus had finished the work of his ministry and had returned to the Father), so that the "old word" becomes a "new word" of God to a new generation. In what follows, we shall seek to determine which of these two approaches seems to have the greater validity.

3

Paul saw an analogy between the structure of Abraham's faith and that of Christians. In the story as we have it, Abraham believed God's promise of an heir and descendants when he was, according to the Biblical story, an old man and Sarah passed the normal child-bearing age. That faith must have been the conviction that God could create life where human possibilities had been exhausted. Christian faith is that God raised to life the Jesus who

---

-canonical Literature" with these remarks: "The historical experience of the Jewish community in the last two centuries BCE certainly affects how Abraham is interpreted for their often conflicted life. . . . As in any age, contemporary experience will affect a community's ways of interpreting biblical texts and imaging characters such as Abraham" (*Abraham*, 152).

3. *Ian Hislop's Olden Days: The Power of the Past in Britain*, a series aired on BBC2 in April 2014, provided an interesting example from "secular" English/British history. The aim of this program was to show "how and why throughout our history we have continually plundered the olden days to make sense of and shape the present." In particular, Hislop showed that the figures of King Arthur and King Alfred were both reinterpreted in different ways in Medieval, Tudor, Georgian, and Victorian times, while Winston Churchill appealed to the story of King Alfred to inspire the nation in the dark days of 1940. It seemed to me that there was something in the stories/legends associated with these two figures of the past which, nonetheless, provided the stimulus for the reinterpretation. Writers looked back into the past in order to address the present and future of English/British society.

had died, was dead, and had been buried. The analogy between the apparently hopeless situation of childless human parents wanting a family and the post-crucifixion situation is this: while there is no possibility of new life from human resources, God's life-giving power can create life from nothing/from death.

Paul's use of Abraham and, specifically, the promise that in his descendants all humanity would be blessed—an aspect of the Abrahamic story not particularly stressed by early Judaism—in order to defend the inclusion of Gentiles within the people of God, was a picking up of a facet of the tradition and developing it in a new situation. An old tradition was revivified and actualized in the context of the first century AD. Just how the framers of Genesis 12:3 envisaged the blessing reaching the peoples of the world may well be beyond recovery. Perhaps later, as suggested by Isaiah 2:2–4 and Micah 4:1–3, there was the concept of the eschatological pilgrimage of the Gentiles to Jerusalem to worship the God of Israel. Paul's application of the idea present in Genesis 12:3 to his own day and the Christian mission to the Gentiles reveals a creative thinker who interacts with tradition and brings something new out of it.

The allegorical approach to the Old Testament, which fed Christian devotion and spirituality for centuries, has been set aside in favor of a more literal, historical approach in large sections of the church for some time now. Thus, it is unlikely that anyone preaching today would wish to follow Paul's allegorization of Hagar and Sarah as equivalents to contemporary Judaism and Christianity respectively (in fairness to Paul, this passage is unusual and rather stands out as an exception to his approach elsewhere).

On the other hand, the pilgrimage theme is one which still strikes a spiritual cord with a great many Christians (even if John Bunyan's *Pilgrim's Progress* is not read nowadays as once it was, when it enjoyed a popularity second only to the Bible itself in many households). *Hebrews*' use of this motif will no doubt be much used in preaching and meditation. Preachers may well exploit the analogy between Abraham uprooted from his homeland and family and going on a journey and the Christian responding to the call of the Gospel without knowing in advance what that call might involve. Preachers might have some hesitation, however, in describing Abraham and others from OT days as those who saw the heavenly City from afar. That the Hebrew tribes people of the patriarchal age believed in an afterlife and a heavenly abode would not be accepted by OT scholars, and the text of Genesis 12–25 itself does not give any indication that this was the view shared by the patriarch himself.[4] His desire for an heir is explicable in terms of people "living on" (as it were) through their descendants.

People today might possibly see Abraham's nomadic wandering as a type of pilgrimage, always on the go and never actually arriving, but that the writer envisaged a celestial city like Bunyan's Pilgrim would seem to impose a Christian garment on him and be another venturing down an allegorical road over which scholarship has to some extent put the sign "No entry." Even here, however, it is worth noting that the Alexandrian tradition, of which Philo was the most notable exponent, had paved the way for the kind of approach which we see in Hebrews: Philo allegorized Abraham's journeys as the journey of the soul.

But is there anything more specific in the Genesis story which might have caught the attention of the writer of the letter to the Hebrews and which he might have reflected on and developed? Two points might be made here. Firstly, it is surely not without significance that when Abraham was negotiating with the Hittites of Hebron in order to purchase a burial site for Sarah, he is recorded as saying to them: πάροικος και παρεπίδημος εγω ειμι μεθ'υμων ("I am an alien and stranger among you") (Gen 23:4 LXX). Hebrews 11:13 used ξενοι και παρεπιδημοι of the patriarchs in a probable allusion to the Genesis verse.[5]

Secondly, Richardson has suggested that Hebrews reasoned that if God had withheld the inheritance of the land from Abraham in his lifetime, i.e., in the present age, then God would have to give it to Abraham in the age to come.[6] In the words of Jesus, Abraham is depicted as enjoying a post-mortem existence of blessedness (the poor man Lazarus is said to be in the bosom of Abraham), while also Abraham, Isaac, and Jacob are envisaged at the future banquet in the glorious Kingdom of God.

Once more, if Richardson is right, we could say that there was something in the tradition, reflection on which (within a certain exegetical approach) led to a development such as we see in Hebrews 11.

---

4. In his otherwise very helpful exposition of how the section Hebrews 11:1–12:3 might "speak" to Christians in today's world (under the heading "Bridging the Horizons"), DeSilva does not tackle this problem unfortunately. DeSilva especially handles in a challenging manner the concept of being a foreigner in this world rather than a rooted citizen and points out how useful and inspiring it would be for us to have a series of contemporary examples of faith as a source of inspiration to us.

5. So Spicq. *Hébreux*, 2:350; Bruce, *Hebrews*, 304; Montefiore, *Hebrews*, 196; Attridge, *Hebrews*, 330; Lane, *Hebrews*, 2:357; Weiss, *Hebräer*, 591; Ellingworth, *Hebrews*, 594; Grässer, *Brief an die Hebräer*, 3:138; DeSilva, *Perseverance*, 399.

6. Richardson, *Pioneer*, 189–92. It is to Richardson's great credit that he has tackled this issue, which so many pass over in silence.

There is also the idea that Abraham was convinced that God was able to raise from the dead, which was a basic conviction of Judaism (11:19a). The author does go on immediately (v. 19b) to say that Abraham, figuratively speaking, received him [Isaac] from the dead.[7] Again, we have to ask whether there was anything in the Genesis story which might have suggested this interpretation to the author. Bruce[8] suggested that Hebrews took Abraham's words to his servants in Genesis 22:5, "I and the lad will go yonder, and we will worship and *come again to you*," to mean that Abraham believed that after he had sacrificed his son, God would raise him to life again. On the level of the narrative, Abraham's words served to conceal from his servants his real intention. A Christian interpreter in the first century AD could well seize on the words at another level, as suggested by Bruce.

However, it is one thing to *explain* how a writer like the author of Hebrews developed his interpretation in the first century AD. It is an entirely different matter to preach that interpretation as if it were based on the data provided by the Genesis narrative. So, how does the modern preacher deal with this issue? In preaching, one approach which would preserve the preacher's integrity and yet enable preaching on a passage like Hebrews 11:8–16 to take place, might be as follows. The author of the Letter to the Hebrews seems to have combined two approaches to looking at time and history.[9] There is what we might call "the horizontal line" approach which sees history in terms of two ages, as having a beginning (Creation) and proceeding to a divinely intended goal (the End of all things and the establishment of the Kingdom of God)—a view often thought to be characteristic of the Hebrew approach. The other approach might be called "the vertical line" approach and thinks in terms of spheres above/below or heavenly/earthly—often regarded as typical of the Hellenistic approach, though a too rigid separation of Hebraic and Hellenistic cannot be sustained.[10] We might say that the author of Hebrews has proceeded rather like a musical composer who takes a piece of music composed by someone else and produces

---

7. The ὅθεν could refer back to the phrase "from the dead" (so Westcott, *Hebrews*, 360) or could be used inferentially (which is frequent in Hebrews—see 2:17; 3:1; 7:25; 8:3; 9:18. So Spicq, *Hébreux*, 2:354; Montefiore, *Hebrews*, 198; Grässer, *Brief an die Hebräer*, 3:149n58; Attridge, *Hebrews*, 335; Lane, *Hebrews*, 2:347, 362; Weiss, *Hebräer*, 597–98; Ellingworth, *Hebrews*, 603 (probably, though also conceding that both senses might be intended); Koester, *Hebrews*, 491.

8. Bruce, *Hebrews*, 311–12.

9. See, e.g., Mackie, *Eschatology and Exhortation*.

10. A "diatasis" between the heavenly-eternal and earthly-transitory can be found in the wisdom tradition of the Old Testament and early Judaism. For a discussion of this, see Maier, *Mensch und freier Wille*.

a "Variation on a Theme."[11] The new product is recognizably related to the original, but a new element has been introduced. The author of Hebrews has taken the story of Abraham's wanderings with the hoped-for goal of having descendants and possessing land (the horizontal line) and produced a "Variation on a Theme" (the vertical line). In this new "Variation," the convictions of having a future and the goal of the wanderings have become a heavenly land or home or city. The author of Hebrews has thus made the story of Abraham into a parable of the journey of the believer(s) through this earthly life with all its trials and temptations, to God's city in the heavenly or transcendent sphere.[12]

This will not convince people of a very conservative-fundamentalist persuasion who interpret the Genesis story of Abraham through the lens of Hebrews 11, though, perhaps, it stands some chance of being listened to without antagonism or dismay. There could be a recognition that the preacher is handling the Scriptures with respect and seeking the living word of God within them,[13] and there would still be a fundamental point of agreement that we are on a pilgrimage and that the OT characters have to some extent trodden the way before us. On the other hand, for people of an enquiring mind, it may be a means of helping them to appropriate the passage in Hebrews 11 without a feeling of unreality about the author's interpretation.

James's position is one with which Paul would have agreed substantially. After all, Paul did say in his letter to the Galatians that in Christ Jesus neither circumcision nor uncircumcision counted for anything, but faith working itself out in love (5:6). In James's letter, Abraham believed God's word, and his obedience to God in his willingness to offer up Isaac demonstrated his faith-in-action, his faith-expressing-itself-in-deeds. James sees faith as something which develops and matures on its way to perfection (2:22; 1:2-4). Faith does have something to do with justification (2:20-26), but not faith on its own (2:24). Faith expresses itself in deeds of obedience to God and love towards the neighbor (cf. 2:8; 1:27). It is God's implanted word which saves (1:21; cf.

11. Dandved, *World of Music*, 2119, comments on "Variations on a Theme": "Originally, the variations were obtained by embroidering the theme with a variety of trills and runs, its rhythmic and harmonic foundation remaining unaltered. But the variations of the Classical period involved changes to the theme itself."

12. This might be akin to the way in which Richard Hays has called Paul's way of reading Scripture as that of "a poetic preacher," who "finds in Scripture a rich source of image and metaphor that enables him to declare with power what God is doing in the world in his own time" (*Conversion of the Imagination*, xvi).

13. The preacher would be operating with what Richard Hays has called "A Hermeneutic of Trust," as opposed to what he calls "the corrosive hermeneutic of suspicion which has come to dominate the modern academy" (*Conversion of the Imagination*, xv).

1:18), and we need to receive God's grace in humility (4:6). Final justification is almost a process, beginning in faith in God and Jesus Christ and translating that faith into obedience and charitable deeds.

The linking of Genesis 15 and 22, something already carried out in early Judaism, is a reasonable step for the interpreter of Genesis to take. The demand to offer Isaac represented a test of Abraham's trust in God, for Isaac was the destined bearer of the promise. The Biblical author of Genesis 22 was silent about Abraham's feelings and emotions. Sufficient that Abraham did what God commanded. (Genesis 22:2 gives the command; 22:3 announces the execution of the command.) In the end, God stayed the execution and rewarded Abraham with a renewed promise of blessing, descendants, and blessing for the nations "because you have obeyed my voice" (vv. 15-18).

James, and Jewish interpreters before him, did not query that God had tested Abraham in making the demand on him to offer his son, Isaac. Many modern Christians find it completely unacceptable that God should make such a demand on any human being. Henton Davies in his commentary on Genesis put it this way: "Did Abraham's conviction or the writer's account of that conviction correspond to a real divine request? Did God make, would God in fact have made, such a demand upon Abraham, or anyone else except himself? There are those of course who would accept the command literally. Our answer however is no. Indeed what Christian or humane conscience would regard such a command as coming from God?"[14] It is only right that such questions should be faced and discussed in a pastorally sensitive manner, though arguably this issue belongs in sermons or Bible studies on Genesis rather than on James.

The essentially practical bent of James no doubt makes its appeal in an age which emphasizes social involvement rather than doctrinal matters. The

---

14. Henton Davies, *Genesis*, 198. Note: this commentary was part of the Broadman Bible Commentary and published by the Broadman Press in conjunction with the Southern Baptist Convention. It was commissioned before the convention became dominated by the extreme fundamentalist wing. Among its other contributors were R. E. Clements, G. R. Beasley-Murray, and R. P. Martin. It is indicative of the sensitive nature of questions like this that Dr. Henton Davies got into trouble for this comment, which caused offense to very conservative Southern Baptists. As a result of a motion of censure in the Southern Baptist convention, the commentary was in fact removed from circulation and another author commissioned to write a new commentary on Genesis for the series.

Other modern writers have used terms like "child abuse" for what Abraham subjected Isaac to in his willingness to sacrifice him. See Fretheim, *Abraham*, 119-24, for a discussion and reference to recent writers raising such issues.

As for those who today preach or lead bible study groups, questions like these can and ought to be raised and discussed in a helpful and non-threatening manner.

present era is one which stresses praxis rather than evincing interest in what Christians believe doctrinally.

The conviction of *Luke-Acts* that the promises to Abraham have found fulfillment in one who was Son of David, Jesus, presents us with a concept of the history of God's saving activity. It begins with Abraham, continues in the story of Israel and reaches a climax with the birth, ministry, death, resurrection, and exaltation of Jesus. Luke is a Biblical historian. In a real sense, he continues the OT histories by telling the story of Jesus and then something of the story of how the good news was taken from Jerusalem out of Israel and into the non-Jewish world, to Rome, the capital of the Roman Empire. Luke keeps the Hebraic roots of the Christian movement firmly before us. There is continuity as well as discontinuity with the past. The Christian faith builds on the old, draws the best from it, and completes it.

Luke's emphasis is a reminder to the Christian church of our day that we cannot and dare not forget or neglect our roots. In practice,[15] one suspects that there is a good deal of the approach of Marcion around today. Especially in Britain, it is increasingly the case that churches have only one service,[16] and, if ministers follow a lectionary, it tends to be the New Testament that is preached on. This leads to a neglect of the Old Testament. This is to be regretted. Luke's insistence on the people of God beginning from Abraham and continuing in the followers of Jesus the Messiah is a conviction that we need to hold on to and live by.

We come to *John's Gospel*. Of John's two emphases, his use of Abraham as a witness to the messianic ministry of Jesus represents a problem for us today, partly because it depends on a Jewish tradition interpreting the sleep of Abraham Genesis 15, a tradition with which most Christians are unfamiliar and which would count in their eyes as embroidering the original story. Yet John's claim here is in line with the early Christian emphasis that the life, death, and resurrection of Jesus was in accordance with the Scriptures. Apart from specific passages which John claims to be fulfilled in Jesus and apart from symbols found in the OT which he claimed prefigure Jesus and were fulfilled in him, John could be said to personalize the idea of Scripture as a witness to Jesus. Thus both Abraham and Isaiah are said to have "seen" Jesus' day or his glory, and to have borne witness to him. In addition, Moses is said to have written about him. John's is very much a Christological interpretation

---

15. What follows reflects on the British scene. I have no acquaintance with the American scene.

16. This is not only true of the Free Churches but also even Anglican churches, especially in rural areas. Even where a parish church does have more than one service, if there are different preachers, the impression I have gained is that they tend to choose the NT passages to preach on.

of the OT, and Christians down the ages have very much lived from this approach. John has fed into that conviction.

The other aspect raises acute problems for Christians today, especially after the Holocaust and the realisation that some Christian writers including Martin Luther and some highly respected philosophers like Hegel, Kant, and Heidegger of the nineteenth and twentieth centuries (to mention but a few) have said some horrible and wholly unjustifiable things concerning Jews, which may have fed into the thinking of some pro-Nazi adherents and sympathizers. Even bearing in mind what we wrote about the inappropriateness of describing John as anti-Jewish, to a great many people the language of John 8 seems like demonizing the Jews and remains unacceptable.

What we have in John 8 is what has been described as "a dualism of decision." One is either in one sphere or the other. (Although there is a predestinarian strand in John, it should not be isolated and given sole prominence. John stresses the invitation to or demand for faith, while there is also a universal strand. Each of these strands—predestination, believing, universalism—must be given due weight in assessing the evangelist's thought.)[17] But one can pass from one sphere to the other. Destiny is not fixed irrevocably.

If, with the idea of "decision" in mind, one turns back to the story of Abraham, then a case can be made out that Abraham at points was confronted with the need to make a decision for or against God, for or against obeying God's command. Thus, Abraham responded positively to the command to go forth from his land and family (Gen 12:1). Lot made the wrong decision to choose the plain of Jordan (Gen 13).[18] Abraham responded positively to God's promise of an heir and descendants (Gen 15:1-6). He obeyed, albeit with a heavy heart, the divine command to expel Hagar (Gen 21), and then obeyed the command to sacrifice Isaac, the supreme test (Gen 22). Abraham was faced by existential choices and decisions.

To be a true child of Abraham is, it could be maintained, to make right decisions for God, to obey Him, to embrace His will. The Jews in John 8 are faced with a choice—to commit themselves more deeply to the one in front of them, who is the Word made flesh, "the Stranger from Heaven," the Son of God from above. Yet he appears to be the son of Joseph and Mary whom people know (6:42). This is the enigma of Jesus of Nazareth. Can people see the divine in the human? The choice faces people—to believe or not to believe.

---

17. I have commented on these strands in John's Gospel in my *Cross in the Johannine Writings*, 193-94.

18. Though primarily a story about the peaceful resolution of a quarrel, the editor who put in chapter 13, to prepare for 18:16–19:29, emphasizes the wickedness of Sodom.

One reveals one's parentage by one's choice, by believing or not believing. Will one follow in the steps of Abraham or not? Subsumed under the larger category, this becomes—is one a child of God or the devil?

The objection to this is due to a number of factors. Firstly, there is a dislike of dualistic language per se, as too restrictive, as too "black and white," and not allowing enough for "shades of grey," for those less than clear cut areas of life. Secondly, a dislike of using language like the devil or the demonic, for fear of being taken literally in an age when such views have long been abandoned.[19] Finally, there is the fear of creating an unbridgeable gulf between oneself/one's church and those to whom one is referring, and closing off possible rapprochement and/or reconciliation.

These are points well made. Yet, in the end, whatever language we use, and sensitivity in language is necessary, there is something inherent in the Gospel which does demand a decision, and John's Gospel constantly emphasizes this need in its use of the verb "to believe" and synonyms. If we are to be true to that Gospel, we cannot eliminate the note of challenge in it, or it will be a bowdlerized version of it. John's Gospel is a constant reminder that the Gospel is challenge.

Finally, what of *the author of Matthew's Gospel*? It cannot be said that the Abrahamic tradition has left a big mark on his handling of his version of the gospel story. Abraham, Isaac, and Jacob are important figures in his tradition. They will have a leading place in the messianic banquet of the future, and Matthew believes that people from the nations will join them in that state of blessedness. The church of Jesus has the task laid upon it by its Lord of making the nations disciples of Jesus, and thus participating in the divine purpose of bringing about the blessing promised through Abraham to them. Contemporary Christians vary in how they think, if at all, of the future Kingdom of God, and some may even query the idea of mission to the non-Christian world. Those for whom the message of the Bible is authoritative will no doubt treasure the idea that blessing for the nations was part of the divine purpose from the beginning, and not some afterthought, and will acknowledge the church's ongoing responsibility to spread the gospel in today's world.

A brief word about Matthew's extremely critical stance towards the Pharisees and their scribes, and his warning to his congregation against being drawn into their approach to the Law. The charge of "hypocrisy"

---

19. I recall hearing the late Revd. Dr. Leslie Weatherhead, the famous Methodist preacher and psychologist, say in a sermon, "Cancer was spawned in hell." I doubt if he believed in a literal hell and probably the congregation who knew him personally would not have assumed that he was speaking literally. But he certainly made his point dramatically and eloquently!

dominates his criticism of the Jewish leaders of his day, and, in its way, is almost as severe as the Fourth Evangelist's criticism of "the Jews." What we have said above in discussing John's Gospel applies here. Though this blanket criticism fits into the polemical approaches of their day, those involved in Jewish-Christian dialogue obviously do not find it helpful.

4

Our contention would be that, on the whole, the uses which the NT writers made of Abraham find points of contact in the Biblical narrative or the post-Biblical development of it. They were creative in their handling of the story, but tradition afforded the basis on which their creative handling took place. Their interests obviously played a part, but these interests have, on the whole, not led to violence being done to the story of Abraham. This assertion rests on the assumption that, whatever his faults, whatever doubts he and indeed Sarah may have had, *on the whole* the picture of Abraham which emerges from Genesis 12–25 is of a person who ventured forth into the unknown (as it were), and, while never possessing a permanent dwelling in the land of Canaan, persisted in continuing in that direction which first led him out of his native land and into Canaan. He never turned back and returned from where he came.

Paul's concentration on Genesis 15 and his ignoring of Genesis 17 is an example of how one aspect of tradition is evaluated as that through which a word of God for a new era emerges, while the stress on circumcision has to be set aside because it is considered no longer to accord with what God wants. The concentration on one area of tradition to the exclusion of another is not to be considered as purely arbitrary. Flebbe has shown that Paul argued on the basis of many Scriptural passages (and not just on Christological grounds) to defend his assertion that we are set in the right before God on the basis of His gracious acceptance and that God intended that His saving purpose should extend world wide and not just be confined to Israel.

There is perhaps some irony in the fact that while the allegorical approach (a major way in which Christians have held on to the Old Testament down the centuries) does not find favor with so many moderns, the concept of the pilgrimage to the heavenly city is one which continues to resonate with many Christians today. This gives us a counter balance to the increasing secularism and consumerism of modern society; the widespread desire for instant self gratification; the loosening of those bonds which unite people in neighborhoods and societies/nations; the devaluation of ideas of duty, obligation, and responsibility and the stress on rights; the tendency to judge a person by their monetary remuneration rather than what they contribute to the good of others; the desire to escape the signs of growing older and appear youthful. The pilgrimage idea reminds us of the transcendental dimension of life. It gives meaning and purpose to living.

The other themes drawn out by the NT writers are ones which nourish and challenge, nurture, and inspire us, as we seek to work out what it means today to be loyal to the God of Abraham who revealed Himself in Jesus of Nazareth.

5

There remains another issue to be considered. If the case which we have put forward that the NT writers handled tradition in a creative way but were in fact drawing out something present in that tradition, what of today? Are we bound by the ways in which they interpreted the tradition? With the closure of the canon, have their ways of interpreting the Abrahamic story laid down the parameters within which the modern preacher must keep? Can the modern preacher go beyond their lines of interpretation? It must be stressed that we are here thinking of the New Testament passages. That the Genesis stories in their own right provide a rich vein for drawing out a "word of God" for today has been shown by not a few studies which have taken the Abraham stories in particular or the patriarchal narratives in general and drawn out implications for the people of God today.

The question which we have posed may be a case of where "the spirits" divide. Attitudes to Scripture will no doubt come into play. For those with what may be for convenience termed a very "conservative" or "evangelical" approach to Scripture may well incline to the view that the modern preacher should keep within the lines of interpretation which the Biblical writers have mapped out. Others of a less conservative and more "liberal" approach to Scripture may feel less inhibited.

One example springs to mind. The writer of 1 Peter praised Sarah for the fact that she obeyed Abraham and held her up for emulation by Christian wives within the congregation to which the letter was written. While today some Christian writers, both female and male, still uphold this as an ideal in Christian marriage, the idea of the "subjection" of a wife to her husband is unlikely to appeal to a majority of women. If we test Scripture by Scripture, we might well feel that Paul's statement that "There is neither Jew nor Greek, slave nor free, male nor female, but you are all one in Christ" (Gal 3:28), whether a pre-Pauline creation taken over and endorsed by the apostle or a Pauline ad hoc creation, should operate as a yardstick by which we judge the relevance of statements like 1 Peter 3. While Paul in Galatians was speaking of the Christian community ("in Christ"), there is no reason why the gist of what he said is not also applicable to society at large.

As to the major directions of the New Testament interpretation of Abraham—the Christological, soteriological, ecclesiological, ethical, and missiological—these certainly remain fundamental for preaching today. They touch on such vital aspects of the gospel that to neglect or exclude them would seriously impoverish our presentation of the Christian message and our fidelity to the apostolic foundation of that message. Equally, as the modern interpreter grapples with the text and seeks to be faithful to it while applying it to the ever changing circumstances of life, he or she finds the text of Genesis about Abraham becomes both a human word and yet also a word of God, as members of the Jewish and Christian communities of faith have found in the past. They find afresh the truth of that great word issued to the company of believers, whom we know as the "Pilgrim Fathers," by their minister, John Robinson, before they set sail for America in 1620: "The Lord has more truth and light yet to break forth out of His holy Word."

Excursus: Abraham in the Apostolic Fathers

1. The First Epistle of Clement

ALTHOUGH NOT PART OF the New Testament, 1 Clement was probably written approximately around the same time as the Gospel of Matthew and the Fourth Gospel. It was written by Clement on behalf of the Church in Rome to the church at Corinth, encouraging it to reinstate elders who had been deposed from office. It is generally dated to ca. 96 AD.[1]

After condemning jealousy and envy because of their disastrous effects both on God's people and on secular societies (3–9), Clement went on to appeal for obedience to God's excellent and glorious will (9.1), and backed up this appeal by examples from the OT Scriptures. In the first place, he mentioned three persons (Enoch, Noah, Abraham), each of whom was described as having been found either righteous or faithful.[2] He mentioned Enoch's righteousness displayed in his obedience (9.3) and the faithfulness of Noah (9.4) who in his generation preached the rebirth of the world (παλιγγενεσια).

---

1. This widespread view has been challenged. See, e.g., Wagner, *Anfange*, 219–30, for a review of the arguments put forward against a date just after the assassination of Domitian. He himself believes that we should be cautious about fixing the date between 70 and 97/98, while believing that a date in the 70s is a possibility.

2. ευρεθεις or ευρεθη, plus either δικαιος or πιστος.

Then Clement devoted chapter 10 to Abraham. After mentioning that Abraham was called "friend" (viz. of God), he went on to stress that Abraham was found faithful πιστος εν τω αυτον υπηκοον γενεσθαι τοις ρημασιν του Θεου. How is this articular infinitive construction to be translated; what is its relation to the main verb; and what is the significance of the aorist infinitive within the construction? Abraham showed his faithfulness to and trust in God when he obeyed God's words (10.1). God's word or words came first, then Abraham's response. This obedient trust was shown in the first place by the fact that Abraham left his land and kindred and his father's house in order that he might inherit what God promised him (10.2),[3] Genesis 12:1–3 being then quoted (10.3). First came the divine intervention: God commanded and at the same time made promises. Then Abraham responded in trust and obeyed.

This is then followed (10.4–6) by two further quotations from Genesis: God's promise that He would give to Abraham the Land, at the time when Abraham and Lot parted company (Gen 13:14–16), and then again when God assured Abraham that he would indeed have descendants as numerous as the stars of heaven (Gen 15:5–6). These quotations helped to stress the greatness of God's promise—extensive land and numerous descendants. There is no indication of the earlier controversy of "justification."

It is possible that Clement chose the example of Abraham's separation from Lot because in Jewish tradition Lot was considered to be guilty of selfishness in choosing the best land.[4] Clement said that Abraham separated from Lot (whereas in the Genesis account Lot separated from Abraham according to Gen 13:14). He may have had in mind those guilty of ejecting the lawfully appointed elders from their office. They were, in his view, guilty of selfish pride and arrogance. If so, Abraham is an example of virtue. There is possibly the implication that he put family concord above his own personal advantage.

Clement concluded by saying: "Because of his faith and hospitality a son was given to him in his old age, and through obedience he offered him as a sacrifice to God on one of the mountains which (God) had shown him" (10.7). The reference to hospitality is to the incident when Abraham entertained the three strangers in Genesis 18, during which they gave Abraham a promise that Sarah would have a son within the year (18:10, 14), while it also provided a means of transition to his next set of examples,

---

3. There is an implicit contrast between the little land, a family lacking in influence, and a small household which Abraham left and what was held out to him in the promises of God, though as Lona, *Der erste Clemensbrief*, 197, points out, "inheritance" and "promise" do not play as significance a role for Clement as they did for the apostle Paul.

4. Cf. Philo, *Migr.* 148–50.

in connection with whom he mentioned hospitality (Lot [11.1] and Rahab [12.1]). Clement also got in a reference to Abraham's obedience to God's command to offer Isaac (made to test him according to the Genesis account, although this is not specifically mentioned by Clement).

Thus Clement ended this chapter, as he began it, with references to Abraham's πιστος/πιστις and υπακοη (vv. 1-2, 7). Lona notes the nearness of Clement to the Jewish standpoint exemplified in 1 Maccabees 2:52; Sirach 44:20; and also James 2:21-23.[5]

Subsequent examples are Lot, whose hospitality and godliness are specified (11.1), and Rahab, who was saved from the destruction of Jericho and its inhabitants because of her faith and hospitality (δια πιστιν και φιλοξενιαν [12.1]).[6] After quoting Jeremiah 9:23-24 and words of Jesus from Luke 6:31, 36-38, Clement encouraged obedience to the hallowed words of Jesus in all humility (13.3), and then made an appeal: "Therefore, brothers, it is right and pleasing (δικαιον και οσιον) to God that we should obey Him rather than follow those who have become leaders in arrogance and a rebellion motivated by detestable jealousy" (14.1). To follow these men was to expose oneself to a great danger (v. 2).

This appeal reveals that all along Clement has had in mind the aim of reversing the deposition of the appointed elders and their reinstatement. Abraham, then, is one among a number of Old Testament examples adduced by Clement in pursuance of this aim.

The use of Abraham and Rahab in chapters 10 and 12 (admittedly broken up by the reference to Lot in chapter 11) reminds us of their juxtaposition in James 2:21-24 and 25, while in Hebrews 11 both Abraham and Rahab figure (vv. 8-12, 17-19, and 31 respectively) with Abraham's faith and obedience being stressed, while Rahab is distinguished from the disobedient in Jericho who perished.

There are two main possibilities: Clement drew on Hebrews, or that Hebrews, James, and Clement drew on a common Christian tradition in which Abraham and Rahab both figured. We need not pursue this question here.

---

5. Lona, *Der erste Clemensbrief*, 199.

6. Chadwick, *Justification by Faith and Hospitality*, 281-85, speculates ("not more than a guess") that some visiting Christians at Corinth accepted hospitality from the deposed clergy rather than the new, and that this was used by the former to reaffirm their position, while the rest of the church reacted in a hostile manner, which left an unfavorable impression on the visitors. Beyschlag, *Clemens Romanus*, 39, dismisses Chadwick's theory as a fanciful hypothesis with minimal basis in the text. Lona, *Erste Clemensbrief*, 209-210, is more favorably disposed to it.

EXCURSUS: ABRAHAM IN THE APOSTOLIC FATHERS

Abraham also received mention a little later in 1 Clement 17.2. The section began with the exhortation to be imitators of those who proclaimed the coming of the messiah, while going around wearing goatskins and sheepskins. Clement specifically mentioned the prophets Elijah, Elisha, and Ezekiel and those who have had a good testimony (17.1). The verb μαρτυρειν afforded the opportunity of mentioning other OT characters, beginning with Abraham. "Abraham had received a glorious witness[7] and was called the friend of God. With humility, while gazing on the glory of God, he said, I am dust and ashes." The reference is to the occasion when Abraham was interceding with God for Sodom (Gen 18:17–33, esp. v. 27). Humility is another virtue prized by Clement, exemplified above all by Christ and here by Abraham, and conducive to peace and harmony in the church (cf. 16.1-2, 17; 19.1; 21.8; 30.3). People like Abraham are worthy models to be imitated in their humility.

After mentioning Job, Moses, and David as further examples of humility (17.3-18.17), Clement sought to apply the implications of his examples. Such humble people have through their obedience benefited not only the present but also the past. "Since we have received a share in many, great, and glorious deeds, let us make haste to return to the goal of peace which was handed on to us from the beginning, and let us look to the Father and Creator of the entire cosmos and let us adhere to His sublime and extraordinary gifts of peace (and) to His kindnesses" (19.2).

Later (30.1-7), Clement advocated pursuing holiness of behavior and avoiding the kind of faults which cause discord and rebellion. The congregation should seek what made for concord. They should aim to be justified by works and not by words. It is qualities like forbearance, humility, and gentleness which are blessed by God (ηυλογημενοις υπο του Θεου [v. 7]). And it is God's blessing (ευλογια) that Christians should seek (31.1). In order to do so, it is a good thing to study what are the ways in which that blessing may be received. Here the record of Scripture helps (31.1). "Why was our father Abraham blessed? Was it not because he did what was right and true, through faith?" (v. 2). Here the reference is couched in general terms, but Clement may have in mind God's promise to bless Abraham because he was willing to offer up his only son (Gen 22:16).[8] Then followed comments on Isaac's willingness to be sacrificed and Jacob's humility, as a result of which the twelve tribes of Israel were given to him (31.3-4).

---

7. For this translation, see Bauer, *Lexicon*, 498.

8. Cf. Lona, *Der erste Clemensbrief*, 340, though Flüchter, *Anrechnung*, 120, is inclined to think of Genesis 15:6, because of the earlier use of it in chapter 10.

Then Clement pointed to the magnificence of the gifts which God gave (32.1), and went on to specify what Jacob (as the progenitor of the twelve tribes) received (32.2). From Jacob came Israel's cultic officials (priests and Levites), the Lord Jesus on the physical side,[9] and kings, rulers, and governors from Judah (the Davidic dynasty). The rest of Jacob's tribes are also held in great honor. "They all, therefore, were glorified and magnified, not through themselves or their own works or the righteous activity which they did, but through His will" (32.3). This is followed up by a statement with something of a Pauline flavor, which applied to the Christian community: "We also, therefore, who have been called through His will in Christ Jesus, are not justified through ourselves or through our wisdom or piety or works done in holiness of heart, but through faith, by which almighty God has justified all[10] from the beginning" (32.4).

This is not the place to consider the juxtaposition of the two emphases "justified by works and not by words" (30.3) and "justified by His [God's] will/by faith" (32.3, 4). Suffice to say that Clement seems to stand close to James in his combination of the two.[11]

We note that Abraham was described quite naturally, as it were, as "our father" (31.2). Abraham is the spiritual father of all Christians. Believers of all generations constitute one family.

There is a general reference to the fathers at 60.4: "Give us and all who dwell on earth harmony and peace as You gave to our fathers, when they called on You in faith and truth with holiness." A participial construction is attached, which may be variously interpreted. It may have a temporal sense—"while we are obedient to Your almighty and most excellent Name and to our rulers and governors on earth,"[12] or a final sense—"in order that we might be obedient, etc.,"[13] or possibly an imperatival sense—"Let us be obedient, etc."[14] The reference to "the fathers" probably includes more than the first three patriarchs of Israel.

---

9. Through the Christological statement, Christians share in the story of Jacob, says Prostmeier, *Barnabasbrief*, 345.

10. I.e., those saved, as maintained by Knopf, *Der erste Clementsbrief*, 98.

11. For two opposing views on whether Clement really understood justification by grace through faith, see Torrance, *Doctrine of Grace*, 44–55; Lawson, *Theological and Historical Introduction*, 42–44.

12. Lightfoot, *Apostolic Fathers*, 83.

13. Lona, *Der erste Clemensbrief*, 585.

14. So Knopf, *Der erste Clementsbrief*, 145. For the imperative use of the participle, see Daube, *Participle and Imperative*, 467–88; Moule, *Idiom Book*, 179–80.

Summary

Clement regards the OT as a Christian book which offers numerous examples of godly men and women who provide worthy examples of virtuous behavior for the Christian community to follow. Of these Abraham is a prominent example. Worthy to be called the friend of God (10.1; 17.2), he was a man faithful and obedient to God (10.1, 7), given to hospitality (10.7) and a man of humility before God (17.2). Because he did what was right, he received God's blessing (31.2).

He is regarded as "our father" (31.2), and is obviously included in the reference to "our fathers" in the prayer at 60.4 which Clement probably draws from the current worship of the church.

In Clement's use of Abraham, there is no sign that the Pauline controversy about justification was a live issue. Clement had his eyes on the problem of the ejection from office of elders at Corinth. He asserted that Abraham's faith produced works of righteousness and truth which led to blessing, and, in this combination of faithfulness plus works, he was a model for current Christians. In this stress, Clement stood close to Jewish tradition which saw the patriarch as the great example of righteous behavior.

2. The Letters of Ignatius[15]

Ignatius only refers to Abraham once, and then together with Isaac and Jacob.

In his letter to the Philadelphians, Ignatius was concerned with those who in his opinion overemphasized the Jewishness of the Christian faith.

> Do not listen to anyone who expounds Judaism to you: for it is better to hear Christianity from a circumcised person than Judaism from someone who is uncircumcised. If neither speaks of Jesus Christ, they are, as far as I am concerned, tombstones and graves of the dead, on which are written only human names. (6.1)

---

15. The Seven Letters of the so-called Middle recension of Ignatius's correspondence—as he was on his way as a prisoner to Rome to face probable martyrdom—are now widely accepted as genuine. For a discussion, see Schoedel, *Ignatius of Antioch*, 1–7. These letters are usually dated to the reign of the Emperor Trajan, sometime between 110 and 117, perhaps nearer to the beginning rather than the end of this period. Recently, Stewart, *Original Bishops*, 239–40, has argued for a date towards the end of the reign of the Emperor Hadrian, when Hadrian was on his way back to Rome after his suppression of the Jewish Revolt of 132–35. The issue of date does not really affect our discussion in any fundamental way.

Ignatius appears to be taking exception to some involvement with Judaism and its practices. He did concede, however, that a Jew who has become a Christian can speak about the faith, but he is opposed to a Gentile who has not been circumcised speaking about things connected with the Jewish faith, i.e., presumably a Gentile Christian who has never been circumcised has become attracted to some aspects of Judaism and speaks warmly of them. For Ignatius, this latter type of person inevitably obscured the primacy of Jesus Christ.

A little later, Ignatius appealed to the church not to do anything in a spirit of partisanship,[16] but to act in accordance with Christ's teaching (κατα χριστομαθιαν),[17] and then went on to refer to a discussion that had occurred in the church. Ignatius must have expressed a particular view, to which some[18] had responded "Unless I find (it) in τα αρχεια, I do not believe (it) in the gospel" (8.2). When Ignatius answered "It does stand written," they replied, "That is the question."[19] Then Ignatius wrote that for him Jesus Christ, was the αρχεια: "the inviolable αρχεια are his cross and his death and resurrection and faith which comes through him." By all this he wants to be justified through their prayers (8.1).

What, then, are τα αρχεια? We may assume that the phrase is referring to the Old Testament Scriptures.[20] Ignatius countered the Philadelphians with whom he was discussing, with the assertion that "the archives" were the death and resurrection of Jesus and the faith that stemmed from him and his ministry. That is, Jesus Christ had become the touchstone rather than the Old Testament.

Then Ignatius acknowledged that the priests of the Old Testament were good, but even better was "the high priest to whom is entrusted the Holy of Holies [by which phrase he of course meant Jesus Christ], to whom the hidden (secrets) of God have been entrusted" (9.1). Here Ignatius was working with something like the Christology of Hebrews, which envisaged Jesus our High Priest as having entered the Holy of Holies, meaning Heaven,

---

16. So Schoedel, *Ignatius*, 207, renders κατ'εριθειαν, and this seems to fit the context admirably (rather than "selfish ambition").

17. Or "in accordance with discipleship to Christ." See Bauer, *Lexicon*, 895.

18. Presumably, these were people in some way connected to those referred to earlier in chapter 6.

19. Literally, "It lies before us" (προκειται). See Bauer, *Lexicon*, 714.

20. There are good reasons for assuming this interpretation. Firstly, Ignatius's reply γεγραπται is the formula for quoting the OT. Secondly, Schoedel, *Ignatius* 207-9, has adduced examples from Josephus and Philo for regarding the OT Scriptures as parallel to public records (archives). Schoedel believes that those whom Ignatius met at Philadelphia were exegetically more expert than he was.

and indicating the presence of God, on our behalf. In that sense, he could be said to have been entrusted with this crucially important "spiritual space."

Ignatius followed this up with the assertion that Jesus Christ was the door to God the Father. He was the door through which Abraham and Isaac and Jacob and the prophets and the apostles and the church entered the presence of God: all these enter into the unity of God (9.1).

In what follows, Ignatius asserted that the gospel contains something distinctive (εξαιρετον), viz. the presence of the saviour, our Lord Jesus Christ, his passion and resurrection. The beloved prophets directed their proclamation toward him. The gospel is the consummation of immortality. "All things are good if you believe with love." (9.2).

Whatever the exact background to Philadelphians 8–9 may have been, it is reasonably clear that Ignatius wished to establish that Jesus Christ was the key to the Old Testament, rather than the other way round.[21] Rather than force Jesus into a pre-existing mold, he was the key to it. That he was thus pre-eminent is shown by the fact that Abraham and other Old Testament worthies, together with members of the church, only come to God through him.

We may also say that Ignatius was claiming that the OT worthies were Christians.[22] In thus enunciating this claim he was following in the wake of many NT writers.

3. The Epistle of Barnabas

The epistle of Barnabas is an extremely anti-Jewish writing. The author in effect denies that the Jewish people were ever the people of the Covenant (the sin of the Golden Calf in effect nullifying their intended status). He alleged that they consistently misunderstood God's command and took literally what He had intended spiritually. Jewish institutions like sacrifice, fasting, circumcision, covenant, sabbath, and temple are reinterpreted, while, by means of midrashic exegesis, baptism, Lord's Supper, and the passion and cross of Christ were extracted from passages in the OT. He used allegorical interpretation of the OT Scriptures in order to wrest them away from the Jews and advance the claim that they belonged to Christians, not to the Jews.[23]

---

21. According to Schoedel, *Ignatius*, 211, preoccupation with Scripture from any standpoint other than Christ is irrelevant.

22. See Meinhold, *Studien zu Ignatius von Antiochien*, 41, who sees in this claim to the OT worthies the consciousness of the superiority of Christianity over Judaism.

23. For the dating of Barnabas to 130–132, see the detailed discussion in Prostmeier,

There is a reference at 5.5-7 to the fact that the prophets were inspired by the Lord Jesus to prophesy concerning himself. The Lord Jesus was manifested in the flesh in order that he might destroy death and reveal the resurrection from the dead. At the same time, he redeemed the promise made to the fathers, and, while preparing for himself a new people during his time on earth, he showed that he would exercise (the final) judgment. What Barnabas seemed to have in mind by fulfilling the promise made to the fathers is the creation of the church, the new people. This seems confirmed by what he said in chapter 6. At 6.8, he quoted the command, from Exodus 33:1, 3, to enter the good land which God had promised to Abraham, Isaac, and Jacob, and argued that this promise of the land had been fulfilled for Christians. Barnabas identified Christ with the land (v. 9), asserted that Christians had been recreated (v. 13), and equated this new creation with entry into the promised land: "We are the ones whom he has led into the good land" (6.16c). The promise made to the patriarchs beginning with Abraham was intended for Christians, not the Jews.

In his discussion of the ritual of sprinkling the ashes of the red heifer over the Israelites (8), we have what Prigent describes as a typological midrash on Numbers 19.[24] The calf is interpreted as Jesus (8.2); those who do the sprinkling are interpreted as the Twelve who were given authority by Jesus to preach the forgiveness of sins and the purification of the heart (8.3). Then Barnabas asked why those who do the sprinkling are three in number? He gives the answer "For a witness to Abraham, Isaac, and Jacob, because they are mighty with God" (8.4). As there is a difference in the numbers between 8.3 and 8.4, it looks as if 8.4 is an expansion by Barnabas of a tradition which was at Barnabas's disposal,[25] and yet his mention of the number three without any further explanation could suggest that his readers know this number also.[26] Prostmeier suggests that the greatness of the patriarchs lies in the fact that they had been given prophetic foreknowledge of Jesus and his cross and the superiority of the church over the Jewish people (e.g., 9.7; 11.9; 13.2.7).

Barnabasbrief, 111-19, esp. 118-19. For an earlier dating to the reign of Trajan, see Carleton Paget, *Epistle of Barnabas*.

24. Prigent, *Barnabé*, 114.

25. Prigent, *Barnabé*, 112-13; Wengst, *Tradition*, 33. Prostmeier, *Barnabasbrief*, 329n51, who rejects Windisch's explanation of a secondary gloss, also argues for different explanations standing side by side.

26. Prostmeier, *Barnabasbrief*, 329.

EXCURSUS: ABRAHAM IN THE APOSTOLIC FATHERS

We may surmise that the purpose of this explanation was to claim the patriarchs for the Christian church.[27] Barnabas in effect was saying that they belonged to us, and Scripture rightly understood bears witness to them.

Barnabas also referred to Abraham and his story in a section devoted to discussing what was the real intention of God behind the command concerning circumcision (9).[28] Barnabas began with a series of texts which mention the circumcision of the ears and of the heart. His aim was to show that while physical circumcision was not really intended by God; that the Jews misunderstood His intention and emphasized the physical aspect,[29] whereas God intended a spiritual meaning, the "circumcision" of the ears and the heart (9.1, 4); and that God had circumcised the ears of Christian believers in order that they might hear the word and believe (v. 4). Sensing an objection ("But you will say . . ."), Barnabas denied that circumcision was given to the Jews as a "seal" (as Gen 17:11 suggested) and pointed out that other nations practiced circumcision but did not belong to God's covenant (v. 6).

Thus, as Hvalvik has pointed out, Barnabas has both contrasted the two peoples, Jews and Christians, and redefined the meaning of circumcision.[30]

At this point,[31] Barnabas mentioned that Abraham was the one who was the first to institute circumcision[32] and that he carried out circumcision λαβων τριων γραμματων δογματα (v. 7). By this phrase Barnabas indicated that Abraham was given an understanding[33] of what "the three letters" indicated. This is backed up by a reference to Genesis 17 where Abraham circumcised the 318 males in his household (the quotation combined Genesis 17:23 and 14:14, the latter being the actual source of the number 318). He said that in the act of circumcising, Abraham was in fact looking ahead to Jesus, under the inspiration of the Spirit (v. 7). Barnabas interpreted allegorically the three letters, which stand for three numbers which make up 318. The Greeks indicated the numerical value ten by the letter Iota, and that of

---

27. Cf. Hvalvik, *Struggle*, 186, without specific reference to 8.4: "It was thus important to make sure that he had Abraham's support."

28. At 8.7, Barnabas claimed that Christians had been able to understand the symbolism of the wool and hyssop in the OT, whereas these matters were dark to the Jews "because they did not hear the voice of the Lord." He continued in 9.1, "Again He said concern the ears, how it is our heart which He has circumcised."

29. Barnabas said that the Jews were led astray by an evil angel (9:4).

30. Hvalvik, *Struggle*, 185.

31. Both Prigent, *Barnabé*, 58–59, and Wengst, *Tradition*, 36, believe that 9.7-9 is probably the work of Barnabas himself (whereas 9.1–3 comes from a written source used by Barnabas).

32. For this sense of περιτομην δους, see Bauer, *Lexicon*, 192.

33. For the meaning of δογμα as indicating an understanding or knowledge of Scripture, see Hvalvik, *Struggle*, 50; Prostmeier, *Barnabasbrief*, 367n59.

eight by letter Eta. With these two letters ιη, Barnabas saw Jesus signified. When he turned to the three hundred, the numerical value of which is represented by the letter tau, Barnabas added "the cross εν τω Τ ημελλεν εχειν την χαριν." This phrase could mean that the grace (of salvation) came about through the cross, not through circumcision, and so it is taken by Windisch and Prostmeier in their commentaries.[34] Torrance maintained that we should translate the phrase as "the cross was to find acknowledgment in the tau."[35] While this would certainly fit the context nicely, there does not seem evidence to justify his claim that this is in accord with the ordinary sense current at the time.[36] For Barnabas, the letter Tau was reminiscent of the cross. And so "The episode was not meant to be "the institution" of circumcision in the flesh, but was a prophecy about Christ."[37]

In this way, Barnabas got Jesus on the Cross from the passage. God[38] "revealed Jesus in the two letters and in the remaining one the cross" (9.8). Barnabas added, "No one received from me more reliable teaching;[39] but I know that you are worthy" (9.9).

Barnabas referred to Abraham again in 13.7. Barnabas had raised the questions whether Jews or Christians were the true heirs of the inheritance promised by God and whether the covenant belonged "to us or to them" (13.1). The question of covenant is dealt with in chapter 14, while chapter 13 handles that of the inheritance. He mentioned two cases where the younger sons had precedence over the older ones. The first example was Jacob whose superiority over Esau was predicted. Barnabas said that his addressees should understand that the Lord showed that this people [the Church] was greater than the other [the Jews] (v. 3).[40] The incident had a revelatory quality.

---

34. Windisch, *Barnabasbrief*, 356; Prostmeier, *Barnabasbrief*, 350, 370.

35. Torrance, *Doctrine of Grace*, 109 (following Cunningham, *Dissertation*).

36. There is no evidence in *LSJ*, *MM*, or the Zimmerli-Conzelmann article, "χαρις κτλ," *TWNT* 9:372–91, to support Torrance's claim.

37. Hvalvik, *Struggle*, 186.

38. Prostmeier, *Barnabasbrief*, 370, appears to take Abraham as the subject of δηλοι, and, in support, this could claim the assertion that Abraham was looking forward to Jesus (9.7). On the other hand, the Lord is the author of all the quotations from Scripture in 9.1–5, and the Lord is, therefore, presumably intended in the threefold occurrence of λεγει in verse 8 in connection with the numbers 318, 18, and 300, respectively. In addition it was from the Lord that Abraham received understanding of these numbers (9.7). It seems reasonable to suppose that the Lord is the subject of the very next statement with δηλοι.

39. See Bauer, *Lexicon*, 162, for this rendering of γνησιωτερον λογον.

40. "As Paul in Gal 4:22–31 set the Jews to Ishmael, Barnabas sets them to Esau" (Windisch, *Barnabasbrief*, 376).

EXCURSUS: ABRAHAM IN THE APOSTOLIC FATHERS

The same is true for the second example, when Jacob gave the blessing of his right hand to the younger grandson, Ephraim, and not the older Manasseh. While Joseph tried to guide his father's hand of blessing to Manasseh, Barnabas said that Jacob saw through the Spirit the type of the people who should come afterwards, and when Joseph protested at what his father was going to do, Jacob said, "I know, my child, I know, but the older will serve the younger, and he [Ephraim] will be blessed"[41] (13.2–5). Jacob was gifted by the Spirit with prophetic insight and foresaw what would happen in the future—the church would be the people blessed by God. The word "type" reinforces the prophetic character of Jacob's action and words. Barnabas concluded with the remark "Note in which (persons) He has established that this people [viz. Christians] should be first and the heir of the covenant" (v. 6).

Thus, these two incidents were proof for Barnabas that the Jews were never God's people and were never the intended recipients of God's promise of an inheritance. These events from Scripture prove that the Church was the true and only people of God.

Barnabas backed up these two illustrations with what God said to Abraham[42] when (or because[43]) he alone believed and it was counted to him for righteousness, which clearly is a reference to Genesis 15:6.[44] God said: "See, I have appointed you, Abraham, the father of nations who believe in God while uncircumcised"[45] (v. 7). Barnabas was not concerned

---

41. The context demands that only Ephraim received the blessing; so rightly Hvalvik, *Struggle*, 130; Prostmeier, *Barnabasbrief*, 461, and against the translation (e.g., Lightfoot, *Apostolic Fathers*, 282) which sees Manasseh referred to in the ουτος. The general comment of Robertson is helpful: "There is continuation, not opposition, in the use of και δε" (*Grammar*, 1185). A good example from the NT would be Luke 1:76, where the baby John (the Baptist) is addressed. The hymn is being continued, but there is no opposition with what precedes, and it would be entirely inappropriate to translate with "and you also" as if the savior from the house of David were the prophet of the Most High and John the Baptist were to be ranked with him. There is also no opposition with what precedes in the use of και δε in Matthew 10:18; 16:18; John 6:51; 15:27; Acts 22:29.

42. The somewhat elliptical δια του Αβρααμ εμνησθη indicated that something had been recalled through Abraham: this could be "this people" [the church] (as Windisch, *Barnabasbrief*, 377; Prostmeier, *Barnabasbrief*, 462, suggest) or the claim that God has appointed the church to be the heir of the covenant (as Hvalvik, *Struggle*, 85, thinks), both of which had just been mentioned in the previous sentence.

43. Flüchter, *Anrechnung*, 119, takes μονος πιστευσας in a causal sense.

44. Flüchter, *Anrechnung*, 119, sees the use here of τιθεναι τινα εις τι as equivalent to λογιζεσθαι with a double accusative.

45. The δι'ακροβυστιας is the genitive of attendant circumstances. The reference to father of many nations is an allusion to Genesis 17:5.

to argue (as Paul was) for the justification of those who are uncircumcised solely on the basis of God's grace and their faith, but he was concerned with the issue of who were the children of Abraham, who were the people of God. This was claimed for Christians—apparently Gentile Christians, as at any rate there is no mention of Jewish Christians.[46] The promise to Abraham was realized in the church.

We may note in passing that in 13.1-7 Barnabas mentioned all three of the earliest patriarchs: Isaac (vv. 2-3), Jacob (vv. 4-5), and Abraham (vv. 6-7). Abraham is the chief of Barnabas's witnesses: "If, therefore, (this people) is mentioned through (the story of) Abraham, we have the perfection of our knowledge" (v. 6). It was clearly important for Barnabas that he could claim the support of Abraham for his position, and this illustrates that Abraham continued to be important for Christians both on the level of community instruction and reassurance and on the level of debate with Jewish opponents.

Summary

For Barnabas there is no "salvation history" from Abraham through Israel to the church. The Jewish people had ceased to be the people of God at Sinai when they worshipped the Golden Calf. Barnabas pursued his purposes of claiming for the church the promises, the Scripture, the covenant, the title of "people of God." They did not belong, and had never belonged, to the Jewish people. All these things were destined for the church. The figure and story of Abraham was pressed into the service of this overriding aim. Abraham was depicted as some one gifted by the inspiration of the Spirit with prophetic insight and understanding. As a result he foresaw both Jesus and his cross (9.7-9) and received a revelation that the people of God would be drawn from Gentile (uncircumcised) believers (13.7). From the story of Abraham, then, Barnabas derived proof of his position that the church of his day was the true people of God, brought into being within God's purposes by the sacrificial death of Jesus (cf. 5.7; 6.9, 11, 16).

4. Summary

We may briefly summarize what the Apostolic Fathers offer in respect to the figure of Abraham.

---

46. Hvalvik, *Struggle*, 193-94. See also 44, 148.

Abraham is regarded as the spiritual father of Christians (Clement, Barnabas). He is an example worthy to be emulated in the combination observable in his life of faithfulness and works, rewarded with God's blessing (Clement). Inspired by the Spirit with prophetic insight, he knew from the start what God intended with the rite of circumcision (Barnabas). For both Clement and Barnabas the OT is a Christian book, but Barnabas's approach of denying it completely to the Jews reflects a sharp and bitter controversy with Jewish opponents in his milieu, wherever that may have been. Ignatius maintains that OT worthies like Abraham enter the kingdom through the door which is Christ.

Bibliography

Abegg, Martin G. "Paul and James on the Law in Light of the Dead Sea Scrolls." In *Christian Beginnings and the Dead Sea Scrolls*, edited by John J. Collins and Craig A. Evans, 63-74. ASBT. Grand Rapids: Baker Academic, 2006. .

Adams, Edward. "Abraham's Faith and Gentile Disobedience: Textual Links between Romans 1 and 4," *JSNT* 65 (1997) 47-66.

Alexander, T.Desmond. "Abraham Re-Assessed Theologically. The Abraham Narrative and the New Testament Understanding of Justification by Faith." In *He Swore an Oath. Biblical Themes in Genesis 12-50*, edited by Richard S. Hess et al., 7-28. 2nd ed. Carlisle: Paternoster, 1994.

Allen, Leslie C. *Ezekiel 20-48*. WBC 29. Dallas: Word, 1990.

Allo, E.B. *Saint Paul: Seconde Épître aux Corinthiens*. EB. 2nd. ed. Paris: Gabalda, 1956.

Attridge, Harold W., *Hebrews*. Hermeneia. Philadelphia: Fortress, 1989.

Aune, David E. *Prophecy in Early Christianity and the Ancient Mediterranean World*. Grand Rapids: Eerdmans, 1983.

———. "Romans as *Logos Protreptikos*." In *The Romans Debate*, edited by Karl P. Donfried, 278-96. Rev.ed., Peabody, MA: Hendrickson., 1991.

Avemarie, Friedrich. "Erwählung und Vergeltung. Zur optionalen Struktur rabbinischer Soteriologie," *NTS* 45 (1999) 108-26.

———. "Die Werke des Gesetzes im Spiegel des Jakobusbriefs. A Very Old Perspective on Paul," *ZTK* 98 (2001) 282-309.

Avemarie, Friedrich, and Hermann Lichtenberger, eds. *Bund und Tora. Zur theologischen Begriffs-geschichte in alttestamentlicher, frühjudischer und urchristlicher Tradition*. WUNT 92. Mohr: Tübingen, 1996.

Bachmann, Michael. *Anti-Judaism in Galatians? Exegetical Studies on a Polemical Letter and on Paul's Theology*. Grand Rapids: Eerdmans, 2008.

———. "Bermerkungen zur Auslegung zweier Genetivverbindungen des Galaterbriefes: "Werke des Gesetzes" (Gal:2.16 u.ö.) und "Israel Gottes" (Gal.6:16)." In *Umstrittener Galaterbrief. Studien zur Situierung der Theologie des Paulus-Schreiben*, edited by Michael Bachmann and Bernd Kollmann, 95–118. BTS 106. Neukirchen-Vluyn: Neukirchener, 2010.

———. "Zur Argumentation von Galater 3.10–12." *NTS* 53 (2007) 524–544.

Bachmann, Michael, and Bernd Kollmann, eds.*Umstrittener Galaterbrief. Studien zur Situierung der Theologie des Paulus-Schreibens*. BTS 106. Neukirchen-Vluyn: Neukirchener Theologie, 2010.

Backhaus, Knut. *Der Hebraerbrief.* RNT. Regensburg: Friedrich Pustet, 2009.

———. "Das Land der Verheissung: Die Heimat der Glaubenden im Hebräebrief," *NTS* 47 (2001) 171–88.

———. *Der neue Bund und das Werden der Kirche. Die Diathke-Deutung des Hebräerbriefs im Rahman der frühchristlichen Theologiegeschichte*. NA NF 29. Münster: Aschendorff, 1996.

———. "Das wandernde Gottesvolk–am Scheideweg. Der Hebraerbrief und Israel." In *"Nun Steht aber diese Sache im Evangelium . . ." Zur Frage nach den Anfängen des christlichen Antijudaismus*, edited by Rainer Kampling, 301–20. Paderborn: Schöningh, 1999.

———. "Per Christum in Deum. Zur theozentrischen Funktion der Christologie im Hebräerbrief." In *Der lebendige Gott. Studien zur Theologie des Neuen Testaments. Festschrift für Wilhelm Thüsing zum 75. Geburtstag*, edited by Thomas Söding, 258–84. Münster: Aschendorff, 1996.

Balch, David L., ed. *Social History of the Matthean Community. Cross-Disciplinary Approaches*. Minneapolis: Fortress, 1991.

Baltzer, Klaus. *The Covenant Formulary in Old Testament, Jewish, and Early Christian Writings*. Philadelphia: Fortress, 1971.

Bammel, Ernst. "Gottes ΔΙΑΘΗΚΗ (Gal.iii:15–17) und das jüdische Rechtsdenken," *NTS* 6 (1959–60) 313–19.

Barclay, John M.G. "Believers and the "Last Judgment" in Paul: Rethinking Grace and Recompense." In *Eschatologie-Eschatology*, edited by Hans-Joachim Eckstein et al., 195–208. WUNT 272. Tübingen: Mohr Siebeck, 2011.

———. " "By the Grace of God I am what I am:" Grace and Agency in Paul and Philo." In *Divine and Human Agency in Paul and His Cultural Environment*, edited by John M.G. Barclay and Simon J. Gathecole, 140–57. London: T. & T. Clark, 2006.

———. "Do We Undermine the Law? A Study of Romans 14:1–15:6." In *Paul and the Mosaic Law*, edited by James D.G. Dunn, 287–308. Grand Rapids: Eerdmans, 2001.

———. " "I will have mercy on whom I have mercy:" The Golden Calf and Divine Mercy in Romans 9–11 and Second Temple Judaism," *Early Christianity* 1 (2010) 82–106.

———. "Mirror Reading a Polemical Letter: Galatians a Test Case." *JSNT* 31 (1987) 73–93.

———. *Obeying the Truth. A Study of Paul's Ethics in Galatians*. SNTW. Edinburgh: T. & T. Clark, 1988.

———. *Paul and The Gift*. Grand Rapids: Eerdmans, 2015.

———. "Paul's Story: Theology as Testimony." In *Narrative Dynamics in Paul*, edited by Bruce W. Longenecker, 133–56. Louisville: Westminster/John Knox Press, 2002.

———. "Unnerving Grace. Approaching Romans 9-11 from the Wisdom of Solomon." In *Between Gospel and Election. Explorations in the Interpretation of Romans 9-11*, edited by Florian Wilk and J.Ross Wagner, 91-109. WUNT 257. Tübingen: Mohr Siebeck, 2010.

———. "Who was Considered an Apostate in the Jewish Diaspora?" In *Tolerance and Intolerance in Early Judaism and Christianity*, edited by Graham N. Stanton and Guy Stroumsa, 80-96. Cambridge: Cambridge University Press, 1996.

Barrett, C. Kingsley. *Acts*. 2 vols. ICC. Edinburgh: T. & T. Clark, 1994, 1998.

———. "The Allegory of Abraham, Sarah, and Hagar in the Argument of Galatians," in *Essays on Paul*, 154-70. London: SPCK, 1982.

———. *A Commentary on The Epistle to the Romans*. BNTC. London: A. & C. Black, 1957.

———. *The First Epistle to the Corinthians*. BNTC. London: A. & C. Black, 1968.

———. *Freedom and Obligation. A Study of the Epistle to the Galatians* London: SPCK, 1985.

———. *The Gospel according to St. John*. 2nd ed., London: SPCK, 1978.

———. *The Gospel of John and Judaism*. London: SPCK, 1972.

———. "The Interpretation of the Old Testament in the New." In *Cambridge History of the Bible 1: From the Beginnings to Jerome* edited by Peter R. Ackroyd and Christopher F. Evans, 377-411. Cambridge: Cambridge University Press, 1970.

———. "Paul and the "pillar" apostles." In *Studia Paulina, in Honorem J. de Zwaan Septuagenerii*, edited by Jon N. Sevenster and W.Cornelius van Unnik, 1-19. Haarlem: Bohn, 1953.

Bassler, Jouette M. *Divine Impartiality. Paul and a Theological Axiom*. SBLDS 59. Chico, CA: Scholars, 1982.

———., ed.. *Pauline Theology, Volume I: Thessalonians, Philippians, Galatians, Philemon*. Minneapolis: Fortress, 1991.

Bauckham, Richard *James*. NTR. London: Routledge, 1999.

Beare. Francis W. *The Gospel according to Matthew*. Oxford: Blackwell, 1981.

Beasley-Murray, George R. *Baptism in the New Testament*. London: Macmillan, 1962.

———. *John*. WBC 36. Waco, Texas: Word, 1987.

Behm, Johannes. διατίθημι διαθηκη, *TDNT* 2.104-34.

Beker, Christian, "The Faithfulness of God and the Priority of Israel in Paul's Letter to the Romans." In *The Romans Debate*, edited by Karl P. Donfried, 327-32. Rev. ed. Peabody, MA: Hendrickson, 1991.

Benoit, Pierre. "L'enfance de Jean-Baptiste selon Luc 1," *NTS* 3 (1956-57) 169-94.

Berger, Klaus. "Abraham in den paulinischen Hauptbriefen," *MTZ* 17 (1966) 47-89.

Bergmeier. Roland. *Gerechtigkeit, Gesetz und Glaube bei Paulus. Der judenchristliche Heidenapostel im Streit um das Gesetz und seine Werke*. BTS 115. Neukirchen-Vluyn: Neukirchener Theologie, 2010.

Betz, Hans D. *Galatians*. Hermeneia. Philadelphia: Fortress, 1979.

———. "In Defense of the Spirit: Paul's Letter to the Galatians as a Document of Early Christian Apologetics." In *Aspects of Religious Propaganda in Judaism and Early Christianity*, edited by Elizabeth Schüssler Fiorenza, 99-114. Notre-Dame: University of Notre Dame Press, 1976.

Bieringer, Reimund, and Didier Pollefeyteds. *Paul and Judaism. Crosscurrents in Pauline Exegesis and the Study of Jewish-Christian Relations*. LNTS 463. London: Bloomsbury T. & T. Clark, 2012.

Bihler, Johannes. *Die Stephanusgeshichte*. MTS HA 30. München: Max Hueber, 1963.
Black, Matthew. *An Aramaic Approach to the Gospels and Acts*. 3rd ed., Oxford: Clarendon, 1967.
———. *Romans*. NCB. London:Oliphants, 1973.
Blank, Josef. *Krisis. Untersuchungen zur johanneischen Christologie*. Freiburg: Lambertus, 1964, 231–51.
Blanton IV, Thomas R. *Constructing a New Covenant. Discursive Strategies in the Damascus Document and Second Corinthians*. WUNT 2.233. Tübingen: Mohr Siebeck, 2007.
Blaschke, Andreas. *Beschneidung. Zeugnisse der Bibel und verwandter Texte*. TANZ 28. Basel: Francke, 1998.
Blass, Friedrich, and Albert Debrunner, translated and revised by Robert W. Funck. *A Greek Grammar of the New Testament*. Cambridge: Cambridge University Press, 1961.
Bloch, Renée. "Midrash." In *Approaches to Judaism: Theory and Practice*, edited by W.S. Green, 29–50. BJS 1. Missoula, MT: Scholars, 1978.
Blocher, Henri. "Justification of the Ungodly (*Sole Fide*): Theological Reflections." In *Justification and Variegated Nomism II. The Paradoxes of Paul*, edited by Donald A. Carson et al., 465–500. Tübingen: Mohr Siebeck, 2004.
Bockmuehl, Marcus. "Abraham's Faith in Hebrews 11." In *The Epistle to the Hebrews and Christian Theology*, edited by Richard Bauckham et al., 364–73. Grand Rapids: Eerdmans, 2009.
———. *Revelation and Mystery in Ancient Judaism and Pauline Christianity*, 1990. Reprint, Grand Rapids: Eerdmans, 1997.
Bonnard, Pierre. *L'Épitre de Saint Paul aux Galates*. CNT 9. Neuchatel-Paris: Delachaux & Niestlé, 1953.
Boobyer, George H. "Mark 12:35–37 and the Preexistence of Jesus in Mark." *ExT* 51 (1939–40) 393–94.
Borgen, Peder. *Bread from Heaven. An Exegetical Study of the Concept of Manna in the Gospel of John and the Writings of Philo*. SNT 10. Leiden: Brill, 1965, 99–146.
———. *Early Christianity and Hellenistic Judaism*. Edinburgh: T. & T. Clark, 1996.
———. "Some Hebrew and Pagan Features in Philo's and Paul's Interpretation of Hagar and Ishmael." In *The New Testament and Hellenistic Judaism*, edited by Peder Borgen and Soren Giversen, 151–64. Aarhus: Aarhus University Press, 1995.
Bornkamm, Gunter. *Studien zu Antike und Urchristentum*. 2nd ed. Munich: Christian Kaiser, 1963.
Bornkamm, Gunter, et al. *Tradition and Interpretation in Matthew*. London: SCM, 1963.
Brawley, Robert L. "Discoursive Structure and the Unseen in Hebrews 2.8 and 11.1: A Neglected Aspect of the Context." *CBQ* 55 (1993) 81–98.
Broer. Ingo. "Die Erscheinung des Auferstandenen vor Paulus bei Damaskus." In *Umstrittener Galaterbrief*, edited by Michael Bachmann and Bernd Kollmann, 57–93, B-TS 106. Neukirchen-Vluyn: Neuchener, 2010.
Brooks, Stephenson H. *Matthew's Community. The Evidence of his Special Sayings Material*. JSNTSS 16. Sheffield: JSOT, 1987.
Brown, Raymond E. *The Birth of the Messiah: A Commentary on the Infancy Narratives in Matthew and Luke*. New York: Doubleday, 1977.
———. *The Community of the Beloved Disciple. The Life, Loves, and Hates of an Individual Church in New Testament Times*. New York: Paulinist, 1979.

———. *The Gospel according to John*. Anchor Bible 29–29A. New York: Doubleday, 1966; London: Chapman, 1971.
———. *An Introduction to the Gospel of John*. Edited by Francis J. Moloney. ABRL. New York: Doubleday, 2003.
Bruce, Frederick F., *The Epistle to the Galatians*. NIGTC. Exeter: Paternoster, 1982.
———. *The Epistle to the Hebrews*. NLCNT. London: Marshall, Morgan & Scott, 1964.
Bruin, Tom de. *The Great Controversy. The Individual's Struggle between Good and Evil in the Testaments of the Twelve Patriarchs and in their Jewish and Christian Contexts*. NTOA/SUNT 106. Göttingen: Vandenhoeck & Ruprecht, 2015.
Bryant, Robert A. *The Risen Crucified Christ in Galatians*. SBLDS 185. Atlanta: SBL, 2001.
Bultmann, Rudolph. *The Gospel of John*. Oxford: Blackwell, 1973.
———. *The History of the Synoptic Tradition*. Oxford: Blackwell, 1963.
Burchard, Christoph. *Der Jakobusbrief*. HNT 15.1. Tübingen: Mohr Siebeck, 2000.
Burger, Christoph. *Jesus als Davidssohn. Eine tradionsgeschichtliche Untersuchung*. FRLANT 98. Göttingen: Vandenhoeck & Ruprecht, 1970.
Burton, Ernest W. *The Epistle to the Galatians*. ICC. Edinburgh: T. & T. Clark, 1920.
Cadbury, Henry J. *The Making of Luke-Acts*. London: SPCK, 1958.
———. *The Style and Literary Method of Luke*. HTS 6. Cambridge: Havard University Press, 1920.
Caird, George B. "*Just Men Made Perfect*." LHQR (1996) 89–98.
———. *New Testament Theology*. Edited by Leonard D. Hurst. Oxford: Clarendon, 1994.
———. *Principalities and Powers. A Study in Pauline Theology*. Oxford: Clarendon, 1956.
———. "The Exegetical Method of the Epistle to the Hebrews." *CJT* 5 (1959) 44–51.
———. *The Language and Imagery of the Bible*. London: Duckworth, 1980.
Calvert-Koyzis, Nancy. *Paul, Monotheism and the People of God: The Significance of Abraham Traditions for Early Judaism and Christianity*. JSNTSS 273. London: T. & T. Clark, 2004.
Cargal, Timothy B. *Restoring the Diaspora. Discoursive Structure and Purpose in the Epistle of James*. SBLDS 144. Atlanta: Scholars, 1993.
Carson, Donald. *The Gospel according to John*. Leicester: InterVarsity; Grand Rapids: Eerdmans, 1991.
———. (ed. et al). *The Paradoxes of Paul*, Vol. 2 of *Justification and Variegated Nomism*. Grand Rapids: Baker Academic, 2004.
Carter, Warren. "Matthean Christology in Roman Imperial Key: Matthew 1.1." In *The Gospel of Matthew in its Roman Imperial Context*, edited by John Riches and David C. Sim, 143–65. London: T. & T. Clark, 2005.
Catchpole, David R. "The Answer of Jesus to Caiaphas (Matthew 26:64)." *NTS* 17 (1971) 213–26
Chae, Daniel J.S. *Paul as Apostle to the Gentiles. His Apostolic Self-Awareness and its Influence on the Soteriological Argument in Romans*. PBTM. Carlisle: Paternoster, 1997.
Cheung Luke.L. *The Genre, Composition and Hermeneutics of James*. PBTM. Carlisle: Paternoster, 2003.l
Christiansen, Ellen J. *The Covenant in Judaism and Paul. A Study of Ritual Boundaries as Identity Markers*. AGAJU 27. Leiden: Brill, 1995.

Ciampa, Roy E. *The Presence and Function of Scripture in Galatians 1 and 2.* WUNT 2.102. Tübingen: Mohr Siebeck, 1998.
Clark, Kenneth W. "The Gentile Bias in Matthew." *JBL* 66 (1947) 165-72.
Clements, Ronald E. " 'A Remnant Chosen by Grace.' (Romans 11:5)." In *Pauline Studies. Essays presented to Frederick F. Bruce*, edited by Donald A. Hagar and Murray J. Harris, 106-21. Exeter: Paternoster, 1980.
Compton, R.Bruce. "James 2.14-26 and the Justification of Abraham." *Detroit Baptist Seminary Journal* 2 (1997) 19-45.
Conzelmann, Hans. *The Theology of Saint Luke* (London: Faber and Faber, 1960).
Cosgrove, Charles H. *The Cross and the Spirit. A Study in the Argument and Theology of Galatians.* Macon, GA: Mercer University Press, 1988.
Cranfield, Charles E.B. "Paul and the Law." *SJT* 17 (1964) 43-68.
———. Romans. 2 vols. ICC. Edinburgh: T. & T. Clark, 1975, 1979.
Cranford, Michael. "Abraham in Romans 4: The Father of all who Believe." *NTS* 41 (1995) 71-88.
Creed, John M. *The Gospel according to St. Luke.* London: Macmillan, 1953.
Crossby, Michael R. *The Rhetorical Composition and Function of Hebrews 11. In the Light of Example Lists in Antiquity.* Macon, GA: Mercer University Press, 1988.
Croy, N. Clayton. *Endurance in Suffering: Hebrews 12:1-13 in its Rhetorical, Religious, and Philosophical Concerns.* SNTSMS 98. Cambridge: Cambridge University Press, 1998.
Cullmann, Oscar. *Christ and Time. The Primitive Christian Conception of Time and History.* London: SCM, 1951.
———. Salvation in History. NTL. London: SCM, 1967.
Cummins, Stephen A. *Paul and the Crucified Christ in Antioch. Maccabean Martyrdom and Galatians 1 and 2.* SNTSMS 114. Cambridge: Cambridge University Press, 2001.
Dahl, Nils A.. "The Story of Abraham in Luke-Acts." In *Studies in Luke-Acts*, edited by Leander E. Keck and J. Louis Martyn, 139-58. Nashville: Abingdon, 1966.
———. "The Future of Israel," *Studies in Paul: Theology for the Early Christian Mission*, 137-58. Minneapolis: Augsburg, 1977.
Das, A. Andrew. *Paul, the Law, and the Covenant.* Peabody, MA: Hendrickson, 2001.
Daube, David *The New Testament and Rabbinic Judaism.* London: Athlone Press, 1956.
Dautzenberg, Gerhard. "Der Glaube im Hebräerbrief." *BZ* 17 (1973) 161-77.
Davids, Peter. *The Epistle of James.* NIGTC. Grand Rapids: Eerdmans, 1982.
Davies, William D. *The Gospel and the Land. Early Christianity and Jewish Territorial Doctrine.* Berkeley: University of California Press, 1974.
———. *Jewish and Pauline Studies.* London: SPCK, 1984.
Davies, William D. and Dale C. Allison. *Matthew.*3 vols. ICC. London: T & T, 1988-1997.
Davis, C.T. "Tradition and Redaction in Matthew 1:18-2.23." *JBL* 90 (1971) 404-21.
Deines, Roland, and Karl-Wilhelm Niebuhr (eds). *Philo und das Neue Testament. Wechselseitige Wahrnehmungen.* I. Internationales Symposium zum Corpus Judaeo-Hellenisticum 1.-4. Mai 2003, Eisenach/Jena. WUNT 172. Tübingen: Mohr Siebeck, 2004.
De Jonge, Marius, and Adam S. van der Woude. "11 Q Melchizedek and the New Testament." *NTS* 12 (1965-66) 301-26.
Delling, Gerhard. τέλος κτλ, *TDNT* 8.49-57.

DeSilva, David A. *Despising Shame. Honor Discourse and Community Maintenance in the Epistle to the Hebrews.* SBLDS 152. Atlanta: Scholars, 1995.

———. *Perseverance in Gratitude. A Socio-Rhetorical Commentary on the Epistle 'to the Hebrews'* " Grand Rapids: Eerdmans, 2000.

Deutsch, Celia. *Hidden Wisdom and the Easy Yoke. Wisdom, Torah and Discipleship in Matthew 11:25-30.* JSNTSS 18. Sheffield: JSOT, 191987.

Dibelius, Martin, "Jungfraunsohn und Krippenkind. Untersuchungen zur Geburtsgeschichte Jesu im Lukas-Evangelium." In *Botschaft und Geschichte*, edited by Gunter Bornkamm, 1-78. Vol.1 of *Gesammelt Aufsätze*.Tübingen: Mohr, 1953.

———. *The Pastoral Epistles*. Edited by Heinrich Greeven. Hermeneia. Philadelphia: Fortress, 1972.

Dietzfelbringer, Christian. *Die Berufung des Paulus als Ursprung seiner Theologie.* WMANT 58. Neukirchen: Neukirchener-Vluyn, 1985.

———. *Das Evangelium nach Johannes.* ZB. 2nd ed. Zürich: ZVZ, 2004.

———. *Paulus und das Alte Testament. Die Hermeneutik des Paulus, untersucht an seiner Deutung der Gestalt Abraham.* THE 95. München: Chr. Kaiser, 1961.

Di Mattei, Steven. "Paul's Allegory of the Two Covenants (Gal. 4:21-31) in the Light of First-Century Hellenistic Rhetorical and Jewish Hermeneutics." *NTS* 52 (2006) 102-22.

Dodd, Charles H. "Behind a Johannine Dialogue," *More New Testament Studies*, 41-57. Manchester: Manchester University Press, 1968.

———. "The Prophecy of Caiaphas: John 11:47-53." In *More New Testament Studies*, by Charles H. Dodd, 58-68. Manchester: Manchester University Press, 1968.

Donaldson, Terrence L. *Paul and the Gentiles. Remapping the Apostle's Convictional World.* Minneapolis: Fortress, 1997.

Donfried, Karl P. *The Romans Debate.* Rev. ed. Peabody, MA: Hendrickson, 1991.

———. "False Presuppositions in the Study of Romans." In *The Romans Debate*. edited by Karl P. Donfried, 102-25. Rev. ed. Peabody, MA: Hendrickson, 1991.

Drane, John. Paul: *Libertine or Legalist? A Study in the Theology of the Major Pauline Epistles.* London: SPCK, 1975.

———. "Why did Paul Write Romans?" In *Pauline Studies. Essays Presented to F.F. Bruce,* edited by Donald A. Hagner and Murray J. Harris, 208-27. Exeter: Paternoster, 1980.

Drury, John. *Tradition and Design in Luke's Gospel. A Study in Early Christian Historiography.* London; Darton, Longman & Todd,1976.

Duling, D.C. "The Therapeutic Son of David: an Element in Matthew's Christological Apologetic." *NTS* 24 (1978) 392-409.

Dunn, James D.G. *Baptism in the New Testament.* SBT 15. London: SCM, 1970.

———.*A Commentary on the Epistle to the Galatians*. BNTC. London: A & C Black, 1993.

———. "The Dialogue Progresses." In *Lutherische und Neue Paulus-Perspektive*, edited by Michael Bachmann, 389-430. WUNT 182. Tübingen: Mohr Siebeck, 2005.

———. "The Incident at Antioch (Gal. 2:11-18)." In *Jesus, Paul and the Law. Studies in Mark and Galatians,* by James D.G. Dunn, 129-82. London: SPCK, 1990.

———. *Jesus, Paul and the Law. Studies in Mark and Galatians.* London: SPCK, 1990.

———. "The Narrative approach to Paul: Whose Story? In *Narrative Dynamics in Paul. A Critical Assessment*, edited by Bruce W. Longenecker, 217–30. Louisville: Westminster John Knox, 2002.
———. *The New Perspective on Paul*. Grand Rapids: Eerdmans, 2005.
———. *The Parting of the Ways*. London: SCM, 1991.
———. (ed). *Paul and the Mosaic Law*. WUNT 89, 1996. Reprint, Grand Rapids: Eerdmans, 2001.
———. *Romans*. 2 vols. WBC 38A-38B. Dallas: Word, 1998.
———. *The Theology of Paul the Apostle*. Grand Rapids: Eerdmans, 1998.
———. *Unity and Diversity in the New Testament*. London: SCM, 1977.
Dupont, Jacques. "The Conversion of Paul, and its Influence on His Understanding of Salvation by Faith." In *Apostolic History and the Gospel. Biblical and Historical Essays Presented to F.F. Bruce*, edited by W. Ward Gasque and Ralph P. Martin, 176–94. Exeter: Paternoster, 1970.
Eastman, Susan. *Recovering Paul's Mother Tongue. Language and Theology in Galatians*. Grand Rapids: Eerdmans, 2007
Eckert, Jost. *Die urchristliche Verkündigung im Streit zwischen Paulus und seine Gegnern nach dem Galaterbrief*. Regensburg: Pustet, 1971.
Ego, Beate. "Abraham als Urbild der Toratreue Israels. Traditionsgeschichtliche Überlegungen zu einem Aspekt des biblischen Abrahamsbildes." In *Bund und Tora, zur theologischen Begriffsgeschichte in alttestamentlicher, frühjüdischer und urchristlicher Tradition*, edited by Friedrich Avemarie and Hermann Lichtenberger, 25–40. WUNT 92. Tübingen: Mohr, 1996.
Eisenbaum, Pamela. *The Jewish Heroes of Christian History. Hebrews 11 in Literary Context*. SBLDS 156. Atlanta: Scholars, 1997.
Elliott, Mark W., and al, eds. *Galatians and Christian Theology. Justification, the Gospel, and Ethics in Paul's Letter*. Grand Rapids: Baker Academic, 2014.
Evans, Craig A., ed. *The Interpretation of Scripture in Early Judaism and Christianity. Studies in Language and Tradition*. JSPPS 33. 2000. Reprint London: T. & T. Clark, 2004.
Evans, Christopher F. *Saint Luke*. TPINTC. London: SCM, 1990.
Farris, Stephen. *The Hymns of Luke's Infancy Narratives. Their Origin, Meaning and Significance*. JSNTSS 9. Sheffield: JSOT, 1985.
Fee, Gordon D. *The First Epistle to the Corinthians*. NICNT. Grand Rapids: Eerdmans, 1987.
Feldman, Louis H. and Gohei Hataeds. *Josephus, Judaism, and Christianity*. Detroit: Wayne State University Press, 1987.
Fitzmyer, Joseph A. *The Acts of the Apostles*. AB 31. New York: Doubleday, 1998.
———. "Further Light on Melchizedek from Qumran Cave 11." *JBL* 86 (1967) 25–41.
———. *The Gospel according to Luke*. 2 vols. AB 28A-28B. New York: Doubleday, 1981, 1985.
Flebbe, Jochen. *Solus Deus. Untersuchungen zur Rede von Gott im Brief des Paulus an die Römer*. BZNW 158. Berlin: de Gruyter, 2008.
Flüchter, Sascha. *Die Anrechnung des Glaubens zur Gerechtigkeit. Auf Weg zu einer sozialhistorisch orientierten Rezeptionsgeschichte von Gen 15:6 in der neutestamentlichen Literatur*. TANZ 51. Tübingen: Francke, 2010.

Foerster, Werner. "Abfassungszeit und Ziel des Galaterbriefes." In *Apophoreta. Festschrift für Ernst Haenchen*, edited by Walter Eltester and Franz Heinrich Kettler, 135-41. BZNW 30. Berlin: Töpelmann, 1964.
Foster, Paul. *Community, Law and Mission in Matthew's Gospel*. WUNT 2.177. Tübingen: Mohr Siebeck, 2004.
France, Richard T. *Matthew*. TNTC. Leicester: IVP, 1985.
———. *Matthew–Evangelist and Teacher*. Exeter: Paternoster, 1989
Frankemölle, Hubert. *Der Brief des Jakobus*. ÖTKNT 17/1-2. Gütersloh: Güterslohverlag, 1994.
———. *Jahwebund und Kirche Christi. Studien zurline Form- und Traditionsgeschichte des "Evangelium" nach Matthäus*. NA nf 10. Munster: Ashendorff, 1974.
———. "Völker-Verheissung (Gen 12-18) und Sinai-Tora im Römerbrief. Das "Dasszwischen" (Röm. 5:20) als hermeneutischer Parameter für eine lutherische oder nichtlutherische Paulus-Auslegung." In *Lutherische und Neue Paulusperspektive*, edited by Michael Bachmann, 275-307. WUNT 182. Tübingen: Mohr Siebeck, 2005.
Fredriksen, Paula. "Judaism, Circumcision of the Gentiles and Apocalyptic Hope. Another Look at Galatians 1-2." *JTS* 42 (1991) 533-64.
———. "Judaizing the Nations. The Ritual Demands of Paul's Gospel." *NTS* 56 (2010) 232-52.
Fuhrmann, Sebastian. *Vergeben und Vergessen. Christologie und Neuer Bund im Hebräerbrief*. WMANT 113. Neukirchen-Vluyn: Neukirchener, 2007.
Fuller, Reginald H. *The Foundations of New Testament Christology*. London: Lutterworth, 1965.
Fung, Ronald Y-K. "Justification by Faith in 1 & 2 Corinthians." In *Pauline Studies, presented to F.F. Bruce on his 70th Birthday*, edited by Donald A. Hagner and Murray J. Harris, 246-61. Grand Rapids: Eerdmans, 1980.
Gager, John G. *Reinventing Paul*. Oxford: Oxford University Press, 2000.
Gale, Aaron M. *Redefining Ancient Borders. The Jewish Scribal Framework of Matthew's Gospel*. New York: T. & T. Clark, 2005.
Garleff, Gunnar. *Urchristliche Identität in Matthäusevangelium, Didache und Jakobusbrief* BVB 9. Münster: LIT, 2004.
Garlington, Don. *Faith, Obedience and Perseverance. Aspects of Paul's Letter to the Romans*. 1994. Reprint, Eugene, OR: Wipf & Stock, 2009.
Garnet, Paul. "Qumran Light on Pauline Soteriology." In *Pauline Studies. Essays presented to F.F. Bruce*, edited by Donald A. Hagner and Murray J. Harris, 19-31. Exeter: Paternoster, 1980.
Gaston, Lloyd. "Abraham and the Righteousness of God." *HBT* 2 (1980) 39-68.
———. "Messiah of Israel as Teacher of the Gentiles: The Setting of Matthew's Christology." *Interpretation* 29 (1975) 24-40.
———. *Paul and the Torah*. Vancouver, BC: University of British Columbia Press, 1987.
Gathecole, Simon J. "Justified by Faith, Justified by his Blood." In *The Paradoxes of Paul*, edited by Donald A. Carson et al., 147-84. Vol. 2 of *Justification and Variegated Nomism*. Tübingen: Mohr Siebeck, 2004.
———. *Where is Boasting? Early Jewish Soteriology and Paul's Response in Romans 1-5*. Grand Rapids: Eerdmans, 2002.
Gaventa, Beverley R. "Galatians 1 and 2: Autobiography as Paradigm." *NT* 28 (1986) 309-26.

———. "The Singularity of the Gospel: A Reading of Galatians." In *Thessalonians, Philippians, Galatians, Philemon*, edited by Jouette M. Bassler, 147–59. Vol. 1 of *Pauline Theology*. Minneapolis: Fortress, 1991.

Georgi, Dieter. *Die Gegner des Paulus im 2. Korintherbrief. Studien zur religiösen Propaganda in der Spätantike*. WMANT 11. Neukirchen-Vluyn: Neukirchener, 1964.

———. *The Opponents of Paul in Second Corinthians*. Philadelphia: Fortress, 1986.

Gheorghita, Radu. *The Role of the Septuagint in Hebrews. An Investigation of Its Influence with Special Reference to the Use of Hab. 2:3–4 in Heb. 10.37–38*. WUNT 2.160 Tübingen: Mohr Siebeck, 2003.

Gibbs, John M. "Purpose and Pattern in Matthew's Use of the title "Son of David." " *NTS* 10 (1964) 446–464.

Gnilka, Joachim. "Der Hymnus des Zacharias." *BZ* 6 (1962) 215–38.

———. *Das Matthäusevangelium* 2 vols. HTKNT 1.1–2. Freiburg: Herder, 1986, 1988.

Gombis, Timothy G. "Arguing with Scripture in Galatia: Galatians 3:10–14 as a Series of Ad Hoc Arguments." In *Galatians and Christian Theology. Justification, the Gospel, and Ethics in Paul's Letter*, edited by Mark W. Elliott et al., 82–90. Grand Rapids: Baker Academic, 2014.

Goppelt, Leonard. *Apostolic and Post-Apostolic Times*. London: A. & C. Black, 1970.

———. "Paulus und Heilsgeschichte. Schlussfolgerungen aus Röm.4 und 1Kor.10.1–13." In *Christologie und Ethik. Aufsätze zum Neuen Testament*, by Leonard Goppelt, 220–33. Göttingen: Vandenhoeck & Ruprecht, 1968.

Gray, Patrick. *Godly Fear. The Epistle to the Hebrews and Greco-Roman Critiques of Superstition*. SBLAB 16. Leiden: Brill, 2004.

Grässer, Erik. *Der Alte Bund im Neuen. Exegetische Studien zur Israelfrage im Neuen Testament*. Tübingen:Mohr, 1985.

———. *Aufbruch und Verheissung. Gesammelte Aufsätze zum Hebräerbrief*. Berlin: de Gruyter, 1992.

———. *Der Brief an die Hebräer*. 3 vols. EKKNT 17.1–3. Zürich: Benziger, 1990–97.

———. Die antijüdische Polemik im Johannesevangelium. In *Der Alte Bund im Neuen. Exegetische Studien zur Israelfrage im Neuen Testament*, by Erik Grässer, 135–53. Tübingen:Mohr, 1985.

———.Die Juden als Teufelsohne in John 8:37–47. In *Der Alte Bund im Neuen. Exegetische Studien*

———. *Der Glaube im Hebräerbrief*. MTS 2. Marburg: Elwert, 1965.

Grindheim, Sigurd. *The Crux of Election. Paul's Critique of the Jewish Confidence in the Election of Israel*. WUNT 2.202. Tübingen: Mohr Siebeck, 2005.

Grundmann, Walter. *Das Evangelium nach Lukas*. TKNT 3. Berlin: Evangelische Verlagsanstalt, 1959.

Gundry, Robert H. "Grace, Works, and Staying Saved." *Biblica* 66 (1985) 1–38.

———. *Matthew. A Commentary on his Literary and Theological Art*. Grand Rapids: Eerdmans, 1982.

———. *The Use of the Old Testament in St. Matthew's Gospel*. SNT 18. Leiden: Brill, 1967.

Haacker, Klaus. "Verdienste und Grenzen der "neuen Perspektive" der Paulus-Auslegung." In *Lutherische und Neue Paulusperspektive. Beiträge zu einen Schlüsselproblem der gegenwartigen exegetischen Diskussion*, edited by Michael Bachmann, 1–15. WUNT 182. Tübingen: Mohr Siebeck, 2005.

Haenchen, Ernst. *The Acts of the Apostles. A Commentary*. Oxford: Blackwell, 1971.
———. "Matthäus 23." *ZThK* 48 (1951) 38–63.
Hagner, Donald A. and Murray J. Harris, eds. *Pauline Studies. Essays presented to F.F. Bruce*. Exeter: Paternoster, 1980.
Hahn, Ferdinand. "Genesis 15:6 im Neuen Testament." In *Probleme Biblischer Theologie. Festschrift Gerhard von Rad*, edited by Hans W. Wolff, 90–107. München: Kaiser, 1971.
———. *The Titles of Jesus in Christology. Their History in Early Christianity*. London: Lutterworth, 1969.
Hamann, Henry Paul. "Faith and Works: Paul and James." *LTJ* 9 (1975) 33–41.
Hamm, Dennis. "Faith in the Epistle to the Hebrews: The Jesus Factor." *CBQ* 52 (1990) 270–91
Hansen, G. Walter. *Abraham in Galatians, Epistolary and Rhetorical Contexts*. JSNTSS 29. Sheffield: Sheffield Academic, 1989.
Hanson, Anthony T. "Abraham the Justified Sinner." In *Studies in Paul's Technique and Theology*, by Anthony T. Hanson, 52–66. London: SPCK, 1974.
———. *The Living Utterances of God. The New Testament Exegesis of the Old*. London: Darton, Longman and Todd, 1983.
———. *Studies in Paul's Technique and Theology*. London: SPCK, 1974.
———. *Studies in the Pastoral Epistles*. London: SPCK, 1968.
Hardin, Justin K. *Galatians and the Imperial Cult. A Critical Analysis of the First-Century Social Context of Paul's Letter*. WUNT 2.237. Tübingen: Mohr Siebeck, 2008.
Harnack, Adolph von. "Das Magnifikat der Elisabeth (Luk.1:46–55) nebst einigen Bermerkungen zu Luk 1 und 2." *SKPAWB* 27 (1900) 538–66.
Harrisville, Roy A. *The Figure of Abraham in the Epistles of St. Paul . In the Footsteps of Abraham*. San Francisco: Mellen Research University Press, 1992.
Hartin, Patrick J. *A Spirituality of Perfection. Faith in Action in the Letter of James*. Collegeville, MN: Liturgical Press (Michael Glazier), 1999.
———. "Ethics in the Letter of James, The Gospel of Matthew, and the Didache: Their Place in Early Christian Literature." In *Matthew, James, and Didache. Three Related Documents in their Jewish and Christian Settings*, edited by Huub van de Sandt, and Jürgen K. Zangenberg, 289–314. Symposium 45. Atlanta: SBL, 2008.
———. *James*. SP 14. Collegeville, Minnesota: Liturgical Press, 2003.
———. *James and the Q Sayings of Jesus*. JSNTSS 47. Sheffield: Sheffield Academic Press, 1991.
Harvey, Anthony E. "Forty Strokes Save One: Social Aspects of Judaising and Apostasy." In *Alternative Approaches to New Testament Study*, edited by Anthony E. Harvey, 79–96. London: SPCK, 1985.
———. *Jesus and the Constraints of History*. London: Duckworth, 1982.
Hayes, Christine E. *Gentiles Impurities and Jewish Identities. Intermarriage and Conversion from the Bible to the Talmud*. Oxford: Oxford University Press, 2002.
Hays, Richard B. *The Conversion of the Imagination. Paul as Interpreter of Israel's Scripture*. Grand Rapids: Eerdmans, 2005.
———. *Echoes of Scripture in the Letters of Paul*. New Haven: Yale University Press, 1989.
———. *The Faith of Jesus Christ. The Narrative Substructure of Galatians 3.1–4.11*. BRS. 2nd ed., Grand Rapids: Eerdmans, 2002.

———. "'The Righteous One' as Eschatological Deliverer: Hermeneutics at the Turn of the Ages." In *The New Testament and Apocalyptic*, edited by Joel Marcus and Marion L. Soards, 191-215. Sheffield: JSOT, 1988.

Heckel, Theo K. *Der innere Mensch. Die paulinische Verarbeitung eines platonischen Motivs.* WUNT 2.53. Tübingen: Mohr, 1993.

Heckel, Ulrich. *Der Segel im Neuen Testament.* WUNT 150. Tübingen: Mohr, 2002.

Heil, Christoph. *Die Ablehnung der Speisegebote durch Paulus. Zur Frage nach der Stellung des Apostels zum Gesetz.* BBB 96. Weinheim: BRLTZ Athenum, 1994.

Heilgenthal, Roman H. *Werke als Zeichen. Untersuchungen zur Bedeutung der menschlichen Taten im Frühjudentum, Neuen Testament und Frühchristentum.* WUNT 2.9. Tübingen: Mohr, 1983.

Held, Heinz-Joachim. "Matthew as Interpreter of the Miracles Stories." In *Tradition and Interpretation in Matthew*, edited by Gunter Bornkamm et al., 165-299. London: SCM, 1963.

Hengel, Martin and Anna Maria Schwemer, *Paul Between Damascus and Antioch. The Unknown Years.* London: SCM, 1997.

———. *The Pre-Christian Paul.* London: SCM, 1991.

Héring, Jean. *L'Épitre aux Hébreux.* CNT 12. Neuchâtel: Delachaux et Niestlé, 1954.

Hill, David. *Greek Words and Hebrew Meanings.* SNTSMS 5. Cambridge: CUP, 1967.

Hoffmann, Paul. *Studien zur Theologie der Logienquelle.* NTAbh NF 8. Munster: Aschendorff, 1972.

Hofius, Otfried. "Das Evangelium und Israel. Erwagungen zu Römer 9-11." In *Paulusstudien* by Otfried Hofius, 175-202 WUNT 51. 2nd. ed. Tübingen: Mohr Siebeck, 1994.

———. "Gal.1:18 ιστορησαι Κηφαν." In *Paulusstudien*, by Otfried Hofius, 255-67. WUNT 51. 2nd ed. Tübingen: Mohr Siebeck, 1994.

———. *Katapausis. Die Vorstellung vom endzeitlichen Ruheort im Hebräerbrief.* WUNT 11. Tübingen: Mohr, 1970.

———. *Paulusstudien.* WUNT 51. 2nd ed. Tübingen: Mohr Siebeck, 1994.

———. "Rechtfertigung des Gottlosen" als Thema biblischer Theologie." In *Paulusstudien* by Otfried Hofius, 121-47. WUNT 51. 2nd. ed. Tübingen: Mohr Siebeck, 1994.

———. *Der Vorhang vor dem Thron Gottes. Eine exegetisch-religionsgeschicht-liche Untersuchung zu Hebraer 6: 19f und 10:19f.* WUNT 14. Tübingen: Mohr, 1972.

Holladay, Carl H. *Theios Aner in Hellenistic Judaism. A Critique of the Use of This Category in New Testament Christology.* SBLDS 40. Missouola, MT: Scholars for SBL, 1977.

Hollander, Harm W. "The Testing by Fire of the Builders' Works." *NTS* 40 (1994) 89-104.

Holtz, Traugott. *Untersuchungen über die alttestamentlichen Zitate bei Lukas.* TU 104. Berlin: Akademie-Verlag, 1968.

Hooker, Morna D. "Adam in Romans 1." *NTS* 6 (1959-60) 297-306. Reprint, *From Adam to Christ. Essays on Paul*, by Morna D. Hooker, 73-84. Cambridge: Cambridge University Press, 1990.

———. *From Adam to Christ. Essays on Paul.* Cambridge: Cambridge University Press, 1990.

———. "A Further Note on Romans 1." *NTS* 13 (1966-67) 181-83. Reprint, *From Adam to Christ. Essays on Paul*, by Morna Hooker, 85-87. Cambridge: Cambridge University Press, 1990.

———. ""Heirs of Abraham": the Gentiles' Role in Israel's Story." In *Narrative Dynamics in Paul. A Critical Assessment*, edited by Bruce W. Longenecker, 85-96. Louisville: Westminster John Knox, 2002.

———. "Interchange in Christ." *JTS* 22 (1971) 349-61. Reprint, *From Adam to Christ. Essays on Paul*, by Morna D. Hooker, 13-25. Cambridge: Cambridge University Press, 1990.

———. "Paul and Covenantal Nomism." In *Paul and Paulinism: Essays in honour of C.Kingsley. Barrett*, edited by Morna D. Hooker and Stephen G. Wilson, 47-56. London: SPCK, 1982. Reprint, *From Adam to Christ*, by Morna D. Hooker, 155-64. Cambridge: Cambridge University Press, 1990.

Hoppe, Rudolf. "Paränese und Theologie im Galaterbrief-eine Profilskizze." In *Umstrittener Galaterbrief*, edited by Michael Bachmann and Bernd Kollmann, 207-30, B-TS 106. Neukirchen-Vluyn: Neuchener, 2010.

Horn, Friedrich W. "Juden und Heiden, Aspekte der Verhaltnisbestimmung in der paulinischen Briefen. Ein Gesprach mit Krister Stendahl." In *Lutherische und Neue Perspektive*, edited by Michael Bachmann, 17-39. WUNT 182. Tübingen: Mohr Siebeck, 2005.

Horrell, David G. "Paul's Narratives or Narrative Substructure? The Significance of "Paul's Story." " In *Narrative Dynamics*, edited by Bruce W. Longenecker, 157-71. Louisville: Westminster John Knox, 2002.

Hoskyns, Edwin C., *The Fourth Gospel*. Edited by Francis N. Davy. 2nd ed. London: Faber and Faber. 1947.

Howard, George. "Christ the End of the Law." *JBL* 88 (1969) 331-37.

———. *Paul: Crisis in Galatia. A Study in Early Christian Theology*. SNTSMS 35. 2nd.. ed., Cambridge: Cambridge University Press, 1990.

———. "Romans 3.21-31 and the Inclusion of the Gentiles." *HTR* 63 (1970) 223-33.

Hübner, Hans. *Gottes Ich and Israel. Zum Schriftgebrauch des Paulus in Römer 9-11*. Göttingen: Vandenhoeck & Ruprecht, 1984.

———. *Law in Paul's Thought. A Contribution to the Development of Pauline Theology*. SNTW. Edinburgh: T. & T. Clark, 1984.

Hummel, Reinhart. *Die Auseinandersetzung zwischen Kirche und Judentum im Matthäusevangelium*. BET 33. München: Kaiser, 1963.

Hunn, Debbie. "Debating the Faithfulness of Jesus Christ." In *The Faith of Jesus Christ. The Pistis Christou Debate. Exegetical, Biblical, and Theological Studies*, edited by Michael F. Bird and Preston M. Sprinkle, 15-31. Milton Keynes: Paternoster, 2009.

Instone-Brewer, David. "James as a Sermon on the Trials of Abraham." In *The New Testament in its First Century Setting. Essays on Content and Background in Honour of B.W. Winter on his 65th Birthday*, edited by P.F. Williams et al., 250-68. Grand Rapids: Eerdmans, 2004.

Isaacs, Marie E. *The Concept of the Spirit*. HM 1. London: Heythrop College, 1976.

Jackson-McCabe, Matt. *Logos and Law in the Letter of James. The Law of Nature, the Law of Moses, and the Law of Freedom*. SNT 100.Leiden: Brill, 2001. Reprint Atlanta: SBL, 2010.

Jacobs, Irvine. "The Midrashic Background for James 2:21-3." *NTS* 22 (1975-76) 457-64.

Jeremias, Joachim. "Αβρααμ. *TDNT* I.8-9.
———. "Μωυσης," *TDNT* 4.848-73.
———. *The Prayers of Jesus*. London: SCM, 1967.
Jervell, Jacob. *Die Apostelgeschichte*. KEKNT. Göttingen: Vandenhoeck & Ruprecht, 1998.
———. "Following the Argument of Romans." In *The Romans Debate*, edited by Karl P. Donfried, 265-77. Rev. ed. Peabody, MA: Hendrickson, 1991.
———. *Luke and the People of God. A New Look at Luke-Acts*. Minneapolis: Augsburg, 1972.
———. *The Theology of the Acts of the Apostles*. Cambridge: Cambridge University Press, 1996.
Jeska, Joachim. *Die Geschichte Israels in der Sicht des Lukas*. Göttingen: Vandenhoeck & Ruprecht, 2001.
Jewett, Robert. "The Agitators and the Galatian Congregation." *NTS* 17 (1970-71) 198-212.
———. "Following the Argument of Romans." In *The Romans Debate*, edited by Karl P. Donfried, 265-77. Rev.ed Peabody, MA: Hendrickson, 1991.
———. *Romans. A Commentary*. Hermeneia. Minneapolis: Fortress, 2006.
Johnson, E. Elizabeth. *The Function of Apocalyptic and Wisdom Traditions in Romans 9-11*. SBLDS 109. Atlanta, Georgia: Scholars, 1989.
Johnson, Luke T. *The Acts of the Apostles*. SP 5. Collegeville, MN: Liturgical Press 1992.
———. *Brother of Jesus. Friend of God. Studies in the Letter of James*. Grand Rapids: Eerdmans, 2004.
———. *The Letter of James*. AB 37A. New Haven: Yale University Press, 1995.
Johnson, Marshall D. *The Purpose of the Biblical Genealogies*. SNTSMS 8. Cambridge: Cambridge University Press, 1969.
Kampling, Rainer, ed. *Ausharren in der Verheissung. Studien zum Hebräerbrief*. SBS 204. Stuttgart: KBW, 2005.
———. "*Nun Steht aber diese Sache im Evangelium . . . " Zur Frage nach den Anfängen des christlichen Antijudaismus*. Paderborn: Schöningh, 1999.
———. "Sich dem Rätsel nähern. Fragen zu den Einleitungsfragen des Hebräerbriefes." In *Ausharren in der Verheissung. Studien zum Hebräerbrief*, edited by Rainer Kampling, 11-34. SBS 204. Stuttgart: KBW, 2005.
Karris, Richard J. "*Romans 14:1-15:13 and the Occasion of Romans*." In *The Romans Debate*, edited by Karl P. Donfried, 65-84, 125-27. Rev.edn. Peabody, MA: Hendrickson, 1991.
Käsemann, Ernst. *Commentary on Romans*. London: SCM, 1980.
———. "Justification and Salvation History." In *Perspectives on Paul*, by Ernst Kasemann, 60-78. NTL. London: SCM, 1971.
———. *New Testament Questions for Today*. London: SCM, 1979.
———. *Perspectives on Paul*. NTL. London: SCM, 1971.
———. *The Wandering People of God*. Minneapolis: Augsburg,1984.
Kaut, Thomas. *Befreier und befreites Volk. Traditions- und redaktionsgeschichtliche Untersuchung zu Magnifikat und Benedictus im Kontext der vorlukanischen Kindheitgeschichte*. AM: BBB 77. Frankfurt am Main: Anton Hain, 1990.
Kaylor, R.David. *Paul's Covenant Community. Jew and Gentile in Romans*. Atlanta: John Knox Press, 1988.

Kertelge, Karl. *"Rechtfertigung" bei Paulus. Studien zur Struktur und zum Bedeutungsgehalt des paulinischen Rechtfestigungsbegriffs.* NA NF 3. 2nd. ed. Münster: Aschendorff, 1971.

Kilgallen, John. *The Stephen Speech.* AB 67. Rome: Pontifical Biblical Institute, 1976.

Kilpatrick, George D. *The Origins of the Gospel according to St. Matthew.* Oxford: Clarendon, 1946.

Kim, Seyoon. *The Origin of Paul's Gospel.* Reprint, Grand Rapids: Eerdmans, 1982.

———. *Paul and the New Perspective. Second Thoughts on the Origin of Paul's Gospel.* Grand Rapids: Eerdmans, 2002.

Kingsbury, Jack Dean. *Matthew. Structure, Christology, Kingdom.* Reprint, London: SPCK, 1976.

Klaiber, Walter. *Rechtfertigung und Gemeinde. Eine Untersuchung zum pauliinischen Kirchenverstandnis.* FRLANT 127. Göttingen: Vandenhoeck & Ruprecht, 1982.

Klein, Gunter. "Exegetische Probleme in Römer 3:21–4:25. Antwort an U. Wilckens." In *Rekonstruktion und Interpretation*, by Gunter Klein, 170–79. BET 50. München: Chr. Kaiser, 1969.

———. "Galater 2:6–9 und die Geschichte der Jerusalem Urgemeinde." In *Rekonstruktion und Interpretation. Gesammelte Aufsätze zum Neuen Testament*, by Gunter Klein, 99–128. BET 50. München: Chr. Kaiser, 1969.

———. "Heil und Geschichte nach Römer iv." *NTS* 13 (1966–67) 43–47.

———. "Individualsgeschichte und Weltgeschichte bei Paulus." In *Rekonstruktion und Interpretation. Gesammelte Aufsätze zum Neuen Testament,* by Gunter Klein, 180–224. BET 50. München: Chr. Kaiser, 1969.

———. *Rekonstruktion und Interpretation. Gesammelte Aufsätze zum Neuen Testament.* BET 50. München: Chr. Kaiser, 1969.

———. "Römer 4 und die Idee der Heilsgeschichte." In *Rekonstruktion und Interpretation. Gesammelte Aufsätze zum Neuen Testament* by Gunter Klein, 145–69. BET 50. München: Chr. Kaiser, 1969.

Koch, Dietrich-Alex. *Die Schrift als Zeuge des Evengeliums. Untersuchungen zur Verwendung und zum Verständnis der Schrift bei Paulus.* BHTh. 69. Tübingen: Mohr, 1986.

Koester, Craig R. *Hebrews.* AB 36. New Haven: Yale University Press, 2001.

Konradt, Matthias. ""Die aus Glauben, diese sind Kinder Abrahams" (Gal.3:7). Erwägungen zum galatischen Konflikt im Licht frühjüdischer Abrahamtraditionen." In *Text, Ethik, Judentum und Christentum, Gesellschaft. Ekkehard W. Stegemann zum 60. Geburtstag*, edited by Gabrielle Gelardini, 25–48. Vol.1 of *Kontext der Schrift* Stuttgart: Kohlhammer, 2005.

———. *Israel, Church, and the Gentiles in the Gospel of Matthew.* Waco: Baylor University Press, 2014.

———. *Israel, Kirche und die Völker im Matthäusevangelium.* WUNT 215. Tübingen: Mohr Siebeck, 2007.

Koester, Helmut. "Die Auslegung der Abraham-Verheissung in Hebräer 6." In *Studien zur Theologie der alttestamentlichen Uberlieferungen. Festschrift für Gerhard von Rad*, edited by Rolf Rendorff and Klaus Koch, 95–109. Neukirchen-Vluyn: Neukirchener, 1961.

Kraus, Wolfgang. "Gottes Gerechtigkeit und Gottes Volk. Ökumenisch-ekklesiologische Aspekte der New Perspective on Paul." In *Lutherische und Neue Paulusperspektive*, edited by Michael Bachmann, 329–47. Tübingen: Mohr Siebeck, 2005.

Kreuzer, Siegried. ""Der den Gottlosen rechtfertigt" (Röm.4:5). Die frühjüdische Einordnung Gen 15 als Hintergrund fur das Abrahambild und die Rechtfertigungslehre des Paulus." *TB* 33 (2002) 208-19.

Kruiji, Th.de. *Der Sohn des lebendigen Gottes. Ein Beitrag zur Christologie des Matthäusevangeliums.* AB 16. Rome: Pontifical Biblical Institute, 1962.

Kuhn, Karl Georg, "προσηλυτος." *TDNT* 6.727-44.

Kümmel, Werner G. " 'Das Gesetz und die Propheten gehen bis Johannes'–Lukas 16:16 im Zusammenhang der heilsgeschichtlichen Theologie der Lukasschriften." In *Verborum Veritas. Festschrift G. Stahlin,* edited by Otto Böcher and Klaus Haacker, 89-102. Wuppertal: Brockhaus, 1970.

———. *Heilsgeschehen und Geschichte.* Marburg: Ewart, 1965.

———. "Individualgeschichte" und "Weltgeschichte" in Gal.2:15-21." In *Christ and Spirit in the New Testament in honour of C.F.D Moule,* edited by Barnabas Lindars and Stephen S .Smalley,157-73. Cambridge: Cambridge University Press, 1973.

———. *Introduction to the New Testament.* London: SCM, 1966.

———. "παρεσις und αφεσις." In *Heilsgeschehen und Geschichte,* by Werner G. Kmmel, 260-70. Marburg: Ewart, 1965, 260-70.

Kuss, Otto. "Der Verfasser des Hebraebriefes als Seelsorger." In Aufsätze zur Exegese des Neuen Testaments, by Otto Kuss. 329-58. Vol. 1 of *Auslegung und Verkundigung.* Regensburg: Pustet, 1963.

Kwon, Yon-Gyong. *Eschatology in Galatians. Rethinking Paul's Response to the Galatian Crisis.* WUNT 2.183. Tübingen: Mohr Siebeck, 2004.

Laato, Timo. *Paul and Judaism. An Anthropological Approach.* SFSHJ 115. Atlanta: Scholars, 1995.

Lane, William L. *Hebrews.* 2 vols. WBC 47A-47B. Nashville: Nelson, 1991.

Lategan, B.C. "The Argumentative Situation of Galatians." In *The Galatians Debate,* edited by Mark D. Nanos, 383-95. Peabody, MA: Hendrickson, 2002.

Laub, Franz. *Bekenntnis und Auslegung. Die paränetische Funktion der Christologie im Hebräerbrief.* BU 15. Regensburg: Friedrich Pustet, 1980.

Laurentin, René. *Structure et Théologie de Luc I-II.* EB. Paris: Gabalda, 1957.

Laws, Sophie. *The Epistle of James.* BNTC. London: A. & C. Black, 1980.

Lee, Chee-Chiew. *The Blessing of Abraham, the Spirit, and Justification in Galatians. Their Relationship and Significance for Understanding Paul's Theology.* Eugene, OR: Pickwick, 2013.

Levenson, Jon D. *The Death and Resurrection of the Beloved Son. The Transformation of Child Sacrifice in Judaism and Christianity.* New Haven: Yale University Press, 1993.

Lewis, Charlton T. and Charles Short. *A Latin Dictionary.* Oxford: Clarendon, 1879.

Lightfoot, Joseph B. *St. Paul's Epistle to the Galatians.* 4th Ed. London: Macmillan, 1874.

Liddell, Henry G., et al. *A Greek-English Lexicon.* Oxford: Clarendon, 1968.

Limbeck, Meinrad. *Die Ordnung des Heils. Untersuchungen zum Gesetzesverständnis des Frühjudentums.* KBANT. Düsseldorf: Patmos, 1971.

Lincoln, Andrew T. "Abraham Goes to Rome: Paul's Treatment of Abraham in Romans 4." In *Worship, Theology and Ministry in the Early Church. Festschrift for Ralph P. Martin,* edited by M.J. Wilkins and T. Paige, 163-79. JSNTSS 87. Sheffield: JSOT Press, 1992.

———. *The Gospel according to Saint John.* BNTC. London: Continuum, 2005.

———. *Paradise Now and Not Yet. Studies in the Role of the Heavenly Dimension in Paul's Thought with Special Reference to his Eschatology.* SNTSMS 43. Cambridge: Cambridge University Press, 1981.

———. "The Stories of Predecessors and Inheritors in Galatians and Romans." In *Narrative Dynamics in Paul. A Critical Assessment*, edited by Bruce W Longenecker, 172–203. Louisville: Westminster John Knox, 2002.

———. *Truth on Trial. The Lawsuit Motif in the Fourth Gospel.* Peabody, MA: Hendrickson, 2000.

Lindars, Barnabas. *The Gospel of John.* NCB. London: Oliphants, 1977.

Lindemann, Andreas. *Paulus im ältesten Christentum. Das Bild des Apostels und die Rezeption der paulinischen Theologie in der frühchristlichen Literatur bis Marcion.* BHT 58. Tübingen: Mohr, 1979.

Linebaugh, Jonathan A. *God, Grace, and Righteousness in Weisdom of Solomon and Paul's Letter to the Romans. Texts in Conversation.* SNT 152. Leiden: Brill, 2013.

Loader, William R.G. *Sohn und Hoherpriester. Eine traditionsgeschichtliche Untersuchung zur Christologie des Hebräerbriefes.* WMANT 53. Neukirchen-Vluyn: Neukirchener, 1981.

Lodge, John G. "James and Paul at Cross-Purposes? James 2:22." *Biblica* 62 (1981) 195–213.

Lohmeyer, Ernst. "Gesetzewerke." *ZNW* 28 (1929) 177–207.

———. *Das Evangelium des Markus.* KEKNT. Göttingen: Vandenhoeck & Ruprecht, 1951.

Lona, Horacio E. *Abraham in Johannes 8. Ein Beitrag zur Methodenfrage.* EHS 23.65. Bern: Herbert Lang, 1976.

Longenecker, Bruce W. "Defining the Faithful Character of the Covenant Community. Galatians 2:15–21 and Beyond." In *Paul and the Mosaic Law*, edited by James D.G. Dunn, 75–97. Grand Rapids: Eerdmans, 2001.

———. *Eschatology and the Covenant. A Comparison of 4 Ezra and Romans 1–11.* JSNTSS 57. Sheffield: JSOT, 1991.

———, ed. *Narrative Dynamics in Paul. A Critical Assessment.* Louisville: Westminster John Knox, 2002.

———. "Sharing in their Spiritual Blessings? The Stories of Israel in Galatians and Romans." In *Narrative Dynamics in Paul. A Critical Assessment*, edited by Bruce W. Longenecker, 58–84. Louisville: Westminster John Knox, 2002.

———. *The Triumph of Abraham's God. The Transformation of Identity in Galatians.* Edinburgh: T. & T. Clark, 1998.

Longenecker, Richard N. "The "Faith of Abraham" Theme in Paul, James and Hebrews: A Study in the Circumstantial Nature of New Testament Teaching." *JETS* 20 (1977) 203–12.

———. *Galatians.* WBC 41. Nashville: Nelson, 1990.

———, ed. *The Road to Damascus. The Impact of Paul's Conversion on His Life, Thought and Ministry.* MNTS. Grand Rapids: Eerdmans, 1997.

Lorenzen, Stefanie. *Das paulinische Eikon-Konzept. Semantische Analysen zur Sapientia Solomonis, zu Philo und den Paulusbriefen.* WUNT 2.250.Tübingen: Mohr Siebeck, 2008.

Lübking, Hans-Martin. *Paulus und Israel im Römerbrief.* EHS 23.260. Frankfurt am Main: Peter Lang, 1986.

Lüdemann, Gerd. *Early Christianity according to the Traditions in Acts.* London: SCM, 1989.
———. *Opposition to Paul in Jewish Christianity.* Minneapolis: Fortress, 1989.
Lührmann, Dieter. *Galatians. A Continental Commentary.* Minnesota: Fortress, 1992.
Lull, David J. "The Law was our Pedagogue: A Study in Galatians 3:19-25." *JBL* 105 (1986) 481-98.
———. "Salvation History: Theology in 1 Thessalonians, Philemon, Philippians, and Galatians." In *Pauline Theology I.*, edited by Jouette M. Bassler, 247-65. Minneapolis: Fortress, 1991.
———. *The Spirit in Galatia. Paul's Interpretation of Pneuma as Divine Power.* SBLDS 49. 1980. Reprint, Eugene, OR: Wipf & Stock, 2006.
Luz, Ulrich. *Das Geschichtsverständnis des Paulus.* BET 49. München: Chr. Kaiser, 1968.
———. "Eine thetische Skizze der Matthäischen Christologie. In *Anfänge der Christologie. Festschrift für Ferdinand Hahn zum 65. Geburtstag*, edited by Cilliers Breytenbach and Henning Paulsen, 221-35. Göttingen: Vandenhoeck & Ruprecht, 1991.
Lyons, George. *Pauline Autobiography. Toward a New Understanding.* SBLDS 73. Altanta: SBL, 1985.
Maier, Gerhard. *Mensch und freier Wille. Nach den jüdischen Religionsparteien zwischen Ben Sira und Paulus.* WUNT 12. Tübingen: Mohr, 1971.
Malina, Bruce J. *The New Testament World. Insights from Cultural Anthropology.* London: SCM, 1983.
Manson, Walter. *The Epistle to the Hebrews.* London: Hodder and Stoughton, 1951.
Manson, W. Thomas. "The Problem of the Epistle to the Galatians." In *BJRL* 24 (1940) 59-80), in *Studies in the Gospels and Epistles*, by Thomas W. Manson, 168-89. Manchester: Manchester University Press, 1962.
———. *The Sayings of Jesus.* London: SCM, 1949.
———. *Studies in the Gospels and Epistles.* Manchester: Manchester University Press, 1962.
Marshall, I. Howard. *The Gospel of Luke.* NIGTC. Exeter: Paternoster, 1978.
———. "A Response to A.T. Lincoln: The Stories of Predecessors and Inheritors." In *Narrative Dynamics in Paul. A Critical Assessment*, edited by Bruce W. Longenecker, 204-14. Louisville: Westminster John Knox, 2002.
———. "Soteriology in Hebrews." In *The Epistle to the Hebrews and Christian Theology*, edited by Richard Bauckham et al., 253-77. Grand Rapids: Eerdmans, 2009.
Martin, Ralph P. *2 Corinthians.* WBC 40. Waco: Word, 1986.
———. *James.* WBC 48. Waco: Word, 1988.
Martin-Achard, Robert. *A Light to the Nations.* Edinburgh: Oliver and Boyd, 1962.
Martinez, Florento Garcia. "4QMMT in a Qumran Context." In *Reading 4QMMT: New Perspectives on Qumran Law and History*, edited by John Kampen and Moshe J. Benstein, 1-27. SS2. Atlanta: Scholars, 1996.
Martyn, J. Louis. "The Covenants of Hagar and Sarah." In *Faith and History, Essays in honor of Paul W. Meyer*, edited by John T. Carroll et al, 160-92. Reprint, Eugene, OR: Wipf & Stock, 2004.
———. *Galatians.* AB 33A. New Haven: Yale University Press, 1997.
———. *History and Theology in the Fourth Gospel.* New York: Harper & Row, 1968.
———. *Theological Issues in the Letters of Paul.* Edinburgh: T. & T. Clark, 1997.

Marxsen, Willi. "Sündige tapfer. Wer hat sich beim Streit in Antiochien richtig verhalten?" *EK* 20 (1987) 81–84.
März, Claus-Peter. *Studien zum Hebräerbrief*. SBA NT 39. Stuttgart: KBW, 2005.
Mason, Jason. *Divine and Human Agency in Second Temple Judaism and Paul. A Comparative Study*. WUNT 2.297. Tübingen: Mohr Siebeck, 2010.
Matlock, R. Barry. "Saving Faith: The Rhetoric and Semantics of pi/stij in Paul." In *The Faith of Jesus Christ. The Pistis Christou Debate. Exegetical, Biblical, and Theological Studies*, edited by Michael F. Bird and Preston M. Sprinkle, 73–89. Milton Keynes: Paternoster, 2009.
Maynard-Reid, Pedrito U. *Poverty and Wealth in James*. Eugene, OR: Wipf & Stock, 2004.
Mayor, Joseph B. *The Epistle of James*. 2nd ed. London: Macmillan, 1897.
McGlynn, Moyna. *Divine Judgment and Divine Benevolence in the Book of Wisdom*. WUNT 2.139. Tübingen: Mohr Siebeck, 2001.
McKelvey, Robert J. *Pioneer and Priest. Jesus Christ in the Epistle to the Hebrews*. Eugene, OR: Pickwick, 2013.
Meeks, Wayne A. *The First Urban Christians. The Social World of the Apostle Paul*. New Haven: Yale University Press, 1983.
———. "On Trusting an Unpredictable God: A Hermeneutical Meditation on Romans 9–11." In *Faith and History. Essays in Honor of Paul W. Meyer*, edited by J. T. Carroll, 105–24. Reprint, Eugene, OR: Wipf & Stock, 2004.
Merk, Otto. *Handeln aus Glauben. Die Motivierungen der paulinischen Ethik*. MTS 5. Marburg: Elwert, 1968.
Meyer, Ben F. *The Early Christians. Their World Mission & Self-Discovery*. Reprint, Eugene, OR: Wipf & Stock, 2008.
Michel, Otto. *Der Brief an die Hebräer*. KEKNT. Göttingen: Vandenhoeck & Ruprecht, 1960.
Minde, H.-J. van der. *Schrift und Tradition bei Paulus. Ihre Bedeutung und Funktion im Römerbrief*. PTS 3. München: Schöningh, 1976.
Minear, Paul S. "Luke's Use of the Birth Stories." In *Studies in Luke-Acts. Essays presented in honor of Paul Schubert*, edited by Leander E. Keck and J. Louis Martyn, 111–130. Nashville: Abingdon, 1966.
———. "A Note on Luke 22:36." *NT* 7 (1964) 128–34.
———. *The Obedience of Faith. The Purposes of Paul in the Letter to the Romans*. SBT 2.19. London: SCM, 1971.
Mittmann-Richert, Ulrike. *Magnifikat und Benedictus. Die ältesten Zeugnisse der judenchristlichen Tradition von der Geburt des Messias*. WUNT 2.90. Tübingen: Mohr Siebeck, 1996.
Mitternacht, Dieter. "Foolish Galatians? A Recipient-Orientated Assessment of Paul's Letter." In *The Galatians Debate. Contemporary Issues in Rhetorical and Historical Interpretation*, edited by Mark D. Nanos, 408–33. Peabody, MA: Hendrickson, 2002.
Moloney, Francis. *The Gospel of John*. SP 4. Collegeville, MN: Liturgical (Michael Glazier), 1998.
Montefiore, Hugh W. *The Epistle to the Hebrews*. BNTC. London: A. & C. Black, 1964.
Morales, Rodrigo J. *The Spirit and the Restoration of Israel. New Exodus and New Creation Motifs in Galatians*. WUNT 2.282. Mohr Siebeck: Tübingen, 2010.

Morgan-Wynne, John Eifion. *Paul's Pisidian Antioch Speech (Acts 13)*. Eugene, OR: Pickwick, 2014.
Morland, Kjell Arne. *The Rhetoric of Curse in Galatians. Paul Confronts Another Gospel*. ESEC 5. Atlanta: Scholars, 1995.
Morris, Leon. *The Epistle to the Romans*. Grand Rapids: Eerdmans, 1988.
———. *The Gospel according to Matthew*. Grand Rapids: Eerdmans, 1992.
Morrison, Michael D. *Who needs a New Covenant? Rhetorical Function of the Covenant Motif in the Argument of Hebrews*. PTM 85. Eugene, OR: Pickwick, 2008.
Mosser, Carl. "Rahab Outside the Camp." In *The Epistle to the Hebrews and Christian Theology*, edited by Richard Bauckham et al, 383–404. Grand Rapids: Eerdmans, 2009.
Motyer, Stephen. *Your Father the Devil? A New Approach to John and the Jews*. PBM. Carlisle: Paternoster, 1997.
Moule, Charles F.D. *An Idiom Book of New Testament Greek*. 2nd. ed. Cambridge: Cambridge University Press, 1959.
Moulton, James H. *A Grammar of New Testament Greek* Vol.1. Edinburgh: T. & T. Clark, 1906.
Moulton, James H. and George Milligan. *The Vocabulary of the New Testament, illustrated from the Papyri and other Non-Literary Sources*. London: Hodder & Stoughton, 1914–29.
Moxnes, Halvor. *Theology in Conflict. Studies in Paul's Understanding of God in Romans* SNT 53. Leiden: Brill, 1980.
Müller, Christian. *Gottes Gerechtigkeit und Gottes Volk. Eine Untersuchung zu Römer 9–11*. FRLANT 86. Göttingen: Vandenhoeck & Ruprecht, 1964.
Müller, Paul-Gerhard. *ΧΡΙΣΤΟΣ ΑΡΧΗΓΟΣ. Der religionsgeschichtliche und theologische Hintergrund einer neutestamentlichen Christusprädikation*. EH 23.28. Bern: Herbert Lang, 1973.
Munck, Johannes. *Christus und Israel. Eine Auslegung von Röm 9–11*. AAU 28.3. Aarhus: Universitetsforlaget, 1956.
———. *Paul and the Salvation of Mankind*. London: SCM, 1959.
Mussner, Franz. *Der Galaterbrief*. HTKNT 9. Freiburg: Herder, 1974.
———. *Der Jakobusbrief*. HTKNT 13.1. 4th ed. Freiburg: Herder, 1981.
Nanos, Mark D., ed. *The Galatians Debate. Contemporary Issues in Rhetorical and Historical Interpretation*. Peabody, MA: Hendrickson, 2002.
———. *The Irony of Galatians. Paul's Letter in First-Century Context* Minneapolis: Fortress, 2002.
———. *The Mystery of Romans. The Jewish Context of Paul's Letter*. Minneapolis: Fortress, 1996.
———. "What Was at Stake in Peter's "Eating with Gentiles" at Antioch?" In *The Galatians Debate. Contemporary Issues in Rhetorical and Historical Interpretation*, edited by Mark D. Nanos, 282–318. Peabody, MA: Hendrickson, 2002.
Nauck, Wolfgang. "Zur Aufbau des Hebräerbriefes." In *Judentum-Urchristentum-Kirche. Festschrift für Joachim Jeremias*, edited by Walter Eltester, 199–206. BZNW 26. Berlin: Töpelmann, 1960.
Nepper-Christensen, Poul. *Das Matthäusevangelium. Ein Judenchristliches Evangelium?* ATD. Aarhuis: Universitetsforlaget, 1958.

Neubrand, Maria. *Abraham-Vater von Juden und Nichtjuden. Eine exegetische Studie zu Röm 4*. Würzburg: Echter, 1997.

Nickle, Keith F. *The Collection. A Study in Paul's Strategy*. SBT 48. London: SCM, 1966.

Nickelsburg, George W.E. *Resurrection, Immortality, and Eternal Life in Intertestamental Judaism and Early Christianity*. HTS 56. Expanded ed. Cambridge, MA: Harvard University Press, 2006.

Niebuhr, Karl-Wilhelm. *Heidenapostel aus Israel. Die jüdische Identität des Paulus nach ihrer Darstellung in seinen Briefen*. WUNT 62. Tübingen: Mohr, 1992.

Nienhuis, David R. *Not by Paul Alone. The Formation of the Catholic Epistle Collection and the Christian Canon*. Waco: Baylor University Press, 2007.

Nolland, John. *Luke*. 3 vols. WBC 35A-35C. Dallas: Word, 1989-93.

Novenson, Michael V. *Christ among the Messiahs. Christ Language in Paul and Messiah Language in Ancient Judaism*. Oxford: Oxford University Press, 2012.

———. "Paul's Former Occupation in *Ioudismos*." In *Galatians and Christian Theology. Justification, the Gospel, and Ethics in Paul's Letter*, edited by Mark W. Elliott et al, 24-39. Grand Rapids: Baker Academic, 2014.

O'Brien, Peter. "Was Paul converted?" In *The Paradoxes of Paul*, edited by Donald A. Carson et al., 361-91. Vol.2 of *Justification and Variegated Nomism*. Tübingen: Mohr Siebeck, 2004.

O'Neill, John C. *The Recovery of Paul's Letter to the Galatians*. London: SPCK, 1972.

Overman, J.Andrew. *Matthew's Gospel and Formative Judaism. The Social World of the Matthean Community*. Minneapolis: Fortress, 1990.

Painter, James. *Just James. The Brother of James in History and Tradition*. Edinburgh. T. & T. Clark, 1999.

Penna, Romano. "The meaning of παρεσις in Romans 3:25c and the Pauline Thought on the Divine Acquittal." In *Lutherische und Neue Paulusperspektive*, edited by Michael Bachmann, 251-74. WUNT 182. Tübingen: Mohr Siebeck, 2005.

Penner, Todd C. *The Epistle of James and Eschatology. Re-reading an Ancient Christian Letter*. JSNTSS 121. Sheffield: Sheffield Academic, 1996.

———. *In Praise of Christian Origins. Stephen and the Hellenists in Lukan Apologetic Historiography*. ESEC 10. London: T. & T. Clark, 2004.

Pesch, Rudolph. *Die Apostelgeschichte*. 2 vols. EKKNT 5.1-2. Dusseldorff: Benziger, 1986.

Philip, Finny. *The Origins of Pauline Pneumatology*. WUNT 2.194. Tübingen; Mohr Siebeck, 2005.

Piper, John. *The Justification of God. An Exegetical and Theological Study of Romans 9:1-23*. 2nd.ed. Grand Rapids: Baker Academic, 1993.

Plummer, Alfred. *The Gospel according to S. Luke*. ICC. 2nd ed. Edinburgh: T. & T. Clark, 1898.

Popkes, Wiard. *Adressaten, Situation und Form des Jakobusbriefes*. SBS 125/126. Stuttgart: KBW, 1986.

———. *Der Brief des Jakobus*. THNT 14. Leipzig: Evangelische Verlagsanstalt, 2001.

Porter, Stanley E. and Andrew W. Pitts. "Πιστις with a Preposition and Genitive Modifier: Lexical, Semantic, and Syntactic Considerations in the πιστις χριστου Discussion." In *The Faith of Jesus Christ. The Pistis Christou Debate. Exegetical, Biblical, and Theological Studies*, edited by Michael F. Bird and Preston M. Sprinkle, 33-53. Milton Keynes: Paternoster, 2009.

Pratscher, Wilhelm. *Der Herrenbruder Jakobus und die Jakobustradition.* FRLANT 139. Göttingen: Vandenhoeck & Ruprecht, 1987.
Prostmeier, Ferdinand R. *Der Barnabasbrief.* KAV 8. Göttingen: Vandenhoeck & Ruprecht, 1999.
Rahles, Alfred. *Septuaginta.* Edited by Robert Hanhart. Stuttgart: Deutsche Bibelgesellschaft, 2006.
Räisänen, H. "Galatians 2:16 and Paul's Break with Judaism." *NTS* 31 (1985) 543–53.
———. *Paul and the Law.* WUNT 29. Tübingen: Mohr, 1983.
Reicke, Bo. "Der geschichtliche Hintergrund des Apostelkonzils und der Antiocha-Episode, Gal. 2:1–14." In *Studia Paulina in honorem J. de Zwaan Septuagenarii*, edited by Jon N. Sevenster and W. Cornelius van Unnik, 172–87. Haarlem: Bohn, 1953.
Reinbold, Wolfgang. "Zur Bedeutung des Begriffes "Israel" in Römer 9–11." In *Between Gospel and Election. Explorations in the Interpretation of Romans 9–11*, edited by Florian Wilk and J.Ross Wagner, 401–16. WUNT 257. Tübingen: Mohr Siebeck, 2010.
Reinmuth, Eckart. *Geist und Gesetz. Studien zu Voraussetzungen und Inhalt der paulinischen Paränese.* TA 44. Berlin: Evangelische Verlagsanstalt, 1985.
———. *Pseudo-Philo und Lukas. Studien zur Liber Antiquitatum Biblicarum und seiner Bedeutung für die Interpretation des lukanischen Doppelwerks.* WUNT 74. Tübingen: Mohr, 1994.
Rhee, Victor Sung-Yui. *Faith in Hebrews. Analysis within the Context of Christology, Eschatology and Ethics.* SBL 19. Frankfurt-am-Main: Peter Lang, 2001.
Richard, Earl. *Acts 6:1–8.4. The Author's Method of Composition.* SBLDS 41. Missoula, MT: Scholars, 1978.
Richardson, Christopher A. *Pioneer and Perfecter of Faith. Jesus' Faith as the Climax of Israel's History in the Epistle to the Hebrews.* WUNT 2.338. Tübingen: Mohr Siebeck, 2012.
Richardson, Peter. *Israel in the Apostolic Church.* SNTSMS 10. Cambridge: Cambridge University Press, 1969.
Riches, John, and David C. Sim, eds. *The Gospel of Matthew in its Roman Imperial Context* ECIC (JSNTSS 276). London: T. & T. Clark, 2005.
Rigaux, Beda. *Les Épitres aux Thessaloniciens.* EB. Paris: Gabalda, 1956.
Rissi, Mathias. *Die Theologie des Hebräerbriefes. Ihre Verankerung in der Situation des Verfassers und seiner Leser.* WUNT 41. Tübingen: Mohr, 1987.
Rochfuchs, Wilhelm. *Die Erfüllungszitate des Matthäus-Evangelium. Eine biblische-theologische Untersuchung.* BWANT 8. Stuttgart: Kohlhammer, 1969.
Robinson, John A.T. *Jesus and His Coming. The Emergence of a Doctrine.* London: SCM, 1957.
———. *Redating the New Testament.* London: SCM,1976.
Robinson, William C. *Der Weg des Herrn. Studien zur Geschichte und Eschatologie im Lukas-Evangelium. Ein Gesprach mit Hans Conzelmann.* TF 36. Hamburg: Herbert Reich, 1964.
Roloff, Jürgen. *Die Apostelgeschichte.* NTD 5. Göttingen: Vandenhoeck & Ruprecht, 1981.
Rose, Christian. *Die Wolke der Zeugen. Eine exegetisch-traditionsgeschichtliche Untersuchung zu Hebräer 10:32–12:3.* WUNT 2.60. Tübingen: Mohr, 1994.

Rosner, Brian S. *Paul and the Law. Keeping the Commandments of God.* NSBT 31. Nottingham: Apollos, 2013.

———. *Paul, Scripture, and Ethics. A Study of 1 Corinthians 5–7.* BSL. Reprint. Grand Rapids: Baker Books, 1999.

Rost, Leonard. *Judaism Outside the Hebrew Canon.* New York: Abingdon, 1976.

Rowland, Christopher C. *The Open Heaven. A Study of Apocalyptic in Judaism and Early Christianity.* London: SPCK, 1982.

Rowley, Harold H. *The Missionary Message of the Old Testament.* London: Carey Press, 1944.

———. *The Relevance of Apocalyptic. A Study of Jewish and Christian Apocalypses from Daniel to Revelation.* New & rev. ed. London: Lutterworth, 1963.

Saldarini, Anthony J. *Matthew's Christian Jewish Community.* Chicago: University of Chicago Press, 1994.

Salevao, Iutisone. *Legitimation in the Letter to the Hebrews. The Construction and Maintenance of a Symbolic Universe.* JSNTSS 219. Sheffield: Sheffield Academic, 2002.

Sanders, Edward P. *Paul and Palestinian Judaism. A Comparison of Patterns of Religion.* London: SCM, 1977.

———. *Paul, the Law and the Jewish People.* London: SCM, 1983.

Sanders, John N.-Mastin, B. *The Gospel according to St. John.* BNTC. London: A. & C. Black, 1968.

Sandmel, Samuel. *Philo's Place in Judaism. A Study of Conceptions of Abraham in Jewish Literature.* Cincinnati: Hebrew Union College Press, 1956.

Sänger, Dieter. "Die Adresse des Galaterbrief. Neue (?) Überlegungen zu einem alten Problem." In *Umstrittener Galaterbrief. Studien zur Situierung der Theologie des Paulus-Schreiben,* edited by Michael Bachmann, and Bernd Kollmann, 1–56. BTS 106. Neuchirchen-Vluyn: Neukirchener Theologie, 2010.

———. *Die Verkündigung des Gekreuzigten und Israel. Studien zum Verhältnis von Kirche und Israel bei Paulus und im frühen Christentum.* WUNT 75. Tübingen: Mohr, 1994.

Sauer, Georg. *Jesus Sirach/Ben Sira.* ATD Apokryphen Band 1. Göttingen: Vandenhoeck & Ruprecht, 2000.

Sayler, Gwendolyn B. *Have the Promises Failed? A Literary Analysis of 2 Baruch.* SBLDS 72. Chico, California: Scholars, 1984.

Schäfer, Ruth. *Paulus bis zum Apostelkonzil. Ein Beitrag zur Einleitung in den Galaterbrief, zur Geschichte der Jesusbewegung, and zur Pauluschronologie.* WUNT 2.179. Tübingen: Mohr Siebeck, 2004.

Scharlemann, Martin H. *Stephen: A Singular Saint.* Analecta Biblica 34. Rome: Pontifical Biblical Institute, 1968.

Schenck, Kenneth. *Cosmology and Eschatology in Hebrews. The Settings of Sacrifice.* SNTSMS 143. Cambridge: Cambridge University Press, 2007.

Schiffman, Louis H. "The Place of 4QMMT in the Corpus of Qumran Manuscripts." In *Reading 4QMMT. New Perspectives on Qumran Law and History,* edited by John Kampen and Moshe J. Bernstein, 81–98. SBLSS 2. Atlanta: Scholars, 1996.

Schlatter, Adolf. *Der Evangelist Matthäus. Seine Sprache, Seine Ziel, Seine Selbstständigkeit.* Stuttgart: Calwer, 1948.

Schlier, Henrich. "ανατελλω ανατολη." *TDNT* 1.351–53.

———. *Der Brief an die Galater.* KEKNT. 5th ed. Göttingen: Vandenhoeck & Ruprecht, 1971.

Schliesser, Benjamin. *Abraham's Faith in Romans 4. Paul's Concept of Faith in the light of the History of Reception of Genesis 15:6.* WUNT 2.224. Tübingen: Mohr Siebeck, 2007.

Schmid, H.H. "In Search of New Approaches in Pentateuchal Research." *JSOT* 3 (1977) 33–42.

———. *Der sogenannte Jahwist: Beobachtungen und Fragen zur Pentateuch-forschung.* Zürich: TVZ, 1976.

Schmid, Josef. *Das Evangelium nach Lukas.* RNT 3. 4th rev. ed, Regensburg: Pustet, 1960.

Schmitt, Rainer. *Gottesgerectigkeit-Heilsgeschichte-Israel in der Theologie des Paulus* EHS 23.240. Frankfurt am Main: Peter Lang, 1984.

Schnabel, Eckhard J. *Law and Wisdom from Ben Sira to Paul.* WUNT 2.16. Reprint, Eugene, OR: Wipf & Stock 2011.

Schnackenburg, Rudolph. *The Gospel according to St. John.* 3 vols. London: Burns & Oates, 1968–82.

Schneider, Gerhard. *Die Apostelgeschichte.* 2 vols. HTKNT 5.1–2. Freiburg.

———. "Die Davidssohnfrage (Mk.12:35–37)." *Biblica* 53 (1972) 65–90.

Schneider, Johannes. "σταυρος." *TDNT* 7.572–84.

Schnelle, Udo. *The History and Theology of the New Testament Writings.* London: SCM, 1998.

———. "Mutz ein Heide erst Juden werden, um Christ sein zu können?" In *Kirche und Volk Gottes. Festschrift für Jürgen Roloff zum 70. Geburtstag*, edited by Martin Karrer et al., 93–109. Neukirchen-Vluyn: Neukirchener, 2000.

Scholtissek, Klaus. "Den Unsichtbaren vor Augen' (Hebr.11:27). Die Ecclesia ab Abel im Israelkapitel des Hebräerbriefes." In *Ausharren in der Verheissung. Studien zum Hebräerbrief*, edited by Rainer Kampling, 135–64. SBS 204. Stuttgart: KBW, 2005.

Schramm, Brooks. *The Opponents of Third Isaiah. Reconstructing the Cultic History of the Restoration.* JSOTSS 193. Sheffield: Sheffield Academic Press, 1995.

Schrenk, Gottlob. "πατηρ κτλ." *TDNT* 5.945–1022.

Scroggs, Robin. "Salvation History: The Theological Structure of Paul's Theology (1 Thessalonians Philippians and Galatians)." In *Pauline Theology I*, edited by Jouette M. Bassler, 212–26. Minneapolis: Fortress, 1994.

Schulz, Siegfried. *Q, Die Spruchquelle der Evangelisten.* Zürich: TVZ, 1972.

Schunack, Gerd. "Exegetische Beobachtungen zum Verstandnis des Glaubens im Hebräerbrief. Eine kritische Anfrage." In *Texte und Geschichte. FS Dieter Lührmann*, edited by S. Maser and E. Scharb, 208–32. MTS 50. Marburg:Elwert, 1999.

———. *Der Hebräerbrief.* ZB NT 14. Zürich: TVZ, 2002.

Schürmann, Heinz.. *Kommentar zu Kap. 1:1–9:50.* Vol.1 of *Das Lukasevangelium.* HTKNT 3. Freiburg: Herder, 1969.

Schweizer, Eduard. *Matthäus und seine Gemeinde.* SBS 71. Stuttgart: KBW, 1974.

Scott, James M. *Adoption as sons of God. An Exegetical Investigation into the Background of ΥΙΟΘΕΣΙΑ in the Pauline Corpus.* WUNT 2.48. Tübingen: Mohr, 1992.

———. " 'For as many as are of Works of the Law are under a Curse' (Galatians 3:10)." In *Paul and the Scriptures of Israel*, edited by Craig A. Evans and James A. Sanders, 187–221. JSNTS 83. Sheffield: Sheffield Academic, 1993.

———. "Paul's Use of Deuteronomic Tradition." *JBL* 112 (1993) 645–665.
Seifrid, Mark A. *Christ, Our Righteousness. Paul's Theology of Justification.* Leicester: Apollos, 2000.
———. "Paul's Use of Righteousness Language Against his Hellenistic Background." In *The Paradoxes of Paul*, edited by Donald A. Carson et al., 39–74. Vol.2 of *Justification and Variegated Nomism.* Grand Rapids: Baker Academic, 2004.
———. "Righteousness Language in the Hebrew Scriptures and Early Judaism." In *The Complexities of Second Temple Judaism*, edited by Donald A. Carson et al., 415–42. Vol.1 of *Justification and Variegated Nomism.* Grand Rapids: Baker Academic, 2001.
Siegert, Folker. *Argumentation bei Paulus gezeigt an Röm 9–11.* WUNT 34. Tübingen: Mohr, 1985.
Siker, Jeffrey S. *Disinheriting the Jews. Abraham in Early Christian Controversy.* Louisville: Westminster John Knox, 1991.
Silberman, Lou H. "Paul's Midrash: Reflections on Romans 4." In *Faith and History. Essays in honor of Paul W. Meyer,* edited by John T. Carroll et al., 99–104. 1994. Reprint, Eugene, OR: Wipf & Stock, 2004.
Silva, Moisés. "Faith versus Works of Law in Galatians. In *The Paradoxes of Paul*, edited by Donald A. Carson et al, 217–48. Vol. 2 of *Justification and Variegated Nomism.* Grand Rapids: Baker Academic, 2004.
———. *Interpreting Galatians. Explorations in Exegetical Method.* 2nd ed., Grand Rapids: Baker Academic, 2001.
Sim, David C. *Apocalyptic Eschatology in the Gospel of Matthew.* SNTSMS 88. Cambridge: Cambridge University Press, 1996.
———. *The Gospel of Matthew and Christian Judaism. The History and Social Setting of the Matthean Community.* SNTW. Edinburgh: T. & T. Clark, 1998.
———. "Rome in Matthew's Eschatology." In *The Gospel of Matthew in its Roman Imperial Context*, edited by John Riches and David C. Sim, 91–106. ECC (JSNTSS 276). London: T. & T. Clark, 2005.
Smith, Barry D. *What must I Do to be Saved? Paul Parts Company with his Jewish Heritage.* NTM 17. Sheffield: Sheffield Phoenix, 2007.
Snodgrass, Klyne R. "Justification by Grace–to the Doers: An Analysis of the Place of Romans 2 in the Theology of Paul." *NTS* 32 (1986) 72–93.
Söding, Thomas. "Die Antwort des Glaubens. Das Vorbild Abrahams nach Hebr 11." *IKZ* 24 (1995) 394–408.
———. "Glaube, der durch Liebe wirke. Rechtfertigung und Ethik im Galaterbrief." In *Umstrittener Galaterbrief. Studien zur Situierung der Theologie des Paulus-Schreibens*, edited by Michael Bachmann and Bernd Kollmann, 165–206. BTS 106. Neukirchen-Vluyn: Neukirchener, 2010.
———. "Zuversicht und Geduld im Schauen auf Jesus. Zum Glaubensbegriff des Hebraerbriefes." *ZNW* 82 (1991) 214–41.
Spicq, Celsus. *L'Épitre aux Hébreux.* EB. Paris: Gabalda, 2 vols.1952–1953.
Sprinkle, Preston M. *Law and Life. The Interpretation of Leviticus 18:5 in Early Judaism and in Paul.* WUNT 2.241. Tübingen: Mohr Siebeck, 2008.
———. *Paul & Judaism Revisited. A Study of Divine and Human Agency in Salvation.* Downers Grove, IL: InterVarsity Academic, 2013.
Stanley, C.D. *Arguing with Scripture. The Rhetoric of Quotations in the Letters of Paul.* London: T. & T. Clark, 2004.

Stanton, Graham. *A Gospel for a New People. Studies in Matthew*. Edinburgh: T. & T. Clark, 1992.

———. "The Gospel of Matthew and Judaism." *BJRL* 66 (1983–84) 264–84.

———, ed. *The Interpretation of Matthew*. IRT 3. London: SPCK, 1983.

———. The Law of Moses and the Law of Christ." In *Paul and the Mosaic Law*, edited by James D.G. Dunn, 99–116. Grand Rapids: Eerdmans, 2001.

Stanton, Graham, and Guy G. Stroumsa, eds. *Tolerance and Intolerance in Early Judaism and Christianity*. Cambridge: Cambridge University Press, 1996.

Stauffer, Ethelbert. *New Testament Theology*. London: SCM, 1955.

Stendahl, Krister. *Paul among the Gentiles*. London: SCM, 1977.

———. " "Quis et Unde." An Analysis of Matthew 1–2." In *Judentum, Urchristentum, Kirche, Festschrift Joachim Jeremias*, edited by Walter Eltester, 94–105. BZNW 26. Berlin: Topelmann, 1964.

———. *The School of St. Matthew and Its Use of the Old Testament*. ASNU 20. 2nd ed. Lund: Gleerup, 1968.

Still, Todd D. "Christos as Pistos: The Faith(fulness) of Jesus in the Epistle to the Hebrews." *CBQ* 69 (2007) 746–55.

Stolle, V. "Nomos zwischen Tora und Lex. Der paulinische Gesetzsbegriff und seine Interpretation durch Luther in der zweiten Disputation gegen die Antinomer vom 12. Januar 1538." In *Lutherische und Neue Paulusperspektive*, edited by Michael Bachmann, 41–67. WUNT 182. Tübingen: Mohr Siebeck, 2005.

Stolz, Lukas, *Der Höhepunkt des Hebräerbriefs*. WUNT 2.463. Tübingen: Mohr Siebeck, 2018.

Stowers, Stanley K. *The Diatribe and Paul's Letter to the Romans*. SBLDS 57. Atlanta: Scholars, 1981.

———. *A Rereading of Romans. Justice, Jews, and Gentiles*. New Haven: Yale University Press, 1994.

Strathmann, Hermann. *Das Evangelium nach Johannes*. NTD 4. Göttingen: Vandenhoeck & Ruprecht, 1959.

Strauss, Mark L. *The Davidic Messiah in Luke-Acts. The Promise and its Fulfilment in Lukan Christology*. JSNTSS 110. Sheffield: Sheffield Academic, 1995.

Strecker, Georg. *Der Weg der Gerechtigkeit. Untersuchung zur Theologie des Matthäus*. FRLANT 82. 2nd ed. Gottingen: Vandenhoeck & Ruprecht, 1966.

Streeter, Burnett H. *The Four Gospels. A Study of Origins*. Rev.ed. London: MacMillan, 1930.

Stuhlmacher, P. *Gerechtigkeit des Gottes bei Paulus*. Göttingen: Vandenhoeck & Ruprecht, 1965.

———. *Revisiting Paul's Doctrine of Justification by Faith: A Challenge to the New Perspective. With an Essay by Donald A Hagner*. Downers Grove, IL: InterVarsity, 2001.

Tannehill, Robert C. *The Gospel according to Luke*. Vol. 1 of *The Narrative Unity of Luke-Acts. A Literary Interpretation*. FFNT. Philadelphia: Fortress, 1986.

———. "The Magnificat as Poem." *JBL* 93 (1974) 263–75

Taylor, Vincent. *The Gospel according to St. Mark*. London: Macmillan, 1953.

Theobald, Michael. "Abraham-(Isaak -)Jakob. Israels Väter im Johannesevangelium." In *Israel und seine Heilstraditionen im Johannesevangelium*, edited by Michael Labahn et al., 158–83. Paderborn: Schöningh, 2004.

---. "Abraham sah hin . . . Realitätssinn als Gütesiegel des Glaubens (Röm.4:18-22)." In *Studien zum Römerbrief*, by Michael Theobald, 398-416. WUNT 136. Tübingen: Mohr Siebeck, 2001.

---. *Das Evangelium nach Johannes. Kapitel 1-12.* RNT. Regensburg: Friedrich Pustet, 2009.

---. "Glaube und Vernunft. Zur Argumentation des Paulus im Römerbrief" (1989). In *Studien zum Römerbrief*, by Michael Theobald, 417-31. WUNT 136. Tübingen: Mohr Siebeck, 2001

---. *Herrenworte im Johannesevangelium*. HBS 34. Freiburg: Herder, 2002.

---. " "Dem Juden zuerst und auch dem Heiden." Die paulinische Auslegung der Glaubensformel Röm.1:3f" (1981). In *Studien zum Römerbrief*, by Michael Theobald, 102-118. WUNT 136. Tübingen: Mohr Siebeck, 2001.

---. "Der Kanon von der Rechtigkeit (Gal.2:16; Röm.3:28). Eigentum des Paulus oder Gemeingut der Kirche?" (1999). In *Studien zum Römerbrief*, by Michael Theobald, 164-225. WUNT 136. Tübingen: Mohr Siebeck, 2001.

---. " 'Der strittige Punkt' (Rh. a Her.1.26) im Diskurs des Römerbriefes. Die propositio 1.16f. und das Mysterium der Erretung ganz Israels" (1999). In *Studien zum Römerbrief*, by Michael Theobald, 278-323. WUNT 136. Tübingen: Mohr Siebeck, 2001.

---. *Studien zum Römerbrief*. WUNT 136. Tübingen: Mohr Siebeck, 2001.

---. "Verantwortung vor der Vergangenheit. Die Bedeutung der Traditionen Israels für den Römerbrief" (1982). In *Studien zum Römerbrief*, by Michael Theobald, 15-28. WUNT 136. Tübingen: Mohr Siebeck, 2001.

---. "Warum schrieb Paulus den Romerbrief?" (1983), *Studien zum Römerbrief*, 2-14. WUNT 136. Tübingen: Mohr Siebeck, 2001.

Thielman, Frank. *From Plight to Solution. A Jewish framework for Understanding Paul's View of the Law in Galatians and Romans*. SNT 61. 1989. Reprint, Eugene, OR: Wipf & Stock, 2007.

---. *Paul and the Law. A Contextual Approach*. Downers Grove, IL: InterVarsity Academic, 1994.

Thiessen, Matthew. *Contesting Conversion. Genealogy, Circumcision, & Identity in Ancient Judaism and Christianity*. Oxford: Oxford Unkversity Press, 2011.

---. *Paul and the Gentile Problem*, Oxford: Oxford University Press, 2016.

Thompson, James W. *The Beginnings of Christian Philosophy. The Epistle to the Hebrews*. CBQMS 13. Washington, DC: Catholic Biblical Association of America, 1982.

Thrall, Margaret E. *2 Corinthians*. 2 vols. ICC. Edinburgh: T. & T. Clark, 1994, 2000.

Thusing, Wilhelm. " "Lasst uns hinzutreten..." (Hebr 10:22). Zur Frage nach dem Sinn der Kulttheologie im Hebräerbrief." In *Studien zur neutestamentlichen Theologie*, edited by Thomas Söding, 184-200. WUNT 82. Tübingen: Mohr, 1995.

---. ""Milch" und "feste Speise" (1 Kor. 3:1f und Hebr 5:11-6:3). Elementarkatechese und theologische Vertiefung in neutestamentlicher Sicht." In *Studien zur neutestamentlichen Theologie*, edited by Thomas Söding, 23-56. WUNT 82. Tubingen: Mohr, 1995.

Thyen, Haerwig. *Das Johannesevangelium*. HzNT 6. Tübingen: Mohr Siebeck, 2005.

Tiede, David L. *The Charismatic Figure as Miracle Worker*. SBLDS 1. Missoula, MT: SBL, 1972.

Tobin, Thomas H. *Paul's Rhetoric in Context. The Argument of Romans*. Peabody, MA: Hendrickson, 2004.

Tomson, P.J. *Paul and the Jewish Law. Halakha in the Letters of the Apostle to the Gentiles.* CRINT 1. Assen, Maastricht: Van Gorcum, 1990.

———. "Transformation of post-70 Judaism: Scholarly Reconstructions and Their Implications for our Perception of Matthew, Didache, and James." In *Matthew, James, and Didache. Three Related Documents in Their Jewish and Christian Settings,* edited by Huub van de Sandt and Jürgen.K. Zangenberg, 91–121. Symposium 45. Atlanta: SBL, 2008.

Trilling, Wolfgang. "Der Einzug im Jerusalem Mt. 21:1–17." In *Neutestamentliche Aufsätze. Festschrift für Josef Schmid,* edited by J. Blinzer et al., 303–9. Regensburg: Friedrich Pustet, 1963.

———. *Das wahre Israel.* SANT 10. 3rd ed. München: Kösel, 1964.

Tsuji, Manabu. *Glaube zwischen Vollkommenheit und Verweltlichung. Eine Untersuchung zur literarischen Gestalt und zur inhaltlichen Kohärenz des Jakobusbriefes.* WUNT 2.93. Tübingen: Mohr, 1997.

Turner, Nigel. "The Relation of Luke I and II to Hebraic Sources and to the Rest of Luke-Acts." *NTS* 2 (1955–56) 100–109.

Tyson, J.B. "Paul's Opponents in Galatia." *NT* 10 (1968) 241–54.

Van de Sandt, Huub and Jürgen K. Zangenberg, eds. *Matthew, James, and Didache. Three Related Documents in Their Jewish and Christian Settings.* Symposium Series 45. Atlanta: SBL, 2008.

van der Minde, Hans-Jürgen. *Schrift und Tradition bei Paulus, Ihre Bedeutung und Funktion im Römerbrief.* PTS 3. München: Schöningh, 1976.

Vanhoye, Albert. *La Structure Littéraire de l'Épitre aux Hébreux.* SN 1. Paris: Desclée de Brouwer, 1962.

———. "Un médiateur des anges en Ga 3:19–20." *Biblica* 59 (1978) 403–11.

VanLandigham, Chris. *Judgment & Justification in Early Judaism and the Apostle Paul.* Peabody, MA: Hendrickson, 2006.

Van Tilborg, Sjef. *The Jewish Leaders in Matthew.* Leiden: Brill, 1972.

Verseput, Donald J. "Reworking the Puzzle of Faith and Deeds in James 2:14–26." *NTS* 43 (1997) 97–115.

Vielhauer, Philip. "Das Benedictus des Zacharias (Lk 1:68–79)." *ZThK* (49) 1952.

Vogel, Manuel. *Das Heil des Bundes. Bundestheologie im Frühjudentum und im frühen Christentum.* TANZ 18. Tübingen: Francke, 1996.

Vögtle, Anton. "Die Genealogie Mt.1:2–16 und die matthaïsche Kindheitsgeschichte." *BZ* 8 (1964) 45–58, 239–62; *BZ* 9 (1965) 32–49.

———. "Messiasbekenntnis und Petrusverheissung. Zur Komposition Mt. 16:13–23." *BZ* 1 (1957) 252–72; *BZ* 2 (1958) 85–103.

———. "Zur Problem der Herkunft von Mt.16:17–19." In *Orientierung an Jesus,* edited by Paul Hoffmann, 372–93. Freiburg: Herder & Herder, 1973.

Von Dobbeler, Axel. *Glaube als Teilhabe. Historische und semantische Grundlagen der paulinischen Theologie und Ekklesiologie des Glaubens.* WUNT 2.22. Tübingen: Mohr Siebeck, 1987.

Voss, J.S. "Die Hermeneuitische Antinomie bei Paulus (Galater 3:11–12; Römer 10:5–10)." *NTS* 38 (1992) 254–70.

Wakefield, Andrew H. *Where to Live. The Hermeneutical Significance of Paul's Citations from Scripture in Galatians 3:1–14.* SBLAB 14. Atlanta: SBL, 2003.

Walker, Rolf. *Die Heilsgeschichte im ersten Evangelium.* FRLANT 91. Göttingen: Vandenhoeck & Ruprecht, 1967.

Wall, Robert W. *Community of the Wise. The Letter of James*. NTC. Valley Gorge, PA: Trinity, 1997.
Walter, Nikolaus. "Die 'als Säulen Geltenden' in Jerusalem–Leiter der Urgemeinde oder exemplarisch Fromme?" In *Kirche und Volk Gottes. Festschrift für Jürgen Roloff zum 70. Geburtstag*, edited by Martin Karrer et al., 75–92. Neukirchen-Vluyn: Neukirchener, 2000.

———. "Zur Interpretation von Römer 9–11." *ZTK* 81 (1984) 172–95.

Ward, Roy B. "Partiality in the Assembly." *HTR* 62 (1969) 87–97.

———. "The Works of Abraham." *HTR* 61 (1968) 283–90.

Watson, Francis. *Paul and the Hermeneutics of Faith*. London: T. & T. Clark, 2004.

———. *Paul, Judaism and the Gentiles. Beyond the New Perspective*. Grand Rapids: Eerdmans, 2007.

Wehnert, Jürgen. *Die Reinheit des "christlichen Gottesvolkes" aus Juden und Heiden. Studien zum historischen und theologischen Hintergrund des sogenannten Aposteldekrets*. FRLANT 173. Göttingen: Vandenhoeck & Ruprecht, 1997.

Weiss, Hans-Friedrich. *Der Brief an die Hebräer*. KEKNT 13. Göttingen: Vandenhoeck & Ruprecht, 1991.

Weiss, Konrad. "Φερω κτλ." *TDNT* 9.56–59.

Wenger, Stefan. *Der wesenheit gute Kyrios. Eine exegetische Studie über das Gottesbild im Jakobusbrief*. ATANT 100. Zürich: TVZ, 2011.

Wenk, Matthias. *Community-Forming Power. The Socio-Ethical Role of the Spirit in Luke-Acts*. JPTS 19, 2000. Reprint London: T. & T. Clark, 2004.

Westerholm, Stephen. *Perspectives Old and New on Paul. The "Lutheran" Paul and His Critics*. Grand Rapids: Eerdmans, 2004.

White, John L. *The Apostle of God. Paul and the Promise of Abraham*. Peabody, MA: Hendricksen, 1999.

White Crawford, Sidnie. *Rewriting Scripture in Second Temple Times*. SDSSRL. Grand Rapids: Eerdmans, 2008.

Whitlark, Jason A. *Enabling Fidelity to God. Perseverance in Hebrews in Light of the Reciprocity Systems of the Ancient Mediterranean World*. PBM. Milton Keynes: Paternoster, 2008.

Wider, David. *Theozentrik und Bekenntnis. Untersuchungen zur Theologie des Redens Gottes im Hebräerbrief*. BZNW 87. Berlin: De Gruyter, 1997.

Wiefeld, Wolfgang. "The Jewish Community in Ancient Rome and the Origins of Roman Christianity." In *The Romans Debate*, edited by Karl P. Donfield, 85–101. Rev.ed. Peabody, MA: Hendrickeson, 1991.

Wieser, Friedrich E. *Die Abrahamvorstellungen im Neuen Testament*. EHS 23.317. Bern: Peter Lang, 1987.

Wikenhauser, Alfred. *Das Evangelium nach Johannes*. RNT 4. Regensburg: Friedrich Pustet, 1961.

Wilckens, Ulrich. "Die Bekehrung des Paulus als religionsgeschichtliches Problem." In *Rechtfertigung als Freiheit. Paulusstudien*, by Ulrich Wilckens, 11–32. Neukirchen-Vluyn: Neukirchener, 1974.

———. *Der Brief an die Römer*. 3 vols. EKKNT 6.1–3. Neukirchen-Vluyn: Neukirchener, 2003–13.

———. *Das Evangelium nach Johannes*. NTD 4. Göttingen: Vandenhoeck & Ruprecht, 2000.

———. "Die Rechtfertigung Abrahams nach Römer 4." In *Rechtfertigung als Freiheit. Paulusstudien*, by Ulrich Wilckens, 33–49. Neukirchen-Vluyn: Neukirchener, 1974.

———. *Rechtfertigung als Freiheit. Paulusstudien*. Neukirchen-Vluyn: Neukirchener, 1974.

———. "Über Abfassungszweck und Aufbau des Römerbriefs." In *Rechtfertigung als Freiheit. Paulusstudien*, by Ulrich Wilckens, 110–70. Neukirchen-Vluyn: Neukirchener, 1974.

———. "Was heisst bei Paulus: "Aus Werken des Gesetzes wird kein Mensch gerecht"?" In *Rechtfertigung als Freiheit. Paulusstudien*, by Ulrich Wilckens, 77–109. Neukirchen-Vluyn: Neukirchener, 1974.

———. "Zu Römer 3:21–4:25. Antwort an G. Klein." In *Rechtfertigung als Freiheit. Paulusstudien*, by Ulrich Wilckens, 50–76. Neukirchen-Vluyn: Neukirchener, 1974.

Wilk, Florian, et al., eds. *Between Gospel and Election. Explorations in the Interpretation of Romans 9–11*. WUNT 257. Tübingen: Mohr Siebeck, 2010.

Williamson, Ronald. *Philo and The Epistle to the Hebrews*. ALGHJ 4. Leiden: Brill, 1979.

Wilson, Todd A. *The Curse of the Law and the Crisis in Galatia. Reassessing the Purpose of Galatians*. WUNT 2.225. Tübingen: Mohr Siebeck, 2007.

Winninge, Mikael. *Sinners and the Righteous. A Comparative Study of the Psalms of Solomon and Paul's Letters*. CB. NT 26. Stockholm: Almquist & Wiksell, 1995.

Winter, Bruce W. *Philo and Paul among the Sophists. Alexandrian and Corinthian Responses to a Julio-Claudian Movement*. 2nd. ed. Grand Rapids: Eerdmans, 2002.

Winter, Paul. "Magnificat and Benedictus–Maccabean Psalms?" *BJRL* 37 (1954–55) 328–47.

Wischmeyer, Oda. "Wie kommt Abraham in den Galaterbrief? Überlegungen zu Gal.3:6–29." In *Umstrittener Galaterbrief. Studien zur Situierung der Theologie des Paulus-Schreiben*, edited by Michael Bachmann and Bernd Kollmann, 119–63. BTS 106. Neukirchen-Vlkuyn: Neukirchener, 2010.

———. "Römer 2:1–24 als Teil der Gerichtsrede des Paulus gegen die Menschheit." *NTS* 52 (2006) 356–76.

Wisdom, Jeffrey R. *Blessing for the Nations and the Curse of the Law. Paul's Citation of Genesis and Deuteronomy in Gal. 3: 8–10*. WUNT 2. 133. Tübingen: Mohr Siebeck, 2001.

Witherington, Ben. *The Acts of the Apostles. A Socio-Rhetorical Commentary*. Grand Rapids: Eerdmans, 1998.

———. *Grace in Galatia. A Commentary on Paul's Letter to the Galatians*. London: T. & T. Clark, 1998.

Worthington, Jonathan D. *Creation in Paul and Philo. The Beginning and the Before*. WUNT 2.317. Tübingen: Mohr Siebeck, 2011.

Wright, N.Thomas. *The Climax of the Covenant. Christ and the Law in Paul's Theology*. Edinburgh: T. & T. Clark, 1991.

———. "Messiahship in Galatians?" In *Galatians and Christian Theology. Justification, the Gospel, and Ethics in Paul's Letter*, edited by Mark W. Elliott et al., 3–23. Grand Rapids: Baker Academic, 2014.

———. *The New Testament and the People of God*. London: SPCK, 1992.

———. *Paul and the Faithfulness of God*. 2 vols. Christian Origins and the Question of God 4. SPCK: London, 2013.

———. *Paul: Fresh Perspectives*. London: SPCK, 2005.
———. *Pauline Perspectives. Essays on Paul, 1978-2013*. London: SPCK, 2013.
———. *What Saint Paul Really Said. Was Paul of Tarsus the real Founder of Christianity?* Oxford: Lion, 1977.
Yeung, Maureen W. *Faith in Jesus and Paul. A Comparison with Special Reference to "Faith That Can Remove Mountains" and "Your Faith Has Healed/Saved You."* WUNT 2.147. Tübingen: Mohr Siebeck, 2002.
Yinger, Kent L. *Paul, Judaism, and Judgment according to Deeds*. SNTSMS 105. Cambridge: Cambridge University Press, 1999.
Young, Norman H. "Paidagogos: The Social Setting of a Pauline Metaphor." *NT* 29 (1987) 150-76.
Zeller, Dieter. *Charis bei Philon und Paulus*. SBS 142. Stuttgart: KBW, 1990
———. *Juden und Heiden in der Mission des Paulus. Studien zum Römerbrief*. FzB 8. Stuttgart: KBW, 1973.
Ziesler, John. *The Meaning of Righteousness in Paul. A Linguistic and Theological Enquiry*. SNTSMS 20. Cambridge: Cambridge University Press, 1972.
Zimmermann, Heinrich. *Das Bekenntnis der Hoffnung. Tradition und Redaktion im Hebräerbrief*. BBB 47. Köln-Bonn: Hanstein, 1977.

Bibliography for Excursus on Abraham in the Apostolic Fathers

Bauer, D.Walter. Die Briefe des Ignatius von Antiochia und der Polykarpbrief. In *Die Apostolischen Väter*, edited by Hans Lietzmann. HzNT. Ergänzungsband. Tübingen: Mohr, 1923.
Beyschlag, Karlmann. *Clemens Romanus und der Frühkatholizismus*. BHT 35. Tübingen: Mohr, 1966.
Carleton Paget, James. *The Epistle of Barnabas*. WUNT 2.64. Tübingen: Mohr, 1994.
Chadwick, Henry. "Justification by Faith and Hospitality." In vol.4 of *Studia Patristica*, edited by F.L. Cross, 281-85. TU 79. Berlin: Akademie-Verlag, 1961.
Daube, David. "Participle and Imperative in 1 Peter." Appended Note in E.G. Selwyn, *The First Epistle of St. Peter*, 467-88. London: MacMillan, 1946.
Flüchter, Sascha. *Die Anrechnung des Glaubens zur Gerechtigkeit. Auf Weg zu einer sozialhistorisch orientierten Rezeptionsgeschichte von Gen 15:6 in der neutestamentlichen Literatur*. TANZ 51. Tübingen: Francke Verlag, 2010.
Hvakvik, Reidar. *The Struggle for Scripture and the Covenant. The Purpose of the Epistle of Barnabas and Jewish-Christian Competition in the Second Century*. WUNT 2.82. Mohr: Tübingen: 1996.
Knopf, Rudolph. Der erste Clemensbrief. In *Die Apostolischen Väter*, edited by Hans Lietzmann. HzNT. Ergänzungsband. Tübingen: Mohr, 1923.
Lawson, John. *A Theological and Historical Introduction to the Apostolic Fathers*. New York: Macmillan, 1961.
Lightfoot, John B. *The Apostolic Fathers*. Edited and Completed by J.R. Harmer. London: Macmillan, 1898.
Lona, Horacio E. *Der erste Clemensbrief*. KAV 2. Göttingen: Vandenhoeck & Ruprecht, 1998.
Meinhold, Peter. *Studien zu Ignatius von Antiochien*. Wiesbaden: Franz Steiner, 1979.

Prostmeier, Ferdinand R., *Der Barnabasbrief.* KAV 8. Göttingen: Vandenhoeck & Ruprecht, 1999.
Prigent, Pierre. *L'Épître de Barnabé I-XVI et Ses Sources.* EB. Gabalda: Paris, 1961.
Schoedel, William R., *Ignatius of Antioch.* Hermeneia. Philadelphia: Fortress, 1985.
Torrance, Thomas F., *The Doctrine of Grace in the Apostolic Fathers.* Edinburgh: Oliver & Boyd, 1948.
Wengst, Karl. *Tradition und Theologie des Barnabasbriefes.* AK 42. Berlin-New York: Walter de Gruyter, 1971.
Windisch, Hans. *Der Barnabasbrief.* In *Die Apostolischen Väter*, edited by Hans Lietzmann. HzNT. Ergänzungsband. Tübingen: Mohr, 1923.

Index of Modern Scholars

Aageson, J. W., 79, 83
Abbott-Smith, G., 100
Adams, Edward, 105, 108
Allen, Leslie C., 264
Allo, E. B., 88
Attridge, Harold W., 168–69, 171, 174–75, 178–80, 183, 185, 189, 194, 196, 200–201, 318
Aune, David E., 92

Bachmann, Michael, 26, 50–52, 64, 158–59
Backhaus, Knut, 165–66, 169, 171–73, 179, 181–82, 187, 196, 201
Bammel, Ernst, 60
Barclay, John M. G., 4, 6–7, 9, 11, 18, 33, 37, 39, 41, 46, 61, 64–65, 71, 75, 77, 79, 91–94, 97–8, 107, 110–11, 114, 121–22, 129–31, 134, 137, 141–42, 154, 156
Barrett, C. Kingsley, 6, 12, 29–30, 32–33, 35, 38–39, 68, 70, 75–76, 83, 87–88, 95–96, 111, 114, 119, 130, 134, 136, 138, 267, 276–77, 279–81, 284–86
Bassler, Jouette M., 57, 93
Bauckham, Richard, 204–6, 213

Bauer, Walter, 12, 34, 41, 90, 100, 121, 155, 162, 174, 206–7, 217, 277–80, 309, 331, 334, 337–38
Beasley-Murray, George R., 70, 193, 279, 282, 285–86, 321
Beare, Francis W., 293, 296, 305, 311
Behm, Johannes, 80
Beker, J. Christian, 92, 143, 146, 162
Benoit, Pierre, 240, 247–48, 250
Berger, Klaus, 1–2, 48, 54, 56, 61, 67, 83, 84, 86, 94, 116, 123, 130
Bergmeier, Roland, 107
Betz, Hans-Dieter, 6, 13, 20, 29, 33–35.41, 44, 53, 55, 60, 61, 64, 75–76, 79–80
Beyschlag, Karlmann, 330
Bird, Michael F., 6, 149–50
Blaschke, Andreas, 9, 267
Black, Matthew, 114, 119, 136, 183
Blass, Friedrich-Albert Debrunner, 118, 121, 123, 181, 186, 212, 240, 244
Blocher, Henri A. G., 107
Bonnard, Pierre, 6, 13, 32, 34–35, 68, 75
Borgen, Peder, 78
Bornkamm, Gunter, 25, 310
Boobyer, George H., 26
Brawley, Robert L., 178

Brewer, David I., 58, 76
Brooke, Stephenson H., 310
Brown, Raymond E., 240, 247–49, 254, 259, 272–73, 285, 293–95, 305
Bruce, Frederick F., 5–6, 16, 20, 29–34, 38, 44, 55–57, 61, 63–65, 68, 75, 79–80, 88, 166, 169, 172–75, 179, 183, 189, 194, 267, 318
Bultmann, Rudolf, 123, 153, 238, 274, 278–80, 284–85, 289
Burchard, Christoph, 204–6, 211–12, 217
Burger, Christoph, 296
Burton, Ernest W., 29, 32–34, 59–60, 64–65, 80–81, 83

Cadbury, Henry J., 239, 259
Caird, George B., 5, 9–10, 133, 167, 179.188, 299
Cargill, Timothy B. 211–12, 217
Carleton Paget, James, 336
Carson, Donald A., 276, 285
Carter, Warren, 293–94, 305
Catchpole, David R., 298
Chadwick, Henry, 330
Chae, Daniel J. S., 93, 108, 115, 117
Christiansen, Ellen J., 77
Clark, Kenneth W., 311
Clements, Ronald E., 321
Conzelmann, Hans, 241–42, 338
Cosgrove, Charles H., 3, 46
Cranfield, Charles E. B., 25, 96, 99, 104, 107, 114, 119, 123–25, 129–30, 136–38, 144, 154
Creed, John M., 239, 256, 259
Crompton, R. Bruce, 211, 218
Crosby, Michael R., 179–80
Cullmann, Oscar, 153, 155
Cummins, Stephen A., 6, 13, 29

Dahl, Nils A., 136
Das, A. Andrew, 19, 21, 23–24, 38, 45–46, 53
Daube, David, 5, 332
Dautzenberg, Gerhard, 170, 190
Davids, Peter, 204–6, 210–12, 217, 219–20, 225
Davies, William D., 311

Davies, William D.–Dale C. Allison, 293–6, 300–302, 304–6, 309
Davis, C. T., 293
De Boer, Marinus, 19
Delling, Gerhard, 168, 188–89, 208
De Roo, Jacqueline C. R., 26–27, 99, 107
DeSilva, David A., 166, 168–70, 172, 175, 178, 180–81, 183, 187, 189, 196, 318
Deutsch, Celia, 310
Dibelius, Martin, 204, 211, 213, 223, 226, 238, 254
Dietzfelbringer, Christian, 8–11, 272, 275–76, 279, 284, 287
Di Mattei, Steven, 76–78
Dix, Gregory, 16
Dodd, Charles H., 119, 136, 258, 273, 282
Donaldson, Terence L., 8, 11, 38, 41, 46, 114
Donfried, Karl P., 92, 98
Drane, John, 64, 68, 74, 144
Drury, John, 259
Duling, D. C., 303, 305
Dunn, James D. G., 5–6, 8, 11, 13, 15–20, 29–34, 37, 41, 44–45, 55–57, 60–61, 64–67, 72, 75, 79–80, 92–93, 95–96, 98, 100, 102, 104, 112, 114–16, 119, 123–25, 128–31, 134, 136–38, 140–41, 144, 149–50, 154–56, 223–24
Du Plessis, Paul J., 208
Dupont, Jacques, 11

Eastman, Susan, 80–84
Edgar, David H., 204
Eichrodt, Walter, 241
Eisenbaum, Pamela, 180, 197–98, 201
Ellingworth, Paul, 168–69, 172, 174, 179–80, 183, 318–19
Elliott, Mark W., 20
Ellis, E. Earle, 250, 259
Esler, Philip F., 4–5, 10, 13–14, 43, 47–48, 56, 61–62, 64–65, 76–77, 284, 287
Evans, Christopher F., 236, 249, 252, 256, 259

INDEX OF MODERN SCHOLARS

Farris, Stephen, 239-40, 247-48, 250, 259
Fee, Gordon D., 68-70, 87, 89,
Fischer, Ulrich, 269
Fitzmeyer, Joseph A., 175, 236, 245, 249, 252, 256
Flebbe, Jochen, 96, 98, 101, 107-8, 112-14, 116, 121-22, 125, 127, 129-32, 138, 140-43, 146
Fluchter, Sascha, 206, 213, 331, 339
Foster, Paul, 316
France, Richard T., 297, 309, 311
Frankemolle, Hubert, 41, 204-6, 208, 211, 213, 214-16, 218-19, 221-22, 293-94, 301, 305-8
Fretheim, Terence, 315, 321
Fung, Ronald Y-K., 87-89
Furman, Sebastian, 171-73, 175

Gamble, Harold, 92
Garleff, Gunnar, 221
Gaston, Lloyd, 4, 19, 28, 31, 34, 62, 97, 99, 103-4, 311
Gathercole, Simon J., 95, 107, 112
Gaventa, Beverley R., 7
Georgi, Dieter, 1
Gheorgitta, Radu, 177
Glombis, Timothy C., 30-32
Gnilka, Joachim, 239-40, 244-45, 250-52, 293-97, 299, 303-6, 309
Goppelt, Leonard, 153, 156
Grasser, Erik, 58, 64, 166-67, 169-70, 172-4, 179-80, 183, 190-91, 194-96, 203, 239, 241, 262, 265-66, 289, 318-19
Grundmann, Walter, 236, 245, 250, 259
Gundry, Robert H., 301, 303

Haacker, Klaus, 10-11, 132
Haenchen, Ernst, 13, 267, 297
Hahn, Ferdinand, 107-8, 240, 259
Hamm, Dennis, 189, 194
Hamann, Henry Paul, 216
Hanson, Anthony T., 150, 280
Hanson, G. Walter, 30, 41, 43-44, 49, 55-56, 60-61, 65, 71, 84, 107
Hardin, Justin K., 84
Hare, Douglas, 310

Harrisville, Roy A., 123
Hartin, Patrick J., 204-6, 208, 210, 218
Harvey, Anthony E., 33
Hays, Richard B., 35, 38, 55, 57-60, 76-79, 82-84, 99, 126, 149-51, 162, 167, 184, 188, 320
Heckel, Ulrich, 126
Heiligenthal, Roman H., 25, 206, 212, 220, 275-78
Held, Heinz-Joachim, 301-3
Hengel, Martin, 16
Henton Davies, Gwynne, 321
Herford, R.Travers, 226
Hering, Jean, 169
Hertzberg, Hans W., 257
Hill, David, 87-88
Hofius, Otfried, 12, 108, 112, 128, 136, 139, 172, 194
Hoffmann, Paul, 309
Holtz, Traugott, 265
Hooker, Morna D., 33, 56, 88, 92, 154, 156, 163
Hoppe, Rudolf, 6
Horrell, David G., 75, 154, 156, 163
Hoskyns, Edwin C., 284-86
Hubner, Hans, 64, 74, 107, 144
Hughes, Philip E., 88
Hummel, Reinhart, 296, 311
Hunn, Debbie, 151
Hvalvik, Reidar, 33-40

Jackson-McCabe, Matt A., 207, 213
Jacobs, Irvine, 219
Jeska, Joachim, 163
Jewett, Robert, 92, 104, 112-13, 115, 117, 119, 123, 126, 129-33, 136, 138-40
Johnson, E. Elizabeth, 128
Johnson, Luke T., 204, 206, 208, 212, 221, 229, 267
Johnson, Marshall D., 294-95
Johnson-Hodge, Caroline, 141

Kampling, Rainer, 167
Karris, Richard J., 92
Kasemann, Ernst, 29, 43, 88, 96, 104, 107, 114-16, 119-21, 123, 132, 134, 136, 138, 144, 156, 181

INDEX OF MODERN SCHOLARS

Kaut, Thomas, 239–42, 250, 252–56
Kaylor, R. David, 96, 116
Kilpatrick, George D., 310
Kim, Seyoon, 11, 46, 54, 128
Kingsbury, Jack D., 299–300, 305
Kittel, Gerhard, 227
Klein, Gunter, 19–21, 29–33, 99, 124, 153, 156–58, 160, 213
Klijn, A. J., 276
Knopf, Rudolph, 332
Koch, Dietrich-Alex, 38, 42, 45, 52, 55, 64, 78, 83, 94, 101, 133, 142, 223
Konradt, Matthias, 38, 43, 46, 79, 312–13
Koester, Craig R., 169, 172, 174, 178–80, 183, 187, 319
Koster, Helmut, 171–75, 178, 196
Kraus, Wolfgang, 7
Kreuzer, Siegfried, 105
Kruijf, Th.de., 298
Kummel, Werner G., 18–20, 29, 32, 68, 153, 156 , 165, 242
Kuss, Otto, 167
Kwon, Yon-Gyong, 3–4

Lampe, Peter, 52
Lane, William L., 168–69, 172, 175, 183, 185, 189, 196, 318–19
Lategan, B. C., 61
Laub, Franz, 167, 172, 175, 179–80
Laurentin, Pierre, 258
Laws, Sophie, 204, 206, 210, 212–13, 215–17, 220, 223
Lawson, John A., 332
Lee, Chee-Chiew, 36, 45, 48, 54, 56
Leenhardt, Franz J., 96, 107, 119, 125, 136, 138
Levenson, Jon D., 186
Liddell, Henry C. et al., 34
Lightfoot, John B., 29, 33–34, 56, 65, 68, 75, 332, 339
Lincoln, Andrew T., 79–80, 107, 146, 154, 156, 279–80, 283–85, 288–89
Lindars, Barnabas, 22, 279, 285
Lindemann, Andreas., 215, 218, 224
Linebaugh, Jonathan A., 3
Loader, William, 167, 169

Lodge, John G., 218
Lohmeyer, Ernst, 28, 298
Lona, Horacio E., 274–77, 329–32
Longenecker, Bruce W., 4, 75, 156
Longenecker, Richard N., 5–6, 13, 29, 32, 34, 45, 56, 60, 64–65, 68, 75–76, 78–79, 83–84
Lubking, Hans-Martin, 128–29, 131, 134–35
Luhrmann, Dieter, 32, 64
Lull, David J., 66, 154, 156
Luz, Ulrich, 11, 45, 58–61, 64, 98, 225, 296
Lyons, George, 4, 7

Mackie, Scott D., 172, 319
Maier, Gerhard, 319
Manson, Thomas W., 16, 309
Marshall, I. Howard, 13, 154, 156, 189, 236, 239, 244–45, 249, 252, 259
Martin, Ralph P., 2, 5–6, 204–6, 210, 212, 217, 219, 321
Martinez, Florento Garcia, 26
Martyn, J. Louis, 6–7, 18–20, 28–29, 38–40, 45–46, 55–56, 58, 60–64, 67–68, 72, 75–80, 83–84, 154, 156, 158
Marxsen, Willi, 16
Marz, Claus-Peter, 167
Mason, Rex A., 234
Matera, F., 54
Matlock, Barry R., 67, 150
Maynard-Reid, Pedro, 204
McKelvey, Robert J., 167, 173, 175, 180–81, 189
Meeks, Wayne A., 92
Meinhold, Peter, 335
Merk, Otto, 6
Metzger, Bruce M., 124, 240
Meyer, Ben F., 21
Michel, Otto, 96, 100, 114, 119, 123, 125, 132, 136, 138, 163, 168–69, 171–72, 179–80, 183, 196, 200
Minear, Paul S., 25, 239, 242
Mitternacht, Dieter, 70
Mittmann-Richert, Urike, 240, 247–50, 256–60, 262

Moloney, Francis J., 273, 277, 279, 283–85
Montefiore, Hugh, 166, 169, 172–74, 179, 189, 196, 318–19
Moo, Douglas J., 206
Morales, Rodrigo J., 35
Morgan, Teressa, 192, 196
Morland, Kjell Arne, 4, 32–35, 44, 53
Morris, Leon, 114, 123, 125, 136, 138, 297, 309
Morrison, Michael D., 167, 181
Mosser, Carl, 179
Moule, Charles F. D., 176, 182, 236, 332
Moulton, James H., 185
Moulton, James H.-George Milligan, 82, 178
Moxnes, Halvor, 38, 65, 97–98, 108, 115, 117–18, 121, 125, 169
Muller, Christian, 128
Munck, Johannes, 4, 16
Mussner, Franz, 5–6, 13, 18, 31–33, 44–46, 56, 60–61, 65–66, 68, 75, 77, 79–80, 83–84, 204, 206, 215, 218–19, 221, 225

Nanos, Mark D., 2–5, 14–17, 70
Nauck, Wolfgang, 165
Nepper-Christensen, Poul, 311
Neubrand, Maria, 98–99, 102, 107, 109, 111–15, 117–18, 122–25
Nickelsburg, George W. E., 276
Nickle, Kenneth F., 16
Niebuhr, Karl-Wilheim, 1–2, 7–8, 98, 128
Niehoff, Maren, 77
Nienhuis, David R., 204, 206, 212–13, 218, 220
Nietzel, H., 213
Nolland, John, 236, 245, 249, 252, 256, 259
Novensen, Michael V., 104

O'Brian, Peter, 107
O'Neill, John C., 64
Overman, J. Andrew, 312

Painter, John, 204
Penna, Romano, 107

Penner, Todd C., 204, 225
Pesch, Rudolph, 267
Petersen, David L., 234
Piper, John, 128–29, 134
Pitts, Andrew W., 150
Plummer, Alfred, 226, 249, 256
Popkes, Wiard, 204, 206, 209, 211, 213–15, 217–18, 220–22, 225
Porter, Stanley, 150
Pratscher, Wilhelm, 204, 315
Prigent, Pierre, 336–37
Prostmeier, Ferdinand, 332, 335–39

Raisanen, Heikki, 65, 74
Reicke, Bo, 16
Reinbold, Wolfgang, 131–32
Reinmuth, Eckart, 95
Redditt, Paul L., 234
Rhee, Victor (Sung-Yul), 191
Richardson, Christopher A., 169, 175.179–80, 182–83, 189, 194, 318
Richardson, Peter, 75
Rissi, Matthias, 169, 191
Robertson, A. T., 82, 339
Robinson, John A. T., 68, 298
Robinson, William C., 242
Rochfuchs, Wilhelm, 295
Roloff, Jurgen, 16, 267
Rose, Christian, 178–81, 183–84, 186, 189, 191, 194
Rowland, Christopher C., 62

Saldarini, Anthony J., 312
Salevan, Iutisone, 185
Sanders, Edward P., 44–47, 64–65, 67
Sanders, J.N. – B.A. Masten, 284
Sandy, William-Arthur C. Headlam, 114, 125
Sanger, Dieter, 4, 36, 43, 46, 48, 53, 92, 97, 107, 112, 120, 128, 135
Schafer, Ruth, 7, 9, 12–15, 18
Schiffman, Louis H., 27
Schlatter, Adolf, 132, 285, 309
Schlier, Heinrich, 5–6, 12–13, 31, 33–34, 44, 56, 61, 75, 249
Schliesser, Benjamin, 98, 109, 111–12, 115–16, 123–24

INDEX OF MODERN SCHOLARS

Schmid, Josef, 249, 259
Schmidt, Karl, 295
Schmithals, Walter, 16
Schmitt, R., 124, 146, 160, 163
Schnackenburg, Rudolf, 273–75, 277, 279–80, 282, 284–86
Schneider, Johannes, 189, 267, 295
Schnelle, Udo, 13, 20, 68, 204–5, 218
Scholtissek, Klaus, 174, 179–80, 184, 191–92, 195, 199
Schrenk, Gottlob, 265
Schroeder, William R., 333–35
Schultz, Siegfried, 309
Schunack, Gerd, 191–92
Schutz, John Howard, 16
Schurmann, Heinrich, 236, 240, 249, 252, 259
Schwartz, Daniel R., 27
Schweizer, Eduard, 309
Scott, James M., 72
Scroggs, Robin, 39, 154, 156
Seifrid, Mark A., 38
Siegert, Folker, 51, 128–29, 133, 137–38
Siker, Jeffrey S., 41, 60, 85, 137, 282–83
Silva, Moises, 12–13, 22
Sim, David, 312
Smith, Barry D., 35, 45–46, 94
Soding, Thomas, 37, 165, 169, 176, 178–80, 183–84, 187, 189, 191, 194, 203
Spicq, Celsus, 168–69, 172–73, 178, 189, 196, 202, 318–19
Sprinkle, Preston, 11, 52, 64, 149–50
Stanton, Graham, 39, 64, 309, 311–12
Stauffer, Ethelbert, 180
Stendahl, Krister, 293, 304
Stewart, Alistair C., 333
Still, Todd D., 189, 194
Stolle, Volker, 10
Stolz, Lukas, 166
Stone, Michael E., 276
Stowers, Stanley K., 93, 96–97, 101
Strecker, Georg, 309, 311
Streeter, Burnett H., 298
Stuhlmacher, Peter, 21, 29, 88, 92

Tannehill, Robert C., 259
Taylor, Vincent, 298

Theobald, Michael, 92, 95–96, 122, 124, 140, 144, 204, 219–20, 272–76, 279–80, 282, 284–87
Thielman, Frank, 20–22, 33, 46, 53
Thiessen, Michael, 39, 76–77, 93–94, 232, 267
Thompson, James W., 180, 191
Thomson, Peter, 204
Thorsteinsson, Runar M., 93
Thrall, Margaret E., 88
Thuren, Lauri, 10, 46, 61, 64, 69
Thyen, Haerwig, 274
Tilborg, Sjet van, 311
Tobin, Thomas H., 10, 79, 91, 97, 100, 112, 116, 123
Torrance, Thomas F., 332, 338
Trilling, Wolfgang, 304, 307–10
Tsuji, Manabu, 204–5, 210, 220
Turner, Nigel, 239

Ulrichs, Karl F., 19, 44, 149–52

Vanhoye, Albert, 63, 169, 173
Van der Woude, Adam S., 175
Vielhauer, Philip, 238, 243, 250
Verseput, Donald J., 212, 215
Vogel, Manuel, 40, 78–79, 83–84, 240, 252, 267
Vogtle, Anton, 293–95, 305
Von Dobbler, Axel, 38, 104, 107, 117, 125
Von Harnack, Adolph, 239, 259
Von Rad, Gerhard, 7, 121, 174

Wachob, Wesley Hiram, 204
Wagner, Jochen, 128, 328
Wakefield, Andrew H., 38, 42, 45–48, 55
Wall, Robert W., 204, 206–9, 211–13, 220
Walter, Nicholaus, 13, 137
Ward, Roy B., 206
Watson, Francis, 9, 16–17, 25, 28, 32, 38, 53–54, 92, 95, 105, 107, 119, 128, 134–35, 138, 140, 150–51, 156
Wehnert, Jurgen, 15–16

INDEX OF MODERN SCHOLARS

Weiss, Hans Friedrich, 165, 167, 169, 172–74, 179–80, 183, 186, 318–19
Wenger, Stefan, 207, 211, 214, 216–18
Wengst, Karl, 336–37
Wenk, Matthias, 262
Westcott, Brooke Foss, 169, 172–74, 196, 319
Westerholm, Stephen, 19, 22, 25, 29, 45–46, 53–54, 67–69, 104, 112
Whitlark, Jason A., 189, 194
Wider, David, 167, 178
Wiefel, Wolfgang, 92
Wieser, Frierich Immanuel, 1, 102, 113, 116, 120, 126, 139, 148–49, 180
Wikenhauser, Alfred, 284
Wilckens, Ulrich, 11, 25, 30, 93–94, 96–97, 99, 107, 109, 111, 114, 119, 124, 131–32, 136, 147, 153, 225, 284
Wilk, Florian, 128
Williamson, Paul R., 121
Williamson, Ronald, 202
Wilson, R. R., 295
Windisch, Hans, 180, 336, 338–39
Winter, Paul, 239, 253
Wisdom, Jeffrey R., 14, 42–44, 49–50, 64, 71, 84
Wischmeyer, Oda, 37
Witherington, Ben, 7, 20, 29, 31–33, 35, 56, 60, 73, 79, 80, 84, 154
Wright, N. Thomas, 8, 10–11, 27, 36–37, 39, 42, 46–47, 59, 64, 75, 88, 93, 95, 99, 101–3, 109–10, 118–19, 128

Yinger, Kent L., 93
Young, Norman A., 66

Zeller, Dieter, 39, 41, 95, 97, 108, 124, 128
Ziesler, John, 25, 96, 114, 136–38, 144
Zimmerli, Heinrich, 338
Zimmermann, Heinrich, 165, 176

Index of Biblical and Extra Biblical Writings

(Where a section appears in italics, individual verses have not been itemized—they will be easily found. Where they occur elsewhere they are listed)

Genesis

1.5	102
1.8	102
1.10	102
2.2	166
11.30	81
12–25	325
12.1–3	43, 139, 171, 202, 294
12.1	180, 321
12.1–3	329
12.1–4	102, 278
12.3	42–43, 65, 142, 265, 306
12.7	57, 117, 181
12.7–8	103
12.8	180
13	321, 323
13.8	160
13.14–16	329
13.14–17	181
13.15	57
13.15–16	117
14	166, 175
14.14	327
14.18–19	175
15	325
15.1–6	43, 103, 183, 278, 321
15.4	132, 185
15.4–5	40, 109
15.5	118, 123, 134, 139, 161
15.5–6	102, 107–8, 202
15.6	26, 37–40, 42, 58, 96, 102, 107, 109, 111, 118, 125–26, 142, 148, 151, 217, 219, 225, 229–30, 331

Genesis (continued)

15.7	117
15.7–19	39
15.7–21	107
15.8	181
15.9–21	284
15.13	58, 72, 106
15.13–14	266
15.18	139, 261
15.18–19	244
16.15	131
17	39, 325
17.2–6	183
17.4–16	261
17.5	108, 120, 122, 142, 161
17.7	57
17.8	58, 180
17.9–14	232
17.10–14	267
17.11	327
17.14	267
17.16	82, 240
17.16–17	183
17.16–19	132
17.17	183, 275, 284
17.19–21	132
17.23	337
18.1–8	278
18.7	276
18.8	42–43, 65
18.10	131, 183, 329
18.10–14	132
18.14	131, 329
18.15	125
18.16–19.29	323
18.17–33	331
18.18	142
19.20	174
21.1–3	131
21.5	171
21.9	83
21.11–12	75
21.12	83, 130–32, 145, 160, 185
21.13	75
21.22	321
22.1–19	278
22.2–3	321
22.5	187, 319
22.12	219
22.15–18	244, 321
22.16	331
22.16–18	132, 139, 172
22.17	134, 137, 170
22.18	264
23.4 (LXX)	318
24.1	284
24.7	57
24.37	180
25.2	75, 131
25.3	133
25.20	171
25.26	171
26.2–5	139
26.4	264
28.4	265
29.32	258
30.1–8	275
30.13	258

Exodus

3.6	163
3.12	266
3.14	285
4.22	278
12.26–27	260
12.40	107
13.8	260
13.14	260
14.19	63
23.7	106
23.17	108
23.20–21	63
32.8	49
32.34	63
33.1, 3	336
34.7	106

Leviticus

12.3	267
16	193

INDEX OF BIBLICAL AND EXTRA BIBLICAL WRITINGS 385

18	193
18.3	119
18.5	23, 51–53, 86
19.18	207, 221, 223
20.22–23	23
20.26	23

Numbers

14.1–24	195
19	336
24.17	249
35.25–26	174

Deuteronomy

4.1	228
4.5	228
5.1	228
5.27	228
4.42	174
6.1	228
6.4	214, 221
9.6	49
11.19	260
14.12	278
18.15	264
19.5	14
21.23	5
27.15–26	23
27.16	26, 57
27.26	22, 45–46, 51, 54–55, 65, 86, 207
29.4	135
30.1–10	108
30.11–14	47
31.9–13	228
32.2	62
32.43	140
34	283

Joshua

2.11	220
4.6–7	260
6.22–25	220

Ruth

4.12	293

1 Samuel

2.1–10	257
2.2	256

1 Regn. (LXX)

2.2	256–57

2 Samuel

5.2	294–95
5.8 (LXX)	303
7	26, 235
7.12–14	58

2 Kings

2.11	234

4 Kings (LXX)

5.7	121

1 Chronicles

2.1–15	293

2 Chronicles

20.7	219

Psalms

2.7	268
8.3 (LXX)	304
8.5–7	166–68
14.3	106
16.11	245
16.33–37	268
18.49	140
18.51	245
28.9	245

Psalms (continued)

29.10	245
30.13	245
32 (LXX31).1–2	111–12, 142
35.28	245
40.6–8	166–67
41.13	245
45.17	245, 260
48.13	260
61.8	245
72.19	245
78.4, 6	260
78.67—72	294
79.13	260
85.9–13	161
89	235, 257
89.1	260
89 (LXX88). 11	257
90.14	247
95.7–11	166
102.12, 18	260
106.20	9
106.31	26
110 (LXX109).1	296, 299, 304
110.4	166–67, 171–73, 176
111 (LXX110).9	256
117.1	140
119.93	65
132	235
135.13	260
145.4–9	161

Proverbs

3.1	228
3.4	228
3.11–12	166
3.29–31	228
6.23	65

Isaiah

1.10	288
2.2–4	317
7–12	258
7.14	202, 258, 292, 299
7.14 (LXX)	279
12	259
8.14	135, 162
9.1–6	248
9.1–7	250
9.2	246, 258
9.11	235
10.3	174
10.22–23	134
11.1	104
11.10	141
26.20	177
28.12	227
28.16	135, 151, 162
29.10	135
29.13	227
29.18–19	302
35.4, 5	302
40.1–2	81
40.3	247
41.4	285
41.8	168, 219
41.9	122
41.13	169
43.10	285
44.22	108
45.21	161
45.21–23	10
46.4	285
46.12–13	108
46.13	161
48.1	280
48.12	122, 285
49.1–6	9
49.14–16	81
49.17–26	81
50.1–3	81
51.1–8	103
51.3	81
51.4, 5	82
51.5–6	161
51.7–8	82
51.10	82
52.1–2	81
52.6	286
52.7–10	81

INDEX OF BIBLICAL AND EXTRA BIBLICAL WRITINGS

53.5	127	6.3	199
53.13	127	6.7	199
54.1	77, 81–83, 156	7.13	299
55.3	268		
56.1	161	## Hosea	
59.20–21	132, 138, 159		
59.26	131	1.2	278
61.1	302	1.10	3
66.7–14	82	2.6	278
		9.7	228
## Jeremiah		11.1	122, 278
		11.8–9	104
1.4–10	9		
7.13	228	## Joel	
9.23–24	330		
11.16	122	1.3	260
23.5	249		
23.5–6	252	## Amos	
29	205		
31.9	3, 278	2.6–8	227
31.31–34	166–67, 190	4.4	227
31.31	94		
31.33	94	## Micah	
31.34	94, 108, 159		
		4.1–3	317
## Ezekiel		5.2	294
		7.20	244, 257
10–11	309		
11.19–20	69, 94	## Habakkuk	
16	278, 288		
30.5	264	2.3–4	166, 177, 179–80
33.23–29	227	2.4	51–54, 86, 142, 150
33.31	227		
34.10–16	241	## Zephaniah	
34.23–24	241, 252		
34.25–31	241	3.17	256
36.16–36	108		
36.25	193	## Zechariah	
36.26	69		
36.26–27	94	3.8	248–49
37.24	241, 252	6.12	248–49
		9.9	303
## Daniel		14.9	10
2.23	199		
3.35	219		
5.13	199		

Haggai

2.6	166–67

Malachi

1.2–3	133
1.6	278
2.17	233
2.17–3.5	234
3.1	247
3.1–5	233, 236, 246
4.5–6	233–34, 236, 246

Apocrypha and Pseudepigrapha

Apocalypse of Abraham

8.15	106
9.6	219
10.6	219
29.14–31	284
30–31	284

1 Baruch

2.9	65
4.1	65, 119

2 Baruch

4.1–7	80
4.2	182
4.4	284
78–86	205
79	276

Book of Biblical Antiquities (Pseudo-Philo)

18.5	186
23.6	284
40.2	186

1 Enoch

62.5	309
69.6	280
90.28–32	80
90.29	182

2 Enoch

31.6	280

4 Ezra

3.14	219, 284
3.25–27	276
7.17	65
7.21	65
7.26	80
7.116–26	119
8.52–53	80
9.38—10.57	80
10.25	182
14.30	65, 119

Joseph & Asenath

8.10–11	121
12.1	121
20.6	121

Jubilees

11.15–17	106
11.16–17	214
11.18–21	107
12.1–8	214
12.17–21	214
14.21	183
16.16–18	75
19.9	219
19.15–29	171
21.1–3	101
22.10—23.3	171
22.16	16
30.20	219

INDEX OF BIBLICAL AND EXTRA BIBLICAL WRITINGS

Letter of Aristeas

139	22
142	22

1 Maccabees

2.52	103, 217, 219, 224, 330

2 Maccabees

1.1–9	205
1.10—2.18	205
7.39	186

4 Maccabees

7.18–19	187
16.25	187
17.12	187
18.23	187

Pirque Aboth

1.15	225
1.17	225–26
2.7	65
2.8	119

Psalms of Solomon

14.2	65, 119
17	251
17.15	264

Testament of Abraham

13.1	219

Testament of Levi

18.10–11	187

Testament of Naphtali

1.10	275

Wisdom of ben Sirach

2.1–18	205
15.11–20	205
17.1	65
18.30–31	205
34.21–22	207
44.19–21	103, 217
44.20	330
44.20–21	219, 267
44.21	260
44.50	260
45.5	65

Wisdom of Solomon

2–5	187
2.24	280
11.8–10	19
12.20–22	19
13.1–5	62

Josephus

Jewish Antiquities

1.154	106

Jewish War

2.153	186

Philo of Alexandria

Allegorical Laws

3.203–8	171

Abraham

69–72	106
170	219
262–73	103
273	171

Migration of Abraham

148–50	329

INDEX OF BIBLICAL AND EXTRA BIBLICAL WRITINGS

Virtues

212–16	106

Rewards and Punishments

79	225
177	108

Questions and Answers on Genesis

4.180	171

Sacrifices of Cain and Abel

93–94	171

Genesis Rabbah

44.25	284

Qumran Writings

Damascus Document

1.4–5	27
5.5–6	26

4Q Flor.

1.11	249

4Q 174

2.2–4	26

4Q 252

2.8–10	107

4QMMT

	26, 312

New Testament

Matthew's Gospel

1.1	263, 291, 294, 310
1.17	292–93, 305
1.18	292
1.18–21	292
1.18–25	279, 301
1.20	304
1.20–21	301
1.21	306
1.23	279
1.24–25	292
2.1–12	310
2.2	294
2.15	299
3.7	288
3.8–9	306
3.17	299
4.3, 6	299
5–7	226
7.16	225
7.21	226
7.24	226
7.26	226
8.1–4	301
8.5–13	306
8.11–12	306, 310
9.27	301–2, 305
10.5–6	309
10.18	339
11.2	295, 302
11.5	302
11.27	300
12.22–30	302
12.23	305
12.39	308
13.13	305
14.22–23	300
14.33	300
15.21–28	302
15.22	302, 305
15.28	302
16.13–23	295
16.16	300
16.16–21	295
16.18	339

16.21	296
20.29–34	302
20.30–31	305
21.5	303
21.9	303, 305
21.12–14	303
21.14–16	304
21.15	305
21.15–16	304
21.28–32	226
21.41	308
21.43	307
22.1–14	308
22.23–33	307
22.32	310
22.41–46	295
22.42	296, 304
22.45	305
23.1–33	227
23.1–6	297
23.7–10	297
23.37	305
23.38	309
23.39	309
24.5	295
24.23	295
26.64	298, 300, 304
27.17	299
27.19	308
27.24–25	308
27.39–44	308
27.52	308
27.62–66	308
28.15	308
28.16–20	306, 309–10
28.18	304

Mark's Gospel

1.4	246
1.44–45	301
3.21	21
7.26	302
8.29	300
8.30	295
9.1	282
10.27	125
10.46–52	301–2
11.9	303
11.12	149
12.18–27	307
12.28–34	207, 224
12.35	296
12.35–37	295–96
14.36	125
14.62	300
16.8	308

Luke's Gospel

1	233–38
1–2	231, 261
1.5–20	233
1.5–25	238
1.7	246
1.13–17	234
1.14–17	241
1.16–17	232, 246
1.17	250
1.20	232
1.26–33	234
1.26–38	279, 280
1.26–38, 46–55	253–61
1.27	259
1.31–33	253, 256
1.32	232, 237, 250–51
1.34	259
1.34–38	235
1.39–45	232, 248, 254
1.41–45	255
1.42–43	235
1.43	246
1.43–45	235
1.46–55	232, 235
1.47–55	235
1.48	256
1.49	235, 255
1.51–53	262
1.51–55	236
1.54–55	261, 264
1.57	257
1.57–66	232, 237
1.57–67	251
1.57–80	238

Luke's Gospel (continued)

1.64	243
1.65–66	237
1.66	238
1.67	244
1.67–79	232, 237
1.69–73	237
1.69–79	239–53
1.71	237
1.72–73	238, 261, 264
1.73	261
1.73–74	237
1.74–77	262
1.76–79	237, 242
1.77	261
1.78–79	237
1.80	232
2.8–14	232
2.25–32	232
2.28–35	236
2.32	261
2.36–38	232
2.38	236
2.40	232
2.49	232
3.3	246
3.7	28
3.7–9	242
3.8	262, 275, 282, 306
3.34	263
6.20–49	226
6.31	330
6.36–38	330
6.46–49	226
7.1–10	306
7.18	295
10.25–37	207, 224
11.29	288, 306
11.39–47	227
11.39–48	288, 306
11.52	227, 247, 288, 306
13.16	263
13.28–29	269, 306–7
14.27	133
16.19–31	187
16.23	269
16.23–31	269
16.24	262
16.30	262
19.9	263
19.45	303
20.27–40	307
20.37–38	269
22.31–32	21
22.66–68, 70	298
23.43	187
24.34	21
24.44	234

John's Gospel

1.14	287
1.17	270
2.23–25	273
3.16–21	242
3.35	286
4.12	281
4.22	289–90
4.46–54	273
4.48	273
4.50–52	273
5.17–18	277
5.18	277
5.19–29	282
5.21–23	286
5.23	282
5.24	274
5.26–27	286
5.28–29	285
5.39	270
5.45–47	270–71
6.5	339
6.30–35	270
6.38	276, 286
6.42	323
6.57	286
6.60–66	273
6.63	274
6.68	274
7.1	277
7.1–9	21
7.25	277
7.30	277
7.33	276

INDEX OF BIBLICAL AND EXTRA BIBLICAL WRITINGS 393

8	323	20.30–31	272, 274
8.12–20	289	21.15–17	21
8.17	270		
8.20	277		
8.29	280		

Acts of the Apostles

8.30	272
8.30–36	274
8.31	271–73
8.31–47	273–81
8.31–36	272
8.37	272
8.37–59	272
8.42–47	282
8.42	272
8.48	272
8.48–49	282
8.48–59	281–87
8.58	287
9.1	303
9.12	270
9.18	152
10.24–38	298
10.34	270
10.34–36	277
10.34–38	289
10.37–38	272
12.23	283
12.31	276
12.34	243
12.41	285
12.42	272
12.42–43	270
12.48	274
13.1	276
13.3	276
14.2	276
14.10	274
14.10–11	272
14.24	274
14.30	276
15.3	274
15.7	274
15.27	339
16.1–4	270
16.11	276
16.28	276
17.1	283
17.11	274

1.14	260
1.16	253
2.38–42	265
3.1	303
3.13	263
3.18	253, 264
3.19	265
3.19–20	264
3.21	252–53, 264
3.22–23	264
3.25	265
3.25–26	264
4.25	253
5.30	263
7.2	107, 262–63
7.2–7	266
7.17	267
7.32	263
7.38	103
8	267
9.15	9
13	163
13.17	263
13.22	268
13.23–25	246
13.26	268
13.38–39	268
20.32	262
22.14	262
22.15	9
22.21	9, 263
22.29	339
26.6–7	268
26.17–23	9
26.23	268

Letter to the Romans

1.1–15	91
1.3	158
1.3–4	104, 140, 296–97
1.5	8, 91

INDEX OF BIBLICAL AND EXTRA BIBLICAL WRITINGS

Letter to the Romans (continued)	
1.8–15	90
1.9–12	91
1.11	123
1.14–15	91
1.16–17	92, 107, 142, 157
1.17	96
1.18–23	105–6
1.18—3.20	92
1.18–32	92–94
1.19–21	95
1.20	123
1.20–21	125
1.21	125, 140
1.32	28
2.1	93
2.1–5	93
2.1–11	225
2.6	24
2.7–8	229
2.11	93, 95
2.12	28
2.13	24, 93, 225
2.14	28
2.14–15	25, 94
2.15	25, 28
2.17–20	101
2.17–24	93, 96, 158
2.17–29	229
2.21	93
2.21–23	24, 93–94
2.23–24	94
2.24	140
2.25	24
2.25–28	115
2.27–29	94
2.28	281
3.1–2	158
3.1–8	128
3.2	152
3.8	29, 223
3.8–10	223
3.9	115, 158
3.9–10	106
3.9–20	59, 95, 140
3.10	215
3.10–18	94
3.19	2
3.19–20	106, 115
3.20	150, 223
3.21	95–96, 107, 144, 157, 163
3.21–22	152
3.21–26	95, 127, 143, 145
3.21–31	97, 151
3.22	150
3.22–26	109
3.22–31	109
3.23	59, 106, 115, 155
3.24	9, 120, 225
3.24–25	20
3.25	150
3.25–26	151, 158
3.26	123, 225
3.27–29	95
3.27–30	97
3.27–31	97, 101, 127
3.27—4.2	96
3.27—4.25	97
3.28	111–12, 220, 225
3.29–30	96
3.31	53, 96, 144
4.1–5	98–111
4.1–8	97
4.1–25	12, 142–43
4.2–3	220
4.3	151, 218
4.4–5	122
4.5	225
4.6	86
4.6–8	111–13
4.6–8	162
4.9	151
4.9–12	113–17
4.9–10	40, 104, 161
4.9–12	145, 157
4.11	123
4.11–12	143
4.12	149
4.13–16d	117–20
4.13	104
4.13–16	143
4.15	28, 144

4.16	123, 143–44, 149, 220	9.5	158, 261
		9.6–8	115
4.16e–22	120–25	9.6–18	161
4.17–18	144, 161	9.7	145, 160
4.17–25	145	9.8	145
4.18	123, 161	9.27–29	162
4.19	160	9.32–33	152, 162
4.20–21	143	10.1	
4.23–25	125–27	10.1–2	159
4.23–25	161	10.2–3	93
4.25	20, 145	10.9	214
5.1	225	10.16–17	152
5.9	225	10.21	59, 162
5.12	59, 155	11.1	158
5.12–21	128, 155	11.1–2	115
5.13	119	11.4–5	59
5.15	155	11.11	115, 123, 159
5.15–21	9	11.13	91
5.17	155	11.13–14	103
5.19	150	11.13–32	91
5.20	119, 144, 163	11.17–19	91
5.21	59	11.17–24	72
6.1	223	11.23	116, 125, 159
6.1–11	32	11.26	115
6.12	123	11.26–27	111, 159
6.18	146	11.28–29	115
6.21	146	11.29	158
7.1–6	72	12.1–16.29	91
7.4	123	12.6–8	212
7.5	144	13.8–10	144
7.6	144	14.1—15.13	91
7.7–11	119	15.7–13	139–41
7.10	28, 100	15.5–6	125
7.12	142	15.7–12	148
7.14	144	15.12	104, 158
7.21	100	15.14–21	91
8.2	146	15.16	91
8.3	119	15.20	90
8.4	94, 145	15.22	90
8.18–23	146	15.23	146
8.29	123	15.24	90–91
8.30	225	15.25–27	90
9.1	281	15.27	159
9.4–5	281	15.28	90
9–11	128–39	15.30–31	16–17
9.1–5	159	16	92
9.4–5	129		

1 Corinthians

1.9	202
1.18–25	15
1.22–23	243
1.22–24	104
1.30	70, 87
2.1–5	157
3.10	8
5.13	69
6.2	72
6.11	20, 70, 87, 225
6.12	223
6.12–20	223
7.19	68
8.7–13	223
8.8	23
9.1–2	8
9.7	152
9.8	145
9.9	69
9.18	123
9.20	104
9.26	155
10.1–11	162
10.4	104
10.6	123
10.13	202
10.23	223
11.23	123
11.26	115
11.28–29	115
11.33	123
12.4–11	212
13.7	152
15.1–11	19
15.3	20–21
15.3–4	252
15.3–8	8
15.7	21
15.10	8
15.56	68

2 Corinthians

1.4	123
1.18	202
1.20	104
3.3	69
3.6	69
3.7	69
3.8	69
3.9	69, 87
3.9–11	162
3.10	69
3.11	69
3.14	80
4.4–6	8
4.6	163
5.14–15	87, 89
5.17–21	87
5.21	88–89
9.19–23	103
11.1—12.13	1
11.3	280
11.13–15	289
11.22	1
11.24	103
11.24–29	83
11.32–33	9

Galatians

1–2	3
1.1	34
1.4	53, 74
1.6	49
1.6–7	4
1.6–9	6, 49
1.8–9	4
1.11–12	7, 12, 41
1.13	34
1.13–14	33
1.15	7–8
1.15–16	7, 41
1.15–24	13
1.16	9, 85
1.16–17	12
1.17—2.10	14
1.18—2.10	12
1.21–24	12
2.1–2	75
2.1–10	13
2.2	42
2.3–6	13

INDEX OF BIBLICAL AND EXTRA BIBLICAL WRITINGS 397

2.4	14	3.13–14	33, 145
2.4–5	23	3.14	79, 86, 143, 150
2.5	42	3.14–15	85
2.7	151	3.15	156, 161
2.7–8	159	3.15–20	57–64
2.7–9	13	3.16	142, 144, 154, 157, 225
2.9	159		
2.11–14	32, 67	3.16–22	143
2.11–15	23	3.17	80
2.11–21	14, 17–18	3.17–18	144
2.14	18	3.18	144
2.15	18–19, 30, 74	3.18–22	80
2.15–17	31	3.19	157, 159
2.15–21	37	3.21—4.6	65–6, 70–76
2.16	20–21, 23, 28–29, 31–32, 45, 49, 86, 143, 150–51, 220	3.21–23	144
		3.22	151
		3.22–24	143, 162
2.17	29	3.22–25	78
2.17–18	31	3.22–28	86
2.18	31	3.23	156
2.19	24, 32–33, 143	3.23–25	104
2.19–20	12, 34	3.24	223
2.20	86, 151	3.25	144
2.21	34	3.28	197, 326
3.1	4, 35	3.29	86, 169
3.2	3	4.1–3	86
3.1–5	*36–37*	4.1–7	78
3.1–5	57	4.3	62, 156
3.2	3, 45, 50, 57, 79	4.4	62
3.2–5	5, 24	4.4–5	158
3.5	35, 50	4.4–7	56
3.6	142	4.5	49
3.6–9	36, 41, 86	4.8	3, 67
3.6–12	86	4.8–10	62
3.6–14	*37–57*	4.8–11	86
3.6–29	5	4.9	5, 62
3.7	80, 85, 143	4.9–10	157, 159
3.7–8	71	4.10	5
3.8	31, 142–43, 158, 160	4.12—5.1	84
		4.17	6
3.8–14	33	4.21–31	66, 131, 154, 338
3.8–22	162	4.21–31	75–84
3.9	143, 157	4.21—5.1	145, 158
3.10	24, 28, 33	4.25	66–67
3.10–14	36	4.27	156
3.10–12	24	5.1	73
3.11	142, 160	5.2–4	4
3.13	79	5.3	51, 207

Galatians (continued)

5.7	3
5.10	4
5.12	4
5.13	73, 84
5.13—6.2	84
5.13-14	64
5.14	144, 223
5.15	6
5.20	5
6.12	6
6.12-13	4
6.12-15	84
6.12-17	19
6.13	49, 51

Ephesians

4.6	215

Philippians

1.10	122
3.2	289
3.5	10, 130
3.6	47
3.19	289
3.20-21	198

1 Thessalonians

1.9	215
2.4	152
2.14-16	83, 159
5.3	155
5.24	202

2 Thessalonians

3.3	202

1 Timothy

2.5	215
2.14	280

2 Timothy

1.12	125
3.5	224

Letter to the Hebrews

1.1-2	192
1.1-11	191
1.1—4.13	165
1.3	167, 189, 191
1.4	168
1.4-14	167
1.5-13	191
1.13	174, 191
2.1	166
2.1-3	166
2.5-18	168-69
2.9	184, 195
2.10	189
2.17	189-90, 319
2.18	194
3.1	184, 191, 319
3.2	150, 190
3.3	167
3.6	166, 195
3.7—4.11	181
3.12	166, 195-96
3.14	166
3.16-19	196
3.19	195
4.1	192, 198
4.2	196
4.6-11	198
4.8	167
4.9	171
4.12-13	192
4.14	172, 191, 195
4.14-15	191
4.14-16	194
4.14—10.18	165
4.15	194
4.16	194
5.6	173
5.9	189
5.12	166
6.1	190
6.1-8	170

6.9–10	170	10.39	176
6.10	166	11.1	176, 193, 202
6.11	195	11.6	202
6.11–12	166	11.7	194, 198, 200
6.12	192	11.8	196, 201–2
6.13–20	170–75	11.8–9	201, 224
6.13–14	201	11.8–12	230
6.15	192, 202	11.8–16	319
6.17	192	11.9	192, 201
6.18	195	11.9–10	200
7.1–3	*175–76*	11.10	171, 194, 200, 202
7.1–10	172, 176, 201	11.11	103, 200–202
7.1–10.18	198	11.13	170, 192, 194
7.5–10	176	11.13–16	200, 202
7.6	192	11.14–16	194
7.7	176	11.15	202
7.15	319	11.16	174
7.17	172–73	11.17	192
7.19	194	11.17–19	201, 230
7.20–21	173, 175	11.19	125, 200, 202, 319
7.25	173, 189, 194	11.20–22	200
7.28	173, 175, 189	11.23–26	198
8.1	191	11.24–25	198, 200
8.1—10.18	166	11.25	199
8.3	319	11.25–27	194
8.6	192	11.26–27	200
9.11–15	182	11.27	200, 202
9.15	192	11.28	198
9.18	319	11.29	198
9.24–26	189	11.31	224, 230
9.28	177	11.33	192
10.1–18	166	11.33–38	199
10.12	189	11.38	198
10.16–17	166	11.39	170, 192
10.19	182, 194	11.40	172, 176
10.19–20	199	12.1	176
10.19—12.3	166	12.1–2	193
10.19—12.29	176	12.1–3	166, 176
10.19—13.17 or 25		12.2	167, 184, 194
	165	12.2–4	194
10.22	193	12.4	166
10.22–23	195	12.4–13	166
10.23	166, 183, 191	12.7–11	166
10.25	166, 174	12.12–13	194
10.32—12.3	176–97	12.22–24	80
10.32–34	166	12.25–29	166, 174
10.32—12.17	176	12.28	192
10.36	192	13.7	166, 193

Letter to the Hebrews (continued)

13.8	194
13.10–14	167
13.13	181
13.14	171, 198
13.22–25	166
13.24	167

Letter of James

1.1	204–5
1.2–4	208, 216, 218, 321
1.2–18	206
1.3	205, 216
1.4	209
1.5	216
1.6	208
1.7–8	216
1.9–11	208
1.12	208
1.13	205
1.16	205, 216, 222
1.17	216
1.18	208
1.18–25	220
1.19	205
1.21	208, 321
1.22	222
1.22–25	208
1.25	210
1.27	208, 321
2.1	205, 215
2.1–13	206–9
2.2–4	215
2.5	215
2.8	210, 220, 223, 321
2.8–13	223
2.11	223
2.12–13	211, 225
2.14–17	205
2.14–26	206, 208–9, 223, 225
2.14–26	209–222
2.14	225
2.15	205
2.21–23	330
2.21–24	230
2.22	103, 229, 321
2.24	225, 321
3.1	205
3.1–12	223
4.4	216
4.6	216
4.8	216
5.12	205
5.15	216
5.19	205

1 Peter

3	327

1 John

1.9	202
3.17	221

The Book of Revelation

2.9	289
3.9	289
20.4	72
21.2	80, 182
21.10	80

Apostolic Fathers

1 Clement

3–9	328
9.1, 3, 4	328
10.1	219, 329, 333
10.2–3	329
10.4–6	329
10.7	329, 333
10.12	224
11.1	330
12.1–2, 7	330
13.3	330
14.1–2	330
16.1–2, 17	331
17.1	331

17.2	219, 331, 333	6.8	336
17.3—18.17	331	6.9	336, 340
19.1	331	6.11	340
19.2	331	6.13	336
21.8	331	6.16	336, 340
30.1–7	331	8.2–4	336
31.2	332–33	8.7	337
32.1–4	332	9.1	337
60.4	332–33	9.1–5	338
		9.4, 6	337

Ignatius of Antioch

Philadelphians

		9.7	336–37
		9.7–8	338
6.1	333	9.7–9	340
8.2	334	9.8–9	338
9.1	334–35	11.9	336
		13.1	338
		13.1–7	340
		13.2–7	339

Letter of Barnabas

		13.3	338
		13.7	338
5.5–7	336	14	338
5.7	340		

www.ingramcontent.com/pod-product-compliance
Lightning Source LLC
Chambersburg PA
CBHW071228290426
44108CB00013B/1334